FIST–FIGHTS IN THE KITCHEN:

Manners and Methods in Social Research

FIST–FIGHTS IN THE KITCHEN:

Manners and Methods in Social Research

Edited by George H. Lewis
University of the Pacific
Stockton, California

Goodyear Publishing Company, Inc.
Pacific Palisades, California

Library of Congress Cataloging in Publication Data

Lewis, George H. comp.
Fist-fights in the kitchen.

1. Social sciences–Methodology. 2. Social science research. I. Title
H61.L49 300'.1'8 74-76450
ISBN 0-87620-326-8

Current printing (last digit): 10 9 8 7 6 5 4 3 2 1

ISBN: 0-87620-326-8

Library of Congress Catalog Card Number: 74-76450

Y-3268-3

Printed in the United States of America

To Both Sides Now....

Contents

PREFACE xi

INTRODUCTION 1

METHODOLOGY AS A CHANGING FIELD OF SPECIALIZATION 3
Irwin Sperber

PART ONE: THINGS OLD, NEW, BORROWED AND BLUE—WEDDING SOCIOLOGY AND SCIENCE 15

Topic I: The Methods (and Madness) of Science 17

BASIC ORIENTATIONS TOWARD THE SCIENTIFIC METHOD 23
Gideon Sjoberg and Roger Nett

THE PROBLEM OF DEFINITION: WHAT IS X? 48
Anatol Rapoport

THE SUBSTANCE OF SOCIOLOGICAL THEORY 56
Norman K. Denzin

Dissection I: Causes, Concepts, and Definitions

BATWINGED HAMBURGER SNATCHER 74
Dan O'Neill

Topic II: Tumbling Dice and City Blocks: Probability and Sampling 83

THE POPULATION AND SAMPLING 87
Sanford Labovitz and Robert Hagedorn

SAMPLING CHART 94
Russell L. Ackoff

RELATIONAL ANALYSIS: THE STUDY OF SOCIAL ORGANIZATIONS WITH SURVEY METHODS 97
James S. Coleman

Dissection II: Samples, Sponsors and Self-Esteem

HOW GOOD ARE THE RATING SERVICES? 108
Richard I. Evans

PART TWO: DIFFERENT STROKES–STRATEGIES OF RESEARCH 119

Topic III: Game Plans and Options 121

APPROXIMATIONS TO KNOWLEDGE 126
Eugene J. Webb, Donald T. Campbell, Richard D. Schwartz and Lee Sechrest

Dissection III: Multiple Operationism: The Case of Field Experiments

MODELS AND HELPING: NATURALISTIC STUDIES IN AIDING BEHAVIOR 152
James H. Bryan and Mary Ann Test

Topic IV: Four Walls Do Not an Experiment Make 165

THE EXPERIMENT 169
Barry F. Anderson

LABORATORY EXPERIMENTS 176
Leon Festinger

ON THE SOCIAL PSYCHOLOGY OF THE PSYCHOLOGICAL EXPERIMENT: WITH PARTICULAR REFERENCE TO DEMAND CHARACTERISTICS AND THEIR IMPLICATIONS 183
Martin T. Orne

Dissection IV: On the Conduct of Experiments

NUREMBERG CODE 196

Topic V: Survey Research: Inner Views or Outer Thoughts? 198

PERSPECTIVES ON INTERVIEWING 202
Raymond L. Gorden

THE INTERVIEW/QUESTIONNAIRE SCHEDULE: AN EXAMPLE AND COMMENTS 217
William J. Goode and Paul K. Hatt

THE PROBLEM OF NONRESPONSE IN SURVEY RESEARCH 225
Calvin M. Endo

Dissection V: Why Should I Scratch Your Back?

POWER AND PURPOSE IN SURVEY RESEARCH (IF YOU GOT THE MONEY, HONEY, I GOT THE TIME) 240
John D. McCarthy and M. Barbara McCarthy

Topic VI: Naturalistic Inquiry: Roles, Rules and Ruses in the Field 250

OBSERVING DEVIANCE 255
Jack D. Douglas

WHEN PROPHECY FAILS 277
Leon Festinger, Henry W. Riecken and Stanley Schachter 277

A COMMENT ON DISGUISED OBSERVATION IN SOCIOLOGY 290
Kai T. Erikson

FIELD NOTES 299
John Lofland

Dissection VI: View From the Other Side

BARROOM SOCIOLOGY 309
Piri Thomas

Topic VII: One Way Mirrors, Four Way Streets: Unobtrusive Measures 316

A. I Only Know What I Read in the Paper: The Written Record 318

THE CRITICAL ANALYSIS OF DOCUMENTARY EVIDENCE 319
David C. Pitt

Dissection A:

THE CONNECTICUT SPEED CRACKDOWN: A STUDY OF THE EFFECTS OF LEGAL CHANGE 332
H. Laurence Ross and Donald T. Campbell

B. The Bugs Are Taking Over: Disguised Observation 341

PATRONS OF ADULT BOOKSTORES AND MOVIES 343
The Report of the Commission on Obscenity and Pornography

Dissection B:

THERE ARE SMILES... 349
Ray L. Birdwhistell

C. When a Girl Sees the Handwriting on the Wall, She's in the Wrong Bathroom: Physical Trace Analysis 357

POP ICONOLOGY: LOOKING AT THE COKE BOTTLE 361
Craig Gilborn

Dissection C:

POGO 372
Walt Kelly

PART THREE: FIST-FIGHTS IN THE KITCHEN 375

Topic VIII: Data Processing and Presentation: What Is Lost in Translation 377

HIRED HAND RESEARCH 380
Julius Roth

THE CASE OF THE INDIANS AND THE TEEN-AGE WIDOWS 396
A. J. Coale and F. F. Stephan

SCIENTIFIC FICTION AS FACT: A CASE STUDY IN THE PERPETUATION OF ERROR 407
Larry T. Reynolds

Dissection VIII: What Is Lost in Translation?

GREAT BOOKS AND SMALL GROUPS: AN INFORMAL HISTORY OF A NATIONAL SURVEY 413
James A. Davis

Topic IX: Ethics and Politics of Social Research–Mutually Exclusive? 428

THE RIGHTS OF THE SUBJECT IN SOCIAL RESEARCH: AN ANALYSIS IN TERMS OF RELATIVE POWER AND LEGITIMACY 432
Herbert C. Kelman

LIFE AND DEATH OF PROJECT CAMELOT 465
Irving Louis Horowitz

Dissection IX: Methods for What?

A MANIFESTO FOR SOCIOLOGISTS: INSTITUTION FORMATION–A NEW SOCIOLOGY 481
Henry Etzkowitz and Gerald M. Schaflander

Preface

Social scientists are at last beginning to recognize as important two facts concerning academic treatment of social science research methods: first, that methods are most often abstracted from the total fabric of social science and taught in the intellectual and moral isolation of "methods" courses; and second, that in this imposed isolation (and perhaps to a great extent because of it) most learning materials designed for the beginning student take one of two highly inappropriate forms. The most common is the "cookbook" text that lists (as an example) the "four cardinal rules for conducting an experiment," to be memorized *in order.* (The books seldom mention the fact that any researcher who insists on following these rules "by the numbers" usually winds up with no more than a rigid mess.) Students exposed to courses emphasizing this type of textual material tend to emerge, as an old Yankee adage reads, "knowing everything, but not *realizing* a damn thing."

On the other hand, anthologies have been constructed to counter this cookbook approach and allow the student to get his/her hands dirty in *real* truth. Unfortunately, the well-intentioned editors tend to draw their material from the professional journals of the field and thus their books emerge as collections of articles originally written by and for academic peers—an unfortunate situation for the apprehensive undergraduate novice assigned the book.

This anthology is an attempt to bridge the gap between cookbooks and collections of methodologically advanced articles. At the same time, the book is also designed to put methodology back in the social picture; I have attempted to relate research methods to social science as a whole and most especially to its theoretical and ethical components.

Fist-Fights in the Kitchen is a compilation that will, I hope, aid the beginning student in gaining a realistic appreciation of the scientific method in the social sciences—an appreciation based on understanding and linkages with the student's own world view and frame of reference. The book consists of papers and essays illustrating the scientific method, uses of sampling, operational alternatives, experiments, interviewing, participant observation, nonparticipant observation, and assorted research problems. Alternative views of each problem are illustrated and special attention is devoted to ethical considerations. More concisely, the book points out not only how the abstract logic of science suggests certain sets of "best" research procedures for studying the social world, but also how the social world makes it impossible to follow through completely on these "best" procedures. The actual process of research is, above all else, a pragmatic and compromising one. This, of course, raises the issue of ethics—an issue that, although missing from many research monographs, texts and anthologies, is an integral part of the research process conceived as a social act.

Fist-Fights in the Kitchen is divided into three major sections: the wedding of sociology and science; differing strategies of research; and ethics, politics, and data presentation. Each major section is divided further into a number of topic areas, or chapters. The topics included are those I feel are the most important involved in the actual *doing* of social research.

Each topic consists of a brief explanation of the issues involved and a perspective from which to view the body of the chapter; a list of suggested readings designed for those who are stimulated to pursue the topic further; a set of carefully chosen articles (many from "nonprofessional" sources) designed to *clearly* present the issues and controversies involved; and a dissection piece.

The dissection reflects its topic and is presented without leading questions or "points to keep in mind." It is an entity, designed to be attacked with knowledge gleaned from earlier portions of the chapter. As such, the dissection piece should challenge the student to develop as a guilty participant (not an innocent bystander) in his/her studies and ultimately, in the research process itself.

There are nine topic areas covered in this book. In considering one topic per week, *Fist-Fights* easily adapts itself to a quarter system. By following up on topics and pursuing actual research as one goes along, the book gives room for a flexible semester plan in which it can be utilized as one of several learning resources. In this way I feel it affords both the instructor and the student the degrees of freedom necessary to learn, as opposed to simply teaching and being taught.

At this point, one traditionally acknowledges the intellectual, financial, and personal debts incurred in creating one's manuscript, in hopes these debts will somehow be accounted for and repaid if only placed in print. Realizing that this is impossible, I still feel compelled to mention *especially* the Faculty Research Committee of the College of the Pacific, without whose enthusiastic encouragement this book may well never have been written, and Sue MacLaurin, for her help in producing the book.

The study of man contains a greater variety of intellectual styles than any other area of cultural endeavor. How different social scientists go about their work, and what they aim to accomplish by it, often do not seem to have a common denominator . . . Let us admit the case of our critics from the humanities and from the experimental sciences: Social science as a whole is both intellectually and morally confused. And what is called sociology is very much in the middle of this confusion.

C. Wright Mills
Images of Man

If you can't stand the heat, you better get out of the kitchen.

Harry S. Truman
Remarks at the Wright Memorial
December 17, 1952

INTRODUCTION

Methodology as a Changing Field of Specialization

Irwin Sperber

Methodology is no longer conceived as a narrow field of technical specialization in the social sciences, and it is rapidly losing the mystique according to which "hard scientists" and "hard data" are alone admissible to its purview. Its importance has become increasingly evident to epistemologists and sociologists of knowledge as well as to students of systematic and historical approaches to social theory. It increasingly reflects the trends toward polarization within the social sciences. Marxist *versus* pluralist theory, activism *versus* aloofness, explicit moral commitment *versus* value-neutrality, ethnomethodology and participant-observation *versus* quantification and experimentalism illustrate some of the major forces now at work in the sociological profession and methodology in particular. The following outline may help orient the reader to the range of topics and problems of importance in assessing these forces, and point out several issues which require much attention in the 1970s in methodological discussions. The long-overdue return of methodological discussions to their humanistic and epistemological genesis in the searching monographs of Emile Durkheim (*Rules of Sociological Method*), Max Weber (*Methodology of the Social Sciences*), and the much misunderstood René Descartes (*A Discourse on Method*) now seems possible. Such a pursuit of critical and historical self-awareness by the researcher also now promises to be amended by a recognition of his own responsibility, as a citizen as well as a scientist, for the social consequences of his procedures and the substantive findings to which they give rise.

VARIETIES OF RESEARCH PROCEDURE AND THE IMPORTANCE OF METHODOLOGY AS A SPECIAL FIELD OF SOCIOLOGICAL STUDY: The Overriding Criterion of "Meaning and Prediction" in Choosing among Procedures

An intellectual perspective through which methodology can be viewed as a major area of concern in sociology includes the following themes.

There are ever-increasing varieties and numbers of research procedures in the social sciences; each procedure entails specific gains and losses when employed to solve a given substantive problem. Which method is most useful under a given set of conditions? What are the possible differences in one's findings which would arise if an alternative method were employed to solve the same problem? What are the kinds of events and meanings in social life to which a given method is sensitive or insensitive? What kinds of events are assumed to be typical or representative of social reality according to a given method? These are some key questions to which methodology is addressed.

Because of the tendency to emphasize proficiency in quantitative and survey research in sociology, a misleading stereotype of the methodologist as a narrowly trained statistician or technician is sometimes uncritically accepted. Actually, the competent methodologist must seek a sense of critical self-awareness through an appreciation of (a) the subtle interdependence of theoretical perspectives, specific hypotheses and research procedures, (b) the far-reaching interdependence of the economic and political institutions and the agencies and personnel engaged in applied research, and (c) the world-view and specific biases of the methodologist himself as a participant in the social order he presumes to study. Far from being a narrowly trained or unreflective technician, the methodologist must in principle and in practice strive to understand the bearing of the history of social thought (including the history of methodology itself) on his discipline, the nature and varieties of sociological theory, the relationship between sociological inquiry and the social order, and the need to keep one's mind open to the possibilities of bias and negative evidence even when a set of findings seems to be technically flawless. In addition to the ability to carry out various types of research, then, the methodologist must have a working knowledge of historical issues arising in his own discipline and a willingness to engage in rigorous self-criticism at all phases of his own research. An important step toward such self-criticism is to pose to oneself the various thematic questions indicated in the immediately preceding paragraph. Indeed, those questions cannot be adequately answered if the aforementioned scholarly and reflective capacities are neglected. For example, one must be aware of the theoretical perspective and underlying assumptions most closely associated with a given method of research in order adequately to identify the kinds of events assumed to be typical of social reality according to that method. One must recognize the ideological components or connotations associated with a particular procedure in order to identify the kinds of negative evidence most likely to be systematically obscured by the application of that procedure to the testing of even the most objectively formulated hypotheses.

A methodologist who selects or advocates a particular research procedure because he happens to be most proficient in its technical execution is still obliged to indicate straightforwardly the relevance of this procedure to the hypothesis under investigation as compared with other procedures which may be more relevant but less mastered than the one chosen. This obligation is only rarely fulfilled in published research reports of qualitative as well as quantitative findings.

When the relevance of two or more methods to a given hypothesis seems roughly equal, another criterion can be employed in making one's selection. *The procedure most likely to yield the data which enable the researcher to understand the meaning of participation and communication from the subjective standpoint of the actors (persons or groups) under study is the procedure of choice.* To understand the meaning of group life from the standpoint of social participants is to be capable of making an informed prediction about their probable responses to a given set of contingencies and therefore to be in a position to construct reliable predictive models of behavior regarding the persons or groups under study. If the evaluation of procedures according to other criteria is difficult or indecisive, or if one procedure is markedly superior to others according to this "meaning and prediction" criterion, then the researcher is generally justified in allowing this criterion primarily to guide his choice. This criterion is an important and usually neglected approach to the reconciliation of the symbolic interactionist, *verstehen*, and statistical schools of thought in methodology.

THE PHILOSOPHY OF SCIENCE AND THE DIVERSE MEANINGS OF THE CONCEPT OF "RELATIONSHIP" IN SOCIOLOGICAL RESEARCH

The philosophy of science, or what Popper views as "the logic of scientific discovery," offers many formal guideposts to the evaluation of the reliability of research findings and the adequacy of the procedures and assumptions by which the findings are obtained. A number of logicians, mathematicians, and social statisticians have called attention to the importance of not only satisfying the explicit and implicit requirements about the nature of quantitative data but also stating explicitly how the researcher has in fact satisfied these requirements in his particular study.

Formulation of unambiguous categories, replicability of observations, attainment of the necessary level of precision to warrant ordering the data with a given scale, sensitivity to negative or unanticipated evidence, clarity in the hypothesis or causal relationship to be investigated, sufficient sample size, minimization of nonrandom error in the collection and analysis of data, and allowance for the operation of random error are among the requirements for the proper interpretation of statistical tests of significance and many measures of association. But few research reports dealing with these tests and measures accord attention to all of these requirements. Frequently, the scientific audience is assured of the sufficiency of sample size and the allowance for the operation of random error but is given little basis to believe that the other requirements are entirely (or even partially) satisfied. Because many seemingly meticulous research reports fail to show whether these requirements have been met, the dimensions and implications of such a failure are an important area of concern in methodology.

Moreover, the elements of formal logic common to all types of sociological research, such as the logical possibility of disproving a substantive hypothesis and the operational translatability of an empirical claim into the testable form "if A . . . then B," are cases in point of the application of scientific method to the social sciences.

The logical differences between a statistical correlation and a causal relationship, and the differences between the magnitude and direction of an apparent association, have been emphasized by Hume, Nagel, Blalock, Costner, and Somers. Some philosophers of science and sociologists (Popper, Hayek, Kuhn, Selvin, Lynd, Mannheim, Mills) also call attention to the differences between the *validity* of an assertion and the importance it may or may not have. This is often expressed as the distinction between the statistical significance and substantive importance of a relationship–the difference between trivia and socially relevant knowledge–and recently emphasized by spokesmen of the new sociology.

THE HISTORY OF METHODOLOGY AND THE HISTORY OF IDEAS:
Continuities and Discontinuities in the Advancement of Sociological Inquiry

The sociological thought of St. Simon, Comte, Marx and Durkheim emerged in the context of Enlightenment philosophy and in an effort to solve the problem of (1) improving the reliability of methods of research used to obtain knowledge about social progress and (2) identifying the social and cognitive processes by which such knowledge is acquired, interpreted and applied to the goal of social progress. To know the history of research procedures is to know why some problems rather than others persist or are ignored;

this leads to methodological self-awareness. As Max Weber and Karl Mannheim clearly recognized, the methodological self-awareness of the researcher is a necessary factor in establishing whatever reliability his findings may have. The perspectives of Condorcet and Fourier, for example, deserve far more attention than they are now given because they represent major efforts to use social statistics in the service of radical humanistic values and because their influence in contemporary sociology is virtually nil; they are rarely mentioned even in textbooks on the history of statistics and methodology in the social sciences.

Unfortunately, the history of methods of research, unlike history of sociological theory, has not received the systematic attention which an appreciation of the interdependence between research and theory would seem to warrant. (a) One can examine the insights and oversights made by pioneering social analysts from the standpoint of their methodological strategies and assumptions. (b) One can identify the continuities and discontinuities in the adherence to comparative methods (such as those of Aristotle, Thucydides, Toynbee, Weber, and Kroeber); quantitative methods (of Conring, Fourier, Condorcet, Quetelet, Tarde, LePlay, Stouffer, Lazarsfeld, Hyman); introspective and participant-observation methods (of Socrates, Augustine, Rousseau, Freud, Cooley, Thomas and Znaniecki, Whyte, Goffman, Piaget); and various dialectic and synthetic methods (of Fanon, Marx, Adorno, Durkheim, Schurmann, Horney). Although these methods often overlap in the work of a particular researcher, one can fruitfully inquire into the historical patterning by which some methods rather than others rise to and fall from prominence as well as the world-views and manifest reasons advanced by the practitioners themselves in justification of such shifting methodological emphases.

THE LIFE HISTORY OF A RESEARCHER: His Specific Skills and Limitations Matched to Appropriate Methods of Research

The life history of a researcher, particularly his training experience, self-image, world-view, psychological capacities for empathy and introspection, and the primary and secondary socialization experiences which molded these capacities, can heavily influence the decision to engage in qualitative or quantitative research. These aspects of one's life history can influence the prospects for successful or unsuccessful results in pursuing qualitative or quantitative research. In addition to an emphasis on the alternative methods of research available for the solution of a given problem, a major task of methodology is *to furnish guideposts to the fruitful matching of a researcher's capacities and the alternative methods most suitable for him in solving the problem.* Although all researchers should be aware of a wide spectrum of qualitative and quantitative methods, extremely few social scientists have been equally masterful in or comfortable with all methods. The very fact that such men as Goffman and Selvin both engage in empirical research into leadership while neither employs the other's procedures is one among many cases in point which could be given. The task for methodology, then, is (a) to identify the aforementioned guideposts and (b) to develop ways by which one's special research capacities can be maximized, limitations and insensitivities minimized, and methodological self-awareness continually exercised in the course of ongoing research.

SOME GENERAL AND SPECIFIC DISTINCTIONS BETWEEN QUALITATIVE AND QUANTITATIVE RESEARCH

After taking into account the points of similarity and logical complimentarity in qualitative and quantitative research, the varieties of each type of research should be differentiated and the special advantages and limitations associated with their use given critical scrutiny. The ways in which various qualitative and quantitative methods are used in different phases of a given research project, such as the use of intensive interviewing in field work prior to the formulation of a questionnaire in the design of survey research, also warrant formal explication.

The varieties of qualitative research include introspection (which can encompass the exercise of reflective intelligence in the symbolic interactionist sense and interpretive free association in the psychoanalytic sense); participant-observation and *verstehen** research; detailed content and documentary analysis; imaginary experiments and "ideal type" analysis; comparative and historical analysis of unique or complex events not readily amenable to quantification. These approaches are not mutually exclusive.

*Participant-observation research is most closely associated with the Chicago school of thought, especially with Mead, Cooley, Dewey, Faris, Wirth and Blumer. It is also traditionally associated with the work of Weber, Dilthey, Simmel and their followers. The latter scholars are primarily concerned with *verstehen* (use of "imaginary experiments" or creative reconstructions of historical events) for the development of empathetically sensitized concepts and the testing of hypotheses.

One might argue that a working definition of qualitative research is that it deals with data which are *relatively* unamenable to standardization, replication, and quantification. The distinction between qualitative and quantitative research would then be merely a question of the degree to which the data are quantifiable. Unfortunately, such an approach tends to obscure the special problems incurred in each type of research and to overlook the role of the researcher (including his own temperamental and cultural characteristics) in various research settings. These special problems and the role of the researcher are central to methodology.

The varieties of quantitative research include experimental or "laboratory-controlled" observations; survey research; assembly and use of census data; the development and application of various statistical tests, magnitudinal measures of association and directional indicators of causal relationship or asymmetry between variables. Among the major cautions which must be kept in mind when evaluating the reliability of quantitative findings are: the need to avoid the fallacies of confounding individual and group data (the "ecological fallacy" and the "nosnibor fallacy" named after Robinson); the temptation to overlook the probability and capacity for the redefinition of attitudes and values in the interaction among social selves despite the apparent rigor with which attitudes and values are measured; the importance of determining whether formal assumptions have in fact been met by the researcher who uses a given test of significance or level of measurement to establish a hypothesized relationship.

Although many types of quantitative research rely upon data gathered by interviewers using structured questionnaires, the fact remains that very little attention is accorded to the evaluation of the risk of systematic bias (a major source of nonrandom error) when statistical relationships are reported to the scientific audience. Although many types of qualitative research depend upon information obtained in open-ended interviews with respondents in their "natural" social context, a similarly scant degree of attention is accorded to the risk of bias on the part of the field worker or participant-observer who gathers and classifies such data. While there are several treatises and manuals which provide suggestions on the minimization and evaluation of such risk in qualitative and quantitative research, such risk is candidly discussed with an instructive rarity and brevity in published research reports. A task of the methodologist, then, is to evaluate these risks even when a research report ignores or obscures their presence. Although one cannot generalize *a priori* about the reliability of a given finding on the basis of any single criterion, there is probably a close and direct relationship between (a) the degree to which the risk of bias is ignored, obscured or lightly dismissed by a researcher and (b) the probability that such a risk is present, high, and an important contribution to the unreliability of the findings included in the research report. A systematic methodological study of this relationship (which I believe is closer and more direct than a researcher might wish to concede in his own work) would itself be a major contribution to our knowledge of the effect of bias on the reliability of a given research finding in qualitative and quantitative research.

Another problem inherent in the social context of the interview is to assess the importance and typicality with which a respondent redefines his attitudes, including his definition of the questions and answers arising from the interview, in open-ended and highly structured interview settings. The interview itself may have an effect on the respondent's attitudes toward the topics about which he is questioned. The process by which attitudes are made into salient objects and redefined by the respondent—who is a social self whether or not the researcher acknowledges this fact—is often extremely difficult to identify and estimate.

The aforementioned cautions are applicable to many forms of qualitative research which deal with the characteristic attitudes and values regarding the distribution of such structural resources as wealth, power and prestige and the perceptions which a social participant has of himself and others in various settings.

Even if one's findings seem to support a given hypothesis at a high level of statistical significance, at least two possibilities must be taken into account before the findings can be properly interpreted.

1. If a certain set of findings becomes known to the kind of persons who had been under study, such persons might alter their behavior in protest of, sympathy with, or other response to those findings. Many research findings have built-in tendencies, both actual and potential, to bring about social changes which lead to the inapplicability or inaccuracy of what had originally been a reliable characterization of events. Unless a researcher specifies both the likelihood that his findings may affect the behavior under study *and* the pattern or patterns of change which may ensue, there is little reason to believe that his findings are an accurate long-term characterization of the behavior even though extremely precise indices and rigorous interval scales are used in his report.
2. The risk that an apparent relationship or measure of association is the result of random error (the operation of chance or random fluctuations in one's sample) can be accurately evaluated by the performance of an appropriate test of significance. However, such a test cannot indicate the risk that the relationship is the result of *non*random error in the sampling of a population, coding of data, and ordering of categories. Such a test can only indicate the mathematical probability that random variation could have produced a relationship as strong as the one obtained in a large number of trials or "dry runs." Unless the researcher actually demonstrates the steps he took to minimize the influence of ideological bias and technical inadvertence in the course of his research, there is little reason to assume that he did in fact take these steps and that his findings are substantively reliable; the presentation of some obtained relationship at the .01 or even the .001 level of significance does not warrant a relaxation of methodological skepticism regarding the reliability (as opposed to precision *per se*) of the findings in question.

As previously mentioned, the aforementioned possibilities are usually ignored in research reports in the sociological literature and, indeed, in virtually all of the scholarly journals in social science. Since a qualitative researcher is also faced with the possibilities that his findings will affect his subject matter and that his observations are systematically biased or obtained from a study of unique or unrepresentative behavior, he has certain problems in common with the social statistician. A sociological analysis of conditions under which a researcher is most and least likely to acknowledge and solve these problems is as important to the methodologist as to the sociologist of knowledge.

THE PLACE OF SOCIOLOGICAL RESEARCH IN MODERN SOCIETY

The major decisions affecting the political, economic, educational, medical and military institutions in modern society are increasingly legitimized by sociological expertise and research findings obtained through contracts, consultantships, retainers, or other special arrangements between a funding agency and a researcher. The researcher often relies upon large research institutes as his "base of operations." Specific kinds of technical facilities and professional hierarchies prevail in such research bureaus. What are the intended and unintended consequences of (a) the high or low reliability of any research findings presented; (b) the problems which are systematically raised or neglected by the researcher; (c) the social manipulation or "social engineering" by commercial and governmental agencies which solicit and utilize the findings; (d) the assumptions, if any, about the nature of social reality, human personality, the Cold War, and the distribution of political power generated by or inherent in these arrangements? Does the fact that a given research project is classified as "secret" or carried out in the interest of national security affect the reliability of prospective findings? What are the consequences, if any, of these arrangements for the development of the community of scholarship so essential to the public criticism and dialogue which make scientific progress possible? These are among the queries that have been raised by Popper, Cicourel, Mannheim, E. Becker, P. Goodman, Mills, Merton, Horowitz, and acknowledged by Lazarsfeld to be of great significance in the future of sociological research.

The pervasiveness of the "publish or perish" outlook of many universities, the emphasis on vertical career mobility, the occasional tendencies toward scientism, and a frequently uncritical acceptance of models in the physical sciences for purposes of sociological research (most explicitly advocated in Lundberg's *Can Science Save Us?*) have contributed to the likelihood that the truth-content and social relevance of one's findings are not the uppermost aims of every researcher. A task for methodology is to ascertain whether and to what degree this likelihood exists in different types of research and its implications for the reliability of a specific set of findings. Such a task can be approached in terms of the following illustrative and leading questions.

(1) Do researchers follow up their recommendations for supplementary inquiry or "implications for future research" which are often routinely included at the conclusion of their published research reports? (2) Do theories which have been found to be based on spurious evidence continue to be uncritically accepted? (For example, Max Weber's thesis in *Protestant Ethic* continues to be widely acclaimed as if it is flawless despite the fact that Weber relied heavily on the statistical data in Offenbacher's work which Samuelson has shown to be unsound).

To the extent that recommendations for further research are not followed up and refuted theories or unsound findings continue to be espoused, one can infer that irrationality is present in the working procedures and assumptions in such an intellectual discipline. An ultimate task of methodology is to estimate the prevalence of these conditions and to indicate ways to eliminate or reduce it wherever possible.

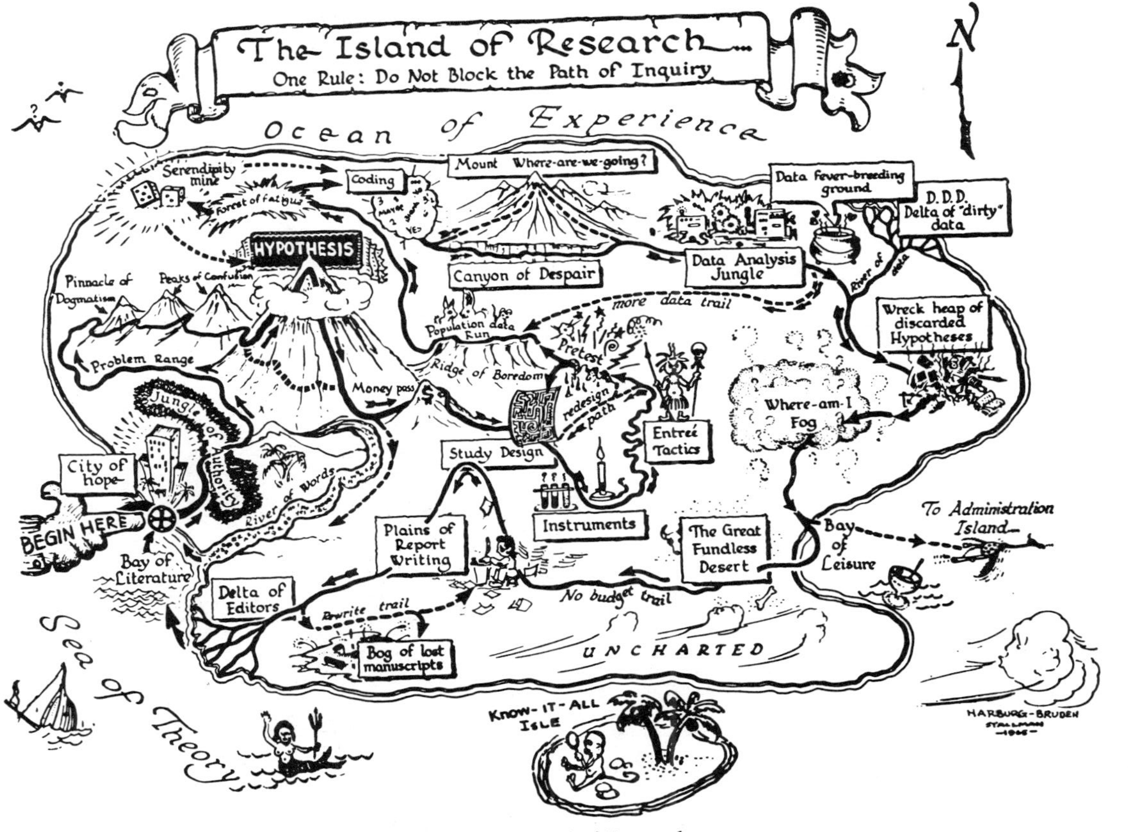

Figure 1. The Island of Research

PART ONE:

Things Old, New, Borrowed and Blue—Wedding Sociology and Science

In attempting to assume the stance of a physical science, we have necessarily assumed its epistemology, its assumptions about the nature of knowledge and the appropriate means of knowing, including the rules of scientific evidence. . . . One of the consequences of using the natural science model was to break down human behavior in a way that was not only artificial but which did not jibe with the manner in which the behavior was observed. . . . We concentrate on consistency without much concern with what it is we are being consistent about or whether we are consistently right or wrong. As a consequence we may have been learning a great deal about how to pursue an incorrect course with a maximum of precision.

Irwin Deutscher
Words and Deeds: Social Science and Social Policy

TOPIC I: The Methods (and Madness) of Science

To a very great extent the term "science" is reserved for fields that do progress in obvious ways. Nowhere does this show more clearly than in the recurrent debates about whether one or another of the contemporary social sciences is really a science. . . . Can a definition tell a man whether he is a scientist or not? If so, why do not natural scientists or artists worry about the definition of the term? Inevitably one suspects that the issue is more fundamental. Probably questions like the following are really asked: Why does my field fail to move ahead in the way that, say, physics does? What changes in technique or method or ideology would enable it to do so?

Thomas S. Kuhn
The Structure of Scientific Revolutions

I.

As Irwin Sperber mentions in the introductory article, sociologists have paid little attention to the history of methodology and the development of their strategies of attack (most of which have been borrowed—to use a polite term—from the natural and physical sciences). The result is, of course, a situation where researchers learn how to drive the car but have absolutely no idea as to the principles behind its operation. If it breaks down, no one knows how to fix it. Many younger academics today feel the discipline has broken down. Many are seeking the knowledge necessary to replace flat tires on the sociological bandwagon with their own brand of tiger paws.

The point of this is that an awareness of what the scientific method is and what it is not is crucial if one is planning to use this method to study some aspect of the world. Traditionally, sociologists have accepted the scientific method as *the* means by which to gather information about the social world. Today, the issue of whether or not the method is appropriate to the problems it is applied to is being raised. "We may have been learning a great deal about how to pursue an incorrect course with a maximum of precision," says Irwin Deutscher. If sociologists continue to ignore the history and nature of methodology and the scientific method, they will never emerge from this cul-de-sac.

Gideon Sjoberg and Roger Nett realize the problem, and in *A Methodology for Social Research*, attempt to present a sociological explanation for the development of the scientific method in the West. They employ a "sociology of knowledge" approach to delineate the rise of rationalism in Europe, and trace the basis for the scientific method back to the melding of abstract conceptual thought of the elite with the grounded and manipulative behavior of the lower class artisans and merchants in the crucible of the French Revolution. Sjoberg and Nett go on to discuss the nature of theory and data in the social sciences. They point out that in present-day sociology there still exists a basic distinction between those interested mainly in abstract conceptualizing (general theorists) and those interested in actual human behavior and "grounded" data collection and handling (empiricists). As James Davis puts it in a later article in this book:

> By and large, the fashionable people in sociology are the "action painters" who dribble their thoughts on the canvas of the journals, unrestrained by systematic evidence, while at the opposite pole there are hoards of "engineers" who grind out academic development housing according to the mechanical formulas of elementary statistics texts. It is not easy to steer between these two courses.

To be methodologically prepared in sociology is to recognize and understand this gap between theory and research, an issue Norman K. Denzin discusses in his article, "The Substance of Sociological Theory."

II.

Denzin points to Herbert Blumer's discussion of what is wrong with sociological theory.* Contemporary theory, Blumer charges, has become divorced from the empirical world; has rested heavily on the importation of images, models, and metaphors from other sciences; and is incapable of utilizing available empirical observation.

> Social theory in general shows grave shortcomings. Its divorcement from the empirical world is glaring. To a preponderant extent it is compartmentalized into a world of its own, inside of which it feeds on itself. . . .Further, when applied to the empirical world social theory is primarily an interpretation which orders the world into its mold, not a studious cultivation of empirical facts to see if the theory fits. . .[1]

Blumer's point, that abstract theory divorced from the real world can be meaningless, is echoed in another medium by the artist Joseph Kosuth.

*Note that Denzin uses a much more restrictive definition of social theory than do Sjoberg and Nett. Denzin's definition is similar to Sjoberg and Nett's description of logico-deductive theory–to their way of thinking, only one type among many.

> When Washington's new Protetch–Rivkin Gallery held an exhibit of conceptual art not long ago, Mr. Kosuth contributed a series of labels bearing declarative sentences such as "Logicians who eat pork chops are not likely to lose money." The propositions are pure nonsense, having nothing to do with logicians or pork chops in the real world. Neither do they add up to anything. They form, rather, a self–contained system not unlike a series of propositions in geometry. This demonstrates Mr. Kosuth's contention that art is a closed system, referring only to itself.[2]

Transferring this argument to the arena of social theory, do closed theoretical systems refer to reality any more often? Herbert Blumer feels that unless the concepts that form the propositions of the system are clearly specified and grounded in reality, the answer is probably no.

> The heart of the difficulty, Blumer suggests, lies in the current status and use of the sociological concept. A concept must meet three simple rules: (1) it must clearly point to a class of objects; (2) it must permit distinctions between that class and other classes; and (3) it must direct empirical activity. When these rules are met the concept serves three important functions: (1) it opens areas of empirical inquiry; (2) it directs concrete observations through the use of different research methods; and (3) it opens the door for theoretical development. By permitting data to be gathered, data that are conceptually relevant, hypotheses can be put to test.[3]

In order to clarify and specify concepts, sociologists have to define them. Definition is the process of communication: of showing someone else what is in your head; how you view the world. A concept, specified by a symbol or a word, can mean many things, depending on who is defining it and how.

> "When I use a word," Humpty Dumpty said, in a rather scornful tone, "it means just what I choose it to mean–neither more nor less."
>
> "The question is," said Alice, "whether you *can* make words mean so many different things."
>
> "The question is," said Humpty Dumpty, "which is to be master–that's all."[4]

Being master includes knowing how you are defining the word. Denzin notes three differing types of definition: nominal, real, and operational. Anatol Rapoport, in his selection, "What Is X?" makes an important distinction between nominal and real definitions on the one hand (which he labels as "verbal") and operational definitions on the other. Operational definitions serve to specify sharply the meaning of symbolic and theoretical concepts as they apply to the real world. As such, these definitions are the connecting links between the abstract symbolic systems of words, concepts, and propositions and the real world of empirical events.

Rapoport feels that operational definitions are the answer to the problem of bridging the gap between theory and research. Denzin, however, urges caution in this regard. His view encompasses more of a gradual sensitization of concepts, rather than immediate operationalization.

> By *sensitizing concepts* I refer to concepts that are not transformed immediately into *operational definitions*. . . . An operational definition defines a concept by stating how it will be observed. Thus if I offer an *operational definition* for intelligence, I might state that intelligence is the score received on an I.Q. test. But if I choose a *sensitizing approach* to measuring intelligence, I will leave it nonoperationalized until I enter the field and learn the processes representing it and the specific meanings attached to it by the persons observed. . . . Sensitizing a concept permits the sociologist to discover what is unique about each empirical instance of the concept while he uncovers what it displays in common across many different settings. . . . Ultimately all concepts must be operationalized. . .The sensitizing approach merely delays the point at which operationalization occurs.[5]

Concepts are the building blocks for propositions, or hypotheses: the stuff of social theory. In the model on the next page, the operational definition should be considered a two-way street.

III.

Theory and research are so interwoven in actual practice that it is impossible to give "rules" for which comes first and in what order each should be considered (although some texts attempt to do just this). As Robert Merton has stated, sometimes theory comes first; sometimes research. Merton's discussion of the place of research and research methods in this interactive process of investigation holds that research can:

1. *initiate* theory, especially if the data from the real world are unanticipated and thus lead to new theoretical connections and ideas (the process of serendipity);
2. *reformulate* theory, if new data reveal weaknesses in the existing arrangement of propositions and hypotheses;
3. *deflect* theory, or change the focus of theoretic interest as new research (and research techniques) suggest differing avenues of investigation; and

Figure 2. Formal Theory and Its Links to the Real World

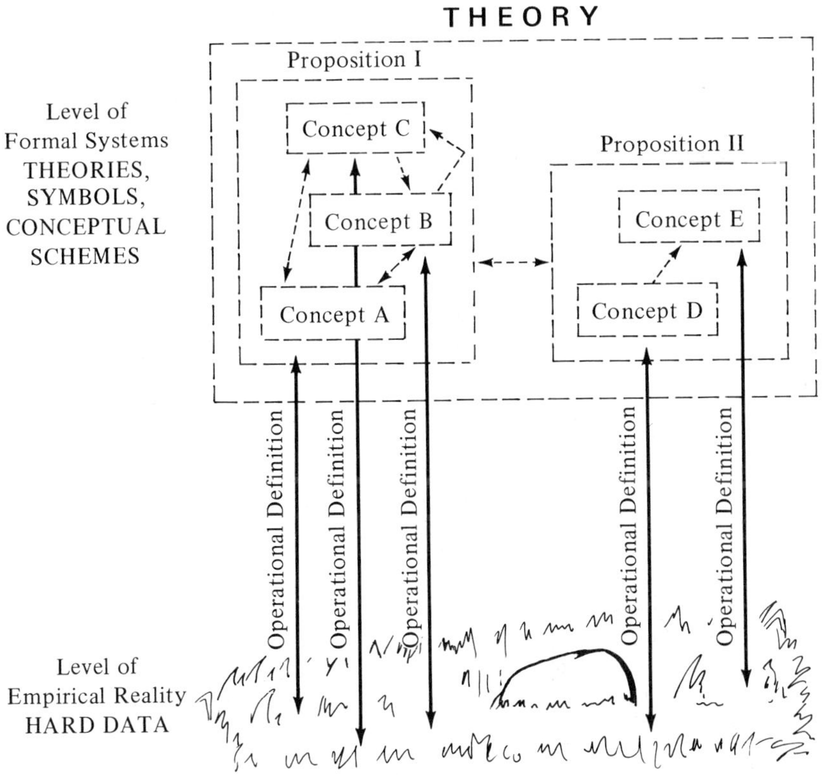

4. *clarify* theory and the concepts involved in the theoretical systems.[6]

So it is no one-way street, as the compartmentalization of "theory" and "methods" in separate courses in most sociology departments might lead you to suspect. The two are inextricably intertwined in practice. Sophisticated methodological procedures are needed so that one can recognize anomalous findings. Sophisticated theory needs to exist so that there will be something to test.[7]

NOTES

1. Herbert Blumer, "What Is Wrong With Social Theory?" *American Sociological Review* 19 (February 1955): 3.
2. Bill Marvel, "Art That Isn't There," *The National Observer,* July 1970.

3. Norman K. Denzin, *Sociological Methods: A Sourcebook* (Chicago: Aldine, 1970), p. 48.
4. Lewis Carroll, *Complete Works of Lewis Carroll* (New York: Random House, 1936), p. 14.
5. Norman K. Denzin, *The Research Act* (Chicago: Aldine, 1970), pp. 14–15.
6. Robert K. Merton, *Social Theory and Social Structure* (New York: Free Press, 1957), p. 103.
7. Herbert H. Hyman, "Reflections On the Relations Between Theory and Research," *The Centennial Review* 7 (Fall 1963): 431–53.

SUGGESTED FURTHER READING

Catton, William J. *From Animistic to Naturalistic Sociology.* New York: McGraw–Hill, 1966.

Cohen, Morris, and Nagel, E. *An Introduction to Logic and Scientific Methods.* New York: Harcourt, Brace and World, 1960.

DiRenzo, Gordon. *Concepts, Theory and Explanation in the Behavioral Sciences.* New York: Random House, 1967.

Glazer, Barney G., and Strauss, Anselm L. *The Discovery of Grounded Theory.* Chicago: Aldine, 1967.

Kuhn, Thomas S. *The Structure of Scientific Revolutions.* Chicago: University of Chicago Press, 1962.

Merton, Robert K. *Social Theory and Social Structure,* pp. 85–117. New York: Free Press, 1957.

Popper, Karl. *The Logic of Scientific Discovery.* New York: Basic Books, 1959.

Rapoport, Anatol. *Operational Philosophy.* New York: Harper and Bros., 1953.

Reichenbach, Hans. *The Rise of Scientific Philosophy.* Berkley: University of California Press, 1951.

Stinchcomb, Arthur. *Constructing Social Theories.* New York: Harcourt, Brace and World, 1968.

Zetterberg, Hans L. *On Theory and Verification in Sociology.* Totowa, N.J.: Bedminster Press, 1965.

Basic Orientations Toward the Scientific Method

Gideon Sjoberg and Roger Nett

A brief sketch of the history of the scientific enterprise provides us with a perspective on modern science and at the same time serves as a backdrop against which we can review the basic postulates underlying the scientific method as well as the conceptions of theory and data among sociologists

SCIENCE HAS A HISTORY[1]

If science today embodies an approach to knowledge that is far more disciplined and calculated than the ordinary inclinations of humans, it has become so only after a slow passage through many painful stages of development. The earliest step, taken in some remote prehistoric age, was the discernment of predictable patterns in the natural environment. Even this bit of knowledge proved useful to man in his efforts to push outward the very narrow confines nature imposed upon his activity. Earliest man, like his modern descendants functioned with a mixture of idealism and realism.

Preliterate man's advances, over several millennia, occurred mainly in two spheres: technology (which includes not only material objects such as tools but also the objective knowledge of how to use them) and social organization. The roster of technological inventions is long: These range from the primeval use of fire to the extraction and working of metals and the development of techniques in animal husbandry and agriculture. These technological innovations both depended upon and led to the creation of complex social organizations. For example, large-scale irrigation systems seem to have required the coordinated activity of hundreds of persons operating under an effective leadership. In turn, the economic surplus made possible by such irrigation systems permitted the development of specialists who could direct activities in the technological sphere.

Out of some of those human settlements with a more complex social organization cities ultimately emerged. Concomitantly, the expanding body of knowledge now demanded, and made possible, a small literate group with sufficient leisure time to sustain and add to the society's accumulated body of learning. It is with the rise of cities and the formation of a literate urban elite that civilization, as we know it, evolved.

The invention of writing, among other factors, accelerated greatly the tempo of social and technological change. The impetus given to human knowledge and intellectual activity by the ability to maintain records cannot be overestimated.[2] The written word not only enabled man to build more readily upon his achievements, but it also facilitated greatly the diffusion of learning across regions and across cultures.

From the time of the emergence of the earliest cities about 5500 years ago up to the scientific and industrial revolution in Europe a few centuries ago, advances occurred on many fronts. As we review the course of man's creativity since the dawn of recorded history, we are impressed by his inventions in the realm of abstract thought. The development of the concept of zero and of such logical systems as that of Aristotle laid the groundwork for the modern scientific revolution. Nor should we minimize the contributions of speculative philosophy. Although many theories closed men's eyes to new ideas and knowledge, speculative thought, on the whole, extended man's range of curiosity, to the profit of later generations seeking to break through the stubborn crust of ignorance.

Alongside these more abstract contributions to human thought, which arose primarily out of society's intellectual or learned class, were the more practical technological contributions of the artisans and merchants. Particularly within the urban environment, the commingling of men of diverse perspectives sparked the formation of new ideas and techniques. Arising out of these preindustrial cities, too, were certain major feats of engineering, such as the aqueducts and roads of the Roman Empire.[3] And not to be overlooked were the improvements in weaponry, which made possible the expansion and destruction of empires. In turn, of course, these technological achievements rested upon advances in man's organizational skills and knowledge.

Although a considerable accretion of knowledge occurred before the dawn of the "modern era," preindustrial civilized societies, those in China, India, the Middle East, and even in Europe, were fundamentally distinct in form, if not in content, from the social orders that took shape in Western Europe after the sixteenth century with the beginning of the scientific and industrial revolution.

In the preindustrial civilized order the nature of thought and action was intimately linked with the society's social structure, notably the power structure, and overall value orientation. Thus, the literati, the small learned group who made up an important segment of the privileged elite, were little interested in applying their ideas to problems on the practical and mundane level. Typically, these persons were either part of or strongly influenced by the religious structure, one that was committed to perpetuating the traditional, sacred body of learning, not to the formulation of new ideas or critical evaluation of the learned heritage.

Just what was the traditional system of knowledge? Primarily it reflected a particular orientation to the social and physical environment. Generally, these latter were assumed to be fixed and immutable, beyond man's immediate control. Indeed, the natural order was viewed as sacrosanct: One could seek to manipulate it only with dire consequences. The educated man, therefore, typically did not experiment either with nature or with society. Instead, he sought to adapt himself to forces whose workings were beyond his immediate comprehension.

Quite in harmony with this conceptualization of reality are magical practices, utilized in varying degrees by all ranks of the preindustrial civilized order. We must recognize that there is a fundamental distinction between magic and science. Magical practices are predicated upon the assumption that man cannot intervene directly in the functioning of the natural order; rather he seeks to adjust to the natural order and, with the aid of supernatural forces, to maintain the "balance" in nature or restore this balance when "evil" forces have acted to upset it.

The history of medicine, for example, exemplifies the general failure of the literati to seek to manipulate nature directly. In China, India, and traditional Europe complicated medical theories were developed to explain the functioning of the human body. But rarely were these theories tested against reality. Not only did learned men assume that they could not change the sacred and/or natural order directly, but they had a disdain for physical labor, for such was considered the proper activity of the lower classes and outcaste groups. Consequently, the early physicians and scholars in the field of "physiology" and medicine rarely resorted to dissecting human or animal cadavers in order to acquire new knowledge or verify existing theories. Hippocrates, although he treated biological factors in naturalistic terms by removing them from the realm of the sacred, nevertheless shied away from the dirty business of dissection. Even Galen, the Roman physician whose writings on anatomy remained the final authority on the subject for thirteen centuries, used only animals to check his theories about the functioning of the human body. When finally his ideas were tested in the sixteenth century by Andreas Vesalius, the first scholar to systematically dissect and study the human cadaver, they did not stand up. The struggles of Vesalius with his empiricist views against the traditions of the ages (for example, to obtain cadavers he often had to resort to theft) have recently been detailed in a compelling manner by O'Malley, a medical historian whose work sheds much light on the evolution of modern science.[4]

But the field of medicine is only one among many that have undergone marked revision since the preindustrial civilized period. Although the Greeks made progress in other realms of natural science, it was typically in areas such as astronomy or botany where considerable description could be accomplished with little need to experiment. To be sure, some historians of science, such as De Solla Price,[5] see certain Greeks as manipulating the natural order to a degree; however, we side with Gillispie, who, among other scholars, stresses the fundamental novelty of the modern scientific revolution:

> Greek science was subjective, rational, and purely intellectual. It started inside the mind whence concepts like purpose, soul, life, and organism were projected outward to explain phenomena in the familiar terms of self-knowledge. . . . Greek science scarcely knew experiment and never thought to move beyond curiosity to power. Modern science, on the other hand, is impersonal and objective. . . . Modern science has not abandoned rationality, but it is first of all metrical and experimental. Related to this is its association with technology as a continuation of that generalized thrust toward mastery of the world which began in the West with the Renaissance.[6]

And bear in mind that the intellectual activity of classical Greece was far advanced over the efforts of earlier preindustrial societies which erected large-scale barriers against any independent probing of the sacred or natural order. If the progress of the Greeks has seemed impressive it is because their activities so markedly contrasted with what had transpired before as well as with what was accomplished during many centuries afterward. Their attainments in the field of "science," however, are all too readily exaggerated.

But what about the nature of social science in preindustrial civilized orders? Here some of the same patterns obtained as in natural science. The philosophical skills of various intellectuals—their contributions in the moral, theological, and philosophical realms—rank in the forefront of man's most constructive endeavors. The great religions of the modern world all have been associated with major intellectual achievements of one sort or another. At the same time, the heavy commitment of the intellectual elite in the preindustrial order to the sacred learning tended to vitiate the evolution of any social science—of any "objective" and "value-free" enterprise geared to accumulating knowledge and discovering principles grounded in empirical reality, by which man could manipulate his social environment and thus command a higher degree of control over his own destiny. Instead, the intellectuals, dominated usually by the priestly group, were intent upon upholding traditional values. And given the nature of the social order to which they belonged, one that resisted rapid social change, the intellectuals were able to isolate themselves from conflicting cultural values and, therefore, many of the issues that trouble modern thinkers.

Here again we can cite deviations from the general pattern, notably in classical Greece. The works of certain Greek theorists suggested important leads for later social scientists. The Arabs, too, had their social philosopher, Ibn Khaldun, who wrote such discerning commentaries on the social order of his time that some scholars believe that he, as much as anyone, is entitled to be called the "founder of sociology."[7] Still, in all the varied writings that have come out of preindustrial civilized societies one searches in vain for certain of the crucial tenets that form the basis of modern social science.[8]

Twentieth-century social science and the fledgling endeavors of the preindustrial era differ fundamentally in the kinds of data employed. In most preindustrial urban societies the literati compiled histories, but these were primarily genealogies or records of the leading families and the royal court. Governments amassed certain kinds of data on the operation of the system, materials which are of some sociological value today. And of course there were accounts of military and other events of significance for the society.[9]

But there was a remarkable lack of interest in the society's lower class and outcaste groups. The few records that exist are apt to be the observations of foreign visitors. For the most part, the educated groups rarely interested themselves in the commoners, some of whom were so far below the elite that they hardly held the status of human beings.

Indeed, few scholars wrote about the social order at all, excepting again certain major military, political, and social events. Their all-consuming interests, as we intimated earlier, lay in philosophical and theological issues. Of course, the fields of theology, philosophy, and logic all border on what we consider to be social science, but major efforts at objectively describing or analyzing a society's social structure are rare indeed. Furthermore, the theoretical treatises were often cast in highly stylized and abstruse language. The intellectuals were writing only for themselves and for God–not for the common man, who, in any case, was unable to read or write.

So much for the upper class and its orientation toward social and natural phenomena. The numerically dominant section of society was made up of the lower class and certain outcaste groups, who carried out the menial and defiling tasks and made possible the leisure enjoyed by the literate, privileged elite. In addition, various practical pursuits, including the work of artisans and merchants, were essential if the social system was to be sustained. What is significant is that these practical tasks often involved some manipulation of the natural order. Thus, for example, it fell to members of the lower class, such as barbers, to engage in bloodletting and other crude forms of surgery. The tools that have come down to us from the preindustrial past are mute testimony to the creativity that existed in the practical, workaday world–creativity that had little or no grounding in theory–as the ordinary man attempted, through trial and error, to construct and perfect devices to help him in his battle against nature. Again let us stress that this practical knowledge on the part of the common man was seldom, if ever, conjoined with the theoretical insights of the intellectuals.

Yet the centuries did witness a considerable accumulation of both theory and practical knowledge within the context of preindustrial civilized societies.[10] It was this knowledge that finally laid the basis for the scientific revolution which began to take shape in the fourteenth and fifteenth centuries in Western Europe and culminated in what is termed the industrial revolution.[11] The striking advances that led to the formation of modern science resulted from a merging of theory, or abstract conceptualization (earlier the exclusive province of scholars), with more practical pursuits (the domain of artisans and members of certain service groups). The process, however, was a slow and painful one. Students of the history of engineering argue that even in seventeenth-century Europe most engineering activities were still being carried out largely on an "inductive," hit-or-miss, trial-and-error basis, with little theoretical foundation.[12]

It is significant that the crucial interplay between the theoretical and practical traditions took place at the time of the breakup of the medieval world. As men shed much of their belief in absolutes, they became more willing to attempt to manipulate and control the physical and the social orders for their own ends. In turn, experimentation with the "natural order" led to the introduction of new and heretical ideas. But the traditional social structure did not take kindly to this undermining of the established system of knowledge, with its particular world view. The Catholic Church, for example, often reacted strongly against these new developments–note the severe pressures exerted on Galileo Galilei.[13] Various forms of social control, some subtle and others not so subtle, ranging from censorship and ostracism to capital punishment itself, were employed to stem the flow of ideas that were eroding the fundamental premises of the medieval world.

The crumbling of the old order was fostered and intensified by the heightened contacts with diverse cultures that characterized the golden age of exploration. Europe after the fourteenth century became a receptacle for new ideas that were carried back by travelers from strange and distant lands. Inevitably this growing awareness of the existence of diverse customs hastened the secularization process. In time, scholars such as Vico and Montesquieu began to reflect upon the reasons for the differing customs and beliefs in other parts of the world. This process led intellectuals to see their own society in different perspective. The foundation for a science of society, as we know it, was being laid.

Although scholars from almost all parts of Europe contributed to the intellectual renaissance, it was in England and northwestern Europe that the scientific and industrial revolution finally came into its own. In England the conditions were even more propitious than on the Continent. The British value system, including that of the Puritans, may, as Merton suggests, have provided a fertile seedbed for the growth of science.[14] But more significantly, the hiatus between the social classes and the intellectual's separation from the world of practical affairs were not so marked in England as in the more tradition-bound countries on the Continent. And England's contacts with the outside world, reinforced by her growing dependence upon trade, did much to further this atmosphere of change.

The scientific-industrial revolution was destined to affect the entire world. It brought about drastic changes in the European social structure and set the stage for a permanent, ongoing revolution. Indeed, science can be viewed as a social movement in its own right. Scientific activity has for some centuries been supported by a loose, though effective, social organization, and its supporters have had an ideology of their own, tinged with a utopian dream of a more perfect society. If we accept Feuer's somewhat controversial thesis, the supporters of the scientific revolution, as it faltered and was revived in different times and places, had a strong commitment to a "hedonist-libertarian" ethic. Feuer, moreover, contends that only when scientists became firmly committed to such a value system did science really begin to prosper.[15]

The scientific-industrial revolution made social science possible, but the emergence of a true science of society was perhaps more directly abetted by what can be viewed as a byproduct of this scientific-technological change: namely, the French Revolution. Without doubt, much of European sociology in the 1800s was a reaction to the upheaval that followed from the destruction of traditional authority and power structures.[16]

Such a context makes it easier to understand why the social movement that carried forward the scientific-industrial revolution engendered counter-movements of its own. Some of these appeared in the early stages of modern scientific development, during the Renaissance; others came to the fore during the French Revolution; still others were reflected in the negative reaction to Darwinism during the nineteenth century.[17]

Although significant pockets of resistance to the application of the scientific method persist,[18] particularly with respect to social data, the goals and ideals of science have become legitimized in the industrial-urban orders of the West. The physical sciences have achieved startling results, and significant advances are apparent in social research as well.[19]

But at the very time that science has emerged victorious, serious questions are being raised about its proper place in society. Whereas in the nineteenth century a significant number of intellectuals looked to science for a utopian solution to human ills, there are fewer today who would argue that salvation will come solely through the advancement of the scientific method.

World War II, and the events surrounding it, did much to erode the utopian elements in scientific thinking. It became clear that empirically verified knowledge about the social and physical orders could assist various types of nations in attaining their particular goals–be they Nazi Germany's destruction of the European Jews or America's use of nuclear weapons in defeating Japan.

The Nazis employed the advances of natural science, as well as some of the principles we associate with scientific management, to engineer one of the greatest feats of mass destruction in human history: the systematic elimination of five to six million Jews, plus several million Poles, Russians, and other non-Aryans. Hilberg, perhaps more than any other scholar, has documented the Nazis' use of scientific knowledge as a means for achieving "the final solution to the Jewish problem."[20] So too, the development of nuclear weapons has posed a dilemma unique in the history of science. Ironically, scientists are now able to destroy the very social structure that has made the advancement of science possible.

THE BASIC POSTULATES OF SCIENCE

An understanding of the history of science is essential for any analysis of the fundamental premises of the scientific method. For the premises (or postulates) of the method one employs are in part a product of one's image of the evolution of the scientific enterprise.

Actually, there are efforts afoot to reevaluate the premises of science and the scientist's relationship to the products of his method. As some scholars have come to recognize, the invention of nuclear devices capable of destroying the scientific community itself immediately outdated traditional formulations.

In light of the evidence, it would be a mistake to confuse scientifically based knowledge with wisdom, as did some of the utopian thinkers of the nineteenth century. Wisdom involves sound ethical direction, the exercise of good taste, and distinguishing the worthwhile from the not so worthwhile. The scientific method (in the narrow sense) does not tell us how to use empirically verified knowledge other than to further the ends of science; however, by utilizing more of the empirically validated knowledge and less of the unverified and often fiat knowledge of other epistemologies the cause of humanity may be advanced.

It is by detailing the premises of the scientific method, as we shall now attempt to do, that we can gain a more adequate understanding of this method and its place in modern society.

Like the logical positivists, we believe in the unity of science; but our formulation differs considerably from theirs. The logical empiricists have conceived of this unity in terms of a common method; the natural and social sciences are seen as similar because they employ similar procedures in their research.[21] Our belief in the unity of science, however, is derived from assumptions on a higher level of abstraction (or generality).

A minimum set of assumptions (often left unstated) which underlie the application of the scientific method are (1) that there exists a definite order of recurrence of events, (2) that knowledge is superior to ignorance, (3) that a communication tie, based upon sense impressions, exists between the scientist and "external reality" (the so-called "empirical assumption"), and (4) that there are cause-and-effect relationships within the physical and the social orders. Moreover, (5) there are certain "observer" assumptions: (a) that the observer is driven to attain knowledge by his desire to ameliorate human conditions, (b) that the observer has the capacity to conceptually relate observations and impute meanings to events, and (c) that society will sustain the observer in his pursuit of knowledge. These assumptions, which the scientist more or less takes for granted, are in the last analysis largely understandable as "functional fictions." Their usefulness in the acquisition of knowledge is the primary raison d'être.

The Assumption of Order in the "Natural" World

Science, in so far as it seeks to generalize and predict, depends upon the existence of some degree of order in the physical or social world under study. That which it cannot describe as a manifestation of regularity it must define as some describable departure from regularity. Such reasoning assumes that events are ordered along certain dimensions. To be sure, all systems of knowledge rest upon the assumption of order in the universe, but this may be of greater significance for science than for other systems of knowledge. After all, scientists spend most of their time differentiating among classes of relative uniformity and relating these one to another. Even within a rapidly changing, revolutionary system there is a degree of order. And change itself displays patterns that can be described and analyzed.

The assumption of order leads the social scientist, if he is to remain a scientist, to eschew historicism. Those who advocate the historicist position in its extreme form assume that every cultural system must be studied as a separate entity and that, moreover, no regularities obtain across cultures. Of course, even the historicist admits there is a uniformity of sorts, for he recognizes that each system has its own laws of development.

The notion of order is closely related to the concept of a "natural universe." In our sketch of the history of science, we observed that a major breakthrough occurred when scholars were able to conceive of the physical and social environments in naturalistic terms, that is, as functioning independently of factors in the spiritual realm. This was an essential step in modern man's development of the means to manipulate and positively control aspects of the social and physical spheres.

In contrast, when one assumes the presence of "supernatural forces," one opens up the possibility of capricious change that cannot be studied via scientific procedures–let alone controlled to any degree. In the days when men, including scholars, perceived of their environment as laden with spirits, friendly or hostile, any direct manipulation of these (as opposed to magical practices, which usually attempt to correct the imbalances in nature through indirect means) was assumed to have grave consequences for all concerned. Today scientists believe that they can manipulate and control the natural and social worlds.[22] Concern with nonnatural forces becomes the province of other epistemologies—theology and philosophy.

Knowledge as Superior to Ignorance

This assumption underscores the fact that the chief goal of science is the search for knowledge. It is perhaps the key premise underlying all scientific activity.

The contention that knowledge is eminently preferable to ignorance does not imply that all the mysteries of the universe can or ever will be resolved; rather the scientist assumes that his knowledge of the social and physical worlds can be continually enlarged, at times by accretion, at other times via more revolutionary thrusts.

Of necessity the pursuit of knowledge rests upon the somewhat arbitrary assumption that knowledge is to be desired even where the short-range consequences of new ideas or data are emotional or social trauma for individuals or for the broader society. A corollary of this assumption is that the alternative to knowledge—ignorance—is undesirable and even detrimental to man's well-being. From this it follows that man could overcome the threat of nuclear war, not by lapsing back into ignorance but by acquiring more adequate knowledge.

The assumption that knowledge is superior to ignorance frequently places those who support the scientific method at odds with the proponents of those epistemologies who define knowledge according to their own particular criteria. Certainly the ideal that human dignity is enhanced when man is restless, inquiring, and "soul-searching" conflicts with a variety of belief systems that would strive toward a closed system, one based on absolute truth. The history of modern science and its clash with absolute systems bears testimony to this proposition.[23]

The concept of the happy, ignorant, implicitly trusting individual doing what arbitrarily assumed authority tells him to do is challenged by the central notion of the scientific method—that knowledge is superior to ignorance. This is the main reason why persons who already "know" and feel no need for further inquiry are threatened by the ongoing scientific revolution. It is also the reason why persons disposed to political authoritarianism must argue that science, already too strong to dispose of, should at least be kept on a leash, so that if "wrong" knowledge develops, it can be outlawed or suppressed, or at least condemned as heresy.

The assumption that knowledge is clearly preferable to ignorance ranges scientists against those groups that glorify "closed systems"—those that encourage bookburning, censoring, and antiintellectualism in general. And science, to survive, must deplore any censoring even of persons who speak out against science in the name of other epistemologies. It follows from this position that science gives man more credit for the ability to judge matters for himself and arrive at decisions based upon his own interpretation of the evidence than is normally granted by the adherents of other epistemologies. For science is fundamentally optimistic about human capacities. It is no mere happenstance that modern science and mass democracy are intimately associated. Democracy, in theory, calls for an open society, with an emphasis upon human dignity. This reinforces some of the assumptions that underlie the scientific method. In turn, the scientific method with its negation of absolutes lends support to democracy.

That the scientific method is also processual and dynamic leads it to clash with many traditional epistemologies. Science must always assume that its findings are tentative, that new evidence may change or even reverse existing theoretical formulations. An important corollary to this is that science cannot harbor fanaticism, that scientists must sustain a highly rational orientation toward their subjects of study and toward any new evidence that is brought to light. Only thereby can science sustain the ideal of knowledge as paramount.

With respect to the preservation of the scientific method, the skeptical outlook toward absolute truth is both a strength and a weakness. It is a strength in the sense that presumably rational man will in the long run act to correct his own errors. It is a weakness in that scientists, not being so confident of the validity of their own assertions as is the general public, may, in those frequent periods when social crises threaten public security, be overrun by absolutists. Science is often temporarily helpless when its bastions are stormed by overzealous proponents of absolute systems of belief.

The Empirical Assumption

Science assumes that a communication tie between man and the external universe is maintained through his own sense impressions. Knowledge is held to be a product of one's experiences, as facets of the physical, biological, and social world play upon the senses. Negatively stated, this premise denies that knowledge about the world is instinctive or inborn, that knowledge necessarily precedes experience. Such an assumption is not unassailable, for it depends upon one's definition of "knowledge." Still, from a historical perspective, the notion that knowledge is based upon some form of empirical test was a reaction against the belief that knowledge, particularly moral understanding, has been innate in human beings. Today almost all learning theory is based upon the "empirical" assumption.

Cause-and-Effect Relationships

Although the concept of "cause and effect" has been the target of considerable criticism since Hume first argued that no one can observe "causation," although a number of scientists have chosen not to write in cause-and-effect terms, and although numerous thorny issues have been involved in the use of this concept even among those scholars who concede its existence, it is still difficult, and often well-nigh impossible, to avoid the assumption that some kind of cause-and-effect relationship does exist. Implicit in the application of the scientific method is the notion that some events occur prior to or concurrently with others and that the former have an impact upon the latter, thereby generating, or causing, specific reactions.

Observer Assumptions

Much less emphasized, but equally essential to the success of the scientific method, are certain assumptions about the scientist himself—what we call "observer assumptions."

We have already mentioned that one of the premises underlying science is the superiority of knowledge over ignorance. Closely related to this premise is the notion that scientific activities in the long run benefit the scientist-observer and his social order. Although conceivably a scientific method that is not dedicated to humanistic goals might develop, the fact remains that science is man's own creation and he is therefore likely to apply the scientific method in terms of his own interests, or, more accurately, in terms of what he perceives to be his own interests. Man, therefore, seems motivated to acquire scientifically based knowledge by the desire to ameliorate his own social condition. Much historical evidence can be adduced in support of the proposition that numerous scientists have been motivated by the belief that science would eventuate in some kind of utopia. Although the specific content of this utopian dream varies considerably, almost always the ideal condition is one that emphasizes freedom, the dignity of man, and the like. Implicit here is the notion that science is not a dehumanizing activity but on the contrary permits man to fulfill some measure of his nobler capacities.

A second observer assumption is that man is or can be made a proper instrument for performing the ratiocinations involved in the application of the scientific method. It is assumed that he can observe, relate, and impute meanings to events—that he can remember, compute, imagine, compare, differentiate, integrate, and thereby place events in their proper perspective.

If man is incapable of performing these tasks, then the requirements of the scientific method are unrealistic and he might as well resign himself to more suitable epistemological undertakings. However, even where man's innate capacities are limited, he may still possess the wherewithal to create instruments that extend his capabilities or in other ways reduce the restrictions placed upon the exercise of his talents. Indeed man has, by recognizing his own weaknesses and then seeking to circumvent them, greatly advanced the cause of science.

A third observer assumption is that the social conditions essential for the application of the scientific method can be sustained. These include not only tolerance of free inquiry but such positive conditions as provision of the machinery and other facilities to meet the needs of scientific endeavor and the presence of a climate of opinion that permits the scientist to function without undue strictures or political pressures. Scientists, like the clergy, may be toughened by persecution, but they hardly flower under it. The necessary conditions for science do not, however, include passivity in the sociopolitical realm, for scientists may have to assume an active role in developing and maintaining the social circumstances conducive to the scientific enterprise.

Implications

We have attempted to isolate those premises underlying the scientific method that are *common* to both the natural and the social sciences. The common assumptions should be kept in mind as we build up to our main thesis: namely, that major differences exist between the natural and the social sciences *in the application* of the scientific method.

Also, looking back upon the premises underlying the scientific method, we must emphasize the limitations these impose upon the activities of scientists. Science does not and cannot reach beyond its own assumptions. It is therefore inadequate for dealing with ultimate causes and other problems so dear to human beings. As with all fields of knowledge, an understanding of the premises permits one to comprehend both the weaknesses and the strengths of the scientific method.

THE NATURE OF THEORY AND DATA

Our sketch of the development of modern science emphasized that its emergence can be traced to that point in time and space when speculative thought and theorizing became systematically linked with empirical data on the technological level, in the practical, workaday world. Theory, as a system of concepts or ideas, is of course not unique to science but is basic to all systems of philosophy and religious thought.

An essential difference, perhaps the only one, between theories in science and in other belief systems lies in the method of validation employed. Scientific theories are necessarily subject to validation through empirical observation, not by fiat or on the basis of tradition.

Although scientists would agree that theory and data are essential features of the scientific method, they disagree, as have philosophers since the days of Hume and Kant, over the relative weight to be assigned to each and over the relationships between the two. Herein we are concerned with the nature of theory and of data in modern sociology and in social science more generally.

The Nature of Scientific Theory

Today most social scientists speak glowingly of the utility of theory. Yet, when we seek an answer to the question, "What is meant by theory in social science?" we encounter definitions that are contradictory or, at best, ambiguous. Moreover, such terms as "theory," "theoretical orientation," "theoretical frame of reference," "theoretical sketch," or "model" are on occasion employed synonymously, at other times with only fine shades of difference.

One group of social scientists would identify, at least implicitly, any kind of conceptualization with theory. Such concepts as "status," "role," "culture," or "public opinion," when defined and utilized in the interpretation of research materials, are equated with social theory. In this sense, theory comes to be defined as almost any thought process as opposed to the observation of facts *per se*. Although all theory involves conceptualization, and although concepts are the building blocks for theory, to equate conceptualization in general, or isolated concepts in particular, with scientific theory seems inutile.

Another group of social scientists tends to identify theory with the writings of classical scholars such as Marx, Weber, Durkheim, Pareto, and Spencer.[24] Granted that modern sociologists frequently overlook some of the advances made by earlier scholars, equating the "history of ideas" with social theory can serve little purpose.

Still other social scientists attempt to define or identify theory in more rigorous terms. To them the term "theory" is applicable only to a "formal" or "logico-deductive" system, one that involves a set of postulates from which testable hypotheses (or propositions) can be derived. In this category belong sociologists such as Zetterberg, Homans, and Schrag,[25] who reason, in lesser or greater degrees, along the lines of such philosophers of science as Popper and Hempel,[26] the latter in turn have taken modern physics as the "model" to emulate. . . . Writers who equate theory with a logico-deductive system often refer to other conceptual systems as "theoretical orientations," "frames of reference," or "theoretical sketches."

This narrow definition of theory, though it has some appeal, raises difficulties of its own. By relegating to the class of "nontheory" all conceptualizations other than the logico-deductive sort, sociologists may inhibit rather than advance the cause of science. Such thinking would lead us to reject certain kinds of logical systems—notably the logic of the dialectic—as inappropriate to social investigation and would blind us to certain types of conceptualizations that have proved useful for coping with specific problem areas. Most significant of all, the narrow definition of theory advocated by Zetterberg,[27] among others, ignores the assumptions scientists make about their data, assumptions that do much to structure the total research process and the interpretation of one's results. . . .

In a broad sense, a scientific theory serves to link apparently discrete observations. More specifically, it refers to a set of logically interrelated "propositions" or "statements" that are "empirically meaningful," as well as to the assumptions the researcher makes about his method and his data. Thus, there are three dimensions to theory in science: (1) the broad logical structure, or the form; (2) the generalizations or propositions concerning the patterning of the empirical world (the specific content); and (3) the assumptions regarding the scientific method and the nature of the data.

We equate theory neither with isolated concepts nor with logico-deductive systems. Rather, our definition is broad enough to encompass such classificatory schemes as those of Parsons (his pattern-variable or system-problem formulations)[28] as well as the more rigorous logico-deductive schemes. Obviously, theories may take different forms: They may be rigorous or loose, general or specific, and so on.

Moreover, our definition of theory includes an aspect of theory building which, as suggested above, has been slighted by methodologists and philosophers of science: the assumptions that scientists make concerning their methods and their data.[29] These assumptions cannot be relegated to the sphere of "metatheory," or theorizing about theory, since they affect the nature of one's propositions and, more specifically, the very selection of the problem and collection and analysis of the data. For example, sociologists who conceive of social reality as fluid and constantly evolving are committed to a set of research procedures that tend to be rejected by those who see social relationships as fundamentally stable and fixed. The general disregard of this dimension of theory building. . .has done much to hinder the advance of methodology in sociology.

To reduce the terminological confusion in this area, we should also comment briefly upon concepts such as "model" and "explanation." Some writers use these as synonyms for theory. Yet the term "model," for instance, has acquired a number of rather different meanings.[30]

Sociologists often speak of a "model" in common-sense terms: as something to be emulated. Thus, Communist China has become a model of economic development for certain recently emergent nations. But a model may also refer to a miniature physical representation of reality, as in chemistry. Or the sociologist's sociogram serves as a physical representation or model for a small group.

A number of writers conceive of this representation in conceptual rather than physical terms. It is in this sense that a model is frequently equated with a logico-deductive system.[31] But even within this framework finer distinctions can be made. For instance, the economist Papandreou distinguishes between a model and a theory. For him a theory is a logico-deductive system that can be falsified, whereas a model is a conceptual system that cannot be falsified but is capable only of empirical confirmation.[32]

The notion of "explanation,". . .is frequently used as a synonym for theory: often, theory = logico-deductive system = explanation.[33] Although theories have explanatory power, the notion of theory, as we have defined it, encompasses more than explanation: It includes in addition the underlying premises.

The Nature of Data

From the time of Durkheim and his concern with "social facts" up to the present day, a long-standing controversy has been brewing over just what is the proper field of study for the sociologist. Most would agree that the sociologist does not study biological or physical phenomena but concentrates upon social or cultural data. But what are social or cultural data? What is a social or cultural fact?

The concept "fact" is not easy to define. The field of philosophy contains a considerable body of literature on the subject, and a controversial one at that. Moreover, what is a fact for a particular social scientist is a product of his own theoretical assumptions. Durkheim's well-known dictum, "Consider social facts as things,"[34] is a case in point. In this utterance Durkheim was reacting to the subjectivist orientation of the utilitarians of his time, and he was intent upon placing sociology on a scientific footing. Although scholars quarrel over the precise meaning of Durkheim's maxim, it seems clear that for Durkheim social facts were external to the observer and the actor alike, and they were capable of being observed in a highly objective manner.

More narrowly, Brodbeck defines a fact as follows: "A 'fact' is a particular thing, a characteristic, event, or kind of event, like Johnny's I.Q. or the proportion of home owners, or the size of the Republican vote. To state a fact, then, is to state that a concept has an instance or a number of instances."[35] Implicit in Brodbeck's definition is the notion that a fact is conceptually defined or ordered. More broadly, these sense impressions can be transformed via concepts into statements or propositions (for example, "There are over 180 million people in the United States") which then are viewed as facts.

Yet problems remain. There are, after all, different kinds of facts: those that are general and those that are specific, those that are positive and those that are negative. Kenneth Burke, among others, has stressed the role of the negative in human symbol systems.[36] The idea of "nothingness" seems to be central to much of social experience. Social scientists cannot ignore the existence of negative facts. Nonaction is a negative fact (or nonevent) that may have considerable relevance for social inquiry. The failure of a citizen to vote or of the groom to kiss the bride are illustrative of such negative facts in American society.

But to get at the facts, just what do social scientists observe? They observe physical behavior, such as walking, waving of the arms, facial expressions, and patterned sounds, and the results of physical behavior, such as writing or tools. Yet these physical movements (or the products thereof) are meaningful to the observer only in terms of his own conceptualization and acquired knowledge of the actor's interpretation of them. Scientists thus observe in terms of some conceptual system—some set of common understandings—which orders or connects disparate physical movements, movements which are taken as indicators of underlying patterns.[37]

Some radical empiricists (including the materialists among them) would remove the subjective element, or meaning, entirely from sociological investigation.[38] Although in so doing they are perpetuating a theoretical perspective that reaches back over several centuries of social thought, the evidence. . . is ranged against the validity of such a viewpoint. To deny the legitimacy of the subjective as an area of scientific investigation is to downgrade the role of conceptualization and ultimately of the scientific method itself.

Relationships Between Theory and Data

It is difficult, if not impossible, to discuss in any meaningful way the role and nature of theory without giving some consideration to the role and nature of data, and vice versa. But which has priority in the research process: theory or data? Undoubtedly the social scientist's particular theoretical assumptions mold the formulation of his problem and even structure the findings. The phenomenologist and the extreme empiricist will inevitably arrive at different conclusions. More generally, those scientists who work within the Kantian tradition give priority to concepts and theory, whereas those who are committed to the views of Locke and Hume and their contemporary expositors stress observation and data rather than theory. In practice, most researchers tend to be either neo-Kantians or neo-Humeans.

A comparison of the writings of Lazarsfeld and Parsons sheds light on one dimension of the theory-data controversy within sociology. Parsons, a champion of the relative priority of theory, has been responsible for sensitizing several generations of sociologists to the crucial role of theory in social research.[39] Examining the functions of theory, he recognizes it as a beacon researchers employ when charting a course through the murky depths of social systems. One must know what to study and what not to study. Theory, moreover, becomes essential when we seek to interpret our observations. And it is theory that illuminates the gaps in our observations of the social world.

The function of theory in structuring the researcher's observations is readily grasped when we compare the divergent approaches of different scientists toward a particular complex of social activities[40]—for instance, the fishing patterns of a tribe of South American Indians. A medical doctor might examine the effect of the tribe's fishing habits upon the people's diet, whereas a geographer could study the fishing patterns from the perspective of the group's adaptation to the physical environment. Or one ethnologist might consider their activities from the viewpoint of the society's economic system, while another might examine their interrelationships with, say, religious ritual and beliefs.

Although sociologists such as Lazarsfeld do not question the significance of theory, their emphasis is upon the role of data in the scientific process. Consequently, Lazarsfeld tends to utilize "natural classes" in his research.[41] He would, when carrying out a public opinion study, for example, employ a classification scheme that reflects the natural breaking points within his data.

Parsons, on the other hand, in examining the same materials, would tend to impose his own classificatory system upon them. Of course, Lazarsfeld's so-called natural classes are partly a product of his theoretical commitment, for he would not utilize or perhaps even recognize those classes that fall outside his own conceptual or theoretical framework.

The split between those scientists who stress theory over those who emphasize observation (or data) reflects to some degree the cleavage between scholars who are committed to a logico-deductive approach in science and those who are oriented toward discovery. . . . More generally, Merton,[42] among others, has, in an effort to build a bridge between the theoreticians and the empiricists, argued at some length that theory and data are in constant interaction. Such a position is widely acclaimed today. But the idea of such interaction has become almost a cliché in some circles. We can readily concur that it is inherent within the scientific method, but in reality we know little about the specific content or form of this interplay between theory and data.

An understanding of the relationship of theory and data rests in large part upon a firm grasp of the nature of perception. For it is perception that connects the data with one's conceptual knowledge of the latter. Perception media are the senses by which human beings see, hear, touch, smell, and taste. There are at least three aspects to this process: (1) the quality of man's perception media, (2) the impact of conceptualization upon perception, and (3) the nature of the data being studied.

A major deterrent to scientific inquiry lies in the selective quality of the senses. Roughly speaking, the senses pick up some sound waves, light waves, odors, and so on, emanating from or reflected by physical objects, but fail to pick up others. We must either remain oblivious to the latter or infer their presence via instruments or, in some instances, deduce their existence from other observable phenomena. Some of the limitations upon human observation have been examined by psychologists. Although methodologists have given little attention to the latter's findings, the experiments of psychologists have certainly elucidated some of the barriers to human perception. One of them is the "Three Men" test, whereby the placement of three individuals with respect to certain geometrical configurations leaves the observer with the impression that they are of different sizes, even though "in reality" all three are the same.[43] We also have experiments in which lines of the same length appear to observers to be of differing lengths, simply because of the manner in which the lines are portrayed.

A second and more insidious kind of influence upon perception stems from one's own conceptual system. Clearly, we perceive objects or behavior largely in terms of prior conceptualizations or categories. This proposition has been documented by crosscultural research.[44] A number of studies have supported the idea that persons in different cultures may perceive the color spectrum, geometric forms, etc. somewhat differently. So, too, they may classify and impute meaning to particular human behavior in rather different ways. Yet if persons from divergent cultures perceived in radically divergent ways one could not distinguish between total failure of communication and total difference in perception. It is because we perceive and respond essentially alike that we can take note of the differences that result.[45]

The impact of conceptualization upon perception *within* broad cultural systems has also been documented through various experiments. For instance, several groups of observers are told different stories about a given picture before they are shown the object. As we might expect, the different groups perceive the picture in terms of patterns that reflect the themes they have been told the picture portrays. This line of reasoning also suggests the crucial influence of the "social situation" upon perception. That an individual's perceptions of objects or of the behavior of other persons is structured by his "expectations" of others has been a conclusion of a number of social psychologists.[46]

Actually, there appear to be various levels of "consciousness" with respect to one's conceptual categories. Some phenomenologists seem rightly to distinguish between those situations wherein a person can conceptualize his observations and disseminate them to others and those wherein a person is "intuitively aware" of objects or reactions but is unable to conceptualize, order, and communicate what he "observes." One may, for example, walk into a room after, say, a year's absence and be aware that changes have occurred in the arrangement of the furniture, and even communicate this awareness to others, but be unable to specify the particular rearrangement that has occurred. Field workers, thus, may be aware of patterns long before they are able to specify or order their observations into well-defined categories.

These fine distinctions aside, it is the overall impact of one's conceptual system upon perception that makes a sociology of knowledge orientation so essential to the methodology of social research. We have already suggested that a significant part of the scientist's overall environment is made up of the concepts held by other persons in his sociocultural milieu. These concepts have an empirical existence of their own in the sense that they are discoverable and can be communicated. It is the scientist's total conceptual environment, not just the concepts he acquires during his scientific training, that structures his observations. For us, the sociology of knowledge perspective is a methodological device that serves to objectify this broader conceptual system so that we may properly gauge its impact upon the scientific observer.

A third element of the perception process is "what is observed." The research of social psychologists lends support to the proposition that, where one's "reality" being observed is relatively fixed or stable, the influence of other persons' conceptual orientations upon one's own observations will be less than where this reality lacks any well-defined reference points and is highly amorphous.[47] We would therefore expect the degree of consensus among scientists to vary with the amount of stability and permanence in the social order they are studying.

But the relationships of conceptualization to perception and to the social environment itself are more complex than we have indicated. There is another element that enters into the picture: language (the nature of which has also been the subject of considerable debate). Following Saussure,[48] we define "language" as a system of signs that link concepts to specific sounds or sequences of sounds. One can hear or utter given sounds, yet fail to attach any specific concepts, or meaning, to these, if he lacks knowledge of the language, or system of signs.

Language, as a system of linguistic signs that serves to convey meaning among speakers, has a structure of its own. This structure, which includes phonemic, morphemic, and syntactic patterns, seems to influence the perception process and conceptualization itself. The perception of certain aspects of social reality may be more readily achieved through some kinds of structural systems than through others. And although. . .it is easy to exaggerate the impact of different language structures upon conceptualization, that they may differentially shape thought patterns in some areas is a proposition that cannot be ignored.

In the end, the broader theoretical system, the specific concepts contained therein, and the language which conveys these concepts all interact in complex ways. Refinement of isolated concepts can lead to improvements in the overall theoretical system, and in turn improvements in the latter may help to refine certain concepts, and, in the process, one's perception of particular phenomena. Moreover, refinement in the system of linguistic signs can lead to advances both in the concepts and in the broader theory, as occurred, for example, in Europe with the adoption of the Hindu–Arabic decimal system in place of the unwieldly Roman numerals. This change did much to facilitate the breakthroughs in mathematics that came in the succeeding centuries. Of course, these achievements in mathematics itself were made possible only by the much earlier reduction of spoken language to written form. And without the invention of writing, science as we know it could never have developed. For writing enabled man to greatly transcend the very narrow limits of his own memory span and to build upon the accumulated knowledge over the millennia.

Ultimately, if we are to understand more fully the relationships between theory and data, we must have a better grasp of the conceptualization process. With a sounder knowledge of conceptualization, we could effect many improvements in the scientific method. The ongoing research in psychology may help scientists widen their grasp of this knotty problem. Certainly, the studies in concept formation by Piaget, Bruner, and so on have blazed a trail through this area that methodologists should not ignore.[49]

So too, the efforts that have been made to apply our knowledge of computers—by drawing an analogy between these and the human brain—to the study of thought and the thinking process will in due time also expand our knowledge of conception (as well as perception). As Goldstine observes:

> Many workers in the field are at present trying to explore what is called artificial or machine reasoning or intelligence. In effect they are trying to see how far a computer can go in doing tasks which we normally class as human ones. . . . It is characteristic of all these efforts, though, that so far the investigators have been unable to deduce any general principles from their results.[50]

Yet eventually this work will likely extend our understanding of the rudiments of conceptualization and in turn of the scientific method itself.

NOTES

1. Our discussion in this section is based on the multivolume work of Charles Singer *et al.* (eds.), *History of Technology* (Fair Lawn, N.J.: Oxford, 1954–1958); A. C. Crombie (ed.), *Scientific Change* (New York: Basic Books, 1963); Gideon Sjoberg, *The Preindustrial City* (New York: Free Press, 1960); and others.
2. Although preliterate man's thought system has been a complex one, it is obvious that it is literate (especially literate–industrial) man who evaluates the preliterate's world view in terms of some broad perspective. The reverse is simply not possible. For literate man possesses the advantage of written records. These provide him with a scope and a vision that can never be attained merely through reliance upon the spoken word. Nor could mathematics or logic ever have reached their current heights without the use of writing, a medium by which one is able to recall (and recheck) complex thought processes.
3. See, e.g., James Kip Finch, *The Story of Engineering* (Garden City, N.Y.: Doubleday, Anchor Books, 1960).
4. C. D. O'Malley, *Andreas Vesalius of Brussels, 1514–1564* (Berkeley: University of California Press, 1964).
5. Derek J. de Solla Price, *Science Since Babylon* (New Haven: Yale, 1961).
6. Charles C. Gillispie, *The Edge of Objectivity* (Princeton, N.J.: Princeton, 1960), 10.
7. Pitirim A. Sorokin, Carle C. Zimmerman, and Charles J. Galpin (eds.), *A Systematic Source Book in Rural Sociology,* vol. 1 (Minneapolis: University of Minnesota Press, 1930), 54.
8. Of course, modern social science did not develop in a vacuum. Thus John Howland Rowe, "The Renaissance Foundations of Anthropology," *American Anthropologist, 67* (February, 1965), 1–20, believes that Renaissance writers were instrumental in creating a "perspective distance" by which antiquity or more recent cultures could be understood.
9. See e.g., D. G. E. Hall (ed.), *Historians of South East Asia* (London: Oxford, 1961). Cf. C. H. Philips (ed.), *Historians of India, Pakistan and Ceylon* (London: Oxford, 1961); and W. G. Beasley and E. G. Pulleybank (eds.), *Historians of China and Japan* (London: Oxford, 1961). There are of course differences among traditional civilized societies, but the patterns enumerated above generally hold.

10. The manner in which knowledge has been accumulated and sustained is itself worthy of study. Knowledge has followed the spread of empires. Thus, after the "fall" of Greece and Rome, many of the ideas and tools that were employed therein were not only preserved but elaborated upon by peoples in the Eastern Roman Empire and the various empires that arose in the Arab world. A number of these ideas and inventions were reintroduced into Europe especially after the tenth century, there to form the basis of the scientific and industrial revolution that followed some centuries later.
11. A number of historians distinguish between the scientific and the industrial revolutions. See J. Bronowski and Bruce Mazlish, *The Western Intellectual Tradition* (New York: Harper & Row, Harper Torchbooks, 1962), chap. 7. Scholars assign different dates to the origins of the scientific revolution. Some date it as early as the fourteenth century and some as late as the sixteenth. Herbert Butterfield, *The Origins of Modern Science,* rev. ed. (New York: Collier, 1962), places its beginnings at about 1300. Almost all writers view the industrial revolution as having begun in eighteenth-century England. Although the distinction between the scientific and the industrial revolutions is analytically useful for some purposes, we view the two as part of one process, with the industrial revolution an extension of the scientific one.
12. See, e.g., A. Rupert Hall, "Engineering and the Scientific Revolution," *Technology and Culture, 2* (Fall, 1961), 333-341.
13. See, e.g., Ludovico Geymonat, *Galileo Galilei,* trans. by Stillman Drake (New York: McGraw-Hill, 1965); and Giorgio de Santillana, *The Crime of Galileo* (Chicago: University of Chicago Press, 1955).
14. Robert K. Merton, *Social Theory and Social Structure,* rev. ed. (New York: Free Press, 1957), chap. 18. The reasons for (or preconditions of) the scientific-industrial revolution have been a matter for wide debate. Merton's thesis has been subject to extended discussion. For a relatively recent bibliographical guide to the controversy, see Joseph Ben-David, "The Scientific Role: The Conditions of Its Establishment in Europe," *Minerva, 4* (Autumn, 1965), 54.
15. Lewis Feuer, *The Scientific Intellectual* (New York: Basic Books, 1963).
16. See, e.g., Robert A. Nisbet, *The Sociological Tradition* (New York: Basic Books, 1966), chap. 2; and Bruce Brown, "The French Revolution and the Rise of Social Theory," *Science and Society, 30* (Fall, 1966), 385-432.
17. See, e.g., Charles C. Gillispie, "Science in the French Revolution," in Bernard Barber and Walter Hirsch (eds.), *The Sociology of Science* (New York: Free Press, 1962), chap. 5; and John C. Greene, *Darwin and the Modern World View* (New York: New American Library, Mentor Books, 1963).
18. See, e.g., Giorgio de Santillana, "Galileo and J. Robert Oppenheimer, Jr., " *The Reporter, 17* (Dec. 26, 1957), 10-18.
19. The development of systematic social research, which sets off the twentieth from the nineteenth and earlier centuries, is beginning to be documented. See, e.g., A. Oberschall, *Empirical Social Research in Germany,*

1848-1914 (New York: Basic Books, 1965); and Paul F. Lazarsfeld, "Notes on the History of Quantification in Sociology–Trends, Sources and Problems," *Isis, 52* (June, 1961), 277-333. See other articles in this issue of *Isis* for the history of quantification in psychology and economics.

20. Raul Hilberg, *The Destruction of the European Jews* (Chicago: Quadrangle Books, 1961). Hilberg describes in great detail how the Nazis relied upon the advances in natural science and upon rational bureaucracy (with its stress upon efficiency) in their killing center operations (esp. chap. 9).
21. This view finds expression in the writings of many philosophers of science. See, e.g., Carl G. Hempel, *Aspects of Scientific Explanation* (New York: Free Press, 1965); and the writings of such sociologists as George A. Lundberg, *Foundations of Sociology* (New York: Macmillan, 1939), and William R. Catton, Jr., *From Animistic to Naturalistic Sociology* (New York: McGraw-Hill, 1966).
22. Most social scientists–positivists and nonpositivists alike–seem to agree that some manipulation or control of the social order is possible. But the positivists or naturalists also are committed to a deterministic conception of the social world. Man simply responds to the course of events. We believe that one consequence of man's ability to use scientific knowledge to control his sociocultural milieu is that he can at times transcend what appear to be deterministic situations.
23. Cf. R. E. Gibson, "Our Heritage from Galileo Galilei," *Science, 145* (Sept. 18, 1964), 1271-1276.
24. See, e.g., Margaret Wilson Vine, *An Introduction to Sociological Theory* (New York: Longmans, 1959). The work of Andrew Hacker, *Political Theory* (New York: Macmillan, 1961), also seems to belong to this tradition.
25. Hans L. Zetterberg, *On Theory and Verification in Sociology,* 3rd ed. (Totowa, N.J.: Bedminster, 1965); George C. Homans, "Contemporary Theory in Sociology," in Robert E. L. Faris (ed.), *Handbook of Modern Sociology* (Chicago: Rand McNally, 1964), chap 25; Clarence Schrag, "Elements of Theoretical Analysis in Sociology," in Llewellyn Gross (ed.), *Sociological Theory: Inquiries and Paradigms* (New York: Harper & Row, 1967), 220-253.

    Merton, *op. cit.,* 96 ff., has on occasion identified theory with the logico-deductive system. However, . . . this reasoning is by no means similar to the logic of the structural-functional orientation which Merton has so ardently championed.
26. Karl R. Popper, *The Logic of Scientific Discovery* (New York: Wiley, Science Editions, 1961); Hempel, *op. cit.* Also, R. B. Braithwaite, *Scientific Explanation* (New York: Cambridge, 1953).
27. Zetterberg, *op. cit.*
28. Talcott Parsons, *The Social System* (New York: Free Press, 1951), and his "General Theory in Sociology," in Robert K. Merton *et al.* (eds.), *Sociology Today* (New York: Basic Books, 1959), chap. 1.
29. Our usage of the term "assumption" differs from that of Schrag, *op. cit.,*

221 ff. Schrag distinguishes between two kinds of generalizations or propositions: (1) descriptions of previous observations and (2) "lawlike assumptions" about events not yet observed or examined. He uses the term "assumption" specifically in this context. Our usage is more theoretical and on occasion more "philosophical" in nature.

30. For a discussion of the use of the concept, "model," see May Brodbeck, "Models, Meaning, and Theories," in Llewellyn Gross (ed.), *Symposium on Sociological Theory* (New York: Harper & Row, 1959), chap. 12. Cf. Merle B. Turner, *Philosophy and the Science of Behavior* (New York: Appleton-Century-Crofts, 1967), chap. 9; E. A. Gellner, "Model (Theoretical Model)," in Julius Gould and William L. Kolb (eds.), *A Dictionary of the Social Sciences* (New York: Free Press, 1964), 435; and Michael Banton (ed.), *The Relevance of Models for Social Anthropology,* A.S.A. Monographs 1 (London: Tavistock, 1965).
31. Not all social scientists equate the notion of conceptual model with the logico-deductive formulation. Some seem to identify "model" with one's assumptions about data and method, as, e.g., M. Brewster Smith, "Anthropology and Psychology," in John Gillin (ed.), *For a Science of Social Man* (New York: Macmillan, 1954), 64-66. And Karl W. Deutsch, "On Communication Models in the Social Sciences," *Public Opinion Quarterly, 16* (Fall, 1952), 356, sees models as structures of symbols and operating rules which are supposed to match certain relevant points in an existing structure or process.
32. Andreas G. Papandreou, "Explanation and Prediction in Economics," *Science, 129* (Apr. 24, 1959), 1096-1100. He writes "Economists construct models, not theories. Their models may be confirmed by reference to empirical data, but they cannot be refuted. Therefore, they are strictly explanatory in character" (1099).
33. See, e.g., Hempel, *op. cit.*
34. Emile Durkheim, *The Rules of Sociological Method,* trans. by Sarah A. Solovay and John H. Mueller, 8th ed. (New York: Free Press Paperback, 1964), 14.
35. Brodbeck, *op. cit.,* 377.
36. Kenneth Burke, "Definition of Man," *Hudson Review, 16* (Winter, 1963-1964), 498-503 and his *Grammar of Motives* (Englewood Cliffs, N.J.: Prentice Hall, 1945), 294-297.
37. See, e.g., Karl Mannheim, *Essays on the Sociology of Knowledge,* trans. and ed. by Paul Kecskemeti (New York: Oxford, 1952), 53-63; and Harold Garfinkel, "Common-Sense Knowledge of Social Structures: The Documentary Method of Interpretation," in Jordan M. Scher (ed.), *Theories of the Mind* (New York: Free Press, 1962), 689-712.
38. One current effort to eliminate the subjective element in scientific inquiry is that of Otis Dudley Duncan and Leo F. Schnore, "Cultural, Behavioral, and Ecological Perspectives in the Study of Social Organization," *American Journal of Sociology, 65* (September, 1959), 132-146. The authors point to the ecological approach as nonsubjective, while admitting that the subjective enters into, say, the behavioral orientation.

39. Charles Ackerman and Talcott Parsons, "The Concept of 'Social System' as a Theoretical Device," in Gordon J. DiRenzo (ed.), *Concepts, Theory and Explanation in the Behavioral Sciences* (New York: Random House, 1966), chap. 2. In this essay co-authored with Ackerman, Parsons contends that "We select, we ascribe importance; and both our selection and our ascription of importance are in a sense unnatural since the array of reality itself does not supply the criteria for the selection or the ascription" (26), a perspective that diverges considerably from that enunciated by Lazarsfeld.
40. Cf. Ely Devons and Max Gluckman, "Conclusion: Modes and Consequences of Limiting a Field of Study," in Max Gluckman (ed.), *Closed Systems and Open Minds* (Edinburgh: Oliver & Boyd, 1964), 158 ff. "The different social and behavioural sciences are in the main distinguished not by the events they study but by the kinds of relations between events which they seek to establish" (160).
41. See, e.g., Paul F. Lazarsfeld and Allen H. Barton, "Some General Principles of Questionnaire Classification," in Paul F. Lazarsfeld and Morris Rosenberg (ed.), *The Language of Social Research* (New York: Free Press, 1955), esp. 91–93.
42. Merton, *op. cit.,* chap. 3.
43. See, e.g., M. L. Johnson Abercrombie, *The Anatomy of Judgment* (New York: Basic Books, 1960), 30–31.
44. See the review of the literature, as well as the original research that was conducted, by Marshall H. Segall *et al., The Influence of Culture on Visual Perception* (Indianapolis: Bobbs-Merrill, 1966). This is a truly valuable work.
45. Fred L. Strodtbeck, "Considerations of Meta-Method in Cross-Cultural Studies," *American Anthropologist, 66,* part 2 (June, 1964), 225. This issue of the *American Anthropologist* is a special publication, "Transcultural Studies in Cognition," ed. by A. Kimball Romney and Roy Goodwin D'Andrade.
46. See, e.g., A. Paul Hare (ed.), *Handbook of Small Group Research* (New York: Free Press, 1962), 26 ff.; Renato Tagiuri and Luigi Petrullo (eds.), *Person Perception and Interpersonal Behavior* (Stanford, Cal.: Stanford, 1958).
47. See, e.g., Muzafer Sherif and Carolyn W. Sherif, *An Outline of Social Psychology,* rev. ed. (New York: Harper & Row, 1956), 81 ff., 103 ff., *passim.*
48. Ferdinand de Saussure, *Course in General Linguistics,* trans. by Wade Baskin (New York: Philosophical Library, 1959).
49. For a brief survey of some of this literature, see Roger Brown, *Social Psychology* (New York: Free Press, 1965), chap. 7.
50. Herman H. Goldstine, "Computers and Perception," *Proceedings of the American Philosophical Society, 108* (August, 1964), 290.

The Problem of Definition: What is X?

Anatol Rapoport

It is remarkable how frequently the same problems recur in the history of man. The most ancient myths, fairy tales, and proverbs often apply, with only slight modifications, to present-day events. In the old tales of malicious gods and demons one finds the perennial problem of human survival in the face of hostile nature. There are, in stories of invisibility gadgets, flying carpets, seven-league boots, and horns of abundance, dreams of technological miracles. There is incessant concern with guessing the future, as in tales of oracles and seers; with family relations, as in stories of the wicked stepmother or the disinherited youngest son; with the frailties of human nature, such as now are the concern of psychiatrists, as in the animal fables common to so many cultures; with rules of living, as in proverbs; with social problems, as in tales of the abuse of privilege by proud and wicked kings.

With one class of problems, however, our forefathers were not nearly as preoccupied as we are. These are problems of communication and understanding. The Genesis story of the Tower of Babel is a notable early exception. It may have had its roots in an actusl crisis, a result of importing large numbers of workers or slaves from distant lands. On the whole, however, language awareness is largely absent in ancient folklore. When Aladdin (presumably a Persian) visits the Chinese princess, the question never arises as to how they are able to converse. They just do. Although the heroes of fairy tales do an enormous amount of traveling, interpreters are generally not mentioned. Communication with foreigners, gods, devils, sphinxes, and beasts, appears to encounter no linguistic obstacles whatever.

On rare occasions, one does find a folk tale which reveals insight into the problems of communication—sometimes an insight which goes far beyond the mere recognition, as in the Tower of Babel story, of linguistic differences. The following ancient anecdote is probably of Indian origin.

> A blind man asked someone to explain the meaning of "white."
>
> "White is a color," he was told, "as, for example, white snow."
>
> "I understand," said the blind man. "It is a cold and damp color."
>
> "No, it doesn't have to be cold and damp. Forget about snow. Paper, for instance, is white."
>
> "So it rustles?" asked the blind man.
>
> "No, indeed, it need not rustle. It is like the fur of an albino rabbit."
>
> "A soft, fluffy color?" the blind man wanted to know.
>
> "It need not be soft either. Porcelain is white, too."
>
> "Perhaps it is a brittle color, then," said the blind man.

This story goes to the core of the matter. It illustrates the impossibility of communication between two people who have not shared a common *experience.* From the point of view of operational philosophy, this is perhaps the most fundamental philosophical problem.

LANGUAGE AS AN ORGANIZATION OF EXPERIENCE

I will begin to discuss the problem of communication by proposing a rather unconventional classification of languages. I will suppose that people are potentially able to speak the same language to the extent that they share certain areas of common experience. Let us see how that compares with the usual classifications (as made by linguists).

The fact that you and I both speak English means this: If we make a list of all the words you use in your speech from day to day and all the words I use from day to day, we will find that practically all the words each of us uses will be found in a standard English dictionary. Do we then speak the same language? We ordinarily assume that we do.

But look at it this way. To determine whether you and I speak the same language, let us leave the dictionary (a third party) out of it and compare our verbal outputs with *each other.* If we do, we will probably find that although our verbal outputs overlap, the correspondence is never exact. There will almost certainly be words which one of us uses and the other does not—and if our backgrounds differ markedly, the differences may be very great. The usual way of stating this fact is to say that we have different "vocabularies." But then one might ask at what point a difference in "vocabularies" amounts to a difference in "language."

Dr. X understands the *Journal of Cellular and Comparative Physiology*, but the *Racing Form* is a complete mystery to him. Mr. Y conducts his business with the aid of the *Racing Form*, but he may not understand a single line of the *Iliad*, even if it is in "English," which Mr. Y insists is his mother tongue. The fact that Dr. X, sitting next to Mr. Y at a lunch counter can ask Mr. Y to pass the mustard and be understood still does not establish that they speak the "same language." If it did, we would have to say that Mr. Y speaks the same language as Señor Z, who comes to see Mr. Y daily. However, Mr. Y would not understand a word of what Señor Z sings to Señorita Q out on the breakwater on a summer night.

There are, of course, explanations for these discrepancies. We say that the scientist's vocabulary is "specialized"; that the bookie speaks only "a little Spanish," just enough to do business with Señor Z, etc. But there is also another way to look at these matters, a more radical way. This is to recognize that the conventional division of languages into groups (Indo-European, Semitic), families (Teutonic, Slavic), and species (English, German) does not serve *all* purposes of communication study. Such classifications, although useful to the professional linguists, are not particularly helpful in the construction of a theory of communication—and a theory of communication is essential to a general theory of knowledge. The linguist's classifications do not, for example, deal with scientific, underworld, commercial, and other jargons which are based on specific areas of experiences shared by groups of people engaged in common activities.

The importance of jargons in the study of communication is beginning to be recognized. There have been serious and semiserious studies of slang, teenage "jive," "legalese," and "federalese." With increasing frequency one reads in the press comments such as these: "In the jargon of Soviet officialdom this means. . . ." or "Translated from diplomatic parlance into plain English, this means. . . ." Periodically articles appear in scholarly and scientific journals deploring the mushrooming of specialists' jargons, which make communication between one scholar or scientist and another practically impossible. To complicate matters, jargons do not necessarily involve many artificial or unfamiliar words. The mathematician, for example, uses words like "group," "ring," "blanket," "loop," "lattice," "ideal," "normal," "singular," "measure" to denote matters which are almost as difficult to explain to someone who is not a mathematician as it is to explain the meaning of "white" to a blind man.

This discrepancy between the seeming simplicity of some kinds of words and the difficulty of communicating their meaning indicates that the meanings of words are not in the words themselves but in the experiences behind them. This sounds so obvious as to seem trite. Yet the fact remains that until recently the main efforts of the students of language have been directed to the analysis of its purely formal aspects, such as phonetics, grammar, and syntax. Only in the last half century or so, with the advent of semantics and metalinguistics, has a concerted effort been made to study language as related to man's experience.

Studying the relation of language to human experience is a major concern of operational philosophy. Operational philosophy views any language as *a certain way of organizing experience.* This view emphasizes the psychological and cultural aspects of language rather than its formal aspects.

To regard languages as ways of organizing experience is to look at them from what is called a *metalinguistic* point of view, as contrasted with the point of view customary in traditional linguistics. In daily life, as in traditional linguistics, we say that the German mystic and the German empiricist "speak the same language"; metalinguistically speaking, we would have to say that they speak different languages, since they organize their experiences in entirely different ways. Similarly the Japanese physicist and the Swedish physicist, even if they have difficulty in asking each other to pass the mustard, may be said to "speak the same language" in their scientific communication, since they organize the same kind of experience in the same kind of way. From the point of view of metalinguistics, it is easy to understand why an American mathematician with a dictionary and a little effort can read a mathematical paper in a Russian journal; and why an English-speaking jazz enthusiast, speaking to an English-speaking lover of Viennese waltzes, cannot make himself understood. Important in the sense of this definition is not the repertory of symbols on which experiences are mapped (vocabularies) but the repertories of the experiences themselves and especially the way experiences are organized (orientation). Once one has had a certain experience or has succeeded in organizing one's experiences in a certain way, it is a simple matter to put a label on it. It is usually much more difficult to do the opposite, namely to enlarge one's experience to fit a label.

To illustrate, take the word *kis.* If you don't happen to know Hungarian, it means nothing. Once it is translated (*kis* means small) one more word is added to your vocabulary with very little effort on your part. But now take the term *standard deviation.* You may know the meaning of both English words which comprise the term, but unless you know quite a bit of mathematics and some rudiments of statistics, it might take you *months* to learn the meaning of this term in the sense of knowing how and when to use it. In the case of the (linguistically) foreign word "kis," you are only enlarging your vocabulary to cover a familiar experience. In the case of the (linguistically) non-foreign terms "standard deviation," you are enlarging your experience to fit words that are familiar in appearance only.

DEFINITION

The process of making a word usable is called *definition.* Obviously, if people speak the same language (the "same" in the strictest sense of the word, that is, sharing not only the same vocabularies but also the same experiences), the need for definition does not arise. The need for a definition becomes felt only if one's vocabulary is inadequate to name a new experience, or if one is faced with a word which does not occur in one's vocabulary. This need can be expressed in the question "What is X?"

Note that "What is X?" can have at least two different kinds of meaning. If X stands for "this," that is, refers to some object or situation, it is the *word* which is missing. Such are the questions of a child about the objects around him, the questions of a person examining the construction of a machine, or the questions of someone learning to speak a foreign language by pointing to objects and learning their names, as Gulliver did on his travels.

On the other hand, if X stands for a word, it is the *experience* (meaning) which is missing. Such are the questions of someone learning a foreign language by reading with the help of a dictionary.

Now the question "What is this?" is easily answered if "this" refers to something tangible. The answer is just the appropriate word. The question "What is X?" where X stands for a word is not so easy to answer effectively, that is, to relate the word to the experience of the questioner. We have seen how difficult, if not impossible, it is at times to extend or to reorganize someone else's experience. Even when there are no conceptual difficulties, that is, when words have simple referents, referents are not always at hand. One cannot exhibit a printing press, an iceberg, a diplomat, and a hippopotamus in one's living room in answer to a youngster's demand for definitions.

To get around this difficulty, there are verbal definitions. If the direct purpose of a definition is to link a word with an experience (either by naming an experience at hand or by letting the questioner experience what the word stands for), then verbal definitions are necessarily indirect. Verbal definitions, after all, link only words with words. They may be nonetheless effective if the defining words are somehow closer to the questioner's experience than the words defined. For instance, if someone learns French, his question "What is 'vie'?" refers to a foreign word. The answer "life," gives him the equivalent in English, and that is sufficient if the word "life" *is* linked with his experience, that is, *means* something to him. Similarly, if the weather is not right for a trip to the zoo, one may define the hippopotamus by a description.

In many cases such undurect definitions do the job. They lose their significance, however, if the words used in the definitions stand no closer to experience than the word defined. Such definitions preserve their form but lose their content. Webster's *New International Dictionary* (second edition), for example, defines *love* as "A feeling of strong personal attachment induced by that which delights or commands admiration, by sympathetic understanding, or by ties of kinship; ardent affection; as, the *love* of brothers and sisters."

Definitions that do *not* bring the word closer to the hearer's experience are not confined to dictionaries. They constitute a goodly portion of our formal education. "A peninsula is a body of land surrounded on all sides but one by water"; "A democracy is a form of government in which the people rule"; "A noun is a name of a person, place, or a thing" are all shabby but remarkably viable examples of classroom knowledge. The worship of verbal definitions stems from a tenacious notion that "to define a thing is to know it."

An operational philosophy of knowledge reflects certain attitudes toward these two separate meanings of the question "What is X?"

If X stands for an unnamed thing, the question can be taken to be a request to name it and nothing else. To supply a name commonly used to refer to the thing is to answer the question. The answer adds no knowledge beyond the knowledge of common usage. It enables the questioner to *refer* to the thing named.

If X refers to a word, the question can be taken for a request to describe or to elicit an *experience*, to which the word refers.

Obviously, then, verbal definitions which do not bring words closer to experience fail to achieve their purpose from the operational point of view. Why, then, does the notion that to "define something is to know it" persist? It persists because it has deep roots in our philosophy of knowledge, roots which stretch to the Middle Ages, when European universities were founded. According to this so-called Aristotelian philosophy of knowledge, to know means to *classify*, and a correct verbal definition *gives the appearance* of classifying the thing defined.

The view that knowledge is primarily a skill at classifying (as the knowledge of the collector undoubtedly is) implies that there is a third meaning to the question "What is X?" The question is then a request to inform about the *nature* of X, about what X is like. It is clear that from an operational point of view such information can be supplied only by some sort of experience with X. A classification, which is a purely verbal act, does not *by itself* supply such experience or add to experience already at hand. Thus defining murder as "malicious, premeditated homicide" does not in itself tell us anything about murder that we did not know before. The only way to find out more about murder is to study the circumstances under which it is committed, the persons who commit it, etc.

In all three cases, therefore, to answer the question "What is X?" from an operational point of view means to make some connection between a word and experience, not merely between a word and other words. Even if the answer is in terms of words alone, these words should be chosen according to the likelihood that they bring the term defined closer to the experience of the questioner.

Confusing one meaning of the question with another leads to frequent miscarriages of communication. For instance, a man contemplating a curious gadget may ask, "What is this?" His question may be taken as a request for a name, so that the answer "This is a parapetaculator" seems appropriate. However, the question might have been asked in another sense, for example, "What is this gadget *used* for?" in which case the answer given carries no meaning at all. Such misunderstandings are not serious if they are cleared up by further questioning.

Unfortunately, our educational system places such emphasis on the importance of knowing names of things that our appetite for knowledge (experience) with which we begin our lives is often channelized into an appetite for names. All too often "This is a parapetaculator" or its equivalent is taken to be the complete and final answer to the question "What is this?"

Failure to keep in mind that meaning means the link between words and experience has been at the root of the sterility of most traditional philosophy. The failure is a reflection of the long preoccupation of philosophers with the *formal* aspect of the question "What is X?" that is, with the form of the answer rather than its content (meaning).

A prescribed form for answering the question "What is X?" was given by Aristotle in his rule for making definitions: name the class to which the thing defined belongs and differentiate it from the other members of its class. In this sense, the Webster Dictionary definition of "love" is a valid definition, since love is classified as a "feeling" and differentiated from other feelings.

The danger in such definitions is in that they *look* like definitions. They purport to explain meaning without indicating any connection between things defined and experience. Similar definitions (often enlarged into dissertations) constitute a great part of what has gone under the name of philosophy. One finds in philosophy discussions about the nature of space and time, of virtue and sin, of causality and will, or the microcosm and macrocosm, of thesis and antithesis. One searches usually in vain for indications of how these words reflect common human experiences.

It is not necessary to look into books on philosophy to find words without referents. Any commencement speech, sermon, newspaper editorial, or radio commercial follows the same philosophic tradition of reinforcing the delusion that anything which is talked about is real: success, charity, public opinion, and four-way indigestion relief. Indeed, nothing is easier than to "define" these noises so as to make it appear that they mean something.

What is success? Success is the attainment of one's ideals.

What is charity? Charity is the practice of Christian attitudes.

What is public opinion? Public opinion is the prime mover of public policy in a democracy.

What is four-way indigestion relief? Four-way indigestion relief is a gentle action which alkalizes the system, purifies the blood, activates the bile, and helps Nature to reestablish equilibrium.

Operational philosophy reflects an altogether different attitude toward the question "What is X?" We have already seen how the various meanings of that question are distinguished. Fundamental in that distinction is a recognition that the question "What is X?" is a particular kind of social act. It is a request *to share experience.* Now, experience can be shared only on the basis of a *common experience.* Therefore any definition must rest on a basis of common experience shared by the giver and the receiver of the definition. This interpretation of the question "What is X?" implies that the answer must be tailored to fit the experience of the questioner. The expression "as impossible as explaining colors to a blind man" reflects this point of view.

It follows that there can be no completely general rule for making definitions. The making of pedagogically or heuristically useful definitions is an "art" rather than a "science." That is to say, the choice of a good definition is more often guided by intuitive feelings about the needs of a particular situation rather than by application of well-defined principles.

Thus, if a child asks "What is time?" it is probably best to talk of days and nights, summers, and winters, to call his attention to the effects of age, to teach him how to cross days off on a calendar while waiting for chicks to hatch, etc. If an experimental physicist asks "What is time?" a good answer is "That which is measured by a clock." But if a theoretical physicist asks "What is time?" the most meaningful answer is "The independent variable in the differential equations of motion." Each definition is geared to a specific set of experiences.

In our discussion, there will be a great deal to say about the so-called operational definition, of which the experimental physicist's definition of "time" is an example. The importance of operational definitions became expecially apparent in the beginning of this century when it seemed that some of the most established notions of the most firmly established branch of science (time, space, causality) were about to be overthrown. The preoccupation with operational definitions and their philosophical consequences (which logical positivists call "logical analysis") has marked the birth of modern operational philosophy and has determined its view toward the most fundamental of philosophical problems–the nature of reality.

The Substance of Sociological Theory

Norman K. Denzin

THE SUBSTANCE OF SOCIOLOGICAL THEORY

In his indictment of modern sociological theory in 1954, Herbert Blumer traced sociologists' inability to develop sound theory to a misunderstanding of concepts. This charge is still valid and is compounded by a number of other difficulties. Perhaps most basic is a misunderstanding of what theory is and what theory consists of.

Social Theory Defined

Surely the most voiced concept in modern sociology, the term *theory* has had attached to it multiple levels of meaning and interpretation. Models are called theories, classical sociological criticism passes for theory, and so do conceptual frameworks and interconnected sets of propositions. To paraphrase Homans, theory refers to a set of propositions that are interrelated in an ordered fashion such that some may be deducible from others thus permitting an explanation to be developed for the phenomenon under consideration (1964, p. 951). A theory is a set of propositions that furnish an explanation by means of a deductive system. Theory is explanation. Durkheim's theory of suicide in Spain conforms to the above specifications (see Homans, 1964, p. 951). It states that: (1) In any social grouping, the suicide rate varies directly with the degree of individualism (egoism); (2) the degree of individualism varies with the incidence of Protestantism; (3) therefore, the suicide rate varies with the incidence of Protestantism; (4) the incidence of Protestantism in Spain is low; (5) therefore, the suicide rate in Spain is low.

General Characteristics of Social Theory

From this example I can now describe the central features of social theory. It consists first of a set of concepts that forms a conceptual scheme. Some of these concepts, as Homans notes, are descriptive and serve to show what the theory is about (individualism, suicide, and Protestantism). Others are operative or relational and specify empirical relationships between other elements in the theory (rate and incidence, when combined with suicide and Protestantism, specify such relationships; Durkheim's theory predicts conditions under which suicide rates would be high and low by specifying the relationship between individualism and religion). But taken alone, "a conceptual scheme is insufficient to constitute a theory [Homans, 1964, p. 952]." A theory must contain a set of propositions or hypotheses that combine descriptive and relational concepts. Propositions state a relationship, such as "suicide rates vary directly with the degree of egoism in a society." Propositions must describe a relationship between two or more elements in a conceptual scheme.

Unfortunately, a set of propositions taken alone does not constitute a theory either. The set must be placed in a deductive scheme. Durkheim achieved this feature by deducing his proposition three from propositions one and two. Proposition five, in turn, is derived from three and four. "When propositions are so derived they are said to be explained and a theory is nothing if it is not explanation [Homans, 1964, p. 952]."

When a deductive system provides explanation, it also permits prediction. That is, while Durkheim explained the low rate of suicide in Spain by his theory, he could also have predicted suicide rates elsewhere.

> If, for instance, one did not know what the suicide rate in Eire was, but did know that the incidence of Protestantism was low, this proposition, together with proposition 3, would allow one to predict that the suicide rate there was low too [Homans, 1964, p. 952].

Theory, as I have defined it meets the goals of sociology. It permits the organization of descriptions, leads to explanations, and furnishes the basis for the prediction of events as yet unobserved. Only when all of these features are present will social theory be said to exist; the absence of any element renders the final product something less than theory. Given this position, it is clear that contemporary sociology has few, if any, theories (but see Berger, Zelditch, and Anderson, 1966, for exceptions to this conclusion). There exist, instead, small attempts at theory, many conceptual frameworks, a few propositional systems without deductive schemes, and, more often than not, vague explanations that bear little formal relationship to theory. Before I turn to these misrepresentations, it is necessary to treat each element in a theoretical system.

THE CONTENT OF THEORIES

Concepts

As an image of reality, concepts are perhaps the most critical element in any theory. Yet while one function of theory is to identify concepts for examination, the concept itself may turn back on a theory and become the major flaw in an otherwise excellent system. This is often the case in theoretical systems with vague, ill-defined or inappropriately measured concepts.

A concept carries with it what all definitions of social objects contain: It designates and suggests a plan of action toward some social object. For example, the concept of self, which occupies a central position in the interactionist framework, is seen as a series of definitions persons hold toward themselves as social objects. Sociologists interested in observing this object have typically assumed that one strategy is to ask persons who they are. This simple question elicits self-definitions and can be seen as following from the definition given that object in the interactionist perspective.

When placed within a theoretical system, concepts become its major designating units. Concepts *define* the shape and content of theories. In the example from Durkheim, his major descriptive concepts were suicide, individualism, and Protestantism.

In addition to their designating function, concepts perform at least three other functions (Blumer, 1931). First, they introduce a new orientation or point of view into the scientific process. Second, they serve as tools or as means of translating perceptions of the environment into meaningful scientific dialogue and operations. Third, they make possible deductive reasoning and, thus, the anticipation of new experience and perceptions.

As a source of new perspectives, scientific concepts carry a double meaning: as a way of looking at things, and as a way of bringing things into existence. Through scientific conceptualization the perceptual world is given an order and coherence that could not be perceived before conceptualization. The concept enables the sociologist to capture a moment of reality and give it a common quality. While scientific action cannot precede conceptualization, the most critical function of the concept is that it permits the scientist, in a community of other scientists, to lift his own idiosyncratic experiences to the level of consensual meaning. It also enables him to carry on an interaction with his environment; he indicates to himself what a concept means and acts toward the designation of that meaning. Scientists are continually assessing the meanings imputed to concepts—assessing them against their relationships to theories, their ability to be perceived by others, and their ability to facilitate understanding and explanation. The concept thus acts as a sensitizer of experience and perception, opening new realms of observation, closing others. That is, to conceive and perceive an object in one manner precludes conception from another, and this is the dilemma of the sociologist (and of all sciences in general). To restrict, for example, observations of the social self to answers given to the question "Who am I?" means that the self is perceived and analyzed in terms of this question and not by another. The need for triangulation is again apparent; sociologists must approach the empirical world from as many methodological perspectives as possible.

The second function, that of a *tool*, is best understood when it is recognized that the concept suggests operational activity the scientist undertakes as he gathers observations. When I say the self is measured by answers to the question "Who am I?" test I am utilizing a concept in this instrumental fashion–that is, I am directing concrete empirical activity toward that event. The success of the activity is measured by the extent to which concrete observations of the concept can be made. If such observations cannot be made, conception of the object is lacking. The valued concepts in sociology should be those that both release empirical activity and facilitate new sensitizing perceptions of reality.

It is often the case that a concept cannot be directly observed–its existence must be inferred, as when the sociologist attempts to discuss nonbehaviorally observable events such as symbols, attitudes and selves. When the existence of a concept must be inferred, the usual canons of observation must be replaced by the criteria of explanation. The scientist must ask himself, "If I infer this process to occur, can I develop better explanations than if I did not make such an inference?" If the answer is yes, then the scientist is said to be employing hypothetical and noncontingent or nonempirically observable concepts.

It matters little whether sociological concepts designate empirically observable or empirically inferred events. If the product of the inference or observation is better sociological theory, the concept has served a useful purpose. Often in the early phases of a concept's development, inferences, not observations, will be dictated, since conceptualizations typically come before operationalizations and observations. The act of measurement and observation may at first be crude and inexact, but in time methods of observation will develop, and perhaps become standardized. This has been the case with the concept of "self." For many years its existence was inferred, seldom observed. With the development of the "Who am I?" test, a method of observing it was finally available.

Too often, however, strategies of measurement are taken as ends in themselves and the theoretical role of the concept is ignored. Since so many key sociological concepts can be only inferred, many analysts feel that moderate advances can be made by developing empirical tools to measure at least some components of these vague concepts. Unfortunately, as Blumer has argued, this strategy avoids the issue. Commenting on the attempts of sociologists and psychologists to operationalize the concept "attitude," he notes:

> The clarification of concepts is not achieved by . . . inventing new technical instruments or by improving the reliability of old techniques—such instruments and techniques are neutral to the concepts on behalf of which they may be used. The clarification of concepts does not come from piling up mountains of research findings. As just one illustration I would point to the hundreds of studies of attitudes and the thousands of items they have yielded; these thousands of items of finding have not contributed one iota of clarification to the concept of attitudes. By the same token, the mere extension of research in scope and direction does not offer in itself assurance of leading to clarification of concepts. These various lines of endeavor, as the results themselves seem abundantly to testify, do not meet the problem of the ambiguous concept [1954, pp. 5-6].

For operationalizations of concepts to be of use, their role as a source of deductive systems must be utilized. By observing several discrete instances of a concept, sociologists are able to move beyond them to problems that transcend them. This was the major achievement of Goffman in his analysis of stigma. . . .He began with a vague definition of this concept (strained interaction) and observed that varieties of this process occurred in such areas as race relationships, crime and delinquency, social disorganization, and mental illness. By combining observations from these other settings, he was able to abstract a series of propositions that explained behavior in more than one situation. As an example, he observed that under conditions of strained interaction the stigmatized person was led to categorize the audiences he would come in contact with. Some audiences were informed of the stigmatizing conditions, some shared the condition, and others were not informed. From this observation a number of propositions were developed to specify the form and shape of interaction taken by the stigmatized person.

Ideally, the sociological concept permits new perceptions of reality by opening previously unexplored avenues of action. Once this occurs the concept will specify lines of empirical activity. If this happens, the sociologist will place his observations into propositional schemes of reasoning—in short, into theory. At each of these steps theory and methodological activity take on increasing importance. Research methods serve to operationalize the concept; theory both stimulates new concepts and provides a framework within which emergent propositions are placed.

Scientific versus Everyday Concepts

While all concepts propose lines of action toward social objects, scientific concepts must meet certain criteria. They must be consensually defined within the community of scientists. When Durkheim states that suicide rates vary by the degree of egoism, it is assumed that other sociologists know what he means. Everyday concepts seldom possess this quality; often they are not consensually defined and most frequently they refer to what is sensed, not what is analyzed. Furthermore, the everyday concept lacks the development toward systematization that the scientific concept must have. In short, the scientific concept is continually evaluated by the canons of science; the everyday concept is evaluated by its ability to give order to the life of its user–everyday man.

These points can be illustrated by examining the concept "self." For the symbolic interactionist, the self refers to a very special set of events. Within the theoretical system it is accorded high priority and a number of tests and strategies have been developed for its measurement. The "Who am I?" test is but one of many (see Kuhn and McPartland, 1954), in the nearly 80 years symbolic interactionists have struggled with the meaning of this term. Kuhn and McPartland have described the uneven scientific career of this concept as follows:

> Although the self has long been the central concept in the symbolic interaction approach to social psychology, little if anything has been done to employ it directly in empirical research. There are several reasons for this, one of the most important of which is that there has been no consensus regarding the class of phenomena to which the self ought to be operationally ordered. The self has been called an image, a conception, a concept, a feeling, an internalization, a self looking at oneself, and most commonly simply the self (with perhaps the most ambiguous implications of all) [1954, p. 68].

The self as a concept has had a career, even if it has been uneven. Everyday concepts seldom have a life of this order. Blumer notes:

> To my mind, the chief difference is that the abstraction embodied in the common-sense concept is just accepted and is not made the subject of special analysis and study. Consequently abstraction is soon arrested and not pushed to the length that is true in the case of scientific concepts. . . . The common-sense concepts are sufficient for the crude demands of ordinary experience. Minor elements of inconsistency within experiences and a fringe of uncertainty can be ignored and are ignored. Hence experiences that might be productive of more refined abstractions do not arise as problems.
>
> With such a background it is to be expected that "common sense," as the term strongly suggests, refers to what is sensed, instead of what is acutely analyzed [1931, pp. 522–23].

That Blumer's position is correct, is documented when a sociologist proposes to ask an ordinary individual what he means by a common-sense term. The individual takes its meaning for granted, and if pressed for an explanation, is likely to point to the reference of his designation. He is not likely to show how that term relates to several others in a deductive scheme—as a scientist properly would. Hence, while persons daily make references to themselves and in so doing employ the concept self, they do so without the heightened criticalness of the scientist.

But while the scientific concept has a career and is subject to special demands, it still has a great deal in common with everyday concepts. This is so because ultimately the subject matter of sociology is: ". . . precisely the matter about which people have convictions, prejudices, hates, the things about which they praise or blame another." Hence, ". . . it would be rather too much to expect our concepts to be as free of popular feeling and distortion as are most names in chemistry or physics [Hughes, 1952, p. 131]." This points to one of the major problems of sociological concepts—that they are ultimately derived from everyday actions (see Rose, 1960). On the one hand, sociological concepts must have an everyday relevance; on the other hand, they must have a meaning that is strictly and totally sociological. If they do not, they become subject to the same ambiguities of the everyday term.

Concepts, then, are the most important element in a theoretical system. They provide the basis for a theory's operationalizations, open unexplored avenues of analysis, and lead the way to new deductive schemes. Scientific concepts must point clearly to instances of the classes of objects they designate, distinguish the conceptualized objects from other classes of objects, and permit the development of cumulative knowledge that pertains to the class of objects conceptualized (see Blumer, 1955, p. 59). In contrast to everyday common-sense terms, scientific concepts have careers, demand consensual, scientific definition, and are assessed by their ability to fit into and generate theory. They open the way for new perspectives, while common-sense terms only validate and reinforce what is known.

The Definition

Behind most concepts is a definition that permits the sociologist to move from the concept to a single case or instance of it. Definitions intervene between the perception of an instance of a concept and the operational process of acting on that instance. Thus, definitions attached to concepts become critical links in the theory process; they assist in the movement toward the second function of the concept—to facilitate observation. Returning to the example of the self, it can be seen that by defining the self as answers to the "Who Am I?" test the sociologist has moved from his conception of the object to its observation.

Because definitions occupy such an important role in the total structure of a theory, a series of ideal standards or norms are associated with their use. Definitions must be exact and state what they do and do not apply to. To state that the self is measured by answers to the "Who are you?" test precisely designates an empirical referent of that concept. Negative definitions ("The self is not the sum total of the attitudes a person holds") do not provide direct specifications for observation; they only tell what not to look for.

In addition to being exact and positive, definitions should be phrased in precise scientific terminology, not in everyday, common-sense terms. (The scientific definition is subject to the norms of consistency, precision and criticalness.) Finally, definitions should not contain the term they propose to define. A tautological definition defines by naming and serves no designating function. If, for example, the self is defined as "self-attitudes held toward the self," no external referent for its observation is given.

The sociologist may employ three types of definitions as he moves from concepts to observations. First are nominal definitions, which "are declarations of intention to use a certain word or phrase as a substitute for another word or phrase [Bierstedt, 1959, p. 126]." One might, for example, define the concept self by the symbol *S* and use only that symbol when referring to the self. Nominal definitions have three characteristics. As the example indicates, the concept defined has "literally no meaning than that given arbitrarily to it [Bierstedt, 1959, p. 126]." Second, the definition has no claim to empirical verification–it cannot be proven true or false, because by definition it is as it is defined. Third, because nominal definitions are true by definition, they cannot serve as a basis for inference or systematic theory construction. Nominal definitions, while not contributing to empirical verifications of theory, do serve several functions for the sociologist. They represent a way of introducing new terms and concepts into a scientific terminology; they indicate a way by which the sociologist can give special recognition to his concepts; and they "permit us to economize space, time and attention in the same way that abbreviations do [Bierstedt, 1959, p. 131]." In this sense they act as symbols and permit the analyst to state his theory with terms that have precise meaning and brevity. Finally, nominal definitions allow the sociologist to "substitute new concepts for familiar words or ordinary speech that have emotional or other nonlogical connotations [Bierstedt, 1959, p. 131]."

A word of qualification must be inserted regarding this last function, for–as Hughes (1952, p. 131) notes–the act of renaming a social object does not eliminate the fact that it may still carry the same qualities. Still, the chief function and justification of the nominal definition is its ability to provide precise designations of concepts–even if these designations lack a concrete empirical base.

The second major type of definition is the real definition. It differs from the nominal definition because it "operates not only on the symbolic or linguistic level but also on the referential level [Bierstedt, 1959, p. 126]." A real definition gives meaning to a concept by resolving it into its constituent elements. For example, a social group might be defined as a number of persons called members who interact with one another. In this case, the concept is broken into sub-elements (person, member, action). By combining these elements, symbolic meaning is given the term. In addition, specifications for its observation are offered. Real definitions take the form of propositions because they place a number of elements together in a relational system.

The ultimate test of these two types of definitions is quite different. Nominal definitions are tested by their ability to give precise meaning to concepts; real definitions are examined in terms of the empirical observations they generate.

The last major type of definition is operational. This relates a concept to the process by which it will be measured. An operational definition of the self could be responses to the "Who Am I?" test. The concept is defined by a statement that specifies how it will be observed. Like the real definition, the operational definition is tested by its ability to generate concrete observations. It does not contain elements of the proposition, however. The operational form becomes the major way of translating real definitions into empirical units; the stress is once again on the second function of concepts (as tools).

Careers of Concepts and Types of Definitions

It is useful to reconsider the point that scientific concepts have careers and to illustrate the role of definitions at various points in their careers. I suggested earlier that theories contain two basic types of concepts: descriptive and relational or empirical. Descriptive concepts point to the domain of the theory; empirical concepts indicate how it is to be put into propositional form. I also suggested that the best concepts are those that specify new propositions with empirical referents. In the career of a concept it can be seen that the three types of definitions will be of varying value. In its early phase a concept is likely to be defined nominally. This will be the case, for example, when the theorist is struggling to give new meaning to an old concept. (Under other circumstances he may be striving for a precise definition of his concepts and might also turn to the nominal definition.) As the theorist attains greater conceptual clarification, he is likely to move toward real and operational definitions; by this point his concepts will have begun to bear scientific fruit, as demonstrated by his ability to state them in propositions, and as he strives toward this goal, the necessity of empirical observations will become apparent. The concept thus begins its movement into the operational phase. Various tests, questions, and methods of observation will be adopted, as tentative forms of data are brought to bear upon his propositions. In this phase of a theory's development, a relatively balanced proportion of real and operational definitions will be incorporated. An excess of any of the three types hampers a theory's ability to achieve the goals of explanation and prediction. Nominal definitions keep the theory too far from empirical reality; real definitions lack the precise empirical specifications a theory demands; operational definitions alone do not provide the base for theory. There must be a continual interaction between conceptualizations, propositions, and the empirical world.

Since a theory becomes an ongoing form of interaction the scientist carries on between his conceptualizations and his observations of empirical reality, at no point in its career can it be said that conceptualizations end and observations begin. The two processes go hand-in-hand–each contributing equally to the other's growth. Blumer has described this relationship as follows:

> Theory, inquiry and empirical fact are interwoven in a texture of operation with theory guiding inquiry, inquiry seeking and isolating facts, and facts affecting theory. The fruitfulness of their interplay is the means by which an empirical science develops. [1954, p. 1].

If a sociologist forgets that the major goal of his discipline is the development of theory, a process of goal-displacement can occur such that operational definitions and empirical observations become ends in themselves. Placing empirical inquiry above theoretical development represents an undue emphasis on definitive-empirical concepts, with a corresponding deemphasis on sensitizing-generic concepts. By relying solely on concepts that can be easily translated into operational definitions, the sociologist too quickly leaves the world of theory and enters the world of empirical fact. The better strategy is to work slowly and carefully from emergent conceptualizations to empirical observations (the sensitizing approach). . . . The sociologist who adopts this method does not ignore empirical observations–he simply moves more cautiously in his collection and interpretation of them.

The Hypothesis and Proposition

The next element of theory that must be considered is the hypothesis. A hypothesis, or proposition (I view them as identical), is defined as a statement of relationship between two or more concepts. Durkheim's statement that "In any social grouping, the suicide rate varies with the degree of egoism" is a proposition. It expresses an interrelationship between more than one concept. Fundamentally, propositions rest upon the definition and the concept, because, as I have just shown, they combine concepts in an explanatory and predictive manner. A proposition can be no better than the elements that comprise it (concepts and definitions). In turn, concepts can be of no greater utility than the plans of action derived from them. And last, definitions are of little value unless the concepts they define are ordered in a propositional system. There is a complex interdependence between all the elements of theory thus far discussed. A weak concept, definition, or proposition weakens any theory.

Because concepts represent tentative ways of looking at reality, propositions become tentative statements concerning the occurrence and interrelationship of events in the empirical world. Thus, propositions, occupy the same tentative and processual position in theory as concepts and definitions. Durkheim's propositions regarding suicide represent the cardinal feature of all propositions: It states a relationship between two or more concepts where one element in the proposition is assumed to be the cause of another. In Durkheim's first proposition, egoism is assumed to be the cause of suicide. That concept seen as causal is termed a causal, determinant, or independent factor; that concept which is caused is the resultant, caused, or dependent variable. When a proposition states an empirically observable event, the propositions it combines are variables. In some cases these variables will have two values (e.g., present or not present); in other cases they will take values of degree (e.g., greater or less); in still other cases, differences in degree can be expressed in terms of a unit of measurement.

Propositions must meet the following criteria. First, the status of the related concepts must be so clearly defined that it is apparent which is caused and which is causal. Unless a reader can unequivocally determine this, it is difficult for him to work with the proposition. Zetterberg illustrated this rule in his discussion of Max Weber's *The Protestant Ethic and the Spirit of Capitalism.* He noted (1965, p. 67) that Weber's work has been misunderstood because it fails to precisely state its key proposition.

Its proposition is hinted in its very title: the Protestant ethic is the determinant and the spirit of capitalism is the result. There are, however, at least four different ways of specifying the determinant and the result in this proposition. If the terms in italics stand for the variates that may be related, we have these possibilities:

1. The *Protestant* Ethic and the Spirit of *Capitalism*
2. The Protestant *Ethic* and the Spirit of *Capitalism*
3. The *Protestant* Ethic and the *Spirit* of Capitalism
4. The Protestant *Ethic* and the *Spirit* of Capitalism

There are four possible propositions stated in Weber's title. The first suggests a comparison of persons who are Protestants and become capitalists with non-Protestants who become capitalists. The fourth assumes "that some ethical precepts in Protestantism lead to a particular spirit which is manifested in a concern for one's material wealth and prestige [Zetterberg, 1965, p. 68]." Zetterberg suggests that

> All four ways of interpreting the thesis are in varying degrees present in Weber. Also, Weber's critics often touch upon some of these ways of interpreting the thesis in a haphazard way. Thus, claims by his critics that Weber has been proved right or wrong are usually restricted to one or two of these possibilities. Much

> confusion could have been avoided if the determinant and the result of the proposition had been more clearly specified [1965, p. 68].

Second, propositions must be so stated that they can be tested. In general, the more varied the tests of a proposition, the greater its power. This rule suggests that propositions may be tested in more than one way, which is in fact the case, although sociologists commonly assume that empirical verification is the only true test. This is an erroneous assumption, for many propositions combine concepts that have no empirical referents. When propositions combine concepts that have empirically inferred referents, the test of logical consistency may be employed. This test asks whether or not the proposition contains contradictory elements that if logically analyzed could lead to its disproof, a test that is commonly used in purely deductive theory formulations. It will be remembered that Durkheim's theory contains five propositions, two of which are deducible from others. Had Durkheim made an illogical deduction within this system, the proposition so derived could have been immediately disproven. In this sense, "the prime test is that no contradictory inferences can be or are drawn from the theory [Schrag, 1967, p. 250]."

If propositions combine empirical concepts, the test of operational adequacy may be utilized. Unless concepts can be related to observations, the proposition, and ultimately the theory, remain untested (Schrag, 1967, p. 250).

Another test is empirical adequacy. This deals with the degree of congruence between the proposition and empirical evidence. A subsidiary test is the general predictive and explanatory power of the proposition. Not only must it fit the data, but it should cover as many different empirical situations as possible, be as abstract and powerful as possible.

Ideally every proposition should pass each of these tests. The third rule states that propositions should be combined with other propositions so that a deductive theoretical system may be developed. Unless this combination is achieved, the explanatory power of any proposition is greatly reduced. Fourth, propositions should be stated so that they predict and explain the domain specified by the concepts. If they do not, they remain at the level of description and do little to move the sociologist closer toward theory. Fifth, some theoretical propositions must contain higher-order concepts. It is quite easy to formulate propositions of an ordinary nature. These are likely to contain few, if any, higher-order concepts and therefore contribute little to theory development. In Durkheim's theory the proposition that "Spain has a low suicide rate because the incidence of Protestantism is low" is relatively ordinary, although it does permit a body of data to be organized. Durkheim's higher-order proposition concerning rates of suicide and degree of egoism is much more powerful and more adequately meets this test.

Sixth, propositions must be stated in terms of the normal rules of concepts and definitions. They must be positive and not negative; must be precise and stated in scientific terms; must not be tautological; and must be capable of test, be that logical, empirical, or operational. Seventh, propositions must be capable of reflecting both process and stability. The most common propositions in sociology take the form of direct relationships that assume that one variable simply causes variations in another (see Homans, 1964, p. 956–59). Durkheim's proposition concerning variations in suicide rates represents this kind of proposition. It is argued that as rates of egoism change, so too does the rate of suicide. There is nothing inherently wrong with these propositions –the problem is that virtually all of the propositions in contemporary sociology are stated in this form; it is commonly ignored that a large proportion of human behavior involves situations where variables interact and that as one changes value, so too does the other. But this is not a one-way change, as Durkheim assumed in his analysis of suicide. In cases of interaction, variables mutually influence one another.

This rule was discussed . . . when I stated that interaction theory demands propositions of interaction. Becker's analysis of the marijuana user illustrates this type of proposition. The third proposition from his analysis met this rule. It indicated how the attitudes and actions of a marijuana user changed depending on who his interactional partners were. This proposition is a lower-order statement of the prediction that "the actual responses of others toward the individual will effect the behavior of the individual [Kinch, 1963, p. 482]." Remaining consistent with interaction theory it can be predicted that: (1) The reactions of Person A to Person B's definitions of him will alter the definitions of B toward A.

On the concrete level: (2) Nonusers of marijuana will change their attitudes toward the drug and toward users to the extent that they meet users who act favorably in their presence.

Similarly: (3) Marijuana users who favorably influence nonusers are likely to change their definitions of the nonuser and begin to smoke and use the drug with greater frequency in the presence of nonusers.

These three propositions illustrate how interaction may be treated propositionally. They represent interactive propositions and are to be contrasted to the directional statements of Durkheim discussed earlier. Had I confined the above predictions to the directional form I might have stated: (4) The more favorable the attitudes of nonusers of marijuana to the drug, the more frequently users will smoke in the presence of nonusers–a proposition that merely states that as the independent variable (attitudes of nonusers) takes on positive values, the dependent variable (smoking in the presence of nonusers) increases in frequency. Propositions 1–3 significantly differ from 4 because they posit reciprocal changes in each variable such that the value of the independent and dependent variables at any point in time is a function of this interaction. . . .

* * *

Eighth, some propositions should be stated so that they express the temporal and situational context under explanation—even though propositions should be made as abstract as possible—because to understand any relationship it is necessary to understand the context in which it exists. This of course was achieved by Durkheim's lower-order proposition concerning suicide rates in Spain. While his highest-order prediction contained no specific time-place reference, his lower-order ones did. The necessity of expressing these references in the proposition derives from the fundamental fact that the social events sociologists analyze are embedded in ongoing units of social organization, and unless statements concerning the social nexus of these events can be made, propositions are reduced in explanatory power. Blumer has illustrated this point:

> A variable relation states that reasonably staunch Erie County Republicans become confirmed in their attachment to their candidate as a result of listening to the campaign materials of the rival party. This bare and interesting finding gives us no picture of them as human beings in their particular world. We do not know the run of their experiences which induced an organization of their sentiments and views, not do we know what this organization is; we do not know the special atmosphere or codes of their social circles; we do not know the reinforcements and rationalizations that come from their fellows. . . . In short, we do not have the picture to size up and understand what their confirmed attachment to a political candidate means in terms of their experience and social context. This fuller picture of the "here and now" context is not given in variable relations. . . . Yet, as I think logicians would agree, to understand adequately the "here and now" relation it is necessary to understand the "here and now" context. The variable relation is a single relation, necessarily stripped bare of the complex of things that sustain it in a "here and now" context. Accordingly, our understanding of it as a "here and now" matter suffers [1956, p. 685].

Blumer's point is clear—for a proposition to be understood it must contain specifications regarding the situations explained. Becker's analysis of the marijuana user satisfies this rule. At several points his material points to the situated context of marijuana smoking and describes a sequential model for its use. By specifying the time and place of this activity he was able to give substance to his propositions that a user takes on shifting attitudes toward the drug as he moves through the subculture. His situational specifications concerning interaction in "safe" and "unsafe" settings illustrates this feature of the proposition.

Some propositions, because of their abstract nature, will not contain time-place references. These references will appear in the exposition of higher-order propositions and in the derivation of concrete predictions.

I have stated eight rules for the proposition:

1. The causal status of all elements in the proposition must be established unequivocally.
2. The proposition must be stated so that it is testable in more than one way. Common tests include logical consistency, operational, and empirical adequacy.
3. Propositions should be placed within a deductive system.
4. Propositions must predict and explain the domain under analysis.
5. Some propositions must contain at least some concepts of high theoretical value.
6. Propositions must be stated in terms of the normal rules of concepts and definitions.
7. Propositions must be capable of reflecting both process and stability.
8. Some propositions should be expressed in a manner that permits temporal and spatial specifications.

Properties and Types of Propositions

Propositions give theory its quality of explanation. They represent an advance beyond concept development and permit the construction of deductive schemes. The sociologist has at his disposal a number of different types of propositions. Propositions may be categorized in terms of: the number of concepts combined; their causal breadth (e.g., the number of cases explained); the relationship between concepts (e.g., interactive, direct, etc.); the causal status assigned the independent variable (e.g., interchangeable with other independent variables, etc.).

Propositions that combine only two concepts are termed bivariate (as distinguished from multivariate propositions, which combine three or more concepts in a sequential pattern). It might be predicted, for example, that as education increases, upward mobility is enhanced, which increases the probability that one's life style will also change. A sequential explanation is implied in this statement. Education itself is insufficient to explain change in life style; upward mocility must also occur. In general, analysts should strive for multivariate predictions, even while recognizing these could be formulated as a series of bivariate relationships, because (as the earlier discussion of causal propositions indicated) variables other than those explicitly contained in a causal system may be creating the differences observed. Multivariate predictions permit the consideration of additional causal factors.

Propositions may be formed to cover all of the cases analyzed, in which case they are universal, or they may apply to just a proportion of those cases. This is the distinction between universal and conditional predictions. The interactionist favors universal predictions. Blumer offers an example of such a prediction. Paraphrased it reads:

> Objects in the symbolic environment never carry their own meanings–meaning is always conferred upon them through the process of interpretation, definition and interaction[1966, pp. 539–40].

Becker's analysis of the marijuana user also furnishes a universal prediction:

> A potential user must have regular access to the drug and must learn the proper means of acting towards it before he will become a regular user [Becker, 1953].

Conditional predictions cover some sub-class of the events observed. Thus it might be predicted that for males, those exposed to marijuana on a regular basis become regular users of the drug.

The basic flaw with this type of prediction is the question of the remaining females. In the prediction they represent deviant cases. Analysis of such cases can serve two important functions (Kendall and Wolf, 1955, pp. 167–70). First, through deviant-case analysis the researcher is able to uncover additional and relevant factors that could lead to needed theoretical revision. Kendall and Wolf state:

> Through careful analysis of the cases which do not exhibit the expected behavior, the researcher recognizes the oversimplification of his theoretical structure and becomes aware of the need for incorporating further variables into his predictive scheme [1955, p. 168].

Kendall and Wolf offer the example of an investigation directed to the impact of Orson Welles' "War of the Worlds" broadcast. It was predicted that listeners who heard the entire program would understand that Welles was presenting a play. An analysis of cases revealed that 15 percent of those who heard the entire program considered it to be news. Investigation of these cases uncovered the fact that for those listeners interruptions of radio programs with news bulletins was so taken for granted that they did not "hear" Welles' statements describing his report as a play. The final proposition was revised on the basis of these cases to include the listeners' expectation for radio listening, as well as whether or not the entire program was heard.

A second function of deviant case analysis is to refine the measurement of statistical variables used to locate the deviant cases (Kendall and Wolf, 1965, p. 169). Virtually all of modern social research assumes that scales and indices can be constructed to measure complex social events. Many times, however, these scales blur the very distinctions the investigator wishes to establish through his analysis. By analyzing deviant cases, weaknesses of the measurement process can be uncovered. Merton's (1946, pp. 125–30) study of responses to Kate Smith's war bond broadcast illustrates this function of the deviant case. He predicted that listeners who had close relatives in the armed forces would be more likely to buy war bonds. His analysis compared listeners with close relatives in the armed forces with those who did not. While his prediction was largely confirmed, a number of listeners who had brothers, sons, and husbands in the armed forces were not persuaded by the broadcast. Investigation of these deviant cases revealed that his index had misclassified them: The close kin of deviant cases were stationed in the United States and were not seen as in immediate danger. A reclassification confirmed Merton's general prediction. In his study, analysis of deviant cases led to revisions of the measurement index and then to confirmation of the hypothesis.

If the researcher seriously strives for universal propositions, then, his probabilistic predictions can be made universal by analysis of deviant cases. As a general rule I propose analysis of every case initially not covered by a proposition. The functions of deviant-case analysis for subsequent research and theory justify this rule.

Earlier I illustrated the difference between interactive and directional propositions. If the interactionist perspective is only partially adopted, I believe there is sufficient justification for constructing propositions that describe interaction or interdependence between social events. Clearly both types of propositions are needed. Currently, however, there is an underrepresentation of interactive propositions in the literature (Homans, 1964, pp. 958–59).

Many multivariate propositions will assign equal causal status to independent variables. For example, both upward mobility and higher education may, under certain conditions, cause changes in life style. In universal propositions, the investigator assumes that he has isolated the necessary causal variables. When deviant cases are ignored this assurance is often lacking in conditional predictions. The distinction under consideration is the extent to which sociologists can discover necessary and sufficient causes for the social events examined. Necessary conditions predict that whenever a certain event occurs, that which it is assumed to cause will also follow. Sufficient conditions are those that will only cause the event studied. Becker's study of the marijuana user represents an attempt to uncover a series of necessary conditions that led to marijuana use. Regular access to the drug, learning to perceive the drug's effect, and interaction with other users were seen as necessary conditions that cumulatively produced regular drug use; no single condition was sufficient. Seldom will the sociologist find such conditions, because few social events are the product of only one cause.

Given this view of causation, I propose that sociologists need sequential propositions that describe the events necessary for the production of any social process. These must be sequential in the simple sense that all human interaction occurs over time, and they must discover necessary events, because few events are the product of one condition.

REFERENCES

Becker, Howard S. 1953. "Becoming a Marihuana User." *American Journal of Sociology* 59 (Nov.): 235–42.

Berger, Joseph, Zelditch, Morris, Jr., and Anderson, Bo. 1966. *Sociological Theories in Progress.* Boston: Houghton Mifflin.

Bierstedt, Robert. 1959. "Nominal and Real Definitions in Sociological Theory." In *Symposium on Sociological Theory,* Llewellyn Gross, ed., pp. 121–44. New York: Harper and Row.

Blumer, Herbert. 1931. "Science Without Concepts," *American Journal of Sociology* 36 (Jan.): 515–33.

———. 1954. "What Is Wrong With Social Theory?" *American Sociological Review* 19 (Feb.): 3–10.

———. 1955. "Attitudes and the Social Act." *Social Problems* 3 (Summer): 59–65.

———. 1956. "Sociological Analysis and the 'Variable'." *American Sociological Review* 21 (Dec.): 683–90.

———. 1966. "Sociological Implications of the Thought of George Herbert Mead." *American Journal of Sociology* 71 (Mar.): 535–44.

Homans, George Casper. 1964. "Contemporary Theory in Sociology." In *Handbook of Modern Sociology,* R.E.L. Faris, ed., pp. 951–77. Chicago: Rand McNally.

Hughes, Everett C., and Hughes, Helen McGill. 1952. *Where Peoples Meet.* Glencoe, Ill.: Free Press.

Kendall, Patricia L., and Wolf, Katherine M. 1955. "The Two Purposes of Deviant Case Analysis." In *The Language of Social Research,* Paul F. Lazarsfeld and Morris Rosenberg, eds., pp. 167–70. Glencoe, Ill.: Free Press.

Kinch, John W. 1963. "A Formalized Theory of the Self-Concept." *American Journal of Sociology* 68 (Jan.): 481–86.

Kuhn, Manford H., and McPartland, Thomas S. 1954. "An Empirical Investigation of Self-Attitudes," *American Sociological Review* 19 (Feb.): 68–76.

Merton, Robert K. and Kendall, Patricia L. 1946. "The Focused Interview." *American Journal of Sociology* 51 (May): 541–57.

Rose, Edward. 1960. "The English Record of a Natural Sociology." *American Sociological Review* 25 (April): 193–208.

Schrag, Clarence. 1967. "Philosophical Issues in the Science of Sociology." *Sociology and Social Research* 51 (April): 361–72.

Zetterberg, Hans. 1965. *On Theory and Verification in Sociology,* 2nd ed. Totowa, N.J.: Bedminster Press.

Dissection I: Causes, Concepts, and Definitions

Batwinged Hamburger Snatcher

Dan O'Neill

Dan O'Neill. Batwinged Hamburger Snatcher, from *Hear the Sound of My Feet Walking . . Drown the Sound of My Voice Talking,* published by Glide Publications.

THERE ARE MANY THINGS MESSING UP OUR CIVILIZATION TODAY.. EFFECTS OF AN INVISIBLE CAUSE..
I DON'T UNDERSTAND..
HOW CAN YOU..
YOU ARE MORE REAL..
MORE REAL?
MORE REAL THAN ME..
YOU ARE A **BIRD**..
SO..
YOU UNDERSTAND CONCEPTS LINKED TO THE CONCEPT **BIRD**!!

LIKE WHAT?
..YOU DUMMY!! THINK!! THE CONCEPT WORM! NEST!! TREE!!
..YOU ARE A BATWINGED HAMBURGER SNATCHER..
I AM WORSE THAN THAT..
I AM THE ONE AND ONLY BATWINGED HAMBURGER SNATCHER..

SO?
.. SO SINCE I FLY.. A BIRD CONCEPT.. LIKE YOU.. WE CAN BOTH SPEAK OF BIRD CONCEPTS.. WORM.. FOOD.. TREE.. SHELTER.. NEST.. HOME.. LOVE..
YEAH?
.. NOW I CAN HOPE TO SPEAK TO YOU OF A BATWINGED HAMBURGER SNATCHER CONCEPT..
..IF IT'S FIERCE WILL YOU HOLD ME..?

WILL IT CREEP UP.. OR POUNCE FROM THE SKY?
THIS IS EXACTLY WHY I GET STONED A LOT..

I'M TRYING TO EXPLAIN THE NATURE OF HAMBURGER..
I LIKE MUSTARD ON MY HAMBURGERS..
..IF YOU GAVE A WORD ASSOCIATION TEST TO AN INTELLIGENT FOREIGNER..
..AND THEY DO EXIST..
..AND DILL PICKLE.. DON'T FORGET THE DILL PICKLE..
..YOU WOULD FIND AFTER HANDING THEM A LIST OF WORDS ONE ANSWER..
I CAN'T STAND MAYONNAISE ON A HAMBURGER..
IT'S A SHORT LIST..

I'M NOT OVERLY FOND OF KETCHUP, EITHER..
.. HAMBURGER
.. HYDROGEN BOMB
.. MICKEY MOUSE
.. MONEY
.. BIBLE BELT
.. BEAUTY
.. PARANOIA
.. DEATH
.. CHRIST IN HIDING

I GET AN UPSET STOMACH FROM HOTDOGS!!
ALL THESE THINGS MEAN AMERICA..
I USED TO ORDER CHOCOLATE MILK SHAKES WITH MY HAMBURGER..
..NOW I ORDER VANILLA..
..NOW HE ORDERS VANILLA..
WHERE ARE YOU GOING..?
THERE'S ONE THING ON THAT LIST THAT I CAN RESOLVE..

THAT BATWING IS A STRANGE YOUNG MAN..
COME ON OUT OF HIDING! YOU LITTLE CREEPS!

TOPIC II: Tumbling Dice and City Blocks: Probability and Sampling

> But throughout all this (survey research) one fact remained, a very disturbing one to the student of social organization. The ***individual*** remained the unit of analysis. No matter how complex the analysis . . . the studies focused on individuals as separate and independent units. . . . Samples were random, never including (except by accident) two persons who were friends. . . . As a result, the kinds of substantive problems on which such research focused tended to be problems of "aggregate psychology," that is ***within***-individual problems, and never problems concerned with relations between people.
>
> James S. Coleman
> "Relational Analysis"

As one moves from the abstract level of theory to the empirics of data, one immediately confronts a dual problem; what data to observe and whether the observation of these specific data will allow one to make generalizations to other unobserved data of the same type. In general, it is inefficient to observe all examples of a given phenomenon; a procedure for selecting certain of these examples (or units) for observation has to be arrived at. Further, the selection process should ideally produce a sample that is representative of all the data, so that one can make generalizations to the entire population, or class of objects, from which the sample is drawn. For example, if one wished to determine how many Americans watched a given TV show on a certain evening, one would have to determine a method of sampling units from the population (Americans) in such a manner that the responses of individuals in this sample could be considered representative and generalized back to the larger population of *all* Americans—a large order indeed!*

Historically, the problem of how to pick a representative sample has been approached in a number of ways, perhaps the most well-known being the technique of random sampling. Random sampling is based on the laws of probability.

> The earliest faint traces of probability, found in the Orient around 200 BC, were concerned with whether an expected child would be a male or a female. However, the first real cornerstone of the calculus of probability seems to have been laid in Italy when a commentary on Dante's *Divine Comedy* referenced the different

*This is the problem of external validity, to be discussed in more depth under Topic III.

Figure 3. Drawing a Sample

POPULATION

1	2	3	4
5	6	7	8
9	10	11	12
13	14	15	16
17	18	19	20
21	22	23	24
25	26	27	28
29	30	31	32
33	34	35	36
37	38	39	40
41	42	43	44
45	46	47	48

← Generalization?

SAMPLE

6	17	21
29	32	42
43	45	47

← Observation

> throws which could be made with three dice in the game of Hazard. The first mathematical treatment of gambling problems was *Suma* (1494) written by Luca Paccioli (1445–1509). This work gives the first version of the celebrated "problem of points," which concerns the "equitable division of the stakes between two players of unequal skill when the game is interrupted before its conclusion.[1]

Nearly 150 years later (1654), a French gambler, the Chevalier de Méré, in his eagerness to pin down the odds in a variety of gambling games, stimulated the French mathematicians Blaise Pascal and Pierre de Fermat into developing the cornerstones of modern probability theory.*

PROBABILITY SAMPLES

Discussed by Sanford Labovitz and Robert Hagedorn in "The Population and Sampling," a random sample, quite simply, is one drawn in such a way that each element (or unit) of the population has an equal chance of being chosen for the sample. The problem of how to determine an "equal" chance is where probability theory enters in. The various outcomes of a process (like

*It is the important problems that get solved. Sampling techniques were further refined and statistical tests invented (including the famous *t* test) to aid in the production processes of the British Isles Guinness Breweries.

tumbling dice) can be depended upon if and only if they occur equally often in an indefinitely large series of repetitions of the process in question.

> Simple empirical examples of processes whose outcomes are equally likely are (1) tossing a coin (the two outcomes, heads and tails, are equally likely) and (2) tossing a die (the six outcomes, one, two, three, four, five, and six, are equally likely). How do we know that these processes have equally likely outcomes? Only because if we actually do the tossing often enough each outcome will appear approximately as often as each other outcome. . . .[2]

> The basic sampling procedure that is followed in taking a random sample involves two steps, once the population has been defined. The first step is to assemble a list of the objects that are in the population. The second step is to decide, for each object listed, whether or not to include it in the sample; this decision is made on the basis of a random device (such as tossing a coin). Although there are many . . . random devices that could be used, the one in most common use today is the random number table. A random number table is a listing of digits such that the choice of which digit is to be placed in each position is random (that is, such that each digit has a one-tenth chance of being in any given position).[3]

So, if each unit of the population is listed and assigned a number (this list is usually called a *sampling frame*), and each number has an equal chance of being chosen from the table of random numbers (or by a coin flip or a die toss), then each unit of the population has an equal chance of coming up in the sample.

There are many variations upon this method of simple random sampling. Some of these are pointed out in Russell Ackoff's "Sampling Chart," and include *systematic* samples, differing types of *stratified* samples (also discussed by Labovitz and Hagedorn in "The Population and Sampling") and *cluster* samples; where one samples actual *areas* (towns, states, city blocks) rather than individuals.

NONPROBABILITY SAMPLES

James Coleman's remarks at the beginning of this discussion are amplified in his article, "Relational Analysis." It is Coleman's contention that probability samples, resting on the assumptions of independence between sampling units (people) and the equal chance of each unit being chosen for the sample, preclude the study of interaction patterns *between* people–which he claims is the proper subject matter of sociology. After all, if you are choosing people at random you may never come up with two persons in your sample who know each other, so how can you study interaction?

Coleman does not discuss the nonprobability sampling techniques of *judgement* sampling and *quota* sampling mentioned by Ackoff, but he does introduce and suggest use of the techniques of *snowball, saturation,* and *dense* sampling as appropriate to many problems in sociology. But there are grave problems involved in using nonprobability samples, as Labovitz and Hagedorn point out. For example, if the units in the population do not have an equal chance of appearing in the sample, with what faith do you generalize sample results back to your population?

In the final analysis, the "best" sampling technique is the one that works best for the specific research problem in question. Representativeness of sample units is just what you do *not* want if you are studying, say, the power holders in a community. In this case, you are looking for *unique* individuals, not representative ones. Choosing a sampling method is the first strategic decision one must make in the tactical organization of one's research design.

NOTES

1. Arthur L. Dudycha and Linda W. Dudycha, "Beharioral Statistics: An Historical Perspective," in *Statistical Issues*, ed. Roger E. Kirk, (Monterey, Ca.: Brooks/Cole Pub. Co., 1972), p. 3.
2. Theodore R. Anderson and Morris Zelditch, Jr., *A Basic Course In Statistics With Sociological Applications,* 2nd ed., (New York: Holt, Rinehart and Winston, 1968), pp. 195–6.
3. *Ibid*., p. 196.

SUGGESTED FURTHER READINGS

Alpert, Harry. "Some Observations On the Sociology of Sampling," *Social Forces* 31 (1952): 30–33.

Brookover, Linda, and Bach, Kurt W. "Time Sampling As A Field Technique," *Human Organization* 25 (Spring 1966): 64–70.

Kish, Leslie. *Survey Sampling.* New York: Wiley, 1965.

Lazerwitz, Bernard. "Sampling Theory and Procedures," in *Methodology in Social Research,* edited by Hubert A. Blalock and Ann B. Blalock, pp. 278–328. New York: McGraw-Hill, 1964.

Slonim, Morris James. *Sampling.* New York: Simon and Schuster, 1960.

Stephan, Frederick. "History of the Uses of Modern Sampling Procedures," *Journal of the American Statistical Association* 43 (March 1948): 12–39.

The Population and Sampling

Sanford Labovitz and Robert Hagedorn

The *population* refers to the largest body of individuals (or other units) being researched; for example, industrialized societies, urban riots, delinquents, college students, or infants. In the final analysis, the researcher wants to say something about the population. A crucial step in social research is to define the population clearly; a clearly defined population makes the selection of representative samples more probable. Such samples are used to infer characteristics of the part (sample) to the whole (population). In statistical terms, the conclusions of a study are restricted to the specified population. For example, if in 1970 you studied delinquents in Ohio, your statistically based conclusions are restricted exclusively to Ohio delinquents (at that particular point in time). The results may apply to delinquents from other states, but to an unknown degree. Further research is required before inferences may be made to other areas or to a larger or different number of individuals or units.

SAMPLING

A scientist seldom observes a total population, but usually gathers data on a part or *sample*. He then tries to specify something about the population from knowledge of the sample (that is, he infers from one to the other). Some populations can never be studied directly because of lack of accessibility, limited time, or prohibitive cost. For example, no one is presently capable of organizing a study of all inhabitants in the world. Furthermore, certain types of problems require destructive procedures that destroy the unit tested. We would not want to use the total population of electric light bulbs to test their life span, and we would want no more than a small quantity of blood out of the human body to test for the presence of a rare disease (or for that matter, no more than a sample of virgins to test their sexual response). A final reason for sampling is its greater accuracy in problems where it is difficult to reach all members of a population—for example, where individuals are widely dispersed or in relatively inaccessible areas. For these reasons, the issue of sampling and making inferences to populations is a major aspect of the scientific method.

Representativeness

Essentially, inference from samples to populations is a matter of the confidence that can be placed in the representativeness of the sample. A sample is representative to the degree to which it reflects the characteristics of a population. For example, if 10 percent of a population is on welfare, the sample should reflect the same percentage.

It must be stressed that the representativeness of a sample is difficult, if not impossible, to check. Often a sample is taken precisely because an estimate is needed on the *unknown* characteristics of the population. Furthermore, some populations are infinite, or nearly so, which defies accurate knowledge about their characteristics. For these reasons, instead of observing the degree to which a sample is representative, researchers rely upon their confidence in the nature of the sampling procedure (a random sample is considered best). Consequently, in the final analysis, the representativeness of a sample is assumed rather than proved.

It is likely that representativeness is to some extent dependent upon the degree of precision to which the population is specified, the adequacy of the sample, and the heterogeneity of the population. Confidence in the representativeness of a sample is increased if the population is well-defined—for example, if a list is obtained of the names of all males in the United States or all freshmen in universities.

Adequacy is an important consideration only if a very small sample is taken. To be adequate, a sample must be of sufficient size to allow the researchers to have confidence (according to statistical techniques) in the inference. In studying male sexual potency, we would hardly have confidence if four males in the United States were examined and then a generalization was made to all males in the country; or if we were concerned with quality control for canned peaches, we would not have confidence in selecting one can in ten million as representative of all.

Finally, representativeness depends on the heterogeneity of the population. The more alike the units of the population, the smaller the sample can be and still be representative. Compare, for example, taking a sample from a barrel of oil with taking a sample of all the males in the United States. In a chemical laboratory, only a drop of oil is required to analyze the chemical components of the whole barrel.

To increase the chances of obtaining representativeness, a *random* probability sample should be selected from a population. In a random sample, each unit has an equal chance of being chosen, and the selection of any one unit has no effect on the selection of any other. One technique for obtaining a random sample is to take all names of students in an introductory sociology course, place these names on separate pieces of paper and put them into a bowl, mix thoroughly, and blindly select twenty of the slips of paper. Technically, the chosen slip of paper should be replaced into the bowl before the next slip is selected.

Although a random sampling procedure controls for certain types of bias, it does not eliminate error. Sampling error is a major source of unrepresentativeness. For example, it is logically possible (but extremely unlikely) to take a 1 percent sample of adults in the United States and not select anyone over the age of eighty. Since every individual has an equal chance of being chosen, it is also possible to select all males in the sample. This possibility is so remote that it is nearly nonexistent, but the point is that, even with the best sampling procedures, chance produces some error.

Sampling Bias

If a random procedure is not employed, the potential bias of a sample (that is, the degree of unrepresentativeness) is more extensive than is bias from sampling error. For example, in taking some public opinion polls, interviewers are instructed to find a certain percentage of blacks and whites; or Protestants, Catholics, and Jews; or upper-, middle-, and lower-class individuals.* Some interviewers, however, will not go to the toughest lower-class neighborhoods for potential interviewees, nor will they go to the most blighted part of the slums. Consequently, since the extremely poor have little chance of entering the sample, the heterogeneity of the population is not completely represented. With a random sample, however, all names of individuals from all classes have an equal chance of being selected, thus minimizing potential bias.

The poll technique should be differentiated from the stratified random sample, where populations also are first divided into categories (such as upper, middle, and lower classes). Unlike the poll, the next step in stratified random sampling is to take random samples of each category or stratum. There are at least two reasons for selecting a stratified random sample over a simple random sample. First, it ensures that a theoretically important variable will be sufficiently represented in the sample. For example, it permits *oversampling* of numerically small categories, which yields a greater number of cases for

*Usually termed "quota sampling."–Ed.

analysis (e.g., if few Jews are in the population, by stratifying on religion, 90 percent of them can be selected). Second, a stratified random sample increases the homogeneity of the sampled strata, because individuals in each category are alike on the variable selected for stratifying; e.g., all are Jews or are rich.

An example of a rather complex random sample is that used in the Bowerman and Elder study. They took a random sample of a larger sample (selected in the course of another research project) of 19,200 white adolescents from unbroken homes. The larger sample consisted of individuals from the school system (public and parochial) in central Ohio and public schools only in the central region of North Carolina. The resulting data used by Bowerman and Elder represented a 40 percent sample of seventh to ninth grades and a 60 percent sample of tenth to twelfth grades.

Multistage Sampling

To obtain a representative sample, an accurate, up-to-date list of all elements or names in the population is essential; however, population lists usually are nonexistent, incomplete, or out of date. A list of all citizens of the United States simply does not exist, and lists of smaller populations, such as those in telephone directories or automobile registrations, obviously are biased toward those in more economically advantaged positions. Furthermore, as soon as any list is published, and perhaps even before publication, the lists become at least partially out of date. People are born, die, move, get new telephones, buy new cars, etc. Although no list is perfect, as a general rule, the smaller the population, the more likely it is that a list of its members exists and the more accurate the list is likely to be. To take advantage of this fact, multistage area sampling is often employed by the U.S. Census Bureau, among other such groups.

Briefly, to employ this sample design, samples of areas are usually taken first, and then perhaps samples are taken of individuals within areas. To illustrate (although not following the technique of the U.S. Census Bureau), in order to take a sample of the population of the United States, a random sample of states may be taken first. Within states, a random sample (say, 20 percent) of counties is selected, and then a random sample of districts or blocks within the selected counties is taken.* Finally, at the district or block level, adequate lists may exist of the population, and a random sample of these lists can be taken. Although multistage sampling presents a variety of problems, it has proved to be fairly accurate and an adequate way of handling the problem of poor population lists. It also offers the advantages of being a somewhat cheaper method to run than are some other methods; and it facilitates data collection.

*Usually termed "cluster" or "area" sampling.–Ed.

Advantages of Random Sampling

Regardless of the type of random sampling, its use of probability yields two major advantages over nonrandom sampling techniques. First, a probability (random) sample helps control for the researcher's biases. These biases make the sample unrepresentative of the population. We can control such biases, within limits, by selecting the members of the sample purely on the basis of probability, which ensures that each member of the population has an equal chance of being selected. Since each member has an equal chance of being in the sample, biases are avoided that may result from researchers not wanting to interview members of certain races, wanting to avoid slums, or not including someone because he is not at home.

The second advantage of the random sampling technique is that it enables us to state numerically the degree of confidence we have in inferring to the population. A precise notion of the degree of confidence allows one study to be compared with the next. The data in diverse studies therefore are reduced to a comprehensible and comparative form. One consequence of this numerical manipulation is that we can assess the relative merit of two studies.

An Evaluation of Voting Behavior Samples

Some of the problems and uses of sampling are illustrated by evaluating some voting behavior studies. In the past, certain opinion polls have resulted in large inaccuracies. Perhaps the most famous example is the Literary Digest Poll of over two million persons that predicted, in 1936, a landslide victory for Alf Landon over Franklin D. Roosevelt. Of course, the 1936 presidential election overwhelmingly favored Roosevelt. The poll erred by approximately 20 percentage points. The biases in the Literary Digest Poll led to the inaccurate prediction. Among the more flagrant biases were that (1) only Literary Digest and telephone subscribers were polled (which was biased toward the wealthier and more conservative elements of the population) and (2) only a small percentage of those polled returned the mailed questionnaire (those who did not return the questionnaire may have been those least interested in the election or in a Republican victory). The inaccuracies of the poll illustrate dramatically the importance of both the population sampled and the method of observation (in this case, mailed questionnaires).

A second instance occurred in 1948 when polls by Gallup and others also forecasted the wrong winner of a presidential election. Some polls showed that Harry S. Truman would receive less than 45 percent of the popular vote, when in actuality he received about 50 percent and, of course, won the election.

The presidential election polls for 1948 illustrate some of the major problems with *quota sampling* techniques. Quota sampling is based on the premise that we know what the correct variables are. For example, income and religion are related to voting. Therefore, in sampling people to determine how they will vote, we stratify on these variables—that is, we get a percentage of people who are rich and poor and who are Catholic, Protestant, and Jewish. It is quite probable that if we knew the correct variables (related to voting behavior) we probably would not need any polls in order to predict the outcome of elections. All we would need to do is establish the distribution of the variables in the population. For example, if social class is perfectly related to voting behavior, then knowledge of the exact number of voting persons in each class would predict the results. We usually do not, however, know the distribution of many variables in the population that are thought to be predictive. Further, as mentioned earlier, interviewers, in filling their quotas, produce bias by the respondents they select. Too few of the persons interviewed come from the highest and lowest income groups and from the lowest educational groups. Finally, if a trend analysis had been made of the 1948 election polls, it could have been seen that Truman was gaining on Dewey as the election date approached.

Even with a representative and adequate sample, there may be crucial problems of interpretation. Consider, for example, the 1966 contest for governor of California between Ronald Reagan and Edmund G. Brown. The polls did forecast accurately the Reagan victory; however, few polls came anywhere near predicting the large margin of victory by the Republican candidate. Polls generally gave Reagan a margin of victory between 400,000 and 600,000; the election results gave Reagan a margin of victory of nearly 1.5 million votes.

The inadequacies of these polls are to be seen not so much in their design (many of them employed probability sampling) as in their interpretation. First, election polls generally do not indicate who will turn out to vote, but only how people would vote if they did turn out. Second, many people may say they are undecided in the polls, but will vote for a candidate at election time. To interpret the polls accurately, some indication must be given of how the undecided will vote.

Decisions on the Type and Size of the Sample

Let us suppose that the population is limited to undergraduate students at colleges and universities in the United States. Given the large student body this represents, a sample is required. Decisions on the sample must consider the types of colleges and universities, the areas of the United States, the size of the sample of colleges and universities, and the size of the sample of students and professors in any particular college or university. For example, we may want to limit the inquiry to public schools, or just to state colleges, or to schools in the Eastern states, or perhaps to colleges with a student enrollment of over fifteen thousand. Separate decisions may be necessary for each college or university selected. Should you select all students in all courses or just a sample of students and courses? If students (and courses or professors) are to be sampled, how many should be selected, and should the sample be stratified on such characteristics as the student's major (social sciences, physical sciences, humanities, etc.), class standing (freshman, sophomore, junior, and senior), or socioeconomic status? This by no means exhausts all the possibilities, but merely illustrates the complexity of the decision-making process. Depending on the resources, an adequate inquiry may be made only on one or a few colleges. If so, a judicious (nonrandom) selection of colleges may be made. This choice can be made on the most "typical" college in an area. For example, the typical college should be coeducational, around twenty thousand students, and located in an urban area. Once the few colleges are selected, random sampling may be applied to each one.

SUMMARY

Because of lack of accessibility, limited time, or prohibitive cost, some populations cannot be studied unless they are sampled. The purpose of a sample is to have a basis for making accurate statements about the population.

Samples should be representative. A representative sample reflects the characteristics of the population that are crucial to the researcher. Representativeness is partially dependent upon the degree of precision to which the population is specified, the adequacy of the sample, and the heterogeneity of the population. An adequate sample is of sufficient size to allow researchers to have confidence (according to statistical techniques) that the characteristics of the sample are "true" for the population. The more homogeneous the population, the smaller the sample can be and still be adequate and representative.

The two basic types of sampling procedures are random and nonrandom. Random sampling assures that each individual has an equal chance of being chosen, and the selection of any one individual has no effect on the selection of any other. It is preferred over nonrandom procedures because it helps control for certain biases (leading to unrepresentativeness), and it enables us to establish statistically the degree of confidence in our inferences to the population.

REFERENCES

Goode, William J., and Paul K. Hatt. 1952. *Methods in Social Research.* New York: McGraw-Hill Book Company. Chapter 14.

Mueller, John H., and Karl F. Schuessler. 1961. *Statistical Reasoning in Sociology.* Boston: Houghton Mifflin Company. Chapter 11.

Sampling Chart

Russell L. Ackoff

Type of Sampling	*Brief Description*	*Advantages*	*Disadvantages*
A. Simple random	Assign to each population member a unique number; select sample items by use of random numbers	1. Requires minimum knowledge of population in advance 2. Free of possible classification errors 3. Easy to analyze data and compute errors	1. Does not make use of knowledge of population which researcher may have 2. Larger errors for same sample size than in stratified sampling
B. Systematic	Use natural ordering or order population; select random starting point between 1 and the nearest integer to the sampling ratio (N/n); select times at interval of nearest integer to sampling ratio	1. If population is ordered with respect to pertinent property, gives stratification effect, and hence reduces variability compared to A 2. Simplicity of drawing sample; easy to check	1. If sampling interval is related to a periodic ordering of the population, increased variability may be introduced 2. Estimates of error likely to be high where there is stratification effect
C. Multistage random	Use a form of random sampling in each of the sampling stages where there are at least two stages	1. Sampling lists, identification, and numbering required only for members of sampling units selected in sample 2. If sampling units are geographically defined, cuts down field costs (i.e., travel)	1. Errors likely to be larger than in A or B for same sample size 2. Errors increase as number of sampling units selected decreases
1. With probability proportionate to size	Select sampling units with probability proportionate to their size	1. Reduces variability	1. Lack of knowledge of size of each sampling unit before selection increases variability

Type of Sampling	*Brief Description*	*Advantages*	*Disadvantages*
D. Stratified 1. Proportionate	Select from every sampling unit at other than last stage a random sample proportionate to size of sampling unit	1. Assures representativeness with respect to property which forms basis of classifying units; therefore yields less variability than A or C 2. Decreases chance of failing to include members of population because of classification process 3. Characteristics of each stratum can be estimated, and hence comparisons can be made	1. Requires accurate information on proportion of population in each stratum, otherwise increases error 2. If stratified lists are not available, may be costly to prepare them; possibility of faulty classification and hence increase in variability
2. Optimum allocation	Same as 1 except sample is proportionate to variability within strata as well as their size	1. Less variability for same sample size than 1	1. Requires knowledge of variability of pertinent characteristic within strata
3. Disproportionate	Same as 1 except that size of sample is not proportionate to size of sampling unit but is dedicated by analytical considerations or convenience	1. More efficient than 1 for comparison of strata or where different errors are optimum for different strata	1. Less efficient than 1 for determining population characteristics; i.e., more variability for same sample size
E. Cluster	Select sampling units by some form of random sampling; ultimate units are groups; select these at random and take a complete count of each	1. If clusters are geographically defined, yields lowest field costs 2. Requires listing only individuals in selected clusters 3. Characteristics of clusters as well as those of population can be estimated 4. Can be used for subsequent samples, since clusters, not individuals, are selected, and substitution of individuals may be permissible	1. Larger errors for comparable size than other probability samples 2. Requires ability to assign each member of population uniquely to a cluster; inability to do so may result in duplication or omission of individuals
F. Stratified cluster	Select clusters at random from every sampling unit	1. Reduces variability of plain cluster sampling	1. Disadvantages of stratified sampling added to those of cluster properties 2. Since cluster properties may change, advantage of stratification may be reduced and make sample unusable for later research

Type of Sampling	*Brief Description*	*Advantages*	*Disadvantages*
G. Repetitive: multiple or sequential	Two or more samples of any of the above types are taken, using results from earlier samples to design later ones, or determine if they are necessary	1. Provides estimates of population characteristics which facilitate efficient planning of succeeding sample, therefore reduces error of final estimate 2. In the long run reduces number of observations required	1. Complicates administration of fieldwork 2. More computation and analysis required than in nonrepetitive sampling 3. Sequential sampling can only be used where a very small sample can approximate representativeness and where the number of observations can be increased conveniently at any stage of the research
H. Judgment	Select a subgroup of the population which, on the basis of available information, can be judged to be representative of the total population; take a complete count or subsample of this group	1. Reduces cost of preparing sample and fieldwork, since ultimate units can be selected so that they are close together	1. Variability and bias of estimates cannot be measured or controlled 2. Requires strong assumptions or considerable knowledge of population and subgroup selected
1. Quota	Classify population by pertinent properties; determine desired proportion of sample from each class; fix quotas for each observer	1. Same as above 2. Introduces some stratification effect	1. Introduces bias of observers' classification of subjects and nonrandom selection within classes

Reprinted from Russel L. Ackoff, *The Design of Social Research* (Chicago: University of Chicago, 1953), p. 124. By permission of The University of Chicago Press. Copyright 1953 by The University of Chicago.

Relational Analysis: The Study of Social Organizations with Survey Methods

James S. Coleman

Survey research methods have often led to the neglect of social structure and of the relations among individuals. On the other hand, survey methods are highly efficient in bringing in a large volume of data—amenable to statistical treatment—at a relatively low cost in time and effort. Can the student of social structure enjoy the advantages of the survey without neglecting the relationships which make up that structure? In other words, can he use a method which ordinarily treats each individual as an isolated unit in order to study social structure?

The purpose of this paper is to describe some important developments in survey research which are giving us a new way of studying social organization.

It is useful to trace briefly the history of survey research, to indicate how it has grown from "polling" to the point where it can now study problems involving complex human organization. A look at this history indicates two definite stages. The first was a polling stage which was concerned with the *distribution* of responses on any one item: What proportion favored Roosevelt in 1936? What proportion was in favor of labor unions? This type of concern continues even today among pollsters, and to the lay public it is still the function of surveys to "find out what people think" or to see just how many feel thus and so.

Among sociologists, however, this purely descriptive use of survey research was soon supplanted by an *analytical* one. First there began to be a concern with how different subgroups in the population felt or behaved. From this, the analysts moved on to further cross-tabulations. Finally, some survey analysts began, through cross-tabulations and correlations, to study complicated questions of why people behaved as they did. By relating one opinion item to another, attitude configurations and clusters of attitudes emerged; by relating background information to these attitudes, some insight was gained into the *determinants* of attitudes. It was in this analytical stage, then, beyond the simple description of a population, that survey research began to be of real use to social science.

But throughout all this one fact remained, a very disturbing one to the student of social organization. The *individual* remained the unit of analysis. No matter how complex the analysis, how numerous the correlations, the studies focused on individuals as separate and independent units. The very techniques mirrored this well: Samples were random, never including (except by accident) two persons who were friends; interviews were with one individual, as an atomistic entity, and responses were coded onto separate IBM cards, one for each person. As a result, the kinds of substantive problems on which such research focused tended to be problems of "aggregate psychology," that is, *within*-individual problems, and never problems concerned with relations between people.

Now, very recently, this focus on the individual has shown signs of changing, with a shift to groups as the units of analysis, or to networks of relations among individuals. The shift is quite a difficult one to make, both conceptually and technically, and the specific methods used to date are only halting steps toward a full-fledged methodology. Nevertheless, some of these methods are outlined below, to indicate just how, taken together, they can even now provide us with an extremely fruitful research tool. This tool has sometimes been used for the study of formal organization but more often for the study of the informal organization which springs up within a formal structure. In both cases, it shows promise of opening to research problems which have been heretofore the province of speculation.

PROBLEMS OF DESIGN AND SAMPLING

The break from the atomistic concerns of ordinary survey analysis requires taking a different perspective toward the individual interview. In usual survey research and statistical analysis, this interview is regarded as *independent* of others, as an entity in itself. All cross-tabulations and analyses relate one item in that questionnaire to another item in the same questionnaire. But, in this different approach, an individual interview is seen as a *part* of some larger structure in which the respondent finds himself: his network of friends, the shop or office where he works, the bowling team he belongs to, and so on. Thus, as a part of a larger structure, the individual is *not* treated independently. The analysis must somehow tie together and interrelate the attributes of these different parts of the structure.

So much for the basic change in perspective—away from the atomistic treatment of the individual interview, and toward the treatment of each interview as a part of some larger whole. This basic perspective has several implications for the kind of data collected and for the sample design. Perhaps the most important innovation in the kind of data collected is sociometric-type data in the interview, that is, explicit questions about the respondent's relation to other specific individuals. Each person may be asked the names of his best friends, or the names of his subordinates in the shop upon whom he depends most, or any one of a multitude of *relational* questions. For example, in a study of two housing projects by Merton, Jahoda, and West,[1] one way to map out the informal social structure in the community was to ask people who their best friends were. Having obtained such data from all the families in the project, so that each family could be located in the network of social relations in the community, it was then possible to examine the relation between this social structure, on the one hand, and various values and statuses on the other. Specifically, this information allowed these authors to show that in one housing project social ties were based very largely on similarities in background and religion; in the other, social relations were more often built around common leisure interests and participation in community organizations.

More generally, the incorporation of sociometric-type data into survey research allows the investigator to *locate* each interviewed individual within the networks of voluntary relations which surround him. In some cases, these networks of voluntary relations will be superimposed on a highly articulated formal structure. In a department of a business, for example, there are numerous hierarchical levels and there are numerous work relations which are imposed by the job itself. In such cases, sociometric-type questions can be asked relative to these formal relations, e.g.: "Which supervisor do you turn to most often?" or, "Which of the men in your own workgroup do you see most often outside of work?" or, "When you want X type of job done in a hurry to whom do you go to get it done?" or, "When you need advice on such-and-such a problem, whom do you usually turn to?"

Another kind of data is that which refers to some larger social unit. For example, in some research on high schools currently being carried out at The University of Chicago, it is necessary to find the paths to prestige within a school, so that the boys are asked: "What does it take to be important and looked up to by the other fellows here at school?". Then the responses to this question—aggregated over each school separately—can be used to characterize the *school* as well as the individual. Because of this, the question itself makes explicit reference to the school.

But apart from the kinds of data collected, there are also important *sampling* considerations. In this kind of research, it is no longer possible to pull each individual out of his social context and interview him as an independent entity. It is necessary to sample parts of that context as well or, to say it differently, to sample explicitly with reference to the social structure. There are numerous ways of doing this; only a few, which have been successfully tried, are mentioned below.

Snowball Sampling

One method of interviewing a man's immediate social environment is to use the sociometric questions in the interview for sampling purposes. For example, in a study of political attitudes in a New England community, Martin Trow has used this approach: first interviewing a small sample of persons, then asking these persons who their best friends are, interviewing these friends, then asking *them* their friends, interviewing these, and so on.[2] In this way, the sampling plan follows out the chains of sociometric relations in the community. In many respects, this sampling technique is like that of a good reporter who tracks down "leads" from one person to another. The difference, of course, is that snowball sampling in survey research is amenable to the same scientific sampling procedures as ordinary samples. Where the population in ordinary samples is a population of individuals, here it is two populations: one of individuals and one of *relations* among individuals.

Saturation Sampling

Perhaps a more obvious approach is to interview *everyone* within the relevant social structure. In a study of doctors in four communities, *all* the doctors in these communities were interviewed.[3] Sociometric-type questions were then used to lay out the professional and social relations existing among these doctors. This "saturation" method or complete census was feasible there, because the total number of doctors in these communities was small—less than three hundred. But in the study mentioned earlier which used snowball sampling, such an approach would have been practically impossible, for the community was about 15,000 in size. Thus this "saturation sampling" is only feasible under rather special circumstances. A borderline case is the study of high schools mentioned earlier. There are 9,000 students in the ten schools being studied. Only because students are given self-administered questionnaires, rather than interviews, is it possible to use a saturation sample, and thereby characterize the complete social structure.

Dense Sampling

Another approach is to sample "densely." This is a compromise between the usual thinly-dispersed random sample and the saturation sample. An illustration will indicate how this may be useful. In a study of pressures upon the academic freedom of college social science teachers, carried out by Paul Lazarsfeld, at least *half* of the social science faculty in every college in the sample was interviewed.[4] Thus, by sampling densely, enough men were interviewed in each college so that the climate of the college could be characterized, as well as the attitudes of the individual respondent.

Multistage Sampling

Any of the above approaches to sampling can be combined with an element found in many sample designs: the multistage sample. For example, in the academic freedom study referred to above, it would have been impossible to have a dense sample of social science teachers in *all* the colleges in the United States, so a two-stage sample was used: first sampling colleges, and then teachers within colleges. In doing this, of course, the crucial question is what balance to maintain between the sampling of colleges and the sampling of teachers within colleges. Enough colleges are needed to have representativity, yet few enough so that the sampling within each one can be dense. In a study of union politics, reported in *Union Democracy,*[5] we perhaps made a wrong decision: we interviewed in 90 printing shops, spreading the interviews so thinly that only one man out of three–at most–was interviewed within the shop. This meant that we had only a very few interviews in each shop, and could not use the interview material to characterize the climate or atmosphere of the shops, except in the very largest ones.

These sampling procedures are, of course, not the only possible ones. An infinite degree of variation is possible, depending upon the problem and upon the kind of social structure involved. The most important point is that the individual interview can no longer be treated as an independent entity, but must be considered as a part of some larger whole: in the sampling, in the questions asked, and in the subsequent analysis.

ANALYTICAL METHODS

The real innovations in this new kind of research are in the techniques of analysis. I will mention several of these with which I am most familiar, to give an indication of the kinds of problems this research examines and the way it examines them.

Contextual Analysis

The first, and the one closest to usual survey research, might be termed contextual analysis. In essence, it consists of relating a characteristic of the respondent's social context–and the independent variable–to a characteristic of the individual himself.[6] A good example of this occurred in *The American*

Soldier, where the attitudes of inexperienced men, in companies where most others were inexperienced, were compared to attitudes of similarly inexperienced men in companies where most others were veterans. It was found that inexperienced men in green companies felt very differently about themselves, and about combat, than their counterparts in veteran companies. That is, when men were characterized by both individual characteristics and by their social surroundings, the latter were found to have an important effect on their attitudes.

In the union politics study mentioned above, one of the major elements in the analysis was an examination of the effect of the shop context on the men within the shop. We had access to voting records in union political elections for these shops, and these made it possible to characterize the shop as politically radical or politically conservative. and as high or low in political consensus. Then we could examine the different behavior or attitudes of men in different kinds of shops and compute a "shop effect." An example is given in Table 1. Each man is in a shop of high or low political consensus, depending on whether the men in the shop vote alike or are evenly split between the radical and conservative parties. And each man has a certain degree of political activity. In this table, the shop's political consensus and the man's political activity are related. The table indicates that in shops of high consensus, men are politically more active than in shops of low consensus. The inference might be that high consensus provides a kind of resonance of political beliefs which generates a greater interest in politics. In any case, the table exemplifies the use of an attribute of a *shop* related to an attribute of a *man* in the shop. This general kind of analysis, which bridges the gap between two levels of sociological units—the individual and his social context—seems to be a very basic one for this "structural" approach to survey research.

Boundaries of Homogeneity

A second kind of analysis attempts to answer the question: How homogeneous are various groups in some belief or attitude? In a medical school, for example, are a student's attitudes toward medicine more like those of his fraternity brothers or more like those of his laboratory partners? This question,

TABLE 1

		Shops of high political consensus	*Shops of low political consensus*
Percent of men active in union politics		29%	7%
	N	(125)	(28)

incidentally, has been posed in a study of medical students presently being carried out at Columbia University.[7] The answer is, in the particular medical school being studied, that his attitudes are far more like those of his fraternity brothers. In other words, in this medical school, the "boundaries of homogeneity" of certain attitudes about medicine coincide very largely with fraternity boundaries.

The major problems in answering questions of group homogeneity are problems of index construction. Consider the above example: each student has twenty or thirty fraternity brothers, but only three laboratory partners in anatomy lab. How can the effects of variability between groups, due to small numbers in a group, be separated out from the actual tendency toward homogeneity of attitude? It can be done, and indices have been developed to do so. The indices, incidentally, are much like the formulas by which statisticians measure the effects of clustering in a random sample.

An example of group homogeneity may indicate more concretely how this approach can be useful in research. In the study of doctors in four communities mentioned earlier, we were interested in the social processes affecting the physicians' introduction of a new drug into their practices. Through interviewing all doctors and asking sociometric questions in the interview, we were able to delineate seven "cliques" of doctors who were sociometrically linked together. (How to reconstruct such cliques is another problem, which will be considered shortly.) The question, then, became this: At each point in time after the drug was marketed, were cliques homogeneous or not in their members' use or nonuse of the drug? If they were homogeneous, then this was evidence that some kind of social influence or diffusion was going on in relation to the measured sociometric ties. If not, this indicated that the cliques delineated on the basis of questions in the interview had little relevance to drug adoption. Table 2 shows, for several time periods, just how much homogeneity there was in the cliques, beyond that which would arise

TABLE 2

Months after drug was marked	*Amount of clique homogeneity*	*Percent of doctors who had used the drug*
1 months	no homogeneity	14
3	no homogeneity	32
5	no homogeneity	49
7	.07	66
9	.12	71
11	.18	76
13	.03	83
15	no homogeneity	86

by chance. An index value of 1.0 means each clique is completely homogeneous in its use or nonuse of the drug. An index value of 0 means there is no more homogeneity than would arise through chance variation between groups.

Table 2 shows that there was no homogeneity until around seven months after the drug was introduced, that is, until over 50 percent of the doctors had used the drug. The maximum homogeneity was reached at about eleven months, when three-fourths of the doctors had begun to use the drug. Then after that, the homogeneity receded to zero again.

This result helped to reinforce a conclusion derived from other findings in the study: that the social networks measured in the study were effective as paths of diffusion at certain times but not at others. However, apart from the substantive results of the study, this example indicates how such analysis of the boundaries of homogeneity may be useful for the study of the functioning of various social organizations.

Pair Analysis

Neither of the above kinds of analysis has required the use of sociometric-type data. An important kind of analysis which does use such direct data on relationships is the analysis of *pairs.* Here, the pair formed by A's choosing B becomes the unit of analysis. Speaking technically, "pair cards" may be constructed for each sociometric choice, and then these cards used for cross-tabulations. In other words, instead of cross-tabulating a man's attitude toward Russia with his attitude toward the United Nations, we can cross-tabulate the man's attitude toward Russia with the attitude toward Russia of the man he eats lunch with at the cafeteria.

One of the most important problems which has been studied in this way is the similarity or difference in attitudes or backgrounds between the two members of a pair. That is, do people have friendship relations with those who are like them politically, with people of the same age, with persons in the same occupation?

This kind of problem can be illustrated by Table 3, which contains hypothetical data. This table, which looks very much like an ordinary contingency

TABLE 3

		Chosen		
		boy	*girl*	
Chooser	boy	45	15	60
	girl	20	20	40
				100

table, must be treated in a slightly different fashion. It allows us to raise the question: Do boys tend to choose boys more than would be expected by chance? and, do girls tend to choose girls more than would be expected by chance? The answer, of course, depends upon what we take as chance. However, chance models have been worked out, so that one can assign measures of the tendency to choose others of one's own kind. For the above example, this measure (varying between 0 and 1) says that the tendency to in-choice for boys is .38 and that for girls is .17. By comparing such indices for numerous attributes, one could get a good glimpse into the informal social organization of the group. For example, in the medical study mentioned earlier which is being carried out at Columbia University, the values of in-choice tendency for friends shown in Table 4 were found:

TABLE 4

Subgroups	*Tendencies toward in-choice*
Class in school	.92
Fraternity	.52
Sex	.33
Marital status	.20
Attitudes toward national health insurance	.37

By looking at the relative sizes of these index values, we get an idea of just how the informal social relations–that is, the friendship choices–at this medical school mesh with the formal structure, and with the distribution of attitudes.

In the study mentioned above of drug introduction by doctors, these pair relations were used as the major aspect of the analysis: By examining how close in time a doctor's first use of a new drug was to the first use of the doctor he mentioned as a friend, it was possible to infer the functioning of friendship networks in the introduction of this drug.

These examples or pair analysis give only a crude picture of the kinds of problems which can be studied in this fashion. The important matter is to break away from the analysis of *individuals* as units to the study of *pairs* of individuals. To be sure, this involves technical IBM problems and problems of index construction along with conceptual problems, but the difficulties are not great.

Partitioning into Cliques

Another important kind of problem is the partitioning of a larger group into cliques by use of sociometric choices. This problem is a thorny one, for it involves not only the delineation of cliques, but, even prior to this, the *definition* of what is to constitute a clique. Are cliques to be mutually exclusive in membership, or can they have overlapping memberships? Are they to consist of people who all name one another, or of people who are tied together by more tenuous connections? Such questions must be answered before the group can be partitioned into cliques.

A good review of some of the methods by which cliques and subgroups can be treated is presented in Lindzey and Borgotta.[8] The two most feasible of these are the method of matrix multiplication[9] and the method of shifting rows and columns in the sociometric choice matrix until the choices are clustered around the diagonal.[10] This last technique is by far the more feasible of the two if the groups are more than about 20 in size. When the groups are on the order of 100, even this method becomes clumsy. And IBM technique was successfully used in the study of doctors and the study of medical students, both mentioned above, in which the groups were 200–400 in size. At The University of Chicago, a program has been developed for Univac, using a method of shifting rows and columns in a matrix, which can handle groups up to 1000 in size.[11] The necessity for some such method becomes great when, for example, one wants to map out systematically the informal organization of a high school of 1000 students.

CONCLUSION

These four kinds of analysis, contextual analysis, boundaries of homogeneity, pair analysis, and partitioning into cliques, are only four of many possibilities. Several other approaches have been used, but these four give some idea of the way in which survey analysis can come to treat problems which involve social structure. In the long run, these modes of analysis will probably represent only the initial halting steps in the development of a kind of structural research which will represent a truly sociological methodology. In any case, these developments spell an important milestone in social research, for they help open up for systematic research those problems which have heretofore been the province of the theorist or of purely qualitative methods.

There is one new development which should be mentioned, although the frontier is just opened, and not at all explored. This development is the construction of electronic computers with immediate-access storage capacities 100 times the size of an 80-column IBM card. Such computers make it possible, for the first time, to lay out a complex social structure for direct and systematic examination. Instead of examining the similarity of attitudes between socially-connected pairs, after laborious construction of "pair cards," it becomes possible to trace through a whole structural network, examining the points in the network where attitudes or actions begin to diverge. Methods for doing this have not yet been developed but, for the first time, the technical facilities exist, and it is just a matter of time until analytical methods are developed. IBM cards and counter-sorters were methodologically appropriate for the individualistic orientation which survey research has had in the past; electronic computers with large storage capacities are precisely appropriate for the statistical analysis of complex social organization.

Unfortunately, it has not been possible here to present any of the tools discussed above fully enough to show precisely how it is used. In giving a broad overview of a number of developments, my aim has been to point to an important new direction in social research, one which may aid significantly in the systematic study of social organization.

NOTES

1. Robert K. Merton, Patricia S. West, and Marie Jahoda, *Patterns of Social Life: Explorations in the Sociology of Housing,* forthcoming.
2. Martin A. Trow, "Right Wing Radicalism and Political Intolerance: A Study of Support for McCarthy in a New England Town." Unpublished Ph.D. dissertation, Columbia University, 1957.
3. J. S. Coleman, E. Katz, and H. M. Menzel, "Diffusion of an Innovation Among Physicians," *Sociometry,* XX (Dec. 1957).
4. P. F. Lazarsfeld and Wagner Thielens, *The Academic Man: Social Scientists in a Time of Crisis,* The Free Press, Glencoe, Ill.: 1956.
5. S. M. Lipset, M. A. Trow, and J. S. Coleman, *Union Democracy,* The Free Press, Glencoe, Ill.: 1956.
6. Peter Blau has emphasized the importance of such analysis in formal organizations for locating the "structural effects" of a situation upon the individuals in it. See his "Formal Organization: Dimensions of Analysis," *American Journal of Sociology,* LXIII (1957), 58–69.
7. Some of the work in this study (though not the work mentioned here) is reported in P. F. Kendall, R. K. Merton, and G. S. Reader, eds., *The Student Physician,* (New York: Commonwealth Fund, 1957).
8. G. Lindzey ed., *Handbook of Social Psychology,* Addison-Wesley, Cambridge, 1956, Chap. II.
9. See L. Festinger, "The Analysis of Sociograms Using Matrix Algebra," *Human Relations,* II, No. 2 (1949), 153–58 and R. D. Luce, "Connectivity and Generalized Cliques in Sociometric Group Structure," *Psychometrika,* XV (1950), 169–90.
10. C. O. Beum and E. G. Brundage, "A Method for Analyzing the Sociomatrix," *Sociometry,* XIII (1950), 141–45.
11. A description of this program, written by the author and Duncan McRae, is available upon request from the author and the program itself is available for copying, for those who have access to a Univac I or II.

Dissection II: Samples, Sponsors and Self-Esteem

How Good Are the Rating Services?

Richard I. Evans

The recent history of television rating services, as all of you know, has led to a kind of confusion, distortion, and downright frustration on the part of all the important decision makers in the television industry. Some comments (such as the one made by a famous comedian, who asked how his program could be rated when he had never known anyone who had been asked if he watched it) reflect an almost complete lack of knowledge of sampling techniques. In other words, the very basic assumptions of audience research are apparently not very well understood.

Another point of confusion seems to center around the apparent differences in ratings of the same program reported by different rating services. As a result of this, there seems to develop a game of selecting for sales purposes the rating service most favorable to the program being represented by a particular advertising agency or television station. But even then the one selected may prove disappointing at the next comparative go-round, when still another rating service will appear which rates the program higher than the favorable rating service selected the previous month.

Still another point of confusion has centered around the whole concept of audience size as a criterion by which television programs are or should be

From *National Association of Educational Broadcasters Journal (NAEB Journal).* Jan.–Feb., 1961, 39–50. Reprinted by permission of Educational Broadcasting Review.

judged. The widely stated example of the "I Love Lucy" show and Philip Morris cigarettes illustrates this quite well. As you know, "I Love Lucy" was consistently top rated by all of the major rating services for a period of time, but Philip Morris cigarettes, the sponsor's product, continued to stand fourth in national sales throughout the entire period. Finally, the tobacco company cancelled its sponsorship of the program. Perhaps the most optimistic statement in defense of the audience size criterion concerning this was the reported remark by the advertising agency account executive representing the program, who stated that without the program the sales of Philip Morris cigarettes might have actually declined. This implied that the success of the program in terms of audience size contributed to the continuing success of a failing product, a comment undoubtedly not relished by the Philip Morris executives.

I should like to discuss very briefly the major audience rating services, their techniques of contacting the television homes that they select in their respective samples, the nature of their samples, and some of the advantages and disadvantages of their respective approaches. In order to base this analysis on the most fundamental data, we wrote to each of the major rating services and requested as much of this information as they had available. It is interesting to note that some of the rating services were extremely cooperative, supplying comprehensive reports of their sampling and measuring techniques, while others apparently limited their information to advertising "blurbs." In these instances, it was necessary to seek more detailed information about their sampling and measuring instruments from other sources, which may or may not be authoritative or up to date.

The final point in my presentation will be an attempt to look at this problem in general and make some suggestions as to how audience studies in depth could conceivably supply new insights concerning the television audience and their responsiveness to programs in terms of buying behavior with respect to the sponsors' products. Such insights might conceivably challenge the notion that programing policy should bow to the criterion of the size of the audiences which programs can command.

SAMPLING THE AUDIENCE

In attempting to assess audience reaction to a given television program, probably the first question that should be raised is: Who exactly is the intended target for the program? Educational television, for example, as well as some public service programing, is admittedly not designed to attract all interest groups. On the other hand, a good deal of, if not most, commercial programing seems to be designed as a kind of "shotgun" technique to gain viewers simultaneously from as broad a base as possible. In other words, there is no doubt that the average commercial television program is designed to appeal, if possible, to interests in as large an audience as possible. Assuming for a moment that we are now interested in assessing the audience for such a program on one of the major television networks, what we technically define as the universe for the program automatically becomes all of the television homes in the United States. It is apparent that every member of the universe cannot be reached for the purpose of audience studies. Sampling theory would therefore require that a random or truly representative sample of this universe be contacted. Let me illustrate this point with an analogy. If a physician wishes to learn something about the structure of a patient's blood, he does not have to drain all of the blood out of the patient's body and examine it. He can study even a single drop of blood and form an accurate picture of the structure of this patient's blood in general. (Incidentally, this example is not intended to suggest what some of you may already believe—that television rating is a bloody business!)

In theory, a sample is truly representative only if every item in the universe has an equal opportunity to be selected. To insure this, tables of random numbers are typically used. Alphabetical lists of all the items in the universe may be used instead. In some cases, for that matter, all of the items could simply be put into a hat, shaken up, and a sample drawn.

Now, the critical point here is that if every television home in the universe has an equal opportunity of being selected, then, in terms of probability theory, how many television homes have to be selected in order to have a truly representative sample? Here we apply a variation of a statistical formula designed to give us the standard error of a percentage, based on the levels of confidence we desire. For example, in a study that we did of the over 300,000 television homes in the signal area of Channel 8 in Houston, this formula estimated that we would have to interview respondents in approximately 600 homes to be accurate within 5 percent. On a national survey of voters, to take another example, surprisingly great precision could be obtained by sampling in the neighborhood of 10,000 randomly selected voters. Such statistical license to sample, I repeat, can be exercised only when every single item in the universe has an equal opportunity of being selected.

Another very important, fundamental point relative to this problem is that if we are considering a universe of all television homes in the United States, and we draw a sample which represents this large group, then breakdowns in terms of subgroups of the total universe, such as, say, a large metropolitan area like Houston, cannot be reliably estimated from the sample selected for the overall United States universe. In order to get a true representation of the metropolitan Houston area, the universe would now have to be defined, as in our earlier-mentioned Channel 8 study, as the television homes in the Houston signal area, and a sample in terms of this particular universe would have to be drawn. It is entirely possible, for example, that on a national sample of the universe of all television homes in the United States, sampling rigor could be theoretically exercised when only nine or ten television homes in the

Houston area are contacted. This, however, would hardly be a statistically sound basis for making inferences about the Houston market.

These few remarks about the elements of sampling should emphasize the necessity of rigorous adherence to theoretically justified sampling procedures, since any departures from such procedures, slight though they may be, can completely invalidate the significance of the data obtained. Suppose, for example, a certain rating service wishes to obtain a sample for the entire United States. Their statisticians select a random sample based on one of the area sampling methods. They even list the specific television home in every part of the United States that is to be contacted by the interviewer. Now let's assume that, among other things, electronic recording devices must be installed in the television sets in these homes. Certain individuals refuse to allow such devices to be installed in their homes. If the residents of a home that has been selected in the sample refuse to participate, a rating service representative might proceed to knock on doors in the immediate vicinity until more cooperative television viewers are found. This procedure introduces what we technically refer to as a biased sampling error. Without proof, we have no reason to believe that individuals who allow electronic devices to be placed in their homes are basically similar in personality characteristics, such as television viewing behavior, to individuals who do not allow such devices to be placed in their television sets. In this example, we might have a well-defined sample, carefully selected by expert statisticians working out of the rating service headquarters; we might have a very accurate electronic device, at least in the sense of actually recording when and to what channel the television set is tuned; yet all this precision is vitiated by the introduction of a biased sampling error at the field contact level. Many other possible sources of sampling errors in audience research could be cited.

MAJOR RATING SERVICES EVALUATED

Of the marketing organizations engaged in television audience research, four have emerged as the leaders in establishing program ratings. These are the A. D. Nielsen Company, Trendex, the Pulse, Inc., and the American Research Bureau. These organizations are staffed, in my opinion, with competent statisticians and research methodologists trained in such fields as psychology, sociology, and marketing. When critically evaluating the validity of reports by these firms, therefore, one is seldom, if ever, justified in asserting that deficiencies or inaccuracies are due to incompetence or lack of sophistication in the theoretical planning stages of their audience studies. Most of the problems critically affecting validity, as we shall see, appear to emerge in the operational stages of the studies.

Among such possible sources of error in audience studies, one of the most important is the interview instrument itself. Any inaccuracies arising from defects in the structure of the interview form or recording device are referred to as instrument errors. If their form or content tends to bias responses in any way, an instrument error is operative. For example, when the aided recall method is used in an interview, the interviewee is given a list of all the television programs presented in the area on the previous day and asked to indicate those he viewed. He may be inclined to mention programs that he viewed only briefly or inattentively simply because they are listed before him—programs which, without the aided recall technique, he would probably have failed to remember. The fact that he recognizes the name of a program on the list cannot be taken as an indication that he viewed the entire program with attention. This would be particularly true of the advertising message tied in with the program.

The so-called viewing diary is also susceptible to instrument errors since data recording is done entirely by the respondent without supervision. Theoretically, the viewer places the diary on top of his television set and records programs at the time of viewing. Actually, he may not fill in the diary until the end of the week or later, relying on memory when he does so. This time lapse introduces the possibility of faulty recall, which may completely distort the record of his week's viewing.

Another factor affecting the validity of the diary method is what we might call a combination instrument and sampling error. The moment an individual is selected to maintain a diary of viewing behavior, he becomes atypical. As a result, he may alter reports of his viewing to create a particular image of himself, to reflect what he conceives to be his ideal behavior rather than his actual behavior. Such a viewer might actually watch a number of western programs, for example, but omit them from his report, substituting, for the sake of his self-esteem, programs which he believes to have more intellectual or artistic merit.

The A. C. Nielson Company employs an electronic device, the Audimeter, which is attached to the television set and records the time it is turned on and the channel to which it is tuned. Nielsen maintains Audimeters in 1,000 television homes selected on the basis of an approximation of random area sampling. The participating family is paid 25 cents per week and one-half the cost of any set repairs for allowing the Audimeter to be attached to the set.

When first introduced, this device was hailed as the ultimate solution to the problem of accurate audience measurement, one which would insure reliable results. It obviously does not depend on individual recall of programs watched nor does it require any particular effort on the part of the viewer. Yet it soon became evident that this was not the final, foolproof method of audience evaluation. For one thing, the great expense of installing and maintaining the Audimeter makes it economically unfeasible to utilize a sample of the statistically most desirable size. It was soon revealed, moreover, that from 5 to 8 percent of the Audimeters were out of order or not functioning properly at any given time. Another obvious flaw in this instrument is that, even when it is working properly, it supplies only a part of the desired information. While it clearly reveals set operation, it does not indicate who, if anyone, is watching the set, a matter of great importance. As many of you will recall from the old days of radio, almost continuous operation of the radio, whether anyone was listening or not, became a habit in many households, where radio was part of the background of family life. There is already some evidence that a similar habit is being formed with respect to television.

Another limitation of the Audimeter in terms of program planning is that it may take three weeks of more of processing to adequately evaluate the data obtained. Still another criticism, to emphasize an earlier example, which applies not only to the Audimeter but to every method which requires some kind of cooperation from the television viewer, is that, no matter how carefully a sample of television homes is selected, there is always the possibility that some individuals in the sample may be unwilling to cooperate. As a result, the sample actually used is not a sample of all television homes in the universe under consideration but rather a sample of all television homes whose residents are willing to participate in audience studies. This certainly suggests the possibility of a biased sampling error, since one would suspect that individuals who refuse to participate in such studies differ significantly from those who agree to participate.

In recognition of possible sources of error affecting the Audimeter, Nielsen began partially verifying Audimeter results by employing viewing diaries. Again, as noted earlier, viewing diaries also present possibilities of instrument error. Furthermore, since Nielsen apparently uses a relatively small sample in its diary surveys, it would hardly be feasible to analyze the results in terms of national markets. There is no reason to suppose, moreover, that one less than perfect measuring technique, the Audimeter, supplemented by another still less adequate measuring device as used herein, the diary, will necessarily provide a more accurate audience measurement than either technique by itself.

TELEPHONE USED

The late C. E. Hooper pioneered an audience evaluation technique called the telephone coincidental method. Trendex, an offshoot of the old C. E. Hooper group, which apparently no longer specializes in radio and TV audience research, employs the telephone coincidental method in 20 cities throughout the United States. This method has the virtues of easy analysis, immediacy, and great flexibility. The limitations of samples based on telephone listees, however, have been conspicuously apparent at least since 1936, when the *Literary Digest* flatly predicted on the basis of a poll based in part on a sample of telephone homes that Alfred Landon would defeat Franklin Roosevelt in a landslide. In those depression days, of course, telephone subscribers were relatively wealthier, on the whole, than the general population and therefore more likely, in those days, to be Republicans. Today, of course, telephone listees are more representative of the total population, yet samples drawn from telephone subscribers may still reflect definite biases. It is well known, for example, that in many metropolitan areas, new housing developments are often without telephone service for a considerable time. Television viewing behavior in such developments may not be adequately represented in samples based on telephone listees. A still more serious limitation of telephone surveys centers around the "time-of-contact" problem. Telephone calls to viewers for the purpose of surveys can hardly be placed later than, say, 10 P.M. without the risk of disturbing sleeping households and precipitating great wrath.

The Pulse, Inc., bases its ratings on personal interviews using the aided recall type of instrument which was discussed earlier. The sample apparently consists of approximately 8,000 television homes per day. Because of cost considerations involved in such large numbers, such interviews must be completed quickly. Therefore, their aided recall instrument allows for interview lengths of only approximately eight minutes. Such rapid interviewing is open to serious question, since without time to establish sufficient rapport even the most skillful interviewer would be hard pressed to get accurate responses from interviewees. From our own experience in audience research, we discovered that short interviews often result in hasty decisions on the part of interviewees, who invariably sense the "let's get it over with" attitude that interviewers in such situations are prone to project. We noted earlier the possibilities of instrument errors inherent in the aided recall technique in general.

The American Research Bureau has made an especially careful effort to obtain accurate data through utilization of viewing diaries. This organization not only attempts to sample with precision 2,000 representative television homes in the national television market, but also demonstrates sampling precision in local television markets. In an attempt to prevent the development of the artificiality in responses referred to earlier, ARB changes its sample of diary-television homes every month. The viewer is asked to maintain a diary record for one week, recording the name of the program, the time, and the channel when he sets the dial. As suggested earlier, the less conscientious viewers may fill in the required information not after watching each program but at the end of the week, thus introducing the possibility of recall errors. Perhaps the most basic criticism of the ARB method, however, concerns the percentage of diaries returned. Although ARB claims as a selling point that from 60 percent to 70 percent of the diaries are returned each week, the fact that around 35 percent are not returned introduces a very significant biased sampling error. After all, even though a television viewer has agreed to participate in maintenance of a diary, one cannot force him to complete and return the diary, nor can one assume that those who are negligent in this respect do not differ appreciably from those who fully cooperate.

In the last several months, the American Research Bureau has introduced an electronic meter, the Arbitron, which is perhaps the most dramatic development in audience measurement devices to date. These instruments, which are placed in representative television homes, are connected to a central data center in which information concerning the operation of the television sets is instantaneously recorded. With the use of electronic computers, it appears to fulfill the need for immediate audience assessment. However, the elimination of the three-week period for data processing seems to be its only major advantage over the Nielsen Audimeter, since even the most amazing electronic device will not solve the sampling problem created by viewers who simply do not wish to have such devices attached to their television sets because they regard them as an unwarranted intrusion on their privacy. At present the Arbitron is operating, of course, in such a few markets (apparently only seven cities) that it has had only a limited application, so a truly fair evaluation of its potential could not, of course, be made at this time.

PROBLEMS IMPAIR ACCURACY

In this brief discussion of the various audience rating services, we have seen that the methods of every single one of them are susceptible to either instrument or sampling errors. As mentioned earlier, I am convinced that the major audience rating services, without exception, have excellent researchers planning their studies, but because of the nature of the behavior that is being studied–television viewing–the operational end of such research is bound to be affected by the kinds of errors that we mentioned which, unfortunately, cannot be easily offset by even the best planning. Therefore, aside from anything further that can be said about audience ratings, these problems involved in implementing such audience studies tend to seriously impair their accuracy. They also provide at least a partial explanation, of course, of the frequent inconsistencies among the reported results of the various services.

Incidently, another basis for this inconsistency lies in the fact that a kind of rank order of television programs is drawn from the rating data. Since a margin of error has to be contended with in the rating of any specific program during a particular rating interval, such error may cause chance rank order differences among the various rating services. In order to overcome this source of error, it would have to be recognized that comparisons of the rankings of specific programs over several rating intervals to determine long-term trends should ideally be incorporated. In the opinion of Dr. Samuel Becker, chairman of the NAEB Research Committee, such analysis of program rankings would demonstrate greater reliability than could be obtained from making comparisons among the services on the basis of any given week's ratings.

To confound the picture even more, however, the data obtained by the rating services are placed in the hands of individuals who see them in the setting of advertising economics and use them in a manner which tends to distort further the overall picture of audience ratings. If you were the account executive of an advertising agency, the temptation would be great to cite only the results of the rating service which rated your program most advantageously. Moreover, if only national program results are purchased, and these national results are favorable to the program being sold, it might be a great temptation to misrepresent national results as being applicable to certain regions in which sponsorship for the program is sought, when such representation, as we pointed out earlier, is by no stretch of the imagination based on a representative sample. To remedy this situation, most of the rating services also sell regional surveys, of course. But these regional surveys are often sold on a cost-per-sample-television-home basis, which, due to cost-cutting efforts, frequently results in the purchase of rating information not only beset by all of the sampling and instrument errors referred to earlier, but also by the additional problem of samples of inadequate size.

Still another problem in interpretation is the reduction of television ratings to what is technically referred to as a percentile standard score system, which was pioneered by the late C. E. Hooper. This system reduces any audience rating to a kind of percentage basis, with 100 being optimal. The transformation of audience sizes into percentiles leads to an illusion of uniformity which may not be statistically valid. When comparing ratings of 30, for example, on any level, regional or national, we must also take into consideration such problems as the number of viewers or television homes in the universe (depending on which is used as the basis of audience size), the number of television stations in the market, the number of television sets that could be expected to be operating at given times, and so on. You have divided your program schedules into such designations as A, B, and C periods in an attempt to indicate relative numbers of sets that could be expected to be tuned in at various times. Ratings must take such factors into consideration when percentiles are projected into the size of the audience claimed for any program.

It is interesting to note that in the interest of more precision, cumulative viewing patterns are now being considered by some of the rating services. This is important in comparing programs that have multiple weekly presentations with those that have biweekly presentations, and so on.

Another example of the kind of problem that is now recognized by some of the rating services is the factor of overlapping viewing behavior, particularly in the case of longer programs such as the so-called "spectaculars." We know that viewers may watch the first portion of one program, switch to another program, and then later switch back to the original program. This kind of behavior on the part of the viewer cannot be ignored in an adequate evaluation of viewing behavior.

These are all examples of the kinds of complex interaction variables that should be very seriously considered in interpreting rating service results and which further underline the difficulties in correctly applying rating service data. As an approach to solving these problems, a form of motivation research, which has begun to permeate the field of market research generally, is now being employed in television audience studies to a greater and greater extent. The basic assumption underlying motivation research as used here is that data obtained from a smaller number of individuals interviewed intensively, although obviously less representative in terms of sampling size, may reveal significant unique audience interests that, from the standpoint of programing strategy, could be a good deal more valuable than simple quantitative statements of sheer audience size, such as most rating services traditionally report.

If we ponder for a moment the notion of a television program designed as a background for the delivery of advertising messages, we may begin wondering whether the kind of quantitative mass appeal so often employed in program content may not eventually create indifference to the advertising message. The viewer, as he becomes more sophisticated, may begin to perceive the fact that the program is designed for a universal target group. He may then tend to react to the sponsor's messages much as he does to form letters, ignoring them in general as having little interest for him as a unique human being. Is it not possible that advertising messages might be more effective in a context of programing directed to a somewhat smaller audience but clearly appealing to the members of that audience as *individuals?*

An example of characteristics of special audiences was apparent in a recent audience study that we completed under terms of a grant from the National Educational Television and Radio Center. In this study in depth of the educational television audience in the Channel 8 signal area, we discovered as we expected, that the size of educational television audiences was very small–so small, in fact, that our criteria of frequency of viewing had to be very crude. We had to designate as "frequent" viewers those who viewed the station as seldom as two times per week or more. A surprising number of respondents viewed the station as infrequently as once a month. Yet even by our crude definition of frequent viewers, the frequent viewers differed significantly from the infrequent or nonviewers. To quote from our research report distributed by the National Educational Television and Radio Center in 1958,

> The frequent viewer of educational television does seem to differ from the infrequent or nonviewer in that to a statistically significant extent he is more likely to vote more frequently in elections. He actively discusses the content of the educational television programs he watches with friends, and he appears to feel that he benefits from such discussions. His leisure time activity seems to be dominated by participative self-improvement activities. . . . He is generally more active, information-minded, self-improvement-seeking, and civic-minded than the nonviewer. . . . The

> frequent viewer appears to be a viewer who counts in the sense that he is inclined to actually put into practice information that he receives.

As you can see, this picture of a minority audience is very provocative since it suggests that the true impact of educational television programing extends beyond the group of actual viewers. Another illustration of the effectiveness of programing directed to a smaller audience can be found in the loyalty of the growing numbers of FM radio listeners. The members of this audience appear to demonstrate their appreciation of special programing by their response to sponsors' appeals. Most reports indicate that FM listeners are more responsive to advertisers' messages than audiences reached through the typical "shotgun" kind of programing which is intended for almost everybody.

If marketing research organizations would expend as much effort in examining such qualitative aspects of the behavior of television audiences as they do on the usual nose-counting techniques, they would, in my opinion, discover that buying behavior could sometimes be stimulated more successfully by recognizing unique needs of certain individuals in the television audience than by appealing at all times to a mythical common denominator. This is not to say that programing for a mass audience would have no place in the industry but rather it suggests that such upgrading of programing in terms of the interests of different audience groups could not only reduce the intensity of some of the basic criticisms of commercial programing, but also, in the long run, increase the effectiveness of programing as a means of influencing the viewer's buying behavior. This would also, of course, require a vast program for the reeducation of advertisers. At a minimum, however, this appears to be a crucial hypothesis that should be thoroughly tested.

Not everyone will agree with all of the observations I have made. But perhaps one might think seriously about the possibilities for upgrading programing which could result from unshackling ourselves from such a limited criterion of programing success as audience size!

PART TWO:

Different Strokes—Strategies of Research

Every cobbler thinks leather is the only thing. Most social scientists, including the present writer, have their favorite methods with which they are familiar and have some skill in using. And I suspect we mostly choose to investigate problems that seem vulnerable to attack through these methods. But we should at least try to be less parochial than cobblers. Let us be done with the arguments of "participant observation" ***versus*** interviewing—as we have largely dispensed with the arguments for psychology ***versus*** sociology—and get on with the business of attacking our problems with the widest array of conceptual and methodological tools that we possess and they demand.

Martin Trow
"Comment on Participant Observation and Interviewing"

TOPIC III: Game Plans and Options

> Every data-gathering class—interviews, questionnaires, observation, performance records, physical evidence—is potentially biased and has specific to it certain validity threats. . . . No single measurement class is perfect, neither is any scientifically useless. . . . When a hypothesis can survive the confrontation of a series of complementary methods of testing, it contains a degree of validity unattainable by one tested within the more constricted framework of a single method.
>
> Eugene J. Webb, *et al.*
> *Unobtrusive Measures*

Eugene J. Webb, in the above quotation, is setting the stage for his plea for multiple operationism in social research. As he explains elsewhere in *Unobtrusive Measures,* the usual question researchers ask themselves is which one of several available methods is the best for the problem at hand. Webb feels a better question to ask is which *set* of methods is best.

> Once a proposition has been confirmed by two or more independent measurement processes, the uncertainty of its interpretation is greatly reduced. . . . If a proposition can survive the onslaught of a series of imperfect measures, with all their irrelevant error, confidence should be placed in it.[1]

Let me offer an example of Webb's thesis. In the early 1960s a social psychologist at Yale University, Stanley Milgram, began investigating the extent to which an individual will obey the commands of a legitimate authority to inflict painful punishment on another individual.[2] Milgram's sample consisted of nearly 1000 male adults in the New Haven-Bridgeport, Connecticut area. He was careful to sample from a wide range of occupational categories and age levels. Although the real purpose of the experiment was to determine the amount of electric shock a subject would administer to another person when ordered to do so by the experimenter, the subjects were told instead that the experiment was to determine the effects of punishment on memory.

> The naïve subject is told that it is his task to teach the learner a list of paired associates (words), to test him on the list, and to administer punishment whenever the learner errs in the test. Punishment takes the form of electric shock (bogus), delivered to the learner by means of a shock generator controlled by the naïve subject. The teacher (subject) is instructed to increase the intensity of electric shock one step on the generator for each error. The learner, according to plan, provides many wrong answers, so that

> before long the naïve subject must give him the strongest shock on the generator. Increases in shock level are met by increasingly insistent demands from the learner that the experiment be stopped because of the growing discomfort to him. However, in clear terms, the experimenter orders the teacher (subject) to continue with the procedure in disregard of the learner's protests.[3]

There were four experimental conditions under which this activity was performed, having to do with the immediacy of the learner to the subject. One extreme was the remote feedback condition, in which the learner and subject were in adjoining rooms, and at a certain voltage level, the learner began pounding on the wall, pleading he had a heart condition, and begging the subject not to go on with the shocks. At a certain higher voltage level, the learner suddenly became silent. The subject was ordered to continue the shocks at higher voltage levels. At the other extreme was the touch-proximity condition, in which the subject and learner were together in the same room. At a low voltage level, the learner refused to place his hand on the metal shock plate and the subject was ordered to physically force his hand onto the plate and administer the shock. This physical forcing of the learner's hand onto the shock plate against his physical and verbal resistance continued at the higher voltage levels.

The results of Milgram's laboratory experiment?

> With numbing regularity good people were seen to knuckle under to the demands of authority and perform actions that were callous and severe. Men who are in everyday life responsible and decent were seduced by the trappings of authority, by control of their perceptions, and by the uncritical acceptance of the experimenter's definition of the situation into performing harsh acts.[4]

In some cases, up to 65 percent of the subjects tested "went all the way"; delivering to the learner a maximum shock, listed in red under a "danger" sign, of 450 volts. A more specific finding was that the greater the physical distance between learner and subject, the more often the subject would go all the way with the shock treatment. Fewer subjects in the touch-proximity condition (about 30 percent) got to the 450 volt level than in the remote feedback condition (about 65 percent).

Milgram's experiment is one method of testing propositions concerning obedience and authority. The experiment has been criticized by some in terms of its being conducted in the artificial setting of the laboratory. "People wouldn't act that way in real life situations," these persons claim. Here is where Webb's concept of multiple operationism fits in. "Once a proposition has been confirmed by two or more independent measurement processes, the uncertainty of interpretation is greatly reduced."[5] Are there other measurement processes that test Americans' obedience reactions under authority?

During World War II, Brigadier General S.L.A. Marshall conducted field interviews (survey analysis) with 400 companies of infantrymen in the European and Pacific combat areas. His central finding was that,

> on an average not more than 15 percent of the men had actually fired at the enemy positions or personnel with rifles, carbines, grenades, bazookas, BARs, or machine guns during the course of an entire engagement. . . . The best showing that could be made by the most spirited and aggressive companies was that one man in four had made at least some use of his fire power.[6]

However, when Marshall looked at those back of the lines using crew-served weapons, such as artillery, he found little evidence of men unwilling to contribute to firepower.

How can you reconcile the results of these two very different measurement processes, each designed to get at the same phenomenon? As you think about the two studies together, note how much more rich the implications are than those of either study taken separately.

Another example of the method of multiple operationism, or triangulation, is an analysis made of the My Lai trial transcripts as compared to the flight logs and bombing schedules of B-52 crews (analysis of existing records). One would find, in the My Lai transcripts, a good deal of information concerning the reactions of Americans to authority figures when the situation is immediate and the individuals upon whom harm is to be inflicted are close at hand. Conversely, the B-52 crew material would reveal reactions to a situation where the "enemy" is remote and unseen, and the Americans involved are acting as members of a tightly knit group.

There are innumerable other data that could be used to shed further light on this problem. Interviews with war veterans, and with members of the Ohio National Guard concerning the Kent State actions, are but two that come to mind.

THE RANGE OF RESEARCH METHODS

The continuum on the next page is an attempt to map the range of alternative methodologies one can employ in the process of multiple operationalism. Each method has its strengths, each its weaknesses. The purpose of this section of the book, "Different Strokes–Strategies of Research," is to make you aware of both strengths and weaknesses so you can put together intelligent research designs containing mutually-reinforcing methods.

In the article which follows, Eugene J. Webb and his colleagues discuss various methodological options available; focusing especially on the unobtrusive, or nonreactive, measures. Their basic argument is that sociologists have

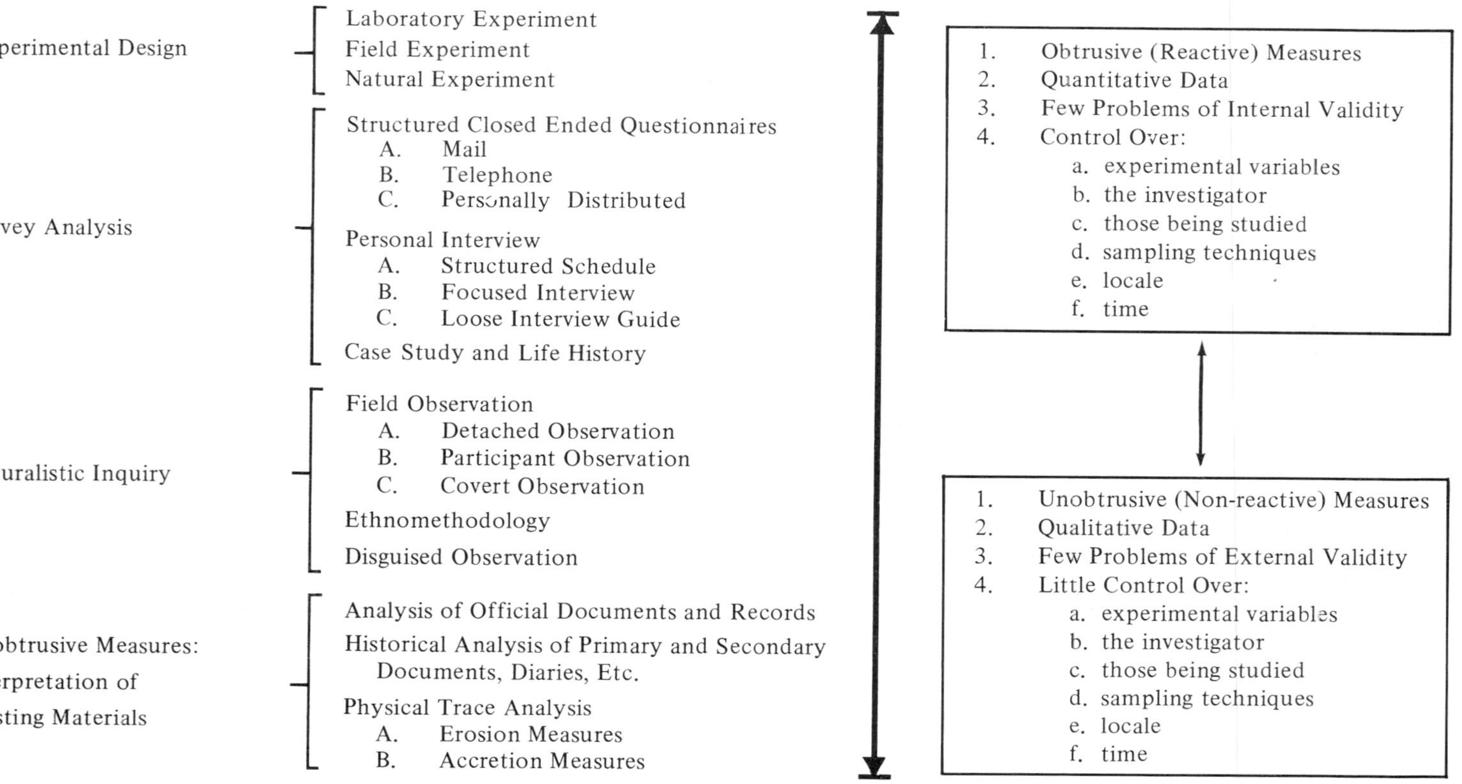

Figure 4. Range of Alternative Methodologies

placed much too much reliance on survey methods *alone* as a means of collecting data, and that the whole range of alternatives should be considered in the spirit of multiple operationism. The discussion generally concerns itself with the various validity problems associated with each type of method employed. (Validity can be defined as, "Are you measuring what you think you are measuring, or is it some unconsidered factor present in the situation that accounts for the measurement?") Read Webb's article with the range of alternative methodologies in mind. What are the strengths and weaknesses of each of these methods, in terms of validity? As you focus more specifically on each class of methods, discussed later, this will be an important article to return to.

NOTES

1. Eugene J. Webb, *et al., Unobtrusive Measures* (New York: Rand, McNally, 1966), p. 3.
2. Stanley Milgram, "Some Conditions of Obedience and Disobedience to Authority," *Human Relations* 18 (1965): 57–75.
3. *Ibid.,* p. 58.
4. *Ibid.,* p. 73.
5. Webb, *Unobtrusive Measures,* p. 3.
6. S.L.A. Marshall, *Men Against Fire* (New York: William Morrow and Co., 1947), p. 54.

SUGGESTED FURTHER READING

Denzin, Norman K. "Strategies of Multiple Triangulation," *The Research Act,* pp. 297–313. Chicago: Aldine, 1970.

Lewis, George H. "Popular Music and Research Design: Methodological Alternatives," *Popular Music and Society* 1, no. 2 (Winter 1972): pp. 108–15.

Miller, Delbert C. *Handbook of Research Design and Social Measurement,* 2nd ed., pp. 1–114. New York: David McKay Co., 1970.

Siever, Raymond. "Science: Observational, Experimental, Historical," *American Scientist* 56, no. 1 (1963): 70–77.

Webb, Eugene J. "Unconventionality, Triangulation, and Inference," *Proceedings of the Invitational Conference on Testing Problems,* October 29, 1966, pp. 34–43.

Approximations to Knowledge

Eugene J. Webb, Donald T. Campbell,
Richard D. Schwartz and Lee Sechrest

* * *

Today, some 90 percent of social science research is based upon interviews and questionnaires. We lament this overdependence upon a single, fallible method. Interviews and questionnaires intrude as a foreign element into the social setting they would describe, they create as well as measure attitudes, they elicit atypical roles and responses, they are limited to those who are accessible and will cooperate, and the responses obtained are produced in part by dimensions of individual differences irrelevant to the topic at hand.

But the principal objection is that they are used alone. No research method is without bias. Interviews and questionnaires must be supplemented by methods testing the same social science variables but having *different* methodological weaknesses.

In sampling the range of alternative approaches, we examine their weaknesses, too. The flaws are serious and give insight into why we do depend so much upon the interview. But the issue is not choosing among individual methods. Rather it is the necessity for a multiple operationism, a collection of methods combined to avoid sharing the same weaknesses. The goal of this monograph is not to replace the interview but to supplement and cross-validate it with measures that do not require the cooperation of a respondent and that do not themselves contaminate the response.

Here are some samples:

. . . The floor tiles around the hatching-chick exhibit at Chicago's Museum of Science and Industry must be replaced every six weeks. Tiles in other parts of the museum need not be replaced for years. The selective erosion of tiles,

From Eugene J. Webb, *et al., Unobtrusive Measures: Nonreactive Research in the Social Sciences,* pp. 1–2; 11–34; 175–81, © 1966 by Rand McNally and Company, Chicago. Reprinted by permission of the publisher. References have been deleted and footnotes renumbered.

indexed by the replacement rate, is a measure of the relative popularity of exhibits.

The accretion rate is another measure. One investigator wanted to learn the level of whisky consumption in a town which was officially "dry." He did so by counting empty bottles in ashcans.

The degree of fear induced by a ghost-story-telling session can be measured by noting the shrinking diameter of a circle of seated children.

Chinese jade dealers have used the pupil dilation of their customers as a measure of the client's interest in particular stones, and Darwin in 1872 noted this same variable as an index of fear.

Library withdrawals were used to demonstrate the effect of the introduction of television into a community. Fiction titles dropped, nonfiction titles were unaffected.

The role of rate of interaction in managerial recruitment is shown by the overrepresentation of baseball managers who were infielders or catchers (high-interaction positions) during their playing days.

Sir Francis Galton employed surveying hardware to estimate the bodily dimensions of African women whose language he did not speak.

The child's interest in Christmas was demonstrated by distortions in the size of Santa Claus drawings.

Racial attitudes in two colleges were compared by noting the degree of clustering of Negroes and whites in lecture halls.

. . . Before making a detailed examination of such methods, it is well to present a closer argument for the use of multiple methods and to present a methodological framework within which both the traditional and the more novel methods can be evaluated. . . .

INTERNAL AND EXTERNAL VALIDITY

Before discussing a list of some common sources of invalidity, a distinction must be drawn between internal and external validity. *Internal validity* asks whether a difference exists at all in any given comparison. It asks whether or not an apparent difference can be explained away as some measurement artifact. For true experiments, this question is usually not salient, but even there, the happy vagaries of random sample selection occasionally delude one and spuriously produce the appearance of a difference where in fact none exists. For the rival hypothesis of chance, we fortunately have an elaborated theoretical model which evaluates its plausibility. A p-value describes the darkness of the ever present shadow of doubt. But for index-number comparisons not embedded in a formal experiment, and for the plausible-rival-hypothesis strategy more generally, the threats to internal validity–the argument that even the appearance of a difference is spurious–is a serious problem and the one that has first priority.

External validity is the problem of interpreting the difference, the problem of generalization. To what other populations, occasions, stimulus objects, and measures may the obtained results be applied? The distinction between internal and external validity can be illustrated in two uses of randomization. When the experimentalist in psychology randomly assigns a sample of persons into two or more experimental groups, he is concerned entirely with internal validity—with making it implausible that the luck of the draw produced the resulting differences. When a sociologist carefully randomizes the selection of respondents so that his sample represents a larger population, representativeness or external validity is involved.

The psychologist may be extremely confident that a difference is traceable to an experimental treatment, but whether it would hold up with another set of subjects or in a different setting may be quite equivocal. He has achieved internal validity by his random assignment but not addressed the external validity issue by the chance allocation of subjects.

The sociologist, similarly, has not met all the validity concerns by simply drawing a random sample. Conceding that he has taken a necessary step toward achieving external validity and generalization of his differences, the internal validity problem remains.

Random assignment is only one method of reaching toward internal validity. Experimental-design control, exclusive of randomization, is another. Consider the case of a pretest-posttest field experiment on the effect of a persuasive communication. Randomly choosing those who participate, the social scientist properly wards off some major threats to external validity. But we also know of other validity threats. The first interview in a two-stage study may set into motion attitude change and clarification processes which would otherwise not have occurred (e.g., Crespi, 1948). If such processes did occur, the comparison of a first and second measure on the same person is internally invalid, for the shift is a measurement-produced artifact.

Even when a measured control group is used, and a persuasive communication produces a greater change in an experimental group, the persuasive effect may be internally valid but externally invalid. There is the substantial risk that the effect occurs only with pretested populations and might be absent in populations lacking the pretest (cf. Schanck & Goodman, 1939; Hovland, Lumsdaine, & Sheffield, 1949; Solomon, 1949). For more extensive discussions of internal and external calidity, see Campbell (1957) and Campbell and Stanley (1963).

The distinction between internal and external validity is often murky. In this work, we have considered the two classes of threat jointly, although occasionally detailing the risks separately. The reason for this is that the factors which are a risk for internal validity are often the same as those threatening external validity. While for one scientist the representative sampling of cities is a method to achieve generalization to the United States population, for another it may be an effort to give an internally valid comparison across cities.

SOURCES OF INVALIDITY OF MEASURES

In this section, we review frequent threats to the valid interpretation of a difference–common plausible rival hypotheses. They are broadly divided into three groups: error that may be traced to those being studied, error that comes from the investigator, and error associated with sampling imperfections. This section is the only one in which we draw illustrations mainly from the most popular methods of current social science. For that reason, particular attention is paid to those weaknesses which create the need for multiple and alternate methods.

In addition, some other criteria such as the efficiency of the research instrument are mentioned. These are independent of validity, but important for the practical research decisions which must be made.

Reactive Measurement Effect: Error from the Respondent

The most understated risk to valid interpretation is the error produced by the respondent. Even when he is well intentioned and cooperative, the research subject's knowledge that he is participating in a scholarly search may confound the investigator's data. Four classes of this error are discussed here: awareness of being tested, role selection, measurement as a change agent, and response sets.

1. THE GUINEA PIG EFFECT–AWARENESS OF BEING TESTED

Selltiz and her associates (1959) make the observation:

> The measurement process used in the experiment may itself affect the outcome. If people feel that they are "guinea pigs" being experimented with, or if they feel that they are being "tested" and must make a good impression, or if the method of data collection suggests responses or stimulates an interest the subject did not previously feel, the measuring process may distort the experimental results [p. 97].

These effects have been called "reactive effect of measurement" and "reactive arrangement" bias (Campbell, 1957; Campbell & Stanley, 1963). It is important to note early that the awareness of testing need not, by itself, contaminate responses. It is a question of probabilities, but the probability of bias is high in any study in which a respondent is aware of his subject status.

Although the methods to be reviewed here do not involve "respondents," comparable reactive effects on the population may often occur. Consider, for example, a potentially nonreactive instrument such as the movie camera. If it is conspicuously placed, its lack of ability to talk to the subjects doesn't help us much. The visible presence of the camera undoubtedly changes behavior, and does so differentially depending upon the labeling involved. The response is likely to vary if the camera has printed on its side "Los Angeles Police Department" or "NBC" or "Foundation Project on Crowd Behavior." Similarly, an Englishman's presence at a wedding in Africa exerts a much more reactive effect on the proceedings than it would on the Sussex Downs.

A specific illustration may be of value. In the summer of 1952, some graduate students in the social sciences at the University of Chicago were employed to observe the numbers of Negroes and whites in stores, restaurants, bars, theaters, and so on on a south side Chicago street intersecting the Negro-white boundary (East 63rd). This, presumably, should have been a nonreactive process, particularly at the predominantly white end of the street. No questions were asked, no persons stopped. Yet, in spite of this hopefully inconspicuous activity, two merchants were agitated and persistent enough to place calls to the university which somehow got through to the investigators; how many others tried and failed cannot be known. The two calls were from a store operator and the manager of a currency exchange, both of whom wanted assurance that this was some university nosiness and not a professional casing for subsequent robbery (Campbell & Mack, in preparation). An intrusion conspicuous enough to arouse such an energetic reaction may also have been conspicuous enough to change behavior; for observations other than simple enumerations the bias would have been great. But even with the simple act of nose-counting, there is the risk that the area would be differentially avoided. The research mistake was in providing observers with clipboards and log sheets, but their appearance might have been still more sinister had they operated Veeder counters with hands jammed in pockets.

The present monograph argues strongly for the use of archival records. Thinking, perhaps, of musty files of bound annual reports of some prior century, one might regard such a method as totally immune to reactive effects. However, were one to make use of precinct police blotters, going around to copy off data once each month, the quality and nature of the records would almost certainly change. In actual fact, archives are kept indifferently, as a low-priority task, by understaffed bureaucracies. Conscientiousness is often low because of the lack of utilization of the records. The presence of a user can revitalize the process—as well as create anxieties over potentially damaging data (Campbell, 1963a). When records are seen as sources of vulnerability, they may be altered systematically. Accounts thought likely to enter into tax audits are an obvious case (Schwartz, 1961), but administrative records (Blau, 1955) and criminal statistics (Kadish, 1964) are equally amenable to this source of distortion. The selective and wholesale rifling of records by ousted political administrations sets an example of potential reactive effects, self-consciousness, and dissembling on the part of archivists.

These reactive effects may threaten both internal and external validity, depending upon the conditions. If it seems plausible that the reactivity was equal in both measures of a comparison, then the threat is to external validity or generalizability, not to internal validity. If the reactive effect is plausibly differential, then it may generate a pseudo-difference. Thus, in a study (Campbell & McCormack, 1957) showing a reduction in authoritarian attitudes over the course of one year's military training, the initial testing was done in conjunction with an official testing program, while the subsequent testing was clearly under external university research auspices. As French (1955) pointed out in another connection, this difference provides a plausible reactive threat jeopardizing the conclusion that any reduction has taken place even for this one group, quite apart from the external validity problems of explanation and generalization. In many interview and questionnaire studies, increased or decreased rapport and increased awareness of the researcher's goals or decreased fear provide plausible alternative explanations of the apparent change recorded.

The common device of guaranteeing anonymity demonstrates concern for the reactive bias, but this concern may lead to validity threats. For example, some test constructors have collected normative data under conditions of anonymity, while the test is likely to be used with the respondent's name signed. Making a response public, or guaranteeing to hide one, will influence the nature of the response. This has been seen for persuasive communications, in the validity of reports of brands purchased, and for the level of antisocial responses. There is a clear link between awareness of being tested and the biases associated with a tendency to answer with socially desirable responses.

The considerations outlined above suggest that reactivity may be selectively troublesome within trials or tests of the experiment. Training trials may accommodate the subject to the task, but a practice effect may exist that either enhances or inhibits the reactive bias. Early responses may be contaminated, later ones not, or vice versa (Underwood, 1957).

Ultimately, the determination of reactive effect depends on validating studies–few examples of which are currently available. Behavior observed under nonreactive conditions must be compared with corresponding behavior in which various potentially reactive conditions are introduced. Where no difference in direction of relationship occurs, the reactivity factor can be discounted.

In the absence of systematic data of this kind, we have little basis for determining what is and what is not reactive. Existing techniques consist of asking subjects in a posttest interview whether they were affected by the test, were aware of the deception in the experiment, and so forth. While these may sometimes demonstrate a method to be reactive, they may fail to detect many instances in which reactivity is a serious contaminant. Subjects who consciously dissemble during an experiment may do so afterward for the same reasons. And those who are unaware of the effects on them at the time of the research may hardly be counted on for valid reports afterwards.

The types of measures surveyed in this monograph have a double importance in overcoming reactivity. In the absence of validation for verbal measures, nonreactive techniques of the kind surveyed here provide ways of avoiding the serious problems faced by more conventional techniques. Given the limiting properties of these "other measures," however, their greatest utility may inhere in their capacity to provide validation for the more conventional measures.

2. ROLE SELECTION

Another way in which the respondent's awareness of the research process produces differential reaction involves not so much inaccuracy, defense, or dishonesty, but rather a specialized selection from among the many "true" selves or "proper" behaviors available in any respondent.

By singling out an individual to be tested (assuming that being tested is not a normal condition), the experimenter forces upon the subject a role-defining decision—What kind of a person should I be as I answer these questions or do these tasks? In many of the "natural" situations to which the findings are generalized, the subject may not be forced to define his role relative to the behavior. For other situations, he may. Validity decreases as the role assumed in the research setting varies from the usual role present in comparable behavior beyond the research setting. Orne and his colleagues have provided compelling demonstrations of the magnitude of this variable's effect (Orne, 1959; Orne, 1962; Orne & Scheibe, 1961; Orne & Evans, 1965). Orne has noted:

> The experimental situation is one which takes place within context of an explicit agreement of the subject to participate in a special form of social interaction known as "taking part in an experiment." Within the context of our culture the roles of subject and experimenter are well understood and carry with them well-defined mutual role expectations [1962, p. 777].

Looking at all the cues available to the respondent attempting to puzzle out an appropriate set of roles or behavior, Orne labeled the total of all such cues the "demand characteristics of the experimental situation." The recent study by Orne & Evans (1965) showed that the alleged antisocial effects induced by hypnosis can be accounted for by the demand characteristics of the research setting. Subjects who were not hypnotized engaged in "antisocial" activities as well as did those who were hypnotized. The behavior of those not hypnotized is traced to social cues that attend the experimental situation and are unrelated to the experimental variable.

The probability of this confounding role assumption varies from one research study to another, of course. The novelty of a test-taking role may be selectively biasing for subjects of different educational levels. Less familiar and comfortable with testing, those with little formal schooling are more likely to produce nonrepresentative behavior. The act of being tested is "more different." The same sort of distortion risk occurs when subject matter is unusual or novel. Subject matter with which the respondent is unfamiliar may produce uncertainty of which role to select. A role-playing choice is more likely with such new or unexpected material.

Lack of familiarity with tests or with testing materials can influence response in different ways. Responses may be depressed because of a lack of training with the materials. Or the response level may be distorted as the subject perceives himself in the rare role of expert.

Both unfamiliarity and "expertness" can influence the character as well as the level of response. It is common to find experimental procedures which augment the experting bias. The instruction which reads, "You have been selected as part of a scientifically selected sample . . . it is important that you answer the questions . . . " underlines in what a special situation and what a special person the respondent is. The empirical test of the experting hypothesis in field research is the extent of "don't know" replies. One should predict that a set of instructions stressing the importance of the respondent as a member of a "scientifically selected sample" will produce significantly fewer "don't knows" than an instruction set that does not stress the individual's importance.

Although the "special person" set of instructions may increase participation in the project, and thus reduce some concern on the sampling level, it concurrently increases the risk of reactive bias. In science as everywhere else, one seldom gets something for nothing. The critical question for the researcher must be whether or not the resultant sampling gain offsets the risk of deviation from "true" responses produced by the experting role.

Not only does interviewing result in role selection, but the problem or its analogues may exist for any measure. Thus, in a study utilizing conversation sampling with totally hidden microphones, each social setting elicits a different role selection. Conversation samples might thus differ between two cities, not because of any true differences, but rather because of subtle differences in role elicitation of the differing settings employed.

3. MEASUREMENT AS CHANGE AGENT

With all the respondent candor possible, and with complete role representativeness, there can still be an important class of reactive effects–those in which the initial measurement activity introduces real changes in what is being measured. The change may be real enough in these instances, but be invalidly attributed to any of the intervening events, and be invalidly generalized to other settings not involving a pretest. This process has been deliberately demonstrated by Schanck and Goodman (1939) in a classic study involving information-test taking as a disguised persuasive process. Research by Roper (cited by Crespi, 1948) shows that the well-established "preamble effect" (Cantril, 1944) is not merely a technical flaw in determining the response to the question at hand, but that it also creates attitudes which persist and which are measurable on subsequent unbiased questions. Crespi reports additional research of his own confirming that even for those who initially say "don't know," processes leading to opinion development are initiated.

The effect has been long established in the social sciences. In psychology, early research in transfer of training encountered the threat to internal validity called "practice effects": the exercise provided by the pretest accounted for the gain shown on the posttest. Such research led to the introduction of control groups in studies that had earlier neglected to include them. Similarly, research in intelligence testing showed that dependable gains in test-passing ability could be traced to experience with previous tests even where no knowledge of results had been provided. (See Cane & Heim, 1950, and Anastasi, 1958, pp. 190–191, for reviews of this literature.) Similar gains have been shown in personal "adjustment" scores (Windle, 1954).

While such effects are obviously limited to intrusive measurement methods such as this review seeks to avoid, the possibility of analogous artifacts must be considered. Suppose one were interested in measuring the weight of women in a secretarial pool, and their weights were to be the dependent variable in a study on the effects of a change from an all-female staff to one including men. One might for this purpose put free weight scales in the women's restroom, with an automatic recording device inside. However, the recurrent availability of knowledge of one's own weight in a semisocial situation would probably act as a greater change agent for weight than would any experimental treatment that might be under investigation. A floor-panel treadle would be better, recording weights without providing feedback to the participant, possibly disguised as an automatic door-opener.

4. RESPONSE SETS

The critical literature on questionnaire methodology has demonstrated the presence of several irrelevant but lawful sources of variance. Most of these are probably applicable to interviews also, although this has been less elaborately demonstrated to date. Cronbach (1946) has summarized this literature, and evidence continues to show its importance (e.g., Jackson & Messick, 1957; Chapman & Bock, 1958).

Respondents will more frequently endorse a statement than disagree with its opposite (Sletto, 1937). This tendency differs widely and consistently among individuals, generating the reliable source of variance known as acquiescence response set. Rorer (1965) has recently entered a dissent from this point of view. He validly notes the evidence indicating that acquiescence or yea-saying is not a totally general personality trait elicitable by items of any content. He fails to note that, even so, the evidence clearly indicates the methodological problem that direction of wording lawfully enhances the correlation between two measures when shared, and depresses the correlation when running counter to the direction of the correlation of the content (Campbell, 1965b). Another idiosyncracy, dependably demonstrated over varied multiple-choice content, is the preference for strong statements versus moderate or indecisive ones. Sequences of questions asked in very similar format produce stereotyped responses, such as a tendency to endorse the righthand or the lefthand response, or to alternate in some simple fashion. Furthermore, decreasing attention produces reliable biases from the order of item presentation.

Response biases can occur not only for questionnaires or public opinion polls, but also for archival records such as votes (Bain & Hecock, 1957). Still more esoteric observational or erosion measures face similar problems. Take the example of a traffic study.

Suppose one wanted to obtain a nonreactive measure of the relative attractiveness of paintings in an art museum. He might employ an erosion method such as the relative degree of carpet or floor-tile wear in front of each painting. Or, more elaborately, he might install invisible photoelectric timers and counters. Such an approach must also take into account irrelevant habits which affect traffic flow. There is, for example, a general right-turn bias upon entering a building or room. When this is combined with time deadlines and fatigue (Do people drag their feet more by the time they get to the paintings on the left side of the building?), there probably is a predictably biased response tendency. The design of museums tends to be systematic, and this, too, can bias the measures. The placement of an exit door will consistently bias the traffic flow and thus confound any erosion measure unless it is controlled. (For imaginative and provocative observational studies on museum behavior see Robinson, 1928; Melton, 1933a; Melton, 1933b; Melton, 1935; Melton, 1936; Melton, Feldman, & Mason, 1936.)

Each of these four types of reactive error can be reduced by employing research measures which do not require the cooperation of the respondent and which are "blind" to him. Although we urge more methodological research to make known the degree of error that may be traced to reactivity, our inclination now is to urge the use of compensating measures which do not contain the reactive risk.

Error from the Investigator

To some degree, error from the investigator was implicit in the reactive error effects. After all, the investigator is an important source of cues to the respondent, and he helps to structure the demand characteristics of the interview. However, in these previous points, interviewer character was unspecified. Here we deal with effects that vary systematically with interviewer characteristics, and with instrument errors totally independent of respondents.

5. INTERVIEWER EFFECTS

It is old news that the characteristics of the interviewer can contribute a substantial amount of variance to a set of findings. Interviewees respond differentially to visible cues provided by the interviewer. Within any single study, this variance can produce a spurious difference. The work of Katz (1942) and Cantril (1944) early demonstrated the differential effect of the race of the interviewer, and that bias has been more recently shown by Athey and his associates (1960). Riesman and Ehrlich (1961) reported that the age of the interviewer produced a bias, with the number of "unacceptable" (to the experimenter) answers higher when questions were posed by younger interviewers. Religion of the interviewer is a possible contaminant (Robinson & Rhode, 1946; Hyman *et al.*, 1954), as is his social class (Riesman, 1956; Lenski & Leggett, 1960). Benney, Riesman, and Star (1956) showed that one should consider not only main effects, but also interactions. In their study of age and sex variables they report: "Male interviewers obtain fewer responses than female, and fewest of all from males, while female interviewers obtain their highest responses from men, except for young women talking to young men" (p. 143).

The evidence is overwhelming that a substantial number of biases are introduced by the interviewer (see Hyman *et. al.*, 1954; Kahn & Cannell, 1957). Some of the major biases, such as race, are easily controllable; other biases, such as the interaction of age and sex, are less easily handled. If we heeded all the known biases, without considering our ignorance of major interactions, there could no longer be a simple survey. The understandable action by most researchers has been to ignore these biases and to assume them away. The biases are lawful and consistent, and all research employing face–to–face interviewing or questionnaire administration is subject to them. Rather than flee by assumptions, the experimenter may use alternative methodologies that let him flee by circumvention.

6. CHANGE IN THE RESEARCH INSTRUMENT

The measuring (data–gathering) instrument is frequently an interviewer, whose characteristics, we have just shown, may alter responses. In panel studies, or those using the same interviewer at two or more points in time, it is essential to ask: To what degree is the interviewer or experimenter the same research instrument at all points of the research?

Just as a spring scale becomes fatigued with use, reading "heavier" a second time, an interviewer may also measure differently at different times. His skill may increase. He may be better able to establish rapport. He may have learned necessary vocabulary. He may loaf or become bored. He may have increasingly strong expectations of what a respondent "means" and code differently with practice. Some errors relate to recording accuracy, while others are linked to the nature of the interviewer's interpretation of what transpired. Either way, there is always the risk that the interviewer will be a variable filter over time and experience.

Even when the interviewer becomes more competent, there is potential trouble. Although we usually think of difficulty only when the instrument weakens, a difference in competence between two waves of interviewing, *either increasing or decreasing*, can yield spurious effects. The source of error is not limited to interviewers, and every class of measurement is vulnerable to wavering calibration. Suicides in Prussia jumped 20 percent between 1882 and 1883. This clearly reflected a change in record-keeping, not a massive increase in depression. Until 1883 the records were kept by the police, but in that year the job was transferred to the civil service (Halbwachs, 1930; cited in Selltiz *et al.*, 1959). Archivists undoubtedly drift in recording standards, with occasional administrative reforms in conscientiousness altering the output of the "instrument" (Kitsuse & Cicourel, 1963).

Where human observers are used, they have fluctuating adaptation levels and response thresholds (Holmes, 1958; Campbell, 1961). Rosenthal, in an impressive series of commentary and research, has focused on errors traceable to the experimenter himself. Of particular interest is his work on the influence of early data returns upon analysis of subsequent data (Rosenthal *et al.*, 1963. See also Rosenthal, 1963; Rosenthal & Fode, 1963; Rosenthal & Lawson, 1963; Rosenthal, 1964; Kintz *et al.*, 1965).

Varieties of Sampling Error

Historically, social science has examined sampling errors as a problem in the selection of respondents. The person or group has been the critical unit, and our thinking has been focused on a universe of people. Often a sample of time or space can provide a practical substitute for a sample of persons. Novel methods should be examined for their potential in this regard. For example, a study of the viewing of bus advertisements used a time-stratified, random triggering of an automatic camera pointed out a window over the bus ad (Politz, 1959). One could similarly take a photographic sample of bus passengers modulated by door entries as counted by a photo cell. A photo could be taken one minute after the entry of every twentieth passenger. For some methods, such as the erosion methods, total population records are no more costly than partial ones. For some archives, temporal samples or agency samples are possible. For voting records, precincts may be sampled. But for any one method, the possibilities should be examined.

We look at sampling in this section from the point of view of restrictions on reaching people associated with various methods and the stability of populations over time and areas.

7. POPULATION RESTRICTIONS

In the public-opinion-polling tradition, one conceptualizes a "universe" from which a representative sample is drawn. This model gives little or no formal attention to the fact that only certain universes are possible for any given method. A method-respondent interaction exists—one that gives each method a different set of defining boundaries for its universe. One reason so little attention is given to this fact is that, as methods go, public opinion polling is relatively unrestricted. Yet even here there is definite universe rigidity, with definite restrictions on the size and character of the population able to be sampled.

In the earliest days of polling, people were questioned in public places, probably excluding some 80 percent of the total population. Shifting to in-home interviewing with quota controls and no callbacks still excluded some 60 percent—perhaps 5 percent unaccessible in homes under any conditions, 25 percent not at home, 25 percent refusals, and 5 percent through interviewers' reluctance to approach homes of extreme wealth or poverty and a tendency to avoid fourth-floor walkups.

Under modern probability sampling with callbacks and household designation, perhaps only 15 percent of the population is excluded: 5 percent are totally inaccessible in private residences (e.g., those institutionalized, hospitalized, homeless, transient, in the military, mentally incompetent, and so forth), another 10 percent refuse to answer, are unavailable after three callbacks, or have moved to no known address. A 20 percent figure was found in the model Elmira study in its first wave (Williams, 1950), although other studies have reported much lower figures. Ross (1963) has written a general statement on the problem of inaccessibility, and Stephan and McCarthy (1958), in their literature survey, show from 3 to 14 percent of sample populations of residences inaccessible.

Also to be considered in population restriction is the degree to which the accessible universe deviates in important parameters from the excluded population. This bias is probably minimal in probability sampling with adequate callbacks, but great with catch-as-catch-can and quota samples. Much survey research has centered on household behavior, and the great mass of probability approaches employ a prelisted household as the terminal sampling unit. This frequently requires the enlistment of a household member as a reporter on the behavior of others. Since those who answer doorbells overrepresent the old, the young, and women, this can be a confounding error.

When we come to more demanding verbal techniques, the universe rigidity is much greater. What proportion of the population is available for self-administered questionnaires? Payment for filling out the questionnaire reduces the limitations a bit, but a money reward is selectively attractive—at least at the rates most researchers pay. A considerable proportion of the populace is functionally illiterate for personality and attitude tests developed on college populations.

Not only does task-demandingness create population restrictions, differential volunteering provides similar effects, interacting in a particularly biasing way when knowledge of the nature of the task is involved (Capra & Dittes, 1962). Baumrind (1964) writes of the motivation of volunteers and notes, "The dependent attitude of most subjects toward the experimenter is an artifact of the experimental situation as well as an expression of some subjects' personal need systems at the time they volunteer" (p. 421).

The curious, the exhibitionistic, and the succorant are likely to overpopulate any sample of volunteers. How secure a base can volunteers be with such groups overrepresented and the shy, suspicious, and inhibited underrepresented? The only defensible position is a probability sample of the units to which the findings will be generalized. Even conscripting sophomores may be better than relying on volunteers.

Returning to the rigidity of sampling, what proportion of the total population is available for the studio test audiences used in advertising and television program evaluation? Perhaps 2 percent. For mailed questionnaires, the population available for addressing might be 95 percent of the total in the United States, but low-cost, convenient mailing lists probably cover no more than 70 percent of the families through automobile registration and telephone directories. The exclusion is, again, highly selective. If, however, we consider the volunteering feature, where 10 percent returns are typical, the effective population is a biased 7 percent selection of the total. The nature of this selective-return bias, according to a recent study (Vincent, 1964), includes a skewing of the sample in favor of lower-middle-class individuals drawn from unusually stable, "happy" families.

There are more households with television in the United States than there are households with telephones (or baths). In any given city, one is likely to find more than 15 percent of the households excluded in a telephone subscription list–and most of these are at the bottom of the socioeconomic scale. Among subscribers, as many as 15 percent in some areas do not list their number, and an estimate of 5 percent over all is conservative. Cooper (1964) found an overall level of 6 percent deliberately not listed and an additional 12 percent not in the directory because of recent installations. The unlisted problem can be defeated by a system of random-digit dialing, but this increases the cost at least tenfold and requires a prior study of the distribution of exchanges. Among a sample of known numbers, some 50 percent of dialings are met with busy signals and "not-at-homes." Thus, for a survey without callbacks, the accessible population of 80 percent (listed-phone households) reduces to 40 percent. If individuals are the unit of analysis, the effective sampling rate, without callbacks, may drop to 20 percent. Random-digit dialing will help; so, too, will at least three callbacks, but precision can be achieved only at a high price. The telephone is not so cheap a research instrument as it first looks.

Sampling problems of this sort are even more acute for the research methods considered in the present monograph. Although a few have the full population access of public opinion surveys, most have much more restricted populations. Consider, for example, the sampling of natural conversations. What are the proportions of men and women whose conversations are accessible in public places and on public transport? What is the representativeness of social class or role?

8. POPULATION STABILITY OVER TIME

Just as internal validity is more important than external validity, so, too, is the stability of a population restriction more important than the magnitude of the restriction. Examine conversation sampling on a bus or streetcar. The population represented differs on dry days and snowy days, in winter and spring, as well as by day of the week. These shifts would in many instances provide plausible rival explanations of shifts in topics of conversation. Sampling from a much narrower universe would be preferable if the population were more stable over time, as, say, conversation samples from an employees' restroom in an office building. Comparisons of interview survey results over time periods are more troubled by population instability than is generally realized, because of seasonal layoffs in many fields of employment, plus status–differentiated patterns of summer and winter vacations. An extended discussion of time sampling has been provided by Brookover and Back (1965).

9. POPULATION STABILITY OVER AREAS

Similarly, research populations available to a given method may vary from region to region, providing a more serious problem than a population restriction common to both. Thus, for a comparison of attitudes between New York and Los Angeles, conversation sampling in buses and commuter trains would tap such different segments of the communities as to be scarcely worth doing. Again, a comparison of employees' washrooms in comparable office buildings would provide a more interpretable comparison. Through the advantage of background data to check on some dimensions of representativeness, public opinion surveys again have an advantage in this regard.

Any enumeration of sources of invalidity is bound to be incomplete. Some threats are too highly specific to a given setting and method to be generalized, as are some opportunities for ingenious measurement and control. This list contains a long series of general threats that apply to a broad body of research method and content. It does not say that additional problems cannot be found.

AN INTERLUDE: THE MEASUREMENT OF OUTCROPPINGS

The population restrictions discussed here are apt to seem so severe as to traumatize the researcher and to lead to the abandonment of the method.

This is particularly so for one approaching social science with the goal of complete description. Such trauma is, of course, far from our intention. While discussion of these restrictions is a necessary background to their intelligent use and correction, there is need here for a parenthesis forestalling excessive pessimism.

First, it can be noted that a theory predicting a change in civic opinion, due to an event and occurring between two time periods, might be such that this opinion shift could be predicted for many partially overlapping populations. One might predict changes on public opinion polls within that universe, changes in sampled conversation on commuter trains for a much smaller segment, changes in letters mailed to editors and the still more limited letters published by editors, changes in purchase rates of books on relevant subjects by that minute universe, and so on. In such an instance, the occurrence of the predicted shift on any one of these meters is confirmatory and its absence discouraging. If the effect is found on only one measure, it probably reflects more on the method than on the theory (e.g., Burwen & Campbell, 1957; Campbell & Fiske, 1959). A more complicated theory might well predict differential shifts for different meters, and, again, the evidence of each is relevant to the validity of the theory. The joint confirmation between pollings of high-income populations and commuter-train conversations is much more validating than either taken alone, just because of the difference between the methods in irrelevant components.

The "outcropping" model from geology may be used more generally. Any given theory has innumerable implications and makes innumerable predictions which are unaccessible to available measures at any given time. The testing of the theory can only be done at the available outcroppings, those points where theoretical predictions and available instrumentation meet. Any one such outcropping is equivocal, and all types available should be checked. The more remote or independent such checks, the more confirmatory their agreement.

Within this model, science opportunistically exploits the available points of observation. As long as nature abhorred a vacuum up to 33 feet of water, little research was feasible. When manufacturing skills made it possible to represent the same abhorrence by 76 centimeters of mercury in a glass tube, a whole new outcropping for the checking of theory was made available. The telescope in Galileo's hands, the microscope, the induction coil, the photographic emulsion of silver nitrate, and the cloud chamber all represent partial new outcroppings available for the verification of theory. Even where several of these are relevant to the same theory, their mode of relevance is quite different and short of a complete overlap. Analogously, social science methods with individually restricted and nonidentical universes can provide collectively valuable outcroppings for the testing of theory.

The goal of complete description in science is particularly misleading when it is assumed that raw data provide complete description. Theory is necessarily abstract, for any given event is so complex that its complete description may demand many more theories than are actually brought to bear on it–or than are even known at any given stage of development. But theories are more complete descriptions than obtained data, since they describe processes and entities in their unobserved as well as in their observed states. The scintillation counter notes but a small and nonrepresentative segment of a meson's course. The visual data of an ordinary object are literally superficial. Perceiving an object as solid or vaporous, persistent or transient, involves theory going far beyond the data given. The raw data, observations, field notes, tape recordings, and sound movies of a social event are but transient superficial outcroppings of events and objects much more continuously and completely (even if abstractly) described in the social scientist's theory. Tycho Brahe and Kepler's observations provided Kepler with only small fragments of the orbit of Mars, for a biased and narrow sampling of times of day, days, and years. From these he constructed a complete description through theory. The fragments provided outcroppings sufficiently stubborn to force Kepler to reject his preferred theory. The data were even sufficient to cause the rejection of Newton's later theory had Einstein's better-fitting theory then been available.

So if the restraints on validity sometimes seem demoralizing, they remain so only as long as one set of data, one type of method, is considered separately. Viewed in consort with other methods, matched against the available outcroppings for theory testing, there can be strength in converging weakness.

THE ACCESS TO CONTENT

Often a choice among methods is delimited by the relative ability of different classes of measurement to penetrate into content areas of research interest. In the simplest instance, this is not so much a question of validity as it is a limitation on the utility of the measure. Each class of research method, be it the questionnaire or hidden observation, has rigidities on the content it can cover. These rigidities can be divided, as were population restrictions, into those linked to an interaction between method and materials, those associated with time, and those with physical area.

10. RESTRICTIONS ON CONTENT

If we adopt the research strategy of combining different classes of measurement, it becomes important to understand what content is and is not feasible or practical for each overlapping approach.

Observational methods can be used to yield an index of Negro–white amicability by computing the degree of "aggregation" or nonrandom clustering among mixed groups of Negroes and whites. This method could also be used to study male-female relations, or army–navy relations in wartime when uniforms are worn on liberty. But these indices of aggregation would be largely unavailable for Catholic-Protestant relations or for Jewish–Christian relations. Door-to-door solicitation of funds for causes relevant to attitudes is obviously plausible, but available for only a limited range of topics. For public opinion surveys, there are perhaps tabooed topics (although research on birth control and venereal disease has shown these to be fewer than might have been expected). More importantly, there are topics on which people are unable to report but which a social scientist can reliably observe.

Examples of this can be seen in the literature on verbal reinforcers in speech and in interviews. (For a review of this literature, see Krasner, 1958, as well as Hildum & Brown, 1956; Matarazzo, 1962a). A graphic display of opportunistic exploitation of an "outcropping" was displayed recently by Matarazzo and his associates (1964). They took tapes of the speech of astronauts and ground-communicators for two space flights and studied the duration of the ground-communicator's unit of speech to the astronauts. The data supported their expectations and confirmed findings from the laboratory. We are not sure if an orbital flight should be considered a "natural setting" or not, but certainly the astronaut and his colleagues were not overly sensitive to the duration of individual speech units. The observational method has consistently produced findings on the effect of verbal reinforcers unattainable by direct questioning.

It is obvious that secondary records and physical evidence are high in their content rigidity. The researcher cannot go out and generate a new set of historical records. He may discover a new set, but he is always restrained by what is available. This weakness is not so great as is frequently thought, but it would be naive to suggest that it is not present.

11. STABILITY OF CONTENT OVER TIME

The restrictions on content just mentioned are often questions of convenience. The instability of content, however, is a serious concern for validity. Consider conversation sampling again: if one is attending to the amount of comment on race relations, for example, the occurrence of extremely bad weather may so completely dominate all conversation as to cause a meaningless drop in racial comments. This is a typical problem for index-making. In such an instance, one would probably prefer some index such as the proportion of all race comments that were favorable. In specific studies of content variability over time, personnel-evaluation studies have employed time sampling with considerable success. Observation during a random sample of a worker's laboring minutes efficiently does much to describe both the job and the worker (R. L. Thorndike, 1949; Ghiselli & Brown, 1955; Whisler & Harper, 1962).

Public opinion surveys have obvious limitations in this regard which have led to the utilization of telephone interviews and built-in-dialing recorders for television and radio audience surveys (Lucas & Britt, 1950; Lucas & Britt, 1963). By what means other than a recorder could one get a reasonable estimate of the number of people who watch *The Late Show*?

12. STABILITY OF CONTENT OVER AREA

Where regional comparisons are being made, cross-sectional stability in the kinds of contents elicited by a given method is desirable.

Take the measurement of interservice rivalry as a research question. As suggested earlier, one could study the degree of mingling among men in uniform, or study the number of barroom fights among men dressed in different uniforms. To have a valid regional comparison, one must assume the same incidence of men wearing uniforms in public places when at liberty. Such an assumption is probably not justified, partly because of past experience in a given area, partly because of proximity to urban centers. If a cluster of military bases are close to a large city, only a selective group wear uniforms off duty, and they are more likely to be the belligerent ones. Another comparison region may have the same level of behavior, but be less visible.

The effect of peace is to reduce the influence of the total level of the observed response, since mufti is more common. But if all the comparisons are made in peacetime, it is not an issue. The problem occurs only if one elected to study the problem by a time-series design which cut across war and peace. To the foot-on-rail researcher, the number of outcroppings may vary because of war, but this is no necessary threat to internal validity.

Sampling of locations, such as bus routes, waiting rooms, shop windows, and so forth, needs to be developed to expand access to both content and populations. Obviously, different methods present different opportunities and problems in this regard. Among the few studies which have seriously attempted this type of sampling, the problem of enumerating the universe of such locations has proved extremely difficult (James, 1951). Location sampling has, of course, been practiced more systematically with preestablished enumerated units such as blocks, census tracts, and incorporated areas.

OPERATING EASE AND VALIDITY CHECKS

There are differences among methods which have nothing to do with the interpretation of a single piece of research. These are familiar issues to working researchers, and are important ones for the selection of procedures. Choosing between two different methods which promise to yield equally valid data, the researcher is likely to reject the more time-consuming or costly method. Also, there is an inclination toward those methods which have sufficient flexibility to allow repetition if something unforeseen goes wrong, and which further hold potential for producing internal checks on validity or sampling errors.

13. DROSS RATE

In any given interview, a part of the conversation is irrelevant to the topic at hand. This proportion is the dross rate. It is greater in open-ended, general, free-response interviewing than it is in structured interviews with fixed-answer categories; by the same token, the latter are potentially the more reactive. But in all such procedures, the great advantage is the interviewer's power to introduce and reintroduce certain topics. This ability allows a greater density of relevant data. At the other extreme is unobserved conversation sampling, which is low-grade ore. If one elected to measure attitudes toward Russia by sampling conversations on public transportation, a major share of experimental effort could be spent in listening to comparisons of hairdressers or discussions of the Yankees' one-time dominance of the American League. For a specific problem, conversation sampling provides low-grade ore. The price one must pay for this ore, in order to get a naturally occurring response, may be too high for the experimenter's resources.

14. ACCESS TO DESCRIPTIVE CUES

In evaluating methods, one should consider their potential for generating associated validity checks, as well as the differences in the universes they tap. Looking at alternative measures, what other data can they produce that give descriptive cues on the specific nature of the method's population? Internal evidence from early opinion polls showed their population biases when answers about prior voting and education did not match known election results and census data.

On this criterion, survey research methods have great advantages, for they permit the researcher to build in controls with ease. Observational procedures can check restrictions only for such gross and visible variables as sex, approximate age, and conspicuous ethnicity. Trace methods such as the relative wear of floor tiles offer no such intrinsic possibility. However, it is possible in many instances to introduce interview methods in conjunction with other methods for the purpose of ascertaining population characteristics. Thus, commuter-train passengers, window shoppers, and waiting-room conversationalists can, on a sample of times of day, days of the week, and so on, be interviewed on background data, probably without creating any serious reactive effects for measures taken on other occasions.

15. ABILITY TO REPLICATE

The questionnaire and the interview are particularly good methods because they permit the investigator to replicate his own or someone else's research. There is a tolerance for error when one is producing new data that does not exist when working with old. If a confounding event occurs or materials are spoiled, one can start another survey repeating the procedure. Archives and physical evidence are more restricted, with only a fixed amount of data available. This may be a large amount–allowing split-sample replication–but it may also be a one-shot occurrence that permits only a single analysis. In the latter case, there is no second chance, and the materials may be completely consumed methodologically.

The one-sample problem is not an issuc if data arc used in a clearcut test of theory. If the physical evidence or secondary records are an outcropping where the theory can be probed, the inability to produce another equivalent body of information is secondary. The greater latitude of the questionnaire and interview, however, permit the same statement and provide in addition a margin for error.

So long as we maintain, as social scientists, an approach to comparisons that considers compensating error and converging corroboration from individually contaminated outcroppings, there is no cause for concern. It is only when we naively place faith in a single measure that the massive problems of social research vitiate the validity of our comparisons. We have argued strongly in this chapter for a conceptualization of method that demands multiple measurement of the same phenomenon or comparison. Overreliance on questionnaires and interviews is dangerous because it does not give us enough points in conceptual space to triangulate. . .

This means, obviously, that the notion of a single "critical experiment" is erroneous. *There must be a series of linked critical experiments, each testing a different outcropping of the hypothesis.* It is through triangulation of data procured from different measurement classes that the investigator can most effectively strip of plausibility rival explanations for his comparison. The usual procedural question asked is, Which of the several available data-collection methods will be best for my research problem? We suggest the alternative question: Which set of methods will be best?—with "best" defined as a series which provides data to test the most significant threats to a comparison with a reasonable expenditure of resources.

There are a number of research conditions in which the sole use of the interview or questionnaire leaves unanswerable rival explanations. The purpose of those less popular measurement classes emphasized here to bolster these weak spots and provide intelligence to evaluate threats to validity. The payout for using these measures is high, but the approach is more demanding of the investigator. In their discussion of statistical records, Selltiz and her associates (Selltiz *et al.*, 1959) note:

> The use of such data demands a capacity to ask many different questions related to the research problem. . . . The guiding principle for the use of available statistics consists in keeping oneself flexible with respect to the form in which research questions are asked [p. 318].

This flexibility of thought is required to handle the reactive measurement effects which are the most systematic weakness of all interview and questionnaire studies. These error threats are also systematically present in all observation studies in which the presence of an observer is known to those under study. To varying degrees, measurements conducted in natural settings, without the individual's knowledge, control this type of error possibility. In all of them–hidden observation, contrived observation, trace analysis, and secondary records–the individual is not aware of being tested, and there is little danger that the act of measurement will itself serve as a force for change in behavior or elicit role-playing that confounds the data. There is also minimal risk that biases coming from the physical appearance or other cues provided by the investigator will contaminate the results.

In the observational studies, however, hiding the observer does not eliminate the risk that he will change as a data-collecting instrument over time. Any change, for the better or worse, will introduce shifts that might be erroneously interpreted as stemming from the causal variable. This source of error must be guarded against in the same way that it is in other measurement classes–by careful training of the observer (interviewer), by permitting practice effects to take place before the critical data are collected, and by "blinding" the observer to the hypothesis. There is no way of knowing, of course, whether all reasonable precautions have worked. For this, the only solution is an internal longitudinal analysis of data from a single observer and cross-analysis of data from different observers at various times during the data collection.

Finally, none of the methods emphasized here, by themselves, can eliminate response sets which might strongly influence the character of the data. These must be brought under experimental control by manipulation of the setting itself (as in contrived field experimentation) or by statistical operations with the data if the character of the response sets is known well enough to permit adjustments. With archival records, it may be extremely difficult to know if response sets were operating at the time the data were produced.

These methods also may counter a necessary weakness of the interview and questionnaire–dependence upon language. When one is working within a single society, there is always the question whether the differential verbal skills of various subcultures will mislead the investigator. It is possible, if groups vary in articulateness, to overgeneralize the behavior or attitudes of the group or individuals with the greater verbal fluency. This risk is particularly marked for the interpretation of research reports which employ quotations liberally. The natural tendency of the writer is to choose illustrative quotations which are fluent, dramatic, or engaging. If the pool of good quotations is variable across the subcultures, the reader may mistakenly overvalue the ideas in the quotations, even though the writer himself does not. This is a question of presentation, but an important one because of the disproportionate weight that may be placed on population segments.

The differential capacity to use the language artfully is one source of error, while the absolute capacity of the language to convey ideas is another.[1] This is an issue strongly present in cross-cultural comparisons, where different languages may vary radically as a medium of information transfer. The effect of this is to limit the content possible for study with questionnaires or interviews. If one worked in New Guinea, for example, and had to depend upon the *lingua franca* pidgin widely spoken there, he would find it adequate to indicate an answer to "Where do you keep your fishing nets?" but too gross a filter to study the ethnocentricism of a tribe. Pidgin simply does not possess the subtle gradients required to yield textured responses to questions on attitudes toward neighboring tribes or one's own tribe. Although it is theoretically possible to learn all the regional dialects well enough to be competent in a language, in practice this does not occur. A more pragmatic approach is to search for observational or trace evidence which will document aspects of ethnocentrism (e.g., reactions to outsiders, disposition and use of weapons) and then relate it to the verbal responses in the inadequate pidgin.

One more weakness of the dependence on language is that sometimes there is silence. So long as a respondent talks, glibly or not, in a rich language or not, checks and controls can be worked on the reported content.[2] There are, however, situations in which refusals to cooperate preclude any chance of correcting distorted information. This usually results in a biased research population and not a rejection of all findings, because it is almost always possible to find some people who will discuss any topic. But it can also result in a complete stalemate if only the verbal report is considered as the research instrument.

An amusing example of this inability to get data by verbal report, and a nonreactive circumvention, is provided by Shadegg (1964). In his book on political campaign methods, Shadegg writes of a campaign manager who used every available means to learn the plans of his opponent, who, reasonably enough, was unwilling to grant a revealing interview. One method arranged for procuring the contents of his opponent's wastebasket: "He came into possession of carbon copies of letters . . . memos in the handwriting of his opponent's manager." Admittedly a less efficient method than the interview, it admirably met the criterion of being workable: "It took a lot of digging through the trash to come up with the nuggets. But . . . daily panning produced some very fine gold." The "investigator" did not limit himself to inferences drawn from observations of his opponent's public acts, but was able to develop ingeniously (although perhaps not ethically) a trace measure to complement the observation. Each aided the other, for the observations give a validity check on the nuggets among the trash (Was misleading material being planted?), and the nuggets gave a more accurate means of interpreting the meaning of the public acts.

Evidence of how others are sensitive to wastebaskets is seen in the practice in diplomatic embassies of burning refuse under guard, the discussion of refuse purchase by industrial spies (Anonymous, 1964c), and the development of a new electric wastebasket that shreds discarded paper into unreadable bits.

Generally speaking, then, observational and trace methods are indicated as supplementary or primary when language may serve as a poor medium of information–either because of its differential use, its absolute capacity for transfer, or when significant elements of the research population are silent.

The verbal methods are necessarily weak along another dimension, the study of past behavior or of change. For historical studies, there is no alternative but to rely mainly on records of the past time. Behavioral research on the distant past is rare, however; more common are studies which center on experiences within the lifetime of respondents. For example, there is a large literature on child-rearing practices, in which mothers recollect their behavior of years past. A sole dependence on this type of data-gathering is highly suspect. It may be enough to note that Thomas Jefferson, in his later years, observed that winters weren't as cold as they used to be. Available records could be used to check both Mr. Jefferson and other observers of secular changes in winter's fierceness.

For more current evidence on the fallibility of such recall data, see Pyles, Stolz, and Macfarlane, 1935; McGraw and Molloy, 1941; Smith, 1958; Weiss and Dawis, 1960–all of whom comment on, or test, the validity of mothers' recall of child-rearing practices. Weiss and Dawis wrote, "It is indefensible to assume the validity of purportedly factual data obtained by interview" (p. 384). The work of Haggard, Brekstad, and Skard (1960) and Robbins (1963) suggests that it is a problem of differentially accurate recall. In Haggard's phrase, the interviews "did not reflect the mothers' earlier experiences and attitudes so much as their current picture of the past" (p. 317).

When, through death or refusal, reports of past behavior are unavailable, a proper contingent strategy is to interview others who have had access to the same information, or who can report at second hand. This is very shaky information, but useful if other intelligence is available as a check. For many investigations, of course, the nature of the distortion is itself an important datum and can become a central topic of study when a reliable baseline is possible.[3] If other materials are present, and they usually are in a record-keeping society, the best way to estimate past behavior is to combine methods of study of archival records, available traces, and verbal reports, even if secondhand. Clearly, direct observational methods are useless for past events.

With studies of social change, the most practical method is to rely on available records, supplemented by verbal recall. If one wanted more control over the data, it would be possible to conduct a continuing series of field experiments extending over a long period of years. But the difficulty of such an approach is evidenced by the scarcity of such longitudinal, original-data studies in social science. Forgetting the number of years required, there is the problem of unstable populations over time, a growing problem as the society becomes more mobile. Potential errors lie in both directions as one moves forward or backward in time, and the more practical approach of the two is to analyze data already collected–making the ever present assumption that such are available.

A more integrative approach for studying change is to develop two discrete time series—one based on available records, the other freshly developed by the investigator. With this strategy, it is necessary to have an overlap period in which the relationships between the two series are established. Given knowledge of the relationships, the available records can be studied retrospectively, thereby providing more intelligence than would be possible if they existed alone. Again, there is a necessary assumption: one must be able to reject the plausibility of an interaction between time and the method. If there is any content or population fluctuation beyond chance, such a method is invalid. Diagrammatically, where O is an observation and the subscript n equals new data and a available data:

$$O_{a1}O_{a2}O_{a3}O_{a4}O_{a5}O_{a6}O_{a7}O_{a8}O_{a9}O_{a10}$$

$$O_{n6}O_{n7}O_{n8}O_{n9}O_{n10}$$

A final gain from the less reactive methods is frequently the lower cost of data collection. Many scholars know how to conduct massive surveys which effectively control major sources of error; few do so. This knowledge is an underdeveloped resource. With survey interviews often costing $10 or more apiece, the failure is understandable, however regrettable. When the interview or questionnaire is viewed as the only method, the researcher is doomed to either frustration or a studied avoidance of thoughts on external validity. Peace of mind will come if the investigator breaks the single-method mold and examines the extent to which other measurement classes can substitute for verbal reports. The price of collecting each unit of data is low for most of the methods we have stressed. In some cases, the dross rate is high, and it may be necessary to observe a hundred cases before one meets the research specifications. Nonetheless, even under these high dross-rate conditions, the cost per usable response is often lower than that of a completed interview or returned questionnaire. The lower cost permits flexibility to expand into content and population areas otherwise precluded, and the result of this is to increase the confidence one has in generalizing findings. Just as in the case of studying social change, it may be possible to generate different data series, some based on verbal reports, others based on secondary or observational data. Providing for enough cases of the more expensive procedures to yield a broad base for linkage, the larger number of cases can be allocated to the usually less expensive observational or secondary methods. It is important to note that we add "usually' before "less expensive." The savings are centered in data-collection costs, and it may be that all the savings are vitiated by the elaborate corrections or transformations that a particular data series may require. The cost of materials and analysis is an equivocal area indeed.

In the multimethod pattern of testing, the primary gains coming from the less popular methods are protection against reactive measurement threats, auxiliary data in content areas where verbal reports are unreliable, an easier method of determining long-term change, and a potentially lower-cost substitute for some standard survey practices.

Offsetting these gains, there are associated problems for each of the less popular measurement classes–indeed, if they were less problematic, we would be writing an argument in favor of an increased use of the interview.

The most powerful aspect of the verbal methods–their ability to reach into all content areas–is a soft spot in the hidden-observation, trace, and archival analysis procedures. We have noted remarkably adept and nonobvious applications of data from these sources, but for some content areas, the most imaginative of investigators will have trouble finding pertinent material. Individually, those methods are simply not as broad gauged. . . .

These, then, are the gains; these the losses. There are no rewards for ingenuity as such, and the payoff comes only when ingenuity leads to new means of making more valid comparisons. In the available grab bag of imperfect research methods, there is room for new uses of the old.

NOTES

1. In a similar note on observers, Heyns and Lippitt (1954) ask if the "observer lacks the sensitivity or the vocabulary which the particular observation requires" (p. 372).
2. For an extended discussion of this issue, see Hyman *et al.* (1954) and Kahn and Cannell (1957).
3. The courts have handled secondary information by excluding it under the "hearsay" rule (Wigmore, 1935; Morgan, 1963). Epically put, "Pouring rumored scandal into the bent ear of blabbering busybodies in a pool room or gambling house is no more disreputable than pronouncing it with clipped accents in a courtroom" (Donnelly, Goldstein, & Schwartz, 1962, p. 277). The case from which this is cited is *Holmes*, 379 Pa. 599 (1954).

Dissection III: Multiple Operationism: The Case of Field Experiments

Models and Helping: Naturalistic Studies in Aiding Behavior

James H. Bryan and Mary Ann Test

Recently, concern has been evidenced regarding the determinants and correlates of altruistic behavior, those acts wherein individuals share or sacrifice a presumed positive reinforcer for no apparent social or material gain. Studies addressed to these behaviors have explored both individual differences in the tendency to be altruistic and the situational determinants of such responses. Gore and Rotter (1963) found that students at a southern Negro college were more likely to volunteer for a social protest movement if they perceived sources of reinforcement as internally rather than externally guided. Subjects

NOTE: While Mary Ann Test collaborated with the senior author on Experiment I, the remaining work is the latter's sole responsibility.

From James H. Bryan and Mary Ann Test, "Models and Helping: Naturalistic Studies in Aiding Behavior," *Journal of Personality and Social Psychology* 6, no. 4 (1967): 400–7.

high on internal control were more likely to volunteer as freedom riders, marchers, or petition signers than subjects who perceived others as primary agents of reinforcement. Experimental evidence has been generated supporting the often-made assumption that guilt may serve as a stimulus to altruistic activity. Darlington and Macker (1966) found that subjects led to believe that they had harmed another through incompetent performances on the experimental tasks (three paper-and-pencil tests) were more willing than control subjects to donate blood to a local hospital. Aronfreed and Paskal,[1] and Midlarsky and Bryan (1967) found that children exposed to treatment conditions designed to produce empathy were more willing to donate M&M candies than subjects given control conditions, while Handlon and Gross (1959), Ugurel-Semin (1952), Wright (1942), and Midlarsky and Bryan have found sharing to be positively correlated with age among school-age children. Lastly, Berkowitz and Friedman (1967) have demonstrated that adolescents of the working class and the bureaucratic middle class are less affected in their helping behaviors by interpersonal attraction than adolescents of the entrepreneur middle class.

Three hypotheses have emerged regarding the situational determinants of self-sacrificing behaviors. One suggests that individuals behave in an altruistic fashion because of compliance to a norm of reciprocity. That is, individuals are aware of the social debts and credits established between them, and expect that ultimately the mutual exchange of goods and services will balance (Gouldner, 1960). Berkowitz and Daniels (1964) have suggested that individuals might show a generalization of such obligatory feelings and thus aid others who had not previously assisted them.

A second hypothesis was put forth by Berkowitz and his colleagues (Berkowitz, 1966; Berkowitz & Daniels, 1963; Berkowitz, Klanderman & Harris, 1964; Daniels & Berkowitz, 1963), who have postulated the social responsibility norm. They have contended that dependency on others evokes helping responses even under conditions where the possibility of external rewards for the helper are remote. Using supervisor's ratings of an unknown and absent other to produce dependency, and a box-construction task as the dependent variable, considerable support has been generated for the suggestion that dependency increases helping.

A third major determinant of helping may be the presence of helping (or nonhelping) models. While attention to the effects of models has generally been directed toward antisocial behavior (cf. Bandura & Walters, 1963; Freed, Chandler, Mouton & Blake, 1955; Lefkowitz, Blake & Mouton, 1955), some recent evidence suggests that observation of self-sacrificing models may lead to subsequent succorant behavior by children. For example, Rosenhan and White (1967) have demonstrated that children are more likely to donate highly valued gift certificates to residents of a fictitious orphanage if they have seen an adult do so. Hartup and Coates[2] found that nursery school children who have been exposed to a self-sacrificing peer were more likely to be altruistic than children not so exposed. Test and Bryan[3] found that female college students were more likely to render aid to another in computing arithmetic problems if they saw other people so doing.

The present series of experiments was designed to test the effects of models in natural settings on subject samples other than college or high school students, and in contexts other than a school room or university setting. The first three experiments reported are concerned with the impact of observing helping models upon subsequent helping behaviors, while the fourth is addressed to the influence of interpersonal attraction upon donation behavior.

EXPERIMENT I: LADY IN DISTRESS: A FLAT TIRE STUDY

Few studies have been concerned with the effects of models upon *adults*, and fewer still with the impact of *prosocial* models upon them (Wheeler, 1966). Those that have been concerned with such behaviors have invariably employed college students as subjects. For example, Rosenbaum and Blake (1955) and Rosenbaum (1956) have found that college students exposed to a model who volunteered, upon the personal request of the experimenter, to participate in an experiment would be more likely to consent than subjects not exposed to such a model or than subjects who observed a model refuse to cooperate. Pressures toward conformity in these experiments were great, however, as the request was made directly by the experimenter and in the presence of a large number of other students.

Test and Bryan found that the observation of helping models significantly increased the subsequent offers of aid by observers. However, in that study, subjects were given the task of solving arithmetic problems and then rating their difficulty, a task ordinarily requiring autonomous efforts. Furthermore, the experiment was conducted within a university setting, a context where independence of thought is often stressed. The effects of the model may have been simply to increase the subjects' faith that assisting others was allowed. While questionnaire data of the study did not support this interpretation, such effects could not be ruled out entirely. Thus, it is possible that the model impact was simply a propriety-defining activity which reduced the inhibitions associated with such helping behavior.

In general, then, investigations of modeling that employ adults as subjects and that demand self-sacrifice on the part of subjects are limited in number, exploit strong pressures toward conformity, and rely upon college students as subjects. The present experiment was designed to assess the impact of models upon subsequent spontaneous offers of help in other than a university setting.

Method

The standard condition consisted of an undergraduate female stationed by a 1964 Ford Mustang (control car) with a flat left-rear tire. An inflated tire was leaned upon the left side of the auto. The girl, the flat tire, and the inflated tire were conspicuous to the passing traffic.

In the model condition, a 1965 Oldsmobile was located approximately ¼ mile from the control car. The car was raised by jack under the left rear bumper, and a girl was watching a male changing the flat tire.

In the no-model condition, the model was absent; thus, only the control car was visible to the passing traffic.

The cars were located in a predominantly residential section in Los Angeles, California. They were placed in such a manner that no intersection separated the model from the control car. No turnoffs were thus available to the passing traffic. Further, opposite flows of traffic were divided by a separator such that the first U turn available to the traffic going in the opposite direction of the control car would be after exposure to the model condition.

The experiment was conducted on two successive Saturdays between the hours of 1:45 and 5:50 P.M. Each treatment condition lasted for the time required for 1000 vehicles to pass the control car. While private automobiles and trucks, motorscooters, and motorcycles were tallied as vehicles, commercial trucks, taxis, and buses were not. Vehicle count was made by a fourth member of the experiment who stood approximately 100 feet from the control car, hidden from the passing motorists. On the first Saturday, the model condition was run first and lasted from 1:45 to 3:15 P.M. In order to exploit changing traffic patterns and to keep the time intervals equal across treatment conditions, the control car was moved several blocks and placed on the opposite side of the street for the no-model condition. The time of the no-model treatment was 4:00 to 5:00 P.M. On the following Saturday, counterbalancing the order and the location of treatment conditions was accomplished. That is, the no-model condition was run initially and the control car was placed in the same location that it had been placed on the previous Saturday during the model condition. The time of the no-model condition was 2:00 to 3:30 P.M. For the model condition, the control car was placed in that locale where it had been previously during the no-model condition. The time of the model condition was 4:30 to 5:30 P.M.

Individuals who had stopped to offer help were told by the young lady that she had already phoned an auto club and that help was imminent. Those who nonetheless insisted on helping her were told the nature of the experiment.

Results

The dependent variable was the number of cars that stopped and from which at least one individual offered help to the stooge by the control car. Of the 4000 passing vehicles, 93 stopped. With the model car absent, 35 vehicles stopped; with the model present, 58 halted. The difference between the conditions was statistically significant ($x^2 = 5.53$, corrected for continuity, $df = 1, p < .02$, detailed). Virtually all offers of aid were from men rather than women drivers.

The time of day had little impact in the offering of aid. Fifty vehicles stopped during the early part of the afternoon; none during the later hours. Likewise, difference in help offers were not great between successive Saturdays, as 45 offers of aid were made on the first Saturday, 48 on the second Saturday.

The results of the present study support the hypothesis that helping behaviors can be significantly increased through the observation of others' helpfulness. However, other plausible hypotheses exist which may account for the findings. It is possible to account for the differences in treatment effects by differences in sympathy arousal. That is, in the model condition, the motorist observed a woman who had had some difficulty. Such observations may have elicited sympathy and may have served as a reminder to the driver of his own social responsibilities.

Another explanation of the findings revolves around traffic slow-down. It is possible that the imposition of the model condition served to reduce traffic speed, thus making subsequent stopping to help a less hazardous undertaking. While the time taken for 1000 autos to pass the control car was virtually identical in the model and no-model condition and thus not supportive of such an explanation, the "slowdown" hypothesis cannot be eliminated. Assuming the model effect to be real, one might still argue that it was not a norm of helping that was facilitated by the model, but rather that inhibitions against picking up helpless young ladies were reduced. That is, within the model condition, the passing motorists may have observed a tempted other and thus felt less constrained themselves regarding similar efforts. Indeed, the insistence of some people to help in spite of the imminent arrival of other aiders suggested the operation of motives other than simply helping. Indeed, while the authors did not index the frequency of pick-up attempts, it was clear that a rather large number were evidenced.

Because of the number of alternative explanations, the evidence supporting the hypothesis that the observation of helpers per se will increase subsequent aiding is weak. Experiment II was designed to test further the prediction that the perception of another's altruistic activity would elicit similar behavior on the part of the observer.

EXPERIMENT II: COINS IN THE KETTLE

The investigation was conducted on December 14th between the hours of 10:00 A.M. and 5:00 P.M. The subjects were shoppers at a large department store in Princeton, New Jersey. Observations made on the previous day indicated that the shoppers were overwhelmingly Caucasian females.

A Salvation Army kettle was placed on the sidewalk in front of the main entrance to the store. Two females, both in experimenter's employ, alternatively manned the kettle for periods of 25 minutes. One solicitor was a Negro, the other a Caucasian. Each wore a Salvation Army cape and hat. Although allowed to ring the Salvation Army bell, they were not permitted to make any verbal plea or to maintain eye contact with the passing shoppers, except to thank any contributor for his donation.

The model condition (M) was produced as follows: Once every minute on the minute, a male dressed as a white-collar worker would approach the kettle from within the store and contribute five cents. As the model donated, he started a stopwatch and walked from the kettle toward a parking lot as if searching for someone. He then returned to the store. The following 20-second period constituted the duration of the treatment condition.

Following a subsequent lapse of 20 seconds, the next 20-second period defined the no-model condition (NM). Within any one minute, therefore, both M and NM treatments occurred. There were 365 occasions of each treatment.

It should be noted that it was possible that some subjects in the NM condition observed the contribution of the model or a donor affected by the model. If that hypothesis is correct, however, the effects of such incidents would be to reduce rather than enhance the differences between treatments.

Results

The dependent variable was the number of people who independently donated to the Salvation Army. People obviously acquainted, as for example, man and wife, were construed as one potential donating unit. In such conditions, if both members of a couple contributed, they were counted as a single donor.

Since there were no differences in model effects for the Negro or Caucasian solicitor, data obtained from each were combined. The total number of contributors under the NM condition was 43; under the M condition, 69. Assuming that the chance distribution of donations would be equal across the two conditions, a chi-square analysis was performed. The chi-square equaled 6.01 ($p < .01$).[4]

In spite of precautions concerning the elimination of correlated observations within a treatment condition, it was possible for subjects in any one observational period to influence one another. Such influence may have been mediated through acquaintances not eliminated by our procedures or the observations of others as well as the model donating. A more conservative analysis of the data, insuring independent observation, was therefore made. Instead of comparing treatments by analyzing the number of donors, the analysis used, as the dependent variable, the number of observation periods in which there was a contribution, that is, those periods in which more than one donation occurred were scored identically to those in which only a single contribution was received. Occasions of donations equaled 60 in the M treatment, 43 in the NM condition. The chi-square equaled 2.89 ($p < .05$).

The results of Experiment II further support the hypothesis that observation of altruistic activity will increase such behavior among observers. But the matter is not yet entirely clear, for when the observer saw the model donate he saw two things: first, the actual donation, and second, the polite and potentially reinforcing interaction that occurred between the donor and solicitor. Conceivably, the observation of an altruistic model, per se, who was not socially reinforced for his behavior, would have little or no effect on an observer. The third experiment was designed to examine this possibility.

EXPERIMENT III: COINS IN THE KETTLE II

The experiment was conducted at a Trenton, New Jersey, shopping center from the hours of 10:00 A.M. to 5:00 P.M. Again, the majority of the patrons were Caucasian females. It is likely, however, that these shoppers were of a lower socioeconomic status than those in the Princeton group.

Salvation Army kettles were placed before the main entrance of a large department store (Kettle 1) and a large food center (Kettle 2). The kettles were separated by more than 200 yards. During the first 120 observations (10:00 A.M. to 12:00 P.M.), two male college students, employed by the Salvation Army and wearing its uniform, manned the kettles. The site of the experiment was Kettle 1, except on those occasions where the worker took his "coffee break." At those times, data collection was centered at Kettle 2. An equal number of M and NM conditions were run at each site, although approximately two-thirds of the observational time was spent at Kettle 1. During the remaining 240 observational periods (1:00 P.M. to 5:00 P.M.) the same male worker and his spouse alternately manned Kettle 1. The wife was stationed by the kettle for 136 minutes, the male for 104 minutes. The experiment was conducted only at Kettle 1 during the afternoon period.

Solicitors were told to make no verbal appeals for donations or responses to the model upon his contribution. While they were not informed of the hypothesis underlying the experiment, they may well have deduced it. The model was the same as in Experiment II, and again was dressed as a white-collar worker.

The imposition of the treatment conditions were identical to those described in Experiment I with the following exceptions. Since the kettle was more visible at this site than at the previous one, 30-second rather than 20-second periods were used for each treatment. To simplify the procedures, no waiting periods between treatments occurred. Additionally, after donating, the model would return to the parking lot. There were a total of 360 occasions of each of the M and NM conditions.

Results

The criteria defining a donor were identical to those outlined in Experiment I. Under the M condition, 84 donors were tallied; under the NM treatment, 56. The chi-square value was 4.86 ($p < .025$).

Since it was possible that one donor might have seen a donor other than the model receive social approval from the solicitor, the more conservative comparison of the treatments as outlined in Experiment II was made. That is, treatments were compared by noting the number of observational periods in which any donation occurred. Therefore, those donors who may have been influenced by a contributor receiving the solicitor's thanks were excluded. Of the 360 observational periods under the M condition, there were 75 in which some donation was made. Of the 360 periods, 51 were marked by contributing. Chi-square yielded a value of 5.09 ($p < .011$).

EXPERIMENT IV: ETHNOCENTRISM AND DONATION BEHAVIOR

While Experiment III was conducted to eliminate the solicitor's explicit social approval as a mechanism underlying donation behavior, it is possible that the model's impact was due to the information communicated to the observer regarding the consequence of donations. Work by Bandura, Ross, and Ross (1963), for example, found that children observing a model rewarded for aggression would be more aggressive than children who had observed a model being punished for such behavior. Additionally, considerable data have been gathered with the university laboratory suggesting that interpersonal attraction may greatly influence the helping response. Berkowitz and Friedman (1967), Daniels and Berkowitz (1963), and Goranson and Berkowitz (1966) have suggested that positive affect increases the probability of low payoff helping behavior.

The present experiment was designed to assess the impact of the solicitor's race upon the donation behavior of shoppers. It was assumed that a Negro solicitor would be held in less esteem by Caucasian shoppers than a solicitor of their same race, and that such attitudes would affect contributions. While the applicability of the "consequence to the model" hypothesis in accounting for the model's effect was not tested directly, the study assesses the importance of interpersonal attraction in eliciting charitable behavior.

Method

The experiment was conducted on December 2 and 3 between the hours of 10 A.M. and 6 P.M. at the Trenton area site. The subjects were Caucasion shoppers at a large department store.[5] Three thousand seven hundred and three shoppers were observed; 2,154 females and 1,549 males. In order to reduce the possibility of including the same subject in the experiment on more than one occasion, tallies were made only of exiting shoppers.

Two Salvation Army kettles were placed at two store exits, their location being separated by approximately 75 yards. Two female solicitors, a Negro and a Caucasian, manned the kettles. Both were in their early twenties, wore the uniform of the Salvation Army, and were in the employ of the experimenter. Each was instructed to make no verbal appeals for donations and to avoid eye contact with the shoppers. After a period of 25 minutes, the girls rotated kettle assignments, and during the last 10 minutes of the hour were allowed to take a coffee break. Hence, during a single hour, each solicitor manned both kettles. Each solicitor manned each kettle on seven occasions per day. Thus, each solicitor was observed for a total of 28 observational periods; 14 on each day (seven on each kettle) over a period of two days.

Two observers, each assigned to a particular kettle, tallied the number and sex of the exiting shoppers and contributors during each of the 25-minute periods. In addition, records were kept of the amount of money donated within any period, although it was impossible on this measure to separate those donations made by incoming from outgoing customers.

Results

The dependent variable was the percentage of donors contributing to the kettle within an observational period. That is, observational periods were assigned a percentage donor score. Shoppers within an observational period were treated as a single group, with differences between groups on percentage donor score forming the critical comparisons. The total N of the study was then the 56 observational periods, rather than the 3,703 shoppers. Since the mean group size for the Negro solicitor was 70.32 and for the Caucasian 61.93 (standard deviations equal to 53.33 and 42.98, respectively), it was assumed that the percentage score was relatively stable.

The effects of race, kettle location, and day and their interactions were analyzed by analysis of variance.

As can be seen from Table 1, both the main effect of race and of day were significant. As predicted, the Negro solicitor elicited a statistically significant lower percentage of donors than did the Caucasian. For the Negro solicitor, the average percentage donor score for observational periods was 2.22 ($SD = 2.36$), while for the Caucasian solicitor the average percentage donor score was 3.89 ($SD = 3.60$). Additionally, Saturday shoppers were by and large less generous than Friday customers. The average percentage donor score of the group was 1.73 ($SD = 1.97$) for the Saturday shopper, and 4.38 for the Friday shopper ($SD = 3.52$).

TABLE 1
ANALYSIS OF VARIANCE OF PERCENTAGE DONOR SCORES

	df	*MS*	*F*
Race (A)	1	38.778	4.84*
Day (B)	1	98.315	12.28**
Kettle (C)	1	.018	
A × B	1	1.511	
A × C	1	11.340	
B × C	1	1.031	
A × B × C	1	3.206	
Error	48	8.009	

$^*p < .05$ (2-tailed).
$^{**}p < .01$ (2-tailed).

A second dependent variable was the amount of money donated during each time period. No significant differences were found for race, day, or kettle location.

The present investigation does support, albeit equivocally, the notion that interpersonal attraction may affect donations even when the solicitors are not the eventual recipients of such contributions. While it is possible that race differences simply fail to remind observers of their social responsibilities, it is also feasible that the subjects wanted to avoid interpersonal contact with a minority group member. If this is true, then it is interesting to note that interpersonal attraction may play an important role even in those situations where personal anonymity is high and escape from unpleasant situations easy.

DISCUSSION

The results of the first three experiments clearly replicate those of Test and Bryan and extend the findings over a variety of subject populations, settings, and tasks. The results hold for college students, motorists, and shoppers; in the university laboratory, city streets, and shopping centers; and when helping is indexed by aiding others solve arithmetic problems, changing flat tires, or donating money to the Salvation Army. The findings then are quite consistent: the presence of helping models significantly increases subsequent altruistic behavior.

That generosity breeds generosity is interesting in light of the recent concern with helping behaviors in emergency contexts. Darley and Latané[6] and Latané and Darley[7] have found that subjects are less inclined to act quickly in emergency situations when in the presence of other potential helpers. Whether faced with a medical emergency (a simulated epileptic seizure) or a dangerous natural event (simulated fire), the rapidity with which students sought to aid was reduced by the presence of others. These findings have been interpreted in three ways: as reflecting the subjects' willingness to diffuse responsibility (others will aid); as reflecting their diffusion of blame (others didn't aid either); or as reflecting conformity to the nonpanicked stooges. It is clear that the results of the first three experiments in the present series do not follow that which might be predicted by the diffusion concepts. A giving model apparently does not lend credibility to the belief that others than the self will make the necessary sacrifices. The helping other did not strengthen the observer's willingness to diffuse his social obligations, but rather stimulated greater social responsibility. In light of these results, the delayed reaction exhibited by the subjects tested by Darley and Latané might be best attributable to conformity behavior. As they have suggested, subjects faced with a unique and stressful situation may have been either reassured by the presence of calm others or fearful of acting stupidly or cowardly. Additionally, it is possible that diffusion of responsibility is only associated with anxiety-inducing situations. The current data fail to indicate that such diffusion occurs in nonstressful situations which demand fulfillment of social obligations.

While it appears clear that the behavior of the motorists and shoppers was not dictated by a variety of situational and social pressures usually associated with the study of modeling in adults or experiment in academic settings (Orne, 1962), the mechanisms underlying the effects are not obvious. While the presence of the model in the flat-tire study may have reminded the motorists as to the social responsibility norm, a hypothesis does not appear reasonable in accounting for the results in the coins-in-the-kettle series. The bell-ringing Salvation Army worker, with kettle and self placed squarely in the pathway of the oncoming pedestrian, would seem to be reminder enough of one's obligation toward charity. A priori, it would not appear necessary to superimpose upon that scene the donating other for purposes of cognitive cueing (Wheeler, 1966).

One hypothesis to account for the model effect is that the observer is given more information regarding the consequences of such donation behavior. Experiment IV suggested that solicitor status or personal attraction might operate on donation behaviors even under conditions of personal anonymity and few social constraints. It is possible that the model serves to communicate to the potential donor relevant information concerning the consequences of his act. That is, the model may demonstrate that an approach to the solicitor does not involve an unwanted interpersonal interaction (e.g., lectures on religion).

A second hypothesis to account for the data pertains to the shame-provoking capacities of the model. It is reasonable to assume that most people feel that they are, by and large, benevolent and charitable. Furthermore, it is likely that such a self-image is rarely challenged: first because charitable acts are not frequently required; second, at least in the street scenes employed in the current series of studies, solicitations are made in the context of many nongiving others. That is, a multitude of negative models–of noncharitable others–surround the solicitations in the current series of studies. Indeed, the contexts are such that most people are not helping; many more cars pass than stop to offer aid to the lady in distress; and there are many more people who refuse to put coins in the kettle than those who do. However, the witnessing of a donor, an individual who not only recognizes his social responsibility but in fact acts upon it, may produce a greater challenge to the good self-image of the observer. Acts rather than thoughts may be required of the observer in order to maintain the self-image of benevolence and charity. If such is the case, then the model characteristics most effective in producing prosocial behavior by socialized adults would be those directed toward shame or guilt production (e.g., donations from the poor), rather than those reflecting potential reinforcement power (e.g., donations from the high status).

Whatever the mechanism underlying the model effect, it does appear quite clear that prosocial behavior can be elicited through the observation of benign others.

NOTES

1. J. Aronfreed & V. Paskal. Altruism, empathy and the conditioning of positive affect. Unpublished manuscript, 1965.
2. W. W. Hartup & B. Coates. Imitation of peers as a function of reinforcement from the peer group and rewardingness of the model. Unpublished manuscript, 1966.
3. M. A. Test & J. H. Bryan. Dependency, models and reciprocity. Unpublished manuscript, 1966.
4. All chi–square analyses were corrected for continuity and all tests of significance were one–tailed.
5. As there were very few Negro donors ($N = 7$), analysis was confined to the behavior of Caucasian shoppers.
6. J. Darley & B. Latané. Diffusion of responsibility in emergency situations. Unpublished manuscript, 1966.
7. B. Latané & J. Darley. Group inhibition of bystander intervention in emergencies. Unpublished manuscript, 1966.

REFERENCES

Bandura, A., Ross, D., and Ross, S. Vicarious reinforcement and imitative learning. *Journal of Abnormal and Social Psychology,* 1963, 66, 601–607.

Bandura, A., and Walters, R. H. *Social Learning and Personality Development.* New York: Holt, Rinehart & Winston, 1963.

Berkowitz, L. A laboratory investigation of social class and national differences in helping behavior. *International Journal of Psychology,* 1966, 1, 231-240.

Berkowitz, L., and Daniels, L. Responsibility and dependency. *Journal of Abnormal and Social Psychology,* 1963, 66, 429-436.

Berkowitz, L., and Daniels, L. Affecting the salience of the social responsibility norm: Effects of past help on the response to dependency relationships. *Journal of Abnormal and Social Psychology,* 1964, 68, 275-281.

Berkowitz, L., and Friedman, P. Some social class differences in helping behavior. *Journal of Personality and Social Psychology,* 1967, 5, 217-225.

Berkowitz, L., Klanderman, S. G., and Harris, R. Effects of experimenter awareness and sex of subject and experimenter on reactions to dependency relationships. *Sociometry,* 1964, 27, 327-337.

Daniels, L., and Berkowitz, L. Liking and response to dependency relationships. *Human Relations,* 1963, 16, 141-148.

Darlington, R. B., and Macker, C. E. Displacement of guilt-produced altruistic behavior. *Journal of Personality and Social Psychology,* 1966, 4, 442-443.

Freed, A., Chandler, P., Mouton, J., and Blake, R. Stimulus and background factors in sign violation. *Journal of Personality,* 1955, 23, 499.

Goranson, R., and Berkowitz, L. Reciprocity and responsibility reactions to prior help. *Journal of Personality and Social Psychology,* 1966, 3, 227-232.

Gore, P. M., and Rotter, J. B. A personality correlate of social action. *Journal of Personality,* 1963, 31, 58-64.

Gouldner, A. The norm of reciprocity: A preliminary statement. *American Sociological Review,* 1960, 25, 161-178.

Handlon, B. J., and Gross, P. The development of sharing behavior. *Journal of Abnormal and Social Psychology,* 1959, 59, 425-428.

Lefkowitz, M., Blake, R., and Mouton, J. Status factors in pedestrian violation of traffic signals. *Journal of Abnormal and Social Psychology,* 1955, 51, 704-706.

Midlarsky, E., and Bryan, J. H. Training charity in children. *Journal of Personality and Social Psychology,* 1967, 5, 408-415.

Orne, M. On the social psychology of the psychological experiment: With particular reference to demand characteristics and their implications. *American Psychologist,* 1962, 17, 776-783.

Rosenbaum, M. The effect of stimulus and background factors on the volunteering response. *Journal of Abnormal and Social Psychology,* 1956, 53, 118-121.

Rosenbaum, M., and Blake, R. Volunteering as a function of field structure. *Journal of Abnormal and Social Psychology,* 1955, 50, 193-196.

Rosenhan, D., and White, G. M. Observation and rehearsal as determinants of prosocial behavior. *Journal of Personality and Social Psychology,* 1967, 5, 424-431.

Ugurel-Semin, R. Moral behavior and moral judgment of children. *Journal of Abnormal and Social Psychology,* 1952, 47, 464-474.

Wheeler, L. Toward a theory of behavioral contagion. *Psychological Review,* 1966, 73, 179-192.

Wright, B. A. Altruism in children and perceived conduct of others. *Journal of Abnormal and Social Psychology,* 1942, 37, 218-233.

TOPIC IV: Four Walls Do Not an Experiment Make

The laboratory is but another situation, and the experiment but another episode, within which the "scientist" dwells, negotiating his own identity and providing his own excuses and justifications. And all he gets back in response are the excuses and justifications of his subjects.

Rom Harre'
Sociology of the Absurd,
Introduction

The laboratory experiment, as described in Barry F. Anderson's selection, "The Experiment," is at once the most elegant and error-free method of conducting research. The ideal experiment involves a sample of individuals drawn at random from a population. This sample is divided into two separate and equal groups (usually by a process of randomly assigning individuals to one group or the other). Now, these two groups, ideally the same in all respects, are labeled "control" and "experimental" groups. Each group is exposed to exactly the same conditions (ideally), except for the *one* variable being measured (usually called the independent variable, or IV). The experimental group *only* is exposed to this variable (an electric shock, for example). Then, after exposure, the two groups are measured. Since the two groups were exactly the same at the beginning of the experiment, and exposed to exactly the same conditions during the experiment (except for the shock), then *any differences between the two groups at the close of the experiment must have been caused by the independent variable*–the only different experience of the two groups during the course of the experiment. This, the ideal form of the classical randomized experiment (CRE) can be diagramed in Figure 5, p. 166.*

Ideals and reality seldom mesh perfectly. Although the CRE looks good in theory, there are some problems involved when putting it into practice.

INTERNAL VALIDITY

It is difficult to insure that both the experimental and control groups are exposed to exactly the same conditions during the course of the experiment

*There are many other more complex experimental designs. The CRE, however, is the most basic, simple, and elegant, although there are problems of external validity that it cannot control for.

Figure 5. The Classical Randomized Experiment

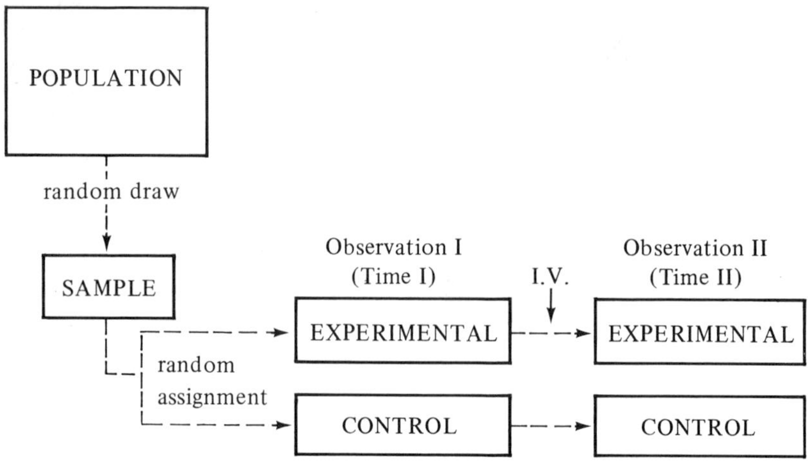

(except for the IV). To be absolutely sure on this count, the two groups would have to be administered to by the same experimenter at the same time and in the same location. Any deviation from this impossible condition of the two groups being in the same place at the same time leaves room for error to creep in. In reality there are many factors other than the independent variable itself that might be influencing the result of the experiment. This is the problem of internal validity: are you measuring what you think you are measuring (the IV), or is it some unknown other factor?

Further problems with internal validity arise because the experiment is a *social* situation. Subjects and observers are both looking for cues as to how to proceed, while at the same time they both have preconceived ideas as to how they *should* act. These cues and preconceived ideas help determine the interaction patterns involved. So again, observed differences between the experimental and control groups may be because of these expectations and interaction patterns, rather than because of the effects of the independent variable. Robert Rosenthal has recalled an instance illustrative of this difficulty: the case of Clever Hans, the horse.

> Hans . . . was that clever horse who could solve problems of mathematics and musical harmony with equal skill and grace, simply by tapping out the answers with his hoof. A committee of eminent experts testified that Hans, whose owner made no profit from his horse's talents, was receiving no cues from his questioners. Of course . . . this was not so, . . . tiny head and eye movements were Hans' signals to begin and to end his tapping. When

> Hans was asked a question, the questioner looked at Hans' hoof, quite naturally so, for that was the way for him to determine whether Hans' answer was correct. Then it was discovered that when Hans approached the correct number of taps, the questioner would inadvertently move his head or eyes upward–just enough that Hans could discriminate the cue. . . .[1]

Some experimenters attempt to control for the subjects' picking up of cues by disguising the purpose of the experiment. Milgram's study of obedience to authority is a good example of this. The procedure is, to say the least, ethically questionable. In fact, the Nuremberg Code For the Conduct of Experiments, established during the trial of Nazi war criminals after World War II, specifically forbids this sort of procedure. Yet it is a common tactic in American social science research. Martin T. Orne discusses the reasons why, as well as looking more closely at the subject-observer relationship, in his article, "On the Social Psychology of the Psychological Experiment." Orne's concern with the influence of observer-subject expectations on the outcome of experiments (labeled the "demand characteristics" of the situation) has been reflected in the work of Robert Rosenthal.

Rosenthal began his studies by conducting laboratory experiments in which two groups of rats with exactly the same "maze intelligence" were presented to observers as "maze bright" and "maze dull." The observers then ran the rats through mazes and, lo and behold, the "maze bright" rats were recorded as performing significantly better than the "maze dull" rats, *even though the rats were exactly the same in maze intelligence.*

Still curious, Rosenthal designed a set of field experiments in the real world to further test his theories. He reasoned, "if rats learn better when their experimenter thinks they will, then children may learn better if their teachers think they will."[2]

> . . . All the children in an elementary school were given an intelligence test which was disguised as a test which would predict academic "blooming." There were 18 classes, three at each of six grade levels. By the use of a table of random numbers, about 20 percent of the children in each class were chosen for the experimental condition. The experimental treatment consisted of telling their teachers that they had scored on the predictive achievement test such that they would show unusual intellectual development within the next academic year. At the end of the academic year the children were retested with the same test of intelligence.
>
> For the 18 classes combined, children whose teachers expected them to gain in performance showed a significantly greater gain in I.Q. than did the control children. . . .[3]

Rosenthal's experiments have shown clearly that people, including observers in experiments, *do* affect the behavior of those with whom they interact because of their expectations of what that behavior will be. In actual practice, such problems of internal validity can significantly affect the outcome of experiments.

EXTERNAL VALIDITY

External validity, or generalizing sample results back to the population, can also be a problem in laboratory experiments. In minimizing problems of internal validity, one creates a laboratory situation with so many things controlled, measured, and parcelled out that the situation is highly artificial and not much at all like the world outside the lab (to which one probably wishes to generalize results). Do Milgram's laboratory experiments, by themselves, show much relation to how people react in real life to authority situations? Leon Festinger addresses himself to some of these problems in his selection, "Laboratory Experiments."

There are two means of conducting experiments that attempt to get closer to real life than the laboratory. One is commonly known as the *field experiment,* and is discussed by Festinger. This is simply an experiment conducted outside the laboratory. In contrast, the *natural experiment,* that Barry Anderson presents in "The Experiment," is a situation in which "nature, not the experimenter, produces the changes" in the independent variable. "In a natural experiment, you manipulate nothing; you merely observe." The field experiment, on the other hand, involves the experimenter manipulating the independent variable in a "real-world" setting.

The strengths of both field and natural experiments are in terms of external validity; however, they both also imply a relaxing of control over sources of internal invalidity—the constant dilemma of those who employ the experimental method.

NOTES

1. Robert Rosenthal, "Unintended Consequences of Interpersonal Expectations, *American Behavioral Scientist* 10, no. 8: (April 1967) 24–26.
2. *Ibid.,* p. 26.
3. *Ibid.*

SUGGESTED FURTHER READINGS

Campbell, Donald T., and Stanley, Julian C. *Experimental and Quasi-Experimental Designs for Research.* Chicago: Rand McNally, 1963.

Fisher, R. A. *The Design of Experiments.* Edinburgh: Oliver and Boyd, Ltd., 1947.
Friedman, Neil. *The Social Nature of Psychological Research.* New York: Basic Books, 1967.
Milgram, Stanley. "Some Conditions of Obedience and Disobedience to Authority," *Human Relations* 18, no. 1 (February 1965): 57–75.
Rosenthal, Robert. *Experimenter Effects in Behavioral Research.* New York: Appleton-Century-Crofts, 1966.
Rosenthal, Robert. *Pygmalion in the Classroom.* New York: Holt, Rinehart and Winston, 1968.
Stouffer, Samuel A. "Some Observations on Study Design," *American Journal of Sociology* 55 (1950): 355–61.

The Experiment

Barry F. Anderson

The experiment may be regarded as a model of the scientific method. It is a miniaturization of the scientific method in that, in its simplest form, it is a procedure for arriving at a single descriptive statement of relationship; and it is an idealization of the scientific method in that it satisfies more fully than any other procedure the requirement of controlled observation. It is the best place to start to get a look behind the generalities, at the actual workings of the scientific method.

THE TRUE EXPERIMENT

According to the principle of controlled observation, for an observation to provide an adequate test of the statement that a change on *A* causes a change on *B,* variable *B* must be observed when different values on variable *A* occur and when all other variables can be discounted as possible causes of whatever

From *The Psychology Experiment* (2nd edition) by Barry Anderson. Copyright 1971 by Wadsworth Publishing Company, Inc. Reprinted by permission of the publisher, Brooks/ Cole Publishing Company, Monterey, California.

change is observed on *B*. Experimental control provides the only certain basis for discounting one variable as a possible cause of a change on another. Because all changes in an experiment are introduced by the experimenter, you can control an indefinitely large number of variables in a true experiment simply by not changing them.

Ideally, to conduct a true experiment you (a) produce a set of conditions and measure variable *B* under these conditions, then (b) reproduce the same set of conditions with just one difference, a change on variable *A*, and measure *B* under these new conditions. You kick the television set, for example, to see whether this will restore the picture. The kick is the one change you have introduced in the situation, and, because you introduced the change yourself, you can be sure what changed and what did not and, hence, what variable to implicate as cause. If the picture comes back on, you can be quite certain that opening the door had nothing to do with it, because you did not open the door; that turning the lights off had nothing to do with it, because you did not turn the lights off; and so on through an indefinitely long list of controlled variables.

The variable that the experimenter changes directly is referred to as the *independent variable* (IV), so named because its value is independently manipulated by the experimenter. The variable that the experimenter examines to see whether it is affected by changes on the IV is called the *dependent variable* (DV), so named because its value is expected to be dependent on the value of the IV. Thus, you might apply heat (IV) to carbon to see whether it will burn (DV), put fertilizer (IV) on mushrooms to see whether they will grow faster (DV), or teach a person something about the scientific method (IV) to see whether this will improve his general reasoning ability (DV). . . .

Each value on the IV that is employed in an experiment defines an *experimental condition.* If one is interested in the effect of instruction in scientific method on reasoning ability, for example. there are any number of different values on the kind of instruction variable one might use: no instruction, reading a book on the scientific method, taking a course in the scientific method, taking a course in logic, taking a course in fifteenth-century Italian painting. In the *simple experiment,* with which we shall be primarily concerned, just two values on the IV, and hence two experimental conditions, are used. In the example, these might be taking a course in logic and taking a course in the scientific method. Notice that the *fewest* experimental conditions an experiment can have is two. Observations under a single condition can result only in state description. For process description, one must observe changes; and, for a change to take place on the IV, there must be at least two conditions.

One of the experimental conditions is often called the *control condition* and the other simply the *experimental condition.* The experimental condition is the one in which the treatment of interest—heat, fertilizer—is administered. The control condition is one that is exactly like the experimental condition except in lacking the treatment of interest. Those variables on which the experimental and control conditions are identical are referred to as *controlled variables* (CVs), hence the name "control condition." The fact that experimental and control conditions are referred to collectively as experimental conditions may seem confusing, but the intended meaning of the term "experimental condition" is usually quite clear from its context. The term "control condition" would ordinarily not be used in describing experiments, such as the one on the scientific method, where two treatments are being compared rather than a treatment being compared with no treatment.

According to the principle of statistical generalization, if one wishes to generalize a descriptive statement to an entire population, the observation should be repeated on an adequate number of members randomly sampled from the population. This introduces another variable into the experiment, the *sampled variable* (SV). The SV usually refers to the objects studied. These might be samples of chemical in a chemistry experiment, plots of land in an agricultural experiment, or subjects in a psychology experiment. The SV is so called because, usually, not all of the objects to which the experiment's conclusions will be generalized are included in the experiment itself; only a limited sample is studied. Though we speak of SV in the singular, an SV such as subjects (hereafter, *S*s) can also be regarded as an indefinitely large collection of variables: height, weight, intelligence, sex, socioeconomic background, and so on.

Thus, every true experiment has an IV, a DV, an indefinitely large number of CVs, and an SV. The main features of an experiment can be conveniently represented in the following kind of diagram:

IV: KIND OF INSTRUCTION

	Logic		*Scientific method*	
S1	80	S7	80	
S2	70	S8	80	
S3	90	S9	90	
S4	80	S10	95	
S5	65	S11	70	
S6	75	S12	80	*DV: Reasoning score*

The IV and the two values on it are identified at the top of the diagram. The *S*s are indicated by the arbitrary numbers *S*1–*S*12. The numbers to the right of the *S*s refer to values on the DV, each number having been obtained by observing the *S* indicated immediately to its left, under the experimental condition indicated at the top of its column. The DV is identified to the right of the diagram. This kind of diagram will be used frequently to represent true experiments. Occasionally, it will be used to represent natural experiments, but this will be done with the understanding that a natural experiment, as will be seen in the next section has no true IV or DV and few or no CVs.

THE NATURAL EXPERIMENT

In order to observe a relationship, one variable must be changed and another observed. In a true experiment, the experimenter produces the changes; in a natural experiment, nature produces the changes. This may seem like a small difference, but it has far-reaching implications.

To make the difference clearer, let us consider how we might conduct both a true experiment and a natural experiment on the question of whether reasoning ability is increased through a college course in the scientific method. In a true experiment, you produce one set of conditions, measure the DV, reproduce the conditions with one difference, and measure the DV again. The first set of conditions in the scientific-method experiment might be described, in part, as follows: an introductory course in scientific method is taught at 9 MWF, during the 10 weeks of winter quarter. A partial description of the second set of conditions would differ from this in only one respect, the value on the IV. It might read: an introductory course in logic is taught at 9 MWF, during the 10 weeks of winter quarter. More complete descriptions would, of course, detail lecturing, problem-set, testing, and grading procedures, yet these procedures would be identical for both conditions.

Establishing the experimental conditions is the first step in manipulating the IV; the second step is administering these conditions to some *S*s, for the experimenter himself must decide not only on the conditions but also on which conditions to administer to which *S*s. More will be said later about assigning *S*s to conditions. For the moment, it will suffice to note that *the defining characteristic of a true experiment is the presence of an IV, that an IV is a variable manipulated by the experimenter, and that manipulation of a variable involves both establishing the experimental conditions and assigning the Ss to these conditions.*

In a natural experiment, you manipulate nothing; you merely observe. What might be done in our scientific-method example is simply to administer a test of reasoning ability to *S*s who had completed courses that could be classified as scientific-method courses and to *S*s who had completed courses that could be classified as logic courses.

In the true experiment, if you found a difference in general reasoning ability between the scientific method *S*s and the logic *S*s, you could safely conclude that kind of instruction was causally related to reasoning ability. In the natural experiment, you could not. The reason is that, in the natural experiment, many other variables were free to change along with, or be *confounded* with, type of instruction—variables that themselves could have produced the observed difference in reasoning ability. It may be that the scientific-method courses were taught at a more favorable time of the day or that more problem sets were assigned in these courses; since you exerted no control over these factors, you do not know. It may be that the brighter students enrolled in the scientific-method courses; again, since you exerted no control over this factor, you do not know. This problem of confounding always exists in natural experiments; it is the problem of the "third factor" in predictive relationships, mentioned earlier. While true experiments yield causal information, natural experiments yield only predictive information.

In a natural experiment, you sample situations rather than produce them. Thus, there are no IVs or DVs, only SVs. The correct terms for the natural experiment analogues of the IV and DV are the *predictor variable* and the *criterion variable*, respectively.

Controls, however, can be introduced into natural experiments; thus, there may be CVs in natural experiments. The procedures for establishing such controls will not be discussed in this book, but the following point is worth making: while the true experiment begins with a situation in which all variables are controlled and allows variation to be introduced one variable at a time, the natural experiment begins with a situation in which all variables are free to vary and allows control to be introduced one variable at a time. This means that in a natural experiment you control only the variables you are aware of, while in a true experiment you control many variables of which you are not even aware. It also means that there are inevitably far fewer controls, and a much greater possibility of confounding, in a natural experiment.

In many cases, you have no choice but to use a natural experiment, for nature makes changes on many variables over which man has no control. Indeed, a number of highly respectable sciences are, of necessity, bound to the use of natural experiments. Astronomy, oceanography, and geology are among these, for it is beyond man's present powers to manipulate the mass of a planet, the temperature of the ocean, or isostatic forces in the earth's crust. In many areas of psychology, as well, the manipulation of variables is either not possible or not ethical, and the natural experiment is the only acceptable alternative. For example, you would not raise children in isolation in order to determine the effects of such isolation on later social behavior.

Even where a choice exists, the natural experiment may be preferable to the true experiment. Especially in the early stages of research in an area, it is good strategy to observe the operation of variables in their natural settings to obtain some estimate of the relative importance of these variables before studying them under the more controlled conditions of the laboratory. Variables that can be made to produce large effects in the laboratory are sometimes relatively unimportant in nature, because their effects are swamped by variables that were controlled in the laboratory setting. Conversely, variables that cannot be made to produce large effects in the laboratory are sometimes of considerable importance in nature. The fear induced by nature on the battlefield or on death row, for example, is far greater than that induced by an experimenter using the strongest electric shock he dares.

Thus, the natural experiment has an important place in science. The person who employs the natural experiment should be aware of its limitations, however, so that he may avoid the false interpretations that so often deceive its users. The limitations of the natural experiment are seen most clearly when it is contrasted with the true experiment, with which we shall be primarily concerned.

EXPERIMENTAL ERROR

A more precise way to characterize the difference between true experiments and natural experiments is to say that (a) in a true experiment, constant error has been eliminated by controlling or randomizing all potential sources of error, while (b) in a natural experiment, the possibility of constant error remains, because little or nothing has been done in the way of control or randomization. Several terms here are in need of definition.

Experimental error exists when a change on the DV is produced by any variable other than the IV. What you are really interested in is the effect of the IV on the DV. When other variables that are causally related to the DV are confounded with the IV, they produce experimental error; they produce differences on the DV between the experimental conditions that add to or subtract from the difference that would have been produced by the IV alone. Experimental error covers up the effect you are interested in and can make it difficult or impossible to assess.

Let us see how this concept might apply to our scientific-method experiment. Let us say that we obtain some *S*s, assign half to a scientific-method course and half to a logic course, and, at the end of the term, measure them all on reasoning ability. There are a number of variables which, unless we are careful, may be confounded with the IV. One is time of day; one course may be taught in the middle of the morning, when students are alert, and the other at the very end of the day. Another is intelligence; students in one course may be brighter than those in the other. Since both of these variables are likely to affect the reasoning score obtained at the end of the term, allowing either to be confounded with the IV is likely to result in experimental error.

There are two kinds of experimental errors: constant error and random error. *An understanding of these kinds of errors and of ways to deal with them constitutes the very basis of experimental reasoning.* A *constant error* is an error that favors the same experimental condition every time the basic experiment is repeated. "Basic experiment" means the experiment as conducted on two *S*s, one in each experimental condition. If 10 *S*s are run, 5 in each experimental condition, then the basic experiment is repeated 5 times. This is often purely a conceptual distinction, for all 10 *S*s may be run at the same time. Any error due to time of day would be a constant error, for whichever course is taught at the more favorable time of day is taught at that time for all *S*s—that is, every time the basic experiment is repeated. The following diagrams show how constant error may distort the true situation.

CONSTANT ERROR

True effect of instruction

Logic		Scientific method	
S1	5	S6	6
S2	5	S7	6
S3	5	S8	6
S4	5	S9	6
S5	5	S10	6

Constant error due to time of day

Morning		Afternoon	
S1	0	S6	-2
S2	0	S7	-2
S3	0	S8	-2
S4	0	S9	-2
S5	0	S10	-2

Resultant scores, in which the true effect is distorted by constant error

Logic in morning		Scientific method in afternoon	
S1	5	S6	4
S2	5	S7	4
S3	5	S8	4
S4	5	S9	4
S5	5	S10	4

A *random error* is an error which, on repetitions of the basic experiment, sometimes favors one experimental condition and sometimes the other, on a chance basis. If *S*s are assigned to conditions randomly, then any error resulting from differences in intelligence will be random error. The following diagrams show how random error may obscure the true situation. For simplicity, only two levels of intelligence are represented.

RANDOM ERROR

True effect of instruction

Logic		Scientific method	
S1	5	S6	6
S2	5	S7	6
S3	5	S8	6
S4	5	S9	6
S5	5	S10	6

Random error due to intelligence

Group A		Group B	
S1	+2	S6	−2
S2	−2	S7	+2
S3	+2	S8	+2
S4	+2	S9	−2
S5	−2	S10	+2

Resultant scores in which the true effect is obscured random error

Logic with group A		Scientific method with group B	
S1	7	S6	4
S2	3	S7	8
S3	7	S8	8
S4	7	S9	4
S5	3	S10	8

Very often, the error from any particular source has both constant and random components. This would be true of the error produced by intelligence if the *S*s volunteered for the conditions and if the brighter *S*s usually, but not always, chose the same course. We shall continue to consider just the pure cases of constant and random error, and it is perfectly legitimate to do so. But we do this with the understanding that the error from any particular source may involve these components in any proportions.

The effect of a constant error is to distort the results in a particular direction, so that an erroneous difference masks the true state of affairs. The effect of a random error is not to distort the results in any particular direction, but to obscure them. Constant error is like a distorting mirror in a fun house; it produces a picture that is clear but incorrect. Random error is like a mirror that has become cloudy with age; it produces a picture that is essentially correct but unclear. . . .

Laboratory Experiments

Leon Festinger

THE RELATIONSHIP BETWEEN LABORATORY EXPERIMENTATION AND THE STUDY OF REAL-LIFE SITUATIONS

In the conducting of research, there should be an active interrelation between laboratory experimentation and the study of real-life situations. It is relatively rare in social psychology that hypotheses, hunches, and recognition of important variables emerge initially from the laboratory; most often they arise in either the formal or the informal study of real-life situations. In studying real-life situations, we are forced to deal with the factors and variables as they exist in all their complexity. Because of this complexity and lack of control, it is rather rare that definitive conclusions and unequivocal interpretations are reached in such studies, but frequently new variables and new hypotheses are brought to our attention. One can take these suggestions, hypotheses, and hunches and use laboratory experimentation to verify, elaborate, and make more secure the theoretical basis for the empirical results which have been obtained.

In the laboratory experiment, sufficient control can be achieved to obtain definitive answers, and systematic variation of different factors is possible. As a result of this greater control, precision, and manipulability, conclusive answers can be obtained and relatively precise and subtle theoretical points can be tested. For example, in a study of the spread of a rumor in a community (3), it was found that the more friends people had, the more likely they were to have heard the rumor. This finding may suggest the hypothesis that friendship reduces restraints against communication of various types of content; or it may suggest the hypothesis that the existence of a friendship makes for an active pressure to communicate; or it may suggest the hypothesis that those who have more friends see more people and spend more time with these people and consequently are more likely to have an opportunity to hear the rumor. In a laboratory experiment it would be possible to set up a situation in which one could, with a high degree of rigor, collect data which would enable one to choose among these possible interpretations. One could, for example, form groups of strangers and friends mixed together in which the amount of contact among members and the opportunity for communication among them were experimentally held constant. The results would enable one to say whether the effect of friendship existed in the absence of differential amounts of contact. It would enable one to accept or reject the third hypothesis stated above. In other groups one could experimentally vary the accessibility of other members for communication to obtain evidence as to whether the friendship represented a decrement in restraint against communication or whether there were actual pressures to communicate in the specific direction of friends.

Such an experiment would undoubtedly be difficult to set up, but, since the major body of this chapter will be devoted to the discussion of how to perform such experiments and how to produce the desired conditions, we shall not, at the moment, go into the details of how it might be done. Let it suffice now to say that in the laboratory, by setting up an artificial situation, we should be able to verify, elaborate, and refine our knowledge so as to increase our understanding of important processes in social life. It should be stressed again, however, that the problem of application of the results of such laboratory experiments to the real-life situation is not solved by a simple extension of the result. Such application requires additional experimentation and study. It is undoubtedly important that the results of laboratory experiments be tested out in real-life situations. Unless this is done the danger of "running dry" or "hitting a dead end" is always present. A continuous interplay between laboratory experiments and studies of real-life situations should provide proper perspective, for the results obtained should continually supply new hypotheses for building the theoretical structure and should represent progress in the solution of the problems of application and generalization.

DIFFICULTIES OF PERFORMING LABORATORY EXPERIMENTS

Laboratory experiments, however, do not represent an easy road to the collection of data for the resolution of theoretical problems. In social psychology they are typically difficult to do, and many dangers are present in their execution. It is extremely difficult to create in the laboratory forces strong enough for results to be measurable. In the most excellently done laboratory experiment, the strength to which different variables can be produced is extremely weak compared to the strength with which these variables exist and operate in real-life situations. One is able to obtain results and to see clearly how these variables operate, in spite of this weakness, because of the increased control one has in the laboratory situation. But it is always possible, even probable, that the factors will be so weak that no differences between conditions experimentally created are apparent in spite of the increased control. Thus, in the setting up of a laboratory experiment, especial care must be taken to make the variables as strong as one possibly can. Unfortunately, one can determine whether or not one has succeeded only after the experiment is over. An exception to this generalization about the weakness of laboratory manipulation can be seen in Asch's use of the announced perceptions of group members (1). This involved, however, the use of seven confederates for a single experimental subject.

Related to the problem of the strength of forces in the laboratory situation is the difficulty of manipulating several variables simultaneously. In the complex field of research with which we are here concerned, it is frequently theoretically important to see the effect of the simultaneous operation of two or more variables. Unfortunately, however, the more variables the experimenter attempts to manipulate, the lower will be the strength of each variable. This is especially true if the manipulation of the variable is to be done by means of verbal instructions to the subjects. The result of this is, at least at the present stage of technical development, that the number of variables which it is possible to manipulate simultaneously in the laboratory is relatively restricted. This will undoubtedly become less true as more powerful techniques of manipulating variables in the laboratory are developed.

These difficulties have an important implication for the conclusions one can draw from the results of laboratory experiments. As in any study, it is possible that the experimenter is dealing with entirely irrelevant variables–that is, there may actually be no relationship among the variables that are being studied. Such a condition would result in negative results–that is, no differences between experimental and control groups. However, we should also find a lack of differences between experimental and control conditions if our experimental manipulations were not sufficiently strong to reveal measurable differences even though such differences really exist. Thus, negative results from a laboratory experiment can mean very little indeed. If we obtain positive results–that is, demonstrably significant differences among conditions–we can be relatively certain concerning our interpretation and conclusion from the experiment. If, however, no differences emerge, we can generally reach no definitive conclusion unless we are quite certain that the manipulation of variables in the experiment was done successfully and adequately. At the present stage of technical development, it is seldom that we can be certain, in the absence of positive results, that our manipulations were adequate. Undoubtedly, as more and more experiments are done, good evidence will become available for believing that a certain manipulation is an adequate one, and then negative results can be interpreted as demonstrating no relationship. At the present time, however, it is all too easy to set up a laboratory experiment which, because of the ineffective manipulation of variables, will show no differences among conditions. It should be stressed again that, at the present stage of technical development, negative results perhaps reveal only the fact that the experiment was not set up carefully and that the experimenter's attempted manipulation of the variables was ineffective.

Keeping in mind these difficulties and the relationship which must exist between laboratory and field investigation, we shall now proceed to a more detailed examination of how laboratory experiments can be performed.

THE DESIGN OF LABORATORY EXPERIMENTS

The first and foremost requirement for a successful laboratory experiment is that the problem be stated in experimental terms. This means, essentially, that there must be a high degree of specificity and clarity in the statement of the problem and in the definition of the variables involved. The foregoing implies that before one can successfully do a laboratory experiment one must already know quite a bit about the phenomena one is investigating.

The process of specifying and clarifying the statement of a problem so that it is amenable to experimental treatment is by no means a simple or easy one. Let us take an example to illustrate the kinds of problems which confront the experimenter at this stage. In a field study of transmission of a rumor in an organization (2), it was observed that communication tended to be directed upward in the organizational hierarchy. This result was explained as depending upon forces acting on members to move upward in the organization; *i.e.*, the upward communication represented substitute movement on the part of the members.

Kelley (4) set out to perform a laboratory experiment to test this hypothesis more thoroughly. At this point the statement of his problem might have been "What direction does communication tend to take in a structured hierarchy?" This statement, however, is still much too general and vague for the purposes of an experiment. An attempt to think in terms of setting up an experiment makes it immediately clear that one must answer questions such as "What exactly is a hierarchy?" and "Exactly what kinds of communication are we talking about?" There are many aspects to what is customarily thought of as a hierarchical structure. Do superior levels in the hierarchy have power over subordinate levels and, if so, what kinds of power? Is each successive level upward in the hierarchy characterized by increased attractiveness of the work, or increased freedom of choice of what work to do, or increased importance of the work? For the purpose of setting up a laboratory experiment, the theory involved and the definition of hierarchy must be made more specific. Kelley chose to establish a hierarchy in the laboratory on the basis of the perceived importance of the job to the subjects, holding the actual attractiveness of the job and the exact work that was done constant for both levels in the hierarchy.

Let us now consider the question of what kind of communication would be expected to go upward in such a hierarchy. It was clear that a distinction had to be made between work-oriented communication, communication of criticism, communication of information, and communication which was irrelevant to the task. It was largely in the last category of communication content that the effect of substitute movement would be expected to appear. Consequently, the experiment was set up to allow and, in fact, to encourage communication of irrelevant content. The final problem in Kelley's experiment was phrased as "What is the direction of irrelevant communication content in a hierarchy based upon perceived differential importance of the task?" This statement was specific enough to permit the design of the actual experiment. This process of clarifying the objectives of the experiment takes considerable time, although it may not take long to describe after it has once been done.

The difficulties of designing a laboratory experiment are by no means overcome when the problem has been specifically defined. There remain the major tasks of inventing measurement devices and techniques for manipulation of variables which will clearly measure and manipulate the variables which have been defined in the statement of the problem. No matter how specifically and clearly the concepts are defined in the statement of the problem, the laboratory experiment cannot be successful unless the measurement and the manipulation of variables actually relate to these defined concepts.

Thus, for example, in the Kelley (4) experiment mentioned above, it was necessary to develop techniques for producing a hierarchy as defined, while other variables, such as the type of work done, power, and attractiveness, would be controlled. The situation created had to be one in which irrelevant communication would occur. Adequate techniques for measuring the amount and direction of communication had to be developed. In the experiment, a two-level hierarchy was established. Each level did exactly the same kind of work, although each was under the impression that the other level was doing something different. High and low hierarchic perceptions were encouraged by the instructions to the subjects: one subgroup was told that its own job was the important one; the other subgroup was told that the job of the other level was the more important. Communication of irrelevant material was encouraged by having all communication carried on in writing and by injecting into the communication stream prepared fictitious notes which were irrelevant in their content, thus encouraging subjects to do such writing themselves. All notes were collected and kept, and thus analysis of the content of the communication, its direction, and amount was possible.

It is rarely safe to assume beforehand that the operations used to manipulate variables will be successful and will tie in directly with the concept the experimenter has in mind. It is a worthwhile precaution to check on the success of the experimental manipulations. In the experiment by Kelley, the subjects were asked a number of questions after the session was over to determine whether or not the manipulation of status in the hierarchy had been successful. It was found that, in terms of their reported perception of status and their desire to be in the other role, the manipulation had created a difference between the two levels. This difference was a relatively small one, however. Small differences in the results could be directly attributed to the small difference in perceived status. When the difference in perceived status was made larger by selecting out those subjects for whom the experimental manipulations were clearly successful, the results become much clearer and more conclusive. If there had been no check on the success of the experimental manipulation, such analysis would have been impossible. It would also have been impossible to attribute unequivocally the inconclusiveness in the results to the relative inadequacy of the experimental manipulation.

The problem of the adequacy of the manipulation of variables may be dealt with in part by preliminary studies. In almost any laboratory experiment, the initial design will have certain inadequacies which will become clear after a few trial experiments. Such preliminary runs are also important to provide practice for the investigator so that his behavior and his instructions become standardized by the time the regular experiments start.

BIBLIOGRAPHY

1. Asch, S.E. Effects of group pressurc upon the modification and distortion of judgments. In Guetzkow, H. (ed.). *Groups, leadership and men.* Pittsburgh: Carnegie Press, 1951, pp. 177–190.
2. Back, K., Festinger, L., Hymovitch, B., Kelley, H., Schachter, S., and Thibaut, J. The methodology of studying rumor transmission. *Hum. Relat.* 1950, *3*, 307–312.
3. Festinger, L., Cartwright, D., Barber, K., Fleischl, J., Gottsdanker, J., Keysen, A., and Leavitt, G. A study of rumor: its origin and spread. *Hum. Relat.,* 1948, *1*, 464–486.
4. Kelley, H.H. Communication in experimentally created hierarchies. *Hum. Relat.,* 1951, *4*, 39–56.

On the Social Psychology of the Psychological Experiment: With Particular Reference to Demand Characteristics and Their Implications

Martin T. Orne

It is to the highest degree probable that the subject['s] . . . general attitude of mind is that of ready complacency and cheerful willingness to assist the investigator in every possible way by reporting to him those very things which he is most eager to find, and that the very questions of the experimenter . . . suggest the shade of reply expected. . . . Indeed . . . it seems too often as if the subject were now regarded as a stupid automaton. . . .

A. H. Pierce, 1908[1]

Reprinted by permission from *American Psychologist* 17 (November 1962), pp. 776–83.

This paper was presented at the Symposium, "On the Social Psychology of the Psychological Experiment," American Psychological Association Convention, New York, 1961.

The work reported here was supported in part by a Public Health Service Research Grant, M–3369, National Institute of Mental Health.

I wish to thank my associates Ronald E. Shor, Donald N. O'Connell, Ulric Neisser, Karl E. Scheibe, and Emily F. Carota for their comments and criticisms in the preparation of this paper.

Since the time of Galileo, scientists have employed the laboratory experiment as a method of understanding natural phenomena. Generically, the experimental method consists of abstracting relevant variables from complex situations in nature and reproducing in the laboratory segments of these situations, varying the parameters involved so as to determine the effect of the experimental variables. This procedure allows generalization from the information obtained in the laboratory situation back to the original situation as it occurs in nature. The physical sciences have made striking advances through the use of this method, but in the behavioral sciences it has often been difficult to meet two necessary requirements for meaningful experimentation: reproducibility and ecological validity.[2] It has long been recognized that certain differences will exist between the types of experiments conducted in the physical sciences and those in the behavioral sciences because the former investigates a universe of inanimate objects and forces, whereas the latter deals with animate organisms, often thinking, conscious subjects. However, recognition of this distinction has not always led to appropriate changes in the traditional experimental model of physics as employed in the behavioral sciences. Rather the experimental model has been so successful as employed in physics that there has been a tendency in the behavioral sciences to follow precisely a paradigm originated for the study of inanimate objects, i.e., one which proceeds by exposing the subject to various conditions and observing the differences in reaction of the subject under different conditions. However, the use of such a model with animal or human subjects leads to the problem that the subject of the experiment is assumed, at least implicitly, to be a *passive responder* to stimuli—an assumption difficult to justify. Further, in this type of model the experimental stimuli themselves are usually rigorously defined in terms of what *is done* to the subject. In contrast, the purpose of this paper will be to focus on what the human subject *does* in the laboratory: what motivation the subject is likely to have in the experimental situation, how he usually perceives behavioral research, what the nature of the cues is that the subject is likely to pick up, etc. Stated in other terms, what factors are apt to affect the subject's reaction to the well-defined stimuli in the situation? These factors comprise what will be referred to here as the "experimental setting."

Since any experimental manipulation of human subjects takes place within this larger framework or setting, we should propose that the above-mentioned factors must be further elaborated and the parameters of the experimental setting more carefully defined so that adequate controls can be designed to isolate the effects of the experimental setting from the effects of the experimental variables. Later in this paper we shall propose certain possible techniques of control which have been devised in the process of our research on the nature of hypnosis.

Our initial focus here will be on some of the qualities peculiar to psychological experiments. The experimental situation is one which takes place within the context of an explicit agreement of the subject to participate in a special form of social interaction known as "taking part in an experiment." Within the context of our culture the roles of subject and experimenter are well understood and carry with them well-defined mutual role expectations. A particularly striking aspect of the typical experimenter-subject relationship is the extent to which the subject will play his role and place himself under the control of the experimenter. Once a subject has agreed to participate in a psychological experiment, he implicitly agrees to perform a very wide range of actions on request without inquiring as to their purpose, and frequently without inquiring as to their duration.

Furthermore, the subject agrees to tolerate a considerable degree of discomfort, boredom, or actual pain, if required to do so by the experimenter. Just about any request which could conceivably be asked of the subject by a reputable investigator is legitimized by the quasi-magical phrase, "This is an experiment," and the shared assumption that a legitimate purpose will be served by the subject's behavior. A somewhat trivial example of this legitimization of requests is as follows:

A number of casual acquaintances were asked whether they would do the experimenter a favor; on their acquiescence, they were asked to perform five pushups. Their response tended to be amazement, incredulity and the question "Why?" Another similar group of individuals was asked whether they would take part in an experiment of brief duration. When they agreed to do so, they too were asked to perform five pushups. Their typical response was "Where?"

The striking degree of control inherent in the experimental situation can also be illustrated by a set of pilot experiments which were performed in the course of designing an experiment to test whether the degree of control inherent in the *hypnotic* relationship is greater than that in a waking relationship.[3] In order to test this question, we tried to develop a set of tasks which waking subjects would refuse to do, or would do only for a short period of time. The tasks were intended to be psychologically noxious, meaningless, or boring, rather than painful or fatiguing.

For example, one task was to perform serial additions of each adjacent two numbers on sheets filled with rows of random digits. In order to complete just one sheet, the subject would be required to perform 224 additions! A stack of some 2,000 sheets was presented to each subject–clearly an impossible task to complete. After the instructions were given, the subject was deprived of his watch and told, "Continue to work; I will return eventually." Five and one-half hours later, the *experimenter* gave up! In general, subjects tended to continue this type of task for several hours, usually with little decrement in performance. Since we were trying to find a task which would be discontinued spontaneously within a brief period, we tried to create a more frustrating situation as follows:

Subjects were asked to perform the same task described above but were also told that when finished the additions on each sheet, they should pick up a card from a large pile, which would instruct them on what to do next. However, every card in the pile read,

> You are to tear up the sheet of paper which you have just completed into a minimum of 32 pieces and go on to the next sheet of paper and continue working as you did before; when you have completed this piece of paper, pick up the next card which will instruct you further. Work as accurately and as rapidly as you can.

Our expectation was that subjects would discontinue the task as soon as they realized that the cards were worded identically, that each finished piece of work had to be destroyed, and that, in short, the task was completely meaningless.

Somewhat to our amazement, subjects tended to persist in the task for several hours with relatively little sign of overt hostility. Removal of the one-way screen did not tend to make much difference. The postexperimental inquiry helped to explain the subjects' behavior. When asked about the tasks, subjects would invariably attribute considerable meaning to their performance, viewing it as an endurance test or the like.

Thus far, we have been singularly unsuccessful in finding an experimental task which would be discontinued, or, indeed, refused by subjects in an experimental setting.[4,5] Not only do subjects continue to perform boring, unrewarding tasks, but they do so with few errors and little decrement in speed. It became apparent that it was extremely difficult to design an experiment to test the degree of social control in hypnosis, in view of the already *very high degree of control in the experimental situation itself.*

The quasi-experimental work reported here is highly informal and based on samples of three or four subjects in each group. It does, however, illustrate the remarkable compliance of the experimental subject. The only other situations where such a wide range of requests are carried out with little or no question are those of complete authority, such as some parent-child relationships or some doctor-patient relationships. This aspect of the experiment as a social situation will not become apparent unless one tests for it; it is, however, present in varying degrees in all experimental contexts. Not only are tasks carried out, but they are performed with care over considerable periods of time.

Our observation that subjects tend to carry out a remarkably wide range of instructions with a surprising degree of diligence reflects only one aspect of the motivation manifested by most subjects in an experimental situation. It is relevant to consider another aspect of motivation that is common to the subjects of most psychological experiments: high regard for the aims of science and experimentation.

A volunteer who participates in a psychological experiment may do so for a wide variety of reasons ranging from the need to fulfill a course requirement, to the need for money, to the unvoiced hope of altering his personal adjustment for the better, etc. Over and above these motives, however, college students tend to share (with the experimenter) the hope and expectation that the study in which they are participating will in some material way contribute to science and perhaps ultimately to human welfare in general. We should expect that many of the characteristics of the experimental situation derive from the peculiar role relationship which exists between subject and experimenter. Both subject and experimenter share the belief that whatever the experimental task is, it is important, and that as such, no matter how much effort must be exerted or how much discomfort must be endured, it is justified by the ultimate purpose.

If we assume that much of the motivation of the subject to comply with any and all experimental instructions derives from an identification with the goals of science in general and the success of the experiment in particular,[6] it follows that the subject has a stake in the outcome of the study in which he is participating. For the volunteer subject to feel that he has made a useful contribution, it is necessary for him to assume that the experimenter is competent and that he himself is a "good subject."

The significance to the subject of successfully being a "good subject" is attested to by the frequent questions at the conclusion of an experiment, to the effect of, "Did I ruin the experiment?" What is most commonly meant by this is, "Did I perform well in my role as experimental subject?" or "Did my behavior demonstrate that which the experiment is designed to show?" Admittedly, subjects are concerned about their performance in terms of reinforcing their self-image; nonetheless, they seem even more concerned with the utility of their performances. We might well expect then that as far as the subject is able, he will behave in an experimental context in a manner designed to play the role of a "good subject" or, in other words, *to validate the experimental hypothesis.* Viewed in this way, the student volunteer is *not* merely a passive responder in an experimental situation but rather he has a very real stake in the successful outcome of the experiment. This problem is implicitly recognized in the large number of psychological studies which attempt to conceal the true purpose of the experiment from the subject in the hope of thereby obtaining more reliable data. This maneuver on the part of psychologists is so widely known in the college population that even if a psychologist is honest with the subject, more often than not he will be distrusted. As one subject pithily put it, "Psychologists always lie!" This bit of paranoia has some support in reality.

The subject's performance in an experiment might almost be conceptualized as problem-solving behavior; that is, at some level he sees it as his task to ascertain the true purpose of the experiment and respond in a manner which will support the hypotheses being tested. Viewed in this light, the totality of cues which convey an experimental hypothesis to the subject become significant determinants of subjects' behavior. We have labeled the sum total of such cues as the "*demand characteristics of the experimental situation*" (Orne, 1959a). These cues include the rumors or campus scuttlebutt about the research, the information conveyed during the original solicitation, the person of the experimenter, and the setting of the laboratory, as well as all explicit and implicit communications during the experiment proper. A frequently overlooked, but nonetheless very significant source of cues for the subject lies in the experimental procedure itself, viewed in the light of the subject's previous knowledge and experience. For example, if a test is given twice with some intervening treatment, even the dullest college student is aware that some change is expected, particularly if the test is in some obvious way related to the treatment.

The demand characteristics perceived in any particular experiment will vary with the sophistication, intelligence, and previous experience of each experimental subject. To the extent that the demand characteristics of the experiment are clear-cut, they will be perceived uniformly by most experimental subjects. It is entirely possible to have an experimental situation with clear-cut demand characteristics for psychology undergraduates which, however, does not have the same clear-cut demand characteristics for enlisted army personnel. It is, of course, those demand characteristics which are perceived by the subject that will influence his behavior.

We should like to propose the heuristic assumption that a subject's behavior in any experimental situation will be determined by two sets of variables: *(a)* those which are traditionally defined as experimental variables and *(b)* the perceived demand characteristics of the experimental situation. The extent to which the subject's behavior is related to the demand characteristics, rather than to the experimental variable, will in large measure determine both the extent to which the experiment can be replicated with minor modification (i.e., modified demand characteristics) and the extent to which generalizations can be drawn about the effect of the experimental variables in nonexperimental contexts (the problem of ecological validity [Brunswik, 1947]).

It becomes an empirical issue to study under what circumstances, in what kind of experimental contexts, and with what kind of subject populations, demand characteristics become significant in determining the behavior of subjects in experimental situations. It should be clear that demand characteristics cannot be eliminated from experiments; all experiments will have demand characteristics, and these will always have some effect. It does become possible, however, to study the effect of demand characteristics as opposed to the effect of experimental variables. However, techniques designed to study the effect of demand characteristics need to take into account that these effects result from the subject's *active* attempt to respond appropriately to the *totality* of the experimental situation.

It is perhaps best to think of the perceived demand characteristics as a contextual variable in the experimental situation. We should like to emphasize that, at this stage, little is known about this variable. In our first study which utilized the demand characteristics concept (Orne, 1959b), we found that a particular experimental effect was present only in records of those subjects who were able to verbalize the experimenter's hypothesis. Those subjects who were unable to do so did not show the predicted phenomenon. Indeed we found that whether or not a given subject perceived the experimenter's hypothesis was a more accurate predictor of the subject's actual performance than his statement about what he thought he had done on the experimental task. It became clear from extensive interviews with subjects that response to the demand characteristics is not merely conscious compliance. When we speak of "playing the role of a good experimental subject," we use the concept analogously to the way in which Sarbin (1950) describes role playing in hypnosis: namely, largely on a nonconscious level. The demand characteristics of the situation help define the role of "good experimental subject," and the responses of the subject are a function of the role that is created.

We have a suspicion that the demand characteristics most potent in determining subjects' behavior are those which convey the purpose of the experiment effectively but not obviously. If the purpose of the experiment is not clear, or is highly ambiguous, many different hypotheses may be formed by different subjects, and the demand characteristics will not lead to clear-cut results. If, on the other hand, the demand characteristics are so obvious that the subject becomes fully conscious of the expectations of the experimenter, there is a tendency to lean over backwards to be honest. We are encountering here the effect of another facet of the college student's attitude toward science. While the student wants studies to "work," he feels he must be honest in his report; otherwise, erroneous conclusions will be drawn. Therefore, if the subject becomes acutely aware of the experimenter's expectations, there may be a tendency for biasing in the opposite direction. (This is analogous to the often observed tendency to favor individuals whom we dislike in an effort to be fair.)[7]

Delineation of the situations where demand characteristics may produce an effect ascribed to experimental variables, or where they may obscure such an effect and actually lead to systematic data in the opposite direction, as well as those experimental contexts where they do not play a major role, is an issue for further work. Recognizing the contribution to experimental results which may be made by the demand characteristics of the situation, what are some experimental techniques for the study of demand characteristics?

As we have pointed out, it is futile to imagine an experiment that could be created without demand characteristics. One of the basic characteristics of the human being is that he will ascribe purpose and meaning even in the absence of purpose and meaning. In an experiment where he knows some purpose exists, it is inconceivable for him not to form some hypothesis as to the purpose, based on some cues, no matter how meager; this will then determine the demand characteristics which will be perceived by and operate for a particular subject. Rather than eliminating this variable then, it becomes necessary to take demand characteristics into account, study their effect, and manipulate them if necessary.

One procedure to determine the demand characteristics is the systematic study of each individual subject's perception of the experimental hypothesis. If one can determine what demand characteristics are perceived by each subject, it becomes possible to determine to what extent these, rather than the experimental variables, correlate with the observed behavior. If the subject's behavior correlates better with the demand characteristics than with the experimental variables, it is probable that the demand characteristics are the major determinants of the behavior.

The most obvious technique for determining what demand characteristics are perceived is the use of postexperimental inquiry. In this regard, it is well to point out that considerable self-discipline is necessary for the experimenter to obtain a valid inquiry. A great many experimenters at least implicitly make the demand that the subject not perceive what is really going on. The temptation for the experimenter, in, say, a replication of an Asch group pressure experiment, is to ask the subject afterwards, "You didn't realize that the other fellows were confederates, did you?" Having obtained the required, "No," the experimenter breathes a sigh of relief and neither subject nor experimenter pursues the issue further.[8] However, even if the experimenter makes an effort to elicit the subject's perception of the hypothesis of the experiment, he may have difficulty in obtaining a valid report because the subject as well as he himself has considerable interest in appearing naive.

Most subjects are cognizant that they are not supposed to know any more about an experiment than they have been told and that excessive knowledge will disqualify them from participating, or, in the case of a postexperimental inquiry, such knowledge will invalidate their performance. As we pointed out earlier, subjects have a real stake in viewing their performance as meaningful. For this reason, it is commonplace to find a pact of ignorance resulting from the intertwining motives of both experimenter and subject, neither wishing to create a situation where the particular subject's performance needs to be excluded from the study.

For these reasons, inquiry procedures are required to push the subject for information without, however, providing in themselves cues as to what is expected. The general question which needs to be explored is the subject's perception of the experimental purpose and the specific hypotheses of the experimenter. This can best be done by an open-ended procedure starting with the very general question of, "What do you think that the experiment is about?" and only much later asking specific questions. Responses of "I don't know" should be dealt with by encouraging the subject to guess, use his imagination, and in general, by refusing to accept this response. Under these circumstances, the overwhelming majority of students will turn out to have evolved very definite hypotheses. These hypotheses can then be judged, and a correlation between them and experimental performance can be drawn.

Two objections may be made against this type of inquiry: *(a)* that the subject's perception of the experimenter's hypotheses is based on his own experimental behavior, and therefore a correlation between these two variables may have little to do with the determinants of behavior, and *(b)* that the inquiry procedure itself is subject to demand characteristics.

A procedure which has been independently advocated by Riecken (1958) and Orne (1959a) is designed to deal with the first of these objections. This consists of an inquiry procedure which is conducted much as though the subject had actually been run in the experiment, without, however, permitting him to be given any experimental data. Instead, the precise procedure of the experiment is explained, the experimental material is shown to the subject, and he is told what he would be required to do; however, he is not permitted to make any responses. He is then given a postexperimental inquiry as though he had been a subject. Thus, one would say, "If I had asked you to do all these things, what do you think that the experiment would be about, what do you think I would be trying to prove, what would my hypothesis be?" etc. This technique, which we have termed the pre-experimental inquiry, can be extended very readily to the giving of pre-experimental tests, followed by the explanation of experimental conditions and tasks, and the administration of postexperimental tests. The subject is requested to behave on these tests as though he had been exposed to the experimental treatment that was described to him. This type of procedure is not open to the objection that the subject's own behavior has provided cues for him as to the purpose of the task. It presents him with a straight problem-solving situation and makes explicit what, for the true experimental subject, is implicit. It goes without saying that these subjects who are run on the pre-experimental inquiry conditions must be drawn from the same population as the experimental groups and may, of course, not be run subsequently in the experimental condition. This technique is one of approximation rather than of proof. However, if subjects describe behavior on the pre-inquiry conditions as similar to, or identical with, that actually given by subjects exposed to the experimental conditions, the hypothesis becomes plausible that demand characteristics may be responsible for the behavior.

It is clear that pre- and postexperimental inquiry techniques have their own demand characteristics. For these reasons, it is usually best to have the inquiry conducted by an experimenter who is not acquainted with the actual experimental behavior of the subjects. This will tend to minimize the effect of experimenter bias.

Another technique which we have utilized for approximating the effect of demand characteristics is to attempt to hold the demand characteristics constant and eliminate the experimental variable. One way of accomplishing this purpose is through the use of simulating subjects. This is a group of subjects who are not exposed to the experimental variable to which the effect has been attributed, but who are instructed to act *as if* this were the case. In order to control for experimenter bias under these circumstances, it is advisable to utilize more than one experimenter and to have the experimenter who actually runs the subjects "blind" as to which group (simulating or real) any given individual belongs.

Our work in hypnosis (Damaser, Shor, & Orne, 1963; Orne, 1959b; Shor, 1959) is a good example of the use of simulating controls. Subjects unable to enter hypnosis are instructed to simulate entering hypnosis for another experimenter. The experimenter who runs the study sees both highly trained hypnotic subjects and simulators in random order and does not know to which group each subject belongs. Because the subjects are run "blind," the experimenter is more likely to treat the two groups of subjects identically. We have found that simulating subjects are able to perform with great effectiveness, deceiving even well-trained hypnotists. However, the simulating group is not exposed to the experimental condition (in this case, hypnosis) to which the given effect under investigation is often ascribed. Rather, it is a group faced with a problem-solving task: namely, to utilize whatever cues are made available by the experimental context and the experimenter's concrete behavior in order to behave as they think that hypnotized subjects might. Therefore, to the extent that simulating subjects are able to behave identically, it is possible that demand characteristics, rather than the altered state of consciousness, could account for the behavior of the experimental group.

The same type of technique can be utilized in other types of studies. For example, in contrast to the placebo control in a drug study, it is equally possible to instruct some subjects not to take the medication at all, but to act as if they had. It must be emphasized that this type of control is different from the placebo control. It represents an approximation. It maximally confronts the simulating subject with a problem-solving task and suggests how much of the total effect could be accounted for by the demand characteristics—assuming that the experimental group had taken full advantage of them, an assumption not necessarily correct.

All of the techniques proposed thus far share the quality that they depend upon the active cooperation of the control subjects, and in some way utilize his thinking process as an intrinsic factor. The subject does *not* just respond in these control situations but, rather, he is required *actively* to solve the problem.

The use of placebo experimental conditions is a way in which this problem can be dealt with in a more classic fashion. Psychopharmacology has used such techniques extensively, but here too they present problems. In the case of placebos and drugs, it is often the case that the physician is "blind" as to whether a drug is placebo or active, but the patient is not, despite precautions to the contrary; i.e., the patient is cognizant that he does not have the side effects which some of his fellow patients on the ward experience. By the same token, in psychological placebo treatments, it is equally important to ascertain whether the subject actually perceived the treatment to be experimental or control. Certainly the subject's perception of himself as a control subject may materially alter the situation.

A recent experiment in our laboratory illustrates this type of investigation (Orne & Scheibe, 1964). We were interested in studying the demand characteristics of sensory deprivation experiments, independent of any actual sensory deprivation. We hypothesized that the overly cautious treatment of subjects, careful screening for mental or physical disorders, awesome release forms, and, above all, the presence of a "panic (release) button" might be more significant in producing the effects reported from sensory deprivation than the actual diminution of sensory input. A pilot study (Stare, Brown, & Orne, 1959), employing pre-inquiry techniques, supported this view. Recently, we designed an experiment to test more rigorously this hypothesis.

This experiment, which we called Meaning Deprivation, had all the *accoutrements* of sensory deprivation, including release forms and a red panic button. However, we carefully refrained from creating any sensory deprivation whatsoever. The experimental task consisted of sitting in a small experimental room which was well lighted, with two comfortable chairs, as well as ice water and a sandwich, and an optional task of adding numbers. The subject did not have a watch during this time, the room was reasonably quiet, but not soundproof, and the duration of the experiment (of which the subject was ignorant) was four hours. Before the subject was placed in the experimental room, 10 tests previously used in sensory deprivation research were administered. At the completion of the experiment, the same tasks were again administered. A microphone and a one-way screen were present in the room, and the subject was encouraged to verbalize freely.

The control group of 10 subjects was subjected to the identical treatment, except that they were told that they were control subjects for a sensory deprivation experiment. The panic button was eliminated for this group. The formal experimental treatment of these two groups of subjects was the same in terms of the objective stress–four hours of isolation. However, the demand characteristics had been purposively varied for the two groups to study the effect of demand characteristics as opposed to objective stress. Of the 14 measures which could be quantified, 13 were in the predicted direction, and 6 were significant at the selected 10 percent alpha level or better. A Mann-Whitney U test has been performed on the summation ranks of all measures as a convenient method for summarizing the overall differences. The one-tailed probability which emerges is $p = .001$, a clear demonstration of expected effects.

This study suggests that demand characteristics may in part account for some of the findings commonly attributed to sensory deprivation. We have found similar significant effects of demand characteristics in accounting for a great deal of the findings reported in hypnosis. It is highly probable that careful attention to this variable, or group of variables, may resolve some of the current controversies regarding a number of psychological phenomena in motivation, learning, and perception.

In summary, we have suggested that the subject must be recognized as an active participant in any experiment, and that it may be fruitful to view the psychological experiment as a very special form of social interaction. We have proposed that the subject's behavior in an experiment is a function of the totality of the situation, which includes the experimental variables being investigated and at least one other set of variables which we have subsumed under the heading, demand characteristics of the experimental situation. The study and control of demand characteristics are not simply matters of good experimental technique; rather, it is an empirical issue to determine under what circumstances demand characteristics significantly affect subjects' experimental behavior. Several empirical techniques have been proposed for this purpose. It has been suggested that control of these variables in particular may lead to greater reproducibility and ecological validity of psychological experiments. With an increasing understanding of these factors intrinsic to the experimental context, the experimental method in psychology may become a more effective tool in predicting behavior in nonexperimental contexts.

NOTES

1. See reference list (Pierce, 1908).
2. Ecological validity in the sense that Brunswick (1947) has used the term: appropriate generalization from the laboratory to nonexperimental situations.
3. These pilot studies were performed by Thomas Menaker.
4. Tasks which would involve the use of actual severe physical pain or exhaustion were not considered.
5. This observation is consistent with Frank's (1944) failure to obtain resistance to disagreeable or nonsensical tasks. He accounts for this "primarily by *S's* unwillingness to break the tacit agreement he had made when he volunteered to take part in the experiment, namely, to do whatever the experiment required of him" (p. 24).
6. This hypothesis is subject to empirical test. We should predict that there would be measurable differences in motivation between subjects who perceive a particular experiment as "significant" and those who perceive the experiment as "unimportant."
7. Rosenthal (1961) in his recent work on experimenter bias, has reported a similar type of phenomenon. Biasing was maximized by ego involvement of the experimenters, but when an attempt was made to increase biasing by paying for "good results," there was a marked reduction of effect. This reversal may be ascribed to the experimenters' becoming too aware of their own wishes in the situation.
8. Asch (1952) himself took great pains to avoid this pitfall.

REFERENCES

Asch, S. E., *Social Psychology* (Englewood Cliffs, N.J.: Prentice-Hall, 1952).
Brunswik, E., *Systematic and Representative Design of Psychological Experi-*

ments with Results in Physical and Social Perception, (Berkeley: University of California Press, 1947, Syllabus Series, no. 304).

Damaser, Esther C., Shor, R. E., and Orne, M. T., *"Physiological Effects during Hypnotically-Requested Emotions," Psychosomatic Medicine* 25 (1963): 334–43.

Frank, J. D., *"Experimental Studies of Personal Pressure and Resistance: I. Experimental Production of Resistance," Journal of General Psychology* 30(1944): 23–41.

Orne, M. T., *"The Demand Characteristics of an Experimental Design and their Implications,"* paper read at American Psychological Association, Cincinnati, 1959a.

Orne, M. T., *"The Nature of Hypnosis: Artifact and Essence," Journal of Abnormal and Social Psychology* 58 (1959b): 277–99.

Orne, M. T., and Scheibe, K. E., *"The Contribution of Nondeprivation Factors in the Production of Sensory Deprivation Effects: The Psychology of the 'Panic Button,'" Journal of Abnormal and Social Psychology* 68 (1964): 3–12.

Pierce, A. H., *"The Subconscious Again," Journal of Philosophy, Psychology, and Scientific Method* 5 (1908): 264–71.

Riecken, H. W., *"A Program for Research on Experiments in Social Psychology,"* paper read at Behavioral Sciences Conference, University of New Mexico, 1958.

Rosenthal, R., *"On the Social Psychology of the Psychological Experiment: With Particular Reference to Experimenter Bias,"* paper read at American Psychological Association, New York, 1961.

Sarbin, T. R., *"Contributions to Role-taking Theory: I. Hypnotic Behavior," Psychological Review* 57 (1950): 255–70.

Shor, R. E., *"Explorations in Hypnosis: A Theoretical and Experimental Study,"* unpublished doctoral dissertation, Brandeis University, 1959.

Stare, F., Brown, J., and Orne, M. T., *"Demand Characteristics in Sensory Deprivation Studies,"* unpublished seminar paper, Massachusetts Mental Health Center and Harvard University, 1959.

Dissection IV: On the Conduct of Experiments

Nuremberg Code

1. The voluntary consent of the human subject is absolutely essential.

This means that the person involved should have legal capacity to give consent; should be so situated as to be able to exercise free power of choice, without the intervention of any element of force, fraud, deceit, duress, over-reaching, or other ulterior form of constraint or coercion; and should have sufficient knowledge and comprehension of the elements of the subject matter involved as to enable him to make an understanding and enlightened decision. This latter element requires that before the acceptance of an affirmative decision by the experimental subject there should be made known to him the nature, duration, and purpose of the experiment; the method and means by which it is to be conducted; all inconveniences and hazards reasonably to be expected; and the effects upon his health or person which may possibly come from his participation in the experiment.

The duty and responsibility for ascertaining the quality of the consent rests upon each individual who initiates, directs or engages in the experiment. It is a personal duty and responsibility which may not be delegated to another with impunity.

2. The experiment should be such as to yield fruitful results for the good of society, unprocurable by other methods or means of study, and not random and unnecessary in nature.

3. The experiment should be so designed and based on the results of animal experimentation and a knowledge of the natural history of the disease or

II Trials of War Criminals before the Nuremberg Military Tribunals under Control Council Law No. 10, The Medical Case 181 (U.S. Government Printing Office, 1949).

other problem under study that the anticipated results will justify the performance of the experiment.

4. The experiment should be so conducted as to avoid all unnecessary physical and mental suffering and injury.

5. No experiment should be conducted where there is an *a priori* reason to believe that death or disabling injury will occur; except, perhaps, in those experiments where the experimental physicians also serve as subjects.

6. The degree of risk to be taken should never exceed that determined by the humanitarian importance of the problem to be solved by the experiment.

7. Proper preparations should be made and adequate facilities provided to protect the experimental subject against even remote possibilities of injury, disability, or death.

8. The experiment should be conducted only by scientifically qualified persons. The highest degree of skill and care should be required through all stages of the experiment of those who conduct or engage in the experiment.

9. During the course of the experiment the human subject should be at liberty to bring the experiment to an end if he has reached the physical or mental state where continuation of the experiment seems to him to be impossible.

10. During the course of the experiment the scientist in charge must be prepared to terminate the experiment at any stage, if he has probable cause to believe, in the exercise of the good faith, superior skill and careful judgment required of him that a continuation of the experiment is likely to result in injury, disability, or death to the experimental subject.

TOPIC V: Survey Research: Inner Views or Outer Thoughts?

Messers. Darwin and Galton have set the example of circulars of questions sent out by the hundreds to those supposed able to reply. The custom has spread, and it will be well for us in the next generation if such circulars be not ranked among the common pests of life.

William James
The Principles of Psychology

The little men in untold legions
Descend upon the private regions.
Behold, my child, the questionnaire,
And be as honest as you dare.

"As briefly as possible, kindly state
Age and income, height and weight.
Sex (M or F); sex of spouse
(spouses—list).
Do you own your house?

How much of your income goes for rent?
Give racial background, by percent.
Have you had, or are you now having
Orgasm? Or thereunto a craving?
Will Christ return? If so, when?
(kindly fill this out in pen)
Do you masturbate? In what style?
(fill and return the enclosed vial)
Do you eat, or have you eaten
Feces? Whose?
And were you beaten?

Was your mother? sister? dog?
(attach descriptive catalogue.)
Have you mystic inspiration?
Our thanks for your cooperation."

Distended now with new-got lore,
Our plump and pleasant men-of-war
Torture whimsey into fact,
And then, to sanctify the act,
Cast in gleaming, ponderous rows,
Ingots of insipid prose.
A classic Paper! Soon to be,
Rammed down the throats of such as we.

Written anonymously (non-respondent #5542) in lieu of a returned questionnaire for Demarath-Lutterman study of campus religion and student values, 1972.

#5542's response is indicative of, at the very least, how many of us *feel* when asked to fill out still another questionnaire. Aside from annoyance (and perhaps anger) at being placed in a position where it is difficult to do anything but allow this "invasion of privacy," many are beginning to question the validity of data obtained in this manner. Under the conditions eliciting #5542's response, how many *others* felt upset enough to distort their answers? The extent of the problem is felt when one considers that 90 percent of sociological data is obtained via questionnaire and interview methods.

Being aware of the problem is not enough. E. E. Evans-Pritchard writes of what is involved in attempting *any* verbal data collection from certain populations–in this case the Nuer tribe of East Africa. Why should we consider the respondents in our own area of research to be any more cooperative?

> Nuer are expert at sabotaging an inquiry and until one has resided with them for some weeks they steadfastly stultify all efforts to elicit the simplest facts and to elucidate the most innocent practices. . . . Questions about customs were blocked by a technique I can commend to natives who are inconvenienced by the curiosity of ethnologists. The following specimen of Nuer methods is the commencement of a conversation on the Nyanding river, on a subject which admits of some obscurity but, with willingness to cooperate, can soon be elucidated.
>
> I: Who are you?
>
> Cuol: A man.
>
> I: What is your name?
>
> Cuol: Do you want to know my *name*?
>
> I: Yes
>
> Cuol: You want to know *my* name?
>
> I: Yes, you have come to visit me in my tent and I would like to know who you are.
>
> Cuol: All right. I am Cuol. What is your name?
>
> I: My name is Pritchard.
>
> Cuol: What is your father's name?
>
> I: My father's name is also Pritchard.
>
> Cuol: No, that cannot be true. You cannot have the same name as your father.
>
> I: It is the name of my lineage. What is the name of your lineage?
>
> Cuol: Do you want to know the name of my lineage?
>
> I: Yes.

> Cuol: What will you do with it if I tell you? Will you take it to your country?
>
> I: I don't want to do anything with it. I just want to know it since I am living in your camp.
>
> Coul: Oh well, we are Lou.
>
> I: I did not ask you the name of your tribe. I know that. I am asking you the name of your lineage.
>
> Coul: Why do you want to know the name of my lineage?
>
> I: I don't want to know it.
>
> Cuol: Then why do you ask me for it? Give me some tobacco. . . .
>
> After a few weeks of associating solely with Nuer one displays, if the pun be allowed, the most evident symptoms of "Nuerosis."[1]

The authors represented in this section realize that interviewing is a social situation and subject to the same sorts of tensions and cross-pressures that all encounters of this sort exhibit; as well as being subject to some tensions quite specific to interviewing as a social form. Norman Denzin has articulated this well.

> The interview situation must be seen as an interactional sequence where one person asks questions and another answers. Yet it is an encounter which has a number of emergent properties about it. Mood, affect, and involvement have to be controlled. Embarassment has to be avoided. Public and socially desirable attitudes have to be probed. Suitable and sufficient time has to be arranged and set aside for asking the relevant questions. Introductions have to be made; entrance into homes, offices, or private settings has to be accomplished. Respondents who refuse to talk, who wander, or who become hostile have to be overcome and manipulated. Guards must be ever set against duping, lying, fabrication, or stereotyping. In short, interviewing is not easy.[2]

Raymond Gorden, in "Perspectives on Interviewing," begins by analyzing how the process is both like and unlike regular communication processes in social systems. Gorden sketches in the types of interview schedules one has as options; and discusses the purposes of interviewing, from discovery to measurement. He concludes by comparing interviews and questionnaires, and suggesting ways these two tools can be used in conjunction with each other.

William Goode and Paul Hatt present a highly structured interview schedule (they note it could as easily be a questionnaire) that has actually been used in a number of important American sociological studies. Goode and

Hatt, in their comments, explain *why* the questions were asked in the way and order in which they were. Are there changes you would make in this schedule if you were to administer it today to a sample of Americans (excluding, for the moment, #5542)?

When utilizing questionnaires, probably the greatest problem of data collection is that of *nonresponse.*

> While occasionally a researcher may administer his research instrument directly to a group of subjects, such as the proverbial class of college sophomores, when other than an availability sample is used, such a procedure is generally unfeasible. Instead, the researcher commonly mails copies of the research instrument to his subjects, who are requested to complete them and to return them by mail. And even the best effort to motivate subjects to cooperate to such an extent is usually less than totally successful. What then are the implications of nonresponse for data analysis and interpretation?[3]

Calvin Endo addresses himself to this question in "The Problem of Nonresponse in Survey Research," attacking the dilemma of how one determines the characteristics of those who don't respond to one's survey to see if they differ from those who do in ways that are important in terms of the problem one is investigating.

Finally, coming full circle, John and Barbara McCarthy, in the Dissection, present in more detail some of the things that are bugging #5542, and why.

NOTES

1. E. E. Evans-Pritchard, *The Nuer* (Fairlawn, N.J.: Oxford, 1940), pp. 12–13.
2. Norman K. Denzin, *Sociological Methods* (Chicago: Aldine, 1970), pp. 185–6.
3. Billy J. Franklin and Harold W. Osborne, *Research Methods: Issues and Insights* (Belmont, Ca.: Wadsworth, 1971), p. 338.

SUGGESTED FURTHER READINGS

Deming, W. Edwards. "On Errors in Surveys," *American Sociological Review* 19 (August 1944): 359–69.

Gorden, Raymond L. *Interviewing: Strategy, Techniques and Tactics.* Hometown, Ill.: The Dorsey Press, 1969.

Manning, Peter. "Problems in Interpreting Interview Data," *Sociology and Social Research* 51 (April 1967): 302–16.

Merton, Robert K., and Kendall, Petricia. "The Focused Interview," *American Journal of Sociology* 51 (1946): 54–57.
Moser, C.A. *Survey Methods in Social Investigation.* London: Heinemann, 1967.
Phillips, Derek L. *Knowledge From What?* Chicago: Rand McNally, 1971.
——. *Abandoning Method.* San Francisco: Jossey-Bass, 1973.
Richardson, Stephen, *et al. Interviewing: Its Forms and Functions.* New York: Basic Books, 1965.

Perspectives on Interviewing

Raymond L. Gorden

To the uninitiated, interviewing is "just talking to people." Perhaps this deceptively simple appearance helps to account for the historically recent advent of systematic attempts to analyze and experiment with the interaction between interviewer and respondent. Since the dawn of civilization, man's survival in organized groups has depended upon his ability to ask a question and get an answer. Even though a certain amount of confusion, distortion, incompleteness and outright lying has always occurred in this communication dyad, there was enough success to keep society functioning. Man became curious about himself and his society and even systematically collected data about human beings in the ancient world, but it is likely that more systematic analysis of this communication process has been done in the last 25 years than in the preceding centuries. . . .

INTERVIEWING COMPARED WITH ORDINARY CONVERSATION

Just as interviewing cannot be divorced from other methods of gaining understanding of human behavior, neither can it be separated from the basic skills of ordinary conversation. Any two-way conversation involves many of the same skills and insights needed for successful interviewing. The main difference is in the *central purpose* of interviewing as opposed to other forms of conversation.

There is a tendency for those faced with the problems of obtaining information on human behavior to vacillate between two views: that interviewing is just talking to people in a spontaneous sociable way or that it is a magical and mysterious formula which allows the interviewer to put away all of his common-sense knowledge, insight and intuition. People with the latter view tend to follow a single "technique" with a slavish rigidity. During the process of training interviewers in industrial, governmental, and educational settings, it is common to hear that "here, we use the _____ technique of interviewing." This blank is filled in with such words as "permissive," "nondirective," "focused," "understanding-listening," "supportive," "depth," "structured," "unstructured," "free wheeling," "subjective," "expressive," "spontaneous," "projective," "phenomenological," "indirect," "transactional," or "psychiatric." The remarkable thing is that the same technique is often used for divergent types of interviewing situations and at all points within a particular interview.

Experience in interviewing, training others to interview, and doing research on interviewing methods, shows that no single approach, style, or technique of interviewing is adequate except within narrow limits. The interviewer should strive to increase his range of techniques and his ability to adapt flexibly to the purposes of the interview and the requirements of the specific situation.

The interviewer should realize the wide range of functions of ordinary conversation and how they relate to interviewing. If this is not done in a self-conscious way, the interviewer may be limited by habits acquired in previous forms of conversation, or be reluctant to use insights or skills learned previously, for fear that they are not "techniques" but merely "common sense.". . .

DIMENSIONS OF INTERVIEWING STYLE

* * *

Scheduled and Nonscheduled Interviews

The completely nonscheduled interview is one in which the interviewer is guided only by a central purpose and must decide for himself the means. In contrast to this, the completely scheduled interview spells out the objectives in terms of specific questions which must be asked in a fixed sequence, using specific words. It may also restrict the respondent by providing answer categories from which he is allowed to select. The schedule to a great extent restricts the techniques used by the interviewer and the form of information given by the respondent.

An interview may be scheduled in varying degrees depending on how many aspects are specified. A schedule may specify (*a*) the content of questions related to the central problem, (*b*) the exact wording of the question, (*c*) any context to be supplied with each question, (*d*) the sequence in which the questions are asked, and (*e*) the answer categories, if any, which are to be used. In the case of the completely scheduled interview, these decisions are made by the person who designs the interview schedule; in nonscheduled interviews, the interviewer himself makes these decisions. To illustrate control of interview style by a schedule, let us look at a completely nonscheduled interview, a moderately scheduled interview, and a highly scheduled interview, all concerned with the same interview topic.

Assume that we wish to discover types of conflict between parents and children and their relationship to juvenile crime. We interview a sample of children who are known to have committed no crimes and a group who have been known to commit several typical juvenile crimes.

THE NONSCHEDULED INTERVIEW

Instructions to the interviewer: Discover the kinds of conflicts that the child has had with the parents. Conflicts should include disagreements, tensions due to past, present or potential disagreements, outright arguments and physical conflicts. Be alert for as many categories and examples of conflicts and tensions as possible.

THE MODERATELY SCHEDULED INTERVIEW

Instructions to the interviewer: Your task is to discover as many specific kinds of conflicts and tensions between child and parent as possible. The more *concrete* and detailed the account of each type of conflict the better. Although there are 12 areas of possible conflict which we want to explore (listed in question 3 below, you should not mention any area until after you have asked the first two questions in the order indicated. The first question takes an indirect approach, giving you time to build up rapport with the respondent and to demonstrate a nonjudgmental attitude toward teenagers who have conflicts with their parents.

1. What sorts of problems do teenagers have in getting along with their parents?

(continued)

(Possible probes: Do they always agree with their parents? Do any of your friends have "problem parents"? What other kinds of disagreements do they have?)

2. What sorts of disagreements do you have with your parents? (Possible probes: Do they cause you any problems? In what ways do they try to restrict you? Do you always agree with them on everything? Do they like the same things you do? Do they try to get you to do some things you don't like? Do they ever bore you? Make you mad? Do they understand you? etc.)
3. Have you ever had any disagreements with either of your parents over:
   a) Using the family car
   b) Friends of the same sex
   c) Dating
   d) School (homework, grades, activities).
   e) Religion (church, beliefs, etc.)
   f) Political views
   g) Working for pay outside the home
   h) Allowances
   i) Smoking
   j) Drinking
   k) Eating habits
   l) Household chores

THE HIGHLY SCHEDULED INTERVIEW

Interviewer's explanation to the teenage respondent: We are interested in the kinds of problems teenagers have with their parents. We need to know how many teenagers have which kinds of conflicts with their parents and whether they are just mild disagreements or serious fights. We have a checklist here of some of the kinds of things that happen. Would you think about your own situation and put a check to show which conflicts you, personally, have had and about how often they have happened. Be sure to put a check in every row. If you have never had such a conflict then put the check in the first column where it says "never."
(*Hand him the first card dealing with conflicts over the use of the automobile, saying* "If you don't understand any of those things listed or have some other things you would like to mention about how you disagree with your parents over the automobile let me know and we'll talk about it.")

Automobile	*Never*	*Only Once*	*More than Once*	*Many Times*
1. Wanting to learn to drive				

(continued)

2. Getting a driver's license
3. Wanting to use the family car
4. What you use the car for
5. The way you drive it
6. Using it too much
7. Keeping the car clean
8. Putting gas or oil in the car
9. Repairing the car
10. Driving someone else's car
11. Wanting to own a car
12. The way you drive your own car
13. What you use your car for
14. Other

(*When the respondent finishes checking all rows, hand him card number 2, saying,* "Here is a list of types of conflicts teenagers have with their parents over their friends of the same sex. Do the same with this as you did with the last list.")

The first of the three examples above does not provide any specific questions to be asked, but merely states the problem for the interviewer, leaving him with the choice of techniques. In the second example, specific questions related to the central problem are provided. The order of the three basic questions is indicated and some possible probes are suggested but not mandatory. Question 3 is followed by a guide of various areas of possible conflict which should be covered by the interviewer. However, neither the actual wording of the questions nor the answer categories are supplied. The third example shows how the information designated by question 3–*a* in the second example is obtained by completely scheduled interviewing in which not only the exact wording of the questions and their sequence is given, but the answers are also structured qualitatively and quantitatively.

As is implied in the examples above, an interview may be scheduled to a consistent degree throughout its total length, or certain portions of it may be more completely scheduled than others. The degree of scheduling of any portion of an interview depends upon the purpose to be achieved. . . .

BASIC OBJECTIVES OF INTERVIEWING

Discovery Objectives

Discovery indicates gaining new consciousness of certain qualitative aspects of the problem. The problem is viewed broadly to include both substantive and methodological aspects of the interview. This will become clearer as the specific discovery functions are described.

LOCATING SPECIAL INFORMANTS

In many types of surveys and community studies where the informants are not all selected by random sampling, a rough-and-ready pilot study is done to locate a certain type of informant. Often there is no need to interview all informants of this class, but several must be located because they have had certain relevant experiences. In this case, the only reason for interviewing more than one is to obtain a more detailed account of the event and to cross-check the accuracy of the informant's observations.

In this type of situation, the interviewer, often a stranger in the community, does not know whether the person he first contacts is one or several steps removed from the type of person he needs to interview. The first informant may be the type of person he is trying to locate, know someone who is, or know someone who knows someone who is. He may or may not wish to help the interviewer find the type of person he seeks. An interviewer studying the conditions which contribute toward peaceful integration of public schools would probably have to do a long series of interviews leading him to the persons involved in bombing the local school board office.

FOCUSING OF THE PROBLEM

It is helpful to think of any study as involving four interrelated levels: first, focusing the problem; second, deciding upon definite types of information relevant to the problem; third, formulating specific questions to be asked in order to obtain relevant information; and fourth, deciding upon the strategy, techniques, and tactics to be used in obtaining answers to the questions. Often it becomes apparent in the early exploratory field work that the problem must be focused more clearly on some specific manifestation of the more general problem being studied.

For example, in a study of intergenerational conflict a few exploratory interviews indicated that most of the conflict which either adults or children could report was within their own family. Therefore, the investigator, decided to focus on parent-child conflict. Further nonscheduled interviews with college students indicated that there was a sudden reduction in parent-child conflict when the children went away to college. This narrowed the focus to high school students living at home. Deeper nonscheduled interviewing showed that it was very difficult to obtain accurate information about conflicts which occurred more than a year in the past. Earlier conflicts were either forgotten or so vaguely remembered that the teenager was unable to give complete information, or he tended to dismiss the whole thing as "just kid stuff" not worthy of discussion. So the quest was further restricted to an analysis of conflicts occurring within the past year. Thus, in this study the nonscheduled interview was used to focus the problem.

DISCOVERING, DEFINING, AND TESTING CATEGORIES

Often the researcher begins a study with certain general ideas of the questions we want to ask, but with little knowledge of categories appropriate for the answers. For example, in a study of the layman's misconceptions of science we first needed to discover the layman's images of science. This necessitated a set of categories within which the images could be arranged. Since the problem called for classifying the images into two dimensions, we devised a tentative *a priori* set of categories which were to be tested in exploratory interviews. The first *a priori* dimension was called "areas of science" and included the physical, biological and social sciences. The second dimension was called "aspects of science" and included the purposes, methods and results of science. Although this system of cross-categorization was relevant to the problem, it was not clear that all the images or misconceptions people could have would fit into this system.

Therefore, using the categories in the exploratory interviewing was avoided by using a very broad open-ended question followed by a series of neutral probes.[1] The opening question was, "What comes to your mind when you think of science?" This would be followed by such neutral probes as, "That's interesting!" "Tell me a little more about that." "I see, now why do you feel that way?" etc. The respondent was allowed to follow his own free association as much as possible and very little topic control was used by the interviewer. These interviews were tape recorded and the content of the responses was analyzed to determine whether the *a priori* categories were sufficient or whether they would need some modification. Certain types of statements made by the respondents were considered very relevant to the problem but did not fall into the *a priori* categories. In the dimension of "areas of science" we found that we needed a fourth category, and in the dimension of "aspects of science" we found we needed two additional categories. Thus, in this case, the nonscheduled interview was used to determine the clarity and adequacy of a set of categories.

Once a system of categories is worked out, it sometimes appears to be "obvious" and therefore possible to have been decided in an *a priori* fashion. In some cases, the system appears to be unnecessarily complex or the definitions seem either too loose or too detailed. The only criteria by which to judge any set of categories arrived at by any method are (*a*) how relevant the categories are to the problem at hand, (*b*) whether the categories include the full-range of relevant responses, and (*c*) how reliably the information can be classified by using the system.

DETERMINING RANGE OF RESPONSE

"Range" refers to quantitative variations in response, in contrast to qualitative categories. To illustrate, in a community study of a village in an underdeveloped area, the interviewer wanted an interview schedule in which he could check the appropriate class interval representing a family's cash income per year. As an American, he would have very little idea of the range needed. Should the item on income run from $25 to $200 per year, $100 to $1,000 per year or $500 to $5,000 per year? In some cases, studies of income have already been done so that exploratory interviewing is not necessary. However, sometimes nothing is published on the problem, or only mean or median figures are given with no range. Here the nonscheduled interview can determine the range of responses.

DETERMINING BEST SEQUENCE OF QUESTIONS

In many interviews there is a natural order in which the various subtopics seem to flow. In some studies the natural flow will follow the same sequence for nearly all respondents. In other cases, it will vary depending upon the type of respondent. For example, Schatzman and Strauss[2] found that this pattern varied with social class. In some cases, the order of the topic will be different for each individual. The best way to discover the natural order of topics and the degree to which a given order is either general or individualized is to interview a small sample, exerting *minimal topic control*. Each respondent is thus allowed to follow his own inclinations. If a given sequence of topics is found to be general, it is then feasible to use a more scheduled interview. The more individualized the pattern appears, the freer should be the topic sequence in the interview schedule.

Exploratory interviews sometimes show that information obtained early in the interview is not valid because a "warm up" period is needed. This gives the respondent time for unhurried reflection and free association. In the interview it is often best to begin by discussing related events which occurred prior to whose which are of central interest to the interviewer. For example, in a study of the effectiveness of an employee information program, the main point was to discover (*a*) the amount of factual information absorbed by the employee, (*b*) his general attitude toward the information meetings, (*c*) the degree to which he believed the information he was given, and (*d*) the degree to which the employee passed the information on to other people.

Since the interview took place many days after the meetings, it was necessary to start with a question which was in itself irrelevant; but since it focused on a time immediately before the events in which the interviewer was interested, it stimulated the respondent's memory and initiated a trend of thought leading to the central focus of the interview. The interview was opened with the question, "How did you first hear about the information meeting?" This was followed by, "What happened at the meeting?" These two questions usually laid a good foundation for obtaining information regarding the respondent's attitudes toward the meeting. The information obtained was probably more valid than it would have been if the first question had been, "How did you like the information meeting you attended last week?" This question asked abruptly before the respondent had an opportunity to "relive" his experience would tend to elicit a response like, "Oh, it was nice," or "I don't really remember much about it."

Similarly, in a study to determine why people bought "Brand X" automobiles, it was found that the respondent could talk more spontaneously about his first purchase of a "Brand X" if a thoughtful, permissive atmosphere was established. The interviewer started with "When did you first drive a car?" and later, "When did you first own a car?" This helped establish a reminiscent mood, sometimes quite nostalgic, which always led smoothly into more recent car-buying episodes. By the time the more recent events were reached, the respondent was becoming aware of changes in his own tastes and motivations in car buying as well as certain consistent patterns. All this provided not only a stimulus to the memory, but also a general *context,* enabling the interviewer to make inferences and pose more searching questions.

DISCOVERING SPECIAL VOCABULARIES

Every social group has its own special vocabulary, or "universe of discourse," which is often not clearly intelligible to outsiders. We are seldom aware of this universe of discourse in our own group unless it is consciously learned as a defense mechanism against the outsider, as is done by professional groups in medicine, education, arts, crafts, and the underworld.

The plumber might complain about the philosophy professor using a lot of "big words," while the plumber himself has a vocabulary equally confusing for the professor. Often these jargons distinguish the initiated from the uninitiated. A person not only has to have the "right ideas," but must also express them in a particular way to be recognized by the group.

These universes of discourse are not always merely a protective jargon, but often provide a type of shorthand or code which may be more efficient and accurate than ordinary language. Special vocabularies are not only associated with professions and occupations, but also with certain social strata and geographical regions.

The nonscheduled interview with minimal topic control is needed to discover these special vocabularies. By carefully listening to the modes of expression the respondent uses to talk about certain topics, the interviewer learns which words can be used in phrasing questions for a more scheduled interview.

DETECTING INHIBITORS AND FACILITATORS OF COMMUNICATION

. . . We will . . . illustrate the need for using nonscheduled interviewing as an aid in mapping out possible trouble spots in the interview as well as possible "spontaneity producers" which might be brought into play. Experience shows us that attempts to empathize with an imaginary respondent to predict his reactions to certain questions sometimes fail completely. Our empathic hunches should be tested in a few exploratory nonscheduled interviews.

As an example, a social worker was interviewing Puerto Ricans in New York to determine the need for aid to dependent children. Three items of information were necessary to estimate the future budget requirements of certain social welfare agencies: whether the woman of the house was married, how many children she had, and the ages of the children. The social worker assumed that the best order of questioning would be as follows:

a. Are you single, married, widowed, separated?
b. (If ever married) How many children do you have?
c. What are the ages of your children?

She had assumed that the first question should precede the second, because a woman would be embarrassed if she first answered she had three children and then was asked whether she was married. To avoid this embarrassment, it was assumed that the respondent with children would falsely report that she was married even if she were not. In this case, however, the interviewer's own cultural values prevented her from empathizing correctly with the respondent.

During a few exploratory interviews the interviewer discovered that there was a large percentage of couples with children who were not legally married. However, these couples did *not* have guilt feelings. If they lied about their marital state, it was usually to avoid embarrassing the interviewer. The longer the common-law couple had been in the United States, the more they were likely to lie about their marital state to those outside the Puerto Rican community. On the basis of this experience, the interviewer decided to reschedule the sequence and phrasing of questions as follows:

a. How old is your oldest child? The next? The next? etc.
b. Are you married, living common-law, or alone?

This order of questioning indicated to the respondent that the interviewer realized there was no necessary connection between having children and being legally married. If, in addition, the interviewer's attitude was not one of condemnation or shock, the respondent was assured that the interviewer "understood" the situation.

The nonscheduled interview frequently discovers unexpected inhibitors or shows that expected inhibitors are not actually present under the conditions of the interview.

In order to understand why people are willing to talk about some things and very reluctant to talk about others, we must be free to explore many avenues of information in addition to those immediately relevant to the subject of the interview. We need to know:

a. how the respondent interprets the interview situation;
b. how we can influence his definition of the interview situation;
c. what "meaning" the information signifies for the respondent in terms of his own ego or social status; and
d. what the respondent can gain by talking to the interviewer.

Sometimes this type of information is obtained through skillful nonscheduled interviewing and sometimes it is stumbled upon by accident. The use of the nonscheduled exploratory interview should considerably increase the probability of obtaining this needed information since, unlike the highly scheduled interview, it does not rule out accidental findings which might be relevant.

Measurement Objectives

It is possible to combine the objectives of discovery and measurement in the same interview; but as more emphasis is placed upon one objective, the other must be subordinated. What style is best for the purpose of measurement? Generally, the scheduled interview, with high topic control, is more efficient and effective in obtaining uniform coverage, precision and reliability of measurement. The measurement is likely to be valid if the interview schedule has been constructed on the basis of results from skillful nonscheduled interviews.

Although the scheduled interview where the measurement objective predominates is used more, there are several situations in which the nonscheduled interview would be capable of more valid measurements if done by a skilled interviewer. This would be true in several types of interview situations where communication barriers would arise if the strictly scheduled interview were used.

One of these situations would be where the *universe of discourse* varies so greatly from respondent to respondent that the interviewer must vary the wording of his question and sequence of probes to fit the understanding of the particular respondent. This might be the case in dealing with topics like toilet training of children, sex behavior among teenagers and adults, and other topics dealing with private spheres of experience.

The nonscheduled interview is also needed where communication on the topic is inhibited by the respondent's *fading memory*. The interviewer must be free to exercise low topic control and to vary the sequence of questions, thus allowing the respondent to follow the natural paths of free association. To further stimulate the memory, the interviewer must be free to probe particular vague points in the story. Also, he must be free to create a mood of thoughtful reminiscence and to return to the same topic several times. In this case, a skilled interviewer can be more effective if he is free to devise his own tactics as the interview progresses.

* * *

A basically different situation in which the nonscheduled interview might be more practical for measurement purposes occurs where the measurement is simple and the respondents so few that the construction of a schedule is not necessary or efficient to validly and reliably rank the respondents on the variable being measured.

In deciding whether a scheduled or nonscheduled interview should be used, one argument advanced is that the nonscheduled interview is dangerous because the interviewer is free to bias the responses. This is true if unskilled, careless, or dishonest interviewers are used. However, bias can also be built into the interview schedule itself, offering the doubtful virtue of uniformity to the bias. We must be careful not to simply trade one source of bias for another. Neither should neatness of the interview schedule, efficiency of coding, or reliability of response be confused with the more important criterion—validity of the information. . . .

INTERVIEW VERSUS QUESTIONNAIRE

Earlier in this chapter when comparing interviewing with other basic methods of information-gathering, we did not mention the questionnaire. The questionnaire is not a separate basic method; it is an *extension* of the interview.

The most essential difference between an interview and a questionnaire is that the interviewer asks the questions orally, while in a questionnaire the respondent reads the questions. There is nothing about the nature or form of the questions or answers which can reliably distinguish the interview from the questionnaire. Thus, according to this minimal definition, an interview can resemble a questionnaire to the point where the differences are insignificant. For example, the principal of a high school requested each of the teachers to distribute 4 x 6 index cards to students at 10 a.m.; each student was to put his full name in the upper left-hand corner and write the numbers from 1 to 5 in the left-hand margin to designate the answers to five questions which were to be asked by the principal over the intercom system. In this way the answers were obtained from 1,000 students simultaneously without having to duplicate 1,000 copies of a questionnaire or to make up the answer sheets. Whether or not this should be called a "group interview" or an "oral questionnaire" is a fruitless controversy.

There are forms of questionnaires which have many of the attributes ordinarily associated with an interview. Typically, we may think of a questionnaire as being sent to the respondent through the mail, but this is not necessary. Instead, the researcher might give it to the respondent personally with an explanation of the purpose of the study and then leave. The respondent might be instructed to mail it back or to finish it by a certain time when the researcher will return and pick it up. Or, the researcher might distribute the questionnaire to a group of people and wait to collect the questionnaires as soon as they are completed. Or, even more similar to the interview situation, one researcher may personally administer a questionnaire to a single person with instructions that, if the respondent has any difficulty interpreting the questions, he should feel free to ask for help. These different ways of administering a questionnaire represent different degrees of opportunity for the researcher to help the respondent interpret the questions and to motivate him to respond to the questionnaire.

Despite the degree to which a questionnaire and an interview may resemble each other, there are certain general differences which must be taken into consideration in choosing between the two modes of gathering information.

Advantages of the Interview

1. The interview provides more opportunity to motivate the respondent to supply *accurate and complete information immediately.* This motivation factor becomes more decisive as the amount of needed information increases, as the degree of answer-structuring decreases, and as the extrinsic rewards for supplying the information decrease. Thus, motivation supplied by an interviewer would not be needed in a case where the respondent merely has to give his name, address and phone number in exchange for a free chance on a $100 thousand lottery. Similarly, the respondent will promptly and accurately fill out an insurance claim form if it is short and simple and the amount to be collected is high. On the other hand, the probability is small that a member of a random sample receiving a form with 200 complex questions about his premarital sex life would supply the information through the mail.

2. The interview provides more opportunity to guide the respondent in his *interpretation* of the questions. This interpretation factor is more important when the questions are complex or abstract and when the literacy level of the respondents is lower. There are cases where the respondents may be completely illiterate or where the reading skill is so low that the probability of understanding the questionnaire accurately is very low. Also, the more varied the respondents in their understanding, interest, and universes of discourse, the more the interviewer is needed to interpret the general purpose of the interview and the meaning of specific questions.

3. The interview allows a greater *flexibility* in questioning the respondent. The more exploratory the purpose, the greater the need for flexibility in determining the wording of the question, the sequence of the questions, and the direction and amount of probing used. When the emphasis is upon discovery as opposed to measurement, we must give serendipity a chance to operate and allow the interviewer to pursue hunches and clues he may get as the interview progresses.

4. The interview allows greater *control* over the interview situation. For example, it may be extremely important in some cases that the respondent deal with questions in a certain sequence, that he answers one question before seeing a subsequent question, or that he does not change the answer to a question in view of the context or clue furnished by a subsequent question. Or it may be necessary that the respondent not consult others in giving his answers. All of these factors can be more clearly controlled in the interview unless we use a personally administered questionnaire in which the researcher stays with the respondent while he answers the questions to one section of the questionnaire before he is given the questions for the next section.

5. The interview provides a greater opportunity to *evaluate* the validity of the information by observing the respondent's nonverbal manifestations of his attitude toward supplying the information. Although it is possible to supply certain cross-checks in questionnaires to detect the respondent who is not serious or who is deliberately lying, it is much simpler to detect, prevent and rectify such attempts by the respondent in the interview. This type of evaluation is particularly important when the subject matter or the circumstances of the interview tend to be controversial or ego-threatening.

Advantages of the Questionnaire

We have mentioned some of the major advantages of interviewing, but there are also several advantages in favor of the questionnaire.

1. The most obvious advantage of the questionnaire is in its *economy.* There are several possible dimensions to this economy. First, if we use mailed questionnaires, we avoid all of the expenses of training and paying interviewers. Also, it eliminates the cost of travel and travel time. This economy becomes more important as the ratio of travel time to interviewing time increases. Thus if we have to ask only two simple questions of a random sample of the United States population, the mailed questionnaire would be infinitely more efficient in getting the questions to the respondents. Another dimension of economy is in the possibility of administering questionnaires to a large group of people simultaneously as, for example, to an audience of a movie.

2. Under certain conditions, the questionnaire can provide a type of *anonymity* not provided by the interview. Occasionally we have circumstances in which the only persons qualified to interview on a topic know all or many of the potential respondents. This was the case when the university foreign student advisors were used to interview Colombian professors regarding their

experiences in teaching foreign students in their classes. Some of the questions dealt with the professors' philosophies and practices in teaching, which, if answered frankly, might be negatively evaluated by the Dean of their department or by the Rector of the university. These particular questions were omitted from the interview but included in a questionnaire which could be returned by mail in a self-addressed stamped envelope directly to the research center which had no connection with the university with which the professor was affiliated.

Combined Use of the Interview and Questionnaire

When we design a research strategy, we must not assume that we need to choose between a mailed questionnaire or an interview. It is possible to collect part of the information in one way and part in the other. Even in those cases where a questionnaire is an appropriate data-gathering instrument and most of the respondents will provide required data, it may be necessary to interview those who would not respond to the questionnaire. In other cases, an interview may be needed to complete or clarify the answers, even though the person did respond to the questionnaire.

Another general way of combining the two is to intersperse a questionnaire with an interview at points where the question or the answer structure is so complex that the respondent could grasp it better in writing. This allows him to re-read it as many times as he wishes and to proceed at his own speed. In some cases, the respondent is given only the answer choices in writing after the interviewer has asked the question orally. . . .

Both the interview and the questionnaire have advantages under certain circumstances, but frequently they are used as complementary instruments. Both may be used to collect related data, or the interview may be used as an exploratory tool in building a valid questionnaire or as an evaluative tool after the data have been collected by questionnaire.

NOTES

1. A "neutral probe" is a one which indicates that the interviewer would like more information on the topic about which the respondent has been speaking, but it does not restrict the scope of the topic because no specific information is requested (for example: "Tell me more about that." "That's very interesting, could you say more about that?").
2. Leonard Schatzman and Anselm Strauss, "Social Class and Mode of Communication," *American Journal of Sociology*, Vol. 60, No. 4 (1955), pp. 329–38.

The Interview/Questionnaire Schedule: An Example and Comments

William J. Goode and Paul K. Hatt

An interview schedule utilized . . . by the National Opinion Research Center is . . . reproduced below with annotations concerning the reasons for the inclusion of each item, as well as the positional aspects of the items.

The purpose of this interview was to ascertain the relative prestige standing of representative occupations in the United States, to discover whether these were constant among major population segments, and to see *why* high prestige was given to some occupations and low prestige to others. Thus the study was of the survey type rather than the closely knit experimental type. Nevertheless there had to be a rationale for the inclusion of each item. It should be kept in mind also, that while this is an interview schedule, with a few minor revisions it could have been a questionnaire, and the same logic would hold in its construction.

Question	*Comment*
1. Suppose some outstanding young man asked your advice on what would be one of the best occupations to aim toward. What *one* occupation do you think you would advise him to aim toward?	1. An opening question which invites the respondent's participation. He is asked to put himself in the position of giving *advice*—surely not a question calculated to arouse hostility. It is also well selected in that it provides a mental set toward the general subject of occupations.

Question / *Comment*

2. What do you think is the most important *single* thing for a young man to consider when he is choosing his life's work?

2. Similar to item 1 in function, thus involving the respondent more heavily in the interview. It follows item 1 because it is a logical extension of that question.

3. Last week, were you working, (keeping house), (going to school), or what?

- Working for pay or profit or doing unpaid family work on farm or in business 1*
- Looking for work 2*
- Had job or business, but did not work because of illness, bad weather, labor dispute, or temporary layoff with definite instructions to return to work within 30 days of layoff . 3*
- Keeping house 4
- Going to school . . . . . 5†
- Permanently unable or too old to work 6
- Retired or voluntarily idle . . 7
- Other main activity (specify) . 8

3. Note here that the major concern of the study is with items 3A and 3B rather than with the main body of that question. The reason for the earlier question (3 proper) is primarily to introduce the other questions without making any assumption that the respondent is employed. To have asked this question directly, that is "What kind of work do you do?" would have been a leading question which would bias the results.

*A. What kind of work do you do?

Job ____________________

Industry ____________________

*If 1, 2, or 3, on Question 3, ask A and B.

†If "Plan to change work" or "Going to school last week," ask 3B1 and 3B2.

3A. This was related to the central problem through the hypothesis that persons of "low" and "high" occupational prestige would react differentially to the prestige pattern of occupations. One finding which bore this out was that people tend to rate their own type of employment higher than others do.

*B. Do you plan to change your general line of work within the next five years?

- Yes . . . . 1†
- No 2
- DK X

3B. This was placed after item 3A because having established the present pattern of employment it is easy to answer a question about the future. Its reason for inclusion was to attempt an estimate of whether the "mobile minded" rated occupations differently from those who were not, as well as to lead up to item 3B1.

†(1). Exactly what occupation do you plan to go into?

3B1. This follows logically from item 3B and its purpose was to dis-

Question / *Comment*

cover what types of jobs represented the majority of "job intentions" among the American population.

†(2). How did you happen to decide on that occupation?

†See footnote, p. 218.

3B2. This also flows logically from item 3B as well as from a "school" answer to item 3. Its purpose was to contribute to our understanding of why people elected to enter certain jobs rather than others.

4. Now I am going to ask you how you would judge a number of occupations. For example, a *railroad brakeman*—which statement on this card (HAND RESPONDENT CARD) best gives *your own personal* opinion of the *general standing of a railroad brakeman?* (PAUSE.) What number of that card would you pick out for him? (RECORD ANSWER.)

1 2 3 4 5 X Railroad Brakeman

Try not to judge a job according to your opinion of some one person you know who has such a job. . . . Now how would you judge a . . . ? (PROCEED THROUGH LIST OF OCCUPATIONS.)

4. By this time the respondent has been involved in the interview, first by giving advice and second by telling something concrete about himself. Now the more difficult part, that of making judgments, is introduced. Note that this is introduced fairly early, before the informant can be fatigued but only after he has already almost committed himself to an interview.

4A.

1 2 3 4 5 X Official of an international labor union
6 7 8 9 0 V Farm hand

---

1 2 3 4 5 X Owner of factory that employs about 100 people
6 7 8 9 0 V Artist who paints pictures that are exhibited in galleries

---

1 2 3 4 5 X Public-school teacher
6 7 8 9 0 V Insurance agent

---

1 2 3 4 5 X Priest
6 7 8 9 0 V Policeman

4A. This begins the listing of the occupations by the prestige ratings, which is the direct approach to the central problem under study—how occupations are rated in the United States today, according to prestige.

The occupations were selected from previous occupational studies and by the judgments of experts, in such a way as to provide as full and representative a listing as possible. Representativeness was considered from two points of view—the number of employed persons covered by the list, and the adequacy of the coverage of the potential range of prestige values.

Question | *Comment*

1 2 3 4 5 X Janitor
6 7 8 9 0 V Trained machinist

1 2 3 4 5 X Traveling salesman for a wholesale concern
6 7 8 9 0 V U.S. Supreme Court Justice

1 2 3 4 5 X Musician in a symphony orchestra
6 7 8 9 0 V Sociologist

1 2 3 4 5 X Automobile repairman
6 7 8 9 0 V Plumber

1 2 3 4 5 X Playground director
6 7 8 9 0 V Government scientist

1 2 3 4 5 X Banker
6 7 8 9 0 V Dentist

1 2 3 4 5 X Radio announcer
6 7 8 9 0 V State governor

4B.

1 2 3 4 5 X Captain in the regular army
6 7 8 9 0 V Restaurant waiter

1 2 3 4 5 X United States Representative in Congress
6 7 8 9 0 V Instructor in the public schools

1 2 3 4 5 X Undertaker
6 7 8 9 0 V Coal miner

1 2 3 4 5 X Newspaper columnist
6 7 8 9 0 V Barber

1 2 3 4 5 X Owner–operator of a lunch stand
6 7 8 9 0 V Civil engineer

4B. This is included to show how informant fatigue was dealt with in so long a schedule. The occupations were listed in *four blocks.* (C and D are not reproduced here.) The *order* of these blocks was rotated by the interviewer. The purpose was to avoid the possibility that bias due to informant fatigue would concentrate on a few occupations. Spreading it around this way helped to preclude any undue influence upon just a few occupations which were listed first.

Question							*Comment*
1	2	3	4	5	X	Night watchman	
6	7	8	9	0	V	Biologist	
1	2	3	4	5	X	Garbage collector	
6	7	8	9	0	V	Garage mechanic	
1	2	3	4	5	X	Tenant farmer–one who owns livestock and machinery and manages the farm	
6	7	8	9	0	V	Accountant for a large business	
1	2	3	4	5	X	Architect	
6	7	8	9	0	V	Railroad section hand	
1	2	3	4	5	X	Psychologist	
6	7	8	9	0	V	Airline pilot	
1	2	3	4	5	X	Manager of a small store in a city	
6	7	8	9	0	V	Bartender	

5. When you say that certain jobs have "Excellent standing," what do you think is the *one main* thing about such jobs that gives this standing?

5. This item is aimed at finding out what people think of as being the *basis* for prestige rankings. It is placed here because the respondent has already made a good many judgments as to the standing of occupations, so that the question is much more concrete than it would have been had it preceded the items on the specific occupations.

6. A good many people don't know exactly what a *nuclear physicist* does, but what is your *general* idea of what he does?

6. This item would not normally be included in a study of this kind since it does not really bear on the central problem. Its inclusion here was purely because of its topical interest.

7. About how much schooling do you think most young men need these days to get along well in the world? (PROBE FOR SPECIFIC ANSWERS.)

7. This item was included to secure a measure of the extent to which people feel that education is necessary to getting ahead vocationally.

Question	*Comment*
8. May I ask your age? ________ Circle if estimated 1	8. This is the first question of the factual as opposed to the opinion items on the schedule. Note that the wording avoids the bluntness of simply asking "How old are you?" The purpose of this item is to test the hypothesis that people of different age groups rate jobs differently. It is also included, as are several of the items in the section, to provide a check on the representativeness of the sample, for we can compare the results with national census data.
9. (ASK EVERYBODY UNDER 45): Did you serve in any of the armed forces in World War II? Yes . . . . 1* No . . . . 2 *(IF "YES," CIRCLE ONE): Army . . 1 Marines . . . 3 Navy . . . 2 Coast Guard . 4	9. This was included to see whether military experience seemed to provide any particular kinds of reactions to the prestige of occupations. This hypothesis was not borne out, and the preliminary findings showing that breakdowns by branch of service yielded such small numbers that these facts were not even tabulated. Except for the purposes of checking the sample this could be considered a wasted item. Almost every schedule or questionnaire will have a least one such result, since it is usually impossible to know enough in advance to include only items which will prove useful.
10. Who is the main earner in your family? Respondent is main earner . . 1 Some other member of family is main earner . . . . . 2* (Relationship to respondent)	10. The purpose of this item is to learn whether the informant is the head of the household. It also seems to introduce the next question concerning the occupation of the head of the household.
*10A. (ASK IF RESPONDENT NOT MAIN EARNER): What kind of work does (he) (she) do? Job________________ Industry ________________	10A. This information is for the purpose of securing an occupational identification of the head of the household, as providing further information on the hypothesis stated above under item 3A.

Question	*Comment*
	Note that, as in item 3A, the question does not ask for occupation but asks for a job description and the kind of industry in which the job is held. This allows for much greater accuracy in recording employment, since occupational designations can be sometimes misleading.
11. What is (was) your father's main occupation? ________________	11. This item was included to gather data on a subarea of interest, that of intergenerational occupational mobility. Thus the answer to this item can be compared with the answer to item 3A. Because of the difficulty of recall it was necessary to ask only for *main occupation* rather than job and industry in this case.
12. What is (was) *his* father's main occupation? ________________	12. The same as item 11.
13. (ASK EVERYONE BUT RURAL FARM QUOTA RESPONDENTS): Do you or your family rent or own the place where you live? Rent . . . . 1* Own . . . . 2† Special conditions (specify) . . . . . . 3 Room and board . . . . . 4 (ENCIRCLE IF RESPONDENT FILLS RURAL FARM QUOTA) 5	13. This item was included as a measure of socioeconomic status and as a check on the representativeness of the sample, while also introducing items 13A and 13B.
*13A. (IF "RENT"): May I ask about how much rent you pay each month? $ ____________	13A and 13B. These are included to test the hypothesis that different levels of socioeconomic status react differentially to the prestige pattern of occupations.
†13B. (IF "OWN"): May I ask about how much you think your house would rent for, unfurnished and without utilities? $ ____________	

Question	*Comment*
14. Do you remember the name of the last school you went to? ______ What was the last grade (or year) you completed in school? Completed college . . . 1 Some college . . . . . 2 Completed high . . . . 3 Some high . . . . . . 4 Completed grammar . . . 5 Five to seven years grammar 6 One to four years grammar 7 No formal schooling . . . 8	14. This item was included to test the hypothesis that amount of education is an important determinant of occupational judgments. Note the way this question is phrased in asking for the name of the last school attended. This serves to introduce the question in a gentle fashion, at the same time so focusing the respondent's attention that an accurate instead of a "stock" answer will be forthcoming. The interviewer, of course, had no actual interest in the name of the school as such. This item also serves as a check on the representativeness of the sample, since the tabulations can be compared with census figures.
15. Did you favor Roosevelt or Dewey in the last Presidential election? Roosevelt . . . . 1 Dewey . . . . 2 Neither . . . . 3 Don't remember X	15. This item was an attempt to link some measure of "liberalism" with patterns of occupational prestige. It did not prove very useful in the analysis.
16. Did you happen to vote, or were you unable to for some reason? Did vote . . . . 1 Didn't vote . . . . 2 Too young to vote . . . . 3 Don't remember X	16. This item was aimed at associating political participation with occupational attitudes, but did not prove very useful. Note, however, the cautious method of phrasing so as to prevent possible embarrassment on the part of the informant.
17. SEX Male . . . . 1 Female . . . . 2 18. RACE White . . . . 1 Negro . . . . 2 19. ECONOMIC LEVEL (Rate everybody) A 1 B 2 C 3 D 4	17, 18, 19 and 20. These items are not asked but are observed by interviewer, in accordance with instructions provided him. Note the completeness of identification which these provide. It is important to have this as complete as the situation will allow, to aid in controlling errors and rechecking where it becomes necessary.

Question	*Comment*
ADDRESS Street ________ City ________ State ______ Interviewer's Signature ______	
20. Record date interview was made:	

The Problem of Nonresponse in Survey Research

Calvin M. Endo

INTRODUCTION

One of the most commonly used methods in sociology, and in several other areas of information gathering as well, is the *survey*. Marketing researchers, public opinion pollsters, politicians, and others routinely rely on this method. A manufacturer uses the survey to determine whether a new product will sell; the newspaper polls the public for opinions on the legalization of marijuana, on the return of the death penalty for certain crimes, and on countless other social issues; and the political candidate relies on a survey of his district to ascertain his chances for success in the upcoming election. Examples of the use of surveys in everyday life are infinite.

Frequently, however, the results of surveys are not consistent with actual outcomes. The no-tar, no-nicotine cigarette made of shredded cabbage, so positively regarded in the preintroductory survey, fails on the market. The

This article was written especially for this volume. Printed by permission of the author.

candidate whose poll a week before the election indicated a win by a 5 percent margin finds himself in the loser's column on election night.

Such cases of inaccurate predictions affect the usefulness and acceptance of the survey as a valid scientific method. For this reason, social scientists devote much time and effort to developing and improving survey procedures in order to increase their accuracy of prediction.

One of the primary explanations for the frequent failure of surveys is inherent in the method itself. That is, there may not be a perfect correlation between a person's attitude—or report of how he will act—and his actual behavior. As long as the researcher insists on predicting a person's future behavior on the basis of his present reports of how he will behave, the researcher will never be able to make predictions with total accuracy. According to this argument, questionnaires are administered and interviews are conducted in artificial situations totally devoid of the actual considerations and pressures that go through the individual's mind when confronted with a situation in which he is called upon to act.

Another explanation for the frequent inaccuracy of results focuses on the problems of the survey sample. The present discussion will attempt to deal with the problem of sampling error in survey research; specifically, the problem of sample bias.

From the sampling standpoint, the problems of the cigarette manufacturer and the political candidate may be due simply to the composition of the groups from which they drew their samples. The cigarette manufacturer, clearly, should survey cigarette smokers and not waste time, money, and effort to obtain a random sample of all residents in a given locality. The candidate should poll only registered voters or, more accurately, those actually planning to vote, and not a sample of all residents of his district.

The key concept is that of *representativeness.* In order to increase the accuracy of prediction to a given population, the researcher must observe—administer questionnaires, personally interview, and so on—a sample of people that is representative of that population. That is, the sample must be a mirror image—reflect the proportionate distribution of types of individuals and characteristics—of the population to which the findings will be generalized.

In survey research, probably the most often used representative sample is the random sample. The logic of random sampling is that of a procedure by which each individual in the population has an equal chance of being selected for the sample. If a random procedure is used, the sample will reflect the characteristics of the population: comparable proportions of upper, middle, and lower class individuals; distribution of males and females; Republicans and Democrats; neurotics and psychotics; and any other characteristic of the population.

Unfortunately, even if the researcher succeeds in drawing a random sample, this does not mean he can stop worrying about the problem of sample bias. One of the primary sources of bias still must be dealt with: that of bias resulting from the refusal or unavailability of individuals selected to participate in the survey. For the present discussion, we refer to such individuals as *nonrespondents* and the resulting bias as *nonresponse bias.* Anyone who has been involved in survey research is acutely aware of the problems of nonresponse to the survey. We are warned constantly of the danger of excluding nonrespondents from analysis. Textbooks make us aware of the high probability of bias in samples having an appreciable proportion of nonresponse. The point generally made is that just having drawn a representative sample is no guarantee of an unbiased sample unless the investigator is successful in maintaining the intactness of the sample. This is done by getting *all* sample subjects to actually participate as respondents.

The extent of this problem seems to be determined partly by the type of data collection instrument being used. Generally speaking, studies using questionnaires, particularly mail questionnaires, are more vulnerable to nonresponse bias than those conducted through personal interviews. The reasons are quite evident. First, it is easier for the subject to ignore the impersonal questionnaire sent through the mail or to leave blank the questionnaire administered to a large group of people at a time, than it is to refuse the request of the personal interviewer to spend a few minutes talking and answering a few questions.

Second, the researcher probably can argue more convincingly for why the subject should participate if he deals with the subject in an interpersonal situation rather than relying on the standardized "incentives" routinely printed on the cover letter of a questionnaire. Simply, the chances of gaining *access* and maintaining good *rapport* with the subject are greater in a personal interview situation.

Furthermore, people seem more willing to be questioned if all they have to do is sit and talk, rather than express their ideas in writing. Also, nonresponse may be more of a factor in mail questionnaire studies than in interviews because reading and writing abilities assume more importance in the former. It is estimated that something of the order of 10 percent of the U.S. adult population is unable to fill out the simplest kind of questionnaire. For complex questionnaires, as typically used in attitudinal surveys, the percentage would be considerably higher.

All this does not mean, of course, that studies conducted through personal interviews are free of the nonresponse problem. For example, there is an important reason for refusing to submit to an interview: the subject cannot be guaranteed anonymity. In fact, the subject may be skeptical even of the interviewer's promise of keeping responses confidential.

Another significant factor affecting nonresponse bias is the nature of the population under investigation. There is evidence to indicate that selected segments of our population are more willing to respond to surveys. Studies focusing on these people can expect relatively high rates of affirmative responses. Conversely, other segments of our society are less cooperative, thus making the problem of sample bias more acute. The following discussion will attempt to identify the characteristics of nonrespondents, assuming that if there is a significant proportion of nonrespondents, the sample will be biased by the underrepresentation of their characteristics. The empirical question is: what characteristics of the population would be underrepresented in the sample because some subjects fail to participate in the study?

CHARACTERISTICS OF NONRESPONDENTS

We are faced with a dilemma when attempting to characterize individuals who do not respond to surveys: to fully answer the question on the characteristics of nonrespondents, we need information which the subjects, by not responding, fail to make available. Consequently, there is very little information, usually no more than demographic data, upon which to base analyses of nonrespondents. Basic demographic data about nonrespondents are often obtainable from other sources such as city directories, school and employment records, and other sources. There are four demographic variables used most often in the analysis of nonrespondents: age, sex, occupation, and educational achievement.

Age

In reviewing results concerning the variable of age, it can be concluded only that there is little consistency among the studies. Several investigators have reported no significant differences in age among subjects who respond early, late respondents, and nonrespondents (Baur, 1947; Newman, 1962; Pace, 1939). Others, such as Lundberg and Larsen (1949), found those who were hard-to-reach to be younger than subjects who responded promptly. Evidence by Gaudet and Wilson (1940) indicates refusals from people of intermediate age, however, Lowe and McCormick (1955) reported a significant rise in the percentage of refusals as age increased. This last finding was supported by Abeles, et al. (1954–55), who found male undergraduates 24 years and older significantly overrepresented among the late respondents and nonrespondents in a study of college students.

Sex

The results on the variable of sex are also inconsistent. Both Gaudet and Wilson (1940), and Lowe and McCormick (1955) used personal interviews to study samples of adults, but had differing results. The former found that refusals tended to come most frequently from housewives, while the latter reported relatively more women than men responded in their study. Lundberg and Larsen (1949) also observed proportionately fewer women among the nonrespondents.

Occupation

No explicit statement can be made concerning the effects of occupation on nonresponse except for high response rates among people from the highest occupational category (professionals and executives). A recent study by Ognibene (1970) indicates that those who respond tend toward more professional jobs and higher incomes. Even this is not unequivocal, however, as some studies have found no differences on the basis of occupation. Robins (1963), in fact, reported refusals significantly *higher* among subjects in white-collar occupations.

Education

The final demographic variable, that of education, seems to be the pivotal factor in distinguishing between respondents and nonrespondents. Studies have substantiated that respondents are more highly educated than nonrespondents. Pace (1939) found for both males and females that a higher percentage of those responding promptly (as compared with nonrespondents) were university graduates. Baur (1947) discovered that subjects with less than a high school diploma responded slowly or not at all, while Lundberg and Larsen (1949) reported that the hard-to-reach were not as likely to seek formal education beyond high school as were respondents.

This writer (Ellis, et al., 1970; Endo, 1967) has uncovered related data. In a study of college undergraduates, I found that those who responded promptly to the survey manifested greater academic potential and achieved higher levels of academic success than those who responded late or not at all. In the area of academic potential, early respondents had higher high school grade point averages (GPA) and higher Verbal and Quantitative Scholastic Aptitude Test scores, while the nonrespondents had the lowest mean scores on these measures. Academic success in college was measured by first-year (freshman) GPA, cumulative GPA, and graduation from the university in a four-year and five-year period. Again, the early respondents had the highest mean GPA, both first-year and cumulative. They also had markedly higher proportions graduating in both four and five years. Late respondents ranked behind the early respondents on these variables, while the nonrespondents manifested a pattern of failure. None of the nonrespondents graduated, even five years after entering the university. Furthermore, their mean first-year and cumulative GPA were significantly lower than the 2.0 average required by the university to maintain full-time student status.

More conclusive data on nonrespondents has been obtained in studies that have gone beyond the basic demographic variables. A review of the research literature uncovers two social-psychological variables that have significant effects on an individual's response to survey research. Empirical results support the conclusions that the greater the person's integration in his social environment (in his community, social organizations, and peer groups), and the greater his interest in the subject matter under study or his knowledge of the agency sponsoring the study, the more likely the person is to respond to the survey.

In considering an individual's degree of social integration, Reuss (1943) indicated that, in a study of former college students, nonrespondents spent a shorter time at the university, obtained fewer credit hours, and received fewer degrees. Furthermore, nonrespondents included more students over 18 years of age at the time they entered college and a lower percentage affiliated with fraternities and sororities. With respect to males, nonrespondents were those who were consistently rated lower by their high school principals in ability to get along with others, initiative, and purposefulness. Apparently, as this study was done in a university setting, the student's integration within this social setting was a salient factor in his/her decision to respond or not to respond.

Other evidence of the importance of this variable can be found in several studies of adults. Donald (1960) discovered that, in her study of members of the League of Women Voters, late respondents and nonrespondents were less involved in the organization and tended to be marginal participators. Lundberg and Larsen (1949) reported that the hard-to-reach included a higher percentage with scores under 16 on Chapin's Social Participation Scale, tended to be younger in age, and included a lower percentage of married people.

With respect to the factor of interest in the subject matter under study and/or knowledge of the sponsoring agency, Reuss (1943) concluded from his study of former college students that loyalty or strength of ties attaching the individual to the institution or the sponsor of the questionnaire seemed to be a factor that favorably influenced questionnaire response. Lawson (1949), in studying attitudes toward gambling, reported that those who feel strongly about gambling, especially those interested in its effects on society or the individual, were more likely to reply to questionnaires on that subject. Suchman and McCandless (1940), studying the radio audience of a child training program, reported that those who knew about the radio program responded to a greater extent than those who had no knowledge of the program. Edgerton, et al. (1947), in their followup of contestants in the First Annual Science Talent Search, indicated that "winner" contestants made almost perfect returns for each of three followup years; "honorable mention" contestants made the next largest percentage; and "others" (also-ran) contestants had the lowest percentage of returns. The voting study of Gaudet and Wilson (1940) revealed that those who refused to respond tended to be disinterested in the election and had very few definite opinions.

Focusing on this factor, Slocum, et al. (1956) have suggested ways of getting reluctant subjects to respond. They suggest that motivation to respond to questionnaires and interviews can be increased by the researcher's conscious effort to: (1) establish an image of the social utility of the survey, in terms of the value system of the society or group under study; and (2) emphasize the special role of each respondent in making possible attainment of the maximum social utility by the survey.

In summary, empirical studies have discovered some differences between respondents and nonrespondents with respect to surveys. Of the demographic variables considered, level of educational achievement is found to be an extremely important discriminator: respondents, particularly those who respond early, are the most highly educated; nonrespondents tend to be the least educated. There is also some hint that one's occupation may have an effect on response. Subjects within the highest occupational level seem inclined to respond in greater proportion than those of other occupational categories. One must remember, however, that the evidence on the effects of occupation is less than conclusive. Indications are that analyses of demographic characteristics between respondents and nonrespondents will yield little in the way of significant findings.

The data suggests that the most important differences between respondents and nonrespondents are social-psychological in nature. Respondents, to a greater degree than nonrespondents, tend to be well-integrated in the community, in various social organizations, and in other social contexts. When studying a sample of community residents, a researcher would probably find, among those responding, a greater proportion of individuals who participate in clubs, charities, and voluntary organizations of various kinds; who are concerned with community problems and issues; and who manifest other indicators of successful integration in the community.

Furthermore, one would find among respondents those who have a particular interest in the subject matter under study and/or those who know the researcher or agency sponsoring the study. Conversely, those who are not interested in the study or who are not acquainted with the research organization would be less likely to cooperate.

The important distinguishing factors between respondents and nonrespondents seem to be those that are unobtainable without directly questioning or observing the individuals. The extent of participation in social groups, feelings of relative social integration or isolation, and attitudes about the particular topic under study, are pieces of information usually unavailable from secondary sources. One can conclude that exclusion from the sample of subjects who are less integrated socially, who have no particular interests or opinions about certain social issues and problems, and who are not interested in the topic under study will have important biasing effects on the research results. Moreover, the extent of bias due to the exclusion of such individuals cannot be measured precisely.

WHAT IS AN ACCEPTABLE RESPONSE RATE?

Despite all the concern and notes of warning, there is curiously little information—let alone agreement—on measurable effects of nonresponse on sample bias. Nor is there any accepted response rate—short of 100 percent—that, if achieved, would assure the researcher of an unbiased sample. This is surely an important consideration for every survey researcher. Some discussion of the topic seems warranted.

In their study of a sample of adults, Gaudet and Wilson found that in numerous instances "refusers" and "unavailables" cancelled each other's influence by following diametrically opposed trends. In the study, the number of unsuccessful contacts was small enough that the influence of nonrespondents was practically unnoticeable. Gaudet and Wilson (1940:777) concluded that ". . . As long as refusals constitute no more than 3 percent and the unavailables 6 percent of the total attempted interviews, and a sufficiently large sample is used, it is unlikely that the loss of unsuccessful contacts will seriously bias the final results." The question that immediately arises is how often do researchers confront such a situation of 9 or 10 percent total nonresponse in a *large* sample survey?

In any event, the above conclusion was supported by Lundberg and Larsen (1949) who attempted a followup of hard-to-reach subjects in a study of adults in Mount Vernon, Washington. They concluded that, on the whole, the personal characteristics of the hard-to-reach were not markedly different from those of the main group studied. The problem with this study was that only 56 percent of the estimated eligible population of Mount Vernon responded to the original study (1739 out of approximately 3100 persons). Of the nonrespondents, a random sample of 200 was drawn for the followup study of hard-to-reach subjects and, of these, only 44 (slightly over 20 percent) were ultimately contacted. This certainly raises some question as to the researchers' statements about nonrespondents.

Abeles, et al. (1954-55) reached a different conclusion in studying a sample of college undergraduates. Using self-administered questionnaires, they found significant differences when comparing those who responded promptly with a combined group of late respondents and those who failed to respond at all. They questioned the assumption, made in studies carried out on college populations, that the percentage of respondents, if reasonably high, is representative of the population under consideration.

My own research (Ellis, et al., 1970; Endo, 1967) involving a sample of college students responding to self-administered questionnaires supported Abeles' conclusion. The results indicated that respondents, including those who responded promptly and others who were late (contacted only through intensive followup efforts), were similar on many demographic and intellectual characteristics. The nonrespondents, however, represented a unique group of students, their unique characteristics having been discussed earlier in this paper. It was also determined that a response rate of about 80 percent was adequate for most research purposes. (Note: Undergraduate populations tend to be much more homogeneous groupings than, for example, a population residing in an urban community. Therefore, it is possible that a response rate of more than 80 percent is needed to obtain a reasonably representative sample of a more heterogeneous population.) An 80 percent return rate is feasible in studies using personal interviews or self-administered questionnaires on a limited sample; however, it does indicate the necessity for more stringent efforts in surveys using mail questionnaires. As the usually accepted margin in mail questionnaire returns is 40 to 50 percent, more intensive and systematic followup efforts are needed to increase the response rate substantially.

As a final note on response rates, another argument should be mentioned: that survey researchers may be placing undue emphasis on 100 percent sample returns (Suchman, 1962). Suchman does not mean we no longer need be concerned with sampling bias, but that we should not automatically assume that just because a sample is biased it is also worthless. We may not place reliance on the frequency distribution of the biased variable, but we may still study how this variable relates to others.

The argument can be presented more clearly with an illustration. A researcher certainly would hesitate to generalize the frequency distribution of socioeconomic status obtained from his biased sample to the population as a whole. Distributions of this and other variables likely do not reflect their proportionate distribution in the larger population. It is still possible, however, to study the relationship in these data between socioeconomic status and voting preference, or attitude toward abortion, or other variables in a meaningful way.

INCREASING THE RESPONSE RATE

I have attempted to show why the problem of bias introduced by nonresponse is worthy of serious consideration. As long as a significant proportion of sampled individuals refuse to participate in a study, the probability of nonresponse bias remains high. This problem has been a concern of researchers for several decades, as evidenced by the dates of some of the references I have cited; yet its elusiveness is shown by the lack of agreement on the extent or magnitude of bias, as well as what sample parameters (characteristics of the subjects in the sample) are particularly affected. The magnitude and direction of sample bias, then, remain problematic.

One obvious solution to this problem is to maximize the response rate. The few empirical studies available indicate that response rates on the order of 80 to 90 percent are needed to insure reasonably representative samples. Those who have undertaken large-scale surveys realize this is easier said than done. The following discussion will present some of my ideas on how to maximize the response rate.

One important factor affecting the response rate is the research instrument itself. Researchers seem to obtain higher percentages of returns when using the personal interview format; conversely, those who use mail questionnaires obtain lower percentages of returns. Self-administered questionnaire studies requiring subjects to appear at designated places and times often get high response rates (depending upon the followup efforts).

The Personal Interview

It is not unusual to get 80 or 90 percent response when people are asked to submit to a personal interview. Such interviews usually do not require a high level of reading and writing abilities, since the person is asked merely to give verbal responses to the interviewer.

The personal interview is also more conducive to gaining access and maintaining rapport, as the researcher confronts each individual face to face. He is able to use all his resources and persuasive ability to convince the person of the importance of participating in the study. Also, from the respondent's standpoint, it is more difficult to refuse the personal appeal of the researcher than it is to throw a mail questionnaire into the nearest wastebasket. Once the researcher has gained access, the problem of rapport is easier to deal with in the personal interaction between interviewer and interviewee than in the interaction between the respondent and the impersonal questionnaire.

All these positive aspects of the interview should be countered by the factor of its higher cost compared with mail questionnaires. Consideration of such costs as time, money, personnel, and other resources must go into the ultimate decision to use the personal interview over some other research instrument.

The Mail Questionnaire

The problem with this method is maximizing response. At least three basic features of this instrument have been discussed extensively in the literature: (1) the "incentive" offered to the subject; (2) length of the questionnaire; and (3) types of postage and addressing used to send the questionnaire.

Various kinds of incentives are used to impress upon subjects the importance of participation in the study. Probably the most effective incentive is money so, not surprisingly, cash payments are frequently offered to increase the response rate. The effect, however, is inconclusive. Dohrenwend (1970–71) offered an honorarium of five dollars to her sample of households drawn from two census tracts in Manhattan. She concluded that such an offer made no difference in completion rates. Scrutiny of her data indicates some differences but, as she claimed, these were not statistically significant. Unfortunately, the lack of significance was partly the result of a small sample size. On the other hand, a small payment of 25 cents accompanying a mail questionnaire significantly increased the response rate for Wotruba (1966). A number of other studies have used cash payments or prizes of various kinds, but there is little agreement about the real effect of such incentives. More important, the question of whether the increase in response rate is worth the cost involved in offering cash or prizes remains unanswered.

A less costly incentive is the cover letter, used to convince subjects to respond to mail questionnaires. Such a letter focuses on the ultimate utility of the research results, and the importance of each subject's participation to the success of the study. As mentioned earlier, Slocum, et al. (1956) suggested the researcher attempt to: (1) establish an image of social utility of the survey in terms of the value system of the society or group under study; and (2) emphasize the special role of each respondent in making possible the attainment of the maximum social utility by the survey.

For selected segments of the population, such as the highly educated, an appeal to the study's contribution to sociological (or scientific) knowledge is sufficient to elicit full cooperation. Such individuals, basically middle-class in outlook, are easy to motivate as they can readily appreciate the importance of basic scientific research.

For other segments of the population, however, it is necessary to justify the importance of the study in terms of more immediate and personal payoff to the subject. The researcher must explain how the subject will ultimately benefit from the participation, or from the research results. Often, this is done by indicating the applicability of the results in dealing with, or solving, problems of personal concern. In my own research, using a statewide random sample of households, the primary objective was to collect socioeconomic information about individuals. The cover letter emphasized the potential contribution of the data to understanding two problems of concern to all: employment, and the high cost of living in this state. It was emphasized that researchers and officials need more information before positive action can be implemented.

Using a variation of this kind of incentive, Champion and Sear (1969) developed two types of cover letters in their study of a sample randomly drawn from three Tennessee cities. One letter was identified as *egoistic* as it emphasized the benefit to the respondent. He was encouraged to use this chance to tell others what he thought about things, that the researchers were interested in what *he* had to say. The second letter was termed *altruistic,* emphasizing the direct benefits accruing to the research organization as the result of the person's response. This letter stressed the opportunity to help someone else. The researchers found a greater response to the egoistic appeal than to the altruistic one among the respondents. Moreover, ". . . Not only were egoistic appeals able to elicit greater responses from all respondents, but they were particularly pertinent where *lower-class respondents* were concerned. Correspondingly, altruistic appeals seemed to be slightly favored by upper-class (high SES) respondents." (Champion and Sear, 1969:339.)

The second feature often discussed is the length of the questionnaire. It is generally believed that response rates are higher for short questionnaires than for long ones. This argument is based on the perceived relationship between length and the time it takes to complete the questionnaire, and its complexity. The shorter the duration and simpler the task, the greater the response rate, or so the story goes.

The relationship between questionnaire length and response rate is much too simple a generalization. If all other variables were held constant, this generalization would probably hold. Unfortunately, the complexity of the relationship is not generally appreciated. Empirical evidence gathered by Champion and Sear (1969), for example, indicates that longer questionnaires (nine pages) tend to be returned more frequently than shorter ones (three pages)! Such a conclusion suggests that a number of factors (along with length) are operating to influence the response rate.

One consideration of the questionnaire itself is the attractiveness of the format. The researcher should make deliberate decisions about the type of printing or duplicating process and the quality of paper with an eye toward creating an attractive instrument. Providing adequate spacing between items for the filling in of responses is another important consideration.

Generally, researchers have felt that the use of more expensive postage (first class postage) increases the response rate. Moreover, hand-stamped questionnaires have a higher return rate than that stamped by a postage meter. Gullahorn and Gullahorn (1959) discovered that the use of special delivery postage elicited responses from those who previously had not responded. Champion and Sear (1969) reported significantly higher response rates using regular and special delivery postage as compared to bulk rate postage. It is assumed that attention to such details would add *importance* and *personalization* to the letter and accompanying questionnaire, thus positively influencing subjects to respond.

Evidence on this factor, again, is not entirely conclusive. Kernan measured the effects of both postage (hand-affixed first class stamp versus bulk rate) and addressing (letter addressed to subject by name versus letter addressed merely to "Occupant"). This resulted in four types of letters: (1) personalized/first class; (2) personalized/bulk rate; (3) occupant/first class; and (4) occupant/bulk rate. Contrary to expectation, there were no significant differences in the response rates, leading Kernan to conclude that "neither personalized addressing nor first-class postage significantly affects response rates to the mailed questionnaire." (Kernan, 1971:421.)

Kernan's results indicate a negative effect of the "personalized touch" to mail questionnaires. Rather than increase the number of respondents, the personalized letters would *suppress* response rates when subjects desire to maintain their anonymity. In this light, he speculates that the similar rates of responses to his four treatments resulted ". . . because of a *combination* of respondents' desire for participation (personalized addressing and/or first-class postage) and anonymity (occupant addressing and/or bulk-rate postage)." (Kernan, 1971:422.)

It should be stressed that response rate is a *cumulative* effect of several factors; questionnaire length in combination with the types and forms of incentive, as well as the type of postage used and the addressing of the envelope.

FOLLOWUPS

Finally, the most important method of maximizing the response rate is a systematic and rigorous followup procedure. The researcher should not plan on just one attempt to elicit responses from subjects unless, of course, he miraculously obtains 100 percent response through the initial contact procedure. Typically, he can expect a relatively low to moderate response rate, depending on whether he uses interviews of questionnaires. In a mail questionnaire study, for example, he can expect about 30 to 40 percent response to the first mailing. Consequently, followup procedures are a routinized part of any study. Sufficient time, funds, and personnel should be allocated for this effort.

Some time after the initial contact–usually in two or three weeks for mail questionnaires, less for personal interviews–the researcher initiates his first followup of all subjects who failed to respond. In the case of personal interviews or questionnaires administered to a large number of subjects at a time, this involves making new appointments with the recalcitrant ones. For mail questionnaires, this involves a second letter with the appropriate incentive and a stronger appeal to the importance of responding. Also included is another copy of the questionnaire, as the individuals surely have discarded the original one.

Again, after an appropriate waiting period, and if resources still permit, a second followup should be attempted. This may involve the same procedures as the first followup, especially in the case of interviews. For mail questionnaire studies, however, the researcher is rapidly approaching a point of diminishing returns, since the number of recalcitrant subjects who will accede at this point is extremely small. He must make a decision as to whether it is worth the high cost to maintain the full-scale followup procedure or to modify it.

Typically, if modification is warranted, it involves a shortening of the original questionnaire to get at a few pieces of information considered vital to the study. Or, the researcher may initiate a telephone interview or personal interview of all or a sample of the recalcitrant individuals, using a shorter list of questions.

Regardless of the number of followup waves included or the form taken, the important point is that such efforts are an integral part of the research design. Systematic and rigorous followup procedures are necessary to bring the response rate up to a minimally acceptable level.

REFERENCES

Abeles, Norman, Iscoe, Ira, and Brown, William F. Some factors influencing the random sampling of college students. *Public Opinion Quarterly* 18 (Winter 1954-55): 419-23.

Andreasen, Alan R. Personalizing mail questionnaire correspondence. *Public Opinion Quarterly* 34 (Summer 1970): 273-77.

Baur, E. Jackson. Response bias in a mail survey. *Public Opinion Quarterly* 11 (Winter 1947): 594-600.

Birnbaum, Z. W., and Sirken, Monroe G. Bias due to nonavailability in sampling surveys. *Journal of the American Statistical Association* 45 (March 1950): 98-111.

Champion, Dean J., and Sear, Alan M. Questionnaire response rate: a methological analysis. *Social Forces* 47 (March 1969): 335-39.

Dohrenwend, Barbara Snell. An experimental study of payments to respondents. *Public Opinion Quarterly* 34 (Winter 1970-71): 621-24.

Donald, Marjorie N. Implications of response for the interpretation of mail questionnaire data. *Public Opinion Quarterly* 24 (Spring 1960): 99-114.

Edgerton, Harold A., Britt, Steuart H., and Norman, Ralph D. Objective differences among various types of respondents to a mail questionnaire. *American Sociological Review* 12 (August 1947): 435-44.

Ellis, Robert A., Endo, Calvin M., and Armer, J. Michael. The use of potential nonrespondents for studying nonresponse bias. *Pacific Sociological Review* 13 (Spring 1970): 103-09.

Endo, Calvin M. *The efficacy of parameter estimates with fallible samples.* Unpublished master's thesis. Eugene, Oregon: University of Oregon, 1967.

Gaudet, Hazel, and Wilson, E. C. Who escapes the personal investigator? *Journal of Applied Psychology* 24 (December 1940): 773-77.

Gullahorn, John T., and Gullahorn, Jeanne E. Increasing returns from nonrespondents. *Public Opinion Quarterly* 23 (Spring 1959): 119-21.

Hansen, Morris H., and Hurwitz, William. The problem of nonresponse in sample surveys. *Journal of the American Statistical Association* 41 (December 1946): 517-29.

Kernan, Jerome B. Are "bulk-rate occupants" really unresponsive? *Public Opinion Quarterly* 35 (Fall 1971): 420-22.

Kish, Leslie. *Survey sampling.* New York: Wiley, 1965.

Lawson, Faith. Varying group responses to postal questionnaires. *Public Opinion Quarterly* 13 (Spring 1949): 114-16.

Lowe, Francis E., and McCormick, Thomas C. Some survey sampling biases. *Public Opinion Quarterly* 19 (Fall 1955): 303-15.

Lundberg, George A., and Larsen, Otto N. Characteristics of "hard-to-reach" individuals in field surveys. *Public Opinion Quarterly* 13 (Fall 1949): 487-94.

Newman, Sheldon W. Differences between early and late respondents to a mail survey. *Journal of Advertising Research* 2 (June 1962): 37–39.

Ognibene, Peter. Traits affecting questionnaire response. *Journal of Advertising Research* 10 (June 1970): 18–20.

Pace, C. Robert. Factors influencing questionnaire returns from former university students. *Journal of Applied Psychology* 23 (June 1939): 388–97.

Parten, Mildred. *Surveys, polls, and samples: practical procedures.* New York: Harper & Row, 1950.

Reuss, Carl F. Differences between persons responding and not responding to a mailed questionnaire. *American Sociological Review* 8 (August 1943): 433–38.

Robins, Lee N. The reluctant respondent. *Public Opinion Quarterly* 27 (Summer 1963): 276–86.

Selltiz, Claire, et al. *Research methods in social relations.* New York: Holt, Rinehart and Winston, 1964.

Slocum, W. L., Empey, L. T., and Swanson, H. S. Increasing response to questionnaires and structured interviews. *American Sociological Review* 21 (April 1956): 221–25.

Suchman, Edward A., and McCandless, Boyd. Who answers questionnaires? *Journal of Applied Psychology* 24 (December 1940): 758–69.

Suchman, Edward A. An analysis of bias in survey research. *Public Opinion Quarterly* 26 (Spring 1962): 102–11.

Wotruba, Thomas R. Monetary inducements and mail questionnaire response. *Journal of Marketing Research* 3 (November 1966): 398–400.

Dissection V: Why Should I Scratch *Your* Back?

Power and Purpose in Survey Research (If You Got the Money, Honey, I Got the Time)

John D. McCarthy and M. Barbara McCarthy

> Because the cooperation of the subjects in the research must be relied upon, all subjects are, in this sense, "volunteers."
>
> J. Richard Udry

It is no accident that social scientists call those who provide them with information, "subjects." Subject cooperation is not characteristic of all methods of evidence gathering in social science. Survey research methodology, however, depends upon the researcher's ability to gain the cooperation of human subjects.

That survey research tools are most appropriate for the study of beliefs, attitudes, and values is widely recognized. If a researcher is interested in discovering how people have actually behaved, asking them is often a poor substitute for direct observation of the behavior of interest. Observing behavior in natural settings, without apprising individuals of the fact that they are un-

This article was written especially for this volume. Printed by permission of the authors.

der observation is, of course, quite time-consuming as the behavior under study may occur infrequently. Consequently, sociologists rely to an overwhelming extent upon survey research tools to gather systematic evidence about human behavior and the functioning of social groups. It has been estimated that approximately 90 percent of the studies reported in sociological journals utilize survey methods (Phillips, 1971). Given this heavy reliance upon these methods, it is important to ask how researchers choose among the wide variety of available survey strategies in planning a research investigation.

The most important criterion in determining survey strategy is consistently said to be the central purpose of the research. Few would deny the central place that purpose *should* play in the choice of survey methodology. It is clear, on the other hand, that several other important factors constrain the easy translation of purpose into method in social research. The most important of these are the costs of research and the power of the researcher over potential subjects. A focus upon such apparently mundane considerations allows a consideration of the effects of the social world of the researcher upon the planning and the execution of survey research.

THE PURPOSES OF THE RESEARCH

The authors of social research methods textbooks are fond of pointing to the overriding importance of "the purposes of the research" in counseling prospective researchers about the design and technique of research. The importance of purpose seems reasonable enough, though it is more difficult to specify what this guideline may mean in actual practice is readily apparent. The most general objective of social research is commonly thought to be some form of understanding of the social world. There is by no means a clear consensus concerning how such an understanding may be accomplished; or how the objective of research, whatever it may be, is related to method. . . .

On her death bed, Gertrude Stein is reputed to have answered Alice B. Toklas' query, "What is the answer?" with, "But what is the question?" If Ms. Stein had responded instead with an answer, we would have most likely remained in the dark regarding the question. Especially since the information sought may come in response to a wide variety of questions, survey researchers believe that there are many ways to ask the same question. The phrasing of a question and the circumstances under which it is asked are subject to major variation. Questions may be asked in written form, as in questionnaires, or in verbal form, as in interviews. Questions may be highly structured with a closed set of alternative responses from which the subject must choose. Questions may be highly unstructured with the subject determining the direction and specificity of response.

Let us briefly consider the investigation of sexual behavior using survey methods. Under some circumstances, sexual behavior may be directly observed, as the work of Humphreys (1970) on male homosexuality in public restrooms and the work of Palson and Palson (1972) on mate swapping demonstrates. However, since the observation of many forms of sexual behavior is almost impossible to accomplish, researchers have relied heavily upon surveys to investigate this phenomenon in modern society. A researcher could conceivably employ any of the variations which have been touched upon. Highly structured questionnaires may be developed to discover if, how often, and under what circumstances premarital coitus is experienced by individuals. The administration of highly structured questionnaires has been used extensively to investigate this topic among groups of college students. On the other hand, almost completely unstructured interviews may be used to investigate similar questions. Cuber and Harroff (1968) typically began their interviews aimed at eliciting knowledge about the sexual behavior of "significant Americans" with the question, "What do you think about marriage?" They used no formal questions, but rather engaged each person in informal conversation on the general subject of men and women and their relationships (1968, p. 8). Allowing respondents, in the comfort of their own homes, this tremendous latitude in determining the content of the interview was very time-consuming for these researchers; some of the interviews required several days to complete.

The possibilities of question phrasing and setting vary widely between the extremes of these illustrations. A researcher must determine which of the many possibilities is most appropriate to the investigation at hand. The considerations of researchers when making these choices are important in understanding the nature of survey research.

Another dimension of purpose is the use to be made of research results, especially since political objectives have become more important *as a result of the growth of evaluation and policy relevant research in the social sciences.* This dimension may operate somewhat independently of purpose as we have thus far discussed it. The anticipated scrutiny of evidence once gathered, and the systematic aversion of social institutions to objective evaluation, influence the researcher as the choice of appropriate methods for an investigation is made. The type of sample, the form of questions, and the content of the questions are constrained by the political uses which will be made of survey evidence.

The Commission on Obscenity and Pornography, for instance, attempted to gather very careful evidence related to the effects of exposure to pornographic material upon individual behavior. Researchers asked very highly structured questions of various samples of the American population in order to specify possible effects (1970). Though in general these researchers concluded that exposure to pornographic material did not produce rapists and perverts, critics of their conclusions pointed out the tentativeness of the results by attacking the adequacy of the evidence. Imagine how easily critics who passionately believe in the pervert-producing potential of pornography could have attacked the evidence presented if it were gathered in interview situations using highly unstructured questions! The anticipation of partisan criticism leads the social science researcher to the use of highly structured questioning procedures whether or not they are appropriate for the problem at hand.

Even though there are no explicitly agreed-upon rules governing the translation of purpose into method, the objectives of the researcher and the possible uses of the gathered evidence influence the choice of available survey methods. However, a number of other factors must be taken into account when this choice is made. One of the most important but least discussed factor is the cost of doing research.

DOLLARS FOR SENSE

Incredible costs are involved in completing some kinds of survey research. Employing a professional research organization to collect interviews from a community sample of subjects, for instance, costs between 50 and 100 dollars for each completed interview; depending upon the length of the interview and the difficulty of locating the subjects. Complicated, lengthy interviews with highly specialized samples may be even more expensive. The realities of such burdensome costs has led Backstrom and Hursh to observe that ". . . cost is the overriding consideration in surveying." (1963; p. 25). National samples employing interviews are just not feasible for the individual researcher who does not have access to a professional organization, although hiring, training, and supervising interviewers for a local community project remains a possibility. The resultant savings, still assuming that interviewers would be reimbursed, may reduce the cost for completed one-hour interviews to less than 20 dollars apiece. Of course, volunteer workers may reduce these costs even further.

In general, the more working hours needed for data collection and data processing, the higher the costs are likely to be in completing a survey. Interviews are more costly than self-administered questionnaires, and community samples of subjects are more costly to contact than institutionalized groups of subjects (such as students, hospital patients, and prisoners). Each question added to an interview schedule or questionnaire adds to the total cost at some point. Additional questions in an interview require more time for each administration and more time for processing before analysis can begin. Processing the response to an unstructured question consumes more time than processing the response to a highly structured question. It is fair to say that the more closely community surveys approximate the accepted cannons of sampling and data collection, the more costly they tend to be.

The high costs of completing community surveys, then, mean that a researcher is heavily dependent upon the availability of funds in order to successfully translate research purposes into actual data collection if these purposes require interviews with community samples. During the last decade, the widely available funds from both public and private sources have enabled some researchers to bear the high costs of community surveys. While it may be true that the institutions which make these funds available exercise some control over the purposes which may be funded and therefore pursued, the researcher's own institutional position, experience, reputation, and relationship with funding sources is important in determining at least the initial access to these funds. Because well-known researchers in prestigious universities and well-respected research organizations are the most likely to gain access to available funds, they are better able to translate research purposes into systematic survey research than are others.

Take, for example, the case of Professor X, whose recent research funding has been described in some detail by Edith Green, Congresswoman from Oregon (1972). Professor X, as a result of his own reputation and his university's reputation, has over a period of years commanded large sums of money from the United States Government to pursue just about any research purpose he determined worthy within the broad area of educational problems. Congresswoman Green notes that Professor X actually used his research funds for purposes rather different than those for which they were granted, but this did not result in any diminishing of his flow of funds. Compare this situation to the financial position of the typical fledgling researcher, who might be an undergraduate student planning an independent study project or a graduate student preparing to engage in research for a doctoral dissertation at a university. The amount of money required for completing a community survey would rarely be available to this novice. If involvement in the activities of someone such as Professor X were not feasible for the beginning researcher, a community survey would be nearly impossible to complete. Without financial sponsorship, even the best of research ideas would flounder upon the realities of cost. For this reason many research ideas can rarely be put to the test by any but the established researcher. That young researchers in American social science research rely so heavily upon data gathered by others or from student subjects is not surprising.

POWER AND EXCHANGE: WHO GETS WHAT IN A SURVEY?

Gaining the cooperation of subjects is rarely discussed as an explicit contingency in planning a research program. It is only when the possible content of survey questions touches upon delicate matters that a concern with subject cooperation becomes explicit. For instance, the study of deviant behavior usually requires the serious consideration of subject cooperation. The researcher expecting cooperation in the direct questioning of a sample of secret homosexuals about their sexual behavior is likely to be disappointed. A recent attempt (Rossman, 1973) to gather information from pederasts about their behavior using the specialized mailing lists of pornography peddlers met with only minimal response. On the other hand, the researcher who gains the cooperation of prison authorities to study individuals who have been imprisoned for pederasty is likely to confront few problems of subject cooperation. The possible risks and rewards of the imprisoned pederast are quite different from those faced by the respectable community member who is also a pederast. It is exactly this problem which brings power to the forefront: how the researcher fits into the risk and reward environment of potential subjects is a crucial consideration in survey planning. It is our contention that researchers subtly and implicitly consider their power relationship with a pool of potential subjects in planning research and in choosing from the range of possible survey techniques. These considerations influence the choice of potential subjects, the content and form of the questions, and the setting in which the questions will be asked. To illustrate this argument, we shall consider in some detail the power relationship between researchers and subjects.

Exchange and Power

Power is commonly defined as "the ability of an individual or group to carry out its wishes or policies, and to control, manipulate, or influence the behavior of others, whether they wish to cooperate or not." (Theodorson and Theodorson, 1969; p. 307.) The exercise of power depends upon the amount and kind of resources under command. There is *persuasive power*, which depends upon an appeal to values and sentiments; *utilitarian power*, which is based upon economic, technical, and administrative resources; and *coercive power*, which relies upon weapons and manpower resources. Coercive power is normally physical force (Etzioni, 1968). It is sometimes difficult to distinguish between utilitarian and coercive power in actual practice. For instance, though most citizens of the United States are unaware of it, their cooperation with the U.S. Bureau of the Census in completing questionnaires is required by law. Ultimately, cooperation could be enforced by the agents of the federal government.

The resources controlled by researchers *vis-a-vis* potential respondents are important when we think of the data gathering encounter as one where the participants exchange resources of one kind or another. The researcher, upon gaining cooperation, also receives the desired information. In this reciprocal relationship, the question remains as to what the respondent gains for being cooperative and granting the required information. Normally, reciprocity in survey research is discussed as a question of subject motivation. A focus on power views the subjects' motivation as a function of the researcher's ability to manipulate rewards and risks for subjects.

A simple utilitarian resource which some researchers may control is money. It is common, for instance, for researchers in university settings to offer monetary rewards for student subject cooperation in experiments and surveys. Though not as common, it is not unheard of to offer money for the cooperation of citizens in community surveys. Indeed, many minority community leaders have argued that community members should deny cooperation to social scientists unless compensation is received, since information about themselves is one of the few resources these individuals possess. Needless to say, survey researchers take a jaundiced view of these demands, because of the enormous additional costs which monetary compensation would entail.

University students are familiar with another resource possessed by many researchers. Grades are often either used as rewards or as punishments to encourage the involvement of students as subjects. Grades may be raised for cooperation or lowered for noncooperation. University researchers regularly gain the cooperation of students for completing questionnaires through their control of classroom activities beyond the crude use of grades. Questionnaires are often passed out for completion during class time with the risks of noncooperation being left ambiguous. As might be expected, students are usually quite cooperative under these circumstances. Incidentally, professorial abuse of students as subjects has led several American universities to protect students from these excesses by university researchers.

In community surveys, on the other hand, subject cooperation cannot normally be gained directly through any command of institutional power. Researchers offer a number of rewards to potential subjects in community surveys, but they are far less able to manipulate risks. The enjoyment of talking about oneself, the importance of involvement in the scientific endeavor, cooperating with a powerful and prestigious community institution, and an appeal to self-interest are the common rewards offered. The use of persuasive power is the most common in this type of research, with the guarantee of anonymity regularly offered as a risk-reducing factor in such an exchange.

Thus far we have considered only the researcher's control over power resources. But because subjects also may control resources, the relationship between the researcher and the subject depends upon the differential in resources between the two. Offering monetary compensation to a millionaire for cooperation would likely be of less utility to the researcher than offering it to welfare recipients. The symbolic reward of involvement in scientific investigation, found useful in many community settings, is not a reward at all when it is offered to those who believe that social scientists are deeply involved in the "communist conspiracy." (McNall, Forthcoming.)

Elites and Prisoners: An Illustration

The argument we have made implies that it is not accidental that social scientists have gathered so much information from institutionalized populations and so little information from elites. Researchers are less likely to have control over subject cooperation, form and content of questions, and setting when attempting to gather information from elites than when studying powerless populations. By comparing the problems of eliciting information from relatively powerless populations (students, mental patients, prisoners, and military personnel) and elites (doctors, lawyers, legislators, business leaders, etc.), we can best demonstrate the importance of power relations to survey research.

The examination of sexual behavior among prisoners (Davis, 1968) is a most relevant study in this regard. Having gained the cooperation of prison officials, this researcher used both questionnaires and extensive interviews to gather the desired information concerning sexual assaults in prison. Further, some of the subjects were administered polygraph tests within the context of the research. The power to elicit complete cooperation (which many institutions have over their members), if lent to or possessed by a researcher, allows for great latitude in technique. Very rigid control may be exercised over the setting under which questions are asked, and the researcher may feel free to ask directly for even sensitive information with little concern about noncooperation. A researcher would probably be quite reticent to administer polygraphs and ask about homosexual rapes in a community survey.

This prison example may represent an exaggerated picture of the power of a researcher to elicit cooperation, but the similar use of rewards and punishments by institutions over their members for research purposes occurs in mental hospitals and military settings and sometimes, although often in more subtle forms, in schools. The most common use is undoubtedly in educational settings.

In contrast, let us view some elite studies to see what kinds of problems researchers often confront in attempting to question powerful people. Hunt, Walke, and Crane (1964), for instance, administered a structured questionnaire to state legislators in several American states and several other countries. Expecting problems of subject cooperation prior to beginning their research, they were surprised at the high rate of cooperation they received. Nevertheless, the sacrifice they were required to make in order to gain this high level of cooperation was to complete a large proportion of the interviews in the lounges of state capitol buildings or on the floors of state legislative chambers. No advantage was claimed for the setting in which the questions were asked, and, indeed, no researcher would choose such a setting for the administration of a structured interview if any choice were involved. The point is that these researchers were required to compromise upon setting in order to obtain cooperation from these powerful subjects.

Another very extensive study of elites, in this case Wall Street lawyers, was accomplished by Erwin Smigel (1964). He found that these subjects were initially quite reticent to cooperate in his study because many of them had little faith or interest in sociology and because the time involved in cooperating was the commodity which they offered clients for sale. It was, therefore, costly for them to spend time answering the researcher's questions. Of course, if the resources had been available, the time required might have been purchased; but Smigel was not graced with such a plethora of resources. The method of study and the sample eventually selected evolved out of the consideration of the difficulties involved in gaining cooperation from this legal elite.

The Cuber and Harroff (1968) study of sexual behavior among elite Americans is another example of a survey begun with the anticipation of problems in obtaining subject cooperation. Though these researchers did not encounter the problems anticipated, their concern was partially responsible for the choice of a highly unstructured interview. They expected that subject cooperation would be enhanced if subjects were given wide latitude in determining the content of the interview situation.

It seems fair to say that unstructured questions are more typically used in studies of elite populations than they are with either community samples or institutionalized populations. In fact, one of the most extensive treatments of the problem of elite interviewing defines an elite interview as unstructured and semidirective (Dexter, 1970). In this regard, Dexter states,

> In elite interviewing . . . the investigator is willing, and often eager to let the interviewee teach him what the problem, the question, the situation, is—to limits, of course, of the interviewer's ability to perceive relationships to his basic problems, whatever these may be. . . . Partly out of necessity, this approach has been adopted much more often with the influential, the prominent, and the well-informed than with the rank and file of a population. (Dexter, 1970; pp. 5–6.)

Research utilizing highly structured interviews to gather information from elites can be and often is done, but this does not render these encounters any less elite interviews. It is, however, precisely the problem of a difference in power which usually requires the researcher to allow the elite individual greater freedom in the encounter. The relative power advantage of the researcher when surveying the average citizen, and even greater power advantage when surveying students and prisoners, allows control in determination of the form and content of the information-gathering encounter.

CONCLUSION

Power, cost, and purpose interact with one another as the choice of survey technique is made. Since under many circumstances economic resources may be used in the exercise of power, access to funds may serve to increase the researcher's power over potential subjects. Unlimited monetary resources do not insure subject cooperation and the researcher's control over setting and the form and content of questions, however. Experienced researchers are well aware of the importance of power and access to funds in making choices among research questions. Nevertheless, systematic consideration of power and money in choice is rare. The recognition and analysis of the operation of these constraints is the best way to begin to transcend their effects upon our understanding of the social world. Social scientists certainly do not lack theoretical and intrinsic interest in the sexual behavior and mental health of the rich and powerful in America. Yet we have far more knowledge of these subjects for poor people, students, minority groups, and prisoners. This is so because, in general, social scientists are powerless and penniless.

REFERENCES

Backstrom, Charles H., and Hursh, Gerald D. *Survey Research.* Evanston, Ill.: Northwestern University Press, 1963.

Becker, Howard S. "Problems of Inference and Proof in Participant Observation." *American Sociological Review* 23 (December 1958): 652–60.

Blumer, Herbert. *Symbolic Interactionism: Perspective and Methods.* Englewood Cliffs, N. J.: Prentice-Hall, 1969.

Cuber, J. F. and Harroff, P. B. *Sex and the Significant Americans.* Baltimore, Md.: Penguin Books, 1968.

Davis, Alan J. "Sexual Assaults in the Philadelphia Prisons and Sheriff's Van." *Transaction* 6 (December 1968): 8–16.

Dexter, Lewis Anthony. *Elite and Specialized Interviewing.* Evanston, Ill.: Northwestern University Press, 1970.

Etzioni, Amitai. *The Active Society.* New York: The Free Press, 1968.

Green, Hon. Edith. "The Educational Entrepreneur–a Portrait." *Public Interest* 28 (Summer 1972): 12–25.

Humphreys, Laud. "Tearoom Trade: Impersonal Sex in Public Places." *Transaction* 7 (January 1970): 10–25.

Hunt, William H., Crane, Wilder W., and Wahlke, John C. "Interviewing Political Elites in Cross-Cultural Comparative Research." *American Journal of Sociology* 70 (July 1964): 59–68.

McNall, Scott G. To be published. *Career of the Radical Rightist: A Case Study of a Radical Political Organization.*

Palson, C., and Palson, R. "Swinging in Wedlock: Mate Swapping." *Society* 9 (February 1972): 28–37.

Phillips, Derek L. *Knowledge For What?* Chicago: Rand McNally and Co., 1971.

____. *Abandoning Method.* San Francisco: Jossey-Bass Publishers, 1973.

Report of the Commission on Obscenity and Pornography. New York: Bantam Books, 1970.

Rossman, Parker. "The Pederasts." *Society* 10 (March/April 1973): 28–35.

Selltiz, Claire, Johoda, Marie, Deutsch, Morton, and Cook, Stuart W. *Research Methods in Social Relations.* New York: Holt, Rinehart and Winston, 1962.

Smigel, Erwin O. *The Wall Street Lawyer.* Glencoe: The Free Press, 1964.

Theodorson, George A., and Theodorson, Achilles G. *The Modern Dictionary of Sociology.* New York: Thomas Y. Crowell Co., 1969.

TOPIC VI: Naturalistic Inquiry: Roles, Rules, and Ruses in the Field

You have been told to go grubbing in the library, thereby accumulating a mass of notes and a liberal coating of grime. You have been told to choose problems wherever you can find musty stacks of routine records based on trivial schedules prepared by tired bureaucrats and filled out by reluctant applicants for aid or fussy do-gooders or indifferent clerks. This is called "getting your hands dirty in real research." Those who thus counsel you are wise and honorable; the reasons they offer are of great value. But one thing more is needful; first-hand observation. Go and sit in the lounges of the luxury hotels and on the doorsteps of the flophouses; sit on the Gold Coast settees and on the slum shakedowns; sit in Orchestra Hall and in the Star and Garter Burlesk. In short, gentlemen, go get the seat of your pants dirty in *real* research.

Robert E. Park
Unpublished statement recorded
by Howard Becker while a
graduate student at Chicago, 1920's.

Naturalistic inquiry, as a method, allows you to get closer to the people you are studying–physically, emotionally and intellectually–than do the techniques of survey analysis. As with most other options, this attribute of naturalistic inquiry has both its good and bad points. The researcher is closer to the actual behavior of individuals, rather than reportage of behavior or artificial laboratory situations; yet at the same time, the researcher has necessarily relaxed control over the situation. Internal validity becomes an important problem, as does the actual time it takes to observe the specific behavior of interest, mixed as it is with all the other free-ranging behavior of individuals in their social situations.

Naturalistic inquiry can be thought of as taking three basic forms; (a) detached observation, (b) participant observation, and (c) covert observation.

DETACHED OBSERVATION

Jack Douglas, in "Observing Deviance," presents this as "the Martian situation," in which the observer remains detached from the situation he is observing and attempts to record an "objective" description of it. Douglas critiques this position because "the Martian researcher would not be able to determine . . . what *the situations for the participants* are, because the situation is almost always meaningful to the participants in terms of unspoken, taken-for-granted meanings."

A humorous example of the sorts of problems involved in describing human behavior from the vantage point of detached observation is that written by Horace Miner. Miner presents an account of various observed customs of the "Nacirema," a North American tribe—as seen from the vantage point of the Martian situation.

> The daily body ritual performed by everyone includes a mouth-rite. Despite the fact that these people are so punctilious about care of the mouth, this rite involves a practice which strikes the uninitiated stranger as revolting. It was reported to me that the ritual consists of inserting a small bundle of hog hairs into the mouth, along with certain magical powders, and then moving the bundle in a highly formalized series of gestures. In addition to the private mouth-rite, the people seek out a holy-mouth-man once or twice a year. These practitioners have an impressive set of paraphernalia, consisting of a variety of augers, awls, probes, and prods. The use of these objects in the exorcism of the evils of the mouth involves almost unbelievable ritual torture of the client . . . The extremely sacred and traditional character of the rite is evident in the fact that the natives return to the holy-mouth-men year after year, despite the fact that their teeth continue to decay. . . .[1]

Detached observers cannot "take the role of the other" in social situations with which they are unfamiliar.

PARTICIPANT OBSERVATION

In order to uncover these "taken-for-granted" meanings, researchers enter the field and actually participate with those they are studying in their social situations. Here, as Douglas points out, the researcher is at first concerned with gaining rapport with the subjects and decreasing their level of suspicion: "managing fronts and establishing trust," as he puts it.

Participant observation is a constantly changing process. Once the researcher has gained trust, he must be adept at shifting his role as the research progresses. Virginia Olesen and Elvi Waik Whittaker have described four differing roles that the participant observer should attempt to move through during the course of his research.[2] From the initial contact of the *surface encounter,* these include:

> *Proffering and inviting,* in which the researcher and those he is beginning to study each present what they feel to be the best "definition of self" for the situation, and ask for same from the other parties in the encounter;
>
> *Selecting and modifying,* in which each party helps select from the many roles and behavior patterns proffered by the other parties, those they feel best fit with *their* definition of how the situation should be structured;
>
> *Stabilizing and sustaining,* in which the agreed-upon meaningful roles and behavior patterns are translated into action in the ongoing social situation. Such stabilization is referred to by Olesen and Whittaker as "balanced instability." They explain what they mean by using their own research with student nurses as an example.

> In situations where shifting role definitions are integrated with institutional expectations, definitions of research or life roles that at the beginning of the research work well enough may not be appropriate later on. In our work we commenced the study by defining ourselves to the students as ignorant laymen who would have to be informed about the hospital, nursing practices, etc. . . . As time went by, however, . . . we . . . absorbed a good deal of rather specific technical information about nursing and medical practice. . . . To continue to proffer the definition of the ignorant layman . . . would have been hypocritical as well as unrealistic, since the students themselves were aware that we were beyond being merely laymen. We thus had to proffer new definitions of ourselves as interested, partially ignorant, somewhat knowledgeable laymen. . . . Similarly, as the students became more knowledgeable as nurses and as they changed certain life roles, perhaps married and had children, they redefined themselves to us.[3]

One should also be aware of the problems of presenting suitable "cooling out" roles as one finishes with data collection and leaves the field behind. Robert Janes has labeled this final role that of the "imminent migrant."

> The final phase, imminent migrant, was initiated by an allusion to an expected date of departure from Riverville. Very quickly, literally overnight, townspeople began a new line of interaction. References to questions about the research findings were made. These remarks occasionally contained a tone of anxiety about what kind of impression the author held about the town. . . . Several parties and dinners . . . were apparently intended to encourage the author to think well of his hosts.[4]

COVERT OBSERVATION

Participant observation also involves another problem. Sometimes called the Heisenberg Principle, this problem involves the fact that, by being a part of the situation, the researcher himself is influencing what goes on.* His very means of studying the situation influence the behavior patterns he is studying. After William F. Whyte had been studying a street corner gang in Boston for some months, his chief informant in the gang told him; "You've slowed me up plenty since you've been down here. Now, when I do something, I have to think what Bill Whyte would want to know about it and how I can explain it. Before, I used to do things by instinct."[5]

One way of minimizing this problem is to participate in covert observation—don't tell those you are studying what you are doing, but instead think up some "excuse" that explains your presence in "real world" terms. Leon Festinger and his associates chronicle just such a study in the selection from "When Prophecy Fails," the study of a social group headed by Mrs. Marian Keech and Dr. Thomas Armstrong, that predicted the destruction of the world and salvation for true believers by The Guardians, beings from outer space.

> PROPHECY FROM PLANET. CLARION CALL TO CITY: FLEE THAT FLOOD. IT'LL SWAMP US ON DEC. 21, OUTER SPACE TELLS SUBURBANITE.
>
> Lake City will be destroyed by a flood from Great Lake just before dawn, Dec. 21, according to a suburban housewife. Mrs. Marian Keech, of 847 West School Street, says the prophecy is not her own. It is the purport of many messages she has received by automatic writing, she says. . . . The messages, according to Mrs. Keech, are sent to her by superior beings from a planet called "Clarion." These beings have been visiting the earth, she says, in what we call flying saucers. During their visits, she says, they have observed fault lines in the earth's crust that foretoken the deluge. Mrs. Keech reports she was told the flood will spread to form an inland sea stretching from the Arctic Circle to the Gulf of Mexico. At the same time, she says, a cataclysm will submerge the West Coast from Seattle, Wash., to Chile in South America.
>
> Lake City *Herald.*[6]

Festinger's selection is important not only in that it presents actual examples of the methods by which one *does* participant observation, but also because it points up the dangers (ethical and otherwise) of this brand of covert research. Jack Douglas discusses this question, as does Kai T. Erikson

*This is a problem in *all* methods of study. It seems most apparent, however, in participant observation.

in his "A Comment on Disguised Observation in Sociology." Erikson contends that disguises "compromise both the people who wear them and the people for whom they are being worn." And yet, as Festinger asks, how else could data of this sort be obtained?

Finally, John Lofland discusses the art of taking field notes. As he states, being an observer is a particular—perhaps absurd—mode of being in the world. "It is a most peculiar kind of social experience, highly subject to a nagging sense of betrayal." Jack Douglas sums up the problems posed by naturalistic inquiry by stating that "reliable understanding demands a hard heart but a supple mind."

NOTES

1. Horace Miner, "Body Ritual Among the Nacirema," *The American Anthropologist* 58 (June 1956): 505.
2. Virginia Olesen and Elvi W. Whittaker, "Role-Making in Participant Observation," *Human Organization* 26 (1967): 273–81.
3. *Ibid.*
4. Robert W. Janes, "A Note on the Phases of the Community Role of the Participant Observer," *American Sociological Review* 26 (June 1961): 446, 450.
5. William F. Whyte, *Street Corner Society,* 2nd ed. (Chicago: University of Chicago Press, 1955), p. 30.
6. Leon Festinger, et al., *When Prophecy Fails* (Minnesota: University of Minnesota Press, 1956), pp. 30–31.

SUGGESTED FURTHER READING

Bruyn, Severyn T. *The Human Perspective in Sociology: The Methodology of Participant Observation.* Englewood Cliffs, N. J.: Prentice-Hall 1966.

Castaneda, Carlos. *The Teachings of Don Juan: A Yaqui Way of Knowledge.* Berkeley: University of California Press, 1968.

Cavan, Sherri. *Liquor License: An Ethnography of Bar Behavior.* Chicago: Aldine, 1966.

Filstead, William J. *Qualitative Methodology: First Hand Involvement with The Social World.* Chicago: Markham, 1970.

Glazer, Myron. *The Research Adventure: Promise and Problems of Field Work.* New York: Random House, 1972.

Humphreys, Laud. *The Tea Room Trade: Impersonal Sex in Public Places.* Chicago: Aldine, 1970.

Lofland, John. *Analyzing Social Settings.* Belmont, Ca.: Wadsworth, 1972.

McCall, George S. and Simmons, J. L. *Issues in Participant Observation: A Text-Reader.* New York: Addison-Wesley, 1969.

Zelditch, Marris Jr. "Some Methodological Problems of Field Studies." *American Journal of Sociology* 67 (March 1962): 566–76.

Observing Deviance

Jack D. Douglas

THE RESEARCH BARGAIN: THE SOCIOLOGIST'S RISKS AND GAINS IN OVERT AND COVERT RESEARCH

All problems of participant-observation involve the nature of the researcher's interaction with the people to be studied. As Martin S. Weinberg and Colin J. Williams have argued in the article entitled "Fieldwork Among Deviants," there are many phases in fieldwork interaction, but, from the researcher's point of view, the first question is: Why do these people agree to be studied? What do they get from allowing themselves to be studied at all? From the point of view of the people to be studied, the question is: Why be studied at all? And this immediately becomes the question: Why is this outsider studying us? Why does he want to talk with us? Why does he want to know things? What is he up to? Rarely does this problem not arise in participant-observer research. . . .

From the very beginning of contact, the researcher has to decide upon the nature of his own involvement, which is of crucial importance in determining whether he can reach a successful research bargain with the group he wants to study. And most important, he must decide at the beginning whether he is going to try to do his research covertly (secretly) or overtly and try to provide some explicit reason for doing it that will both communicate the idea of research to the group and be seen as justified by them.

As one would expect, there has been considerable argument, both among sociologists and those outside the field, over the whole issue of *secret research.* Two fundamental questions are involved in this issue: (1) the question of *effectiveness*—Which provides the more reliable evidence, secret or nonsecret involvement? and (2) the question of *morality*—Is secret research immoral and, if so, should it therefore be rejected by sociologists?

The tradition of field research developed by the Chicago sociologists, which is the only highly developed tradition of field research in sociology, generally involves the assumption that secret methods are both ineffective and immoral. Effectiveness is really the primary issue, since one must first decide that secrecy is somehow effective before he cares whether it is moral. Invalid information, whether morally or immorally obtained, is worthless.

The Chicago field researchers argue that the definition of oneself as a sociological researcher does not bias the observations. They believe that individuals under study may at first find the idea strange and that this may affect their observable behavior, but that they quickly get used to the idea and often forget about it. They believe the sociologist becomes a taken-for-granted presence—that is, *if* he establishes trust and *rapport,* which are, in any case, necessary to his being accepted at all or gaining entrée to the group. Moreover, the Chicago researchers generally argue that defining oneself as a member and trying to do secret research actually make many things unobservable to a researcher. There are things that members would be willing to expose to a trusted individual who is not a member because he will not use the information against members to advance himself in the organization, as ordinary members might do.

But how is one to know that these answers are correct? Howard Becker, probably the best-known member of the Chicago school of the study of deviance, argues that it is generally best to define yourself as a researcher to the group being studied, but at the same time he notes the disagreement that exists over this and has suggested that there may well be situations in which the researcher on deviance must "pass" as one of the deviants. He also notes the lack of good evidence to test the point:

> Supposing you have found your observation post, what role will you play once you are there? The major choices are to disguise yourself as one of the deviants . . . , to be one of the service personnel associated with the location (a waitress in a homosexual bar, for example), or to make yourself known as a researcher. The latter choice gives you great freedom to pursue your scientific interests, for you need not tailor what you do and ask to what would be appropriate to an occupant of either of the other roles, but can instead ask and do a great variety of things, offering science as the justification. Furthermore, you can avoid incriminating or distasteful participation in deviant activities on the reasonable grounds that, while perhaps sympathetic, you are not really "one" yourself. Many researchers feel, however, that to be known as an outsider will severely limit the amount of information one can get. I do not believe the problem that severe, but know of no evidence on the point.[1]

Neither the Chicago sociologists nor anyone else has ever systematically sought to determine the truth of such assumptions by subjecting them to systematic comparisons–that is, by doing research with one method and comparing the results with those obtained by using other methods. Indeed, the whole Chicago tradition has remained very largely an oral tradition that is unexplicated and certainly undemonstrated. Their argument seems to be that their long experience in the field has shown them that the definition of oneself as a researcher does not significantly affect the findings and it may lead to more useful information. This would seem to imply that they have tried it both ways, but this does not appear to have been the case, since they also generally have such strong moral rules against secrecy. They could quite legitimately argue, however, that in some few instances they have studied groups, in which they had previously been involved as members, by explicitly defining themselves as researchers. To some extent, for example, this could be argued for Becker's study of marijuana use among jazz musicians.[2] The researcher had been a member of the same or similar groups for long periods and then did explicitly defined research on them. Presumably, he found no basic differences between his *member knowledge* and his *researcher knowledge.* But there is a problem involved here. For this argument, were it made, would not only imply that one *should* have comparisons with secret research, but that, in fact, in these cases the researchers did *what amounted to secret research,* though without raising a moral issue.

An evaluation of the effectiveness of covert versus overt participant-observer methods is not yet possible, for we know too little about the actual effects of the different methods on the individuals being observed. It will take more systematic comparisons of alternative methods to determine the effectiveness of the methods. Even then there will be some irreducible element of uncertainty, since in order to check the validity of any findings we would have to compare them with what we know to be "true" from some other method, which, in turn, would presuppose that we already know what is a more valid method.

Strictly from the standpoint of effectiveness, it seems apparent that we should remain flexible in our methods.[3] Since some deviant groups are loath to be "revealed" to anyone, it is probable that some forms of information can be gotten only through using secret research. This would necessitate an individual's having a high degree of member knowledge, which he would presumably get only from long involvement with the group *as a member,* either from pervious membership or from a carefully controlled entrance for purposes of research. This approach has serious potential problems; for example, exposure of one's research identity, or "blowing one's cover," could prove dangerous in some cases. But for some purposes researchers may decide that the possible information gained through such risks outweighs the problems. In fact, some sociologists studying deviance have long accepted the risks. Both Howard Becker's study of marijuana use among jazz musicians and Ned

Polsky's study of poolroom hustlers were based largely on their member knowledge gained from years as members of those groups. Laud Humphreys' study of public restroom homosexuality involved the acceptance of the far greater risk of arrest and stigmatization entailed by his becoming a "lookout" for the homosexuals.[4]

Although some of the moral objections to secret research undoubtedly involve considerable academic posing and "priggishness," there are serious moral questions involved that any sociologist considering such methods must certainly face. In a pluralistic society such as ours—but one in which there is nonetheless a strong emphasis on public conformity to the absolute public morality—privacy becomes a highly valued thing.[5] This is especially so today because of the development of technical devices that can secretly circumvent the traditional measures taken to protect privacy. In addition, it is precisely such invasions of privacy that could facilitate the establishment of *technological tyrannies*;[6] and few of us wish to make a contribution toward creating a *1984*.

But while I believe we must take the moral issues seriously and move cautiously to keep from contributing to the forces of technological tyranny, I do concur with James Henslin that we must avoid any form of *methodological puritanism*. Most members of our society believe that the search for truth, while never wholly devoid of personal interests and moral dangers, is justified in itself, but we are all dimly aware of the early doctors who were suspected of ghastly crimes because of their perseverance in exploring the mysteries of the human body. And today, many people still find this secularization—and "desecration"—of our physical being morally repulsive; they cannot appreciate the common medical cast of mind in which gynecological examinations of young girls and autopsies are seen as necessary forms of medical bookkeeping and are assumed to be devoid of all moral significance for the people involved. On the other hand, most of us can also appreciate the moral courage of those early doctors which supported their "immoral" invasions of the body's mysteries, and, while we condemn the scientistic mechanism that makes some doctors blind to our human sensibilities, most of us do support the *moral exceptions* to our usual moral feelings that allow their work to continue.

There is a danger, then, that the use of secret research will encourage a moral blindness and a willingness to *use* people among sociologists, especially among those who already have the scientistic stance. Like all human action, research on deviance involves the possibility of abuse, of going too far. We must specifically guard against such abuse by recognizing it as a danger and instituting measures against it.

As doctors, lawyers, and other professionals have done over the centuries, sociologists must work purposefully to carve out a special *moral niche,* or to construct a *situational morality,* for their research activities. Exceptions to important social rules, such as those concerning privacy and intimacy, must be made only when the research need is clear and the potential contributions of the findings to general human welfare are believed to be great enough to counterbalance the risks. If we can agree that these factors are present (so that we do not run the risk of unleashing "mad social scientists" upon the world to fulfill their own Frankenstein fantasies), then we should have the courage to try to change the morals of our society and to do the research with as little invasion of privacy as possible.

. . . We must try to extend to social scientists the legal protection lawyers and doctors have from prosecution for being accessories to crimes. As Polsky so rightly argues, until we are able to do this, sociologists cannot avoid violating laws against being accessories:

> If one is effectively to study adult criminals in their natural settings, he must make the moral decision that in some ways he will break the law himself. He need not be a "participant" observer and commit the criminal acts under study, yet he has to witness such acts or be taken into confidence about them and not blow the whistle. That is, the investigator has to decide that when necessary he will "obstruct justice" or have "guilty knowledge" or be an "accessory" before or after the fact, in the full legal sense of those terms. He will not be enabled to discern some vital aspects of criminal lifestyles and subcultures unless he (1) makes such a moral decision, (2) makes the criminals believe him, and (3) convinces them of his ability to act in accord with his decision. That third point can sometimes be neglected with juvenile delinquents, for they know that a professional studying them is almost always exempt from police pressure to inform; but adult criminals have no such assurance, and hence are concerned to assess not merely the investigator's intentions but his ability to remain a "stand–up guy" under police questioning.[7]

While it is probable that legal exclusion from prosecution for such "research offenses" will eventually be given, there will be some small risks involved for a long time to come, which will have to be accepted if truthful information is to be gotten.

The case for purposeful involvement in the crimes themselves is very different. Though refusal to at least "go along" to observe the on-site action *might* jeopardize one's research relations and will certainly prevent our knowing what really happens at the scene of a crime, legal defense of such participation does not at present seem possible. In addition, this participation is generally unnecessary and can itself endanger research relations. William Foote Whyte, who took part in the illegal actions of multiple voting with his gang boys, recognized this long ago:

> That was my performance on election day. What did I gain from it? I had seen through firsthand personal experience how repeat-

ing was accomplished. But this was really of very little value, for I had been observing these activities at quite close range before, and I could have had all the data without taking any risk. Actually, I learned nothing of research value from the experience, and I took a chance of jeopardizing my whole study. While I escaped arrest, these things are not always fixed as firmly as the politician's henchmen think they are. A year later, when I was out of town at election time, somebody was actually arrested for voting in *my* name.

Even apart from the risk of arrest, I faced other possible losses. While repeating was fairly common in our ward, there were only relatively few people who engaged in it, and they were generally looked down upon as the fellows who did the dirty work. Had the word got around about me, my own standing in the district would have suffered considerable damage.[8]

THE RESEARCH BARGAIN: THE MEMBER'S RISKS AND GAINS IN THE RESEARCH SITUATION

Whether the researcher uses a *research cover* or explicitly defines his research purposes for the group, once he has answered the group members' first crucial question–What is he up to?–he will be asked the second–What's in it for me? While the economic exchange model of human behavior is a gross distortion of social interaction, nonetheless a primary concern when we first encounter a stranger who seeks to make our acquaintance is the potential value, help, bother, burden, fun, and so on, of this relationship to us: What's in it for me? What good? What harm?

Rosalie Wax has given an excellent outline to this exchange model of the research encounter:

> "Why should anybody in this group bother to talk to me? Why should this man take time out from his work, gambling, or pleasant loafing to answer my questions?" I suggest that as the field worker discovers the correct answers he will improve not only his technique in obtaining information but also his ability to evaluate it. I suggest moreover, that the correct answers to these questions will tend to show that whether an informant likes, hates, or just doesn't give a hoot about the field worker, he will talk because he and the field worker are making an exchange, are consciously or unconsciously giving each other something they both desire or need.
>
> The gifts with which a field worker repays the efforts of his informants will, of course, vary with each investigational situation.

> Some will be simple gifts like relieving boredom or loneliness. Others will be on a more complicated psychological level, like giving an informant who thinks himself wronged an opportunity to express his grievances. And, not infrequently, the field worker who comes to understand why an informant talks to him will not be particularly flattered by this knowledge.
>
> The fact that many informants talk freely because they are lonely or bored is perhaps not sufficiently appreciated by young field workers. Notebooks full of data may be acquired from an elderly person or from an individual who does not get along well in his community. The skill of the interviewer often plays a minor part in the accumulation of these data. The lonely informant has simply found someone who will listen to him.[9]

In general, the specific situation in which any human communication takes place becomes the contextual determinant of the meaning of that communication for the individuals involved. The sociologist seeking information on a group must, therefore, understand the meaningful properties of the situation in which communication occurs for the people with whom he is communicating. This is necessary so that he can analyze the ways in which the situation is determining the meanings of the communications. He must know the properties of the situation not only to determine how "true" the information is but to be able to even determine the meanings of the communications.

Specifically, in studying deviance we must be concerned with determining the meaningful properties of the encounter situation with deviants, especially the *initial encounter situation*–the *entrée situation* in which the sociologist is trying to specify his intentions in such a way that the deviants will find them acceptable and will be willing to give him truthful information. (There will, of course, be a fundamental difference between those situations in which the sociologist is trying to join the group for purposes of secret research and those in which he is trying to define himself for the group as a researcher. There is probably little that can be said of the secret research situation that would be of much help to any researcher. There are, of course, certain obvious things, such as the risk involved in disclosure or the possible problems involved in getting information from someone who simply sees you as another member of the group. Much more can be said about the encounter situation involving an explicit definition of oneself as a social researcher and, since the great mass of social research on deviants will probably continue to be of this sort, this more important situation will concern us here.)

In any situation, there are the inevitable contingencies of human interaction that can in no way be anticipated; for example, the invitations by homosexuals to Weinberg and Williams to "slow dance." The researcher must use common sense in such a situation to accurately manage it. These are, in fact, the most important aspects of any research encounter and, other than such general commentary as this, we necessarily leave them unexplicated. What we must seek in any analysis of the research situation is not specific details on how to handle the situation but general understandings or *research recipes* that the individual can use in constructing effective situational strategies for managing the situation.

As Carol A. B. Warren found during her research into the gay community, *trust* is the crucial factor involved in establishing a research relationship. This is true of the situation of deviance in general. In the deviant encounter situation, the most important factor related to trust is probably the suspicions that deviants might have about the relationship existing between the researcher and the deviants' enemies, especially official control agents. It is, therefore, essential that the researcher in some way convince the people he wants to study that he does not represent the officials and that his future statements about the group will in no way be of value to officials in controlling that group. He accomplishes this partly by his *personal style*—that is, by showing that he is not the kind of person who is apt to cooperate with officials. Although overconcern with the issue would probably be self-defeating by arousing suspicion that, perhaps, the researcher does in fact have something to hide, in most situations of overt research it is important to inform the individuals about his relations to the official world and something about his motives. Taking into consideration the obvious reasons for the deviants' suspicions, it seems likely that the researcher will at various times be subjected to testing, or "sounding," to determine his degree of loyalty to their way of life as opposed to the official way.

Ultimately, of course, actions speak louder than words, and the researcher will have to demonstrate by his actions that he is on the side of the deviants or, at least, not on the side of the officials. Today this generally means showing not only that he won't blow the whistle, but also that he shares the *way of life* of his group. Most importantly, most groups that today would in any way be considered deviant by important segments of our society make a fundamental distinction between the *hip* and the *square* (though the terms vary greatly). The hip are those who know and share, or sympathize with, the way of life of the "deviant" group; the square are those who oppose that way of life, who categorize it as "deviant" by opposing it to their own. The hip way of life includes not only external signs but also the beliefs and feelings of the group that such signs represent. Given the fact that so many deviants assume that they are under siege by the squares, it is highly unlikely that any sociologist would be able to study them without appearing to share to at least some minimal degree their way of life and without appearing to be quite independent of the square world. To most deviants anything else will seem too risky, if not because of potential disclosure to the officials, then because of the implied attack on them that involvement in the square world constitutes.

Our discussion of establishing trust and gaining entrée thus far would seem to fall into the usual mode of treating these subjects in fieldwork analyses, but we must not conclude that this is all there is to trust and maintaining one's research relations. In the traditional treatments of these subjects, once the researcher has established trust and gained entrée, that's all there is to it; he then can spend all his time observing the truth. In fact, as John Johnson has shown in his own studies, field research is a *developmental process*, always changing and fluid.[10] The person who trusts you today may see you as his enemy tomorrow. The person who appears to trust you may be doing so to be better able to hide things from you. Actually, this should not be so surprising, since the same is true of most human relationships. Marriage partners of 25 years, for example, may suddenly find reason to suspect each other and to hide things from each other. There are no easy paths to observing deviant groups, no guarantees that relations once established will not be destroyed or used against the researcher. The researcher must continually deal with the problems of building trust and maintaining his lines of information.

On balance, there might appear to be little reason why deviants would choose to be studied. But there is a crucial aspect to the situation of deviance in our society that makes it very likely that most deviants will in fact want to be studied. And if the researcher can in some way point it out, it seems likely that the deviants will be more willing to participate with him. Like most people, deviants are interested in themselves and see themselves as people whom others would find interesting; as such, they prize publicity highly. But, unlike people defined as "normal," deviants experience a profound public relations problem and are often anxious to have somebody "study them," especially if such study will result in a book. In addition to their desire for the world to see what they are like, they also often want to justify themselves to the world or to show that they are superior to those who consider them "deviants." Even though professional criminals are among the *least* concerned with public relations, Edwin Sutherland, David Mauer, Ned Polsky, and a few others who have sucessfully studied them have found that they too are very interested in being studied and in being written about.[11] In fact, many professional criminals (or exprofessionals) have written their own books.

The nonprofessional deviants are often even more anxious to be studied. A basic reason for their becoming "deviants," for joining the group and accepting the social categorization of themselves as "deviants," is often the desire to show that they are different from the rest of the world, especially the square world. This is especially true today of some young people, such as those who use marijuana or hard drugs. In many cases, the deviance becomes a symbolic device by which they dramatize their rejection of the square (middle-class) world, and by being studied they can communicate their rejection of this world. It becomes a stimulus to self-dramatization and can be extremely valuable to them. This is, presumably, the basic reason why such young deviants today are often very open about their deviance and are willing, even anxious, to be studied–and even, sometimes, to have their names used.

By utilizing this desire on the part of deviants to be studied, to have their way of life openly communicated "like it is" to the rest of society, the sociologist, if he is trusted and respected, can generally get cooperation in his research. As Polsky has shown from his own experience, the barrier against everyday-life studies of deviants has been created almost entirely by sociologists as a result of their own fears of the deviants rather than as a result of deviants' reluctance to be studied.[12]

However, for the researchers, the willingness of deviants to be studied can produce the same kind of difficulties as their fear of exposure. One of the not uncommon problems is the desire of deviants to be paid by the researcher for the information they give when they suspect that the researcher will be writing a book or that the researcher himself is paid for this kind of research. In one instance, a student doing a study of call girls immediately encountered a demand for payment. In such a case, paying for information would defeat the purpose of the research, for it would probably call forth on the part of the deviant extreme dramatizations and fronts common to that form of deviance. Call girls are aware that there are many highly successful and profitable books written about their occupation—books that are successful because they constitute a kind of publicly acceptable pornography. Thus they assume that anyone writing such a book would be interested primarily in lurid descriptions rather than in mundane everyday details, and they would be very apt to strain to find lurid details for a researcher willing to pay. To avoid such presentations of the lives of deviants, the sociologist must avoid paying them or intimating in any way that the research he is doing may prove remunerative. When the student studying call girls told them firmly that he had no money for the research and did not expect to get any (which was in fact the case), he did not face any further problem. They were then willing for him to do the research and were anxious in many ways to tell him about their lives.

The fundamental problem here, however, is the danger that the anxious concern of the deviant to present himself to the rest of the world through the work of the researcher will result in self-dramatizations. Research involving explicit definition of the researcher will always face this problem to some degree, and it can only be solved by comparing the results of such research with those of secret research.

But we have little reason at this time to believe that this *uncertainty effect* —that is, the effect of the method of observation on the resulting observations —or, in this case, the more specific *dramatization effect,* cannot be minimized over the long run by the researcher's simply becoming a taken-for-granted part of the deviant's everyday life. While deviants may never forget that they are more on stage when the researcher is around than otherwise, if the researcher ceases to emphasize his research role and the possible publicity resulting from his research, he can probably recede into the background. The effective solution to this problem of self-dramatization involves the whole question of the degree to which the sociologist participates in the everyday lives of the deviants.

MANAGING FRONTS AND ESTABLISHING TRUST

The deviants' fear of exposure coupled with their desire to be studied can produce a fundamental problem for any sociologist trying to become involved in deviant groups in order to study them. As Dorothy Douglas found, both motives can cause the deviants to use their many *fronts* to lead the sociologist astray, so that the unsuspecting sociologist may get a consistently false idea of what the deviants' lives are like.

As with all individuals, important groups in our society have both friends and enemies. Thus, since a deviant group is one considered by some significant other groups to be deviant, by definition it has enemies who would often be willing to take strong measures against it. Groups legally defined as deviant are in a particularly dangerous situation because they often face real possibilities of official action being taken against them. Even if they are not violating laws, officials may still exercise paralegal controls over them. (For example, most students today appear to agree that police see young people, especially students, as almost all potentially deviant. The young thus feel that even when they are not doing anything the police might legally construe as deviant, the police will investigate and threaten them anyway.)

Because deviant groups face great problems of this sort, they have become especially adept at constructing *fronts* behind which they can carry on their activities. They have become particularly clever at managing what Lofland has very appropriately called "insider information" and "outsider information."[13] Indeed, some deviant groups, such as professional criminals and prostitutes, have developed "lines" for those outsiders who are potentially dangerous to them and have passed these lines down over the centuries. The effectiveness of such lines is shown by the fact that so many outsiders still take them to be truths.

Such ageless fronts can probably be spotted and managed effectively, but most fronts are not so easily managed. Most fronts are created by specific groups to meet specific social situations so that they change rapidly as the social situations change. A kind of *cultural wisdom* can probably be learned about such groups so that one does suspect when he is being given a line, or "put on." But only prolonged association with any particular group can make the sociologist aware of *situational fronts* and allow him to develop effective strategies for dealing with them. Situational fronts are created by individuals out of bits and pieces of old fronts, and out of their own creative thoughts, to deal with the situation-at-hand. These are *idiosyncratic fronts*–or fronts peculiar to an individual or a situation–that can only be spotted if the researcher knows enough about the specific group and, perhaps, even about the specific individual, so that he already knows a good deal of the truth about the group and the individual. Only such specific knowledge of the situation and of the group in-the-situation will allow the student of deviance to *check out* what he is told by individuals in specific situations.

But, unless he is able to gain *initial acceptance* by the group, the researcher could not even participate sufficiently to be able to gain this minimal degree of necessary understanding. Deviant groups appear willing to allow outsiders to observe them in *some* of their activities long before they are willing to let outsiders see *all* of the kinds of things the group is involved in. This constitutes a kind of *limbo membership*, in which an individual is granted tentative acceptance by the group—that is, one sufficient to allow them to evaluate his trustworthiness. No clear line is drawn between insider and outsider information, but tentative acceptance usually means granting the individual the right to exist somewhere between the two. Thus he can observe the group in their everyday lives and can talk with them and be tested by them without gaining so much information as to constitute a real danger to them. An example of a group today that would act this way would be marijuana users, who will discuss at length their use of marijuana without allowing an individual to witness them in possession of it, without naming the other people involved, and, most especially, without telling from whom they buy marijuana or to whom they sell it.

As we have seen earlier, *trust* is the crucial factor in determining if an individual is granted such limbo membership, let alone allowed to participate with the group. *Trust is the basic consideration of any individuals or any group in determining whether they will allow an individual to pierce their public fronts and observe their private behavior.* For those who are deviant, this is an *overriding* concern. They are very conscious of it, and in many cases develop explicit strategies for testing the trustworthiness of individuals.

Deviants also develop many diffuse and specific ideas about personal *styles* and believe that one's style is an adequate *symbolization of one's social purposes*. Personal style thus becomes a crucial determinate for them of whether one can be trusted. Police, for example, are commonly thought to have personal styles that they are unable to hide and that give them away, and any individual showing such personal style is not to be trusted. (This idea seems less important today because police more frequently use undercover agents, who are often former members of deviant groups and who know how to make use of deviant personal styles.) Such personal styles must be effectively managed by the sociologist before he comes into contact with the deviant group, for changes in one's personal style, like changes in one's ideas, will give an impression of inconsistency, which will arouse suspicion among members of the group. (This principle of consistency of personal behavior results primarily from the commonsense assumption that an individual has a *substantial self* that must be the same at all times. When an individual appears to behave inconsistently, then our immediate conclusion is that our former ideas about his substantial self must have been wrong. We then must consider whether he was trying to manipulate our beliefs about him—that is, whether he was putting up a front in our initial encounter with him. Inconsistency gives rise to suspicion, which can only be overcome by moving to a greater synthesis—

that is, moving to an idea of his substantial self that would plausibly include both of the previous impressions we had received of him.)

Once one has managed such problems of initial encounters and has, presumably, established some kind of limbo membership so that he is at least able to observe the group of deviants in their daily lives, the problems of establishing and maintaining trust become more a matter of personal beliefs and personality types than of general symbolic style. Attention to language, hand motions, and so on, could be important. Polsky, however, from his own experience with hustlers and professional criminals, argues that it is ineffective for a sociologist to try to fit in with the group of deviants by using their styles of language. Indeed, this can have exactly the opposite effects from what one intends; a sociologist with little previous involvement with the group he is trying to study and who assumes the linguistic and behavioral styles of that group may be detected and may be seen as attempting to deceive them into believing that he is one of them. Polsky argues convincingly that such dishonesty will destroy the whole relationship. Certainly it is true that any seemingly dishonest use of the deviants' language or life styles will destroy trust and, thus, prevent the sociologists' getting valid information about the group. But there are a great many research situations in which the sociologist has become enough of a member to honestly use the same language and life styles. The use of such language and life styles is part of the fundamental issue of the degrees and kinds of researcher participation in the deviants' lives.

THE DEGREES AND KINDS OF PARTICIPATION

The sociologist's observations of social action involve varying degrees of participation in the action, ranging from no participation to total immersion. Differences in the degree of participation are significant in determining what can be observed and how "objective" the observations are likely to be.

At one extreme would be observation with absolutely no participation. This situation, which Fred Davis has aptly called the "Martian situation,"[14] has never actually been used by sociologists because they always have vast commonsense knowledge of our society before they begin any study, and some of this knowledge will be shared by any subculture. Many sociologists, however, have held it up as an ideal method toward which we should strive. The early form of this minimal-participation method was that adopted by the mechanistic social analysts who sought to study and explain social behavior without any reference to social meanings or to the analyst's commonsensically derived understandings of those meanings. While this particular form of this method is rarely used today, except in some of the atypical mathematical models of social actions, it has been replaced by a modified version, which seeks, ideally, to determine social meanings completely from outside the commonsense understandings of those meanings. The most serious presentation of this ideal is found in the plea for a "presuppositionless" method—that is, a method of observing and analyzing phenomena that would in no way presuppose any basic properties of thought or any ideas about the phenomena. There are some good philosophical critiques of the fundamental weaknesses of this "method" as a philosophical ideal;[15] and these critiques seem to hold for the linguistic analyses that constitute the only Martian method much used in the social sciences today.

At the opposite extreme from the Martian method is the total immersion of the self in the group being studied, an immersion that, at least for its duration, abrogates study *of* the group for experience *in* the group. This is the experience that Kurt Wolff has called *surrender* and that he has described so well for his own experience in a community study:

> It was years before I understood what had happened to me: I had fallen through the web of "culture patterns" and assorted conceptual meshes into the chaos of *love*; I was looking everywhere, famished, with a "ruthless glance." Despite admonitions to be selective and form hypotheses that would tell me what to select, I was not and did not. Another thing I sensed was that I was not content with the probable but wanted to *know*; and I thought I might *know* if, instead of looking for culture patterns, for instance, I looked directly—not through the lens of *any* received notion but the adequate lens that would come out of my being in Loma. "Culture pattern," indeed any conceptual scheme, had come to strike me as something learned *outside* Loma that I would import, impose, and that has been imposed on me. Instead, I was busy, even panicky at times, observing, ruminating, and recording as best I could. Everything, I felt, was important, although the ways in which it was important would yet have to become clear.[16]

"Surrender" has a number of basic meanings for Wolff:

> Its seminal meaning is cognitive love, in the sense in which this is redundant for love. "Surrender" has a military connotation, as well as the sound of passivity, of "giving up." I have therefore thought of other words, such as "abandonment," but this suggests a dissoluteness alien to it; "exposure," but this had a gratuitous ring of exhibitionism; "devotion" or "dedication," but these envisage only an attitude and inappropriately introduce a moral note; "laying oneself open" or "laying the cards on the table," but these, too, convey only part of the meaning—unconditionality or honesty. Thus I have stuck to "surrender." Its meaning of "cognitive love" is seminal because all the other meanings follow from it. Major among them are: total involvement, suspension of received notions, pertinence of everything, identification, and risk of being hurt.[17]

Minimal participation might provide the sociologist with information on deviance. For example, some kinds of ecological information concerning habits of "hanging out," which involve little more than counting appearances at certain spots at certain times, might prove to be of value. But even such observations of events are rarely of interest to us unless we can see the relations between these patterns of events and social meanings. And *social meanings can only be "observed" by using participation, because this is the one way by which we can learn how to relate the perceivable states of communication* (linguistic statements, facial expressions, hand signs, utterances, and so on) *to the internal states of mind and feeling that are the meanings of the external states.*

In order to understand the necessity of such participation, let us consider a version of the Martian method that one might try to use to determine "meanings" without using participation. In this method one tries to get at the observable relations between linguistic statements, body signs, situations, and actions without making use of any direct participation with the individuals involved.

In its ideal manifestation, the first step of this external method would include the exact recording of all verbal and nonverbal communication found in any situation (perhaps by using sound films). The next step would be the preliminary analysis of the patterns of invariant *linguistic items*–that is, words, phrases, sentences, facial expressions, and so forth. Following this, one would analyze such communications to determine the *varying structures* in which these linguistic items appear–that is, one would determine the *usages* (or *constructions*) made with these linguistic items. One would then attempt to determine the relations between the constructions and the general *situations,* or contexts, of the social actors, as defined by the actors. And finally, one would be ready to venture a more general theory relating "meanings" to each other and to actions.

Presumably, such an externalistic approach would have to define "meaning" not in terms of internal states, which is what we mean commonsensically by the term, but in terms of the associations or relations between linguistic and other expressions of the individuals involved, the other kinds of activities they perform (walking, hitting, and so on), and the situations in which these expressions and actions occur. There would be two crucial problems for this would-be Martian researcher. First, the number of possible relations between the various external activities would be infinite because of the great freedom individuals have–and must have because of the infinite complexity of the world we live in–in constructing their activities and because of the openness of the world for each individual. If this infinite complexity is so, it would not be possible to realize the ideal meaning, even with the finest computers. One would have to have prior knowledge of these unspoken devices before he could understand how the individuals construct meaning in their everyday situations.

Second, the Martian researcher would not be able to determine from his exact and total recording of externally perceivable events what the *situations for the participants* are, because the situation is almost always meaningful to the participants only in terms of unspoken, taken-for-granted meanings. The Martian researcher, therefore, would have to know the meanings of the situations to the participants before he could adequately determine the meanings of the events he has witnessed. He could probably only break this chain by asking the participants, and, although this would involve a minimal form of participation, it would still be participation. (We might also add that, *even if* one could approximate this ideal Martian method, the expenditure of human effort would not be worth it, for it is doubtful that one would achieve anything unique by this method.)

Member participation, or previous involvement in the everyday lives of a group of deviants as a member, can be a great help in studying deviants. First of all, it can be an aid in gaining some insight into one of the most crucial problems faced by sociology—the relation between the commonsense experience of everyday social life and the experience of an individual who has received a formalized education in sociology or one of the other social sciences. Formalized education, the academic world, sociological theory, and so on are all basic to the preconceptions with which a social researcher approaches fieldwork. After many years of such training, much of it using technical jargon greatly removed from everyday life, these formalized preconceptions can become so taken for granted that they form an unconscious frame around everyday experience. These preconceptions may prevent the researcher from grasping the meanings that the members may be taking for granted; and the researcher may find that he can "make sense" out of his observations in terms of his own preconceptions rather than in terms of theirs.

Secondly, previous experience with a group of deviants can be extremely important in providing an individual with a "natural" understanding of the deviants' style of life. Such an understanding is of special importance in establishing trust with the deviants. As we have noted, there are a number of useful studies of deviants done by sociologists that have made primary use of earlier *member participation,* though in most instances the sociologists using such insider information have not reported their methods. For example, Marvin Scott's highly interesting interpretation of the deviance of jockeys was based on his long-standing insider experience at race tracks, which occurred well before he thought of becoming a sociologist.[18] Although Scott has not provided us with enough information on the exact ways in which he inferred the existence of jockey strategies, it should be apparent from the work that he could only have gotten at such strategies, and could only have been very sure that they existed—that is, that they are "going through the minds of jockeys" and determining their behavior—through very long and intimate association with people at race tracks.

Regardless of whether the sociologist has had such previous insider experience in the deviant subculture he is studying, he has at least had extensive insider experience in our culture. Since almost all groups of deviants in our culture have only subcultural differences from the general culture, he will already share many understandings with them. The sociologist will necessarily be making primary use of this insider experience in our culture to participate with deviants and to understand the meanings of things to them. His knowledge of the language, American English, is the most obvious and important form of insider information he will be using. But his general understanding of the values of American society, of subcultural styles, of subcultural attitudes toward other subcultures, and so on will also be used extensively. While these understandings are absolutely essential, they may also be the basis for the formation of dangerous preconceptions unless the sociologist is always very careful to assume that the meanings to the members of the subculture must be treated by him as being problematic–that is, he must always be trying to determine how *adequately* these understandings meet the *practicality test:* How effectively can he interact with the members of the group in a given situation?

Any sociological research on deviants requires a great degree of involvement with the deviants, since trust, the important factor, can be established only in this way. Thus, the sociologist studying deviants must live with them much of the time, even if he does not intend to do the research secretly. If, for example, one is to do a valid study of delinquents, then one must participate with the boys, as Carl Werthman did in his study of gang boys;[19] and, if one is going to study the hippies in the Haight-Ashbury, one must live much of the time in the Haight, as Sherri Cavan did.[20] If one cannot live with them or run with them, then one must make use of the next best thing, which is "commuting" or "hanging out" with the deviants. This has, in fact, been the most widely used form of participation with deviants. . . .

This emphasis on "intimacy" and "living with" the deviants does not mean that the sociologist must "surrender," "go native," or become "one of the blood" in order to get at what the meanings of things are to them. Becoming "one of the blood" can be extremely useful to sociologists in gaining insight into those kinds of things that members of any group take completely for granted. Even more significantly, it can provide insight into those kinds of things that are really secrets within the group itself–things that are understood by the members of the group but that are so intimate or so deviant from their own standpoint that they must not be talked about. While this form of "surrender" affords one the easiest source of insight, it does create some of its own problems, especially those of being objective and of being able to observe what the members take for granted–that is, if the sociologist becomes extremely involved as a member it can be difficult for him to see those things which the members themselves find hard to see. While I believe the sociologist can overcome these problems by using *retrospective analysis* of his experience after he is no longer involved and has returned to his identity as sociologist, and while I believe surrender should, consequently, be encouraged as long as his primary identification remains with sociology, it does create its own problems. Moreover, it is probably not necessary for getting at most of the kinds of meanings that concern us.

While most sociologists of deviance in recent years have not believed in surrendering to the deviant groups, many have felt it essential that sociologists *take the side of* or *sympathize with* the deviants. It is precisely because of the fundamentally important distinction between empathy and sympathy, and their often opposite relations to gaining reliable understandings of social meanings, that sociologists must be extremely careful about committing themselves to political interest groups if they want to keep the search for truth about human beings as their primary goal.[21] It is the commitment to narrow political interest groups that makes so many sociologists believe that sympathy is necessary and desirable. If a sociologist has a broader perspective and has a truthful understanding of human actors as his primary goal, such sympathetic concerns for (narrow) moral or political interest groups can be a fundamental failing.

There has always been a very important and influential minority of American sociologists who, primarily because of their liberal and leftist political stances, have tried to take the side of deviants.[22] For example, these sociologists have taken a definite sympathetic attitude toward the lower-class black culture that middle-class people would commonly see as deviant. On the other hand, there have been some areas in which there has been little evidence of this sympathetic stance. For example, sociologists, as one might expect from any middle-class group, have shown little sympathy toward prisoners and "hardened criminals."

It is crucial to realize that this sympathetic stance is very different from participating in a deviant group for purposes of gaining an objective understanding of it. The aim of objective understanding can be defeated by taking the sympathetic stance, especially when it is done primarily for political or ideological reasons. The sympathy that sociologists in our society have shown for various groups of deviants and lower-class people has raised grave dangers of just this sort. Some of the most recent and highly touted studies of the poor, especially of the black poor, have come close to being *romantic justifications of the ways of the poor* to the educated and the middle class. For example, a large portion of *Tally's Corner,*[23] one of the most popular works of social science in many years, consists primarily of trying to justify the activities of the lower-class blacks Eliot Liebow had gotten to know so intimately through his long participation in their everyday lives. Indeed, much of the work is written from the perspective of trying to "tell it like it is" to the middle-class white world. While such writing is a political activity in our society today, it must be seen, too, as a suspect report of actual occurrences in the everyday lives of these people, for it seems unlikely that they spend such a large portion of their lives seeking to justify themselves to the middle-class world. If they did so when Liebow was present, then we must suspect that his being a member of the white middle-class group must have biased the contact situation and must have resulted in the blacks spending much of their time justifying themselves to him as a representative of that group. In that case, the work could not be taken as a valuable scientific study of the everyday lives of these people.

The kind of bias resulting from taking the sympathetic stance is in no way a consequence of using the participant-observer method. There is no evidence to suggest that participation in deviant or lower-class groups necessarily causes one to take the sympathetic stance or that there is more bias in the participant-observer method than in any other. On the contrary, greater bias is more likely to be found when a method other than participant-observation is used. An excellent example of this is Chapter 1 of Kenneth Clark's *Dark Ghetto,*[24] in which an attempt is made to depict the lives of the people of Harlem in New York City. This chapter, entitled "The Cry of the Ghetto," is based on an interview study of members of the Harlem community done by social scientists. The interviews were done in the setting of a social-problems oriented (community action) organization called Haryou, presumably because the social scientists doing the study were primarily concerned with the problematic, or "suffering," aspects of the everyday lives of the residents of Harlem and with ways of getting social and financial support for solving these problems and ending this suffering. The overall effect of the dialogue in the chapter is a dismal picture of everyday life in Harlem. From these selected excerpts, which Clark presumably took from the interviews in order to give some "objective picture" of everyday life, it would seem that the members of the Harlem community spend all their time suffering. They have no ordinary joys, such as having fun with friends, joking with acquaintances, playing with children, making love, drinking with comrades, and so on, which all of us with direct experience with lower-class groups have in the past found to be the dominant aspects of everyday life among these groups.

It seems apparent that the social scientists doing this study were primarily concerned with eliciting support for the particular political programs intended to solve what they defined as social problems. They focus, through the use of the interview method, on the information they expect to use to justify their appeals for these programs. And the interview method, especially when its results are combined with excerpted illustrative material, is extremely amenable to such purposes. The participant-observer study is less amenable, since it has to take into consideration a far wider range of life and is less capable of structuring the situation so that the individuals to be observed respond primarily in terms of those aspects of their lives relevant to suffering.

Taking a sympathetic stance toward deviants is by no means a necessary or even a major cause of bias in studies of deviants, though many sociologists have in recent years come to assume that this is the case. I would suggest that the actual circumstances are the complete opposite of this. Instead of becoming sympathetic toward the group being studied, and thence having great problems of objective reporting, sociologists facing situations in which bias is involved seem *to have already been sympathetic (and often biased) toward the group*. Because of this they have gone out *to "study" the group in order to show that the deviants are "more right" than their attackers*, whom such sociologists often see as *their own attackers as well.* One kind of evidence for this is that the same sociologists can do "studies" showing how "bad" the officials are, even though they do the studies by participating with them. If participation were the biasing factor, rather than previous political and ideological commitments, then these sociologists would, presumably. wind up doing reports on the officials that are quite favorable to them. There are definitely instances of this happening, but it also goes the other way.[25] There are also reports on deviant groups, based on long participation, that are in no way sympathetic; obvious examples would be most of the early ethnographic studies of deviants done in Chicago in the 1920s. Works such as *The Gang* and *Taxi Cab Dance Hall Girls* appear to be neither sympathetic nor unsympathetic. They are a real mixture, probably in the style of much of social-work reporting. But one of the best examples of a work involving high participation without sympathy is the recent work done by Hunter Thompson on *Hell's Angels*. Though not a professional sociologist, Thompson spent a good part of a year or more riding with the Hell's Angels, so that he did far more fieldwork on them than all but a few sociologists have done on any deviant group. The work is in no way a sympathetic report on the Angels. Though he argues that most of the newspaper and political pictures painted of the Angels are completely false, and that the members are certainly not inhuman, his final commentary on the Angels—which came after a stomping they gave him for a minor mistake—is a malediction:

> On Labor Day 1966, I pushed my luck a little to far and got badly stomped by four or five Angels who seemed to feel I was taking advantage of them. A minor disagreement suddenly became very serious.
>
> None of those who did me were among the group I considered my friends—but they were Angels, and that was enough to cause many of the others to participate after one of the brethren teed off on me. The first blow was launched with no hint of warning and I thought for a moment that it was just one of those drunken accidents that a man has to live with in this league. But within seconds I was clubbed from behind by the Angel I'd been talking to just a moment earlier. Then I was swarmed in a general flail. . . .
>
> My next stop was the hospital in Santa Rosa, nearly fifty miles south of the Angel encampment. The emergency-ward waiting room was full of wounded Gypsy Jokers. The most serious case was a broken jaw, the result of a clash earlier that evening with a pipe-wielding Hell's Angel.

> The Jokers told me they were on their way north to wipe the Angels out. "It'll be a goddamn slaughter," said one.
>
> I agreed, and wished them luck. I wanted no part of it–not even with a shotgun. I was tired, swollen and whipped. My face looked like it had been jammed into the spokes of a speeding Harley, and the only thing keeping me awake was the spastic pain of a broken rib.
>
> It had been a bad trip . . . fast and wild in some moments, slow and dirty in others, but on balance it looked like a bummer. On my way back to San Francisco, I tried to compose a fitting epitaph. I wanted something original, but there was no escaping the echo of Mistah Kurtz' final words from the heart of darkness: "The horror! The horror! . . . Exterminate all the brutes!"[26]

Even prolonged participation involving considerable personal involvement can lead to antipathy and negatively biased reporting against the group. It seems likely that the nature of one's initial commitment to studying the group and one's initial sympathies and antipathies toward its way of life become the primary determinants of whether one takes the side of the deviants or the side of their enemies.

Surrender, sympathy, and other forms of identification with the deviants and with their (self-defined) best interests do not seem to be necessary in the way in which some sociologists of deviance have assumed them to be. These various forms of identification are quite different from what earlier sociologists called "empathy." I believe *empathy* is what is needed, rather than sympathy. Empathy is an ability *to feel with*, to see things from the standpoint or perspective of the individual being studied rather than to identify with or act from this standpoint. There is no reason whatsoever to believe that to understand is to sympathize with or to agree with, although this may be necessary for certain individuals because of their own feelings, identifications, and so on. But there is no reason to believe it is true of all individuals. On the contrary, many individuals are able to take the standpoint of others for purposes of understanding it without surrendering to or getting inside it. It is even quite possible for some individuals to empathize with their enemies. Indeed, one would suspect that all great military commanders have had precisely this ability and have tried to train their subordinates to have it so that they could better destroy their enemies. In a way, empathy is a hard-headed stance, while sympathy is an analogous but soft-hearted stance. We must recognize that reliable understanding demands a hard heart but a supple mind. . . .

NOTES

1. Howard S. Becker, "Practitioners of Vice and Crime," in Robert Habenstein (ed.), *Pathways to Data* (Chicago: Aldine, 1970).

2. Howard S. Becker, *Outsiders: Studies in the Sociology of Deviance* (New York: Free Press, 1963).
3. Becker, in Habenstein, *op. cit.*, calls for a similar strategy.
4. Laud Humphreys, *The Tearoom Trade: Impersonal Sex in Public Places* (Chicago: Aldine, 1970).
5. See the discussion of public and private situations in Douglas, *American Social Order.*
6. Technological tyranny is discussed in Jack D. Douglas (ed.), *Freedom and Tyranny* (New York: Random House, 1970).
7. Polsky, *op. cit.*, pp. 133–134.
8. William Foote Whyte, *Street Corner Society* (Chicago: University of Chicago Press, 1955).
9. Rosalie Hankey Wax, "Reciprocity as a Field Technique," *Human Organization*, 11 (1952), pp. 34–37.
10. See John Johnson, "Field Research" (unpublished paper).
11. See, especially, Edwin Sutherland, *The Professional Thief* (Chicago: University of Chicago Press, 1937).
12. Polsky, *op. cit.* Also, see the article in this volume by John Irwin, "Participant-Observation of Criminals."
13. See John F. Lofland, *Doomsday Cult* (Englewood Cliffs, N.J.: Prentice-Hall, 1966).
14. This was in private communication from Fred Davis.
15. See the discussion of this in Jack D. Douglas, *Understanding Everyday Life* (Chicago: Aldine, 1970).
16. Kurt Wolff, "Surrender and Community Study," in Arthur J. Vidich, Joseph Bensman, and Maurice R. Stein (eds.), *Reflections on Community Studies* (New York: Wiley, 1964), pp. 233–263.
17. *Ibid.*
18. Marvin Scott, *The Racing Game* (Chicago: Aldine, 1968).
19. Carl Werthman, "The Function of Social Definitions in the Development of Delinquent Careers," in *Juvenile Delinquency and Youth Crime,* Task Force Report of the President's Commission on Law Enforcement and Administration of Justice (Washington, D.C.: Government Printing Office, 1967).
20. Most of this study has not been published, but part of it appears in Sherri Cavan, "The Hippie Ethic and the Spirit of Drug Use," in Jack D. Douglas (ed.), *Observations of Deviance* (New York: Random House, 1970).
21. I have discussed this crucial point in Jack D. Douglas (ed.), *The Relevance of Sociology* (New York: Appleton-Century-Crofts, 1970).
22. See Howard Becker, "Whose Side Are We On?" *Social Problems,* 14 (Winter 1967), 239–247.
23. Elliot Liebow, *Tally's Corner* (Boston: Little, Brown, 1967).
24. Kenneth Clark, *Dark Ghetto* (New York: Harper & Row, 1965).
25. This is especially obvious from journalistic "exposés" and police investigations that involve undercover work.
26. Hunter S. Thompson, *Hell's Angels* (New York: Random House, 1966), pp. 277–278.

When Prophecy Fails

Leon Festinger, Henry W. Riecken and Stanley Schachter

In most studies that rely heavily on participant observers for collecting data, these observers are known as such to the people being studied. In our investigation of the group which gathered about Dr. Armstrong and Marian Keech, our observers posed as ordinary members who believed as the others did. In short, our investigation was conducted without either the knowledge or the consent of the group members. This situation presented a number of problems that merit detailed discussion.

In our very first contact with the central figures of the group, their secrecy and general attitude toward nonbelievers made it clear that a study could not be conducted openly. Our basic problems were then obtaining entree for a sufficient number of observers to provide the needed coverage of members' activities, and keeping at an absolute minimum any influence which these observers might have on the beliefs and actions of members of the group. We tried to be nondirective, sympathetic listeners, passive participants who were inquisitive and eager to learn whatever others might want to tell us. As we shall point out later, our initial hope—to avoid *any* influence upon the movement—turned out to be somewhat unrealistic for reasons outside our control and inherent in the process of making such a study as this. The other problems of the study were of a more tactical nature: we had to be on the spot whenever something was happening in the group, and we also had to make opportunities for recording our observations before they were forgotten or distorted by subsequent events.

OBTAINING ENTREE

We did not learn of the flood prediction until very late September and, owing to the pressure of other activities, could not arrange direct contact

From Leon Festinger, Henry W. Riecken and Stanley Schachter. *When Prophecy Fails,* University of Minnesota Press, Minneapolis.

with the group until a week later. By the time we had acquired sufficient information to determine that the movement satisfied the conditions necessary to test our hypothesis, it was the beginning of November. Finding suitable observers and giving them even the briefest of training took another week or two, and it was almost that much longer before they could secure entree into the movement in Lake City and Collegeville. All this had to be done with the utmost dispatch, since it was vital to collect as much "pre-disconfirmation" data as possible and we could anticipate needing considerable time to establish ourselves well enough in the group so that we could safely proceed to ask relatively intimate questions of the various members. Finally, the training and supervising of observers was handicapped by the fact that the study was carried on in localities far from our home base.

Our first problem then was to obtain a quick but firm entree into the movement in two distant places. Because of the severe pressure of time we chose whichever technique for introducing observers promised to be most effective. Accordingly, the procedure varied from person to person and place to place. Our initial contact was with Mrs. Keech, whom one of the authors telephoned shortly after the newspaper story about her appeared in late September. He told her his name and said he had called to ask if he might talk with her about some of the things she had told the reporter, especially the matter of the predicted flood and flying saucers. He said he happened to be visiting Lake City "on business" and had telephoned on impulse because he and some friends in his home city had read the story and been interested. Mrs. Keech was reluctant to discuss any of her beliefs over the phone, or to give details on the extent of followership and similar matters. Since the caller could not conveniently visit her at that time he asked her if he might stop in on a subsequent trip and received an affirmative answer.

About ten days later, two of the authors made a trip to Lake City, primarily in order to learn as much as they could about the size of the movement if any, the activities of members, and so forth. One telephoned Mrs. Keech on arrival and made an appointment to call on her the following morning. He represented himself to be a businessman who had occasion to travel a good deal. Mrs. Keech seemed completely incurious about his occupation and readily accepted his statements that he and several of his friends had an "informal group" in Minneapolis that frequently "got together and discussed saucers and things like that."

She willingly began to talk about her experiences with "automatic writing," read aloud at great length from her notebooks full of messages, and, in general, was quite receptive, friendly, and talkative. She did seem reluctant to say much about the flood prediction and had to be questioned extensively before much information emerged. She was evasive on the question of how many "believers" there were in Lake City, and quite adamant in refusing to say what she and her followers (if any) were going to do about preparing for the cataclysm. Fortunately, Daisy Armstrong was present at the interview, visiting Mrs. Keech at the time, and supplied some answers that Mrs. Keech would not. She told the author about the Seekers in Collegeville, and made some reference to going to the Allegheny Mountains in late December.

In all, the author spent three hours interviewing the two women that morning, and returned that evening with his colleague, whom he introduced as a business associate from Minneapolis, for another three- or four-hour talk. Before the authors left, they made sure they could take the initiative to call again in Lake City or in Collegeville when they wanted further information. Thus it was easy to make the acquaintance of these two persons and to establish a basis for future contacts.

One of the authors called on the Armstrongs in Collegeville approximately three weeks later, this occasion having been chosen as the nearest convenient time for a visit, but still not so near the first contact as to arouse any wonder on the part of the Armstrongs about the speed and intensity of our interest in their activities. It was our hope, on this visit, to meet the members of the Seekers and to be invited to attend a meeting. We did meet a number of members and, in talking to the Armstrongs, picked up some important information about their plans for going to a mountain refuge just before the flood was to strike. On the basis of this information we decided to hire local observers in Collegeville, and, accordingly, secured the services of a male student in sociology to make the first approach.

We instructed this observer to attend the open meetings of the "elementary" Seekers . . . at the Community Church and to attempt to get on good terms with Dr. Armstrong, with the aim of being invited to one of the Sunday afternoon meetings of the "advanced" Seekers. We have already reported the difficulty our observer experienced in arousing Dr. Armstrong's interest in him; all his efforts to stimulate an invitation to the "advanced" group meetings were having no success. Time was passing and we were losing opportunities for valuable observation. We therefore decided upon a strategem suggested to us by Dr. Armstrong's inquiry to our observer as to whether he had ever had any "psychic experiences." We decided to equip our representative with an "experience" with the supernatural.

The observer had told Dr. Armstrong of his having spent some time in Mexico, so we borrowed a folktale and set the scene there. The story our observer told was as follows: He and a companion had been driving between two Mexican cities. Toward dusk, they picked up an elderly peasant woman hitchhiking in their direction and let her occupy the rear seat. Soon she was talking to them, a long admonitory monologue full of warnings about disaster ahead. They paid little heed to her, and, after a time, she fell silent and, they assumed, slept. When they reached the outskirts of their home city, they turned to ask where she would get off, and found that she had disappeared! They had not stopped at all, and had been moving at a fast speed; they had heard no door open, no cry or noise of any kind from the rear once the old lady had stopped talking.

Dr. Armstrong's interest was immediately aroused, and he very quickly began to manifest much more friendliness toward our observer, and interest in him. The observer was invited to attend the next meeting of the Seekers at Dr. Armstrong's home and, from the point of view of gaining acceptance for our representative, the strategem was a complete success.

At the same time that we were constructing this scheme for our male observer in Collegeville, we had decided to hire and train a young woman to act in the same capacity. Forewarned by his difficulties in approaching the Armstrongs through the medium of the elementary Seekers, we decided to arm our female observer with a "psychic experience" and to have her go directly to the Armstrong house to tell this story: A few nights previous to her call at the Armstrong home, our observer said, she had had a strange dream that disturbed her a good deal. She had consulted Dr. Armstrong professionally about a year ago, and he had urged her at that time to "get in tune with the universe" and this suggestion had stuck in her mind. Therefore, when she had the puzzling dream she had thought at once of going to him for advice and help. Her dream was as follows: "I was standing on the side of a hill. It wasn't a mountain, and yet it wasn't exactly a hill: and I looked up and there was a man standing on top of the hill with a light all around him. There were torrents of water, raging water all around, and the man reached down and lifted me up, up out of the water. I felt safe."

Mrs. Armstrong's reaction to this story was enthusiastic. She welcomed the observer warmly, and at once began to enlighten her visitor about the protectors from outer space. Within an hour, our observer was informed about the belief system, had been told of the predicted flood, of the mission of the flying saucers, and like matters. When Dr. Armstrong came home from work, his wife proudly presented the observer as one who "had been sent," and the two Armstrongs began to interpret the "dream." During the next few days, our observer was pressed to retell her "dream" several more times to other members of the Seekers and finally was asked to tape-record it so it could be sent to Lake City or played to people in distant places. Again, our scheme had been successful for gaining entree into the group.

Unhappily, it had been too successful, for, in our effort to tailor a story to fit the beliefs of the members of the group, and thus gain their approval for our observers, we had done too well. We had unintentionally reinforced their beliefs that the Guardians were watching over humanity and were "sending" chosen people for special instruction about the cataclysm and the belief system. Dr. Armstrong's initial indifference to the male observer had led us to underestimate the powerful effect of the "dream." In all probability its effect was magnified by coming so close behind the male observer's story (they were separated by only two or three days).

In introducing themselves into the Lake City group, our observers there told stories that were quite unexciting, even commonplace. The male observer told Mrs. Keech that he had read the newspaper story about her in

September and had intended to call on her earlier, but somehow had never got around to it. He had remained interested, however, though he was not quite sure what he wanted to know; he just wanted to know more than the newspaper account had given.

Mrs. Keech's response to this introduction was favorable, though not as enthusiastic as the Armstrongs' welcome of our Collegeville observers had been. She volunteered to tell the observer how she had begun to receive messages, how the messages related to flying saucers, what the significance of many of her writings were, and so on. She spent a couple of hours explaining these things, offered him refreshments, and, when he asked if he might return, told him: "My door is always open. Please feel free to come back."

Our female observer in Lake City was instructed to use a somewhat different approach, in order to avoid stretching a coincidence. She called a day or so before our male observer had and told Mrs. Keech the following story. She had been at a meeting of people interested in ethical and religious problems in the neighborhood where she lived and worked. The discussion had turned to flying saucers and a man seated next to her had remarked that if our observer really wanted to know about flying saucers, she should go visit Mrs. Keech, and had given her Mrs. Keech's address. The observer had thought about this piece of advice for a while and then, on impulse, had come to call. She seemed a little uneasy and said that she felt "sort of silly" and "didn't know exactly why she had come," but was "just curious about flying saucers."

Mrs. Keech again reacted favorably, inviting the young lady into the house to warm herself, and began to talk about flying saucers, about her communication with their occupants, her messages from Sananda, reincarnation, and the like. She told the story of the sice at Lyons field, mentioned the "war" between Atlantis and Mu, and offered to "get a lesson" from Sananda for our observer. In all, she spent about four hours talking about the belief system, without once mentioning the coming cataclysmic flood on December 21. This observer also asked if she might return and Mrs. Keech gave her permission, but warned her to telephone first, so that she would not come at a time when some other student was receiving a lesson.

In spite of the relatively ordinary, nonexotic stories that the Lake City observers told Mrs. Keech she subsequently made much the same use of their appearance on her doorstep as the Armstrongs had with the Collegeville observers. Her imagination embroidered the circumstances somewhat and, within a week of the first observer's call, Mrs. Keech was explaining to other members of the group that a girl had come to her door, upset, excited, wringing her hands, and so terrified that she could not speak; the girl had not known why she had come, and obviously she had been "sent" by the Guardians. Then, Mrs, Keech added, a man had also called, again not knowing why he was there, confused, upset, and unsure of his errand. She elaborated not only the bewilderment and emotionality of the observers but also her own warmth of response and comforting actions toward them. Her account was retold in

Collegeville by the Armstrongs, just as their versions of our observers' visits to them were retold in Lake City. In both cases the visits were given as illustrations that "strange things are happening."

The members of the group who heard these accounts were impressed, it seemed to us, by this upsurge of membership within a few days. There is little doubt that the addition of four new people to a fairly small group within ten days had an effect on the state of conviction among the existing members, especially since the four seem to have appeared when public apathy to the belief system was great and there were very few inquiries or new faces in either Collegeville or Lake City. Most important of all, perhaps, is that the four observers could not be traced through any mutual friends or acquaintances to existing group members and thus the most common and expected channel of recruitment was evidently not responsible for their appearance. It was an unfortunate and unavoidable set of events—we had no choice but to establish local observers in both cities where there were believers, to do it quickly, and to "push" as much as we dared to get our people well enough received so they could begin to move about in the groups, ask questions, and have a reasonable expectation of getting answers. We could not afford to have them remain peripheral members, or strangers, for very long.

One other observer, a man, did not make contact with the group until Christmas Day when he called at the Keech house, saying simply that he had read the newspaper accounts of recent happenings and had come out to learn more about what was going on. He had no problem of entree. As we have already pointed out, he was readily admitted and regarded as a spaceman, even though he told a most straightforward story of his earthly origin and occupation (unemployed IBM operator).

It seems clear that his appearance in the post-disconfirmation stage probably affected the state of conviction too, for he was the only new recruit the group attracted. The group imposed their own meaning on his visits. The new observer was introduced in order to maintain coverage. The regular observers and the authors had been "on duty" nearly full time for nearly ten days at that point, were exhausted, and had personal affairs to take care of.

MAINTAINING MEMBERSHIP

A major problem in acting as an observer was to become friendly enough, well enough accepted and integrated into group activity, to allow one to be present on significant occasions and to ask fairly personal questions of others, while still avoiding any act of commitment, proselyting, indication of conviction, or any act of directing the course of the movement. We have already shown how the mere joining of the group by the observers tended to heighten the conviction of at least the Armstrongs and Mrs. Keech, but a few examples of the kinds of situations the observers faced as members will illustrate the difficulties they encountered and their attempts to cope with them. Actually, we were unable to achieve our goal of complete neutrality. At various points there arose situations in which the observers were forced to take some action and no matter what they might have done, their action would have had some effect on developments in the group.

One of the most obvious kinds of pressure on observers was to get them to take various kinds of responsibilities for recommending or taking action in the group. Most blatant was the situation that one of the authors encountered on November 23 when Marian Keech asked him, in fact commanded him, to lead the meeting that night. His solution was to suggest that the group meditate silently and wait for inspiration. The agonizing silence that followed was broken by Bertha's first plunge into mediumship (see Chapter III), an act that was undoubtedly made possible by the silence and by the author's failure to act himself. Twice again during that long meeting Marian Keech asked the author if he had "brought a message" for the group. By the time of his third refusal to act, he began to be concerned lest his apparent incapacity should injure the carefully nurtured rapport he had established in the group.

Both of our Lake City "local" observers were under pressure at various times in mid-December to quit their jobs and spend all their time with the group. One observer persistently avoided making any statement about his plans; the other waited until the 17th and then announced that her job had been terminated. Yet their evasion of these requests and their failure to quit their jobs at once were not only embarrassing to them and threatening to their rapport with the group, but also may have had the effect of making the members who had quit their jobs less sure they had done the right thing. In short, as members, the observers could not be neutral–any action had consequences.

Another form of demand for action was pressure on all the observers to take a stand when a division of opinion occurred in the group. Illustrative of this is the dilemma which the observers faced when during the meeting of December 4 Bertha brought meat into the Keech home after the Creator had revoked the vegetarian rule. While most members of the group proceeded to eat the meat, Mrs. Keech herself abstained. Any action of the observers had to be a choice between Sananda and the Creator. On this occasion the observers chose to abstain from eating the meat.

Another type of difficulty was faced by the observers when, on occasion, they were forced to deal directly with outsiders. During mid-December, especially from the 18th to the 20th, the Lake City observers were occasionally handed the task of answering the phone. When they could not avoid doing it, they were careful to ask for detailed instructions and meticulously followed them. Once or twice they were asked to discuss the belief system with callers. Ordinarily the observers tried to turn such occasions into interviews with the inquirers, but could not always avoid direct questions from the caller. Such questions were always personally embarrassing but became strategically difficult when a "real" member of the group was in a position to overhear the observer's answer. As far as we can tell, we fumbled our way through these latter crises without positively convincing any caller and without arousing any suspicions among members save those having to do with the observers' intelligence and knowledge of the belief system.

Occasionally the observers' well-hidden network of communication outside the group proved invaluable but led to unintended interpretations among the members of the group. Through these channels the authors learned of two meetings in Lake City that we had not been informed of "officially" by Mrs. Keech and we requested invitations to visit her on these days. It was clear from her subsequent remarks that she regarded our means of anticipating meetings as having supernatural origin. Once we had an observer change a personal plan that he had announced to Mrs. Keech in order to have him attend a meeting where we thought we might be shorthanded. Forced to give some account of his unexpected (and uninvited) appearance he had to say that he had changed his plans on impulse and, again, what might have been regarded by most people as a curious coincidence was interpreted by Mrs. Keech as a significant exercise of influence by the Guardians. It was omniscience of this sort that led Mrs. Keech to suspect that one of the authors had "his own channels of information" to the Guardians.

Finally, we shall describe an incident that strikingly highlights the utter impossibility of avoiding influence on the believers short of absolute refusal to participate in an activity. At the end of the December 3–4 meeting, Bertha sat for "private consultations" between the individual members and "the Creator" who spoke through her. All the observers dutifully asked a question or two of the Creator and accepted the answers passively, quitting the situation as soon as they politely could. The last observer to go through this ritual was not allowed to be merely passive and nondirective, however. The voice of the medium droned on for a few minutes and then said: "I am the Creator." Next the voice asked our observer: "What do you see when I say 'I am the Creator'?" To this the observer replied, "Nothing," whereupon the medium's voice explained: "That's not nothing; that's the void." The medium then pressed further: "Do you see a light in the void?" Our observer struggled with this impasse by answering, "A light in the void?" and got, as a reply, a fuller explanation of the "light that expands and covers the void" together with an increasing flood of elaboration that terminated when the medium called other members into the room and asserted that the observer had just been "allowed to witness Creation"! The medium further stated that this "event" was validation of her speaking with the Creator's voice since, every time her voice said "I am the Creator" our observer saw the vision of Creation! Against this sort of runaway invention even the most polished technique of nondirective response is powerless.

In spite of our best efforts, then, we did have some effects on the movement. We have perhaps overemphasized the effect of the observers by pulling out the major incidents that evidence our influence, but our presence alone, and some of our actions, did lend support to their convictions and their activities. On the other hand, at no time did we exercise any influence whatsoever on proselyting activity. We were meticulously concerned with this point and we were completely successful in avoiding any impact on our major dependent variable.

THE OBSERVERS AND THEIR TASK

All observers were either students or staff members in departments of psychology or sociology, and all had had some previous experience in interviewing and observational technique.

We included one male and one female observer in each local team, so that we could exploit any advantages that a same-sex interviewer has in gathering data from a subject. It turned out to give us certain unanticipated advantages, too, for the female observers were able to pick up a great deal of information as parttime residents of the Keech and Armstrong households, a role that would have been much more difficult for a man to fill.

The assignment handed the observers was necessarily open-ended for the very good reason that the situation they were to observe was extremely fluid and unpredictable. The observers were given very brief "training" in the objectives of the study and instructions about the kinds of information we were most interested in collecting. They were informed that we needed to know, about each individual in the movement, the degree to which he was sincerely convinced of the truth of the various components of the belief system; the kinds of actions he had taken (or failed to take) in committing himself to participation in the movement; and, finally, the extent to which he had engaged in proselyting or propagandizing for the belief system. In addition, the observers were instructed to note any activities or utterances of members that indicated changes or developments in the belief system, in plans for future action (particularly in regard to coping with the cataclysm), and any items of personal history that might throw light on how the members had become interested and active in the movement–especially if these items would throw further light on conviction, commitment, and proselyting. The first objectives of observation, then, were to determine whether or not a group of followers existed, who they were, and how convinced and committed they were.

The second important task, in the early phase of observation, was to discover what actions the members of the movement would take as the date of the cataclysm drew near. We knew that it would be essential to be present during the disconfirmation and recovery phases, and were greatly concerned about the initial plan of the group to go to the "safe places" in mountain ranges. Since we did not know how many people, or who, would be going to any particular place, or how many observers would be needed, we were greatly concerned about personnel, equipment, and travel facilities for accompanying the migrants and living with them for an indefinite period of disconfirmation on the side of a hill in midwinter.

Finally, since the ideology itself seemed changeable, and the inspirations of the leaders unpredictable, we had to be prepared for almost any contingency including the awful possibility that the date would be changed, postponed, or abandoned. It was a nerve-racking uncertainty that stayed with us right up till the midnight vigil on December 20.

Thus the job of observation differed from that encountered in a community study or the study of a stable, organized group holding regular meetings and having a fairly fixed plan of activity. We could not count on the regular recurrence of particular activities or interactions. With the exception of one or two of the Seekers' meeting we rarely knew more than a few days ahead of time when any organized activity would take place, or where it would occur. The leaders themselves were unable to give planful coherence to their activities because of the other-worldly origin of their directives, and invariably shrugged off any question about the future by asserting that they were waiting for orders. Thus we had to grant as much responsibility and autonomy to our observers as possible and depend largely on their own initiative and acquaintance with the local situation to govern their actions. Problems of rigor and systematization in observation took a back seat in the hurly-burly of simply trying to keep up with a movement that often seemed to us to be ruled by whimsy.

For all practical purposes, the period of intensive observation began approximately one month before the predicted flood—i.e., on November 19. Between this date and the end of intensive observation on January 7, we conducted observations in Collegeville on 29 days and in Lake City on 31 days. Some of these visits or contacts were brief—only an hour or two, while others lasted up to 12 or 14 hours of continuous observation. Coverage grew more intensive as the predicted date of the cataclysm drew nearer. In Collegeville there was daily observation from the 9th through the 24th of December, and in Lake City, from the 14th through the 27th of December. In both places there was at least one observer present at almost every waking hour between the 17th and the 22nd. Indeed, for this period, our female observers for all practical purposes resided in the Keech and Armstrong homes. When the Lake City observer told the group on the 17th that she no longer had a job, Mrs. Keech invited her to move in. In Collegeville, when the Armstrongs set out for Lake City on the 13th they simply assumed that our observer there would be willing to stay in their home and help look after their children. This observer was trapped and there was nothing to do about it.

It will be clear from this account of the extent of surveillance that we were fairly successful in arranging to have an observer present at the major events and developments in the movement and, when these were not correctly anticipated, to have someone on the scene shortly afterward to get an account of what had occurred from one or more of the participants. We are sure that we had a representative at every group meeting between the 20th of November and the 7th of January, and the only major "event" we did not cover at first hand was the Christmas carol sing on the lawn in front of Mrs. Keech's house on December 24.

Owing to observer fatigue we have a less complete account than we would like of the meeting (on December 12–13) between Marian Keech and Ella Lowell; but we believe we picked up the essential details and know the significance of the meeting. There were a few minor events during the observation period that we did not cover: one rump meeting at Bertha's home on December 6 (although we heard fairly complete tape recordings of the speeches of Dr. Browning on this occasion); a small private meeting on December 16 following the public lecture to the flying saucer club; and other events of this nature, whose significance was made clear to us by the participants' subsequent accounts.

Thorough coverage was both essential and difficult. Many of our observers' visits produced a relatively low yield of information (though scarcely any were completely barren) simply because nothing new had occurred since their previous call, or the members were engaged in biding their time—a rather unexciting activity. When no special event was taking place, the observers were usually able to draw out background information, cross-check rumors and reports among members, make inquiries about degree of conviction or proselyting activity, and, if nothing better offered itself, continue to build rapport.

The observational scheme was difficult to operate too because of the near impossibility of keeping a fresh, alert observer on duty at all times whenever something was likely to occur. Observing, in this study, was exhausting work. In addition to the strain created by having to play an accepting, passive role vis-à-vis an ideology that aroused constant incredulity, which had to be concealed, observers frequently had to stay in the group for long hours without having an opportunity to record what they learned. Sometimes, the long hours were imposed by Mrs. Keech or Bertha, who would make rules regarding constancy of attendance; sometimes circumstances stuck one observer with his task during a crucial phase when he was unable to summon a relief, or the relief could not appear.

Our observers had their own daily lives to care for as well as the job, and were subject to occasional bouts of illness or fatigue from lack of sleep. The job was frequently irritating because of the irrelevancies (from the point of view of our main interest) that occupied vast quantities of time during the all-night meetings, the repetitiousness of much that was said, and the incoherence of the congeries of beliefs that went into the melting pot of ideology. This last aspect was not only exhausting because of the strain imposed on attention and memory, but irritating because the observers felt responsible for keeping it all straight and setting it down as accurately as possible at a later time.

RECORDING OBSERVATIONS

The data collected by the observers was in the form of anecdotal accounts of events that took place in their presence; reports to them of actions that members had taken earlier or elsewhere; factual or attitudinal data elicited in interviews or conversations with members; and the content of talks or assertions made to the group as a whole. The circumstances of observation made it impossible to make notes openly except on a single occasion, the meeting of November 23, when the Creator ordered notes taken. It was also difficult to make notes privately or secretly, for the observers were rarely left alone inside the house and it was necessary to be ingenious enough to find excuses for leaving the group temporarily. One device used occasionally was to make notes in the bathroom. This was not entirely satisfactory, however, since too frequent trips there would probably arouse curiosity if not suspicion. Sometimes the bathroom was used in relays. On the morning of December 21, for example, when all our observers were very fatigued and unwilling to trust their memory too much, one would go make notes while the others stayed to listen.

Every so often it was possible for an observer to slip out on the back porch to make notes in the dark. During breaks in the meetings the observers would frequently take walks outdoors to get fresh air, thus providing another opportunity. For example, after Dr. Armstrong had finished urging one of the authors to shed his doubts at the critical time of 3:30 A.M. on December 21, Dr. Armstrong went back indoors but the author, pleading that he needed to think alone, stayed outdoors and wrote down the whole episode immediately.

At other times we had to depend upon memory to retain the substance of conversations, interviews and the like until we could dictate these observations into tape recorders. Every observer had access to such a machine, and was under instructions to dictate his observstions as soon as possible after each contact. Ordinarily such dictation could be accomplished within a few hours after leaving the observation site, though from time to time an observer, exhausted by an all-night meeting, had to defer dictation until he had caught up on sleep. The greater part of our data was tape-recorded within three or four hours of the time the observer ended his contact. During the period of round-the-clock coverage of the Lake City group (between the 17th and the 22nd of December), we maintained a temporary headquarters in a hotel about half a mile from Mrs. Keech's home, and the observers kept three tape-recording machines busy absorbing their notes. Most of the material obtained during this time was recorded within an hour after leaving the house.

In all, the reports of the observers filled approximately 65 reels of one-hour tapes, yielding almost 1000 pages of typescript when they were transcribed; in addition, we accumulated about 100 typewritten pages of material that had been directly recorded. This latter material includes a variety of things. When Marian Keech and Dr. Armstrong addressed the Flying Saucer

Club, we arranged to have a special assistant attend this public meeting and he succeeded in recording almost the entire session on a midget tape recorder.

Our verbatim material also includes many phone conversations. From the evening of December 21 on, the group, expecting that orders from the Guardians might come over the phone, tape-recorded every incoming phone call. The group was quite happy to let one of our observers borrow these tapes, which we then transcribed. In addition, our observers in Collegeville were able to transcribe many of the Ella Lowell tapes. We also have verbatim copies and sometimes the originals of many of Mrs. Keech's most important messages.

The material we gathered, therefore, varies in accuracy from verbatim transcriptions or written documents on the one hand to a few reports that are simply summaries of the highlights of very long meetings. For events before the beginning of direct observation we have had to rely largely on retrospective material.

We have quoted directly from documents and firsthand tape recordings, but otherwise have used the direct quotation form only when the observer either had an opportunity to make written notes on a conversation within a few minutes of its occurrence, or when he made an especial point of remembering an important statement verbatim and putting it into his record with assurances to that effect.

SUMMARY

From the foregoing description as well as from the report in the substantive chapters, it should be clear to the reader that the procedures used in conducting this study departed from the orthodoxy of social science in a number of respects. We should like to summarize here some of these departures and the facts that made them necessary.

In the first place, it is clear that we were unable to rely on the standard array of technical tools of social psychology. Our material is largely qualitative rather than quantitative and even simple tabulations of what we observed would be difficult. Owing to the complete novelty and unpredictability of the movement, as well as to the pressure of time, we could not develop standard categories of events, actions, statements, feelings, and the like, and certainly could not subject the members of the group to any standardized measuring instrument, such as a questionnaire or structured interview, in order to compare indices before and after disconfirmation.

Actually we faced as much a job of detective work as of observation. We had to listen, probe, and query constantly to find out in the beginning who the members of the group were, how sincerely they believed the ideology, what actions they were taking that were consonant with their beliefs, and to what extent they were propagandizing or attempting to convince others.

Later, we had to continue to accumulate this sort of data while further inquiring about what was going to happen next in the movement: when there would be another meeting, who was being invited, where the group (or individuals) were going to wait for the flood, and like questions. Furthermore, we had to conduct the entire inquiry covertly, without revealing our research purpose, pretending to be merely interested individuals who had been persuaded of the correctness of the belief system and yet taking a passive and uninfluential role in the group. Our data, in places, are less complete than we would like, our influence on the group somewhat greater than we would like. We were able, however, to collect enough information to tell a coherent story and, fortunately, the effects of disconfirmation were striking enough to provide for firm conclusions.

A Comment on Disguised Observation in Sociology

Kai T. Erikson

At the beginning of their excellent paper on the subject, Howard S. Becker and Blanche Geer define participant observation as "that method in which the observer participates in the daily life of the people under study, either openly in the role of researcher or covertly in some disguised role . . ."[1]

The purpose of this paper is to argue that the research strategy mentioned in the last few words of that description represents a signigicant ethical problem in the field of sociology. In point of sheer volume, of course, the problem is relatively small, for disguised participant observation is probably one of the rarest research techniques in use among sociologists. But in point of gen-

Kai T. Erikson, "A Comment on Disguised Observation in Sociology," *Social Problems,* 14 (Spring, 1967), 366–373. Reprinted by permission of the author and The Society for the Study of Social Problems.

eral importance, the problem is far more serious–partly because the use of disguises seems to attract a disproportionate amount of interest both inside and outside the field, and partly because it offers a natural starting point for dealing with other ethical issues in the profession.

In recent years, a handful of studies have been reported in the literature based on the work of observers who deliberately misrepresented their identity in order to enter an otherwise inaccessible social situation, Some of these studies have already provoked a good deal of comment–among them, for instance, the case of the anthropologist who posed as a mental patient by complaining of symptoms he did not feel,[2] the sociologists who joined a gathering of religious mystics by professing convictions they did not share,[3] the Air Force officer who borrowed a new name, a new birth date, a new personal history, a new set of mannerisms and even a new physical appearance in order to impersonate an enlisted man,[4] and the group of graduate students who ventured into a meeting of Alcoholics Anonymous wearing the clothes of men from other social classes than their own and the facial expressions of men suffering from an unfortunate disability.[5]

In taking the position that this kind of masquerading is unethical, I am naturally going to say many things that are only matters of personal opinion; and thus the following remarks are apt to have a more editorial flavor than is usual for papers read at professional meetings. But a good deal more is at stake here than the sensitivities of any particular person, and my excuse for dealing with an issue that seems to have so many subjective overtones is that the use of disguises in social research affects the professional climate in which all of us work and raises a number of methodological questions that should be discussed more widely.

I am assuming here that "personal morality" and "professional ethics" are not the same thing. Personal morality has something to do with the way an individual conducts himself across the range of his human contacts; it is not local to a particular group of persons or to a particular set of occupational interests. Professional ethics, on the other hand, refer to the way a group of associates define their special responsibility to one another and to the rest of the social order in which they work. In this sense, professional ethics often deal with issues that are practical in their application and limited in their scope: they are the terms of a covenant among people gathered together into a given occupational group. For instance, it may or may not be ethical for an espionage agent or a journalist to represent himself as someone he is not in the course of gathering information, but it certainly does not follow that the conduct of a sociologist should be judged in the same terms; for the sociologist has a different relationship to the rest of the community, operates under a different warrant, and has a different set of professional and scientific interests to protect. In this sense, the ethics governing a particular discipline are in many ways local to the transactions that discipline has with the larger world.

The argument to be presented here, then, is that the practice of using masks in social research compromises both the people who wear them and the people for whom they are worn, and in doing so, violates the terms of a contract which the sociologist should be ready to honor in his dealings with others. There are many respects in which this is true, but I will be dealing here in particular with the relationship between the sociologist and (a) the subjects of his research, (b) the colleagues with whom he works, (c) the students he agrees to teach, and (d) the data he takes as his subject matter.

The first of these points has to do with the responsibilities a sociologist should accept toward other institutions and other people in the social order. It may seem a little cranky to insist that disguised observation constitutes an ugly invasion of privacy and is, on that ground alone, objectionable. But it is a matter of cold calculation to point out that this particular research strategy can injure people in ways we can neither anticipate in advance nor compensate for afterward. For one thing, the sheer act of entering a human transaction on the basis of deliberate fraud may be painful to the people who are thereby misled; and even if that were not the case, there are countless ways in which a stranger who pretends to be something else can disturb others by failing to understand the conditions of intimacy that prevail in the group he has tried to invade. Nor does it matter very much how sympathetic the observer is toward the persons whose lives he is studying: the fact of the matter is that he does not *know* which of his actions are apt to hurt other people, and it is highly presumptuous of him to act as if he does—particularly when, as is ordinarily the case, he has elected to wear a disguise exactly because he is entering a social sphere so far from his own experience.

So the sheer act of wearing disguises in someone else's world may cause discomfort, no matter what we later write in our reports; and this possibility raises two questions. The first, of course, is whether we have the right to inflict pain at all when we are aware of these risks and the subjects of the study are not. The second, however, is perhaps more important from the narrow point of view of the profession itself: so long as we suspect that a method we use has at least *some* potential for harming others, we are in the extremely awkward position of having to weigh the scientific and social benefits of that procedure against its possible cost in human discomfort, and this is a difficult business under the best of circumstances. If we happen to harm people who have agreed to act as subjects, we can at least argue that they knew something of the risks involved and were willing to contribute to that vague program called the "advance of knowledge." But when we do so with people who have expressed no readiness to participate in our researches (indeed, people who would presumably have refused if asked directly), we are in very much the same ethical position as a physician who carries out medical experiments on human subjects without their consent. The only conceivable argument in favor of such experimentation is that the knowledge derived from it is worth the discomfort it may cause. And the difficulties here are that we do not know how to measure the value of the work we do or the methods we employ in this way, and, moreover, that we might be doing an extraordinary disservice to the idea of detached scholarship if we tried. Sociologists cannot protect their freedom of inquiry if they owe the rest of the community (not to mention themselves) an accounting for the distress they may have inadvertently imposed on people who have not volunteered to take that risk.

The second problem with disguised observation to be considered here has to do with the sociologist's responsibilities to his colleagues. It probably goes without saying that research of this sort is liable to damage the reputation of sociology in the larger society and close off promising areas of research for future investigators. This is true in the limited sense that a particular agency–say, for example, Alcoholics Anonymous–may decide that its integrity and perhaps even its effectiveness was violated by the appearance of sociologists pretending to be someone else and deny access to other students who propose to use an altogether different approach. And it is also true in the wider sense that any research tactic which attracts unfavorable notice may help diminish the general climate of trust toward sociology in the community as a whole. So long as this remains a serious possibility, the practice of disguised observation becomes a problem for everyone in the profession; and to this extent, it is wholly within the bounds of professional etiquette for one sociologist to challenge the work of another on this score.

This objection has been raised several times before, and the answer most often given to it is that the people who are studied in this fashion–alcoholics or spiritualists or mental patients, for example–are not likely to read what we say about them anyway. Now this argument has the advantage of being correct a good deal of the time, but this fact does not prevent it from being altogether irrelevant. To begin with, the experience of the past few years should surely have informed us that the press is more than ready to translate our technical reports into news copy, and this means that we can no longer provide shelter for other people behind the walls of our own anonymity. But even if that were not the case, it is a little absurd for us to claim that we derive some measure of protection from the narrowness of our audience when we devote so much time trying to broaden it. The fact is that we are increasingly reaching audiences whose confidence we cannot afford to jeopardize, and we have every right to be afraid that such people may close their doors to sociological research if they learn to become too suspicious of our methods and intentions.

The third objection to be raised here, if only as a note in passing, concerns the responsibilities the profession should accept toward its students. The division of labor in contemporary sociology is such that a considerable proportion of the data we use in our work is gathered by graduate students or other apprentices, and this proportion is even higher for research procedures that require the amount of energy and time necessary for participant observation. Of the dozen or more observers who took part in the studies I have cited, for example, all but one was a graduate student. Now a number of sociologists who have engaged in disguised observation have reported that it is apt to pose serious moral problems and a good deal of personal discomfort, and I think one might well argue that this is a heavy burden to place on any person who is, by our own explicit standards, not yet ready for professional life. I am not suggesting here that students are too immature to make a seasoned choice in the matter. I am suggesting that they should not be asked to make what one defender of the method has called "real and excruiciating moral decisions" while they are still students and presumably protected from the various dilemmas and contentions which occupy us in meetings like this—particularly since they are so likely to be academically, economically, and even psychologically dependent upon those elders who ask them to choose.[6]

The fourth objection I would like to raise here about the use of undercover observation is probably the most important—and yet the most remote from what is usually meant by the term "ethics." It seems to me that any attempt to use masquerades in social research betrays an extraordinary disrespect for the complexities of human interaction, and for this reason can only lead to bad science. Perhaps the most important responsibility of any sociologist is to appreciate how little he really knows about his intricate and elusive subject matter. We have at best a poor understanding of the human mind, of the communication signals that link one mind to another, or the social structures that emerge from those linkages—and it is the most arrant kind of oversimplification for us to think that we can assess the effect which a clever costume or a few studied gestures have on the social setting. The pose might "work" in the sense that the observer is admitted into the situation; but once this passage has been accomplished, how is he to judge his own influence on the lives of the people he is studying? This is a serious problem in every department of science, of course, and a good deal of time has been devoted to its solution. But the only way to cope with the problem in even a preliminary way is to have as clear a picture as possible of the social properties that the observer is introducing into the situation, and this is altogether impossible if we ourselves are not sure who he is. We can *impersonate* other modes of behavior with varying degrees of insight and skill, but we cannot *reproduce* them; and since this is the case, it seems a little irresponsible for a sociologist to assume that he can enter social life in any masquerade that suits his purpose without seriously disrupting the scene he hopes to study.

When people interact, they relate to one another at many different levels at once, and only a fraction of the messages communicated during that interchange are registered in the conscious mind of the participant. It may be possible for someone to mimic the conventional gestures of fear, but it is impossible for him to reproduce the small postural and chemical changes which go with it. It may be possible for a middle-class speaker to imitate the broader accents of lower-class speech, but his vocal equipment is simply not conditioned to do so without arousing at least a subliminal suspicion. It may be possible for a trained person to rearrange the slant of his body and reset his facial muscles to approximate the bearing of someone else, but his performance will never be anything more than a rough imposture. Now we know that these various physiological, linguistic, and kinetic cues play an important part in the context of human interaction, but we have no idea how to simulate them–and what is probably more to the point, we never will. For one thing, we cannot expect to learn in a matter of hours what others have been practicing throughout a lifetime. For another, to imitate always means to parody, to caricature, to exaggerate certain details of behavior at the expense of others, and to that extent any person who selects a disguise will naturally emphasize those details which *he* assumes are most important to the character he is portraying. In doing so, of course, he is really only portraying a piece of himself. It is interesting to speculate, for example, why the Air Force lieutenant mentioned earlier thought he needed to present himself as a near-delinquent youth with a visible layer of personal problems in order to pose as an enlisted man. Whatever the reasoning behind this particular charade, it would certainly be reasonable for someone to suspect that it tells us more about the investigators' impression of enlisted men than it does about the men themselves–and since we have no way of learning whether this is true or not, we have lost rather than gained an edge of control over the situation we are hoping to understand. What the investigators had introduced into the situation was a creature of their own invention, and it would be hardly surprising if the results of their inquiry corresponded to some image they had in advance of the enlisted man's condition. (It is perhaps worth noting here that impersonation always seems easier for people looking down rather than up the status ladder. We find it reasonable to assume that officers "know how" to portray enlisted men or that sociologists have the technical capacity to pose as drunks or religious mystics, but it is not at all clear that the reverse would be equally true.)

This, then, is the problem. If we provide observers with special masks and coach them in the "ways" of the private world they are hoping to enter, how can we learn what is happening to the people who meet them in this disguise? What information is registered in the unconscious minds of the other people who live in that world? How does the social structure accommodate to this peculiar invasion?

It is clear, I think, that something happens–something over which we have no control. Let me relate two incidents drawn from the studies mentioned earlier. The first has to do with the Air Force officer who posed as an enlisted man. In their report of the study, the investigators used several pages of a short paper to describe the elaborate masquerade they had fashioned for the observer and the coaching he had received in the ways of the adolescent subculture. "So successful was the tutoring," reads the brief report, "that when the time for 'enlistment' arrived, the recruiting sergeant . . . suggested that the observer not be accepted by the Air Force because by all appearances he was a juvenile delinquent."[7] And later, during an interview with a service psychologist, the observer was recommended for reclassification on the grounds that he appeared quite anxious over the death of his father. Now these events may indeed suggest that the pose was successful, for the observer *was* trying to look somewhat delinquent and *did* have a story memorized about the death of his father in an auto accident. But who would care to argue that the diagnosis of the sergeant and the psychologist were inaccurate? Surely something was wrong, and if they perceived an edge of uneasiness which reminded them of anxiety or detected a note of furtiveness which looked to them like delinquency, they may only have been responding to the presence of a real conflict between the observer and his mask. We may leave it to the psychoanalysts to ask whether vague anxieties about "killing" one's father are an unlikely impression for someone to leave behind when he is parading around with a new name, a new background, a new history, and, of course, a new set of parents. The authors of the article tell us that the observer "did have something of a problem to transform himself from a 27-year-old college trained, commissioned officer into a 19-year-old, near-delinquent high school graduate," and this is certainly easy to believe.[8] What is more difficult to believe is that such a transformation is possible at all—and if it is not, we can have very little confidence in the information gathered by the observer. Since we do not know to what kind of creature the enlisted men were responding, we do not know what sense to make of what they said and did.

The second example comes from the study of the apocalyptic religious group. At one point in the study, two observers arrived at one of the group's meeting places under instructions to tell quite ordinary stories about their experiences in spiritualism in order to create as little commotion as possible. A few days afterwards, however, the leader of the group was overheard explaining that the two observers had appeared upset, excited, confused, and unsure of their errand at the time of their original visit, all of which helped confirm her suspicion that they had somehow been "sent" from another planet. In one sense, of course, this incident offered the observers an intriguing view of the belief structure of the cult, but in another sense, the leader's assessment of the situation was very shrewd: after all, the observers *had* been sent from another world, if not another planet, and she may have been quite right to sense that they were a bit confused and unsure of their errand during their early moments in the new job. "In both cases," the report informs us, the visits of the observers "were given as illustrations that 'strange things are happening.' "[9] Indeed, strange things *were* happening; yet we have no idea how strange they really were. It is almost impossible to evaluate the reaction of the group to the appearance of the pair of observers because we do not know whether they were seen as ordinary converts or as extraordinary beings. And it makes a difference, for in the first instance the investigators would be observing a response which fell within the normal range of the group's experience, while in the second instance they would be observing a response which would never have taken place had the life of the group been allowed to run its own course.

My point in raising these two examples, it should be clear, is not to insist on the accuracy of these or any other interpretations, but to point out that a wide variety of such interpretations is possible so long as one has no control over the effects introduced by the observer. A company of recruits with a disguised officer in its midst is simply a different kind of organization than one without the same ingredient; a group of spiritualists which numbers as many as eight observers among its twenty or so members has a wholly different character than one which does not–and so long as we remain unable to account for such differences, we cannot know the meaning of the information we collect.

In one of the most sensible pieces written on the subject, Julius Roth has reminded us that all social research is disguised in one respect or another and that the range of ethical questions which bear on the issue must be visualized as falling on a continuum.[10] Thus, it is all very well for someone to argue that deliberate disguises are improper for sociologists, but it is quite another matter for him to specify what varieties of research activity fall within the range of that principle. Every ethical statement seems to lose its crisp authority the moment it is carried over into marginal situations where the conditions governing research are not so clearly stipulated. For instance, some of the richest material in the social sciences has been gathered by sociologists who were true participants in the group under study but who did not announce to other members that they were employing this opportunity to collect research data. Sociologists live careers in which they occasionally become patients, occasionally take jobs as steel workers or taxi drivers, and frequently find themselves in social settings where their trained eye begins to look for data even though their presence in the situation was not engineered for that purpose. It would be absurd, then, to insist as a point of ethics that sociologists should always introduce themselves as investigators everywhere they go and should inform every person who figures in their thinking exactly what their research is all about.

But I do think we can find a place to begin. If disguised observation sits somewhere on a continuum and is not easily defined, this only suggests that we will have to seek further for a relevant ethic and recognize that any line we draw on that continuum will be a little artificial. What I propose, then, at least as a beginning, is the following: first, that it is unethical for a sociologist to *deliberately misrepresent* his identity for the purpose of entering a private domain *to which he is not otherwise eligible;* and second, that it is unethical for a sociologist to *deliberately misrepresent* the character of the research in which he is engaged. Now these negative sanctions leave us a good deal of leeway–more, perhaps, than we will eventually want. But they have the effect of establishing a stable point of reference in an otherwise hazy territory, and from such an anchored position as this we can move out into more important questions about invasion of privacy as an ethical issue.

In the meantime, the time has probably come for us to assume a general posture on the question of disguised participant observation even if we are not yet ready to state a specific ethic, and a logical first step in this direction would be to assess how most members of the profession feel about the matter. I am not suggesting that we poll one another on the merits of adopting a formal code, but that we take some kind of unofficial reading to learn what we can about the prevailing climate of opinion in the field. If we discover that a substantial number of sociologists are uncomfortable about the practice, then those who continue to employ it will at least know where they stand in respect to the "collective conscience" of their discipline. And if we discover that only a scattering of sociologists are concerned about the matter, we will at least have the satisfaction of knowing that the profession—as a profession—has accepted the responsibility of knowing its own mind.

NOTES

1. Howard S. Becker and Blanche Geer, "Participant Observation and Interviewing: A Comparison," *Human Organization* 16 (1957): 28–32.
2. William C. Caudill, *et al.*, "Social Structure and Interaction Processes on a Psychiatric Ward," *American Journal of Orthopsychiatry* 22 (1952): 314–34.
3. Leon Festinger, Henry W. Riecken, and Stanley Schachter, *When Prophecy Fails* (Minneapolis: University of Minnesota Press, 1956).
4. Mortimer A. Sullivan, Stuart A. Queen, and Ralph C. Patrick, Jr., "Participant Observation as Employed in the Study of a Military Training Program," *American Sociological Review* 23 (1958): 660–67.
5. John F. Lofland and Robert A. Lejeune, "Initial Interaction of Newcomers in Alcoholics Anonymous: A Field Experiment in Class Symbols and Socialization," *Social Problems* 8 (1960): 102–11.
6. To keep the record straight, I might add that I first became interested in these matters when I was a graduate student and applied for one of the observer posts mentioned here.
7. Sullivan, *et al., Participant Observation*, p. 663.
8. Stuart A. Queen, "Comment," *American Sociological Review* 24 (1959): 399–400.
9. Festinger, *et al., When Prophecy Fails*, pp. 241–2.
10. Julius A. Roth, "Comments on 'Secret Observation,'" *Social Problems* 9 (1962): 283–4.

Field Notes

John Lofland

For better or worse, the human mind forgets massively and quickly. The people under study forget massively and quickly, too. In order, then, to have any kind of an edge on the participants in articulating and understanding their world, it is necessary to have some means to overcome forgetting. Writing is such a device. Without the sustained writing down of what has gone on, the observer is in hardly a better position to analyze and comprehend the workings of a world than are the members themselves. Writing, in the form of continued notes with which the forgotten past can be summoned into the present, is an absolutely necessary if not sufficient condition for comprehending the objects of observation. Aside from getting along in the setting, the fundamental concrete task of the observer is the taking of field notes. Whether or not he performs this task is perhaps the most important determinant of later bringing off a qualitative analysis. Field notes provide the observer's *raison d'etre*. If he is not doing them, he might as well not be in the setting.

MENTAL NOTES

Let us assume the observer is somewhere—meeting with persons, attending an event, etc. The first step in taking field notes is to evoke one's culturally common sense and shared notion of what constitutes a descriptive report of something happening. From reading newspapers, magazines, and the like, one is already familiar with the character of sheer reportage. It concerns such matters as who and how many were there, the physical character of the place, who said what to whom, who moved about in what way, and a general characterization of an order of events.

The first step in the process of writing field notes is to orient one's con-

From *Analysing Social Structures* by John Lofland. Copyright © 1971 by Wadsworth Publishing Co., Inc., Belmont, California 94002. Reprinted by permission of the publisher.

sciousness to the task of remembering items of these (and, as the research develops) other kinds. This act of directing one's consciousness in order to remember at a later point may be called *mental notes*. One is preparing oneself to be able to put down on paper what he is now seeing.

JOTTED NOTES

If one is writing field notes *per se* only at the end of a period of observation or at the end of a day—which is a relatively typical practice—it will be helpful to preserve these mental notes as more than electrical traces in the brain. Such traces have a very high rate of decay. One way in which provisionally to preserve them is with *jotted notes*. Jotted notes are constituted of all the little phrases, quotes, key words, and the like that one puts down during the observation and at inconspicuous moments in order to have something physically to refer to when one actually sits down to write his field notes. Jotted notes have the function of jogging one's memory at the time of writing field notes.

Many field workers carry small, pocket-sized tablets or notebooks precisely for the purpose of jotting down notes. Any surface will do, however—the cover of a book, a napkin, the back of a pamphlet, etc.

PREVIOUSLY FORGOTTEN

In the field, a present observation will often bring back a memory of something that happened on a previous occasion that one has forgotten to put in his field notes. Include these memories in one's jotted notes also.

DON'T JOT CONSPICUOUSLY

Whether one is a known or an unknown observer, the general rule of thumb is "don't jot conspicuously." Of course, one may also be doing interviewing in the field while observing. In that case, in order to seem competent, one should take notes . . . . In an interaction defined as an interview, the interviewee will expect one to take some kind of notes in order to indicate that you are indeed seriously interviewing him! And there may be other occasions when someone expects one to write something down on the spot.

But in ordinary day-to-day observation it seems wisest not to flaunt the fact that one is recording. If one is a known observer, the observed are already well aware of being observed. One need not increase any existing anxieties by continuously and openly writing down what is being viewed. Rather, jot notes at moments of withdrawal and when shielded: for example, in rest rooms, and sometimes in cars, hallways, and offices, etc. In some settings that have "meetings," members will sometimes themselves make notes. Under such conditions one can feel free to go along with the crowd.

FULLER JOTTINGS

In addition, and before getting to the full field notes, an observer may—on the way home, waiting for a bus, before going to bed, etc.—make more elaborate jottings.

THE FULL FIELD NOTES

At the end of a day (or of a shorter observation period), the observer must cloister himself for the purpose of doing *full field notes.* All those mental notes and jottings are *not* field notes until one has converted them to a running log of observations.

Mechanics

WRITE PROMPTLY

As a general rule, full field notes should be written no later than the morning after observation on the previous day. If one observed only in a morning, then write them up that afternoon. If one observed only in an afternoon, do the notes that evening. The underlying rule is to minimize the temporal span between observation and writing field notes.

Among the useful findings of psychologists is that forgetting is very slight in the first time units after a learning experience but then accelerates in a rather geometric fashion as more time passes. To wait a day or more is to forget a massive amount of material. Happily, it has also been found that memory decays very little during sleep. That is, forgetting has more to do with the acquisition of new experience than with the sheer passage of time. Therefore, it is reasonably safe to sleep on a day's or evening's observations and write them up the first thing the next morning, thus avoiding the necessity of staying up half the night. But if one waits for days, he is likely to remember only the barest outlines of the observation period.

PERSONAL DISCIPLINE AND TIME

Let me not deceive the reader. The writing of field notes takes *personal discipline* and *time.* It is all too easy to put off actually writing notes for a given day and to skip one or more days. For the actual writing of the notes may take as long or longer than did the observation! Indeed, a reasonable rule of thumb here is to expect and plan to spend as much time writing notes as one spent in observing. This is, of course, not invariant. Some observers spend considerably less time and are still able to perform good analysis. Many others have been known to spend considerably more than equal time in writing up their notes. How much time one actually spends depends, too, on the demands of the setting one is observing and the proportion of one's total time being devoted to the study.

But one point is inescapable. All the fun of actually being out and about mucking around in some setting must also be matched by cloistered rigor in committing to paper—and therefore to future usefulness—what has taken place.

DICTATING VERSUS WRITING

Some observers have access to the luxury of dictating machines and transcribing secretaries. And, it seems, talking one's field notes takes much less time than writing them. Such affluents need the same advice here as was given for intensive interviewing: Get the transcriptions as soon as possible and review and pore over them, making further notes in the process. While talking rather than writing saves time, it also removes one from really having to think about what has happened and from searching out analytic themes. Writing rather than talking stimulates thought, or, at least, so it seems for a great number of people.

Since I prefer writing and believe most observers to be poor, I assume, in what follows, writing rather than dictating observers.

HANDWRITING VERSUS TYPEWRITING

I am afraid that an observer should know how to type. Typing is faster than writing, and it is easier to read. As discussed below, copies of the notes are going to be needed. If humanly possible, learn how to type before undertaking any significant piece of field research. I am mindful, nonetheless, that the great works of anthropological field work and works even today are performed well without such an aid. But, then, because many tasks *can* be performed by brute force is not to say that mechanical aids would not help enormously. Thus, one cannot be certain that dictating and computerized transcription will not soon replace typewriting.

NUMBER OF COPIES

Even the least affluent of observers should make at least an original and two carbons of his field notes. The typical practice is to retain one set of notes undisturbed as the running, raw material of observation. Thus, context, sequence, and the like can more easily be summoned up at points of quandary and inquiry at later dates. The other two copies will be literally cut up, filed, and otherwise manipulated . . . .

To the slightly more affluent or resourceful, I should like to recommend a practice described by George McCall. Each day's notes can be typed directly onto ditto, spirit, mimeograph, or other inexpensive duplicating masters.

Whatever number of copies one wants are then made, and the masters retained in case one wants even more copies (McCall and Simmons, 1969:76). In such a way, one attains maximum flexibility in manipulating one's observational material.

What Goes In?

What do field notes consist of? At the most general level they are a more or less chronological log of what is happening, to and in the setting and to and in the observer. Beyond this general statement, the following materials typically and properly appear in field notes.

RUNNING DESCRIPTION

For the most part, they consist of a running description of events, people, things heard and overheard, conversations among people, conversations with people. Each new physical setting and person encountered merits a description. Changes in the physical setting or persons should also be recorded. Since one is likely to encounter the same physical settings and persons again and again, such descriptions need not be repeated, only augmented as changes occur. Observers often draw maps into their field notes, indicating the approximate layouts of locations and the physical placement of persons in scenes, indicating also gross movements of persons through a period of observation.

Since the notes will be heavily chronological, records can be kept of approximate times at which various events occurred.

The writing of running descriptions can be guided by at least two rules of thumb.

> *Be concrete*. Rather than summarizing or employing abstract adjectives and adverbs, attempt to be behavioristic and concrete. Attempt to stay at the lowest possible level of inference. Avoid, as much as possible, employing the participants' descriptive and interpretative terms as one's own descriptive and interpretative terms. If person *A* thought person *B* was happy, joyous, depressed, or whatever, today, report this as the imputation of person *A*. Try to capture person *B's* raw behavioral emissions, leaving aside for that moment any final judgment as to *B's* "true state" or the "true meaning" of his behavior. The participant's belief as to the "true meaning" of objects, events and people are thus recorded as being just that.
>
> *Recall distinctions*. Truman Capote has alleged his ability to recall verbatim several hours of conversation. Such an ability is strikingly unusual. More typically, people recall some things verbatim and many other things only in general. Whether or not one is giving a verbatim account

should be indicated in one's field notes. One might consider adopting notations such as those employed by Anselm Strauss *et al.* in their study of a mental hospital: "Verbal material recorded within quotations signified exact recall; verbal material within apostrophes indicated a lesser degree of certainty or paraphrasing; and verbal material with no markings meant reasonable recall but not quotation" (Strauss, Schatzman, Bucher, Ehrlich, and Sabshin, 1964:29).

PREVIOUSLY FORGOTTEN, NOW RECALLED

As observation periods mount up, one finds himself recalling–often at odd moments–items of information he now remembers that he has not previously entered into the field notes. An occurrence previously seen as insignificant, or simply forgotten, presents itself in consciousness as meriting of record. Summoning it up as best one can, enter the item's date, content, context, and the like into the current day's notes.

ANALYTIC IDEAS AND INFERENCES

If one is working at it at all, ideas will begin to occur about how things are patterned in this setting; how present occurrences are examples of some sociological or other concept; how things "really seem to work around here"; and the like. Some of these ideas may seem obvious and trivial; some may seem far fetched and wild; and many may seem in between. *Put all of them into the field notes.*

The only proviso about putting them in is to be sure to mark them off as being analytic ideas and inferences. This can be done with various characters that appear on a typewriter key board–especially brackets [ ].

When one eventually withdraws from the setting and concentrates upon performing analysis he should thus have more than only raw field material. The period of concerted analysis is greatly facilitated if during the field work itself one is also assembling a background, a foundation of possible lines of analysis and interpretation.

Analytic ideas are likely to be of three varieties. (1) Ideas about the master theme or themes of the study. "What will be the main notions around which all this minutiae is going to be organized?" (2) "Middle-level" chunks of analysis. "Although the topic could not carry the entire analysis, here seems to be developing a set of materials in the field notes that hang together in the following way . . . taking up perhaps 10 to 20 pages in the final report." "Relative to this topic, I want to consider . . ." (3) Minute pieces of analysis. "Here is a neat little thing that will perhaps work out in this way . . . taking a few pages to write up in the final report."

One is very likely to have many more of these memos on analytic directions included in his field notes than he will ever include in the final report. But, by building a foundation of memos and tentative pieces of and directions for analysis, the analytic period will be much less traumatic. Analysis becomes a matter of selecting from and working out analytic themes that already exist. (This is in decided contrast to the pure field note grubber who has no ideas and faces the trauma of inventing analysis during the subsequent period of writing the report. Such people tend not to write the reports or to write highly undisciplined description.)

PERSONAL IMPRESSIONS AND FEELINGS

The field notes are not only for recording the setting; they are for "recording" the observer as well. The observer has his personal opinions of people; he has emotional responses to being an observer and to the setting itself. He can feel discouraged, joyous, rejected, loved, etc. In order to give himself some distance on himself, the observer should also be recording whatever aspect of his emotional life is involved in the setting. If he feels embarrassed, put down, looked upon with particular favor, if he falls in love, hates someone, has an affair, or whatever, this private diary should be keeping track of such facts. Such keeping track can serve at least two important functions. (1) In being at least privately honest with oneself about one's feelings toward objects, events, and people, one may find that some of the participants *also* feel quite similar things and that one's private emotional response was more widespread, thus providing a clue for analysis. In feeling, for instance, that some person in the setting is getting screwed by a turn of events, and getting privately angry over it, one may also discover later that many other people privately felt the same way. And a fact of this kind may lead into important analytic trails. (2) Periodically, one will review his notes, and during analysis one will work with them intensively. A concurrent record of one's emotional state at various past times, might, months later and away from the setting in a cooler frame of mind, allow one to scrutinize one's notes for obvious biases he might have had. One becomes more able to give the benefit of the doubt in cases where one was perhaps too involved or uninvolved in some incident. This running record of one's opinions, impressions, emotions, and the like should, of course, also be labeled as such in the notes.

NOTES FOR FURTHER INFORMATION

Any given day's observations are likely to be incomplete. An account of an incident may lack adequate description of given persons' behavior or their conscious intentions. The event, or whatever, may only be sketchily known. A well-described incident may lead one to want to look for further occurrences of events of that kind. In other words, a given day's notes raise a series of observational questions. It is reasonable to make note of these as one is writing up the notes. One can then review the notes and assemble all these queries as reminders of questions unobtrusively to ask of particular people or of things to look for.

Other Aspects

HOW LONG AND FULL?

There is the inevitable question of how many pages notes should run for a given observation period. It happens that observers differ enormously in the detail and length of their field notes. Some seem to be frustrated novelists and have been known to write 40 or more single-spaced pages on a three-hour period of observation. Other observers might write only a few pages. Here there are no set rules. Settings differ enormously. Observers' verbal compulsions differ enormously. The kinds of phenomena to which observers are sensitive vary quite widely. One possible rule of thumb is that the notes ought to be full enough adequately to summon up for one again, months later, a reasonably vivid picture of any described event. This probably means that one ought to be writing up, at the very minimum, at least a couple of single-spaced typed pages for every hour of observation. It is quite likely that one will want to write much more.

LET IT FLOW

Field notes are typically quite private documents, or at least accessible only to one's trusted friends, as in most team observer situations. One need not attempt, then, always to employ correct grammar, punctuate with propriety, hit the right typewriter keys, say only publicly polite things, be guarded about one's feelings–and all those other niceties we affect for strangers. The object in field notes, rather, is to get information down as correctly as one can and to be as honest with one's self as possible. Since they will *never* be public documents–such as a letter or a paper–one can–to modify a current metaphor–*write on*. Let all those mental and jotted notes flow out, typing like a madman with a compulsion.

Field notes are, after all, behind the scenes. It is at the next stage–concerted analysis–that all of this is processed for propriety.

THEIR WARHOL FLAVOR

I have perhaps made field notes sound intimate and revealing and therefore fascinating reading. To a degree they are. But the overwhelming portion of field notes is constituted of the first category described, "running descriptions." Thus, they are much like the early movies of Andy Warhol. They are largely mundane, uneventful, and dull. Indeed, if they were otherwise, people would simply publish their field notes. It is precisely because they are little in and of themselves that it is necessary to do analysis. Therefore, do not begin by believing that the field work venture and field notes in particular are always zap-zing affairs. Patience, persistence, drudgery, and dullness occur here, as everywhere else in social life. However, take heart. Field work can also be punctuated by periods of elation and joy over events and the occurrence of insights, ideas, and understandings.

FIELD NOTES AS COMPULSION

Take heart, too, in the following likely occurrence. Once a regime of jotting regularly and then making disciplined, full notes is established, it can come to have a demand and a logic of its own. The observer can get to feel that unless something he remembers appears in his full notes he is in peril of losing it. He experiences a compulsion to write it up lest it be lost to him, and he does. Upon reaching that level of felt responsibility for logging information in his field notes, the observer is fully *engaged* in field work.

THE SENSE OF BETRAYAL

Somewhat independently of how much or how little the observer "grooves" with the people observed, some special problems of the observer's orientation arise out of this process of note taking and analysis.

These jottings and cloisterings for drawing up field notes place the observer in a peculiar relation to the people under observation. While they are forgetting and going on to live their lives, he is cloistered somewhere remembering and contemplating their world. Even when an unknown observer, he is playing a different role than they, despite the documentation part of his life not being visible to them. But *he* knows what he is doing. And what he is doing is playing to a different audience. To engage in a regime of documentation and analysis is necessarily to compromise one's local loyalties and intimacies. While the participants forget, the observer remembers.

It happens that participants everywhere do and say many things they would prefer to forget or prefer not to have known, or at least not widely known. In the process of writing up his notes, the observer necessarily violates these participant preferences.

Unless the observer is bent upon presenting the setting in the most self-serving and idealistic fashion, a disparity must necessarily arise. The comprehensive portrait he is likely to present is unlikely to be the one that the participants would want promoted as the best possible public image. The observer is likely to recognize this.

This skewing of understanding becomes all the more poignant because the observer typically forms personal attachments to some, if not all, of the observed. They are likely to confide in him as friends and persons, rather than simply as observed and observer. And, alas, the products of such attachments and diffuseness must go into his field notes and eventually into his reports. The texture of this situation, and one likely upshot, has been most sensitively described by Fred Davis.

> Filling him with gossip, advice, invitations to dinner and solicitations of opinion, they devilishly make it evident that whereas he may regard himself as the *tabula rasa* incarnate upon whom the mysteries of the group are to be writ, they can only see him as someone less detached and less sublime. There then follows for many a fieldworker the unsettling recognition that, within very broad limits, it is precisely when his subjects palpably relate to him in his "out-of-research role" self . . . that the *raison d'etre* for his "in-role" self is most nearly realized; they are more themselves, they tell and "give away" more, they supply connections and insights which he would otherwise have never grasped. (One is tempted to conceive of this moral paradox as the sociologist's original sin, although happily the benign interposition of area sampling, precoded questionnaires and paid interviewers now spare more and more of us from suffering its pangs.)
>
> It is in large measure due to this ineluctable transmutation of role postures in field situations that, when he later reports, the sociologist often experiences a certain guilt, a sense of having betrayed, a stench of disreputability about himself; these despite the covers, pseudonyms, and eletions with which he clothes his subjects. (Or, have I alone heard such "confessions" from fellow sociologists?) In an almost Durkheimian sense, I would hold that it is just and fitting that he be made to squirm so, because in having exploited his non-scientific self (either deliberately or unwittingly) for ends other than those immediately apprehended by his subjects he has in some significant sense violated the collective conscience of the community, if not that of the profession (Davis, 1961:365).

Being an observer, then, is a peculiar—perhaps absurd—mode of being in the world. It is a most peculiar kind of social experience, highly subject to a nagging sense of betrayal. One can begin to experience that nagging sense while doing field notes.

REFERENCES

Davis, Fred, "Comment on 'Initial Interaction of Newcomers in Alcoholics Anonymous,'" *Social Problems,* 8:364–365 (Spring, 1961).

McCall, George, and J. L. Simmons, eds., *Issues In Participant Observation: A Text and Reader,* Reading, Mass.: Addison-Wesley Publishing Co., 1969.

Strauss, Anselm, *et al., Psychiatric Ideologies and Institutions,* New York: Free Press, 1964.

Dissection VI: View from the Other Side

Barroom Sociology

Piri Thomas

That night, after a nap, we walked around the colored part of Norfolk. The night air was cool and everything was living and going someplace. It reminded me of Harlem. We were on our way to the Blue Bell, a place Brew remembered from another life. It had a dance floor, a hot combo, and some rooms nearby for sitting out dances.

It wasn't a big place, but it swung. Inside it was dark except for red and blue light bulbs that gave the walls the shadows of the patrons. Brew and I got to a table and almost right away a waiter came up to us. "May I help you, gentlemen?" he asked.

We gave him our order, and a few minutes later he returned with our drinks. He spoke so well I asked him if he was from New York.

"No," he said, "I'm from Pennsylvania. But I can tell you're from New York, and," he added, looking at Brew, "you're not."

"Yuh right," Brew said, "Ah's a home boy."

"Been here long?" asked the Pennsylvanian.

"Couple of days," I lied. "We're on business. How about you?"

"Well, I've been here–excuse me, somebody's waving for service. Look," he said as he moved away, "I have my relief in a few minutes and if you don't mind, I'll join you for a chat."

We nodded "okay," and the Pennsylvanian saluted his thanks and drifted off through a mass of bodies. I eye-drilled a hole in the dress of a pretty baby leaning on a jukebox across the dance floor. "I'd like to get workin' with her like real fast," I said. "Dig, she got my eye."

From *Down These Mean Streets* by Piri Thomas. (New York: New American Library, Signet Books, 1967), pp. 167–75.

"Well, play it cool," Brew said, " 'cause tha's what she's heah fo', to ketch yo' eye an' yo' bread."

As I rolled my eyes around the broad's curves, the Pennsylvanian returned with fresh drinks. He sat down and told us he had been in Norfolk about three months. He looked about twenty five or twenty six. "I'm writing a book on the Negro situation," he said, "and I came down for the sense of personal involvement. I wanted the feel of what it means for a Negro to live here in the South. Background and such, you know what I mean?"

"Damn, man," Brew said, "yuh sho' coulda picked a tougher place than Norfolk fo' your book. Ah means a place whar you li'ble to get a kick in yuh background."

The Pennsylvanian smiled. "Oh, I'm not looking for that kind of personal involvement," he said. "I'm not seeking violence but rather the warmth and harmony of the southern Negro, their wonderful capacity for laughter and strength, their spiritual closeness to God and their way of expressing faith through their gospel singing. I want to capture on paper the richness of their poverty and their belief in living. I want the words I write to blend with the emotions of their really fantastic ability to endure and absorb the anguish of past memories of the slavery that was the lot of their grandparents. I want to write that despite their burdens they are working with the white man toward a productive relationship."

I glanced at Brew. He was studying the shadows on the walls. I took a good look at the Pennsylvanian. He was tan-colored and not really very negroid-looking. I got a funny, almost proud feeling that I looked more negroid than he did.

The Penn State man continued, "You see, I really feel the large part of the publicity being given the southern situation is adverse and serves only to cause more misunderstanding. I realize that there have been incidents, and white men have been cruel and violent toward the Negro, but only an ignorant and small minority–"

Brew broke in quietly with a wave of his hand, "You not a southe'ner, are yuh?"

"No, I'm not."

"Evah bin down South before?"

"No, I haven't."

"Evah notice any of these problems you was talkin' 'bout up No'th?"

"Well, I suppose there is some bigotry up there, but it's not the same, or at least I find it doesn't have the same meaning as here in the South."

"Ah sees," said Brew, barely hiding a growing disgust. "You-all been any other places inna South?"

"No, but I've been making plans to go to Atlanta, and–"

"You oughta go to some of them small towns whar a rock better fuckin' well know his place."

"Well, I don't think that's totally necessary. The problem of the southern

Negro is the same whether he's in the large cities or in back-wat—I mean, backwood counties. I believe that the southern Negro of today is marshaling his dignity and preparing himself for a great social revolution."

"Yuh-all gonna be a part of it?" Brew asked.

"I certainly feel that my book will contribute in some effective way to the Negro's cause."

"Ah means," said Brew, "if it comes down to fightin' an' havin' black an' white mixing their blood on big city guttahs or goddamn dirt roads?"

"If in looking for a solution to this problem," the Pennsylvanian replied, looking at me, "it comes to the point of violence, I know that many will die, especially Negroes. Those that fight, of course. And that will be their contribution to their cause. Some whites may die, and that will be their contribution to their cause. But it falls to others, black or white, to contribute in some other way. Perhaps one of these ways is by writing. By writing I will be fighting."

"About what? an' foah who?" said Brew. 'Yuh gonna write 'bout Negroes' warmth an' harmony, an' their won'erful ability to laugh an' rejoice, an' that shit 'bout the richness of their poverty? Yuh gonna write 'bout their fantastick 'bility to endure fuck-up mem'ries of slavin' an' smilin'? Prissy, wha's your name? Mine's Brewster, Brewster Johnson."

"My name, Mr. Johnson, is Gerald Andrew West," the Pennsylvanian said in such a way to let Brew know that he didn't like being called "Prissy." It was like the way you let someone know your name when you think he's inferior to you.

There was a fifth of whisky on our table. It hadn't been there before, or had it? It was almost empty, and I felt high, and Brew seemed high too. "You-all don' mind if ah calls yuh by your first name, eh, Ger-rul?" he said.

"If you like—er, Mr. Johnson—I hope I haven't caused any misunderstanding between us. I didn't mean to cause any resentment. I hope . . ."

Brew didn't answer.

"Don't worry, man," I said, "say it like you feel it," and I nudged Brew to keep his cool. He smiled gently, like a hungry tiger, and I knew he'd stay cool. "*Suave, panita,*" I added to Brew.

"Oh, you speak Spanish," Gerald Andrew West said to me, "Mr.—"

"Piri—Piri Thomas. Yeah, I do."

"How wonderful! Are you of Spanish descent?"

"No, just Puerto Rican father and moms."

"I speak a little Spanish, also," said Gerald Andrew West. "*Yo estoy estudiano español.*"

"Ah di'n't order any more drinks," Brew said as another fifth of whisky found its way to the table.

"This is on me, Mr. Johnson. Uh—do you speak Spanish fluently, Mr.—Piri? May I call you by your first name?"

"You 'ready did," said Brew. "Damn p'lite prissy."

I nudged Brew again; he made pop eyes and mumbled, "'Scuse me." Gerald Andrew West looked like he hadn't heard him or like Brew wasn't there.

"Yeah, you can call me Piri–uh, Gerald," I said.

"You know, Piri, I've been taken for Spanish many times, and Indian, too. I know that many dark people say that, but it's really happened with me." Gerald smiled almost too pat and added, "So you're Puerto Rican?"

I looked at the shadows over Brew's head and then at the jukebox. Pretty baby was still leaning on it.

"A-huh," I answered, "Puerto Rican *moyeto.*"

"*Moyeto?* What does that mean?"

"Negro," I said.

"Oh–er–do Puerto Ricans–er–consider themselves–uh–Negro?"

"I can only talk 'bout me," I replied, "but *como es, es como se llama.*"

Gerald thought for a second and translated, "Like it is, is how it's called. Am I right?"

"Word for word, *amigo,*" I said. "I'm a Puerto Rican Negro."

"Wha' kind is you-all, Gerald?" Brew said, smiling.

"What kind of what?" Gerald asked. "I'm afraid I don't understand you, Mr. Johnson."

"Ah means, what kinda Negro is yuh?"

"Oh! I understand now. Well, uh–according to–er–my–according to a genealogical tracer–you know, those people who trace one's family tree back as far as possible–well, according to the one my parents contracted to do the tracing, I'm really only one-eighth colored."

Brew was shaking his head slowly up and down. He made a move with his head at the bottle and Gerald said, "That's what it's there for, Mr. Johnson. By all means, please be my guest and help yourself."

"How's that work?" I asked Gerald. "I mean, tracing and all."

"Well, you see, they check back to your grandparents and get information so they can trace back to your great-grandparents and so on. For example, my great-great-grandfather was an Englishman named Robert West. He was on my father's side. His, wife, my great-great-grandmother, was from Malaya. You can see my eyes have an Oriental cast about them. Well–"

"A-huh, Ah sees," Brew said absently.

"–he–my great-great-grandfather–was a ship's captain and married his wife on one of his trips to Malaya. Then his oldest son, my great-grandfather –his name was Charles Andrew West–married a woman whose father was white and mother was half Negro. They had children and their second son, my father, married my mother, who had Indian blood, from, uh, India, and uh–some Spanish blood and uh–some Negro, colored blood. I–really–I'm so blended racially that I find it hard to give myself to any, ah–well, to any one of the blends. Of course, I feel that the racial instincts that are the strongest in a person enjoying this rich mixture are the ones that–uh–should be followed."

"What is your instinks, ah, Gerald?" asked Brew, staring at our blended friend.

Gerald laughed nice-like and answered, "I–rather–feel–sort of Spanish-ish, if I may use that term. I have always had great admiration for Spanish culture and traditions. I–er–yes–feel rather impulsed toward things Spanish. I guess that's why I have this inclination to learn Castilian. Of course, I don't disregard the other blends that went into the making of me, which–"

"Yuh evah been mistook fo' a Caucasian?" Brew interrupted.

Gerald smiled politely and answered, "Well, like I said, I'm always being mistaken for one of Spanish, uh, origin, or Puerto Rican. It's the same thing, I guess, and–"

Unpolite Brew broke in again, "Ah said *Caucasian.*"

"Er, I rather think that Spaniards, even though some are swarthy like Italians from Sicily, uh–are considered Caucasians. Yes, I probably have been taken for a white."

"How 'bout gittin' mistook fo' a Negro?" Brew asked. He was tight and his voice sounded like it did that day on the stoop in Harlem when he was sounding me on the same subject.

"Well," Gerald said hesitantly, "I've seen looks of doubt, and I've had some rare unpleasant experiences. But I find that I am mostly taken for a Negro by Negroes. I guess there are many like myself who, because of their racial blends, find themselves in the same unique position."

"An' what's your answer when yuh ast?"

"By the Caucasians?"

"Naw! Ah can figger what yuh tells 'em. Ah wanna know what you says to the rock people."

"Why, I say 'yes.' I–er–couldn't possibly say anything else under the circumstances. It would at best create resentment if I attempted to explain that I don't feel 100 percent Negro, since I am only one-eighth Negro."

"Don' yuh-all feel a leetle bit more Negro than that?"

Gerald looked at me for assurance that this wasn't going to be one of those "under the circumstances" situations that would lead to resentment and make his "personal involvement" physically painful. I smiled at him that I'd do what I could to keep everything cool.

"Don' yuh-all feel a leetle bit more Negro than that?" Brew repeated. "Tell me, is the book you're writin' gonna be frum the Negro's point o' view? It's gonna be a great book. Yuh-all fo' sure show the true picture of the workin's toward a productive relationship 'tween the Mistuh Charlies and the rock people. Ah am sure that your book will tru'fully show who all is enjoyin' the producin' part from that there relationship."

Gerald stayed quiet for a long time, then he said, "Mr. Johnson, I'd like to tell you something." For the first time he sounded like he was going to say what he had to and fuck Brew and whatever he thought or whatever he was going to do. Brew looked at him *carapalo*. "I'm not ashamed for the so-called 'Negro' blood in me and neither am I ashamed for what I feel myself to be. Nor how I think. I believe in the right of the individual to feel and think—and choose—as he pleases. If I do not choose to be a Negro, as you have gathered, this is my right, and I don't think you can ask or fight for your rights while denying someone else's. I believe that my book will contribute. I believe that the so-called 'Negro writers' are so damned wrapped up in their skins that they can't see the white forest for the black trees. It's true I don't look like a true Caucasian, but neither do I look like a true Negro. So I ask you if a white man can be a Negro if he has some Negro blood in him, why can't a Negro be a white man if he has white blood in him?"

Gerald tenderly squeezed the flesh of his left shoulder with the fingers of his right hand. I dug the jukebox and its ornament. Brew watched Gerald.

"I believe the Negro has the burden of his black skin," Gerald continued. He was in focus now. "And I believe the white man has the burden of his white skin. But people like me have the burden of both. It's pretty funny, Mr. Johnson. The white man is perfectly willing for people like me to be Negroes. In fact, he insists upon it. Yet the Negro won't let us be white. In fact he forbids it. Perhaps I was a bit maudlin in describing what I was looking for in the southern Negro, and this may have set you against me. But I would like you to know that if, because of genetic interbreeding, I cannot truly identify with white or black, I have the right to identify with whatever race or nationality approximates my emotional feeling and physical characteristics. If I feel comfortable being of Spanish extraction, then that's what I'll be. You might very well feel the same way, were you in my place."

People were still dancing and Gerald was still tenderly squeezing his shoulder. I was thinking that Gerald had problems something like mine. Except that he was a Negro trying to make Puerto Rican and I was a Puerto Rican trying to make Negro.

Gerald got up. "Do you know, Mr. Johnson," he said, "it's easier to pass for white down here than up North. Down here, a white man thinks twice before accusing another white openly of being a Negro for fear of getting slapped with a lawsuit or worse. And the Negro only has to think once for fear of just the 'worse.' But up North it's not an insult according to law, and I've never seen or heard of the 'worse' happening. Anyway, I've come down here to find what I couldn't find up North, and I think I've gotten what I came looking for. I've wanted to taste, feel, and identify with what was fitted for me. Even Negro. But I cannot. Not only do I not feel like a Negro, but I cannot understand his culture or feelings or his special kind of anger. Perhaps it's because I was born and raised in the North and went to white schools and white boys were my friends from childhood. I've mingled with colored boys up North, but I never felt like I was one of them, or they of me. Tonight, Mr. Johnson, I started out of place. The same feeling I've lived with a long time. And I found out tonight that I *am* out of place. Not as a human being, but as a member of your race. I will say that you hit it on the head when you insinuated that I was trying to be a Puerto Rican so I could make the next step to white. You're right! I feel white, Mr Johnson; I look white; I think white; therefore I *am* white. And I'm going back to Pennsylvania and *be* white. I'll write the book from both points of view, white and Negro. And don't think it will be one-sided. That one eighth in me will come through; it's that potent, isn't it?"

Gerald stood there waiting for Brew or maybe me to say something. Brew was looking at a fat broad sitting at the bar. I looked at the jukebox. Gerald smiled at the shadows on the wall and said, "Good night, Mr. Johnson . . . Piri. And good-bye and good luck."

"*Adiós,* Gerald, take it smooth." I waved a hand and wasn't sure I meant it. But I found it hard to hate a guy that was hung up on the two sticks that were so much like mine. Brew just nodded his head and watched a self-chosen white man make it from a dark scene. "Ah guess he's goin' home," he said and downed his drink. "Le's go se what pussy's sellin' fo' by the pound."

I heard Lady Day singing from the jukebox. The broad was still there, still coming on. I thought, *pussy's the same in every color,* and made it over to the music.

TOPIC VII: One Way Mirrors, Four Way Streets: Unobtrusive Measures

PHYSICAL TRACES

It is by the garbage that the janitor judges, and, as it were, gets power over the tenants who high-hat him. Janitors know about hidden love-affairs by bits of torn-up letter paper; of impending financial disaster or of financial four-flushing by the presence of many unopened letters in the waste. Or they may stall off demands for immediate service by an unreasonable woman of whom they know from the garbage that she, as the janitors put it, "has the rag on."

Everett Hughes
Men and Their Work

WRITTEN RECORDS

The obituaries were Poppa Hondorp's measure of human worth. "There's little they can add or subtract from you then," was his view. Poppa's eye had sharpened over the years so that he could weigh a two-and-a-half-inch column of ex-alderman against three-and-a-quarter inches of inorganic chemist and know at a glance their comparative worth.

Richard Stern
Golk

DISGUISED OBSERVATION

The investigators took special precautions to keep subjects ignorant of the fact that their remarks were being recorded. To this end, they concealed themselves under beds in students' rooms where tea parties were being held, eavesdropped in dormitory smoking rooms and washrooms, and listened to telephone conversations.

M. Henie and M. B. Hubble
"Egocentricity In Adult Conversation"

I, as everyone who discusses this subject, am indebted to Eugene J. Webb, *et al.* for their incredible compilation of material, *Unobtrusive Measures: Nonreactive Research in the Social Sciences* (New York: Rand, McNally, 1966).

"Unobtrusive measures" are a *pot pourri* of social science methods which are frequently labeled as nonreactive data, because when these data are created, the individuals have no reason to suspect the material will be used in social research and thus are not reacting to being studied, as are persons exposed to other methods considered in this book.

> Public archival documents represent one major class of unobtrusive measures; the conditions that lead to their production are in no way influenced by an intruding sociological observer. Unobtrusive measures range from the public and private archive to simple behavior observations of persons at work or play, from contrived observations based on mechanical equipment (such as tape recorders and video cameras) to physical trace analysis.[1]

Although there are many problems with these rough measures,* they are an invaluable–and often overlooked–means of obtaining data about the social world. Used in conjunction with data obtained by more "standard" methods, unobtrusive measures can present ingenious complements to a research design.

This section is set up differently than the previous ones since "oddball" measures require different structures. Because of the diversity of these measures, they are presented under three major headings. Each of the three subsections, then, contains an introduction, a descriptive essay, and a Dissection.

NOTES

1. Norman K. Denzin, *The Research Act* (Chicago: Aldine, 1970), p. 260.

SUGGESTED FURTHER READING

Berelson, Bernard. *Content Analysis in Communication Research.* New York: Free Press, 1952.

Birdwhistell, Ray L. *Kinesics and Context.* Philadelphia: University of Pennsylvania Press, 1970.

Campbell, Donald T., *et al.* "Seating Aggregation as an Index of Attitude," *Sociometry* 29 (1966): 1–15.

Gottschalk, Louis, *et al. The Use of Personal Documents in Hisotry, Anthropology, and Sociology.* New York: Social Science Research Council, 1945.

Hall, Edward T. *The Silent Language.* New York: Doubleday, 1959.

*See Webb, *et al.*, "Approximations To Knowledge," (pp. 126-151) for a discussion of the validity problems inherent in these measures.

Hayner, Norman S. "Hotel Life: Proximity and Social Distance," in Ernest S. Burgess and Donald J. Bogue, eds., *Contributions to Urban Sociology*, pp. 314–23. Chicago: University of Chicago Press, 1964.

Kotok, Alan B. "Foreign Nationals and Minority Americans in Magazine Fiction, 1946–1968," in Bernard Rosenberg and David Manning White, eds., *Mass Culture Revisited*, pp. 249–65. New York: Van Nostrand Reinhold Co., 1971.

Webb, Eugene J., *et al. Unobtrusive Measures: Nonreactive Research in the Social Sciences.* New York: Rand McNally, 1966.

A. I Only Know What I Read in the Papers: The Written Record

The use of written records and archival material is probably the best-known type of unobtrusive measure. From diaries to census data, sociologists have long utilized this form of nonreactive data. Because of its long history of use, the strengths and weaknesses of this type of data are probably more generally known than those of some of the other classes of unobtrusive material. David C. Pitt, in "The Critical Analysis of Documentary Evidence," presents these strengths and weaknesses, and makes valuable comparisons between the use of this material and surveys and participant observation. One should be wary, as Pitt points out, in drawing conclusions from documentary evidence alone. In the Dissection piece, "The Connecticut Speed Crackdown," H. Laurence Ross and Donald Campbell show how the sophisticated analysis of official records can reveal a much different picture of reality than their original interpretation. What was at first thought to be an effective legal procedure (an intensive crackdown on speeding in the state of Connecticut) actually reduced the automobile accident rate no more than would have been expected without such a crackdown over the same period of time. Notice how Ross and Campbell operate: utilizing official records over time to set up a "quasi-experimental design" within which to analyze the data.

The Critical Analysis of Documentary Evidence

David C. Pitt

. . . The research worker has to be fully aware of the limits of the kind of evidence he has extracted from the historical record, and particularly the ways in which this evidence compares and differs from data gathered in fieldwork, or from other kinds of sources. This is an essential preliminary to utilizing and integrating historical data into analyses.

ESTABLISHING PROBABILITIES

One obvious difference between historical and fieldwork data is that the latter has usually been gathered by the fieldworker himself. It is firsthand observation, whereas in the historical record the perspective is through somebody else's eyes (primary sources), and information may even be gathered by third or fourth hand (secondary sources). This means that the anthropologist or sociologist using historical documents has to go to some lengths to establish what has been called the "framework of facts," that is, events, incidents, or structural features, and so forth, for which there is a high degree of probability. The research worker cannot go back himself to those events reported; he must rely, therefore, on his ability to evaluate the statements that have been made about the situation. Thus the first concern must be with those factors likely to affect the veracity of these statements.

Before going on, I should emphasize the importance of probability in the framework of fact. In the nineteenth and early twentieth centuries many historians followed Ranke's dictum that the historian's purpose was "simply to show how it really was" (*wie es eigentlich gewesen*), that is, to provide an accurate compilation of past events. It was assumed that there existed some kind of hard core of indisputable facts. Since the late nineteenth century, however, there has been a strong reaction against the Rankian scissors-and-paste history. Many historians have argued that the nature of the facts depends on the interpretation of the historian himself, and some have gone so far as to say that history is quite subjective and that the history of the same events is rewritten by every generation. However, most historians recognize that although there is always a subjective and contemporaneous viewpoint, interpretation rests ultimately on an interaction between the facts, as they probably happened, the historical observer, and the historian's thoughts and present situation (Collingwood 1945, Carr 1964:21). I will return to this important triangle later.

The job of assessing the probability of these kinds of "facts" and the statements made about them is the researcher's initial major task. There are several basic steps in this process.

First, an assessment must be made of how far the document represents an accurate description of the situation, that is, the degree to which the statement about the facts agrees with the facts as they probably happened. To begin with, the research worker must know the details of the document's authorship, the date and place of the events described, and the date when and place where the description was written up. He should try to find out details about the context of the author's observations and recording, the events that were going on around and before the event described and recorded. Necessary, too, is a knowledge of details about the author's life, his attitudes and experiences, and the like. Finally, the research worker must know whether the document is the original description or analysis. If it is not the original, then details on the intermediaries and the circumstances of communication should be known. The job of establishing the physical authenticity of a document is often called external criticism. The analysis of the contents to detect inconsistencies, errors, or falsehoods is the process of internal criticism. Both external and internal criticism play a part in the third and most essential job of evaluation, that is, weighing up the evidence at hand, not only trying to assess more fine degrees of reliability but also interpreting statements, trying to say, that is, what the "evidence" is evidence of (Handlin *et al.* 1966:23). To illustrate the problems involved in these processes, more detailed examples of critical procedures will now be considered.

ORIGINALITY, ERRORS, AND FALSIFICATION

The question of originality is not usually the most serious problem. The kinds of documents relevant to anthropological and sociological research are often the work of firsthand observers. There is not usually the problem, which occurs, for instance, in medieval historiography, of interpreting the fragmented, distorted, or inaccurate commentaries of a string of intermediaries. In many modern political and judicial institutions recording is done *in extenso* in shorthand.

Accidental error and falsification are common occurrences in the historical record. Historians over the years have developed a series of strict critical tests and guidelines for detecting these errors and falsities, either in originals or in copies. The French historical methodologists Langlois and Seignobos (1898: 76) have claimed that "texts degenerate in accordance with certain laws." In fact, most of those "laws" turn on reasonably obvious indications, such as confusion of sense in the document, internal inconsistencies, inconsistencies with known data or other reports, and so forth, nearness to the situation, pressures making for modification. In general, if the research worker is vigilant, skeptical, and well informed on the background to his document, most major errors can be detected.

Similarly, investigation of authorship is not likely to be as great a problem for the anthropologist or sociologist as it is for many historians. Most modern documents are likely to be signed, or, in the case of administration papers, at least initialed, though dating may be more of a problem.

INTERPRETATION OF REPORTING–PRELIMINARY POINTS

A much more significant problem is that historical documents are often summaries after the events and not detailed records of events as they occur. The differences between this aspect of fieldwork and historical data should not be overemphasized, however. It is a difference of degree rather than kind. In fact, the fieldwork record resembles the historical record in important respects, and presents similar problems of verifying or establishing reliability. Many fieldworkers do not record events as they happen–often, in fact, the social situation precludes this–but write up their impressions at the first opportunity, probably, at best, several hours after the event. These notes inevitably contain summaries and abbreviations and may not be consulted again until the fieldworker is writing up his material. At this stage, connections and details which were apparent at the time the summary was written may have been forgotten. The fieldwork record has become, in a sense, a kind of historical document.

However, this time lapse may be much less than in historical writing. Reliability of evidence tends to decrease as the time lapse between the action and the reporting increases, though the human memory is a complex variable. The problem is not quite the same in social survey work. Many questionnaires are filled in on the spot by informants or interviewers. The data recorded, however, are often details of past actions, attitudes, beliefs, or events.

Another variable is the attentiveness of the witness at the time of the action. The story is told (Gottschalk 1945:39) of a psychology professor who started a brawl in his class and then asked the students to write an essay on what had happened. Apart from conflicting accounts, the most important feature of the reports was that nobody noticed that in the middle of the fracas the professor had taken a banana from his pocket, peeled it, and eaten it. Inattentiveness to boring but important detail is not only an historical observer's vice, as many anthropologists who have participated in exciting feasts and ceremonials well know.

In fieldwork also a considerable amount of evidence may come from second hand. Anthropologists try to be participant-observers, but they cannot participate in, or observe, everything. Sometimes the events in the field which the anthropologist wants to see occur simultaneously, and there are many relevant events which occur outside the restricted time-space framework of the fieldwork—or while the fieldworker is in some way incapacitated or otherwise occupied. Information related to these events or facts is gathered by research assistants or local informants. The anthropologist will, even when he is a participant-observer, utilize the ideas and interpretations of other people to help explain what is going on around him.

Similarly, in survey work, information is gathered by intermediary research assistants, often in terms of a highly structured questionnaire which does not allow the recording of unexpected or unwanted, but sometimes relevant, data.

As far as establishing the framework of fact is concerned, a more important difference than the relative proximity of the observer is his subjectivity. It is not that the anthropologist or sociologist is really objective in his selection and interpretation of data. His intellectual attitudes are the product of the conventions of a particular culture and a discipline, and he is constantly interpreting and translating the actuality of the fieldwork situations into these terms. The point is rather that these subjectivities remain substantially the same at the time of recording and analysis. Even if these attitudes undergo some radical change during or after fieldwork, there will presumably be some awareness of the bases of previous subjectivity. The research worker does not have the same knowledge of the subjectivity of those persons who produced the historical record.

The subjectivity in historical documents may well result in an undue concentration on certain features of the social structure, omission of facts which do not support the case being presented, or a willful distortion or invention of facts. The only, albeit partial, solution to this problem is for the anthropologist or sociologist to absorb as much of the relevant literature as he can so that he knows, to some degree, the reporter's frame of mind. For example, an anthropologist attempting to utilize mission records to any degree should read widely in the religious and social history of the period.

In addition, an assessment of the accuracy of a particular document can be achieved by looking critically at the subject matter of the document and its author (for example, is there an official line on the subject?), its intended circulation, its purpose (the most accurate documents are *aide-mémoires* and straight reports), its confidentiality (the more confidential it is, the more truthful it is likely to be), the personal position of the writer and his sympathies and antipathies (even such things as the state of his health), what, if anything, the author has to gain from a particular point of view, and so on. There are also certain conditions favorable to credibility (Gottschalk 1945:43), for example, when the witness is under legal oath, or fears retributions to himself or family for prevarication, or when he is indifferent to consequences and has little desire to please, displease, propogandize, and so forth, or when he has little to gain financially or otherwise, or when the facts are felt to be common knowledge. Finally, it may be possible to discover from other sources something of the writer's ability in, or reputation for, accurate reporting. Some writers are consistently inaccurate. This condition is known to the historians as "Froude's disease"—after the English historian who was "destined never to advance any statement that was not disfigured by error" (Langlois and Seignobos 1898:125). In fact, this condition is rather rare, and a writer's evidence should never be completely rejected because of his reputation but should rather be more carefully scrutinized.

Fortunately, the anthropologist or sociologist does not face the same problems of, for example, the medieval historian, who must be constantly on the lookout for false or missing documents. Most of the documents relevant to anthropological study are housed in secure archives, though local records are particularly likely to have been tampered with.

BIAS

Very often the problem is not as simple as asking whether or not a given statement about a fact is true or false but rather is one of ascertaining the degree of bias in any statement. There can only be a complete record of any given event in a limited sense. For one thing, the semantic constraints in language itself do not allow the same kind of completeness in the documentary record as that recorded, for example, in a photograph or movie. Even in the visual record, the camera cannot be in all places at all times. There is always a viewpoint. In reporting there is always a bias, a priority in the order in which details are noted, a selectivity in impressions recorded, the choice of words, the tone of the writing, and a hundred other subtle points. It should be noted too that bias is not simply to be found in reportage, in the historical observers document, but enters, of course, into the research worker's interpretation and analysis. The first kind of bias I shall term "observer bias" and the second, "interpretational bias."...

One of the most important factors contributing to both observer and interpretational bias is ethnocentrism or lack of cultural relativism. For example, many, probably most, early observers of Afro-Asian people cast their descriptions in terms of their own cultural frameworks. In some cases this led to what might be called the "backward primitive" complex, the description of institutions in deprecatory terms, constantly emphasizing inferiority and difference vis-à-vis European models. Usually, on those occasions when institutions were favorably compared, it was in terms of their similarity to highly regarded idealized European institutions. . . .

Another factor likely to increase observer bias is what might be called expediency. Most observers live or work not only in a general cultural context but also within a specific institution. Within these institutions there are numerous demands and pressures for particular kinds of attitudes in reporting. The missionaries provide a good example of the effects of this kind of pressure. Especially in official reports, it was often expected that a missionary would write of the native religion in terms of its heathenism and to emphasize satanic and magical influences. Many missionaries in official reports also often exaggerated the virtues of converts and vices of nonconverts, who are portrayed as poor, inferior, and unhappy because of their beliefs. As we have noted, however, this institutional pressure did not stop the missionaries from writing relatively unbiased accounts when outside official focuses of interest or areas of control. Additionally, as in the case of spotting errors, observer bias may be due to such factors as particular quirks in the author's personality.

Interpretational bias is always present to some degree. In a recent paper Raymond W. Mack (M. Sherif and C. W. Sherif 1969:52) points out that the great majority of sociological investigation is colored by ethnocentrism and professional pressures and conventions. At some point the theoretical tools which the observer uses impart a bias to the research. In the documentary part of research work the selection of documents and methods of interpretation inevitably colors the ultimate analysis. Models, methods, and materials are inextricably intertwined, and the best the research worker can do is be aware of the bias, constantly adjusting theoretical approaches as new empirical material emerges.

Bias is also present when the observer records the facts himself. The observer cannot record everything he sees or hears. Even a camera records only one angle and a tape recorder one or a small number of proximate voices on a single theme. In any case these more complete recording devices yield too much data, and the bulk of fieldwork data must be selective notetaking. In this selection the observer must choose between different places and times, and then between different aspects of events. Most significant of all, during notetaking the form and functions of the notes reflect the observer's own cultural and intellectual background, his prejudices and proclivities. This leads us to a very important point which has been generally overlooked in the literature. Because all records contain some kinds of bias, the differences between amateur and professional sources, or between the records of professionals of different disciplines, are differences of degree not kind. The techniques to be used in utilizing a historical source do not differ fundamentally from the techniques applied to the scrutiny of professional analyses. In all cases a thorough knowledge of the context of the document's authorship, and of the author's cultural and intellectual background, is the essential prerequisite for accurate interpretation.

However, this is not all that is needed. As I have said, the major procedures in dealing with bias are similar to the procedures involved in the establishment of the probability of facts. In fact, the higher the probability of facts, the lower the level of bias is likely to be. Important too is the author's own awareness of his bias. If this awareness is not present, or is misconstrued, then the research worker has the assessment to do. This requires more than knowledge of context. It necessitates a high degree of absorption in, or sympathy with, the historical observer. Barzun and Graff (1957:163) describe this process as one of triangulation, the points being the research worker (A), the historical observer (B), and the objects which he describes (C).

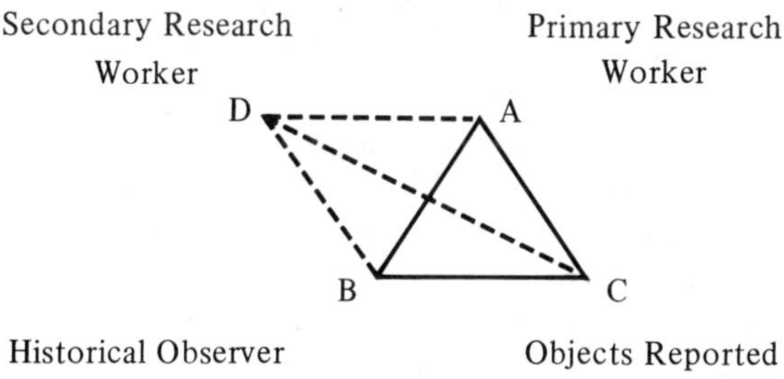

All evaluations then are made through this triadic perspective, which minimizes the size of both research worker and observer bias. The use of triadic, tetradic, or higher order processes is especially important in analyzing secondary sources, that is, those which are not the product of the original observer. Some historians have felt that historical writing, and especially secondary reportage, is highly subjective, being intrinsically different among different authors, particularly if they lived in different times, places, or cultural contexts. We can clearly see that this is not the full story. In any triangle B and C remain constant, and even if it is not possible to bypass A—that is, to go back to the originals, D, B, C—then A is just one of three additional variables. . . .

CORROBORATION

The detection of errors, falsifications, biases, or distortions, and the like is a major historical method in establishing the probability of facts, or rather the compatability of the probable actuality and the statements about it. Equally important is verification, notably through the corroboration of evidence.

If many people record an event or feature in the same or similar ways, without collaboration, the degree of probability increases, but just how many witnesses constitute a critical mass is debatable. It may be difficult to establish the independence of witnesses, as they may be only repeating one another. Also, to a considerable extent, the existence of multiple recordings depends on the size of the documentary record. The anthropologist may be faced with a solitary record, especially in the early days of contact in many areas. If there is only one record there can be no corroboration, though there can be no contradiction either. Corroboration through alternative sources is more important in relatively recent times when there has been a multiplicity of institutions (and records) concerned with a single fact. For instance, newspaper records of recent events often help fill out official files.

The contemporary research worker also has means of corroborating evidence not usually utilized by historians, that is, through informants or through oral history and tradition. Informant history provides corroboration for several important kinds of documentary fact. Most significantly, great events (great political or religious occasions, rites of passage, natural disasters, periods of deprivation or personal distress) in the life of the society or person are remembered vividly and in detail.

The reliability of an informant's evidence is something the research worker comes to know as he comes to know the informant and his culture. Reliability is likely to increase as rapport with local society increases. But accuracy of evidence is affected by factors other than personal reliability. There are limits to personal memory. These constraints do not vary directly with time elapsed, though all things being equal, events of long ago are remembered less well than very recent events. Some people, however, have prodigious memories, and many can recall vividly a single or small number of details. . . .

The techniques for studying myth have relevance for our interest in historical criticism. Anthropologists particularly have to deal with recorded myths that describe possible events. It becomes necessary then to recognize when an account is mythical. This may be a simple task if the myth contains impossible or extremely unlikely events (such as men living forever, or humans existing in animal form), but all myths contain some probable and possible facts. Moreover, it is possible that all historical accounts contain mythical elements. Levi-Strauss (1970:12–13) implies that this is why there are different and contradictory descriptions of the same event (for example, the French Revolution).

Critical methods, particularly corroboration, can get around some of these problems. More significantly, myth (like music) occurs usually as a complex interrelated arrangement of units and not as a single unit within an historical account. Myths then, even when concerned with historical or possible events, can often be recognized by their general shape, and perhaps by other features such as their anaclasticism (Levi-Strauss 1970:5).

Despite the chances of corroboration, there will always remain a large body of unverified evidence, of possible facts. The assessment of probability may be assisted by circumstantial evidence, by how well one fact fits in with others of greater probability. Interpretational as well as circumstantial evidence is also important. A great many historical facts owe their credibility, as Professor Carr has pointed out (1964:12), to the fact that they fit in with this or that theory or thesis. However, it is important for the research worker to try and use other validity tests before this one.

COVERAGE DEFICIENCIES

Another very important difference between documentary and fieldwork or survey data relates to the coverage of reporting. On the one hand; in the fieldwork situation or in a survey, the data recorded is, to a considerable extent, the fieldworker's choice. Certainly there may be subjects, places, or times which are temporarily restricted, but at least the fieldworker has a definite schedule of information he wants. On the other hand, the documentary record represents other peoples' choices of data to be recorded and preserved.

Inevitably, the historical record, vis-à-vis the fieldwork or survey record, contains certain gaps and deficiencies. These gaps are of several kinds. First, there are the gaps imposed in the public archives on the time availability of documents or their confidentiality. Second, there are the gaps created by the accidental or deliberate destruction of papers. This is especially a problem in local archives, where records are simply not kept or are periodically weeded. Third, there are the gaps created by the research worker himself through his unconscious or conscious selection of documents to be looked at or facts to be recorded. Fourth, there are the gaps created by the selectivity of the reporters.

The reportage of any event is recorded in a qualitatively different way by anthropologists or sociologists, on the one hand, and by officials, missionaries, and such, on the other hand. Officials' notes are not destined to become learned monographs but are utilized for specific reports. Seldom will the reporter either indulge in recording inconsequential details or allow his imagination to explore possible explanations of an event, a characteristic of many anthropological fieldwork notebooks. Many times in the record, in fact, an observer will stop short, or describe a highly significant event in agonizingly generalized terms. This generality is particularly unfortunate in two important respects. Personal and place names may be omitted from the historical record far more often than they would be in fieldwork reporting. Certainly, persons in high political offices may be named, though there is a tendency to use general descriptive terms—chief, leader, prince, and so forth. Generality is much more marked as one descends the social scale, or as one moves outside the focuses of political power.

In addition, there are subject concentrations stemming from bias or job considerations—for example, administration records focus on political activities, and mission records on processes of religious change. Other deficiencies may result because reporters have inadequate knowledge of the local language or customs.

As a consequence of all this, subjects of great interest recorded and detailed in the field are inadequately covered in the historical record. One good example is kinship data; another is material on personality. Both these fields have been neglected by historians, not in the least because of lack of documentary evidence. On the other hand, recent work by Eric Erikson (1959) and Alain Besançon (1967) have shown the possibilities of psychoanalytical history using letters and literature.

The quantitative historical record is in some ways less deficient in certain respect vis-à-vis the field record than the qualitative record. This is partly because in many official organizations the collection of statistics is, or was, an important function. Possibly, it is also a result of the fact that anthropologists have used relatively simple quantitative fieldwork techniques and have fewer expectancies in this respect. There has been a certain suspicion about statistics (especially by British social anthropologists), and very detailed statistical coverage, even for a small unit, is a great time- and resource-consuming task.

Nevertheless, there are important gaps and deficiencies in the quantitative historical record. Censuses have only been conducted at long intervals in many parts of Afro-Asia, using different enumeration techniques and areas at different times and thus making analysis very difficult. The unreliability of such statistics may also be considerable. Often all that remains are the bare figures for a territory or district in a year, the detailed returns on which these returns were based having been destroyed or lost. Once again, statistics are usually only available insofar as they have a use in the political apparatus, and the categories are those which are officially understood, approved, or recognized. Hence important frequencies (for example, illegal marital forms or important class or traditional distinctions) may not be recorded.

To some extent the problems arising from faulty coverage can be ameliorated in much the same way as corroboration is achieved. Informant history particularly may be used to plug certain gaps or provide extra material. Informants may be not only people from the local society but also persons involved in the administration or mission machinery. Retired people, especially, freed from organizational pressures, may well be prepared to provide valuable information. Fortunately, also, when there is a multiple recording of events, the gaps in one record may not be replicated in another. For example, some material from confidential documents is often contained in open files. Local archives have usually less stringent rules on time limits. Newspaper files are again very useful for the contemporary period.

Generality may be more difficult to counter. But the anonymity of the local area or special group can sometimes be penetrated through special records. For example, historian George Rudé (1958) has been able to examine in detail (through the skillful use of police records) the social characteristics of the "crowd," the lower classes who participated in some of the violent events of the French Revolution. This kind of record, especially in periods of stress or strain (rebellions, revolutions, riots, depressions, and so forth), can be of critical importance since great detail is present, and since at such times important aspects of the social structure are dramatically revealed. Unfortunately, these documents often have a short life expectancy or are kept in the most confidential places.

INFERENCE

Historians have also used another method to get around some of the problems raised by gaps and deficiencies in the record, that is, inference, or extended interpretation. Through inferential methods relationships between, or the consequences of, known facts or events can be assessed. Quite often in historical studies a relationship is assumed if there is a coincidence in time between two events. . . .

Another kind of extended interpretation used by historians is what is usually called "content analysis" (North *et al.* 1963, Berelson 1952). In this method it is postulated that the frequency of occurrence in a text of a word, theme, character, concept, or item (Berelson 1952:135) can be correlated with a given social fact. Content analysis lends itself to quantification and has been used particularly in political studies, but potentially, content analysis can be used in a wide variety of problems. A good example of the sophisticated use of this technique is a recent study of family patterns in eighteenth-century America (Lantz *et al.* 1968). In this study Lantz and his colleagues used fifteen magazines (comprising 546 issues) which were published in New England in the period 1741-1794. Their main object was to provide data on key features of the American family such as the romantic love complex and marital motives, freedom of mate choice, husband-wife and parent-child relations, and sexual standards in the preindustrial period. In discussing "romantic love," the authors first picked out the number of times romantic love is discussed in the magazine articles as the motive for marriage vis-à-vis other motives, such as wealth or status. They find that romantic love far outweighs the other motives and conclude, contrary to many traditional views, that notions of romantic love preceded industrialization.

Gaps in statistical information pose special problems. However, there are inferential mathematical techniques (for example, multivariate analysis) for providing estimates to fill certain gaps resulting from incomplete time or spatial coverage. The relative validity of these estimates is ultimately dependent on the volume of the data, and in many cases in Afro-Asia, particularly, there simply are not enough data. Frequently, for example, there are general historical statistics which are not, however, broken down for the geographical or subject areas in which the research worker is interested. In these cases it may be possible to provide some kind of local estimate, if the relationship between the local and general statistics is known at more than one point in time, and if there have been no dramatic changes in the local area or in its relationship with other areas. If, let us say, per capita income or output in our village are approximately *x percent* below the national mean during the fieldwork period, and if there are no reports of dramatic changes in the village economy during the previous periods, then it is probable that village wealth has remained of this order. In this case, it may be possible to extrapolate local figures from national figures for earlier periods.

The analysis of demographic changes almost always requires a good deal of statistical inference. Census information, at best, is usually taken at ten-year intervals, and in early periods of contact even simple estimates of numbers may be hundreds of years apart. Even if we leave aside the knotty problems of differential reliability of sources, and even if we work in a period where census material is available at ten-year periods, the assumption is often made that the demographic characteristics at any point in time vary directly in relation to the characteristics at the census dates. Where there is reliable and frequent evidence, this is probably a reasonable assumption, but such inferences may be meaningless, especially in early periods. . . .

REFERENCES

Barzun, J., and Graff, H. *The Modern Researcher*. New York: Harcourt, 1957.

Berelson, B. *Content Analysis in Communication Research*. Glencoe, Ill.: Free Press, 1952.

Besançon, A. *Le Tsarevitch Immolé*. Paris: Plon, 1967.

Carr, E. H. *What Is History?* Hamondsworth: Penguin, 1964.

Collingwood, R. *The Idea of History*. New York: Oxford University Press, 1945.

Erikson, E. H. *Young Man Luther: A Study in Psychoanalysis and History*. London: Faber, 1959.

Gottschalk, L., Kluckholm, C., and Angell, R. *The Use of Personal Documents in History, Anthropology, and Sociology*. New York: Social Science Research Council, 1945.

Handlin, O., *et al. Harvard Guide to American History*. Cambridge, Mass.: Belknap, 1966.

Langlois, C. V., and Seignobos, C. *Introduction to the Study of History*. London: Duckworth, 1898.

Lantz, H. R., Britton, M., Schmitt, R., and Snyder, E. C. "Preindustrial Patterns in the Colonial Family in America: A Content Analysis of Colonial Magazines." *American Sociological Review* 33, no. 3: 413–26, 1968.

Levi–Strauss, C. *The Raw and the Cooked*. London: Cape, 1970.

North, R. C., Holsti, O. R., Zaninovich, M. G., and Zinnes, D. A. *Content Analysis*. Evanston, Ill.: Northwestern University Press, 1963.

Rudé, G. *The Crowd in the French Revolution*. London: Oxford, 1958.

Sherif, M., and Sherif, C. W. *Interdisciplinary Relationships in the Social Sciences*. Chicago: Aldine, 1969.

Dissection A:

The Connecticut Speed Crackdown: A Study of the Effects of Legal Change

H. Laurence Ross and Donald T. Campbell

In 1955, the state of Connecticut introduced a campaign to reduce highway fatalities through enforcement of speed limit laws. We report here the results of a study of this campaign, with two goals in mind. First, with our methodology we wish to illustrate some pitfalls of uncritical interpretations of change and to demonstrate some more dependable ways in which to evaluate the effects of changes in law and other systems of social control. Second, although our findings are limited to the case at hand, we wish to suggest some problems and unforeseen results that may accompany attempts to change behavior by law enforcement.

Automobile accidents caused 324 deaths in Connecticut in 1955. This was a record high for the decade of the fifties. As the hazardous Christmas holidays approached, Governor Abraham Ribicoff initiated an unprecedented attempt to control traffic deaths by law enforcement, in the form of a crackdown on speeders. He acted in the belief that excess speed was a common contributing factor in traffic deaths, that control of speed would result in diminished fatalities, and that this control could be accomplished by enforcing speed limits. On December 23, Governor Ribicoff announced that in the future all persons convicted of speeding in Connecticut would have their licenses suspended for thirty days on the first offense, with longer periods of

From H. Laurence Ross and Donald T. Campbell, "The Connecticut Speed Crackdown: A Study of the Legal Effects of Change," in *Perspectives on the Social Order,* 2nd ed., ed. H. L. Ross.

suspension for repeating offenders. The decree was put into force through the Governor's power of appointment over local judges, who were told that reappointment in 1957 would be denied to those who appeared lax in conviction of speeders, or who did not recommend to the Motor Vehicle Department the suspension of drivers' licenses for this offense.

In the first three months of 1956, license suspensions for speeding numbered 2,855, an increase of almost 2,700 over the corresponding period in 1955. There were 10 fewer fatalities, and 765 fewer arrests for speeding. The Governor was quoted as saying: "This is positive proof that operators are not only driving slower, but are driving better."

By the end of June there were 22 fewer fatalities than in the first six months of 1955, representing a 15 percent reduction. Suspensions for speeding had risen from 231 to 5,398, and arrests had declined from 4,377 to 2,735. Ribicoff announced: "Connecticut has succeeded in stopping the upward surge in highway deaths, and in the first six months of this year, contrary to the national trend, we have saved lives. Fewer people died on the highways this year than in the same period last year, in Connecticut. We did it by enforcing the law, something the safety experts said couldn't be done because the people wouldn't be behind it."

In the late summer Connecticut experienced a very high number of traffic fatalities, and by the beginning of September deaths almost equaled those of the previous year. However, fatalities were fewer in the fall, and by the end of the year Connecticut counted a total of 284 traffic deaths, as compared with 324 in 1955. Governor Ribicoff concluded: "With the saving of 40 lives in 1956, a reduction of 12.3 percent from the 1955 motor vehicle death toll, we can say the program is definitely worthwhile."

Our study of the Connecticut speed crackdown is based on analysis of mileage death rates, i.e., the number of deaths per 100 million miles driven in the state. This corrects for the fact that more deaths would be expected in Connecticut during the decade merely because more miles were being driven.

Figure 1 presents the mileage death rates for Connecticut for the years 1955 and 1956, on which Governor Ribicoff based his claims for the effectiveness of his program. If we think of these data as similar to a classical experiment, the 1955 data constitute a pretest, the crackdown is like an experimental treatment, and the 1956 data constitute a posttest.[1] Governor Ribicoff believed the difference between the pretest and the posttest to be the effect of the treatment, an inference that might be valid if the study had truly been a classical experiment, subject to controls and randomization of extraneous variables. As the latter was not the case, this situation, which we term "quasi-experimental," requires independent evidence to rule out several possible alternative explanations of the observed difference. Some of these, briefly stated, are as follows:

Figure 1. Pre- and Posttest Measures of Connecticut Traffic Fatalities per 100 Million Driver Miles.

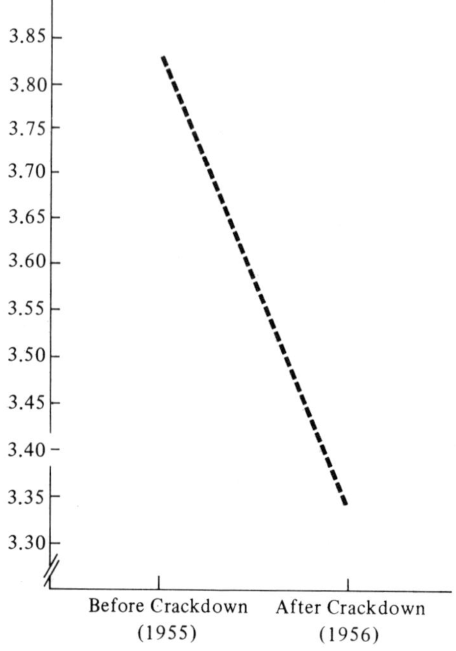

1. History. This term denotes specific events, other than the treatment, occurring between the pretest and posttest, which might independently account for the change. For instance, 1956 might have had less snow and ice than 1955, this fact rather than the speed crackdown producing the lower death rate.

2. Maturation. This term is taken from psychology, where it refers to changes correlated with the passage of time per se, such as growing older or more tired. Its use is not limited to organic changes, however. Maturation may refer to any general, secular, time-linked changes not the result of discrete events. Potential causes of the change in the Connecticut death rate subsumed under this heading are improved roads and more competent medical care.

3. Testing. A change may occur as a result of the pretest, even without the treatment. In the present instance, the assessment of the death rate for 1955 constitutes the pretest. It is conceivable that publicizing the high death rate for that year may have changed driver caution, and hence changed the death rates for the following year.

4. Instrumentation. This term refers to a shifting of the measuring instrument independent of any change in the phenomenon measured. Such changes are common in sociology, for example, artificial rises in crime rates which occur due to changes in the administration of police records.

5. Regression. Statistical theory tells us that when a group is selected for study because of extreme scores on one test, their scores on a subsequent test will tend to be less extreme, merely as a statistical artifact. As high accident rates for 1955 were cited to justify the crackdown, lower rates for 1956 would be expected due to regression.

6. Instability. A ubiquitous problem in quasi-experimentation is to distinguish "true" changes in a measure from random changes due either to a small population base on which observations are made or to large numbers of change-producing events which, taken individually, we have called history.

The plausibility of these alternative explanations can be evaluated by the systematic use of series of data which are commonly available to the researcher in the situations similar to this. If data are gathered for the years directly prior to and following the treatment, they are usually available for other years as well. A fairly long sequence of observations before and after the treatment allows us to apply the logic of the quasi-experimental model termed the Interrupted Time-Series Design. Figure 2 presents the relevant data for Connecticut.

Figure 2. Interrupted Time-Series Presentation of Connecticut Traffic Fatalities per 100 Million Vehicle Miles.

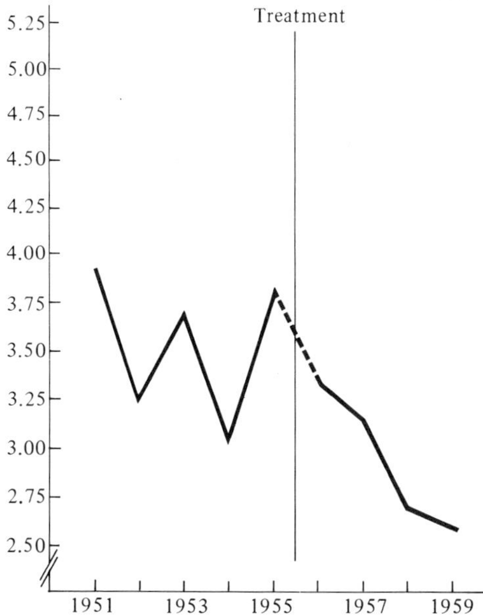

The data of Figure 2 help us to evaluate maturation and, on certain assumptions, testing as causes of the observed change of Figure 1. For these explanations to be plausible, the observed change should be part of a long-term, secular trend. They would be implausible—and our preferred explanation in terms of the treatment would be more plausible—if an abrupt change took place at the time of treatment and nowhere else in the series. Unfortunately for Governor Ribicoff's claims, the changes in 1955–1956 seem to be well in accord with these alternative explanations. The fact that 1955–1956 is the third abrupt downward jump in five years, and the smallest of the three, certainly argues against imputing any special causal effects to events occurring at that point.

The likelihood of regression is also supported by the data of Figure 2. The largest upswing in the series occurs in 1954–1955, just prior to the crackdown. This peak is seen even more strongly in the raw death statistics, presented for comparison in Figure 2a. It thus seems quite likely that the high figures of 1955 caused the crackdown, and thus less likely that the crackdown caused the low figures of 1956, for such a drop would have been predicted on grounds of regression in any case.

The graphic presentation of the precrackdown years provides evidence of the general instability of the accidental death rate and makes the supposed effect of Figure 1 now look trivial. Box and Tiao[2] have developed an analytical technique for estimating and making inferences about change in the level

Figure 2a. Interrupted Time-Series Presentation of Traffic Deaths in Connecticut (Raw Figures).

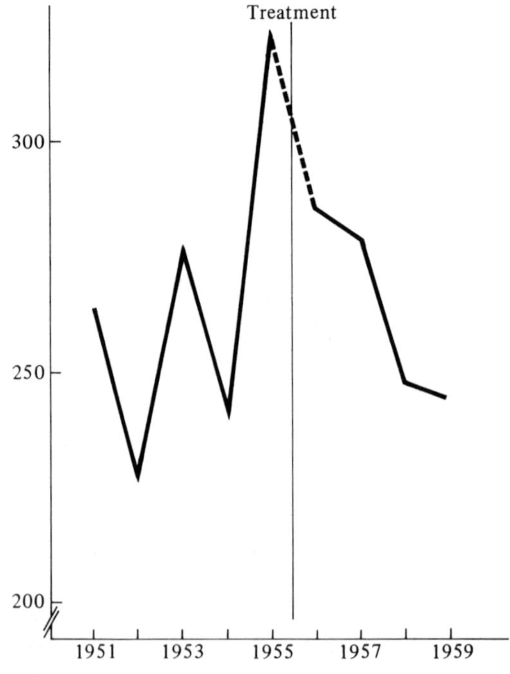

of a nonstationary time series, and this technique was applied to our data (in monthly units) by Gene V. Glass.[3] The test was unable to show a significant shift at the time of the crackdown.

In the case at hand it was possible to improve on the methodology discussed up to now by constructing a type of control group of adjacent and similar states: New York, Massachusetts, Rhode Island, and New Jersey. This is a Multiple Time-Series Design. It provides a quasi-experimental control for history, which is not possible with single Interrupted Time-Series, and acts as an additional check on maturation, testing, and instrumentation. The data are presented in Figure 3. A significant fact in this comparison is that prior to the crackdown Connecticut's rate is rising relative to the other states, but afterwards its rate is falling. Glass's analysis applied to these data does show a statistically significant reduction in fatalities associated with the speed crackdown. However, the change appears minute, and the continuing possibility of regression as a cause of the shift renders enthusiastic support of the hypothesis very difficult.

Some additional analyses were made to illustrate further the use of time-series methodology, and to show that the crackdown had a real effect in the

Figure 3. Multiple Time-Series Comparing Connecticut Fatalities with Those of Four Comparable States.

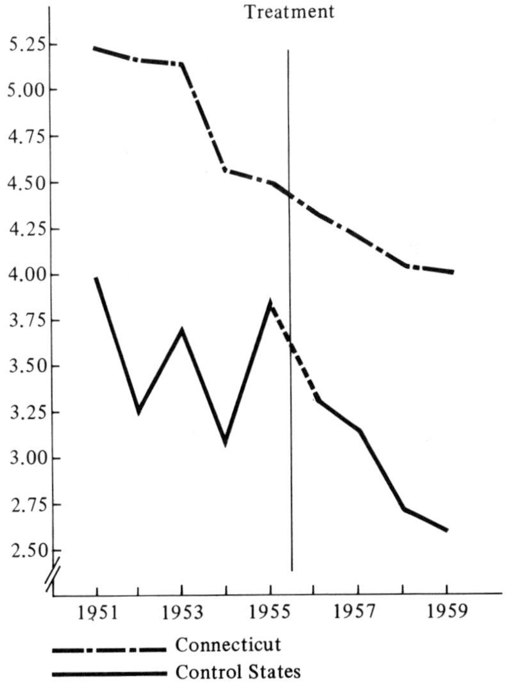

legal system and that it produced some unanticipated and unintended consequences. No control-state figures were obtained, but the single-state time-series are quite convincing.

Figure 4 provides evidence that the crackdown was put into effect as indicated by a great increase in suspensions of licenses for speeding.

Figure 4. Suspensions of Licenses for Speeding, as a Percentage of All Suspensions.

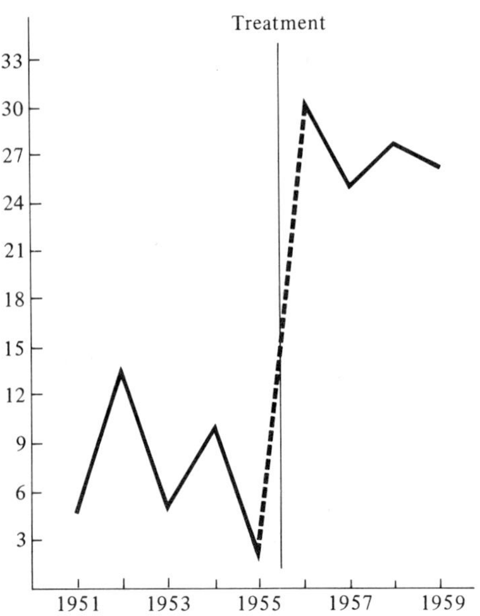

Figure 5 plots the percentage which speeding violations constitute of all traffic violations. This shows a decline, ostensibly due to greater conformity to speed limits, although it is also likely that policemen and prosecutors were more willing to overlook minor infractions or to charge them as something else.

Figure 6 concerns persons whose licenses were further suspended because they were convicted of driving with a suspended license. As a percentage of all suspensions, this jumps from an almost consistent zero to some 4 to 6 percent. Our interpretation of this phenomenon is that automobile transportation has become a virtual necessity for many residents of the diffusely settled megalopolitan region that includes Connecticut and that these people are willing to risk very severe punishments in order to continue daily routines that involve driving.

Figure 5. Speeding Violations, as a Percentage of All Traffic Violations.

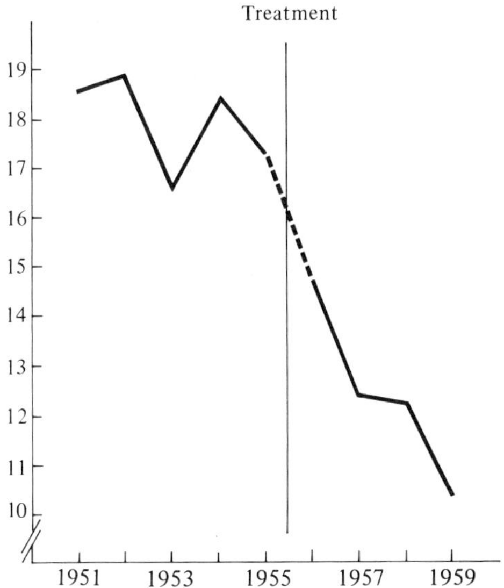

Figure 6. Arrested while Driving with a Suspended License, as a Percentage of Suspensions.

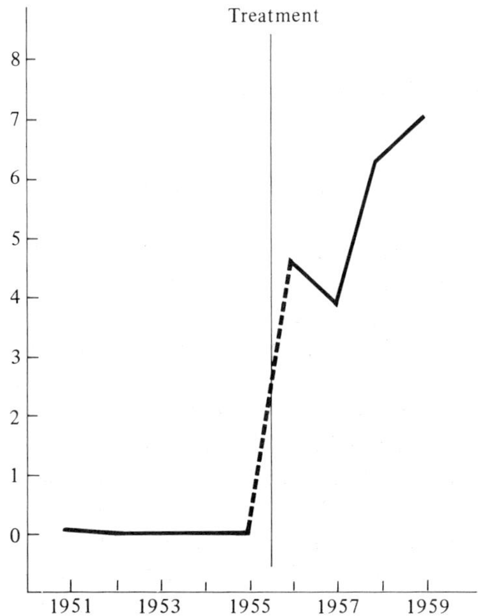

Figure 7 shows a reaction of the legal system to the administratively imposed crackdown. Even with fewer speeding violations reaching the courts, the courts were more lenient in their handling of these cases, as expressed by proportions of not-guilty judgments. Such leniency could be the result of

Figure 7. Percentage of Speeding Violations Judged Not Guilty.

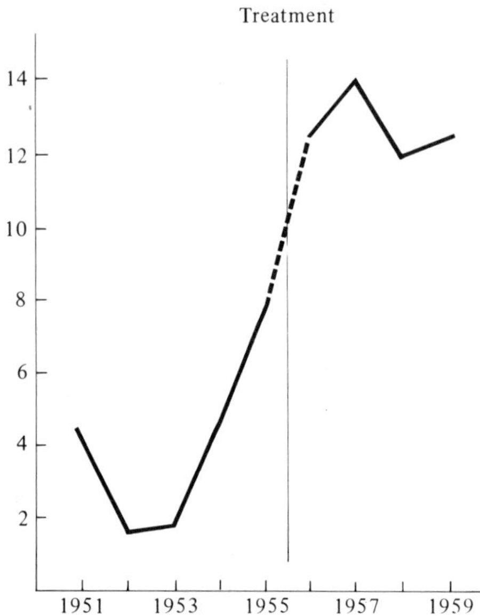

more generous handling by judges and prosecutors or of more vigorous defenses by the accused because more is at stake. The two effects shown in Figures 6 and 7 indicate a vitiation of the punitive effects of the crackdown in a society that acknowledges dependence on automobile transportation.

In conclusion, our analysis has shown that the Connecticut crackdown on speeding was a substantial enforcement effort, though its most punitive aspects were mitigated in practice by fewer arrests and convictions and by a willingness of some people to drive with suspended licenses. As to its effects, we are forced to conclude that they comprised no substantial reduction in traffic fatalities.

More important, we believe, than the specific findings of the study is the methodology here exemplified. While the social scientist cannot as a rule truly experiment on a societal scale, abrupt focused social change is continually going on, especially in the legal realm, and it can be evaluated by the careful researcher despite the lack of classical controls. We hope that familiarity with quasi-experimental techniques such as Time-Series will increase the ambitions as well as the results of sociologists who study societal changes.

NOTES

1. Quasi-experimental methodology is discussed in, e.g., Donald T. Campbell and Julian S. Stanley, "Experimental and Quasi-experimental Designs for Research on Teaching," in Nathan L. Gage, Ed., *Handbook of Research on Teaching*, Chicago: Rand McNally, 1963, pp. 171–246; Donald T. Campbell, "From Description to Experimentation: Interpreting Trends as Quasi-experiments," in Chester W. Harris, Ed., *Problems in Measuring Change*, Madison: University of Wisconsin Press, 1963; Donald T. Campbell and Keith N. Clayton, "Avoiding Regression Effects in Panel Studies of Communication Impact," *Studies in Public Communication*, No. 3, Chicago: Department of Sociology, University of Chicago, 1961, pp. 99–118, reprinted in Bobbs-Merrill Reprints in Sociology as S-353.
2. E. P. Box and G. C. Tiao, "A Change in Level of a Non-stationary Time Series," *Biometrika* 52 (1965), pp. 181–192.
3. Gene V. Glass, "Analysis of Data on the Connecticut Speeding Crackdown as a Time-Series Quasi-experiment," Research Paper #1, Laboratory of Educational Research, University of Colorado, July, 1967.

B. The Bugs Are Taking Over: Disguised Observation

This form of data collection is one in which "the observer has no control over the behavior or sign in question and plays an unobserved, passive, and unobtrusive role in the research situation."[1] Much data of this sort is caught by recording devices such as tape recorders and cameras. In fact, to insure nonreactivity in some instances, the recording device is left behind and hidden—to be retrieved at some later date.[2]

Many times data that would be otherwise unobtainable because of individuals' refusals to respond can be collected by means of disguised observation, though this tactic does raise the issue of ethics.[3] This was the problem faced by the President's Commission assigned to study obscenity and pornography in the country. How could they obtain data on who the patrons of "adult" bookstores and movies actually were? Although not addressing themselves to the ethics of this sort of data collection, the Commission Report does show the effectiveness of disguised observation in obtaining such data. Note also that the few incidents of response obtained via interview methods tended to support the findings obtained by disguised observation; another example of the power of multiple operationism as a research technique.

Ray Birdwhistell, in the Dissection, "There are Smiles," presents the pursuit of an hypothesis concerning human body motion communication; from simple observation of smiles and the recording of them, to document (photo) analysis, and even to the study of infant smiles under more stringent (yet unobtrusive) laboratory conditions. Other examples of disguised observation, mentioned earlier by Eugene Webb in "Approximations to Knowledge,"[4] include measuring the degree of fear induced by a ghost-story-telling session by measuring the shrinking diameter of a circle of seated children, and the degree of customer interest in jade by notation of pupil dilation. Consultation with the FBI would produce, I am sure, many more examples of this research technique in action.

NOTES

1. Eugene J. Webb, *et al., Unobtrusive Measures* (Chicago: Rand McNally, 1966), p. 112.
2. Perhaps the device is activated by sound, or turned on in a pre-determined random pattern (random sampling of time) rather than just letting it record everything that does not occur.
3. See the articles in this book by Kai T. Erikson (pp. 290-298) and Herbert C. Kelman (pp. 432-465) for discussions of this issue as it pertains to disguised observation.
4. "Approximations To Knowledge," pp. 126-151.

Patrons of Adult Bookstores and Movies

The Report of the Commission on Obscenity and Pornography

The "consumer of pornography" has been a vague and shadowy concept in American folk myth, not well defined but nevertheless obviously an undesirable type. Yet, in spite of the debate regarding the legal control of obscenity that has been growing the past 15 years, not one empirical study had been reported on the characteristics of people who bought erotic materials when the Commission came on the scene. The Commission has funded a few pilot studies of the patron of adult bookstores and movie theaters, and these together begin to sketch in a more definite image of the "consumer of pornography."

From *The Report of the Commission on Obscenity and Pornography*, "Patrons of Adult Bookstores and Movies," Washington, D.C. United States Government Printing Office, 1970. Edited version.

ADULT BOOKSTORE PATRONS

Massey (1970) observed 2,477 people who entered two bookstores carrying sex-oriented materials in Denver, Colorado. The observations were made over a six-day period in August 1969. One of the stores carried exclusively sex-oriented materials, while the other was a segregated section of a larger bookstore-newsstand. The sex-oriented sections were clearly marked "for adults only." Trained observers attempted to classify each patron in terms of sex, age, ethnic group membership, type of dress and the presence or not of a wedding band.

The patrons were almost exclusively male. Almost three-quarters (74 percent) were estimated to be in the age range of 26-55, while 22 percent were 21-25, and 4 percent were over 55; less than 1 percent were possibly under 21. Eighty-nine percent of the patrons were white, 4 percent black, and 5 percent Spanish-American. Over half the sample were casually dressed, 26 percent wore suits and 13 percent were blue-collar workers; the remainder were soldiers, students, tourists, hippies and clergymen. One-third of the patrons whose left hands were observable had on wedding bands. Jewelers estimate that roughly half of married males wear wedding bands, so well over half of these patrons were probably married.

Massey also inserted postcards in the purchases of 500 customers asking for demographic information. Only 52 of these postcards were returned, but the results were very similar to the observations. The purchaser who returned the postcard was male, age 26-35, had some education beyond high school, was married, a resident of the city, had an annual income of $10,000-$15,000, and had a professional or white-collar occupation. . . .

Massey attempted to interview some of the patrons, but soon gave up. The customers were quite skittish and generally silent while in the store; they appeared poised for flight. If someone spoke to them, they tended to respond in monosyllable and move away. Customers did not interact with each other and interacted with the cashier-clerks as little as possible. . . .

Booksellers' descriptions of their customer populations were quite consistent with the objective observations. Most of the stores claim a steady clientele who buy materials regularly, as well as transients who rarely come in more than once, but no estimates of the proportions of these two types could be made.

Nawy (1970) observed 950 customers in 11 adult bookstores in San Francisco. Only 3 percent of these were females and they were mostly accompanied by a male escort. About 8 out of 10 of the customers were over 25 years old and less than 1 percent were possibly under 18. The ethnic composition of the customers approximated the ethnic composition of San Francisco as given in the United States Census; predominantly white with a small proportion of blacks and orientals. Middle-class customers, as indicated by dress style, predominated. It is estimated, based on the number of wedding bands observed, that most customers were married. Nine out of ten shopped alone. Approximately one customer in every five made a purchase.

Winick (1970a) reports observations of 1800 patrons of bookstores, 300 in each of six cities; Mid-town Manhattan, Los Angeles, Chicago, Detroit, Atlanta, and Kansas City. Ninety-nine percent of the patrons were male. Approximately 80 percent were white, 15 percent black, and smaller percentages were Spanish-American and oriental. The variations across cities in ethnic composition of customers seemed to reflect the differing ethnic composition of the cities. . . . The age distribution was roughly the same across the cities. Twenty-six percent of the patrons wore business clothes, 41 percent casual, and 33 percent work clothes; few military uniforms were observed. There were considerable variations from city to city regarding costume: Atlanta, New York, and Kansas City had lower proportions of business attire and higher proportions of work clothes; Chicago and Los Angeles had higher proportions of business attire. The observers estimated the social class of the patrons as 44 percent lower class, 47 percent middle class, and 8 percent upper middle class. The downtown Manhattan figures inflated the lower class proportions considerably. Almost all (96 percent) shopped alone.

The profile of the patron of adult bookstores that emerges from these observations in different parts of the United States is: white, middle aged, middle class, married, male, dressed in business suit or neat casual attire, shopping alone. . . .

ADULT MOVIE THEATER PATRONS

Winick (1970a) observed 5,000 customers of adult movie theaters in nine different communities that provided a considerable spread of size, geographic, cultural, ethnic, and socioeconomic characteristics. The observations in eight of these locations were relatively consistent, but one was quite different from the others. We will describe the results of the observations on the eight and then discuss the ninth location.

Seventeen percent of the attendees were estimated to be in the age category 19-27, 32 percent in the 28-40 category, 41 percent in the 41-60 age group, and 10 percent were estimated to be over 60 years old. These figures did not vary significantly from city to city. Eighty percent were white, 14 percent black, 5 percent Spanish-American, and 2 percent oriental. These figures did vary from city to city, but the variation appears to reflect the ethnic makeup of the community. Ninety-eight percent of the patrons were male; more females were observed in suburban locations than in downtown locations. All the females were with a male escort or in a mixed-gender group. Ninety percent of the men attended alone. Attending alone was even more characteristic for the downtown theaters; roughly 15 percent of the patrons of neighborhood theaters attended in groups of two or more males.

Twenty-nine percent of the patrons were estimated to be lower class, 55 percent middle class, and 16 percent upper middle class. These proportions differed widely from situation to situation reflecting the character of the area in which the theater was located. For example, 62 percent of the patrons of New York neighborhood theaters were lower class, 69 percent of those in Kansas City were middle class, and 48 percent of patrons of New York suburban adult theaters were upper middle class. Forty-one percent wore suits and ties, 50 percent wore neat casual clothes, and 10 percent wore work clothes. This also varied by community. Downtown and suburban theaters had more suits and ties and neighborhood theaters had more work clothes; Los Angeles had more casually dressed patrons. Approximately 15 percent of the customers scrutinized the outside display and a similar proportion exhibited a conflicted demeanor in entering the theater. Very few juveniles were observed looking at the displays outside the theater.

The one theater whose patrons did not fit this general description was a theater in a relatively small city that contained several colleges. The patrons of this theater were more likely to be younger, white, and casually dressed; there was also more attendance of male-female couples.

Winick (1970b) also conducted interviews with 100 patrons of an adult movie theater which provided validation for the classifications based on external observation. He classified each of the patrons in terms of age, ethnicity, and social class on the basis of external observations before the interview and then again after the interview on the basis of the interview data. The two sets of classifications correspond very closely, the main difference was reclassification of a few cases from upper middle class to middle class. These data confirm the possibility of making such judgments accurately from external observation and heightened our confidence in the descriptions provided by such observations.

Nawy (1970) observed a total of 2,791 customers at three adult theaters in San Francisco. Ninety-seven percent of these customers were male. Blacks are underrepresented and Chinese overrepresented in comparison to their population in the city. Thirty-nine percent wore suit and tie, 49 percent wore neat casual clothes, 6 percent were dressed in sloppy casual clothes, 4 percent were in "hip" costumes, and 2 percent in blue collar work clothes. Thirty-one percent wore a wedding band, 58 percent did not, and 11 percent could not be observed; this provides an estimate that about 60 percent are married based on the assumption that half of married men wear wedding bands. Eighty-five percent of the customers entered the theater alone, 6 percent were with the opposite sex, and 8 percent were in a group of the same sex. Twenty-three percent of the patrons appeared to be regular customers.

Nawy (1970) also collected questionnaire data from 251 of these adult movie theater patrons. The demographic data of this questionnaire sample is very similar to the description of the total sample of patrons based on external observation. . . . Thus, the external observations are validated and amplified by the self reports.

Patrons of adult movie theaters may be characterized on the basis of these observations to be predominantly white, middle class, middle aged, married, males, who attend alone. This contrasts very much with the characteristics of patrons of general movie theaters who tend to be young heterosexual couples (Yankelovich, 1968).

Nawy (1970) reports that his observations revealed that over half of the adult movie theater business is conducted during the 9:00 a.m. to 5:00 p.m. working day. This may be less true for neighborhood and suburban theaters than for downtown theaters. This business pattern contrasts sharply with that of the general motion picture theaters which often do not open until 6:00 p.m. . . .

INTERVIEW AND QUESTIONNAIRE STUDIES OF CONSUMERS OF EROTIC MATERIALS

Several investigators (Goldstein, *et al.,* 1970; Massey, 1970; Nawy, 1970; Winick, 1970b) have attempted to study patrons of adult bookstores and adult movie theaters. All have reported a great deal of difficulty in securing the cooperation of members of these potential subject populations. Customers in adult bookstores appear more reluctant to participate in a study than patrons of adult movie houses. The response rates in the successful studies were all less than 50 percent. This low response rate may introduce an undetermined bias into the results because those who agree to filling out the questionnaire or to the interview may be different in some other way from those who do not agree to participate. The distribution of demographic data on the people who participated in the more intensive studies is very similar to that found for the larger samples of observed customers, however; this would suggest that the other data may be fairly representative, too. . . .

REFERENCES

Finkelstein, M. M. Traffic in sex-oriented materials, Part I: Adult Bookstores in Boston, Massachusetts. *Technical reports of the Commission on Obscenity and Pornography*, Vol. 4. Washington, D.C.: U. S. Government Printing Office, 1970. (a)

Finkelstein, M. M. Traffic in sex-oriented materials, Part II: Criminality and organized crime. *Technical reports of the Commission on Obscenity and Pornography*, Vol. 2. Washington, D.C.: U. S. Government Printing Office, 1970. (b)

Kutschinsky, B. Pornography in Denmark: Studies on producers, sellers, and users. *Technical reports of the Commission on Obscenity and Pornography,* Vol. 4. Washington, D.C.: U. S. Government Printing Office, 1970.

Massey, M. E. A market analysis of sex-oriented materials in Denver, Colorado, August, 1969—A pilot study. *Technical reports of the Commission on Obscenity and Pornography,* Vol. 4. Washington, D.C.: U. S. Government Printing Office, 1970.

Nawy, H. The San Francisco erotic marketplace. *Technical reports of the Commission on Obscenity and Pornography*, Vol. 4. Washington, D.C.: U. S. Government Printing Office, 1970.

Winick, C. A study of consumers of explicitly sexual materials: Some functions served by adult movies. *Technical reports of the Commission on Obscenity and Pornography*, Vol. 4. Washington, D.C.: U. S. Government Printing Office, 1970. (a)

Winick, C. Some observations of patrons of adult theaters and bookstores. *Technical reports of the Commission on Obscenity and Pornography*, Vol. 4. Washington, D.C.: U. S. Government Printing Office, 1970b.

Yankelovich, Inc. Public survey of movie-goers—1967. In *A year in review.* New York: Motion Picture Association of America, 1968, pp. 11–12.

Dissection B:

There Are Smiles...

Ray L. Birdwhistell

Laughing and crying seem to be such universally recognized human expressions that from the beginning of my interest in human body motion communication I was tempted to see these as basic physiologically derived expressions, the study of which could provide us with a starting point for measuring special individual conventionalized behavior. When I began to film real children in real contexts, the temptation remained but the confidence in the method rapidly faded.

As long as we studied the laughing or crying situations as identified by the participants, it was easy to code (linguistically and kinesically) the laughter as laughter, the crying as such. It was not nearly so easy to code the constituents of these contrastive social acts exhibited by an isolated individual whose context was unknown. Since I found the sounds made by persons laughing or crying confusing, I decided to turn to smiling and "sad-faced." The latter category proved impossible to handle, but over the years the question of smiling, of when it is appropriate, and of how the child learns its appropriate employment have remained as concerns—particularly when we are trying to understand the children we see who are, socially and emotionally, seriously distressed and distressing.

Early in my research on human body motion, influenced by Darwin's *Expression of the Emotions in Man and Animals*, and by my own preoccupation with human universals, I attempted to study the human "smile."[1] Without recognizing my own preconceptions, I had been attracted to a simplistic theory which saw "verbal" communication as subject to (and responsible for) human diversification while "nonverbal" communication provided a primitive and underlying base for (and was the resultant of) human unity. Smiling, it seemed to me, provided the perfect example of a behavior bit which in every

From Ray Birdwhistell, "There Are Smiles" in *Kinesics and Context* © University of Pennsylvania Press, Philadelphia, 1970.

culture expressed pleasure (in the jargon which I was using then, "positive response") on the part of the actor. Almost as soon as I started to study "smiling" I found myself in a mass of contradictions. From the outset, the signal value of the smile proved debatable. Even the most preliminary procedures provided data which were difficult to rationalize. For example, not only did I find that a number of my subjects "smiled" when they were subjected to what seemed to be a positive environment, but some "smiled" in an aversive one. My psychiatric friends provided me with a variety of psychological explanations for this apparent contradiction, but I was determined to develop social data without recourse to such explanations. Yet, inevitably, these ideas shaped my early research.

As I enlarged my observational survey, it became evident that there was little constancy to the phenomenon. It was almost immediately clear that the frequency of smiling varied from one part of the United States to another. Middle-class individuals from Ohio, Indiana, and Illinois, as counted on the street, smiled more often than did New Englanders with a comparable background from Massachusetts, New Hampshire, and Maine. Moreover, these latter subjects smiled with a higher frequency than did western New Yorkers. At the other extreme, the highest incidence of smiling was observed in Atlanta, Louisville, Memphis, and Nashville. Closer study indicated that even within Georgia, Kentucky, and Tennessee there were systematic differences in the frequency of smiling; subjects from tidewater Georgia, the Bluegrass of Kentucky and western Tennessee were much more likely to be observed smiling than were their compatriots from the Appalachian sections of their states. If I could have maintained my faith in the smile as a "natural" gesture of expression, an automatic neuromuscular reaction to an underlying and "pleasurable" endocrine or neural state, I would have had a sure measure to establish isoglosses of pleasure with which to map the United States. Unfortunately, data continued to come in.

Almost as soon as I attempted to isolate contexts of propriety for smiling, data emerged which made it clear that while it was perfectly appropriate (as measured by social response) for a young female to smile among strangers on Peachtree Street in Atlanta, Georgia, such behavior would be highly inappropriate on Main Street in Buffalo, New York. In one part of the country, an unsmiling individual might be queried as to whether he was "angry about something," while in another, the smiling individual might be asked, "What's funny?" In one area, an apology required an accompanying smile; in another, the smile elicited the response that the apology was not "serious." That is to say, the presence of a smile in particular contexts indicated "pleasure," in another "humor," in others "ridicule," and, in still others, "friendliness" or "good manners." Smiles have been seen to indicate "doubt" and "acceptance," "equality" and "superordination" or "subordination." They occur in situations where insult is intended and in others as a denial of insult. Except with the most elastic conception of "pleasure," charts of smile frequency clearly were not going to be very reliable as maps for the location of happy Americans.

But what about the "natural" smile of the "happy" infant? (Twenty-five years ago, we believed that babies were not only more "natural" than grown-ups but also more like grown animals and more "primitive." By the time we were ready to forego the term primitive as applicable to non-Western people, we were not ready to give it up as descriptive of Western and non-Western children.) Friends who were studying child development said that as the infant matured past the point where his smiles were grimaces from gas pains he had a natural smile which some felt provided a naturally seductive stance with which to involve adults in care and protection. Others insisted that this infantile smile was a natural expression of pleasure and that, until the adult and peer world converted or suppressed it, the child would continue to smile "naturally" in response to his own euphoria or to situations of social euphoria. Others insisted that while there was a "natural tendency" to smile, this tendency was constrained as the child was conditioned to use the smile as a symbolic cue. That is, the infantile smile, as an organic or physiological and automatic reflex of pleasure, with maturation comes under voluntary control and becomes utilizable as a unit of the communication system. At the other extreme were those who, believing that the fetus resists birth and is born angry, see the infantile smile as descendent from the teeth-baring of an animal ancestry and thus signifying threat. The threat is mediated and the child subjugated by the social insistence upon converting the meaning of the smile from malevolent intent to benevolent intent. Finally, this apparent divergence of opinion is bridged by others who solve such problems by blending the dichotomy and who see man as basically ambivalent. For these persons the smile is a naturally ambivalent gesture which can be and is used to express the gamut of human feelings.

This is not the occasion to review some of the attempts to test these and other dependent hypotheses using caricatures, photos, and smiling models with infants in laboratory conditions. As I have read them I find them indeterminate although interesting. We do not have very reliable information about infant smiling in cultures other than those of the Western world. At the time of this writing I do not know whether infants in all societies smile prior to *any* socialization nor do I know what happens to infants in any particular society who do not smile at all or who smile all the time. On the other hand, there is considerable clinical and anecdotal material to indicate that at least in Western cultures children must learn to smile in appropriate situations. That is, they must learn how and when to smile; if they do not they are somehow isolated for special attention.

It is this latter point which is relevant to our communicational studies. Smiles do not override context. That is, insofar as we can ascertain, whatever smiles are and whatever their genesis, they are not visible transforms of underlying physiological states which are emitted as direct and unmitigated signal forms of that state. And, the fact that subjects are not always aware that they are or are not smiling or are not always skilled enough to emit convincing smiles upon demand does not relegate such smiles into the realm of the psychologist or the physiologist. Linguistic or Kinesic structure is no less orderly because performers are not conscious of their utilization of it.

At this stage of the study of smiling (I am fictionalizing the order of investigation and discovery somewhat for purposes of discussion) it had become clear that not only could I not support any proposition that smiles were universal symbols in the sense of having a universal social stimulus value but, insofar as the study of communication went, my work was only complicated by assumptions about communication as an elaboration of a panhuman core *code* emergent from the limited possibilities of physiological response. However, I could not rid myself of the nagging question occasioned by negative evidence from quite another level. I had talked with a great many anthropologists who had studied in the most widely diversified cultures and *none* reported the *absence of any* smiling from their field work. And, in fact, *none* reported societies in which smiling *never* appeared in situations which could be interpreted as pleasurable, friendly, benevolent, positive, and so on. The question was: Even if smiling does not have the same meaning in every society and is not traceably a direct response to a primitive affective state, doesn't its universal distribution as a facial phenomenon give us the right to call it a universal gesture? Obviously it does if we are speaking at the *articulatory level* of description. That is, if a smile is the bilateral extension of the lateral aspects of the lip region from a position of rest, all members of the species *Homo sapiens* smile.

There then emerges the second question: Does not the fact that smiling in every culture can be *in certain of its contexts* related to positive response indicate that man, as he gained spoken language in a prelanguage situation, utilized this expression as a device for interpersonal constraint (in the Durkheimian sense) and that smiling is a kind of urkinesic form which has been absorbed into human communicational systems as they developed? The only answer that I can give to this is that I don't know. Important as it might be to answer this question, at this stage of research I am not particularly interested in origins or in the ethnography of atavistic or "vestigial" forms. However, I am interested in determining, in a descriptive sense, what it is that we mean when we say that someone "smiled." I am interested in being able to examine the structure of events relevant to "smiling" in order to deal with the social situations of which it is a part.

Over the past decade I have been engaged in intrachannel structural kinesic research. I have become aware that, similar to other "gestures," "smiling" is not a thing in itself. The term "smiling" as used by American informants covers an extensive range of complex kinemorphic constructions which are reducible to their structural components. The positioning of the head, variation in the circumorbital region, the forms of the face, and even general body position can be and usually are involved in the performance and reception of what the informant reports as "smiling." I have learned that "he smiled," as a statement on the part of an American informant is as nonspecific and uninformative as the statement on the part of the same informant that "he raised his voice."

Only by intrachannel analysis have I been able to free myself from an ethnocentric preconception that I know what a smile is. We have not done the semiotic or communication research necessary to establish the range of appropriate social contexts within which to measure the range of consequences (meanings) of the possible range of shapes of "smiles." I think that we know *how* to study "smiling" as a *social* act. However, I don't think we will know what a smile means until we understand, from society to society, its intrachannel role and its contextual variability.

Insofar as I have been able to determine, just as there are no universal words, no sound complexes, which carry the same meaning the world over, there are no body motions, facial expressions, or gestures which provoke *identical* responses the world over.[2] A body can be bowed in grief, in humility, in laughter, or in readiness for aggression. A "smile" in one society portrays friendliness, in another embarrassment, and, in still another may contain a warning that, unless tension is reduced, hostility and attack will follow.

Perhaps it would be useful to discuss the "smile" as a deceptively familiar facial expression. It may be possible through its analysis to make a series of points about so-called gestures and facial expressions. First, what kinds of behavior do we abstract when we say that a man or a woman has a smile on (note the preposition) his or her face? We could, if we wished, make a list of the musculature of the lips and around the mouth. Such a listing might be of interest to an anatomist or to the plastic surgeon attempting to restore expression to a mutilated face or to a neurologist searching for a way to repair the damage of a neural accident. But this is not what we are seeking. Even our most preliminary investigation reveals that the lateral extension of the corner of the mouth or the upward pull on the upper lips, or any combinations of these do not make a recognizable smile. These same activities occur with a snarl or a grimace of pain. The response of an infant to a gas pain seems to involve the same circummouth musculature as the response to its mother.

A detail from a painting which is limited to the behavior immediately associated with the oral cavity is ambiguous. It takes little observation to realize that this ambiguity arises from the fact that our abstraction is partial, that we have inappropriately sliced nature.

It is true that a child can be taught to make a large oval, put a small circle in its center, two small parallel circles just above the central circle and an upwardly curving line below the central circle and the completed figure can be recognized as representing a face. When the abstraction is presented as a whole, the curved line in this drawing can *stand for* a smile. Yet, this figure is more of a statement about the conventional shorthand of cartoons or of Western European childish representation than it is proof that the smile occurs in the mouth. If one belongs to a culture that sustains this abstractional convention, the curved line *stands for* a smile. In other cultures which do not use this total figure for a face or recognize the curved line symbol for a mouth as a mouth, this abstraction is confusing if not downright nonsensical. The particular organization of sounds which are heard as "smile" stands for a particular facial expression only for members of those cultures which have made this arbitrary and conventionalized association between the complex of sounds "Smile" and a particular range of facial expression. Comparably, the curved line is a symbol, carrying meaning only in those societies which have this convention. However, it is very easy to be deceived into believing that because an abstraction can stand for an activity, the abstraction itself is a universal representation of this expression—that a smile, so abstracted, *is* an activity engaged in by the mouth.

Because artistic representation is always, if meaningful, in some sense conventionalized, we must look at faces and not at pictures of faces if we are to abstract and comprehend either "what" a smile is, how it is made up, or what it "means." That is, "smiles" must be studied in their social setting if we are to understand the ranges of meaning humans of a given society convey to each other when they display facial activity.

If a "smile" is not limited to the mouth, what are the physical involvements characteristic of its performance? If we limit our discussion to an American communicating by body motion, we can study this problem along two different but mutually contributive pathways. One of these is to take the mouth behavior which repeatedly appears in that activity which we, as members of an American, diakinesic system recognize as a smile and which our informants identify as a smile, and see where else it appears. By a few comparative operations we can quickly discover that the lips are pulled back, or up and back, in a variety of other facial expressions. That is, even though some degree of movement is required by the lips in order to smile, this same movement is utilized in expressions that could not by the farthest stretch of the imagination be called "smiling." By this operation we recognize that the mouth movement is a segment of a structure that can be used as part of a code and that it is not specifically meaningful in and of itself.

Analogically, we could compare the movement of the lips which is at times used to compose the expression "smile" as a conventionalized body activity, with the long vowel /uw/, which in my dialect stands between the consonantal clusters in the forms "school" and "fool." There is nothing about the /uw/ sound which signifies that these two words have an underlying common identity. By some other operations we might discover that the /uw/ sound is to "school" and "fool" as the /i/ sound is to "skill" and "fill." That is, these are significant pieces of linguistic structure but are not in themselves meaningful.

The lip movements we are discussing are also pieces of structure. They must be combined with other pieces of comparably derived structure to form a meaningful unit of American communicative body movement. By examining the neighborhood of the curved lips, we can discover that this behavior often, *but not always*, occurs with a shifting tonus in the cheek area. It may *or may not* be accompanied by certain changes in the circumorbital region. It may *or may not* be accompanied by a shift in the positioning in the upper and lower lids. There may *or may not* be involvement of the eyebrows, and/or the forehead. Careful observation may reveal that this behavior may be accompanied by a movement of the scalp. The head may *or may not* be tilted. Continuing this same investigation, we can, using our descriptive and abstractive method of search, discover that the shoulders and the arms may *or may not* be involved. The trunk, too, while often not shifting as the lips curve or assume an original "at rest" position, may at times be seen to move. The hips may *or may not* be involved. And, if we are careful enough observers, we may come to recognize that in many of the situations in which we observe mouths curving, the legs and feet can be seen to move in regular and characteristic ways.

By other operations of isolation and contrast we may discover that each of the variables which we have just discussed also may occur without the appearance of a curving mouth. If each of these taken separately or together in a variety of combinations influence the way that people characteristically respond to a particular complex of behavior, we know that we are dealing with pieces of structure. We can surmise that we have begun to isolate some of the building blocks for the system through which Americans communicate with each other. In other words, we have discovered, on the one hand, that the word "smile" is a lexical (verbal) abstraction of very complex behavior and, on the other, that there are, in the American body movement system, events like words, sentences, and paragraphs. We have demonstrated that some order of lip movement seems required in the activity perceived by Americans as a smile. By extensive operations of search, in fact, we will discover that if other pieces of facial behavior are correctly presented there is no need for an actor to either curl or part his lips–a slight softening is sufficient. The observer will report that the actor has "smiled."

While many of the techniques used in the abstraction and analysis of communication systems are relatively new, the insights on which the approach is based have been around for some time.[3] A popular beginning point for those concerned with the history of modern communication theory is Darwin's *Expression of the Emotions in Man and Animals.* In this work, the great biologist attempted to organize an extensive body of observations into some kind of ordered theory about the audible and visible behavior of mammals and the emotional states which induce such behavior. A rigorous observer, Darwin set a model for behavioral description which can be read with profit today.

However, his concern with certain kinds of psychological problems, many of which remain unsolved, vitiated his attempt to regulate his data. In his role as synthesist he was hampered by preconceptions which even the sternest materialists of his day could not avoid.

Inheritance, as Darwin used it, seems at times a genetic, and at other times a social phenomenon. Perhaps it makes little difference to his major thesis which aspects of human behavior are biologically inherited as long as he demonstrates the continuity of the species and the society. However, for certain problems with which the human sciences are concerned today, it makes a great deal of difference whether or not vocal and body motion systems ultimately derive their order from the biological base or are exclusively a product of social experience. Careful reading of Darwin leads one to believe that if he had had some knowledge about social systems or even about the systematic quality of language and its cultural inheritance, he might have unraveled or at least loosened some of these knots himself. Clearly, his work does set the stage for many of the problems with which some anthropologists, the modern ethnologists, and the comparative psychologists are now concerned:

> Are certain kinds of social behavior, particularly gestures, facial expression, and certain sounds, somehow closer to the biological base than others?
>
> Are such behaviors biologically inherited and thus specially revealing as descriptions of the emotional life of certain groups or members within the group?
>
> Are there particular sounds and expressions and gestures which can be studied *in isolation* and which are evidence of particular, predisposing psychological states regardless of the cultural context of their appearance?

Cross-cultural research suggests that the answer to all of these questions is negative. How can we, then, comprehend and rephrase the evident regularities which we observe within particular social groups? And how can we assess the variations within these regularities? Scholars for over a hundred years have been concerned with analyzing the relationship between language and body motion and the personalities which express them. Insightful and even brilliantly intuitive though many of them are, most are directed toward a different order of data than we are developing here. They were largely concerned primarily with isolated examples of vocalic variation or gesture and posture as expressional behavior; their patent ethnocentrism, atomism, or biologism has precluded rather than encouraged cross-cultural study. With few exceptions, most of the work is not of direct concern to this presentation.

The development of microcultural analysis owes much to the work of

Boas,* Efron (1942), Bateson, Devereux, LaBarre (1949) and Margaret Mead, among others. Mead's work especially has been stimulating to the development of kinesic analysis. Her reappraisal of the Gesellian position on development (1956), her work with Bateson which dramatized the usefulness of the camera as a research tool (1952), and her consistent stress on careful problem arrangement in the analysis of culture and personality data were important contributions to the analytic procedures of kinesics. Several psychologists have also provided hypotheses, the analyses of which have led to the clarification of the linguistic-kinesic approach. Among these are K. Dunlap (1927), M. H. Krout (1933), Otto Klineberg (1927), Gardiner Murphy (1947), John Carroll (1953), and, especially, C. E. Osgood (1954). This is by no means an exhaustive review of the influences contributing to the development of the linguistic-kinesic approach to microcultural analysis. From every discipline making up the behavioral sciences have come insights which lead to the perspective best put by Bateson: "Our new recognition of the complexity and patterning of human behavior has forced us to go back and go through the natural history phase of the study of man which earlier scholars skipped in their haste to get to laboratory experimentation."

NOTES

1. The pages which follow are adapted from "Kinesics, Inter– and Intra–Channel Research," in *Studies in Semiotics,* Thomas A. Sebeok, ed. Social Science Information, International Social Science Council (Paris, Mouton, 1968), Vol. VII–6, pp. 9–26.
2. The following section on smiles is part of a paper "The Artist, The Scientist, and a Smile" presented at the Maryland Institute of Art on December 4, 1964.
3. This selection is adapted from "Paralanguage: Twenty–five Years after Sapir," in *Lectures on Experimental Psychology,* Henry W. Brosin, ed. (Pittsburgh: University of Pittsburgh Press, 1961).

C. When a Girl Sees the Handwriting on the Wall, She's in the Wrong Bathroom: Physical Trace Analysis

The final type of nonreactive measure to be considered is the sketchiest and most ambiguous: that of physical traces left behind by individuals that

*The influence of Franz Boas is expressed in the work of his students, particularly Mead, Sapir, and Efron. Professor Boas was among the first scholars to utilize the movie camera as a field research instrument.

give some clue as to who they were and what they were doing. Physical traces can be thought of as falling in two main types: erosion and accretion measures.

Erosion measures are the natural remnants of activities that have selectively worn certain objects Webb has mentioned the selective erosion of tiles on a museum floor as a measure of the popularity of exhibits. Another erosion measure was utilized in Norman Hayner's study of the "souvenir habit."

> This habit, as defined by a hotel detective, includes "everything from the taking of a carnation from the lobby bouquet to the theft of hundreds of dollars worth of silver and linen at a time." Hayner's study of theft patterns in the urban hotel provided him with a central clue to the motivations and self-conceptions of hotel residents. He pointed to the impersonality that pervades hotel living and suggested that the "souvenir habit" was only one index of the feeling of estrangement and transitoriness that characterizes a large majority of hotel dwellers.[1]

Accretion measures, on the other hand, are natural deposits of objects that individuals have made over time. Webb points to a study in which an investigator wanted to learn the level of whiskey consumption in an officially "dry" town. He did so by counting empty bottles in ashcans. Alan J. Weberman, according to a 1970 Associated Press release, has taken this method a bit further in his studies of the lifestyles of celebrities such as Bob Dylan.

> Still hungry for more information, Weberman strolled past the Dylan house last fall. 'I reached in the garbage can and pulled out a half-finished letter to Johnny Cash. I said, "This is no garbage can, it's a gold mine!"
>
> "After two weeks Dylan got wise. He began to censor his garbage."

Dylan's censorship underscores one of the basic problems with utilizing physical trace analysis—that of *selective deposit. Selective survival* of materials is the second major problem with this sort of data. If it can be eaten, rotted, or reused, it will not show up for analysis.

Physical trace analysis is not all of this "naturalistic" sort. The researcher can intervene and create controlled measures of erosion and accretion. A good example of a controlled measure is Stanley Milgram's "lost letter" technique of data collection.

> At the root, the technique is a simple one. An investigator distributes—drops—throughout a city a large number of letters, addressed and stamped but unposted. A person who comes across one of these "lost" letters on the street must decide what to do: mail it? disregard it? destroy it?

> There is a widespread feeling among people that one *ought* to mail such a letter. . . . In some circumstances, however–as when the letter is addressed to an organization the finder thinks highly objectionable–he may *not* mail it. Thus, by varying the addresses on the letters and calculating the proportion returned for each address, one can measure sentiment toward an organization. . . .
>
> The basic premise of the technique is that [a person's] action will tell us something of how he relates to that object. By mailing the lost letter, he aids the organization in question; by disregarding or destroying the letter he hinders it. And he has defined his relationship toward the organization by the quality of his actions.[2]

Milgram has employed this technique successfully in predicting voting patterns in settings as disparate as New Haven, Connecticut and Hong Kong.

> Other investigators now have used the lost-letter technique to study attitudes toward Vietnam, and the McCarthy-Johnson primary in Wisconsin, with varying results. While the technique seems to reflect gross differences of opinion, it fails to reflect the subtle differences that are more typical of social disagreement. Yet when the study starts with an interesting idea, interesting results sometimes follow. For example, William and Melissa Bowerman, graduate students at Harvard, distributed anti-Nazi letters in Munich, and found a depression in the return of anti-Nazi letters in specific neighborhoods of that city. Thus, they pinpointed the areas of strongest neo-Nazi sentiment. I hope readers traveling to Moscow this summer will not try dropping letters in Red Square. But if you are serious about research . . .[3]

Craig Gilborn presents, in "Looking at the Coke Bottle," the basic techniques of scientific analysis: description, classification, and interpretation. Though these techniques, as applied to physical trace data, have been little used in sociology, they show great promise when considering their possible applications.

Recalling Richard Evans' discussion of TV rating services, as presented earlier in this book, turn to this section's Dissection piece. As Pogo points out, Evans missed an opportunity to apply unobtrusive measures to the problem of who is watching what television show .

NOTES

1. Norman K. Denzin. *The Research Act,* (Chicago: Aldine, 1970).
2. Stanley Milgram, "The Lost Letter Technique," *Psychology Today* (June 1969), pp. 30-31. Reprinted from *Psychology Today* Magazine, June, 1969. Copyright © Ziff-Davis Publishing Company.
3. *Ibid.*

Pop Iconology: Looking at the Coke Bottle

Craig Gilborn

The redoubtable Samuel Johnson was citing a condition and not offering a choice when he wrote in the preface to his *Dictionary* (1755), "I am not yet so lost in lexicography as to forget that words are the daughters of earth, and that things are the sons of heaven." Dr. Johnson did not elaborate about the two realms of words and things, but he may have been acknowledging that words are not capable of translating all of those attributes of an object that are available to, and integrated by, the human senses. The cliché about a picture being worth a thousand words should be enlarged to include things: *Any thing is worth a thousand words.*

Knowledge of an object means that we have had some experience with it, either directly or on some previous occasion with an object that is similar or identical to it. In an earlier article in *Museum News* I tried to convey the complexity and cultivation of this nonverbal knowledge as it is revealed in the performances of such object-centered specialists as the museum curator, the primitive hunter, and the preindustrial men and women whose daily tasks presupposed a vast body of informed, first-hand experience. Narrowing the scope of the earlier paper, I will pick up the discussion at the point in which recent educational theory and practice were said to be seeking to provide students with the kinds of first-hand experiences that challenge and motivate the scholar and scientist in their pursuit of knowledge.[1]

Objects are capable of yielding a considerable amount of information about themselves and the conditions in which they were formed or fashioned. Scholars and scientists in fields such as art history and criticism, archeology,

From Craig Gilborn, "Pop Iconology: Looking at the Coke Bottle," *Museum News*, December, 1968; pp. 12–18.

paleontology, and the life and earth sciences use terms and methodologies appropriate to their respective problems of studying primary, nonverbal data. Without minimizing the differences that exist among these disciplines that take objects for their main source of evidence, it is worth asking whether the analysis of objects may not involve common modes of perception and organization. . . .

The Coke bottle has been manufactured for more than 50 years, a long history by modern standards. The bottle has maintained a continuity of form during this period, but with discernible modifications from which relative and absolute chronologies can be obtained without resorting to any evidence but that presented by a sample of the bottles. Coke bottles are found in large quantities throughout the United States (and in most nations of the world); they are inexpensive, expendable, durable, and possess sculptural and optical qualities of great complexity. Accompanying the Coke bottle is an extensive lore consisting of anecdotes, personal associations, and behavior traits (e.g., the "Coke break") that amount to a "folk" tradition that is truly national in scope. Hence, the bottle is, by any practical educational standard, a model vehicle for the performance of those operations which are basic to the systematic analysis of most objects.

A number of operations are involved in the study of objects.[2] Three broad operations, each capable of further subdivision, are identified in the sequence in which they are generally carried out: description, classification, and interpretation. The charts, pictures, and discussion that follow are based upon these operations as they apply to a study of the "classic" Coca-Cola bottle.

Several cautionary remarks are in order. First, the exercise as outlined below cannot provide all of the experiences that are part of the work that is performed in the field. For instance, description for the archaeologist frequently includes an entire site, not simply the objects uncovered in the site. Occasionally, however, archaeologists must work without a true archaeological context, as when artifacts or other material objects have been scattered by flooding streams or bulldozers. Second, different disciplines place different emphasis upon the operations. Art historians seldom work out classifications, partly because the differences seem so much greater than similarities (especially in the fine or creative arts) and partly because it is presumed that previous scholarship has established classifications that are still useful.

DESCRIPTIVE OPERATION

This operation, as applied to the Coke bottle, would ask the student or team of students to describe the "classic" bottle (identified in fig. 2 as the Type) in terms of its attributes of shape, symbol markings, structural details, material, color, and the like. There are two objectives to this operation. The methodological objectives (1) provide a written and iconic record which can be consulted on other occasions, and (2) involve the student—or the scholar-scientist—as a learner of every detail of the object to be studied. In this exercise the learning objective is to *develop an awareness of the diverse attributional character of objects.*

Believers of the efficacy of words may find the attempt to describe the shape of the bottle to be a humbling experience. Metaphors have been used, but these are dated: "hobble-skirt," so called because of the design of the dresses worn when the classic bottle was introduced; "Mae West" and "hourglass." Hence line drawings are essential (fig. 1), and to these a nomenclature of visible attributes should be assigned. Some of these attributes will be ge-

Figure 1. Iconic Description

105,529
DESIGN FOR A BOTTLE
Eugene Kelly, Toronto, Ontario, Canada, assignor to The Coca-Cola Company, Wilmington, Del., a corporation of Delaware
Application March 24, 1937, Serial No. 68,391
Term of patent 14 years

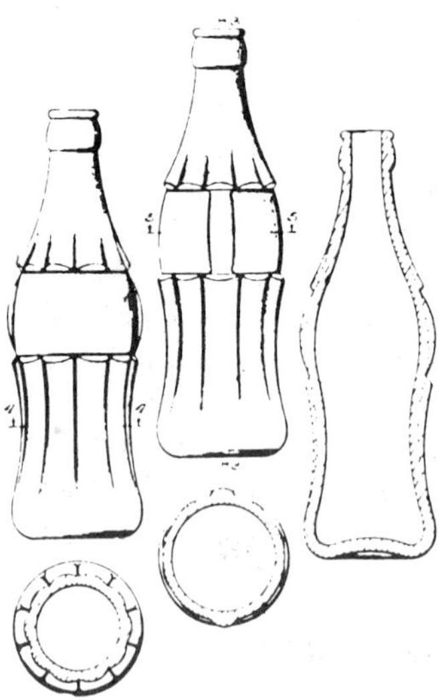

The ornamental design for a bottle, as shown.

neric in that they are expressive of the functional form that we call "bottle," involving the use of such terms as "mouth," "lip," "neck," and so on. There may be collectivities of attributes that indicate sections of the bottle, such as "top zone," "middle zone," or "front" and "back." Some attributes are peculiar to the Coca-Cola bottle itself, especially the shape or design, the signatures "Coca-Cola" and "Coke" (all three trademarked), and the ribs. Some attributes, such as material, color, and weight, cannot be visualized iconically, though they must be a part of any proper description. Signs of wear should be noted if they occur. (In the bottlers' lexicon a "bum" is a bottle that can be safely refilled, but that looks disreputable; a "scuffie" is a bum that is scuffed; and a "crock" is a bum with a chipped bottom.)

During this first operation, students may be given one bottle or one example from each of the three Sub-Types designated in figure 2. The latter choice will raise questions about differences that are to be dealt with in the classificatory operation.

CLASSIFICATORY OPERATION

The difference between description and classification is that the former treats each object as an entity—almost as if each were unique—whereas classification segregates objects on the basis of dissimilar attributes. An assumption at the outset of the classificatory operation is that there is an historical or functional relationship among the objects being classified, so that differences in attributes can be explained in terms of changed behavior or altered conditions, usually as they have taken place over a period of years.

There are two methodological objectives to classification: first, as suggested above, to reveal relationships that are real and not categorical (for example, billiard balls and tomatoes as "round, smooth" objects); and, second, to provide a future reference against which freshly uncovered specimens may be compared and identified or otherwise accounted for. The classification for the classic Coke bottle (fig. 2) serves both objectives by indicating relationships among the Sub-Types and their Variants, and by providing a model for the identification of bottles. Like most classifications, this one is subject to modification or further refinement.

As for the learning objectives to this exercise, there are three that should be mentioned. The first is that while all objects consist of a variety of attributes, *some of these attributes are diagnostic in that they identify groups or differentiate one group from another*. Hence the attributes jointly diagnostic of the Family in figure 2 are the Coca-Cola signature and the shape of the bottle. By contrast, glass is not an attribute diagnostic of the Family, though it is descriptive in that it is an attribute common to all Coca-Cola bottles.

A second learning objective might show *the distinction between relative chronology and absolute chronology*. It is possible to arrange the three Sub-

Types and/or Variants E through K in the sequence in which they were introduced, using internal evidence and the senses (including common sense) as means for proposing, for example, that Blown & Painted (B&P) bottles fall between All-Blown (A-B) and All-Painted (A-P) bottles. Deciding whether

Figure 2. Classification

		Sub-Types	*Diagnostic Attributes*	*Remarks*
Family			(1) "Coca-Cola" trademark and (2) Shape	6½, 10, 12, 16, 26 oz. returnables. Before 1957, beverage available only in 6 oz. bottles.
Types			Above plus (1) "6" or "6½" fl. ozs. or (2) height 7¾ in.	Green glass in America, clear glass for foreign markets (except Japan)
Variants			Above plus All-B B&P, or All-P	
1915	A	Sub-Types	Pronounced bulge	Prototype, designed by A. Samuelson, Terre Haute, Ind., U.S. patent No. 48160. One surviving example illustrated in *The Coca-Cola Bottler,* June, 1967 (p. 102)
1916–23	B	6 ozs – All-Blown	"Bottle Pat'd Nov. 1915"	Slimmed down to accomodate standard bottle filling equipment. Protected by first patent. Mold no., Mfr's mark and year appear either on heel or hobble.
1923–37	C	6 ozs – All-Blown	"Bottle Pat'd Dec. 25, 1923"	U.S. design patent No. 63657
1937–51	D	6 ozs – All-Blown	"Bottle Pat. D–105529"	Empty weight of bottle 14.01 oz., capacity 207.0 c.c. Bottle pat. March 24, 1937. Year-Mfr's Mark-Mold Number confined (?) to hobble.
1951–59	E	6 ozs – All-Blown	(1) "Min contents" "6-fl. ozs" and (2) "In U.S. Patent Office"	Common law rights protection with expiration of patent. Mfr's Mark moved to base, leaving year-mold number on hobble, e.g. "53–21"
1957–65	F	6½ ozs	"6½ Fl. ozs."	Empty weight 13.80 oz., cap. 202.8 c.c. Second shape ever registered as a trademark (1960), protected while it identifies the product. Other trademarks: "Coca-Cola" (1893), "Coke" (1945).

Figure 2. Continued

1958–60 G	Blown and Painted	"Coke" not on throat	Transitional. Bottler's town ceases to appear on G, H, I; re-appears on J and K. Registration dimple appears. Empty Wt. 13.65 oz., Cap. 202.1 c.c.
1958–60 H	Blown and Painted	"Coke" on throat	Transitional. Painted labels appeared in 1956 but writer has seen none dated earlier than 1958.
1961–62 I	All-Painted	"Coke" on throat	
1963–65 J	All-Painted	(1) "Coke" on one panel and (2) "6½ oz." on one panel	Bottler's town re-appears on base of some bottles. Empty Wt. 13.25 oz., cap. 205.0 c.c.
1965– K	All-Painted	"6½ oz." on both panels	Mfr's Marks: © Chattanooga Glass Co.; Ⓘ Owens-Illinois; LG Liberty Glass Co.; L Laurens Glass Works; ⚓ Anchor Hocking.

or not A–B bottles came before A–P bottles might be answered in two ways. One way is inconclusive, though it would probably lead to a correct choice in the case of the Coke bottle: this would see the development of the bottle proceeding from simple to more complex attributes, which would suggest a relative chronology of A–B, B&P, A–P.

The second way involves the use of frequencies of occurrence, the principle being that earlier specimens will be those that are found in fewer numbers. Since all of the classic Coke bottles carry the date of manufacture, it is possible to establish the absolute chronology and the durations of Variants by examining a random sample of bottles and correlating date digits with the Variants. Sufficient numbers of Variants E through K survive to make this frequency analysis possible wherever Coke bottles are found; earlier Variants (A through D) must be identified largely through written and pictorial materials, such as, for example, U.S. patents (fig. 1) and advertisements which illustrate these early Variants being used at times given by the date of publication.[3]

A third learning objective might *indicate the ways in which the systematic analyses of objects are capable of generating information or new knowledge.* The frequency approach, just cited, helps to verify what would otherwise be a highly theoretical classification; the fact that Coke bottles can additionally be dated allows us to visualize the development of the Coke bottle and to raise questions about the possible human motivations or economic principles that lie behind the changes. For example, the sequence and durations of the manufacture of Variant bottles (fig. 3) indicates that while the Coca-Cola

Figure 3. Sequence and Durations (F–K based on frequencies)

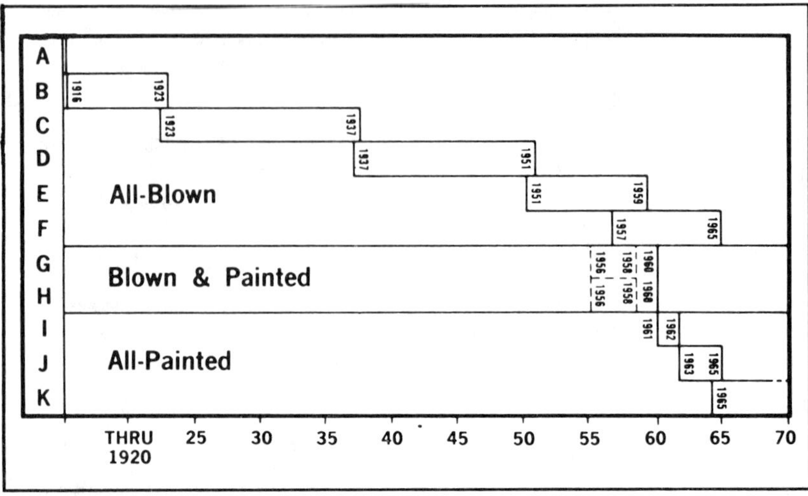

Company introduced Variants one after another, there was considerable overlapping in the durations of manufacture, so that during the years 1958–60 there were four Variants being manufactured. These overlapping durations notwithstanding, the "drift" from blown to painted bottles is apparent in figure 3. The implications of this "drift" are presented in yet another chart (fig. 4), which suggests that some sort of evolutionary principle may have been operative in the changes that have occurred in the Coke bottles of the last ten years or so.

INTERPRETIVE OPERATION

Interpretation is the culminating objective since it addresses itself to the broad question, *What possible meanings can be derived from the products of our labors?*

For some scholars and scientists the objectives of description and classification constitute legitimate ends in their own right. Classification, they might assert, is itself a form of interpretation, though one that imposes conditions upon any attempt to depart radically from recorded data. Others view interpretation as both an opportunity and a responsibility for the informed imagination to depart, if necessary, from facts to levels of generalization that may not be entirely supported by the evidence at hand. Whether the interpretation is modest or daring, a step or a leap from the known to the unknown, will depend upon the nature of the problem and the materials being dealt with,

Figure 4. Interpretation: Evolution Suggested by Linkages

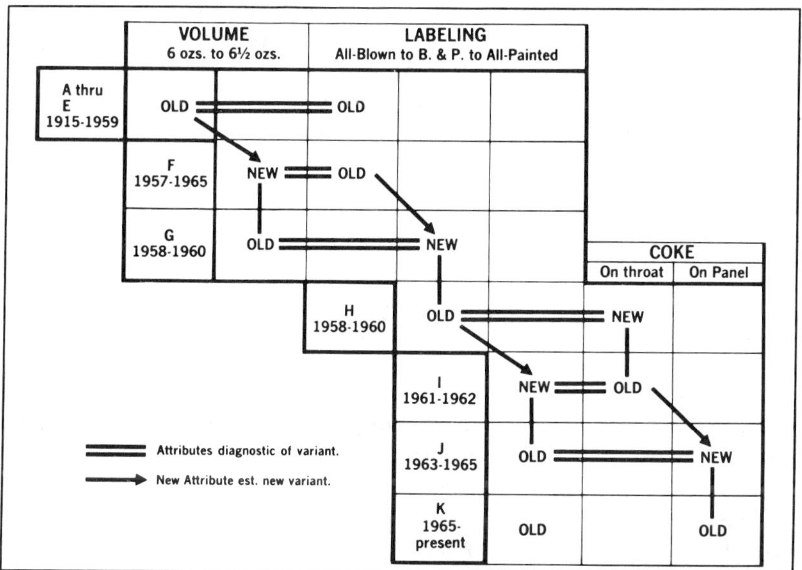

the criteria of truth accepted by the profession involved, and the personal abilities and inclinations of the interpreter.

The following capsule analyses represent three (undefined) levels of generalization.

History

Coca-Cola was invented and first sold in Atlanta, Georgia, in 1886, by a pharmacist, John S. Pemberton.[4] Six years later the business was incorporated as "The Coca-Cola Company;" a year later, "Coca-Cola" was registered in the United States Patent Office. The company adopted an aggressive policy aimed at winning public favor. By 1901 the advertising budget reached one hundred thousand dollars, a sum increased tenfold within the next ten years.

Coca-Cola was first bottled in 1894. Between that year and 1915 the beverage was sold in straight-sided bottles of varying colors and designs. To protect their product from imitators, the company adopted and patented a design devised in 1915 by Alexander Samuelson, an employee of the Root Glass Company, of Terre Haute, Indiana. Except for the slimming down of the initial design and changes in the labeling characteristics, the basic form of the "classic" bottle has remained essentially unaltered.

Presently there are three registered trademarks–"Coca-Cola" (since 1893),

"Coke" (since 1945), and the design of the bottle (since 1960), the last being previously protected by a succession of design patents and common law rights. The bottle is manufactured by six glass companies in 27 factories in the United States. Foreign bottlers obtain their bottles from manufacturers in countries of origin—and with labels in many languages. Nearly 6.6 billion Coke bottles were manufactured between 1916 and 1960 in the U.S. By 1966 the beverage was being sold in 132 countries and territories around the world.

Popular Culture

America's pop artist, flamboyant recorders of the commonplace, singled out the Coke bottle as one of their earliest subjects. The first "pop" depiction of the bottle was Robert Rauschenberg's "Coca-Cola Plan," a sculptural construction of 1958 incorporating three bottles. Among other early treatments was Andy Warhol's large canvas of 1962 illustrating 210 Coke bottles.[5] The bottle's unparalleled success as a commercial and cultural symbol (Raymond Loewy called it the "most perfectly designed package today") is suggested by an egg and a Coke bottle in a still-life painting done for the author by Jonathan Fairbanks. The sacred and the profane are confounded by these juxtapositions, in which the mysteries of art are appropriated by the clutter of everyday life.

The Coke bottle is the most widely recognized commercial product in the world. Only 1 person out of 400 was unable to identify a picture of the bottle in a product recognition study undertaken in 1949.[6] The bottle is one of the few truly participatory objects in the United States and in much of the world. Presidents drink Coca-Cola, so do sharecroppers. Usage cuts across nationalities, social and occupational classes, age groups. The bottle, unlike most other objects which might be regarded as symbols *par excellence* of American culture, is singularly free of anxiety-producing associations. It is regarded with affection by generations of Americans brought up in gasoline stations, boot camps, and drug stores, and evokes pangs of nostalgia when Americans gather in the cafes of Europe and Asia.

Evolutionary Change

Evolution in the biological world has been applied to the civilizations and institutions of the human world. The extra-Darwinian use of evolutionary thought has been largely metaphorical–a means of visualizing the human story as a succession of periods following one another according to some presumed necessary developmental logic. Previous civilizations seem to have passed through periods of youth, maturity, and decay; but is this due to the preconception of historians or is it rather an expression of some profound law governing the development of human societies? Institutions and their products may provide evidence that can be more readily observed than the larger society of which they are a part.

Taking the Coca-Cola bottle, we find that evolution of a sort has taken place, beginning in 1955 when the company introduced bottles that were partially painted. The older all-blown bottle, which had seen service since 1916, remained in production while the company determined the public's response to the greater visibility provided the white label against the brown beverage. Between 1955 and 1965 the company introduced six Variant bottles in succession, each Variant introducing a new attribute (fig. 2). What is interesting–and perhaps significant–is the progression in which a new attribute in an earlier Variant became an old attribute in a later Variant, so that each Variant since 1955 has linked old-new attributes. The relationship is represented in figure 4.

Do these linked attributes indicate the operation of some evolutionary principle? One might say that each change in the Coke bottle is the result of some overall corporate plan, and that the underlying decisions are arbitrary. But corporate decisions are predicated upon the future success of the product in the marketplace. When the product cannot adapt to changing patterns of buying habits, it will fail or become obsolete–the artifactual equivalent of extinction in the natural world.

In the 1950s the Coca-Cola Company was not expanding its sales to the satisfaction of its directors.[7] Other beverage producers were responding to an affluent consumer market that was willing to buy new varieties of flavors in a range of sizes. The Coca-Cola Company met the competitive challenge by adding four sizes of bottles and the metal can to the established "classic" bottle. (The nonreturnable bottles are yet another, more recent, development.)

The old workhorse bottle must have presented a problem: How could it be modified without damaging its demonstrated effectiveness as a seller of Coca-Cola? The answer was a gradual change of the bottle over a ten-year period, retaining the familiar all blown bottle down to 1965 and introducing between 1955 and 1965 a series of painted bottles whose modifications would become familiar and hence acceptable to the public. Raymond Loewy presented the dilemma facing corporate planners and industrial designers when he wrote that the "consumer is influenced in his choice of styling by two opposing factors: (a) attraction to the new and (b) resistance to the unfamiliar."[8] That a degree of stability has been achieved after a decade of change is indicated by the fact that Variant K has been the only "classic" bottle in production since 1966 (fig. 3).

Other questions that invite interpretation are:

> *What are the sensuous* (touch, sight, etc) and psychological qualities that contribute to the effectiveness of the Coke bottle?
>
> *How might archaeologists* of a future millenium use the bottle in reconstructing the events and forces of the twentieth century?
>
> *What kinds of ritualized behavior* accompanies the drinking of Coca-Cola from bottles?
>
> *Compare the changing historic roles* of the Christian cross, the American flag, and the Coca-Cola sign in the non-Western nations of the world.

Several points might be noted in conclusion. While words are not a substitute for first-hand experience, they are the most efficient means of organizing and communicating a part of that experience to oneself and to others. Dr. Johnson's remark, quoted earlier, should be pondered in much the same spirit of humility with which it was written: words and things *are* different, but this is not to say that we must therefore choose between a life of pure conception or of unmediated experiences, a proposition that seems to underlie much of the thinking of those who criticize, and with justice, the traditional emphasis or reliance in education upon responses that begin and end with words, seldom consulting the world of the senses as a point of departure.

The second and third points are related, and they are formulated as questions. Are there common modes of perceiving and organizing evidence in artifacts? The Coca-Cola bottle is exceptional only because it provides opportunities for carrying out so many of the procedures that are part of the analyses of such diverse things as prehistoric pottery, candlesticks, and domestic architecture. Finally, do museums, as repositories of things and of the skills and knowledge which make these things understandable, have a legitimate role to play by clarifying, both for themselves and others, how objects may be used to inform the mind, but without burdening it with information that will be useless or forgotten a few years hence?

NOTES

1. "Words and Machines: The Denial of Experience," *Museum News* 47 (September 1968): 25–29.
2. See, for example, Irving Rouse, "The Strategy of Culture History," in *Anthropology Today* (University of Chicago, 1958), 57–76.
3. See, for example, issues of the *Saturday Evening Post* for July 9, 1932 and August 28, 1937 (Variant C); and for July 30, 1938 and July 24, 1943 (Variant D).

4. The single most complete source of historical information is the fiftieth anniversary issue of *The Coca-Cola Bottler,* LI (April 1959), 243 pp.
5. "Portrait of a Product," *Art in America* 52 (April 1944): 94-5.
6. E. J. Kahn, *The Big Drink* (New York: Random House, 1960), 155-56.
7. Jack B. Weiner, *Dun's Review* 88 (October 1966) p.28ff.
8. *Never Leave Well Enough Alone* (New York, 1951), 279. See, also, Robert W. Sarnoff, "Anatomy of the New Trademark," *Saturday Review* 51 (April 13, 1968): p. 91ff.

Dissection C:

Pogo

Walt Kelly

(2)
BUT RESEARCH SHOWS THAT MOST VIEWERS ARE AVID PEACH EATERS ... SO WE HAVE A VICE-PRES WHO GOES AROUND SPOT-CHECKING GARBAGE CANS ... S'POSE HE FINDS ONE IN FOUR FULL OF PEACH PITS? ...
WE THROWS A TABULATION TEAM IN THERE, THEY COUNT 100 PITS ... THIS MEANS ONE HOUSE IN FOUR THRU THE NATION GOT 100 VIEWERS. WHAT DO YOU THINK OF THAT?
I THINK IT'S BEIN' PERTY CHINCHY WITH THE PEACHES.
(4)
BUT S'POSE SOME SNEAKY, SECRET PEACH EATER, LIKE AN OLD GRAN'PA, SWIPES A DOZEN AND ...
OLD GRAN'PAS DON'T DUMP PITS IN THE GARBAGE ... THEY CHUNKS 'EM UNDER THE BED ...
SO WHEN OUR V.P. CHECKS THE GARBAGE CANS AN' FINDS 100 PITS IN ONE OUT OF FOUR, HE KNOWS EVERY FOURTH HOUSE HAS 100 TV VIEWERS ... THIS WE CALL THE WHOPPER RATING.
YER RIGHT THERE, ANYWAY.

PART THREE:

Fist-Fights in the Kitchen

Much of the controversy among sociologists involves social conflict and not only intellectual criticism. Often, it is less a matter of contradictions between sociological ideas than of competing definitions of the role considered appropriate for the sociologist. . . . These controversies follow the classically identified course of social conflict. Attack is followed by counter-attack, with progressive alienation of each party to the conflict. Since the conflict is public, it becomes a status battle more nearly than a search for truth. . . . The consequent polarization leads each group of sociologists to respond largely to stereotyped versions of what is being done by the other.

Robert K. Merton
"Social Conflict Over Styles of Sociological Work"

TOPIC VIII: Data Processing and Presentation: What Is Lost in Translation

The men in the academy are not unaware that it is one thing to busy oneself with patchy little research projects that don't really harm anyone, but quite another thing for an enthusiast to get so caught up in the commodity values of empiricism as to go out into the world and tell people he's got a salable package. What makes this enthusiasm awkward and dangerous is that people will pay for "right" recommendations, but they will howl like mad at "wrong" or unsuccessful recommendations. The physician who makes a wrong diagnosis has the advantage of polishing off the patient. The sociologist who makes a wrong recommendation has only a life-long embittered opponent. . . . Too many such disastrous decisions, and the sociologist-turned-cynical-money-grubber-turned-guilt-alleviator may arrive at the beginning of the end of Establishment sociology.

Irving Louis Horowitz
"Sociology For Sale"

Research projects are seldom successful in the sense that they neatly follow some preconceived primrose path set up in the researcher's study design. Earlier articles have considered at some length the problems posed "on the line" by subject-investigator interactions. The next step in most sourcebooks on the subject is to consider the ethics and politics of the research process; how these considerations shape the form of the final product. These immensely important issues will be considered in the next chapter. But there is another problem area to be considered first: the handling of data from the stage of its collection to its appearance in final form; tabular or otherwise. Data processing and presentation is usually given minimal treatment (if considered at all) in treatises on research methods.

Julius Roth, in his "Hired Hand Research," properly notes that a great deal of sociological research is condusted within large-scale research organizations. Why, he asks, do not the research findings gleaned *from* sociological studies of other complex organizations also apply to the research organizations built by sociologists?

> In their research methods texts, our students are told a great deal about the mechanics of research technique and little about the social process of researching. What little is said on the latter score consists largely of Pollyannaish statements about morale, honesty, and "proper motivation." It should be noted that appeals to

> morality and patriotism never reduced gold-bricking and restriction of production in industry, even during the time of a world war. There is no reason to believe that analagous appeals to interviewers, graduate students,research assistants, and others who serve as hired hands will be any more effective.

Indeed, Roth's findings in terms of hired hands and the data coding process have been substantiated in other studies. Marvin Sussman and Marie Haug reported up to 18 percent error in the coding of occupations in a study they conducted.[1] They also reported on another, independently conducted, study in which 20 percent error was detected. These findings are similar to those of this author, reported on in an earlier study of the coding process.[2]

Roth comes to the unsettling conclusion that, given the inattention paid to these problems, if there is a good reason to believe significant parts of the research have been carried out by hired hands, then there is also a good reason for discounting "much or all of the results of the study."

A. J. Coale and F. F. Stephan point out that the results of any research project must be interpreted in the light of *all* the operations performed on the data, such as interviewing, coding, recording, punching, sorting, and tabulating. Their article, a "statistical detective story," reveals the fact that there were errors made in transcribing the 1950 US Census data from factsheets to IBM cards. Some data were punched in the wrong columns, resulting in surprising numbers of widowed and divorced 14-year-old boys and young male Indians. Although the U.S. Census Brueau today uses other methods of data transcription, similar problems still exist for many social scientists whose data are yet being transcribed onto IBM cards. And the newer methods of data transcription employed by the Bureau of the Census have their own associated potential sources of error.

Coale and Stephan's article, "The Case of the Indians and the Teen-Age Widows," brings up a further point: the psychological assurance we in this culture tend to get from numbers. For some reason, if data are in numerical form, they seem more "right" to Americans. We are always translating reality into numbers: traffic fatalities, football scores, Vietnam body counts. It works the same way in science. What we should remember is that at some point along the line someone translated real-world data into these numbers. Do we have any reason to trust the judgement and skill that went into this translation? As computer technicians are fond of saying, "G.I.G.O. (Garbage in, Garbage out)."

In looking at another phase of the data dissemination process, Larry Reynolds traces the perpetuation of a scientific fiction from one study to another, fiction never challenged, but repeated so often it is taken as fact. Remarking on his own article, Professor Reynolds notes that:

> the notion of science as a "self-correcting institution" is a handy myth—as handy and as mythical as its economic counterpart, the

> doctrine of a self-regulating market". . . . Given the dominance of the economic over the scientific order . . . sociology as presently practiced is nothing more than one knowledge-producing branch of the market.[3]

Reynolds' feelings seem to square with those of Irving Louis Horowitz, quoted at the beginning of this chapter. Horowitz's point is also relevant in introducing James A. Davis' article, "Great Books and Small Groups," the Dissection at the end of this topic.

NOTES

1. Marvin Sussman and Marie Haug, "Human and Mechanical Error—An Unknown Quantity in Research," *Behavioral Science* 11 (Nov.-Dec. 1967): 55-56.
2. George H. Lewis, *The* STGPROC *System of Data Manipulation by Computer* (CASEA: University of Oregon, 1970). pp. 35–41.
3. Larry T. Reynolds and Janice M. Reynolds, *The Sociology of Sociology* (New York: David McKay, 1970), p. 203.

SUGGESTED FURTHER READINGS

Carter, Reginald K. "Clients' Resistance to Negative Findings and the Latent Conservative Function of Evaluation Studies." *American Sociologist* 6, no. 2 (May 1971): 118-24.

Crespi, Leo. "The Cheater Problem in Polling." *Public Opinion Quarterly* (Winter 1945-46): 431-45.

Dalton, Melville. "Preconceptions and Methods in *Men Who Manage,*" in *Sociologists at Work,* edited by Phillip E. Hammond. New York: Basic Books, 1964, pp. 58–110.

Hart, Clyde W. "Some Factors Affecting the Organization and Prosecution of Given Research Projects." *American Sociological Review* 12 (Oct. 1957): 514-19.

Sussman, Marvin, and Haug, Marie. "Human and Mechanical Error—An Unknown Quantity in Research." *Behavioral Science* 11 (Nov.-Dec. 1967): 55-56.

Hired Hand Research

Julius Roth

CASE I

After it became obvious how tedious it was to write down numbers on pieces of paper which didn't even fulfill one's own sense of reality and which did not remind one of the goals of the project, we all in little ways started avoiding our work and cheating on the project. It began for example when we were supposed to be observing for hour and a half periods, an hour and a half on the ward and then an hour and a half afterwards to write up or dictate what we had observed, in terms of the category system which the project was supposed to be testing and in terms of a ward diary. We began cutting corners in time. We would arrive a little bit late and leave a little bit early. It began innocently enough, but soon boomeranged into a full cheating syndrome, where we would fake observations for some time slot which were never observed on the ward. Sam, for example, in one case, came onto the ward while I was still finishing up an assignment on a study patient and told me that he was supposed to observe for an hour and a half but that he wasn't going to stay because he couldn't stand it anymore. He said he wasn't going to tell anyone that he missed an assignment, but that he would simply write up a report on the basis of what he knew already about the ward and the patients. I was somewhat appalled by Sam's chicanery, and in this sense I was the last one to go. It was three or four weeks after this before I actually cheated in the same manner.

It was also frequent for us to miss observation periods, especially the 8 to 9:30 a.m. ones. We all had a long drive for one thing, and we were all chronic over-sleepers for another. For a while we used to make up the times we

From Julius Roth, "Hired Hand Research," *TAS* 1 (August 1966: 190–96.

missed by coming in the next morning at the same time and submitting our reports with the previous day's date. As time went on, however, we didn't bother to make up the times we'd missed. When we were questioned by our supervisor about the missing reports, we would claim that there had been an error in scheduling and that we did not know that those time slots were supposed to be covered.

There were other ways we would cheat, sometimes inadvertently. For example, one can decide that one can't hear enough of a conversation to record it. People need to think fairly highly of themselves, and when you think that you're a cheat and a liar and that you're not doing your job for which you are receiving high wages, you are likely to find little subconscious ways of getting out of having to accuse yourself of these things. One of the ways is to not be able to hear well. We had a special category in our coding system, a question mark, which we noted by its symbol on our code sheets whenever we could not hear what was going on between two patients. As the purgatory of writing numbers on pieces of paper lengthened, more and more transcripts were passed in with question marks on them, so that even though we had probably actually heard most of the conversations between patients, we were still actually avoiding the work of transcription by deceiving ourselves into believing that we could not hear what was being said. This became a good way of saving yourself work. If you couldn't hear a conversation, it just got one mark in one column of one code sheet, and if you wrote down an elaborate conversation lasting even ten minutes, it might take you up to an hour to code it, one hour of putting numbers in little blocks. In the long run, all of our data became much skimpier. Conversations were incomplete; their duration was strangely diminishing to two or three minutes in length instead of the half-hour talks the patients usually had with each other. We were all defining our own cutting off points, saying to ourselves, "Well, that's enough of that conversation." According to the coding rules, however, a communication can't be considered as ended until the sequence of interaction has been completed and a certain time lapse of silence has ensued.

In order to ensure the reliability of our coding, the research design called for an "Inter–Rater Reliability Check" once every two months, in which each of the four of us would pair up with every other member of the team and be rated on our ability to code jointly the same interaction in terms of the same categories and dimensions. We learned to loathe these checks; we knew that the coding system was inadequate in terms of reliability and that our choice of categories was optional, subjective, and largely according to our own sense of what an interaction is really about, rather than according to the rigid, stylized, and preconceived design into which we were supposed to make a reality fit. We also knew, however, that our principal investigators insisted on an inter–rater reliability coefficient of .70 in order for the research to proceed. When the time came for another check, we met together to discuss and make certain agreements on how to bring our coding habits into conformity for the sake of achieving reliability. In these meetings we would confess our preferences for coding certain things in certain ways and agree on certain concessions to each other for the duration of the check. Depending on what other individual I was to be paired with, for example, I had a very good idea of how I could code in order to achieve nearly the same transcriptions. We didn't end it there. After each phase of a check, each pair of us would meet again to go over our transcriptions and compare our coding, and if there were any gross discrepancies, we corrected them before sending them to the statisticians for analysis. Needless to say, as soon as the reliability checks were over with, we each returned to a coding rationale which we as individuals required in order to do any coding at all—in order to maintain sanity.

CASE II

There didn't appear to be too much concern with the possibility of inconsistency among the coders. Various coders used various methods to determine the code of an open-end question. Toward the end of the coding process, expediency became the keynote, leading to gross inconsistency. The most expedient method of coding a few of the trickier questions was to simply put down a "4" (This was the middle-of-the-road response on the one question that had the most variation.). If the responses were not clear or comprehensible, the coder had two alternatives: on the one hand, he could puzzle over it and ask for other opinions or, on the other hand, he could assign it an arbitrary number or forget the response entirely.

In the beginning, many of us, when in doubt about a response, would ask the supervisor or his assistant. After a while, I noted that quite often the supervisor's opinion would differ when asked twice about the same response and he would often give two different answers in response to the same question. One way the supervisor and his assistant would determine the correct coding for an answer would be to look at the respondent's previous answers and deduce what they should have answered—thereby coding on *what they thought the respondent should have answered,* not on the basis of what he *did* answer. One example that I distinctly remember is the use of magazines regularly read as reported by the respondent being used as a basis on which to judge and code their political views. This, in my opinion, would be a factor in some of the cases, such as the reading of an extreme leftist or extreme rightist magazine, but to use magazines such as *Time* or *Reader's Digest* to form any conclusions about the type of person and his views, I feel is quite arbitrary. Furthermore, I feel questionnaires should be used to see *if* consistent patterns of views exist among respondents and it is not the coder's job to put them in if the respondents fail to!

Some of the coders expected a fixed pattern of response. I, not being sure of what responses meant in a total political profile, treated each response separately—which I feel is the correct way of coding a questionnaire. Others, as I learned through their incessant jabbering, took what they thought was a more sophisticated method of treating an interview. A few would discuss the respondent's answers as if they took one political or social standpoint as an indicator of what all the responses should be. They would laugh over an inconsistency in the respondent's replies, feeling that one answer did not fit the previous pattern of responses.

The final problem leading to gross inconsistency was the factor of time. The supervisor made it clear that the code sheets had to be in the computation center by Saturday. This meant that on Saturday morning and early afternoon the aim of the coders was to code the questionnaires as quickly as possible, and the crucial factor was speed, even at the expense of accuracy. The underlying thought was that there were so many questionnaires coded already (that we *assumed* to be coded consistently and correctly) that the inconsistencies in the remainder would balance themselves out and be of no great importance. I found myself adapting to this way of thinking, and after spending two or three hours there on Saturday morning, I joined in the game of "let's get these damn things out already." It did indeed become a game, with the shibboleth, for one particularly vague and troublesome question, "Oh, give it a four."

CASE III

One of the questions on the interview schedule asked for five reasons why parents had put their child in an institution. I found most people can't think of five reasons. One or two—sometimes three. At first I tried pumping them for more reasons, but I never got any of them up to five. I didn't want (the director) to think I was goofing off on the probing, so I always filled in all five.

Another tough one was the item about how the child's disability affected the family relationships. We were supposed to probe. Probe what? You get so many different kinds of answers, I was never sure what was worth following up. Sometimes I did if the respondent seemed to have something to say. Otherwise I just put down a short answer and made it look as if that was all I could get out of them. Of course, (the director) *did* list a few areas he wanted covered in the probing. One of them was sex relations of the parents. Most of the time I didn't follow up on that. Once in a while I would get somebody who seemed to be able to talk freely without embarrassment. But most of the time I was afraid to ask, so I made up something to fill that space.

Then there was that wide open question at the end. It's vague. Most people don't know what to say. You've been asking them questions for about an hour already. Usually you get a very short answer. I didn't push them. I'd write up a longer answer later. It's easy to do. You have their answer to a lot of other questions to draw on. You just put parts of some of them together, dress it up a little, and add one or two bits of new information which fits in with the rest.

Any reader with research experience can probably recall one or more cases in which he observed, suspected, or participated in some form of cheating, carelessness, distortion, or cutting of corners in the collection or processing of research data. He probably thought of these instances as exceptions—an unfortunate lapse in ethical behavior or a failure of research directors to maintain proper controls. I would like to put forth the thesis that such behavior on the part of hired data collectors and processors is not abnormal or exceptional, but rather is exactly the kind of behavior we should expect from people with their position in a production unit.

The cases I have presented do not constitute proof, of course. Even if I presented ten or twenty more, my efforts could be dismissed as merely an unusually industrious effort to record professional dirty linen (or I might be accused of making them up!) and not at all representative of the many thousands of cases of hired researching carried out every year. Rather than multiply examples, I would like to take a different tack and examine the model we have been using in thinking about research operations and to suggest another model which I believe is more appropriate.

The ideal we hold of the researcher is that of a well-educated scholar pursuing information and ideas on problems in which he has an intrinsic interest. Frequently this ideal may be approximated when an individual scholar is working on his own problem or several colleagues are collaborating on a problem of mutual interest. Presumably such a researcher will endeavor to carry out his data collection and processing in the most accurate and useful way that his skills and time permit.

When a researcher hires others to do the collecting and processing tasks of his research plan, we often assume that these assistants fit the "dedicated scientist" ideal and will lend their efforts to the successful conduct of the overall study by carrying out their assigned tasks to the best of their ability. As suggested by my examples, I doubt that hired assistants usually behave this way even when they are junior grade scholars themselves. It becomes more doubtful yet when they are even further removed from scholarly tradition and from the direct control of the research directors (e.g., part-time survey interviewers).

It seems to me that we can develop a more accurate expectation of the contribution of the hired research worker who is required to work according to somebody else's plan by applying another model which has been worked out in some detail by sociologists—namely, the work behavior of the hired hand in a production organization. First, let us look at one of the more thorough of these studies, Donald Roy's report on machine shop operators.[1]

Roy's workers made the job easier by loafing when the piece rate did not pay well. They were careful not to go over their informal "quotas" on piece rate jobs because the rate would be cut and their work would be harder. They faked time sheets so that their actual productive abilities would not be known to management. They cut corners on prescribed job procedures to make the work easier and/or more lucrative even though this sometimes meant that numerous products had to be scrapped. Roy's calculations show that the workers could have produced on the order of twice as much if it had been in their interest to do so.

But it is *not* in their interest to do so. The product the hired hand turns out is not in any sense his. He does not design it, make any of the decisions about producing it or about the conditions under which it will be produced, or what will be done with it after it is produced. The worker is interested in doing just enough to get by. Why should he concern himself about how well the product works or how much time it takes to make it? That is the company's problem. The company is his adversary and fair game for any trickery he can get away with. The worker's aim is to make his job as easy and congenial as the limited resources allow and to make as much money as possible without posing a threat to his fellow workers or to his own future. The company, in turn, is placed in the position of having to establish an inspection system to try to keep the worst of their products from leaving the factory (an effort often unsuccessful–the inspectors are hired hands, too) and of devising some form of supervision to limit the more extreme forms of gold-bricking and careless workmanship.

Almost all the systematic research on "restriction of output" and deviation from assigned duties has been done on factory workers, office clerks, and other low prestige work groups. This is mostly because such work is easier to observe and measure, but also because much of this research has been controlled in part by those in a position of authority who want research done only on their subordinates. However, there is evidence to indicate that work restrictions and deviations in the form of informal group definitions and expectations are probably universal in our society. They can be found among business executives and in the professions, sports, and the creative arts. They are especially likely to crop up when one is working as a hired hand, and almost all productive activities have their hired hand aspects. A professor may work hard on scholarly tasks of his own choosing and perhaps even on teaching a course which he himself has devised, but he becomes notoriously lax when he is assigned to a departmental service course which he does not like–spending little or no time on preparation, avoiding his students as much as possible, turning all the exams over to a graduate assistant, and so on.

"Restriction of production" and deviation from work instructions is no longer regarded by students of the sociology of work as a moral issue or a form of social delinquency. Rather, it is the expected behavior of workers in a production organization. The only problem for an investigator to work practices is discovering the details of cutting corners, falsifying time sheets, defining work quotas, dodging supervision, and ignoring instructions in a given work setting.

There is no reason to believe that a hired hand in the scientific research business will behave any different from those in other areas of productive activity. It is far more reasonable to assume that their behavior will be similar. They want to make as much money as they can and may pad their account or time sheet if they are paid on that basis, but this type of behavior is a minor problem so far as the present discussion is concerned. They also want to avoid difficult, embarrassing, inconvenient, time-consuming situations as well as those activities which make no sense to them. (Thus, they fail to make some assigned observations or to ask some of the interview questions.) At the same time they want to give the right impression to their supervisors—at least right enough so that their material will be accepted and they will be kept on the job. (Thus, they modify or fabricate portions of the reports in order to give the boss what he *seems* to want.) They do not want to "look stupid" by asking too many questions, so they are likely to make a stab at what they think the boss wants—e.g., make a guess at a coding category rather than having it resolved through channels.

Even those who start out with the notion that this is an important piece of work which they must do right will succumb to the hired hand mentality when they realize that their suggestions and criticisms are ignored, that their assignment does not allow for any imagination or creativity, that they will receive no credit for the final product, in short, that they have been hired to do somebody else's dirty work. When this realization has sunk in, they will no longer bother to be careful or accurate or precise. They will cut corners to save time and energy. They will fake parts of their reporting. They will not put themselves out for something in which they have no stake except in so far as extrinsic pressures force them to. Case No. I is an excerpt from the statement of a research worker who started out with enthusiasm and hard work and ended with sloppy work and cheating when she could no longer escape the fact that she was a mere flunky expected to do her duty whether or not it was meaningful. The coders in Case II soon gave up any effort to resolve the ambiguities of their coding operation and followed the easiest path acceptable to their supervisor. In this case, the supervisor himself made little effort to direct the data processing toward supplying answers to meaningful research issues. We must remember that in many research operations the supervisors and directors themselves are hired hands carrying out the requests of a client or superior as expeditiously as possible.

Many of the actions of hired hand researchers are strikingly analogous to restrictive practices of factory operatives. Interviewers who limit probing and observers who limit interaction recording are behaving like workers applying "quota restriction," and with interacting hired hands informal agreements may be reached on the extent of such restrictions. To fabricate portions of a report is a form of gold-bricking. The collusion on the reliability check reported in Case I is strikingly similar to the workers' plot to mislead the time-study department. Such similarities are no accident. The relationship of the hired hand to the product and the process of production is the same in each case. The product is not "his." The production process gives him little or no opportunity to express any intrinsic interest he may have in the product. He will sooner or later fall into a pattern of carrying out his work with a minimum of effort, inconvenience, and embarrassment—doing just enough so that his product will get by. If he is part of a large and complex operation where his immediate superiors are also hired hands with no intrinsic interest in the product and where the final authority may be distant and even amorphous, quality control of the product will be mechanical and the minimal effort that will get by can soon be learned and easily applied. The factory production situation has at least one ultimate limitation on the more extreme deviations of the hired hands: The final product must "work" reasonably well in a substantial proportion of cases. In social science research, on the other hand, the product is usually so ambiguous and the field of study so lacking in standards of performance that it is difficult for anyone to say whether it "works" or not.

What is more important is the effect of the hired hand mentality on the *nature* of the product. Workmen not only turn out less than they could if it were in their interest to maximize production, but often produce shoddy and even dangerous products.[2] In the case of research, the inefficiency of hired hands not only causes a study to take longer or cost more money, but is likely to introduce much dubious data and interpretations into the process of analysis. Our mass production industrial system has opted to sacrifice individual efficiency and product quality for the advantages of a rationalized division of labor. The same approach has been applied to much of our larger scale scientific research and the results, in my opinion, have been much more disastrous than they are in industrial production with little compensating advantages.

When the tasks of a research project are split up into small pieces to be assigned to hired hands, none of these data collectors and processors will ever understand all the complexities and subtleties of the research issues in the same way as the person who conceived of the study. No amount of "training" can take the place of the gradual development of research interests and formulations on the part of the planner. Since the director often cannot be sure what conceptions of the issues the hired hands have as a result of his explanations and "training," he must make dubious guesses about the meaning of much of the data they return to him. If he attempts to deal with this difficulty by narrowly defining the permissible behavior of each hired hand (e.g., demand that all questions on a schedule be asked in a set wording), he merely increases the alienation of the hired hand from his work and thus increases the likelihood of cutting corners and cheating. As he gains in quantity of data, he loses in validity of meaningfulness.[3]

I do not want to give the impression that the hired hand mentality with its attendant difficulties is simply a characteristic of the large-scale on-going research organization. We may find it at all size levels, including the academic man hiring a single student to do his research chores. The argument may be advanced that assignment of specified tasks by the director of a study is essential to getting the job done in the manner that he wants it done. My answer is that such assignments are often not effectively carried out and it is misleading to assume that they are.

Let me illustrate this point. A researcher wants to do a study of the operation of a given institution. He has some definite notion of what aspects of behavior of the institutional personnel he wants information about and he has some ideas about the manner in which he will go about analyzing and interpreting these behaviors. He finds it possible and useful to engage four trained and interested assistants. Let me outline two ways the study might be conducted.

A. Through a series of discussions, general agreement is reached about the nature of the study and the manner in which it might be conducted. Some division of labor is agreed upon in these discussions. However, none of the field workers is held to any particular tasks or foci of interest. Each is allowed to pursue his data collection as he thinks best within the larger framework, although the field workers exchange information frequently and make new agreements so that they can benefit from each other's experience.

B. The director divides up the data collection and processing in a logical manner and assigns a portion to each of the assistants. Each field worker is instructed to obtain information in all the areas assigned to him and to work in a prescribed manner so that his information will be directly comparable to that of the others. The director may use a procedural check such as having each assistant write a report covering given issues or areas at regular intervals.

Which is the preferred approach? Judging from my reading of social science journals, most research directors would say Method B is to be preferred. Method A, they would maintain, produces information on subjects, issues, or events from one field worker which is not directly comparable to that collected by another field worker. They would also object that if each field worker is permitted to follow his own inclinations even in part, the total study will suffer from large gaps. These accusations are quite true—and, I would add, are an inevitable result of dividing a research project among a number of people. What I disagree with, however, is the assumption that Method B would not suffer from these defects (if indeed, they should be regarded as defects). It is assumed that the assistants in Method B are actually carrying out their assigned tasks in the manner specified. In line with my earlier discussion of the behavior of hired hands, I would consider this highly unlikely. If the information produced by these assistants is indeed closely comparable, it would most likely be because they had reached an agreement on how to restrict production. And, whether the study is carried out by Method A or by Method B, gaps will occur. The difference is that the director of Study A–assuming he had succeeded in making his assistants into collaborating colleagues–would at least know where the gaps are. The director of Study B would have gaps without knowing where they are–or indeed, that they exist–because they have been covered over by the fabrications of his alienated assistants.

It is ironic that established researchers do not ascribe the same motivating forces to their subordinates as they do to themselves. For many years research scientists have been confronting those who pay their salaries and give them their grants with the argument that a scientist can do good research only when he has the freedom to follow his ideas in whatever way seems best. They have been so successful with this argument that university administrations and research organization directorates rarely attempt to dictate–or even suggest–problems or procedures to a researcher on their staff, and the more prominent granting agencies write contracts with almost no strings attached as to the way in which the study will be conducted. Yet research directors fail to apply this same principle to those they hire to carry out data collection and processing. The hired assistant's desire to participate in the task and the creative contribution he might make is ignored with the result that the assistant's creativity is applied instead to covertly changing the nature of the task.

There has been very little discussion in our journals and our books on research methods on the relationship of the hired hand to the data collected. Whatever discussion there *has* been can be found in the survey interview field where there have been some studies of the effect of such demographic factors as age, sex, and race, sometimes measured personality traits, on "interviewer bias." The nature of the interviewer's status in a research organization is seldom discussed in print. The problem of interviewer cheating, although a common subject of informal gossip, is seldom dealt with openly as a serious problem. When Leo Crespi published an article 20 years ago in which he expressed the worry that cheating was seriously affecting the validity of much survey data,[4] those who responded (mostly survey organization executives) stated reassuringly that few interviewers cheated and that they had pretty effective ways of controlling those who did.[5] If the analysis offered in this paper is correct, the first part of this reassurance is almost certainly wrong. The low-level flunky position which most interviewers occupy in survey organizations[6] should lead us to expect widespread deviations from assigned tasks. The survey executives who responded give no convincing evidence to the contrary. As for the second part of the assertion, their descriptions of their control measures indicate that they can hope to block only the cruder, more obvious, and repeated forms of cheating. The postal card followup will catch the interviewer who make contacts, but fabricates demographic data (to fill a spot-check followup interviewing may eventually catch the interviewer who makes contacts, but fabricates demographic data (to fill a quota sample) or completes only part of the interview and fills in the rest in a stereotyped manner later on. (Even here, many of his interviews may be used before he is detected.) However, from the cases of hired hand interviewing which I am familiar with, I would say such crude cheating is not the most common form of cutting corners on the job. Far more common is the kind found in Case III where the interviewer makes his contact, obtains a fairly complete interview, but leaves partial gaps here and there because he found it time-consuming, embarrassing, or troublesome, felt threatened by the respondent, or simply felt uncertain about how the study director wanted certain lines of questioning developed. With a little imagination, such gaps can be filled in later on in a way that is very unlikely to be detected in a followup interview. If, for example, a supervisor in Case III had returned to the respondents and asked them whether the "five reasons" listed on their interview form were accurate reflections of their opinion, probably most would have said yes, and the few who objected to one or two of the reasons could have been dismissed as the degree of change that one expects on reinterview.[7]

Some gimmicks for catching cheaters may even put the finger on the wrong person. Thus, one approach to detecting cheating is to compare the data of each interviewer to the group averages and to assume that if one deviates markedly from the group, he is cheating or doing his work improperly. This reasoning assumes that cheating is exceptional and will stand out from the crowd. I have already suggested that the opposite is often the case. Therefore, if the cheaters are working in the same direction (which is readily possible if they have reached an informal agreement or if the question is of such a nature as to suggest distortion in a given direction), it is the "honest" person who will deviate. In the study alluded to in Case III, for example, one of the interviewers always left spaces open on the "five reasons" item. At one point the director reprimanded him for not obtaining five responses "like the rest of the interviewers." The director preferred to believe that this man was not doing his job right than to believe that all the rest were making up responses.

Large survey organizations have at least made some attempts to control the cruder forms of cheating. In most studies using hired hands, even this limited control is absent. The academic man with one or a few assistants, the research organization study director with one or a few small projects, usually has no routine way of checking on the work of his assistants. If he duplicates much of their work or supervises them very closely, he may as well dispense with their services. If he gives them assignments without checking on them closely, he is in effect assuming that they are conducting their assignment more or less as directed and is accepting their products at face value. This assumption, I assert, is a dubious one. And since it is a common practice nowadays to farm out much of one's research work—quite often to accumulate research grants only to hire others to do the bulk of the work—the dubious nature of hired hand research is a widespread problem in small as well as large scale research, in surveys, in direct observation, and in various forms of data processing.

I do not want to suggest, however, that the major failure of hired hand research is the lack of control of cheating. Rather, the very fact that we are placed in a position of having to think up gimmicks to detect cheating is in itself an admission of failure. It means that we are relying for an important part of our research operation on people who have no concern for the outcome of the study. Such persons cannot have the kind of understanding of the data collection or data-processing procedures which can come only with working out problems in which the researcher has an intrinsic interest and has gone through a process of formulating research questions and relevant ways of collecting and processing data.

I can hear the objection that much social science cannot be done without hired hands. But we should at least be aware of the doubtful nature of some of the information collected in this way and construct our data collection and processing in such a way as to reduce the encouragement of cheating and restriction of production as much as possible (See Crespi's list of "ballot demoralizers."[8]) More important, however, I believe the need for hired hands has been greatly exaggerated. Why, for example, must we so often have large samples? The large sample is frequently a contrivance for controlling various kinds of "errors" (including the "error" introduced by unreliable hired hands). But if the study were done on a much smaller sample by one person or several colleagues who formulated their own study and conducted it entirely by themselves, much of this error would not enter in the first place. Isn't a sample of 50 which yields data in which we can have a high degree of confidence more useful than a sample of 5000 where we must remain doubtful about what it is that we have collected? Often a large-scale study tries to do too much at one time and so ends up as a hodge-podge affair with no integration of ideas or information ever taking place because it is, in effect, *nobody's* study. How often have you read the report of a massive study expending large amounts of money and employing large numbers of people where you were disappointed at the paucity of the results, especially when compared to a far smaller project on a similar issue conducted entirely by one or a few people?

Let me repeat that I am not singling out large-scale operations as the only villains. The current structure of professional careers is such that often small studies are turned over to hired hands. We tend to be rated on how many studies we can carry on at the same time rather than on how thoroughly and carefully we can carry through a given line of research. Soon we find that we do not have time for all of the projects we have become involved in and must turn some over to others of lower professional status. This might not be so bad if we were willing to turn over the research work wholeheartedly. We might simply act as entrepreneurs to funnel funds to others and to provide them with appropriate clearance and an entré to research settings. We can then leave the specific formulation of the problem and procedure (and the credit for doing the work) to the person we have helped out. Such is often done, of course. However, there are many instances in which the senior researcher believes those he has hired cannot be trusted to formulate their own plans, or professional career competition convinces him that he cannot "afford" to give up any of his studies to others. In such cases he is likely to maintain a semblance of control by mechanically structuring a research plan and making assignments to his assistants. This, as I have indicated, is the way to the hired hand mentality with its attendant distortions of research data.

What is a hired hand? So far I have been talking as if I knew and as if the hired hand could readily be distinguished from one who is not. This, of course, is not true. The issue is a complex one and information on it is, by its very nature, not very accessible. It is a crucial question which deserves study in its own right as part of the more general study of the process of "doing research."

Let me attempt a crude characterization of hired hand research, a characterization which hopefully will be greatly refined and perhaps reformulated with further study. A hired hand is a person who feels that he has no stake in the research that he is working on, that he is simply expected to carry out assigned tasks and turn in results which will "pass inspection." Of course, a hired assistant may not start out with the hired hand mentality, but may develop it if he finds that his talents for creativity are not called upon and that his suggestions and efforts at active participation are ignored.

From specific examples from the research world and by analogy from research on hired hands in other occupational spheres, I am convinced that research tasks carried out by hired hands are characterized, not rarely or occasionally, but *typically*, by restricted production, failure to carry out portions of the task, avoidance of the more unpleasant or difficult aspects of the research, and outright cheating. The results of research done in part or wholly by hired hands should be viewed as a dubious source for information about specific aspects of our social life or for the raw material for developing broader generalizations.

Of course, this leaves open the question of what constitutes a "stake in the research" and how one avoids or reduces the hired hand mentality. Again, I have no specific answers and hope that issue will receive much more attention than it has up to now. A stake may mean different things in various circumstances. For graduate students, a chance to share in planning and in writing and publication may often be important. For interviewers or field workers, the determination of the details of their procedure may be crucial. In an applied setting, the responsibility for the practical consequences of the research findings may be most important.[9]

It would also be worthwhile to examine the conditions which make for hired hand research. Here again, I have little specific to say and this subject, too, needs much more investigation. However, I will suggest a few factors I consider important.

Size

Hired hands can be found in research staffs of all sizes from one on up. However, it is clear that when a very small number of researchers are working together, there is a greater possibility of developing a true colleagueship in which each will be able to formulate some of his own ideas and put them into action. The larger the group, the more difficult this becomes until the point is probably reached where it is virtually impossible, and the organization must be run on the basis of hierarchical staff relations with the lower echelons almost inevitably becoming hired hands.

Subordination

If some members of the research group are distinctly subordinate to others in a given organizational hierarchy or in general social status, it will be more difficult to develop a true colleague working relationship than if their status were more closely equal. The subordinate may hesitate to advance his ideas; the superordinate might be loath to admit that his lower–level coworker be entitled to inject his ideas into the plans. Formal super–subordinate relationships can of course be muted and sometimes completely overcome in the course of personal contact, but certainly this is an initial, and sometimes permanent, basis for establishing hired hand status.

Adherence to Rigid Plans

If a researcher believes that good research can be done only if a detailed plan of data collection, processing, and analysis is established in advance and adhered to throughout, he has laid the basis for hired hand research if he makes use of assistance from others who have not participated in the original plan. Sticking to a preformed plan means that others cannot openly introduce variations which may make the study more meaningful for them. Any creativity they apply will be of a surreptitious nature.

In their research methods texts, our students are told a great deal about the mechanics of research techniques and little about the social process of researching. What little is said on the latter score consists largely of Pollyannaish statements about morale, honesty, and "proper motivation." It should be noted that appeals to morality and patriotism never reduced goldbricking and restriction of production in industry, even during the time of a world war. There is no reason to believe that analogous appeals to interviewers, graduate students, research assistants, and others who serve as hired hands will be any more effective. If we want to avoid the hired hand mentality, we must stop using people as hired hands.

Glaser and Strauss state that we regularly "discount" aspects of many, if not most, of all scientific analyses we read because we consider the research designed onesided, believe that it does not fit the social structure to which it was generalized, or that it does not fit in with our observations in an area where we have had considerable experience.[10]

I would like to suggest another area in which we might consistently apply the "discounting process." When reading a research report, we should pay close attention to the description of how the data were collected, processed, analyzed, interpreted, and written up with an eye to determining what part, if any, was played by hired hands. This will often be a difficult and highly tentative judgment, requiring much reading between the lines with the help of our knowledge of how our colleagues and we ourselves often operate. However, we can get hints from such things as the size of the staff, the nature of the relationship of the staff members, the manner in which the research plans were developed and applied, the organizational setting in which the research was done, mention made of assignment of tasks, and so on. If there is good reason to believe that significant parts of the research has been carried out by hired hands, this would, in my opinion, be a reason for discounting much or all of the results of the study.

NOTES

1. Donald Roy, "Quota Restriction and Goldbricking in a Machine Shop," *American Journal of Sociology* 57 (March 1952): 427–42.
2. I want to emphasize once again that in a business setting, supervisors and executives, as well as production line workmen, participate in aspects of the hired hand mentality. None of them may have an intrinsic interest in the quality of the product. (See, for example, Melvin Dalton, *Men Who Manage* (New York: Wiley, 1959), esp. chaps. 7, 8, and 9.) The same is the case in much large-scale research.
3. In this discussion I am assuming there *is* someone (or a small group of colleagues) who has initially formulated the research problem or area of concern because of intrinsic interest and curiosity. In much of our social science research, we do not have even this saving grace and the research is formulated and carried out for various "political" reasons. In such cases, we cannot count on having anyone interested enough to try to turn the accumulations of data into a meaningful explanatory statement.
4. Leo Crespi, "The Cheater Problem in Polling," *Public Opinion Quarterly* (Winter 1945–1946): 431–45.
5. "Survey on Problems of Interviewer Cheating," *International Journal of Opinion and Attitude Research* 1 (1947): 93–107.

6. Julius A. Roth, "The Status of Interviewing," *The Midwest Sociologist* 19 (December 1956): 8–11.
7. I have even heard the argument that it makes no difference if perceptive interviewers make up parts of the interview responses with the help of information from other responses because their fabrications will usually closely approximate what the subject would have said if he could have been prompted to answer. But if we accept this argument, a large portion of the interview should have been eliminated to begin with. It means we already claim to know the nature of some of the relationships which the study is purportedly investigating.
8. Leo Crespi, *op. cit.*, pp. 437–39.
9. The "human relations in industry" movement has given us some useful suggestions about the circumstances which alienate workers and executives, and also ways in which industrial employees may be given a real stake in their jobs. See, for example, Douglas McGregor, *The Human Side of Enterprise* (New York: McGraw–Hill, 1960), Part 2.
10. Barney Glaser and Anselm L. Strauss, "Discovery of Substantive Theory: A Basic Strategy Underlying Qualitative Research," *American Behavioral Scientist* 8 (February 1965): 5–12.

The Case of the Indians and the Teen-age Widows

A. J. Coale and F. F. Stephan

INTRODUCTION

This article, for the most part, is a statistical detective story. It analyzes circumstantial evidence drawn from the 1950 Census of Population of the United States [2, 4, 5]. This evidence conclusively shows, we believe, that there were processing errors affecting a tiny fraction of the basic *P* or *Persons* punch cards which were sorted to provide most of the tabular results of the population census.

The detective story describes the unraveling of a fairly complex pattern of "clues"—an exercise in deduction that may in itself prove an interesting diversion to some readers, as it did to the authors. The story also has practical implications for users of statistical data. Readers interested in these implications, but not in the somewhat complicated story upon which they are based, are referred to the final section beginning on p. 405.

ANOMALOUS DATA ON THE MARITAL STATUS OF TEENAGERS

Our first clue was the discovery in the 1950 Census of Population of the United States of startling figures about the marital status of teenagers. There we found a surprising number of widowed 14-year-old boys and, equally sur-

From *Journal of the American Statistical Association* 57 (June 1962): 338–47.

prising, a decrease in the number of widowed teen-age males at older ages. The numbers listed by the Census [4, tables 103 and 104] were 1,670 at age 14; 1,475 at age 15; 1,175 at 16; 810 at 17; 905 at 18; and 630 at age 19. Not until age 22 does the listed number of widows surpass those at 14. Male divorcés also decrease in number as age increases, from 1,320 at age 14 to 575 at age 17. Smaller numbers of young female widows and divorcées are listed—565 widows and 215 divorcées at age 14. These strange figures, even though they appear in a very minor part of the carefully prepared and widely useful data presented in the Population Census, aroused our curiosity and set us to searching for an explanation.

Our investigation is in no way a reflection on the high quality and established accuracy of the Population Census overall. It merely recognizes that in well organized and competently conducted data collection processes there are still possibilities for error and the progress of statistical data collection consists of discovering such errors to the fullest extent possible and correcting them as opportunities permit.

Errors arising either from ignorance or falsification on the part of the respondent or from carelessness or incompetence on the part of the enumerator are to be expected in any survey, including the decennial censuses. For many decades the Bureau of the Census has tried conscientiously to minimize such errors by its field procedures (including extensive pretesting), by careful design of the census questionnaires, and by its training program for enumerators and crew leaders. Moreover, the Bureau has pioneered in systematic attempts to determine the extent of errors in response and coverage, and has served as a model of objective scientific behavior for collectors of data by including extensive statements about sampling variability, and response and coverage errors in its published tabulations [2, 3, 4, *Introduction*]. However, it appears unlikely that the teen-age widowers are the result of errors by the respondent or the enumerator. Why should more false entries (or responses) of widowed be made at age 14 than at 15, or at age 15 than at 16? The strongly declining pattern of widowhood with age was not present in earlier censuses, as would be expected were the source of the anomaly in the behavior of respondents or interviewers.

Having noted the anomaly in listed marital status Stephan conjectured that the source of the error might be a mistake in punching some of the basic *P* or *Persons* cards which were sorted to provide most of the tabular results of the population census. Coale then joined him in searching out the discoverable effects of such mistakes in punching to provide a test of this hypothesis and also to yield an estimate of the number of cards that may have been affected and the probable causes of the punching error.

If columns 24 to 28 [on the *P* card] were punched one position to the right of the proper set of punches, the following changes would take place on the cards affected:

a) *Relationship to head* would become *race,* with these transformations:

Head of household	becomes	*White*
Wife	becomes	*Negro*
Child	becomes	*Indian*
Son or daughter-in-law	becomes	*Japanese*
Grandchild	becomes	*Chinese*
Parent	becomes	*Filipino*
Other relation	becomes	*Other race*

b) *Sex* would be determined by the entry in the *race* column, with these transformations:

White	becomes	*Male*
Negro	becomes	*Female*

The other racial categories would produce entries in the sex column that would result in the card's rejection as erroneously punched. The result of a discovered punching error might have been either the recognition of the shift in columns or the assignment of a "correct" (male or female) punch in the sex column on the basis of entries in other columns.

c) *the first digit of age* would be determined by *sex,* with these transformations:

Male	becomes	*one* (age in the teens)
Female	becomes	*two* (age in the twenties)

d) *the second digit of age* would be determined by *the first digit of age.*

e) *Marital status* would be determined by *the second digit of age.* The transformations implied by a column shift here are complicated by the fact that the coding of marital status for persons falling in the 20 percent sample was not the same as the coding for nonsample persons. For persons not in the sample, the 1 position in column 29 was to be punched if the person was married, 2 if widowed, 3 if divorced, 4 if separated, and 5 if single.

Additional information regarding presence of spouse was to be coded for married persons in a 20 percent sample of the population.[1] The information was obtained by examination of adjacent lines on the schedule. For sample cards, then, position one should never have been punched, while position six meant married, spouse present, and position seven meant married, spouse absent.

Thus the following transformations are indicated for cards in the 20 percent sample:

Second age-digit of 2 becomes *widowed*
Second age-digit of 3 becomes *divorced*

Second age-digit of 4 becomes *separated*
Second age-digit of 5 becomes *single*
Second age-digit of 6 becomes *married, spouse present*
Second age-digit of 7 becomes *married, spouse absent*

It is not clear what would happen to sample cards subject to a shift of column if the second digit of age were 0, 1, 8, or 9. It would have been reasonable to assign the sample cards punched with a 1 (married) to 6 (married, spouse present) or 7 (married, spouse absent) on the grounds that the puncher had incorrectly punched the sample card by the procedure appropriate for nonsample cards. The cards with punches of 0, 8, or 9 could be regarded only as wrongly punched. Two possible actions could have followed: (1) the column shift may have been detected, and a new card punched; or (2) the cards may have been . . . "assigned to the modal marital status category for persons of their age."–*single* for teen-age males [2, p. 50].

ERRONEOUSLY DESIGNATED TEENAGERS WERE REALLY MIDDLE-AGED MALES

If occasionally cards were erroneously punched one column to the right, the source of erroneously listed teenagers (14–18) would be males in their 40s, 50s, 60s, 70s, or 80s. *Heads of households* would be the source of erroneous *white* teenagers, while all other relationships to the head would produce erroneous *nonwhite* teenagers. White persons would produce *male* teenagers, Negro persons *female* teenagers, and all other races would yield an unacceptable punch in the sex column. Persons aged 42 would be listed as widowed 14-year-olds, 52 as widowed 15-year-olds, etc; while persons aged 43, 53, 63, 73, and 83 would be listed as 14, 15, 16, 17, and 18-year-old divorcés.

In an effort to make a numerical estimate of the errors in classification of marital status, we attempted a rough construction of the number who *should* have been listed as married, widowed, and divorced in some of the teen ages. We might have contemplated an assumption that the proportion in each marital status at each age was the same as in 1940, had there not been a marked increase in the frequency of marriage below age 20 in the decade of the 1940s. We allowed for this increase in early marriage by assuming that the fraction married at ages 14, 15, 16, and 17 for a given color-sex group (e.g. white males) increased by the same multiple as the increase in the fraction married at ages 18 and 19. (The fraction married at these ages in 1950 was not seriously contaminated by the punch-card error, because the source of erroneous cards would be the relatively small number of heads of households in their 80s and 90s.) We also assumed that the widowed and divorced at each age in the range 14–17 changed, as a fraction of the married, in the same proportion as at ages 19 and 20. The resulting estimates of married, widowed and divorced among white males 14–17 are included in Table 1.

Estimates of the "true" number in each marital status based on these assumptions can scarcely be considered precise, and no estimates have been reproduced where the estimated true figure is as much as 50 percent of the number reported in the census. When the estimated true figure is only a small fraction of the number given in the census, imprecision in the estimate is relatively unimportant. Thus if the true number of 14-year-old white male widowers were twice our estimate (implying a 100 percent mistake in estimation), the estimated 1950 Census error would be reduced only from 1515 to 1430.

Actually, the use of 1940 proportions of widowed/married tends to overestimate expected widows in 1950, because it neglects reduction in mortality during the decade, especially maternal mortality. The assumption that the fraction married at 14–17 increased to the same degree as those married at age 19 is harder to appraise. The frequency of teen-age marriage undoubtedly increased, but whether or not the increase was greater at very young ages—14 or 15—than at 19 remains a matter of conjecture.

Moreover, it appears that the proportion widowed/married at early teen ages in the 1940 Census was actually overstated. In 1940, the reported *number* widowed increases steadily with age, but the widowed as a *proportion* of the married descends from 14 to age 19 as follows: 50, 34, 29, 17, 9, and 6 per thousand. When allowance is made for the negative socioeconomic selec-

TABLE 1
U.S. EVER-MARRIED WHITE MALES 14–17 BY MARITAL STATUS, 1950, ACCORDING TO THE 1950 CENSUS, AND TO ESTIMATES BASED ON THE 1940 CENSUS

Age	*14*	*15*	*16*	*17*
Married				
1950 Census	6195	6400	*	*
Estimated from 1940 Census	1765	2465	*	*
Apparent excess in 1950 Census	4430	3935	*	*
Widowed				
1950 Census	1600	1355	1115	720
Estimated from 1940 Census	85	85	135	185
Apparent excess in 1950 Census	1515	1270	980	535
Divorced				
1950 Census	1240	930	730	525
Estimated from 1940 Census	85	135	125	255
Apparent excess in 1950 Census	1155	795	605	270

*At ages 16 and 17 estimated marriages were more than 50 percent of the census figures, and the estimated error was deemed too unreliable to be published.

tion that is probable among those marrying very young, for the likelihood that the young wives are exposed to pregnancy and childbirth at very early ages, and for the doubtless rising probability of widower-remarriage as age of the widower increases from 14 to 19, it is possible to make a case for the validity of figures showing a declining proportion widowed/married as age increases. But the *magnitude* of the reported decline is not credible. Surely most 14-year-old widowers would have been married no more than a year; and the ratio of widowed/married among the 14-year-olds implies a mortality rate 50 to 100 times the rate for adolescent girls in 1940, and 15 to 30 times the maternal mortality rate for white mothers. However, the steeply declining proportion of widowed/married is characteristic of all recent censuses, and the assumption of such a pattern in 1950 may be employed as an approximation not to reality, but to what the census tables would have shown in the absence of a shift of columns in the punching operation.

The persons erroneously classified as white males aged 14, 15, 16, and 17 were presumably white male heads of households in their 40s, 50s, 60s, or 70s. To be reported as a 14-year-old widower, the white male household head would be 42; if 43 he would be reported as a 14-year-old divorcé. No single-year age-distribution by age, sex, color, and relationship to head of household was printed in 1950. However, by interpolation of the proportion by five-year age groups of white male household heads/total white males it is possible to form a close estimate of such a single-year distribution. We can then estimate what proportion of the punch-cards were subject to the column-shift error. The proportions are shown in Table 2. The proportion "shifted" whose age terminates in 2 appears to be somewhat in excess of those with a terminal digit of 3. The persistent difference in the 40s, 50s, 60s, and 70s could scarcely be explained by chance variations in erroneous punching. Perhaps some other source of error swelled the number reported as widowed; perhaps the erroneous "divorced" were more frequently detected by some sort of editing procedure, or perhaps our technique of "updating" the 1940 Census consistently overestimated the true number of divorcés. In any event, it seems clear that some 14 to 20 per 10,000 of the white male household-head punch cards sorted in the 20 percent sample were punched (in at least a portion of the columns) one column to the right of proper position.

Persons erroneously classified as *white females* aged 14, 15, 16, and 17 were (if we accept the hypothesis of a shift in columns) Negro heads of households in their 40s, 50s, 60s, and 70s. Because the true number of married, widowed, and divorced is much higher at the young ages among females than among males, it is not possible to estimate nearly as well the number of errors caused by a shift in columns. However, at age 14 if it is assumed that the change in widowed/married since 1940 was the same as at age 19, the true number of widows would be about 80 at age 14, and the number shifted from Negro male household heads age 42 would be about 400. This constitutes

TABLE 2
PROPORTION OF PUNCH CARDS APPARENTLY SUBJECT TO SHIFT OF COLUMN FOR WHITE MALE HOUSEHOLD HEADS OF VARIOUS AGES

Age of Household Head	*Estimated No. of White Male Household Heads*	*Reported as*	*Estimated Number Erroneously Reported*	*Errors Per 10,000 of Original Cards*
42	822,000	widowers age 14	1,515	18.4
52	650,000	widowers age 15	1,270	19.5
62	478,000	widowers age 16	980	20.5
72	244,000	widowers age 17	535	21.9
42, 52, 62, 72	2,194,000	widowers 14–17	4,300	19.6
43	739,000	divorcés age 14	1,155	15.6
53	613,000	divorcés age 15	795	13.0
63	444,000	divorcés age 16	605	13.6
73	212,000	divorcés age 17	270	12.7
43, 53, 63, 73	2,008,000	divorcés 14–17	2,825	14.1
41, 44, 46, 47	2,760,000	married age 14	4,430	16.1
51, 54, 56, 57	2,342,000	married age 15	3,935	16.8

some 50/10,000 of the estimated 77,000 Negro male household heads aged 42. Similar calculations (still less reliable) indicate an error rate of over 60/10,000 at ages 52 and 62. In short, the proportion of erroneous punch cards for Negro male household heads appears to have been about three times as high as for white male household heads. Of course it is possible that the errors in punching were "bunched," and that the high proportion of errors among cards for Negroes was the result of a fortuitous concentration of errors among cards for geographical areas where Negroes predominate.

WHITE CHILDREN OF HOUSEHOLD HEADS BECOME YOUNG INDIANS

The figures presented above do not give a completely persuasive explanation of the anomalous data on marital status in the 1950 Census. In support of the hypothesis of the shift in columns while punching there is the fairly consistent proportion of estimated erroneous widowed males to the number of white male household heads at ages 42, 52, 62, and 72, and the similar consistency in the proportion of erroneous divorcés to heads at ages 43, 53, 63, and 73. But the two sets of proportions are different, and the proportion of errors among Negro males appears to be several times higher. No complete explanation of these discrepant error rates presents itself. In fact, an especially skeptical reader might question the whole hypothesis of a shift in columns in view of these varying apparent rates of error. However, there is an independent and wholly conclusive reason for believing that a shift in columns *did* occur.

As was stated earlier, a shift of the punches intended for column 24 into column 25 would translate relationships to head of household (other than household head itself) into races other than white. Specifically a white person when relationship to the head was *child* would be coded as a male Indian, while a Negro child of the household head would be coded as a female Indian. If the white child were male, he would appear as an Indian in his teens; if female, as an Indian in his twenties. Since over 99 percent of "children" are under 50, and since the shift transfers first digit of age into the second digit, the erroneous Indians would be 10–14 if really male, and 20–24 if really female.

An examination of the age-distribution of the nonwhite population [5, Table 3] discloses that there are indeed excess Indians at ages 10–14 and 20–24 among both males and females, with more numerous erroneous male than female entries. Moreover, the excess is glaringly apparent in those areas (e.g., Northeastern United States, or North Central Urban) where the true Indian population is a small minority. Thus in the Northeast there are reported 757 male Indians aged 5-9; 1,379 aged 10–14; 668 aged 15–19; 1,297 aged 20–24; and 596 aged 25-29. The erroneous entries at 10–14 and 15–19 are about as numerous in this region as the genuine entries. No "bulges" at 10–14 and 20–24 are to be found in the male Indian population reported in 1940, or in earlier censuses.

EXCESSIVE WIDOWHOOD AND DIVORCE AMONG INDIANS

As a final confirmation that a shift in columns was the cause of these errors, we find anomalous figures of a sort to be expected on this hypothesis in the reported marital status of the Indian population 14–24, 25–44, and 45 and over [5, Table 10]. Included in the reported 14–24 year olds would be erroneous entries caused by the shift in columns. The source of the erroneous cards would be male persons 40 or older whose relation to the head of the household is "child," and female "children" 0–19 years old. The marital status reported for these erroneously entered Indians would depend only on the second digit of age. Those with terminal digits of 2 and 3 would be tabulated as widowed and divorced, with 1, 4, 6, and 7 as married, with 5 as single. If the second digit of age were 0, 8, or 9 the card would be detected as wrongly punched. It could then either have been recognized as subject to a column shift, and a new card punched, or the modal marital status (single) could have been assigned. The marital status anomaly that we expect is an excessive number of widowed and divorced in the age category 14-24, especially among the males. In the whole United States and in every region except the West, where the *true* Indians are most numerous, the widowed and divorced 14-24 year old males are reported (contrary to common sense) as exceeding in number the widowed and divorced females in the 14-24 age group. Moreover, in the Northeast, the reported number of widowed and divorced males 14-24 exceeds those reported at 25-44 by more than two to one.

The number of erroneously reported Indian males 14-24 in the Northeast (substantially equal to those reported as 20-24, since there are so few male "children" in their forties to be shifted into the 14-year-old category) can be estimated by assuming that the ratio of 20-24 year olds to the sum of 15-19 and 25-29 year olds *should* have been the same as in 1940. The estimate on this basis is about 650 erroneously reported. Of these, 2/7 (those with terminal age digits of 2 or 3 rather than 1, 4, 5, 6, or 7) would be reported as widowed or divorced. 2/7 of 650 is about 185. The reported 14-24 year old male widowers and divorcés number 184.

The number of false Indians in the nation can be approximated by the same procedure applied above to the Northeast. The result indicates more than 3,000 white male "children" were erroneously listed as male Indians 10-14, and about 2,000 white female children as male Indians 20-24. These errors constitute more than 15 percent of the true Indians at these ages, but only about 1 per 10,000 of the white "children." Errors in the female Indian age distribution at ages 10-14 and 20-24 are sufficient to cause a visible distortion, but are much fewer than among the males—since the source is male and female Negro "children." The error rate among white children is less than one-tenth that found earlier among the cards of white household heads. Part of this difference in error rate is to be expected on the following basis: an x punch was made in column 46 for cards *not* in the 20 percent sample; cards without the x punch would thus be sorted as sample cards. A shift of columns would put the x punch in column 47 (where it means "same house last year"). Moreover, all of the codes in column 46 except "not working" (code 6) would be translated into acceptable entries in column 47. In short, it appears likely that nearly all of the "shifted" cards would appear in the 20 percent sample, implying that the error rate on sample tabulations is about 5 times that in tabulations of all cards. The remainder of the 10 times difference could be accounted for by the high proportion of "children's" cards that would be coded 6 (not working) in column 45 and rejected when sorted on column 46. On the other hand, most heads of households would be coded 1 to 5 in column 45 and the card would *not* be rejected when sorted on column 46.

SUMMARY AND CONCLUSIONS

We have found conclusive evidence that several thousand of the basic *Persons* cards used in the tabulations of the 1950 Census of Population were subject to a displacement of columns when being punched. The portion affected ranges from about 1/100 of one percent among all cards for white females who were children of the household head to about 5/10 of one percent of the 20 percent sample cards among Negro male household heads. We can account for some of the variation by noting that all of the shifted cards should have been sorted with the 20 percent sample, and by the fact that cards coded as "not working" in column 45 would be rejected. But we are left with residual variations in error rate–Negro errors apparently some two-and-a-half to three times the white, for example–that we cannot explain.

These errors were so infrequent that their effect on the number of cards in the groups from which they were drawn is completely negligible. However, in three instances where the groups into which the erroneous cards were sorted were very small, the effect was anything but negligible. For example, the 1950 Census age distribution of American Indians contains more than 15 percent too many males 10-14 and 20-24; and the number of white males under 17 reported in marital status categories other than "single" was determined more by cards punched in wrong columns than by actual marriages, divorces, and deaths of spouse.

Several practical implications emerge from an appreciation of these errors. First is the importance of the realization that the results of any survey (or indeed of any measurement) must be interpreted in the light of all of the operations–such as interviewing, coding, recording, punching, sorting, and tabulating–that underlie the published figures. It was only through inferring the operational basis of the erroneous classification of teen-age marital status that we were led to anticipate errors in the age-distribution of Indians. We were able to do so only because the Bureau of the Census publishes such a full account of all of its procedures [2], a custom that should be followed by other major data collecting agencies.

A feature of the Census operations that is relevant to the column shift was the verification of punching on a sampling basis by quality control procedures [2, p. 31]. The use of quality control in place of 100 percent verification of punched cards is amply justified by the savings achieved. One hundred percent verification would have about doubled the cost of punching. The consequent reallocation of funds would inevitably have caused other more important deficiencies in the census. But quality control, by its nature, permits a very low, unavoidable rate of occurrence of punching errors. In almost all instances these errors are wholly inconsequential. Through the misfortune that some of the very infrequent unavoidably tolerated errors in punching inflated categories which were themselves very rare, a few tabulated results were, in fact, tangibly distorted.

A further implication, then, is that users must scrutinize numbers in small cells of census tabulations with special care. Leon E. Truesdell pointed out this necessity in 1938, citing as an example the possibility that persons for whom no answer is recorded to a question about reading and writing might be recorded as illiterate. Illiteracy was assumed relatively infrequent in his example, so that a small number of "blanks" counted as "no" might double the apparent incidence of illiteracy [1]. Many other examples could be cited of errors of one sort or another that have a visible effect on small cells. One instance can be observed in the listing of years of school in which enrolled, by single years of age, in the United States in 1950 [4, Table 112]. In the first year of elementary school there are shown 7,790 persons 13 years old, 12,765 14 years old, and 8,885 aged 15. In the second year of elementary school the figures at ages 14, 15, and 16 are 6,980, 11,025, and 6,665. It is almost certain that some students in the first year of *high school* (where the modal age is 14) were erroneously listed as in the first year of elementary school.[2] The proportion of such errors was small, but sufficient to produce a large proportionate inflation of the numbers of reported 14-year-olds in the first year of elementary school. In this article we have merely found an additional source—column shifts—of possible error in the numbers in rare categories in tabulations of survey results.

The Bureau of the Census changed over in 1960 to data sensing machinery to transcribe information onto magnetic tape, and the specific problem of a shift in columns is no longer relevant to census operations. The new set of processing operations poses new problems of error control for the Bureau, and may possibly cause misleading figures to show up in new and unsuspected ways in small cells. Users must continue to regard such data with special care.

NOTES

1. The tables showing marital status by age were based on tabulation of 20 percent sample cards.
2. Enumerators were instructed to code elementary school attendance (in an eight-grade elementary school) as *S*1 to *S*8, and high school attendance as *S*9 to *S*12 [2, p. 55]. An occasional coding of "first year high school" as *S*1 is perfectly understandable.

REFERENCES

1. Truesdell, Leon E. "Residual relationships and velocity of change as pitfalls in the field of statistical forecasting," *Journal of the American Statistical Association* 33 (1938): 373–9.
2. United States Bureau of the Census. *The 1950 Censuses–How They Were Taken.* Washington, D.C.: Government Printing Office, 1955.

3. United States Bureau of the Census. *The Post-Enumeration Survey: 1950.* Bureau of the Census, Technical Paper No. 4, Washington, D.C., 1960.
4. United States Bureau of the Census. *U.S. Census of Population: 1950, Volume II, Characteristics of the Population,* Part 1, United States Summary. Washington, D.C.: Government Printing Office, 1953.
5. United States Bureau of the Census. *U.S. Census of Population: 1950, Volume IV, Special Reports,* Part 3, Chapter B, "Nonwhite Population by Race." Washington, D.C.: Government Printing Office, 1953.

Scientific Fiction as Fact: A Case Study in the Perpetuation of Error

Larry T. Reynolds

One of the principal dictates of the currently dominant, if somewhat shaky, concept of science is that science is a self-correcting institution. However, when one uncovers a case where scientists are engaged in actively perpetuating a "factual fiction," the doctrine of a self-correcting institution becomes highly suspect. Furthermore, when the error is being perpetuated by widely read authors the "factual fiction" becomes both widely and rapidly disseminated. Whenever this is the case, the question can easily become one of self-corrective for whom? The more widely spread the error, the more difficult any self-corrective endeavors become.

The following commentary-narrative attempts to illustrate the process by which an unsubstantiated claim comes to be taken as a "verified fact." The unverified assumption under consideration is that women are capable of making finer visual color discriminations than men.

This paper is a slightly revised version of the author's article, "A Note on the Perpetuation of a 'Scientific' Fiction," *Sociometry* 29 (March 1966): 85–88, and is reprinted by permission of the author and the American Sociological Association.

My first encounter with this particular claim came during the course of a discussion of the relationship between personal values and perceptual processes. Most of those present agreed that women were indeed able to make finer color discriminations than men—presumably this difference arises because of a greater feminine concern with matters of dress and decor which affords the opportunity to practice color discrimination. No one present was able to refer me to any source which would substantiate this claim. Several persons did mention that a similar claim was made by Otto Klineberg in his book *Social Psychology.*[1]

While Klineberg makes a statement supporting feminine superiority in color discrimination, he does not contend that this superiority will persist when color-blindness has been controlled. Klineberg notes: "Studies of sensory capacities have shown women to be slightly superior in color discrimination. . . ."[2] As he fails to refer his readers to these studies, however, it is impossible to ascertain whether or not they controlled for color-blindness.

When such studies did not show up in a survey of the literature, I wrote to M. D. Vernon, a well-known authority on the perceptual processes, asking if she could refer me to any studies reporting feminine superiority in color discrimination. Vernon indicated that she was not familiar with any such studies and stated, further, that she thought it ". . . most unlikely that men without colour defects are inferior to women in colour discrimination."[3] It is interesting to note here how readily a physiologically oriented psychologist who gives scant credit to social factors in influencing perceptual processes is willing to assume that, apart from color-blindness, there are no sexual differences in color perception. As we shall soon see, the evidence in this case is on her side. However, she makes her assumption without being aware of the evidence—perhaps because this assumption of no sex differences is compatable with the larger domain assumptions of her physiological-psychological paradigm. What Vernon has here then is an assumption. She *does not treat* this *assumption as fact*. Such is not the case with the social psychologists—sociologists we are about to look at.

Failing to obtain the information I sought from Vernon, I then wrote directly to Otto Klineberg, asking if he could direct me to his original references. In reply, he stated that he was unable to produce them. He suggested that I contact Anne Anastasi, the noted differential psychologist, as he felt that she ". . . should have a complete bibliography."[4]

In reply to my letter of inquiry, Anastasi noted that she ". . . never had the occasion to survey the literature on sex differences in color discrimination."[5] She stated further that, in the 1949 edition of her *Differential Psychology,* "I refer briefly to sex differences in the incidence of color-blindness and cite one early reference on color discrimination in infancy, but these were only casual and incidental citations." However, on the same page containing these "casual" and "incidental" citations, one finds the following not so casual and incidental statement: "Even among individuals of normal vision, females excel in color discrimination."[6] Like Klineberg, Anastasi fails to refer her readers to the original sources upon which her claim is supposedly based.

Lindesmith and Strauss, in their *Social Psychology,* make reference to feminine superiority in color discrimination, as does Robert Bierstedt in his book *The Social Order.* Bierstedt's is only an incidental reference to color perception, and he does not inform us whether or not he feels this superiority will persist when color-blindness is controlled.[7] However, he does not cite any empirical work to substantiate his claim, thereby making it impossible to ascertain whether he is referring to something other than the lower incidence of color-blindness among females.

Lindesmith and Strauss make the following claim: "A middle-class American woman's color discriminations are richer, more extensive, and far more precise than her husband's."[8] As was the case with Bierstedt, Anastasi, and Klineberg, Lindesmith and Strauss fail to cite empirical support for their contentions.

In the hope that these authors could direct me to a pertinent reference I had missed in my survey of the literature, I wrote to both Bierstedt and Lindesmith, asking if they could substantiate their claims for feminine superiority in color discrimination.

In reply, Bierstedt stated: "Feminine superiority and color perception does not refer only to a lower incidence of color-blindness. Whatever evidence I have for the assertion came almost certainly from *Women and Men,* by Amram Scheinfeld. . . ."[9] In checking Scheinfeld's book, I find that he does make a statement which could be construed as supporting feminine superiority with respect to color discrimination. Scheinfeld states: "Even where only those with normal vision are compared, it appears that the female color response is better."[10] It turns out, however, that what Scheinfeld is refering to is a study by Ruth Staples,[11] a study which deals with *color preference* and not with color discrimination. While Bierstedt has been able to cite the secondary source upon which his contention is supposedly based, examination of this source reveals that it in fact does not support any claim for feminine superiority in color discrimination.

In his return letter, Lindesmith was unable to refer me to any work which would substantiate his claim for feminine superiority in color discrimination. He further stated: "It may be that no empirical studies of the kind you want are in existence. We may have regarded this as something self-evidently true—which, of course, it may not be."[12] Lindesmith has here hit the nail right on the head! Just as Vernon, a physiological psychologist, was ready to assume that there were no sex differences in color discrimination other than color-blindness because her general paradigm plays down the impact of "the social" in shaping perceptual processes; so, too Klineberg, Bierstedt, Lindesmith, and Strauss, all sociologists or social psychologists, are ready to assume that there are sex differences in color discrimination beyond those associated with color-blindness because their general paradigm plays up the impact of social life on biological processes. The point I am trying to make here is that assumptions compatible with one's larger domain assumptions are frequently treated as "self-evidently true" or as already verified facts in cases where there is either no evidence or the evidence runs counter to such assumptions. The tendency for such errors to be perpetuated is perhaps helped along when we read opponents' major theoretical works but ignore their detailed research efforts.

On the possibility that I may have overlooked something pertinent during my first survey of the literature, I now returned for a more intensive review. While this second survey failed to turn up any empirical research supporting the claim for feminine superiority in color discrimination, I was able to locate works refuting such a claim. R. W. Pickford reports in detail a number of studies presenting such evidence. In summarizing these studies, Pickford concludes:

> The experiments reported show no important sex differences in colour sensitivity except those connected with the forms of sex-linked red-green defects . . . apart from the colour-blind and anomalous subjects, men are just as good judges of all colours as women . . . women may be more expert in the use of subtle colour names and they may be more interested in colours than men, owing to tradition and social influences, but they are not fundamentally better at judging colour likeness and differences than men.[13]

Pickford's contention is supported by Henmon when the latter's experiment on school children's ability to discriminate between various hues of the color red failed to produce a significant sex difference.[14]

While it runs counter to the available evidence, the idea that females excel in color discrimination, even when controlling for color-blindness, is apparently widely accepted. The "scientific" perpetuation of errors such as the one reported here should lead one to begin to question such *prime* assumptions of the orthodox scientific community as the notion that science is a self-correcting institution. If scientists, operating without benefit of evidence, accept as fact falsehoods which support their theories and reject as false facts which do not, what are we to conclude about the additional *prime* assumption that the orderly collection, marshalling, and unfolding of "facts" is the real way in which science develops and progresses?

In the last analysis, I suppose a believer of the current scientific orthodoxy could argue that my little exercise here is itself an example of science's self-correcting function and that it helps to "prove" the self-corrective nature of science. A comparison of the large number of students who for years have been exposed to the basic introductory texts by Klineberg, Bierstedt, Anastasi, Lindesmith and Strauss with the students who will just be beginning to read this one should serve as a heady corrective for any such optimism.

A FURTHER NOTE ON SCIENTIFIC FICTION AS FACT*

". . . (T)he time and effort expended by Reynolds in pursuit of the facts is commendable and is the sort of thing that should be done more often . . . it is unfortunate in this case that he is wrong. Both Ligon[1] and DuBois[2] have demonstrated female superiority in differentiating color. Both experimenters used the Woodworth–Wells[3] color–naming and word–reading tests. Whereas Ligon's findings on sex differences were incidental to other objectives, DuBois set out specifically to test sex differences. In addition to the color–naming test and the word–reading test, DuBois used a non–verbal form of the Woodworth–Wells test. Moreover, he discarded subjects who did not show normal color vision on the Ishihara test. Differences in all tests favored the women. . . . While there may be other sources demonstrating the same type of findings the point here is merely to indicate that there is evidence for making the statement about which Reynolds was concerned. . . .

E. Z. Dager
Purdue University

REJOINDER

Basing his argument on the results of the two studies reported in the *American Journal of Psychology,* Edward Z. Dager has taken exception to my contention that the widespread notion of female superiority in color perception is fiction perpetuated as fact. Dager has either misinterpreted the articles that he cites or has misunderstood my original article.

The Ligon study is concerned with color naming and does not directly address itself to sex differences in actual color perception. Even if the study had focused on this problem, its results would still be suspect since color–blindness was not taken into consideration. While DuBois' study did control for defective color vision, it too was concerned with recognition speed, color identification, and color naming, and not with one's ability to make *fine perceptual discriminations* between colors. Neither study presents evidence indicating that females are capable of making finer visual color discriminations than males. Perceptual color discrimination refers to the ability of a subject to indicate that two or more colors, or two or more hues of a color, are or are not identical. This is what I meant by visual color discrimination in my original article, and an apology is in order for not having made it explicit. . . .

However, even if Dager had turned up evidence directly supporting female superiority in color perception, such evidence would not mitigate the main point of my article. There would then be evidence both for and against such a claim. As many a logical positivist has indicated, where consensus is lacking a hard fact cannot be said to exist. The point is . . . that authors have an obligation to either support their contentions with facts or label them as speculations. In this case no author could provide a single relevant reference to support his claim.

Larry T. Reynolds
The Ohio State University

*This dialogue was excerpted from correspondence reacting to Reynolds' original article in *Sociometry,* Vol. 29. The letters in full appear on pages 468 and 469 of that volume.

1. Ernest M. Ligon, "A Genetic Study of Color Naming and Word Reading," *American Journal of Psychology,* 44 (January, 1932), pp. 103–122.
2. Phillip H. DuBois, "The Sex Difference on the Color-Naming Test," *American Journal of Psychology,* 52 (July, 1939), pp. 380–382.
3. P. S. Woodworth, and F. L. Wells, "Association Tests," *Psychological Monographs,* 13 (December, 1911), Whole No. 57, pp. 1–85.

NOTES

1. Otto Klineberg, *Social Psychology* (New York: Henry Holt and Co., 1954).
2. *Ibid.*, p. 227.
3. Letter from M. D. Vernon, December 9, 1963.
4. Letter from Otto Klineberg, December 31, 1963.
5. Letter from Anne Anastasi, January 16, 1964.
6. Anne Anastasi and John P. Foley, *Differential Psychology* (New York: The Macmillan Co., 1949), p. 647.
7. Robert Bierstedt, *The Social Order* (New York: McGraw–Hill, 1963), p. 362.
8. Alfred R. Lindesmith and Anselm L. Strauss, *Social Psychology* (New York: The Dryden Press, 1956), p. 91.
9. Letter from Robert Bierstedt, January 14, 1965.
10. Amram Schienfeld, *Women and Men* (New York: Harcourt, Brace and Co., 1944), p. 79.
11. Ruth Staples, "The Response of Infants to Color," *Journal of Experimental Psychology* 15 (April, 1932): 119–41.
12. Letter from Alfred Lindesmith, January 16, 1965.
13. R. W. Pickford, *Individual Differences in Colour Vision* (London: Routledge and Kegan Paul, Ltd., 1951), pp. 334–35.
14. V. A. C. Henmon, "Sex Differences and Variability in Color Perception," *Colorado University Studies* 7 (1910), pp. 207–14.

Dissection VIII: What Is Lost in Translation?

Great Books and Small Groups: An Informal History of a National Survey

James A. Davis

This is, within the narrow limits imposed by perceptual defense and criminal libel, my recollection of how National Opinion Research Center Survey No. 408, the Great Books study, proceeded from its inception in the summer of 1957 to the publication of a book in 1961. Although I tend to view the chronicle as the struggle of a brave study director against time, money, clients, winter weather, Texas Great Books groups, and NORC's business staff, these events may better be viewed as a reasonably typical case study of how modern social research proceeds in a large nonprofit research organization.

This brings us to the subject of money. I think it may be stated as a matter of indisputable fact that there is no money available in the contemporary United States for unrestricted support of large-scale social research. On occasion, a professor whose work is fashionable or whose years of loyal back-scratching on professional committees is deemed worthy of a reward will receive the munificent unrestricted sum of $1,000 or $2,000, most of which he passes on to subsidize graduate students, but private donors prefer to see their names on university dormitories; the association of sociology and socialism is graven in the minds of congressmen; and foundations have (let us face it) retreated from social research. No one is going to give NORC or similar private institutions the wherewithal to pursue their own research interests at $50,000 per interest. The citizens of Michigan do subsidize the Survey Research Center, and its senior staff members have sabbaticals and swimming pools and who knows what else; but the private, nonprofit research center is in there hustling in the market place along with Ford, General Dynamics, and Joe's Drugstore.

Thus is born "the client," typically a large foundation or a government agency with a particular research question which it feels is worth the exorbitant costs and personal frustrations involved in commissioning research. And with the birth of the client comes the eternal triangle of client, organization, and study director. It is the operation of this triangle which is the key process in the poignant histories of surveys.

Let me begin, however, with a few kind words for clients. As a matter of fact, the client for this study, a foundation executive in one of the many progeny spawned by the Ford Foundation, is a fine guy, and at least prior to his reading of this document, I consider him my friend. But, as we know from introductory sociology, personalities and roles are two different matters. Rolewise, to be a client is somewhat like being a sugar daddy responsible to a board of directors. It is an extraordinarily expensive business, the satisfactions are occasional and fleeting, there is the distinct impression that one is being ruthlessly exploited, and all of this has to be justified at the annual meeting.

At the same time, those in the humanistic studies who are so enraged at the funds they see flowing into social research might momentarily consider how it would be to receive an enormous commission, most of which disappeared into $25 checks to unknown ladies in New Jersey and a mysterious maw called "overhead," and to have the Medici Fund tell you that you could paint anything you liked as long as it matched the rug in their private audience room.

All of this would work out cozily, as it does in business, were it not for the motivations of study directors. There are, I would guess, no more than a hundred people in the country today leading the lives of noisy desperation characteristic of study directors, but they fall into two types. Historically, relatively few study directors in market research and in nonprofit organizations came from graduate study in sociology or social psychology, a Ph.D. in sociology being no more necessary for competence in this area than a degree in electrical engineering. Among NORC's senior study directors, for instance, are non-Ph.D.'s trained in history, anthropology, and undergraduate liberal arts. Into this occupation, however, like locusts, have come the Ph.D.'s. They tend to be ambitious, steely-nerved young men who have worked out the implication of the following propositions: (1) academic success is contingent on research publication, regardless of the topic; (2) young men seldom get research grants on their own; (3) people come to research centers and give them the wherewithal to do large-scale studies.

While the two types of study directors appear indistinguishable to the naked eye, they vary considerably in their view of research and of their jobs. The "old-line" staff tend to identify with the research organization and to gain their rewards from pride in craftsmanship and budgetmanship, reputed client satisfaction, and the feeling that they have contributed to the success of the organization. The new men, however, while often willing to deliver a thorough and honest piece of work for the sponsor, find their major satisfactions in milking the research for journal articles or publications to throw into the potlatch of academia, whence cometh their eventual reward: a research professorship.

I am, in truth, accentuating differences that are far from polar, for most people in research work find their major rewards from intellectual challenge (as well as salaries superior to teaching), and "applied" research is generally more challenging intellectually. That is what I said: applied work is usually more challenging—because there are more definite standards of accomplishment. In social-science theoretical work, the feeling that it "sounds right" or has the requisite polysyllabic mumbo jumbo is the typical yardstick; in "pure" empirical research, if *any* significant correlations can be wrung out, the material is generally publishable; but in applied research, there are rather precise questions at issue and the failure to answer them is painfully apparent. In addition, applied research in government agencies, the larger commercial firms, and centers like NORC is characterized by superior probability sampling, larger samples, better interviewing, more careful control of coding and tabulations, and informal monitoring of the work by colleagues who are specialists in the same area. One wonders why the Ph.D.'s have continual intellectual dissatisfaction in their jobs.

The root of the problem, I think, lies in the differences between generality and specificity. Clients commission research because they are interested in something specific: who has health insurance, whether enough people are training for careers in biochemistry, how much scholarship money is available to graduate students, to what extent people near airports are bothered by jet noise, and so on. Sociology is, however, the enemy of the specific. Even though the facts of social life in modern America are less well documented than the facts of marine life at the bottom of the ocean, the academic sociologist (the ultimate judge, employer, or journal editor whom our young Ph.D. wants to impress) has a phobia against research which "merely" describes. This is "nose-counting," "dust-bowl empiricism," "trivia," and so forth and is not part of the grand scheme for building the science of sociology. That the history of natural science is in the reverse order—theories having been developed to explain facts, rather than facts gathered to ornament theories—weighs little against the pressure of intellectual tradition. Therefore, the academically oriented study director is faced with a dilemma. If he completes his research in such a fashion as to satisfy the sponsors, it will lack academic glamour. If, on the other hand, he completes a piece suitable for academic publication, it will probably tell the sponsor nothing about the questions which led to the research.

If one has attained sufficient eminence, one proceeds to conduct the study as one pleases, considering the client lucky to have his problem studied by an important person, even if in the process the client's problem disappears. For younger people and the struggling research organization, this is a dangerous tactic, and the natural strategy is to attempt both tasks: a specific descriptive report "for the client" and a high-brow article or monograph for the study director's self-aggrandizement. Thus, as well as a description of who gets scholarships comes a test of the theory of relative deprivation among graduate students; along with the descriptive materials on whether poor boys go on to college comes a paper on status crystallization and career choice; along with the statistics on what doctors prescribe brand-X drugs comes a paper on sociometric aspects of innovation; and so on. . . .

Considered, then, as roles, social research is typically conducted by (1) a study director, who may be willing to do what he is paid for, but is more interested in wresting an academic article from the remains, (2) a sponsor, who stokes the fires with money and hopes vaguely that the evasive, fasttalking young man will complete within his lifetime a report bearing vaguely on the topic, and (3) a research organization, beset with financial woes and firmly aware of the fact that the study director (who gets no profits when a study makes money and pays no refund when he runs into the red) is capable of spending the organization into the poorhouse without shedding a tear and in the process alienating the client beyond the point at which he can be persuaded to pony up the deficit.

Let us now see how these three archetypal characters proceeded to produce NORC Survey 408.

I did not have much to do with the Great Books study until it was about six weeks old. During the early summer of 1957, I was away from Chicago doing field work in Ohio for a community study directed by Peter Rossi. Why? Because I had been hired by NORC in the summer of 1957 to direct a study of physicians, which never took place. In order to keep me busy, I had been sent into darkest Ohio as gunbearer for Mr. Rossi, who was stalking community leaders there.

The infant Great Books study had been ushered into the world by Clyde Hart, NORC's director at that time, and the staff at the Fund for Adult Education, my role being that of pediatrician rather than obstetrician.

Had I been in Chicago for every moment of the initial negotiations, I would probably have little more to add to this chronicle than I can from my observation post in a commercial hotel in "Mediana," Ohio. Indeed, the exact origins of this survey, as for many, are a mystery. My hearsay version goes as follows.

The Fund for Adult Education, a subsidiary of the Ford Foundation, had since 1951 been supporting diverse activities in the area of adult education by grants to ongoing study-discussion programs, continuing educational centers, educational-television experiments, and so on. The fund was oriented to action, not research, and had commissioned little or no professional research prior to the Great Books study.

I am told that it came to pass that from within the parent Ford Foundation came word that the time had arrived for the Fund for Adult Education to render an accounting of its stewardship and that the conventional medium for such an accounting was "research." The Fund for Adult Education, not unexpectedly, proceeded to commission a number of studies, of which Great Books was one.

Now, if the Fund for Adult Education was bemused to find itself bankrolling a statistical survey, the object of the inquiry—the Great Books Foundation—was flabbergasted. The foundation, an independent, nonprofit corporation with headquarters in Chicago (which has no connection with Great Books of Western World, a commercial publishing venture), coordinates the national program of Great Books, using a small professional staff and a large number of volunteers. As intellectual types, the personnel of Great Books stand somewhere to the right of Jacques Barzun and Arthur Schlesinger, Jr., in their opinion of sociological surveys; but it is amazing how persuasive a large foundation with a history of generosity can be, so eventually the foundation was persuaded to cooperate. I think it would be fair to say that, while the foundation did provide the requisite liaison to complete the study, its stance was of one about to be photographed with a midget on his lap at a congressional hearing.

At this point, the following parties are involved: NORC, a research organization fully aware that evaluation studies usually make the client look bad; the Fund for Adult Education, an action organization already persuaded of the merits of Great Books, but hopeful of gaining concrete evidence of these merits; and the Great Books Foundation, already persuaded of the merits of its program, but quite doubtful that surveys can measure them.

Here ensued a number of conferences in Chicago and New York, during which the basic framework of the study was established. The only firm agreement prior to that time had been that the study was to be concerned with participants rather than the operations of the foundation and that we were interested in "the effects" of participation in Great Books.

For those of you who have not had the opportunity to read *Great Books and Small Groups,* the Great Books program in 1957 was roughly as follows. In 1957-1958, it consisted of some 1,960 discussion groups dispersed through the United States, with some additional groups in Canada and overseas. Each group meets every other week from September to June, and at each meeting the members discuss a specific selection which they have read before the meeting (e.g., Milton, *Areopagitica;* Tolstoy, *The Death of Ivan Ilyich;* Rousseau, *The Social Contract*). The readings are organized into blocks of one year each and, in theory, should be read in sequence. The groups vary in size (from around 5 to around 35, with an average of 11 in our sample); in sponsorship (most are affiliated with public libraries, but a number are sponsored by churches, business firms, and individuals); and in leadership (some have a single leader, most have two leaders, a few rotate the leadership each meeting). The leaders are not formally trained teachers, but a number have had brief training courses conducted by the foundation. The members do not pay any tuition or get any certificate for completing the program. In fact, no one can complete the program, as additional years of reading are always available. Members are encouraged to buy the inexpensive readings from the foundation but are not required to do so.

It was this program which was to be evaluated, to the end of discovering whether the effects on the participants were such as to justify the continuation or expansion of Fund for Adult Education support. As a separate operation, the Fund for Adult Education commissioned a management-consultant firm to assess the organization of the foundation, market potential for Great Books, and similar internal affairs.

The design of such research falls naturally into two parts, which can be thought of as sampling, in the sense of deciding which people are to be studied and in what numbers; and questionnaire construction, in the sense of deciding what measures to use on the sampled respondents.

Of the two, sampling presented the fewest problems. It so happened that this is one social-science situation for which there is a clear-cut textbook sample design. According to the course I teach in research methods, one should collect a large number of people, arrange for a random subgroup to participate in Great Books, prevent the remainder from participating in the program, and measure both groups on the dependent variables before and after the experiment. (Technically, if you have done it perfectly, you do not need to measure both groups before.) It also so happened that, as usual, the textbook design was out of the question. Such an experimental study would be "possible," although there would be an enormous number of difficulties—making sure that the controls do not get Great Books or equivalent experience, establishing community programs which mask the mechanics of the sample design, and so forth. The major obstacle turned out to be time. We began active work on the study in the late summer of 1957 and had to deliver a report by fall 1958. It would have been plainly impractical (as well as quite expensive) to get a field experiment organized in two months before the 1957–1958 Great Books year got under way and results of a spring–1958 follow-up assessed by fall 1958. In addition, we all agreed that if the program's effects were as expected, some of them might not show up until after several years of exposure to the program.

It was this idea of long-term effects which enabled us to find a compromise design. If it is correct that, unlike indoctrination movies or television debates, the effects of Great Books require a long, long time for their appearance, then beginning participants should make a reasonably good "control group," particularly if the field work could be hurried so that first-year members were reached before they had attended more than one or two meetings. Because, in addition, both beginning and advanced-year members are equally self-selected, this design even has the advantage over a control group of nonmembers in that the latter would necessarily be suspected of less motivation or interest in joining Great Books.

The great problem with this design—and a problem which remained one of the main issues of the research—is that, as compared with a true experiment, the design left open the possibility that advanced-year members differ systematically from beginners, and it would be their other differences which produced any differences in the dependent variables. For example, almost necessarily, advanced-year members are older than beginners, and if age were related to the dependent variables, spurious differences would emerge. While this problem would give nightmares to an experimental purist, by and large it did not bother me too much. I knew that we were going to have sufficient cases so that by cross-tabulations we could control for any differences in gross variables such as age, sex, education, occupation, and so forth. A major pitfall, however, was the problem of retention. Nobody really knew the dropout rates in Great Books, but from all that is known of volunteer organizations, they had to be high. Furthermore, it made plain common sense that retention in the program would be correlated with the dependent variables, for people who were not getting the "effects," whatever they may be, would be prime candidates for dropping out, as in any educational institution. Even worse, there was no way of controlling for dropouts in a sample limited to current members, since we would have to introduce as statistical controls events that had not happened yet. The best we could do was to introduce some questions about intention to continue and use these for controls in comparing beginning and advanced members.

Looking back now, I wonder why we let it go at that. We could have interviewed some ex-members without too much difficulty, but I do not remember that this was seriously raised as a possibility. Perhaps at that time I already had the germ of the idea of a second study to determine actual dropouts; perhaps I did not. At any rate, I am glad now we let it go; for without the continuing problem of attrition, the study would have begun and ended as another evaluation project.

The net result of all of this was a decision to sample from existing discussion groups, stratified to oversample the advanced-year groups wherein lay the pay dirt, if any. At this point, another vital, but not deliberate, decision was made. The Great Books Foundation has no individual membership rolls but merely a rather loose file of group registrations. Given the lack of coercive structure for the program, a number of groups exist without the official blessing of the foundation; and at least in 1957, rather than groups' petitioning Great Books for the right to exist, functionaries of the foundation continually scanned press clippings to find their groups, which were then sent registration materials. If a file of individuals had existed, I do not know whether we would have used it; but having no choice, we sampled groups—a very important decision, as it turned out.

The final crucial decision was an economic one. Because of the money to be saved, we decided to raise the case base by asking entire groups to fill out a self-administered questionnaire at their meeting, gambling that the members would be literate and thus capable of filling out a questionnaire and hopefully sophisticated enough to cooperate with a research project. We also had the naive hope that the foundation would put a little heat on the groups to increase cooperation.

In sum, while from an abstract point of view we should have had a sample of individuals both in and out of the Great Books program, because of a series of unwitting decisions based on practical exigencies we ended up with a sample of discussion groups within the program. We began with the Great Books, but the Small Groups got into the study by default.

While limitations of time and budget usually provide enough restrictions so that sample designs for national surveys amount to choosing among a number of restricted possibilities, when it comes to writing a questionnaire, the sky is the limit; or rather, one's guess as to how lengthy a document the respondents will complete without rebellion is the only boundary. Within this area—and it is amazing how much respondents will actually do for you if approached correctly—we had all of Western culture from which to pick items. It is precisely the major advantage and the major problem of surveys that an enormous amount of information can be collected, the marginal increment in cost for an additional item being very small when compared with the fixed costs of sampling and contacting respondents. At the same time, *the* intellectual challenge in survey analysis is in ordering and synthesizing the diverse information—in this schedule ranging from father's occupation to the respondent's opinion as to whether the course of history is capricious, purposive, or mechanistic. (In case you are curious, 25 percent thought it capricious, 48 percent thought it purposive, 13 percent thought it mechanistic, and 13 percent were "no answer.")

A certain amount of disagreement arose among the parties: the Fund for Adult Education backing two horses, the Great Books Foundation a third, and the study director a dark fourth horse. The first horse was "community participation," a matter of considerable interest to the Fund for Adult Education, which was convinced that participation in Great Books should and maybe even did lead people to become more active in community affairs. The general idea was that after reading, say, the Greek philosophers on the nature of the good society, the Great Books members would be impelled to remodel

Toledo, Ohio, and Minneapolis, Minnesota. The idea met with polite skepticism on the part of Great Books and me.

The Great Books Foundation maintained, and with some justice, I think, that their program did not have any purposes at all, at least in the sense of the sort of thing that can be listed and translated into surveys. With the naiveté of a young man who had read all the texts on evaluation research, I kept hounding the foundation to list–1, 2, 3–the purposes of their program so that they might at least be tried on charges of their own devising. In the face of such pressures for oversimplification, all the foundation staff could come up with was the denial that participants were expected to become more active, passive, liberal, conservative, or anything that directional. Rather, they were expected to become more sophisticated, more critical in their thinking, broader in their approach, and so on, whether or not they chose to favor the left, right, center, or to refrain from community life. In this the participants in the actual survey agreed, the bulk opting for the response, "The Great Books provide an intellectual understanding (of specific social and community problems), but few or no keys to plans for action," as opposed to "Great books provide both an understanding of the problems and a key to plans of action" or "Great Books are not applicable to specific social and community problems." While the foundation opposed the community-participation stress on the basis of intellectual ideology, I was against it on the practical grounds that I doubted we would get any effects. To begin with, I thought that Great Books members were typically fugitives from community life, rather than involved. I was dead wrong, but more on that later. In addition, from all that I knew of the literature, I was sure that class, sex, political preference, for example, played such an important part in community participation that exposure to a reading discussion program could not make much difference. I was perfectly willing to let the facts speak, but I was not going out of my way to disappoint somebody who had given me $40,000 to do research.

At this point, the inevitable answer occurred: to stress both purely intellectual and also community-participation materials. However, this led to a knotty problem of measurement. In assessing community and political involvement, we felt we were on safe grounds, for there is rich experience in survey measurement of such phenomena, and the content is heavily behavioral and hence fairly easy to translate into questions. In the measurement of such things as "critical thinking," "tolerance of ambiguity," "intellectual sophistication," that way madness lies. I was toying with pulling out existing tests of critical thinking and similar measures, and the Great Books Foundation had in desperation proposed that the respondents be given essay examinations which the foundation staff would evaluate, when the Fund for Adult Education split into two spokesmen, with the entrance of the late Carl Hovland, then a consultant to the fund. Hovland, as a psychologist, was highly concerned about the details of testing: whether the tests could be given under standard conditions, timed, collusion prevented, motivation maintained, and so forth. The answer, of course, is that they could not, or at least could not to the satisfaction of a testing specialist. Hovland felt that we might get away with it but that the results could never be sold to a really hostile critic who was oriented to psychological measurement.

The compromise decision actually became a sellout of the Great Books Foundation's position, for on the basis of Hovland's technical doubts, critical thinking and open-mindedness essentially disappeared, except in the form of some very simple attitude and opinion items in which, for example, the respondents were asked to name "any particular authors or schools which you once disliked, but now find more acceptable." Rather, we began to search for some sugar-coated test-oid materials to get at more superficial things. We actually found two good ones, a set of cartoon items (e.g., a gentleman in a nightshirt nailing a paper on a door, to denote Martin Luther posting his theses; a child in diapers composing at the piano, to denote the young Mozart, etc.), which had originally appeared in *Life* magazine, and a marvelous poetry test,[1] developed in the early 1920's by M. R. Trabue and Allan Abbott. Trabue and Abbott presented the original version of a well-known poem, along with versions systematically deformed in aesthetic content, and the respondent was asked to pick the one liked best. We never did find a complete set of the poetry-test items, even by long-distance calls to Prof. Trabue, by then a sprightly emeritus, but we got enough to go into print. In addition, we packed in voluminous materials on reading quality and musical taste and picked a number of items on philosophical points from the work of Charles Morris.

Note what was happening here. What should have been a series of technical measures of cognitive functioning became a set of crude information measures along with considerable materials on aesthetics and ideologies. Part of the shift can be explained by Hovland's technical qualms, part by the inability of the Great Books Foundation to come up with neat objectives for which nice tests exist, but a good proportion came from the wily maneuvers of the study director.

What was I up to? Viewed from the perspective of getting some academic yardage out of the study, Great Books appeared to have three possibilities, of which I picked the wrong one. The first possibility would have been to conduct an evaluation study of such methodological luster that it would attract attention despite the offbeat character of the sample and the stigma of "Adult Education." I knew in my bones that because of the design limitation and the fuzziness of the measures, this one could not make it. Now, get me right. I felt all along that we could deliver useful and valid information to the client on the effects of Great Books (and I think we did), but I doubted that we could get out a study which would be cited as technically outstanding or particularly convincing to a *resistant* reader. This meant that while for report purposes the materials had to yield an evaluation study, for academic purposes I had to find an analytical theme such that the whole sample could be treated as a single group and differences in exposure to Great Books (our analogue of experimental and control groups) ignored.

Looking back now, I think there were actually two possibilities. It turned out that Great Books members are phenomenally active and involved in local community affairs and that we had the makings of a detailed study of community involvement among young, educated, middle-class Americans. Actually, Vickie Beale, who was on the staff, managed to get a good Ph.D. thesis on this theme, but for some reason I did not pick that tack. The third possibility was a detailed analysis of the members' intellectual lives, their tastes, ideologies, philosophical positions, and so forth. I had done a Ph.D. thesis on taste and status symbols, and I have always been fascinated by the writings of Russell Lynes, David Riesman, Eric Larrabee, etc. In the back of my mind, I envisioned the development—from data, mind you—of typologies of kinds of intellectual stances and styles within the Great Books members.

My own proclivities here were reinforced by a marvelous but misleading field experience. Because of the timing of the program, there was no way to see a Great Books group in action before the questionnaire was completed. (My record is still perfect. I have never actually seen a Great Books discussion, despite several years of almost full-time work on this project.) However, in the summer of 1957 Great Books was running a summer program at Aspen, Colorado, which I arranged to visit. While my strongest memory is of the magnificent train ride through the Rockies—a revelation to a midwestern boy—professionally I came away with two hunches. The first was that Great Books tends to attract a social type which can perhaps be described as "isolated intellectuals." It seemed to me that at Aspen a large number of the people I met were extraordinarily well read, very serious, and given to the construction of homemade philosophical systems, without being hooked into the orbit of academic intellectuals or professional creative artists. I do not mean they were screwballs, but they did seem to be the sort of people whose opinions on whether the course of history was purposive might be interesting. Apparently the people who attended that summer conference were quite unrepresentative of the Great Books membership, for the actual survey showed the Great Books participants to be a pretty clean-cut group of PTA joiners and *Time* readers, not much given to the construction of homemade philosophical systems.

I came away with one other impression which did have a pay-off, although indirect. While I have never seen a legal, in-season Great Books discussion, I did watch a number of the sessions in Aspen and tried to make some guesses about the group dynamics beneath the surface of the discussions. It seemed to me that what was going on was a sort of political process in which people would advance ideas, allies would rally to them, and enemies would muster forces against them and that the course of the discussions was heavily influenced by latent attractions and antagonisms among the participants. Mulling this over later in Chicago, I decided to insert some sociometric questions to see whether a member's isolation or acceptance by others in the discussion group affected his reactions to the program. In the back of my mind was the idea that perhaps the discussions worked best when there were fairly "even sides" in the ideological and interpersonal teams. However, the Great Books Foundation vetoed these questions on the grounds that it might produce complaints if members were asked to name their friends and enemies.

The key items in the final study—a series of questions about functional roles in the groups—were actually devised as a substitute. The items asked each member to rate himself and others in the group in terms of such roles as "joking and kidding," "making tactful comments," "providing 'fuel' for the discussion," and others. The logical structure of the items was suggested by the work of Fred Bales. I have never had a course in small groups, but Bales's influence is very strong at Harvard, where I did my graduate work, and a sort of Balesian, functional approach to roles and group dynamics, absorbed by osmosis during graduate-school days, was the only one I knew.

This is the intellectual history of the questionnaire, a lengthy document bearing the stamp of the Fund for Adult Education's interest in community participation, some vestigial traces of the foundation's interest in "critical thinking," a lot of my own penchant for materials on aesthetics and ideologies, and a good bit of information on functional roles, inserted as a substitute for the excised sociometric items.

Were I to recount in detail the field work, coding, key-punching, and card-cleaning which took up the next ten months, this essay would become a book about a book. Let me merely say that with the superb help of Grace Lieberman, Mary Booth, Ursula Gebhard, Joe Zelan, and a charming group of Antioch College cooperators we came into the possession of schedules from over 90 percent of the sampled groups and coded the data from the 1,909 individual respondents onto some dozen decks of IBM cards.

I am also going to gloss over the first report, a bulky, 256-page, single-spaced mimeographed document completed in August 1958. It consisted of (1) a description of the Great Books participants, (2) analyses of the members' reported effects of participation in the program, (3) comparisons between beginning and advanced members in terms of dependent variables, and (4) data on role structures and social correlates of role performance. Vickie Beale, who had joined the project staff in the spring of 1958, analyzed the materials on community participation; Ursula Gebhard had done most of the role analysis, and I did the rest.

Because the report was done under great pressure, the entire analysis and writing being concentrated in a period of about three months, the document was overly long and underly organized. In essence, however, we showed (1) strong differences in knowledge between beginners and advanced-year members, (2) slight differences in attitudes, consistent with the idea of increased tolerance or open-mindedness, and (3) few differences in behavior. Taken together, I feel that the material pretty well showed that exposure to Great Books does add to the intellectual depth and perspective of the members but does not produce striking or consistent effects on behavior, which is, after all, just what the results should be if the program does what its organizers think it does. We also found that, rather than being socially marginal, the Great Books members were highly educated, highly involved in their communities, and *less* upwardly mobile than comparable college graduates. While this may be a comfort to the friends of Great Books, it "did in" my plans for analyzing their intellectual lives. If the members had turned out to have a considerable proportion of homely philosophers, upwardly mobile people, or members of strange cults, the results might have been quite "marketable" because academic sociologists gobble up materials on strange cults and deviant people; but since the participants turned out to be quite typical suburban types, without being statistically representative of suburban types, it would be hard to justify detailed analysis of their tastes and ideologies.

The Fund for Adult Education received the report and must have been clairvoyant, for they gave Great Books a large-scale grant about a month before they saw the results, such being the crucial role that social research plays in decision-making in modern America. . . .

Were I to draw morals from this history, they would be these.

(1) I think the cronicle of *Great Books and Small Groups* illustrates the tremendous importance of technical methodological developments in the substantive development of social science. It is commonly believed that research technology is a mere servant of substantive or theoretical interests. Actually, research technology makes a direct contribution to the content of the field in the same way that the invention of the microscope or radiotelescope shaped the content of physical science, or perhaps more exactly in the same way that Whorfians claim language shapes our thinking. We can ask of the data only questions that can be translated into specific research operations, and until such translations exist, the research questions remain purely ruminative. Thus, the existence of a national research center makes it both possible and inevitable that comparative studies of groups will take place. Thus, the statistics of correlation and partial correlation give meaning to the vague concepts of "cause," "intervening factors," "spurious relationships," and such, and thus, the development of techniques for contextual analysis focuses our attention on "social climates." The history of content in social science is the history of fad, fashion, and momentary preoccupations, but the history of research methods is one of cumulative developments which have enabled us to ask increasingly precise and sophisticated questions about human behavior. In this sense, I believe progress in social science is mostly in the ability to ask questions, not in the ability to foresee the answers.

Second, I think that this cronicle illustrates the ways in which survey analysis is much akin to artistic creation. There are so many questions which might be asked, so many correlations which can be run, so many ways in which the findings can be organized, and so few rules or precedents for making these choices that a thousand different studies could come out of the same data. Beyond his technical responsibility for guaranteeing accuracy and honest statistical calculations, the real job of the study director is to select and integrate. Of all the findings, only some should be selected for presentation, but which ones? Is this particular finding so unimportant that it should be left out as confusing to the reader, or so important that it must be reported even though it will make the results appear terribly complicated? Should we emphasize the smashing difference which is, however, "obvious," or should we give play to the puzzling surprise, even though it produces only a small difference? The 101 (an IBM machine used for cross tabulations) takes independent variables in batches of four; and having listed the seven obvious columns for cross tabulations, which "unobvious" one do you choose as a gamble for the eighth? How much attention shall we give to the client's areas of success and how much to his areas of failure? How much of the data shall we present in the report: so much that no one will read it, or so little that the reader cannot check our conclusions against the evidence? In multivariate analyses, one can produce a large range in percentages either by dividing a very few variables into fine categories (e.g., cutting income by thousands of dollars versus dividing it at the median) or by taking a larger number of items and dichotomizing them. Which is preferable? Statistics books will not help you, for the answers must come from the study director's experience and his intellectual taste, his ability to simplify but not gloss over, to be cautious, without pettifoggery, to synthesize without distorting the facts, to interpret but not project his prejudices on the data. These, I submit, are ultimately aesthetic decisions, and the process of making these decisions is much like aesthetic creation.

But all this should not be construed as support for the fallacious idea that "you can prove anything with statistics." Short of deliberate falsification, statistical data are remarkably resistant, as anyone who has desperately tried to save a pet hypothesis knows. It is almost impossible for two competent study directors to arrive at *contradictory* conclusions from the same data, but it is almost inevitable that they will differ considerably in their emphases, organization, and selection.

Thus, if survey analysis is an art, it is not an art like sculpture or painting, in which one can make almost anything out of the raw materials. Rather, it is an art very much like architecture, in which it is possible to show disciplined creativity by producing elegant structures while working with raw materials characterized by limited engineering properties and for clients with definite goals and finite budgets.

Balance between discipline and creativity is very difficult in social science. By and large, the fashionable people in sociology are "action painters" who dribble their thoughts on the canvas of the journals, unrestrained by systematic evidence, while at the opposite pole there are hordes of "engineers" who grind out academic development housing according to the mechanical formulas of elementary statistics texts. It is not easy to steer between these courses, and I am not claiming that I did so in this study, but my opinion is that the fun lies in trying to do so.

There is a lot of misery in surveys, most of the time and money going into monotonous clerical and statistical routines, with interruptions only for squabbles with the client, budget crises, petty machinations for a place in the academic sun, and social case work with neurotic graduate students. And nobody ever reads the final report. Those few moments, however, when a new set of tables comes up from the machine room and questions begin to be answered; when relationships actually hold under controls; when the pile of tables on the desk suddenly meshes to yield a coherent chapter; when in a flash you see a neat test for an interpretation; when you realize you have found out something about something important that nobody ever knew before—these are the moments that justify research.

NOTES

1. M. R. Trabue and Allan Abbott, "A Measure of the Ability to Judge Poetry," *Teacher's College Record,* XXI (1921).

TOPIC IX: Ethics and Politics of Social Research—Mutually Exclusive?

> Like any other member of an establishment, the sociologist who is a political liberal is expected to lie along with his fellow members of The Establishment, to feel the rightness of their cause and a responsibility for its success. The bias of the sociologist, then, does not derive simply from the fact that it is inherent in the human condition or in sociological research. The sociologist also lies because he is a political person. It would seem, however, that sociologists have no right to be complacent about anything that they, more than others, should have good reason to know makes liars out of them.
>
> Alvin Gouldner
> "The Sociologist As Partisan"

Gouldner's point is well taken. Sociologists are members of social groupings and subject to the same sorts of group pressures as are any individuals, especially when dealing with political issues. When social research gets tied up in the economic and political concerns of organizational society, then one must take a hard look at the actions and rationalizations of social scientists who continue to work within the context of this system.

Many researchers today have begun to take "traditional" sociology to task in just such a fashion. As Herbert Kelman states in "The Rights of the Subject in Social Research," the increased use of social research in our society and its increased relevance to public policy and social decisions have raised concern over the ethical and political implications of such research activities. Social scientists must be wary especially in their examinations of the lives of the poor and powerless, lest the results of their studies be used to control and manipulate those who already occupy the disadvantaged positions in our society. The argument was put well by Martin Nicolaus, speaking to the American Sociological Association at its 1968 convention in Boston, Massachusetts.

> Sociology is not now and never has been any kind of objective seeking–out of social truth or reality. Historically, the profession is an outgrowth of nineteenth–century European traditionalism and conservatism, wedded to twentieth–century American corporation liberalism.
>
> That is to say that the eyes of sociologists, with few but honorable (or: honorable but few) exceptions, have been turned downwards, and their palms upwards.

> Eyes down, to study the activities of the lower classes, of the *subject* population—those activities that created problems for the smooth exercise of governmental hegemony. Since the class of rulers in this society identifies itself *as* the society itself . . . therefore the problems of the ruling class get defined as *social* problems. . . . The things that are sociologically "interesting" are the things that are interesting to those who stand at the top of the mountain and feel the tremors of an earthquake.
>
> Sociologists stand guard in the garrison and report to its masters on the movements of the occupied populace. The more adventurous sociologists don the disguise of the people and go out to mix with the peasants in the "field," returning with books and articles that break the protective secrecy in which a subjugated population wraps itself, and make it more accessible to manipulation and control. . . .
>
> Unlike knowledge about trees and stones, knowledge about people directly affects what we are, what we do, what we may hope for. The corporate rulers of this society would not be spending as much money as they do for knowledge, if knowledge did not confer power. So far, sociologists have been *schlepping* this knowledge that confers power along a one-way chain, taking knowledge from the people, giving knowledge to the rulers.
>
> What if that machinery were reversed? What if the habits, problems, secrets, and unconscious motivations of the wealthy and powerful were daily scrutinized by a thousand systematic researchers, were hourly pried into, analyzed and cross-referenced, tabulated and published in a hundred inexpensive mass-circulation journals written so that even the fifteen-year-old high school dropout could understand it and predict the actions of his landlord, manipulate and control *him?*[1]

Myron Glazer, in a stimulating book (*The Research Adventure*), has cast the problem Nicolaus raises in terms of interpersonal exchange.

> Social scientists often reach understandings with respondents about the limits of their work and the protections to which informants are entitled. When these understandings concerning *personal* reciprocity are not met, social scientists may be justly accused of poor faith. In other instances, researchers adhere to the demands of *group* reciprocity and may decide to modify their own reports in order to protect the identity or legitimate interests of those they have studied. In exceptional circumstances, the investigator may actually put his materials "under lock and key" when the safety of subjects is at stake. These two components of legitimate research reciprocity are not the only instances, how-

> ever, where scholarly findings are adjusted. Respondents or sponsors have also attempted to pressure investigators when research findings seem distasteful to them. *Bureaucratic* reciprocity often occurs when the social scientist is confronted by a powerful host or sponsoring agency.
>
> Gideon Sjoberg explicitly analyzes the tension that, he feels, should exist between the social scientist and those who man the administrative control centers of modern society. Social scientists, he writes, must be committed to research that exposes even the most sensitive areas of a social system. Administrators, on the other hand, are committed to maintaining the system, gathering information that will aid them in this effort, and staving off criticism that will threaten their own position. These two divergent commitments often result in conflict. . . .[2]

The concept holding the above critique together is that of *knowledge as power.* Herbert Kelman, adopting the perspective of power and power differentials in the research process, breaks ethical and political problems down into two general areas: (1) a concern with the *processes* of obtaining the data, and (2) a concern with the *products* of the research: to what use is this knowledge put?

Kelman's discussion of process problems should bring to mind a number of ethical issues raised by authors earlier on in this volume (Martin T. Orne, John and Barbara McCarthy and Kai T. Erikson come especially to mind). What *is* ethical behavior in the data collection process? And, more importantly, can valid data be collected while adhering to ethical standards of conduct?

Irving Louis Horowitz, in "Life and Death of Project Camelot," speaks more directly to Kelman's *product* issue and the maze of political and ethical dilemmas raised by the proliferation of institutionally-sponsored large-scale social research. Can the sort of funding necessary for large-scale research projects be developed without placing the resulting data solely in the hands of a single-interest sociopolitical grouping (in Horowitz's case, studies of political revolutionaries financed by the United States Army)? And, more importantly in Horowitz's eyes, can one escape the censorship of research that large-scale funding implies? "Giving the State Department the right to screen and approve government funded social science research projects on other countries, as the President has ordered, is a supreme act of censorship."

On the other hand, if one followed the strictures layed down by Martin Nicolaus and others *against* studying certain social groupings, is one any more free of censorship in one's research activities?

The Dissection at the close of this topic chronicles one attempt on the part of activist-oriented social scientists to deal with issues raised in the topic. Against what charges will they, in their turn, have to defend themselves?

NOTES

1. Martin Nicolaus, remarks at the American Sociological Association's 1968 convention in Boston, Massachusetts.
2. Myron Glazer, *The Research Adventure* (New York: Random House, 1972), pp. 179–80.

SUGGESTED FURTHER READINGS

Beals, Ralph L. *Politics of Social Research.* Chicago: Aldine, 1968.

Becker, Howard. "Who's Side Are We On?" *Social Problems* 14 (Winter 1967): 239–48.

Horowitz, Irving Louis. *The Rise and Fall of Project Camelot.* Cambridge, Mass.: MIT Press, 1967.

Kelman, Herbert C. *A Time To Speak: On Human Values and Social Research.* San Francisco: Jossey–Bass, 1968.

Phillips, Derek L. *Abandoning Method.* San Francisco: Jossey–Bass, 1973.

Reynolds, Larry T., and Reynolds, Janice M. *The Sociology of Sociology.* New York: David McKay Co., 1970.

Sjoberg, Gideon. *Ethics, Politics and Social Research.* Cambridge, Mass.: Schenkman Publishing Co., 1967.

Stein, Maurice, and Vidich, Arthur. *Sociology on Trial.* Englewood Cliffs, N.J.: Prentice-Hall, 1963.

Vidich, Arthur, Bensman, Joseph, and Stein, Maurice. *Reflections on Community Studies.* New York: Wiley, 1964.

The Rights of the Subject in Social Research: An Analysis in Terms of Relative Power and Legitimacy

Herbert C. Kelman

The increasing use of social research in American society and its increasing relevance to public policy and social decisions have engendered widespread concerns about the ethical implications of such research activities. Briefly, these concerns are of two kinds: (*a*) concerns relating to the *processes* of social research, which are exemplified best by the issue of invasion of privacy and its various ramifications; and (*b*) concerns relating to the *products* of social research, which focus largely on the fear that social research may provide tools for controlling and manipulating human behavior and, more specifically, that these tools may be used by some segments of the society at the expense of others. . . .

The ethical problems surrounding social research, with their direct implications for human freedom, can be conceptualized in terms of the power relationship between the subjects of social research, on the one hand, and the social scientist, as well as the sponsor and user of social research, on the other hand. Ethical problems arise because of the fact that—and to the extent that—the individuals, groups, and communities that provide the data for social research are deficient in power relative to the other participants in the research process. I shall touch occasionally on the power relationships among these other participants themselves—such as that between the researcher and the research sponsor—which raise significant issues in their own right (often with implications for the research subject). The primary focus of the present analysis, however, shall be on the relative power position of the research subject.

THE POWER DEFICIENCY OF THE SUBJECT IN SOCIAL RESEARCH

The power deficiency that often characterizes the subject in social research can be traced to two sources: (*a*) his position of relative disadvantage within the social system—that is, the society in general and the particular organization in which the research is conducted; and (*b*) his position of relative disadvantage within the research situation proper. In other words, subjects for social research tend to be recruited from the relatively powerless segments of the society or organization and thus come into the research situation at a disadvantage. This disadvantage is further exacerbated by their limited power within the structure of the research situation itself.

The Subject's Position within the Social System

A great deal of social research is carried out on groups that are in some sense disadvantaged within the society: children and old people, ethnic minorities and welfare recipients, mental patients and invalids, criminals and delinquents, drug addicts and alcoholics, college sophomores and military recruits. These groups are dependent and powerless by virtue of their age, their physical and mental condition, their economic and political position, their educational level, their social deviance, or their captive status within various institutions.

Various reasons can be cited for the tendency to focus so much social research on disadvantaged groups. To a large extent, this tendency is a reflection of what is taken as problematic within the society and within its research community (cf. Kelman, 1970b, pp. 82–84). Two strands of problem definition seem to be converging on the disadvantaged groups. On the one hand, the established segments of society are concerned with the control of social deviance and the management of social dependency. Insofar as social scientists themselves tend to come from the middle classes, they share this concern. More importantly, however, this concern is part of the mission of many of the agencies, both public and private, that sponsor social research, and is, therefore, reflected in the kinds of research questions to which investigators address themselves and hence the populations from whom they seek their data. On the other hand, many social scientists—and some of the agencies sponsoring social research—are rooted in a tradition of "social problems" research and strongly committed to social welfare and social reform. They are concerned with helping individuals and communities who, for one or another reason, are troubled and powerless. This concern often leads them to focus their research on the disadvantaged groups themselves. In short, social research—whether out of a concern with social control or social change or some combination of the two—often has defined its problems in a way that calls for subjects from among the disadvantaged segments of the society.

Another important reason for the tendency to draw disproportionately on disadvantaged groups in the recruitment of subjects for social research is the greater availability of these groups. Practical considerations of availability of subjects often determine which of a number of potentially relevant populations an investigator studies. In fact, an investigator may study a population less relevant to his problem simply because it is more available, or he even may choose his research problem in terms of considerations of availability, In general, members of disadvantaged groups are more readily available precisely because of their power deficiency. Investigators can induce them more easily to participate in research that members of more powerful groups would find objectionable, and more securely expect them to put up with procedures that higher status subjects would challenge. In most cases, they lack both the ability and the habit of "talking back." Rightly or wrongly, they perceive themselves as having no choice, particularly since the investigators are usually higher in status and since the agencies sponsoring and conducting the research may represent (or at least appear to represent) the very groups on which the subjects are dependent. The link between dependence and availability is, of course, very direct in those situations in which the research is conducted in the context of an institution where the subject is held "captive" or is in a clearly defined position of lower status. The institutionalized child, the hospitalized patient, the prison or reformatory inmate, the army recruit, and the grade school pupil are almost automatically available as subjects for research conducted or approved by institutional authorities. Similarly, though the university is not a "total institution" in the same sense as a mental hospital or a prison (cf. Goffman, 1961), psychological and social research has relied so heavily on college sophomores for its subjects because of their relative availability in that organizational context.

The last examples call attention to the fact that the subject's power deficiency often is based not only on his position in the society at large, but also on his position within the particular organization in which the research is conducted. Typically, research in organizational contexts is sponsored by those in high-status positions who "own" the organization, while the data are obtained from those in low-status positions. For example, social research in industry usually is sponsored by top management, but the data are provided by blue-collar workers and now more frequently by middle-level management. Insofar as the research is related to the way in which the organization is run—to questions of personnel policies, for instance—it has direct consequences for members in lower status positions. Yet the research usually is focused on those issues that top management considers problematic. The less powerful segments of the organization generally lack the familiarity with social research as a potentially useful tool for their own purposes, the financial and manpower resources to carry out such research, and the ability to elicit the ready cooperation of the organization's higher echelons.

The uneven distribution of resources also plays a major role in the selection of societies and communities as subjects for social research. At this level too we find a considerable discrepancy in power between those who conduct social research and those who serve as its subjects. Social scientists from the more affluent and powerful industrialized nations often go to developing countries to carry out their research; very rarely, however, do African, Asian, or Latin American social scientists come to study conditions in the more industrialized parts of the world. Similarly, within the United States, social research often has been carried out by members of the white middle class, collecting their data in black, Puerto Rican, Indian, or poor white communities; very rarely has the pattern been reversed. Thus, within the context of the international system or the national system, we see again that the subjects for social research tend to be drawn from the communities in disadvantaged and relatively powerless positions. The more powerful communities are generally the only ones who have the resources to carry out social research and who are thus in a position to define what is problematic. At the same time, they are better able to resist intrusions from the outside and thus to avoid being studied themselves.

In sum, the subjects in social research tend to be drawn disproportionately from the disadvantaged segments in the society, from the lower status positions in the organizations in which the research is carried out, and from the less affluent and powerful communities in the national and international systems. Their power deficiency within the social system places them at a disadvantage vis-à-vis the more powerful agencies that sponsor and conduct the research. It increases their vulnerability with respect both to their recruitment as subjects and to their treatment in the research situation. That is, they have (or at least feel that they have) less freedom to refuse participation in the research and less leverage to protect themselves against procedures that they may find objectionable. Furthermore, the subjects' power deficiency reduces the likelihood that the products of the research will accrue to their benefit. Their own groups typically have no voice in determining the questions to which the research is to be addressed, in terms of *their* definition of what is problematic, nor do they have the resources to make use of the research findings. Thus, the subjects lack the power to counteract the possibility that the research in which they participate may be irrelevant or even antagonistic to their own interests.

The Subject's Position within the Research Situation

Regardless of his position in society, the subject's position within the research situation itself generally places him at a disadvantage. The investigator usually defines and takes charge of the situation on his own terms and in line with his own values and norms, and the subject has only limited opportunity to question the procedures. This is particularly true when the research is carried out in a setting "owned" by the investigator (such as a research laboratory) and utilizes structured techniques (such as experimental tasks, questionnaires, interviews, or psychological tests). Once a person agrees to come to the laboratory or to carry out a research procedure, he subjects himself to the control of the investigator—as the very use of the term "subject" implies. When the research is carried out in a setting owned by the subject and takes the form of observing the natural flow of ongoing behavior (as in studies of organizations or communities utilizing participant observation), the investigator's control is far less extensive. He is not in a position to structure the behavior of his subjects and he is expected to adhere to the norms of the setting. Yet, even in this type of research, once members of an organization or community open their doors to an investigator, they relinquish a considerable degree of their control to him, since they usually have only limited knowledge of what is being observed and to what use these observations will be put. Of course, if observations are carried out without the subjects' knowledge, then their control of the situation is reduced even further.

The power deficiency of the subject within the research situation derives from the structure of that situation itself, rather than from the subject's position in the society or organization. The situation-linked disadvantage of the subject, however, is especially pronounced if his societal or organizational status is relatively low. Low-status and dependent subjects do not have—or at least do not avail themselves of—the full degree of countervailing power with which the research situation provides the subject. Potentially, the subject's power in his relationship with the investigator is not inconsiderable, since the investigator's ability to carry out his research ultimately depends on the subject's cooperation. Although the subject relinquishes control over the situation once he agrees to participate, he must first be induced to enter into the agreement; and, furthermore, if he finds the situation sufficiently distasteful, he may withdraw from the agreement despite the embarrassment that such a step would entail. But subjects who occupy low-status or dependent positions in the society or organization are less likely to see themselves as having the option to refuse participation in the research, or to withdraw once they have entered the situation.[1] Compared to higher status subjects, they are more reluctant to question or challenge the investigator, and—even if they were inclined to raise questions—they usually have less of the knowledge required to raise them effectively. They still have some power in the situation—the power to undermine the research by providing false information, performing the required task improperly, or engaging in some other form of subtle sabotage. Such efforts at undermining research have become a very real possibility, for example, in laboratory experiments in psychology carried out on college campuses, often with a more or less captive subject population. Typically, however, subjects will not engage in deliberate acts of sabotage, as long as they accept the legitimacy of the investigator and the research situation.

Two closely interrelated factors limit the subject's exercise of power in the research situation: he perceives himself as lacking both the *capacity* and the *right* to question the research procedures. Although the strength of these factors is likely to vary, as we have already seen, as a function of the subject's position in the society or organization, basically they are built into the structure of the research situation. The subject feels that he lacks the capacity to question research procedures because he does not have the necessary informational base for doing so. It is usually presumed, particularly if the research is carried out in an institutional setting (such as a university or a hospital), that the investigator has the credentials required for running the study. If he did not, then presumably he would not be there. Thus, the subject usually takes it for granted that the investigator knows what he is doing and that he is proceeding from information that the subject himself could not possibly have. Not only does the investigator have expertise and specialized knowledge in the field which the subject usually does not possess, but he is also operating in a situation that is constructed entirely by him and defined in his own terms. The investigator is the only one who knows the dimensions of the situation, who knows the nature of the business to be transacted and the way in which it is to be transacted. Under the circumstances, the subject feels that he lacks the information that would enable him to question the investigator's actions, to challenge him, or to disagree with him.

The investigator's specialized knowledge and expertise are a major component of his perceived legitimacy in the eyes of the subject. That is, his expertness contributes to the subject's view that the investigator has the right to set rules and prescribe behavior in this situation, and that the subject, in turn—having submitted himself to the investigator's authority—does not have the right to question these procedures. Clearly, there are limits to what a subject will do without question, and these limits are reached more quickly in some situations than in others and by some subjects than by others. There is considerable evidence, however, that at least in certain laboratory situations, many subjects will engage in behaviors that are highly distasteful and potentially harmful to themselves or to others when such behaviors are required by the experimenter (e.g., Milgram, 1963; Orne & Evans, 1965). At the very least it can be said that, insofar as subjects accept the investigator's legitimacy, they are reluctant to *claim* the right to question his procedures.

The investigator's presumed expertness is one of a number of features of the research situation that jointly enhance his legitimacy in the eyes of the subjects and hence his relative power over them. There are usually indications that the investigator's role is socially recognized and supported. He often carries out the research in the name of or under the sponsorship of an official agency or prestigious institution. When the research actually is carried out in the setting of a university or a hospital or a government facility, then the institutional aura of legitimacy spreads to the research situation. The investigator may also be covered and surrounded by some of the trappings of legitimacy—such as the white coat, the sign on the door, the diploma on the wall, or the expensive equipment. Furthermore, legitimacy that inheres in other institutional roles often is transferred to the research situation; for example, when research on students is carried out or sponsored by a professor, research on patients by a physician, or research on citizens by a government agency, the investigator's legitimacy in the research situation is enhanced by his relationship to the subject outside of the research situation. Finally, a major contributor to the investigator's perceived legitimacy is the acceptance of science as a general value within the society. The subject feels obliged to cooperate with and reluctant to question procedures that are presented to him in the name of science. In the context of a scientific study, he does not feel entitled to challenge the investigator merely because he finds a procedure personally uncomfortable or distasteful.

It is interesting to note that, in some sense, the value society places on science gives the scientific investigator even greater power over his subject than the physician has over his patient in the usual medical relationship. The physician has a great deal of power because he possesses specialized knowledge and expertise that the patient does not have, particularly since this knowledge relates to questions of life and death for the patient; because he is higher in social status than the average patient; and because he is supported fully by the trappings of legitimacy. Yet, the fact remains that the physician's task is to serve the patient and to meet his interests. Ultimately, the patient is expected to follow his instructions because it is in his own interest to do so. The instructions of the scientist, on the other hand, are not even subject to that restriction, since they are legitimized by a social value that supposedly transcends the interests of the indivisual subject. Thus, the subject does not have the "right"—as does the patient—to bring his own interests into consideration. Clearly, the position of greatest power vis-à-vis the subject is held by the medical researcher, since he can draw both on the physician's link to matters of life and death and on the scientist's link to overarching values. The social and behavioral scientist does not have quite as great a power advantage over his subject, but he too operates in a research situation whose structure and governing values make it difficult for the subject to question its procedures. . . .

ETHICAL PROBLEMS RELATING TO THE PROCESSES OF SOCIAL RESEARCH

In speaking of the processes of social research, I refer to the experiences of the specific individuals (or groups or communities) who participate in the research as subjects—who provide the data for it. How are they recruited for the experiment, the survey, or the community study in which they participate? How are they treated in the course of these procedures—that is, what kinds of experience do these represent for them? What are the consequences of their participation for them, both in the short run and in the long run? Questions about the long-run consequences of participation, particularly when these involve consequences for a group or community, overlap with the questions relating to the products of social research to which I shall address myself later. My focus at present, however, is not so much on the consequences of the knowledge (in the sense of a social product) that has been generated by the research and that may now be put to some particular social uses, as it is on the consequences of a group's having participated in the research, having revealed certain information, and having in some sense increased their own vulnerability.

Some Illustrative Problems

Some of the ethical concerns that have been voiced about one or another piece of social research have included the point that it represents an invasion of the subject's privacy, an imposition on him, or an exploitation of him; that it deceives the subject about the true nature of the research; or that participation may be harmful to the subject because it disturbs his psychological well-being or because the data may be used somehow to his disadvantage. Let us examine some of these concerns as they apply to research carried out in different settings.

One of the particular settings to which I have addressed myself in some detail (see, e.g., Kelman, 1968, chap.8) is that of the social-psychological laboratory. My major concern has been with the extensive use of deception in the conduct of laboratory experiments in social psychology (and in certain other areas of psychology as well). Deception is used because many of the phenomena that the psychologist hopes to observe would be destroyed if he revealed the true purpose of the experiment to his subjects. For example, if an experiment were designed to study the conditions under which an individual conforms to the judgments of the majority, knowledge of this fact would so alter the subject's behavior that it would no longer be relevant to the question posed by the experiment. The medical researcher finds himself in a comparable situation when he uses placebos in drug studies: to reveal to a patient that he has been given a placebo would destroy the very reaction for which the placebo is designed to control. In general, however, the situation of the medical scientist is different from that of the behavioral scientist. When he uses deception it is often as a way of assuring readier cooperation on the subject's part. On the other hand, when the behavioral scientist uses deception, it is often integral to the nature of his study. Without deception, it would be impossible—at least within the limits of our current research technology—to obtain the kind of information that many psychological experiments are designed to produce.

Thus, the experimental social psychologist is confronted with a conflict of values. On the one hand, the use of deception is ethically objectionable. On the other hand, however, certain lines of research cannot be pursued without the use of some deception. For those who value these lines of research because they represent contributions to knowledge—perhaps even to the betterment of the human condition—it is difficult, therefore, to take the absolutist position that a psychologist must refrain from using deception in his experiments under any and all conditions. Even granting the relativist position, however, there remains the question of the extent to which deception is used, the circumstances under which it is used, and the way in which it is used. Before deciding to use deception, an experimenter ought to give very serious consideration to three dimensions: (*a*) the importance of the study, which refers not only to its scientific significance (admittedly a subjective judgment), but also to the stage of research that it represents (e.g., exploratory versus final); (*b*) the availability of alternative (deception-free) methods capable of producing at least comparable information; and (*c*) the noxiousness of the deception, which refers both to the degree of deception involved and to the probability of harmful consequences.[2] These three considerations must be put into the balance before deciding on the use of deception. Only if a study is very important and no alternative methods are available can anything more than the mildest form of deception be justified. In other words, even if deception is not eliminated entirely from the repertory of the social psychologist, it ought to be used only in rare cases and under highly circumscribed conditions. What has concerned deeply some critics of deception, like myself, has been the fact that, by the early 1960s, deception in social-psychological experiments had been routinized and escalated to such an extent that it was used as a matter of course and often took rather elaborate forms. Fortunately, the last few years have seen increasing sensitivity to this problem within the field, as part of a general reexamination of the role of experimental methodology (cf. Miller, 1972).

Deception presents special problems when it is used in an experiment that is stressful, unpleasant, or potentially harmful to the subject, in the sense that it may create self-doubts, lower his self-esteem, reveal some of his weaknesses, or create temporary conflict, frustration, or anxiety. By deceiving the subject about the nature of the experiment, the experimenter deprives him of the freedom to decide whether or not he wants to be exposed to these potentially disturbing experiences. It is, of course, true that whenever people engage in social interaction, they risk the occurrence of such experiences. This fact, however, does not in and of itself justify exposing subjects to these risks—without their explicit knowledge—for purposes of social research. In real-life situations, the person engages in social interactions for his own purposes and he takes whatever risks (such as an unexpected blow to his self-esteem) these interactions entail. Similar risks are taken by his partners in the interaction. By contrast, the experimental situation is one that is constructed by the experimenter for his own purposes and in which the subject participates largely for the benefit of the experimenter and as a service to the larger social good that the research is seen to represent. Moreover, the interaction lacks reciprocity since the experimenter does not expose himself to the same kinds of risks as the subject in the interaction proper (although he does, of course, risk his scientific reputation in every experiment he undertakes). Under the circumstances, it is ethically questionable to ask a subject to participate in an experiment that might expose him to potentially disturbing experiences without informing him of the nature of the risks entailed. Questions arise even if the risks are no greater than those involved in day-to-day social interaction; they become especially serious if the experiment is so structured that a higher than usual degree of stress or self-doubt is generated in the subject.

The use of deception presents ethical problems even when the experiment does not entail potential harm or discomfort for the subject. Deception violates the respect to which all fellow humans are entitled and the trust that is basic to all interpersonal relationships. Such violations are doubly disturbing since they contribute, in this age of mass society, to the already powerful tendencies to manufacture realities and manipulate populations. Furthermore, by undermining the basis of trust in the relationship between investigator and subject, deception makes it increasingly difficult for social scientists to carry out their work in the future. Subjects will be less inclined to cooperate in social research and, even if they do participate, to believe the investigator's definition of the situation and thus to react spontaneously within the terms of that definition. The effects of such "pollution" of the research environment are discussed in a paper by Donald Warwick (1971).

The ethical problems often raised by social research manifest themselves more clearly when the research is carried out in a laboratory setting since the setting is almost entirely under the investigator's control and he, therefore, enjoys (as mentioned earlier) a considerable power advantage over the subject. However, similar problems, with varying degrees of severity, can arise when research is carried out in "natural" settings—that is, when the investigator goes to the subject, rather than having the subject come to him. Warwick's paper is devoted to a case study of precisely such a piece of research which combined the methods of participant observation and the survey interview. To be sure, that study is atypical and raises more thorny ethical questions than most studies in its genre do, but it does illustrate that the ethical dilemmas of social research are by no means unique to a particular methodology.

Research based on participant observation inevitably raises some concerns about the invasion of subjects' privacy. When the observation is disguised, these concerns become particularly serious and parallel those raised by deception in the laboratory (see Erikson, 1967). A social scientist, for example, who joins an organization in order to make observations, and misinforms or fails to inform the group about the nature of his activities, clearly is invading his subjects' privacy without giving them any choice in the matter. They may be revealing information that they would not have wanted to reveal to an outsider, particularly if they are deliberately keeping their activities or part of their activities secret. Insofar as the observer pretends to be a member, he deprives the group of the opportunity to decide what to reveal or not to reveal to a nonmember.

Some ethical problems, less severe in nature, arise even if the participant-observer acknowledges his research interest and is accepted in the group on that basis. The role of the participant-observer creates many ambiguities, in that the social scientist is seen as neither a full-fledged member nor a complete outsider. Sometimes, in fact, the observer himself is unclear about his role; he may be a sympathizer or even a genuine member of the organization that he is observing, or he may become committed to it as his research proceeds. In view of these ambiguities, the members of the group may come to accept the observer and act "naturally" in his presence. They may thus reveal information that they might prefer to keep private, not because they are uninformed about the observer's purposes, but because they have learned to ignore him. As a matter of fact, the success of a participant-observer can be measured precisely by the extent to which he stays in the background, without intruding in the normal flow of activities, and is ignored by the members of the group. In and of itself, this state of affairs is not objectionable from an ethical point of view. If the observer has explained fully the purposes of his research, then the group members are aware of his interest in observing the normal, spontaneous flow of their activities. Once they have agreed to this arrangement, it is up to them to take the necessary steps if there are certain aspects of their normal activities that they would rather keep private. Ethical problems arise, however, when the observer deliberately takes advantage of the ambiguity of his role to seduce group members to give him information that they might not have revealed otherwise. This would happen, for example, if by implying a greater level of commitment to the organization than he actually felt, he gained access to esoteric knowledge or to the inner circle of organizational decision making. The temptation to take advantage of the ambiguities inherent in his role places a considerable ethical burden on the participant observer.

Research in natural settings that uses unobtrusive measures—that is, in which the investigator makes systematic observations of some aspect of his subjects' behavior without their awareness that these observations are taking place—presents problems similar to those of unacknowledged participant observation. The ethical issues are less severe when the observations focus on naturally occurring events that are essentially public—for example, on behavior in streets, in trains, in restaurants, or in department stores. In these situations, the subject clearly knows that his behavior is observable by outsiders; what he does not know is that some of these outsiders are there specifically for the purpose of making systematic observations of his behavior. Greater ambiguities arise when the social scientist has gained access to observations that are not generally public, or when he has introduced experimental manipulations into the natural situation.

The experimental manipulation of natural settings may take various forms. In one of the oldest studies in this genre, Hartmann (1936) systematically varied the type of appeal used in political leaflets sent out to different segments of the population in the course of an actual election campaign and then compared the effectiveness of these appeals. In other studies, experimenters stage little happenings in public places or make certain requests of passersby or sales clerks, and then observe their reactions; by varying systematically some aspect of the staged event or of the request, they are able to assess the effects of relevant experimental variables. The use of experiments in natural settings has increased greatly in recent years, partly in response to the increasing realization of the limitations of laboratory experiments in social psychology. Some highly ingenious naturalistic experiments have been and are being carried out, for example, in the area of helping behavior (e.g., Bryan & Test, 1967; Latané, 1970; Piliavin, Rodin, & Piliavin, 1969). Campbell (1969) has argued very persuasively for the value of this type of research in "producing a nontrivial social science [p. 370]." Its unique value, however, rests on the fact that the subject is unaware of his participation in an experiment—and this is precisely one of the more disturbing features of this type of research from an ethical point of view. The laboratory experiment, even when it uses deception, at least gives the subject the chance to decide whether or not to participate; the naturalistic experiment, of the type discussed here, deprives him of that choice.

There is, of course, as Campbell pointed out, considerable variation in the severity of the ethical problems raised by different experiments in this genre. On the one hand, we may have a study in which some minor variations are introduced in an ongoing activity, such as a street collection for a charity or a solicitation of signatures on a petition; the variation may consist in the status of the solicitor (his age, his style of dress) or in the presence of a positive or negative model. This type of study presents no serious ethical problems. The deception and intrusion involved are rather mild since "the experimental treatment falls within the range of the respondent's ordinary experience, merely being an experimental rearrangement of normal-level communications [Campbell, 1969, p. 371]." At the other extreme, to take a hypothetical example, we may have a study in which the experimenter's accomplice feigns a heart attack in a public place under varying experimental conditions and an observer notes the amount and type of help that people offer him. Such a procedure, on the basis of a rather massive deception, places the subject in a situation that may constitute a considerable imposition and that may (whether or not he decides to help the victim) be very disturbing to him—without giving him any choice in the matter at all. The fact that such events may occur naturally does not, of course, justify staging them for research purposes. In the long run, the proliferation of such experiments would add to the already considerable degree of deceit and irrationality that pervades modern life. Increasing public awareness that such experiments are taking place would add not only to the "pollution" of the research environment, which I have already mentioned, but also to the ambiguity of real-life situations that call for helping behavior. In some respects, the long-term implications of active deception in naturalistic experiments are even more disquieting than those in laboratory experiments, since the laboratory at least represents a situation that is by definition isolated from the rest of life and in which the subject is aware that certain unusual procedures are likely to be introduced.

Research based on the use of unobtrusive measures and disguised experimental treatments again presents us with a difficult dilemma. It certainly can be argued that, from a methodological point of view, social research is often at its best when the subject is unaware that he is being studied. Such research also may yield knowledge that may be of great social significance—such as knowledge about the conditions under which people will extend or refuse help to those in need. Yet, there are some difficult ethical problems inherent in this type of research. As in other lines of research, the severity of the ethical problems raised by the research must be weighed against its importance and the unavailability of alternative procedures.

Survey research, which generally is carried out in the setting of the respondent's home, is less beset by problems of deception and disguise than some of the other approaches that have been discussed so far. It may, of course, happen that a survey researcher will misrepresent the organization that is conducting the survey or the overall purpose of the survey. Such misrepresentations, however, are in no way inherent in survey methodology and are frowned upon by reputable survey research organizations. On the other hand, the investigator does not necessarily give the respondent complete information about the study. Although the purpose of the interview is often transparent and the questions straightforward, the interviewer may be pursuing certain specific hypotheses that he does not reveal to the respondent, and he deliberately may introduce some questions that are indirect or that have no obvious relationship to the topic of the interview. As long as the interview is not marked by any major hidden agenda, however, the pursuit of such hypotheses and the use of such questions are well within the terms of the contract formed when the respondent agrees to be interviewed.

There are certain other ethical problems that survey research brings into focus. The mere fact that an interviewer arrives at someone's doorstep to ask questions, often without prior arrangement, may represent an imposition and an unacceptable invasion of privacy. It may place the respondent in a position of being induced to reveal information that he might prefer not to reveal. If he does not have any information about a subject on which he is questioned, or if he lacks an opinion on a matter on which he feels that he is expected to have an opinion (and the very fact that he is asked questions on the topic implies such an expectation), then he may feel embarrassed and exposed and he may experience a lowering of his self-esteem. Sometimes he may feel embarrassed and uncomfortable about the opinions that he does have, since he may feel that the interviewer disapproves of them. A well-trained interviewer, of course, does not communicate disapproval and structures the situation so that the respondent will not experience any embarrassment, but the possibility of such reactions still remains. I do not wish to imply that these are, in most cases, profoundly disturbing experiences; in many respects, as Warwick (1971) has pointed out, the experience of being interviewed may in fact be highly rewarding for the respondent. It must be remembered, however, that survey research does represent some invasion of privacy, which is particularly troublesome if the respondent feels a lack of choice about his participation in the interview. From a broader social point of view, there is also the question of the extent to which the proliferation of survey research may add to the already considerable erosion of privacy in our society.

When interviews, questionnaires, or psychological tests are administered to a delimited population—such as the workers in an industrial firm, the students in a high school, or the welfare recipients in a community—then the problem of anonymity takes on special significance. If an individual's responses became known to the factory management, the school administration, or the welfare agency, they might have potentially damaging consequences for him. Under such circumstances, negligence in protecting the respondent's anonymity would constitute a serious ethical violation. In reporting his findings, the investigator must remove not only the names of the respondents, but also any other information that might—given the context of a delimited organization or community—provide clues to his identity. If, in fact, the data collected are to be used not only for purposes of research, but also for some subsequent decisions about individual respondents—for example, decisions relating to their employment status or their admission to an educational program—then the investigator must make it perfectly clear at the outset that the usual guarantees of anonymity do not hold. It would be very dangerous, from the point of view both of the rights of the subject and of the integrity of social research, for an investigator to countenance any ambiguity between research uses and administrative uses of his procedures.

Even when the anonymity of the individual respondent is clearly assured, the research may have potentially damaging consequences for any group whose data are reported separately. For example, findings in a survey conducted in an industrial organization about the distribution of attitudes in different units may provide the basis for a reorganization or some special treatment of one or another of these units; these changes may or may not be desirable from the point of view of the workers involved. These are the types of concerns that have made some members of the black community wary of questionnaires and psychological tests. They are afraid that responses of blacks (e.g., on children's achievement tests) may compare unfavorably with those of whites (because of biased instruments or for other reasons), and that these findings may then be used to their group's disadvantage in the formulation of policy decisions. The basic concern here, actually, is with the product of the research and the social uses to which it is put—issues that I pursue in a later section. For the present purposes, the main point is that members of a minority group may feel that participation in this type of research would increase their vulnerability, and that these feelings often may be justified. Under the circumstances, it is incumbent upon the investigator to conduct and communicate his research in a way that will minimize the vulnerability of the group he studies, and to afford his potential subjects a genuine choice about their participation in the research.

When research in the black or other minority communities is carried out by white investigators, it also raises special questions about the invasion of the group's privacy and exploitation of its resources by outsiders. These concerns about the danger that information revealed in the course of the research may be damaging to the interests of the community, are very similar to those that have arisen in the context of research in foreign areas. Along with other social scientists, I have been concerned particularly about the implications of research conducted by American or European scholars in developing countries (see Kelman, 1968, chaps. 3 and 4). Some of the problems that arise in this setting have been highlighted by such incidents as Project Camelot (see Horowitz, 1967). In foreign area research, the general concern with invasion of privacy is exacerbated by the fact that the researcher is a foreigner who will report his findings to other foreigners; the subjects easily can feel that they are being treated as specimens to be put on display before a curious audience that may denigrate their way of life because of insufficient understanding of it or sympathy for it. Concern with exploitation arises particularly when investigators from industrialized nations come into less-developed countries to collect data for their own research, often with the help of local resources, and then export these data to advance their own careers abroad without making sure that sufficient benefits accrue to the society providing the data. Finally, there is the concern that research by outsiders in less-developed areas may represent direct or indirect intervention in the affairs of the countries studied, or at least that it may be used, in some fashion, to promote the interests of the more powerful sponsoring country at the expense of the weaker and poorer host country. Project Camelot is a good example of a research program that created resentment and suspicion in Latin America, where many saw it as having been designed for purposes of intelligence and intervention. Although there is no evidence that the project was designed for these purposes, the auspices under which it was organized and the framework within which it was conceived made these suspicions more than reasonable. Much of social research carried out in developing countries has been quite oblivious to these ethical issues, but since the fiasco of Project Camelot they have been discussed widely and considered seriously among social scientists.

My discussion of the many ethical problems engendered by social research in its various settings was not meant to imply that all social research is an ethical morass. I have mentioned various practices and consequences because they can and do occur, not necessarily because they are typical occurrences. Some are fairly widespread, being built into particular traditions; others are quite rare. In large proportions of social research, the subject's treatment can by no means be described as degrading, overly intrusive, or potentially harmful. In fact, participation in social research often may represent an enriching and personally satisfying experience for the subject. In short, I am not proposing that any of the lines of research that I have discussed ought to be abandoned (although some do deserve serious reexamination, from an ethical as well as a methodological point of view). My purpose is to point out ethical pitfalls that call for our active awareness.

There are various ways of looking at the ethical pitfalls that I have enumerated. In keeping with the conceptual orientation of the present article, I shall look at them as questions about the way in which the social researcher uses his power. Research procedures that involve potential ethical violations correspond to illegitimate uses of the investigator's power. When we say that an investigator has invaded a domain that the subject has the right to keep private, or that he has limited the subject's freedom to decide on his own participation or to protect his own interests, or that he has induced the subject to take actions or reveal information that may be personally damaging to him, or that he has been unresponsive to the norms of the group he has studied, we are in effect suggesting that he may have abused his power—that he may have used it in an arbitrary fashion. The legitimate use of power presupposes adherence to shared norms that govern the relationship between the two parties. The central norm governing the relationship of investigator and subject is that of voluntary informed consent, and ethical problems generally arise because this norm has been violated or circumvented. Voluntary consent is impossible to the extent that the subjects constitute a captive audience or are unaware of the fact that they are being studied. Informed consent is impossible to the extent that subjects' participation is solicited under false pretenses or they are deceived about the true nature of the research. If investigators were to adhere scrupulously to the norm of consent and related principles, then most of the ethical problems would be avoided or corrected for readily. The question is how such adherence can be facilitated.

Some Corrective Approaches

. . . Commitment to the principle of voluntary informed consent, however, cannot by itself resolve the major ethical issues, since a great deal depends on the degree to which and the manner in which the principle is implemented. Implementation of the principle is by no means straightfoward; there is no simple, universally acceptable set of rules that can be followed. Total adherence to the principle is impossible if any research is to take place at all. For one thing, many kinds of research—such as research with small children, or research using unobtrusive measures—would have to be ruled out entirely, unless the principle is adjusted to special circumstances. Even if we were prepared to rule out all such research, a literal adherence to the principle would be physically impossible (see Parsons, 1969). The investigator cannot give the subject the precise reason for every question he asks and every procedure he uses, nor can he remove from his sample all those who conceivably might be participating out of some sense of obligation. Thus, the operational meaning of voluntary informed consent must remain in an area of judgment. In implementing the principle, some decision has to be made about what constitutes, under varying circumstances, consent that is sufficiently voluntary and sufficiently informed. Furthermore, implementation usually involves some translation of the principle into a specific procedure, such as the signing of a consent form. Any such procedure easily can become routinized and ritualized, thus pushing the ethical issue just one step further back. That is, it is quite possible for subjects to be deprived of the opportunity for voluntary informed consent to the act of signing the consent forms, as has indeed happened in certain areas of medical research (see, e.g., Lear, 1966).

Since implementing the principle of voluntary informed consent requires subjective judgments and is open to the possibility of routinized tokenism, we clearly need more than a set of formal procedures to insure genuine consent. The atmosphere and structure of the investigator-subject interaction must be such that the subject has both the opportunity and the capacity to make meaningful choices. It is in this context that my earlier remarks about the power relationship between investigator and subject become particularly germane. The subject's relative power deficiency makes it difficult and sometimes impossible to achieve a genuine voluntary informed consent. Power deficiencies deriving from the subject's position in the society or organization tend to militate against *voluntary* consent. Members of low-status or dependent groups are limited (or at least feel limited) in their ability to withhold consent, both at the point of recruitment as subjects and at other choice points throughout the research. Quite often, they do not feel free to refuse participation, to abstain from procedures that they find distasteful, or to withdraw from the study once it is underway. In short, they are less able to mount countervailing power against that of the investigator and thus have less control over their participation and experiences as subjects. Power deficiencies deriving from the subject's position within the research situation proper tend to militate against *informed* consent. Since the research situation is constructed by the investigator and defined in his terms, the subject must depend on him for the information he needs in deciding about his own participation and continuation in the study. His information thus tends to be limited, particularly if he is deceived about the nature of the experiment or kept in the dark about certain features of the situation.

To create the structural conditions for more truly voluntary informed consent, we need collective efforts and institutional mechanisms that will help to overcome the subject's power deficiency by increasing his participation in the research and, most importantly, by providing him with countervailing power in his relationship to the investigator. The need is not just for greater sensitivity and goodwill on the part of the investigator (though these too are essential), but for institutionalized patterns that would define the rights and obligations vested in the role of both investigator and subject. Such patterns would be designed to assure that the norm of voluntary informed consent is adhered to as fully and as scrupulously as possible; and, to the extent that other necessities dictate certain adjustments in adherence to this norm, that such adjustments are kept within the limits of legitimacy. I mention here some of the forms that such institutionalized mechanisms might take. . . .

PATTERNS OF RESEARCH

A major barrier to correcting ethically questionable procedures in social research is the fact that some of these procedures have become institutionalized. For example, the use of deception has been a standard feature of social–psychological experiments for some time; deception experiments have served as the basis for many PhD theses and many journal articles; in fact, some major research traditions are built almost entirely on this procedure. Under these circumstances, even an investigator who has become sensitive to the ethical implications of the procedures he uses and concerned about them finds it difficult to abandon them entirely. He may try to correct for them—as many social psychologists have done, for example, by giving careful attention to the postexperimental feedback, in which they explain to the subjects the nature of the deception and the reasons for its use—but such corrections, though valuable, are designed to retain rather than to abandon the basic procedure. No scientist will give up readily a procedure that has been successful in producing results (both in terms of scientific knowledge and in terms of career advancement). Change does take place, however, within a community of scientists if new procedures are developed and prove to be at least as effective in producing results as the old procedures.

One major corrective approach, then, to the ethical ambiguities of social research is the active development and the institutionalization of alternative research models that call for an ethically sounder relationship between investigator and subject. The models I have in mind can be characterized as *participatory research,* in that they are designed to involve the subject as an active participant in a joint effort with the investigator. The procedures would depend on the subject's positive motivations to contribute to the research enterprise—because he has been persuaded of the importance of the research, or because he finds the procedures intrinsically rewarding, or because he feels that he has a unique contribution to make, or because he has a special stake in the outcome of the investigation. . . .

In experimental social psychology, the search for more participatory research approaches might take the form of further exploration and development of procedures based on some form of role playing (Kelman, 1968, pp. 223–225). In role-playing experiments, observations and data are provided by the subject's performance in what he knows to be a make-believe situation. Subjects can become highly involved in a role-playing experience, both because the laboratory situation may be inherently engrossing and because their interest in actively contributing to the research may have been mobilized. Role-playing experiments may take various forms. Perhaps the simplest form is one that replicates a standard laboratory experiment, except that the subject is told ahead of time that the experimental minipulations are make believe; in other words, the subject is asked to play the role of a subject in a deception experiment.[3] A form of role playing that may on occasion be very elaborate and complex involves laboratory simulation, in which subjects are asked to take roles in a laboratory model of some aspect of the real world (e.g., the roles of political decision makers in the international system); here the subject is asked to play a real-life role, rather than merely the role of a subject. Another variant of role playing makes use of structured game situations, which (like "Monopoly" or other parlor games) can be highly involving, even though the participant knows that "it is only a game." I do not believe that all of the phenomena with which experimental social psychologists have been concerned can suitably be studied through role-playing techniques; I do believe, however, that the potential uses of these techniques are greater than we have realized so far. There is a need to explore the circumstances under which role-playing techniques would be suitable—or more precisely, the specific purposes to which different types of role playing can be applied.

In survey research, it is commonly assumed that "elite interviews"—that is, interviews with political leaders, business leaders, or other high-status personages—require a somewhat different orientation than ordinary interviews. Usually, in structuring such an interview, the interviewer makes it clear to the respondent that he regards him as an expert who can make a unique contribution to the research enterprise by drawing on his special knowledge and experience. The respondent thus becomes an active partner in the research, who gains satisfaction from the utilization of his expertise and the knowledge that he is making a unique contribution. This kind of orientation is characteristic of the interviews conducted by anthropologists with informants in the field (see Mead, 1969). One way of moving in the direction of more participatory research would be to extend this model to all survey interviews—to treat all respondents as elite respondents. To be sure, the respondent in a sample survey is not selected because of his expertise, but he does have special knowledge and experience to bring to the interview. The interview is concerned with his personal opinions, beliefs, and experiences—matters on which he clearly has unique information to contribute. When the interview is oriented toward these special contributions, it becomes more of a partnership in a joint enterprise for the two participants. . . .

None of these examples of participatory research provides a completely satisfactory solution to the ethical dilemmas that have been raised. From a methodological point of view, there are some significant problems that probably cannot be investigated with participatory techniques. Clearly, these techniques are not suited for the study of phenomena that tend to disappear once a person is aware of being observed. Even from an ethical point of view, participatory research is not entirely free of ambiguities. It is possible that these techniques too may become routinized and ritualized, thus creating the impression of participation without genuinely involving the subject in the research process. Nevertheless, the further development and institutionalization of participatory models of social research would provide some meaningful alternatives for those social scientists who are concerned about the unequal relationship between investigator and subject.

PATTERNS OF TRAINING

One of the ways of institutionalizing concern for the rights of their subjects among social scientists is to build it into the definition of their professional role—which in turn means making it an integral component of professional training. Certain ethical concerns—such as respect for confidentiality of subjects' responses—have traditionally been important parts of the normative structure of social research. Other issues, however, have tended to be ignored in the course of professional training; in fact, to become a fully trained social researcher a student often has had to learn to overcome whatever compunctions he might have had about deceiving his subjects or invading their privacy. It is not that social researchers as human beings have been concerned any less with these issues than anyone else; often, however, they have not been concerned with them *as social scientists.* To correct for some of the ethical problems arising in social research, norms for the treatment of subjects must become a central part of the operational code of social scientists, alongside of norms for proper methodology or honest reporting. . . .

ETHICAL PROBLEMS RELATING TO THE PRODUCTS OF SOCIAL RESEARCH

If knowledge is power, then the knowledge produced by social research is, to a large extent, power to control and manipulate human behavior. The production of such knowledge creates difficult ethical dilemmas for the social scientist, particularly when he considers who is likely to use the power to manipulate, over whom, and to what ends. I have discussed some of these general ethical issues elsewhere (Kelman, 1968, chap. 1). For the present purposes, I shall focus more narrowly on the implications of the knowledge produced by social research for the *differential* control of some segments of the population over others—an issue that touches directly on our concern with the rights of the subject.

In general, it can be said that those who produce social research—both the research sponsors and the investigators—are in a position to gain some relative advantage from it. They have the opportunity to define the problem to which the research will be addressed and thus to make it relevant to their particular interests; they also have the capacity and the resources to make use of the research findings. On the other hand, those who supply the data may very well place themselves in a more disadvantageous position. Whatever information they make available about themselves conceivably can be used to control their subsequent behavior. If all segments of a society participated equally as both researchers and subjects, then the relative advantages and disadvantages brought about by these two roles would, in the long run, balance themselves out. Since these roles are not distributed evenly within our society, however —since the less powerful segments of the society provide a disproportionately large number of the subjects and a disproportionately small number of the producers and users of social research—there is a real possibility that social research may serve to strengthen the established segments of the society at the expense of the disadvantaged. Such a possibility raises some difficult questions about the rights of the subject, since his participation in the research may have some damaging consequences for his group.

Considerations of this sort underlie many of the criticisms of social research—or of certain lines of social research—that are being voiced increasingly by activists in the black, the poor, and the student communities. They resent the fact that they are being used as subjects, complaining that "by focusing research attention on them, social scientists are placing them in a position where they can be more readily controlled and manipulated in the interests of the established powers [Kelman, 1970a, p. 97]." I do not feel that there is anything inherent in the nature of social science that works to the disadvantage of the powerless, or that the overall impact of social research has been in that direction. On the contrary, social research is potentially a powerful tool for social change and has in fact made important contributions to that end. Nevertheless, as long as the power relationship between the investigator and the subject remains as imbalanced as it has tended to be, there is a real possibility that social research may further increase the disadvantage of those who are already disadvantaged. I shall mention some illustrative problems and indicate what, in my view, they do and do not imply about the overall impact of social research, before turning to a discussion of some corrective approaches.

Some Illustrative Problems

Perhaps the clearest example of the use of social research by the powerful for the direct manipulation of the powerless is provided by some of the counterinsurgency activities carried on by the United States military and other agencies in developing countries. Project Camelot (see Horowitz, 1967), which has already been mentioned, is by now a classic example of such research, even though it was discontinued before any data actually had been gathered. It is important to recall that Project Camelot was not an operational research program designed to help the United States Army carry out counterinsurgency missions in Latin America; rather, it was designed as unclassified, basic research on the causes and prevention of internal conflict in developing nations. Since the research was sponsored by the Army, however, and since its theoretical questions were formulated within the Army's counterinsurgency framework, there is reason to believe that—whatever the theoretical interests of the investigators may have been—the findings would have been most directly relevant to the Army's counterinsurgency mission. A recent article by Wolf and Jorgensen (1970) provides apparently more blatant examples of the involvement of American social scientists in counterinsurgency programs in Thailand. According to the authors, "these programs comprise efforts at the manipulation of people on a giant scale and intertwine straightforward anthropological research with overt and covert counterinsurgency activities [p. 26]." In sponsoring such programs, the United States government "is less interested in the economic, social, or political causes of discontent than in techniques of neutralizing individual or collective protest [p. 34]." Wolf and Jorgensen cite one research proposal that is designed specifically to help in the development of such techniques. They also describe a "Tribal Data Center," whose purpose is to bring together and process data on tribal villages and their residents and, from all indications, to make these available for counterinsurgency uses. Such data, it seems, are being provided by social scientists, including anthropologists engaged in legitimate ethnographic studies, who may or may not be aware of the uses to which these data may be put. Some of the data requested by the Tribal Data Center, it should be noted, are of a kind that anthropologists traditionally have kept confidential. The information available on these activities is still very sketchy, but they serve to illustrate the possible ways in which data provided by relatively powerless groups may be used to their disadvantage.

The examples from counterinsurgency illustrate the possibility of social research conducted in a way or under conditions that make its products very directly applicable to the control and manipulation of disadvantaged populations, either because the explicit purpose of the research is to provide such information or because the sponsorship of the research makes such application almost inevitable regardless of the purposes of the investigator. There are other kinds of research that do not have this direct link to manipulative activities but whose products could well lend themselves to such purposes. Research on deviant behavior, though it may be completely independent from the operations of any mission-oriented agencies, often is carried out from the perspective of control or prevention of social deviance. As I mentioned earlier, this tendency may reflect the concerns of agencies sponsoring such research, or the concerns of the social scientists themselves. In any event, it influences the kinds of questions to which the research addresses itself and hence the kinds of data that the research produces. For example,

> much of this research focuses on the deviant behavior itself and on the characteristics of the indivisuals and groups that manifest it and the families and neighborhoods in which it is prevalent, rather than on the systemic processes out of which it emerges [Kelman, 1970b, p. 82].

It thus "points more readily to ways of controlling or at best preventing deviant behavior than it does to ways of restructuring the social realities that are indexed by this behavior [p. 83]."

The data produced by such research could be used directly for purposes of control. This can be seen most clearly in connection with political deviants, such as college protesters or ghetto rioters. Some critics have pointed out, for example, that information on the social and psychological characteristics of protesters might be used by college administrations for the purpose of weeding out protest-prone students at the point of admission. Or, information on the involvement of various segments of a ghetto population in riots could be used to break up all groups that potentially might serve as the focal points for a future riot. The control and prevention of riots and destructive forms of social deviance are legitimate social goals, but I am speaking here of attempts to prevent such activities by repressing those who potentially might engage in them—in other words, to prevent the manifestations of violent protest rather than its causes. Such attempts can only increase the disadvantage of the powerless by blocking their efforts to change the conditions of their lives. There are, of course, studies of student protesters (e.g., Flacks, 1967) and of black militants (e.g., Tomlinson, 1970) that are oriented toward social change rather than social control. Even the findings of such studies conceivably could be used for repressive purposes. However, if one goes beyond the possible use of isolated findings, it stands to reason that the products of a research program taking the problem of control of deviance—or more particularly of protest—as its point of departure are more likely in the long run to be used to the disadvantage of the powerless.

This type of research may not only lend itself to direct use in controlling disadvantaged populations but also may have indirect consequences detrimental to the interests of such populations. By focusing on the carriers of deviant behavior (who are drawn most often from the ranks of the poor, the disadvantaged, and the minority groups) such research may reinforce

> the widespread tendency to explain such behavior more often in terms of the pathology of the deviant individuals, families, and communities, than in terms of such properties of the larger social system as the distribution of power, resources, and opportunities [Kelman, 1970b, p. 83].

. . . These issues were at the heart of the debate that was generated by the Moynihan Report on the Negro family (see Rainwater & Yancey, 1967), which emphasized the deterioration of the Negro family as the major obstacle in Negroes' ability to achieve equality. Critics of the report—who included many social scientists—argued that its conclusions about the increasing pathology of the black family were not justified by the evidence and seemed to imply that the weakness of the black family (to whatever extent it does exist) is the cause rather than the effect of blacks' disadvantaged position within the society. They felt that the report could have the consequence (probably unintended) of encouraging national policies that concentrate on efforts to strengthen the black family rather than efforts to provide jobs for black men, to eliminate barriers to economic opportunity, and to correct for inequalities in the distribution of resources.

The debate about the alleged pathology of the black family raises a more general question, going beyond research that focuses on deviant behavior. Some recent critics of social research with black subjects—particularly when it is carried out by white investigators—have taken the position that any research yielding data on the psychological or social characteristics of blacks, which can then be compared with data on whites, is likely to have damaging consequences for the black community. This position was developed, at least in large part, in reaction to Jensen's (1969) lengthy article, which tried to argue that the lower average IQ scores obtained by blacks as compared to whites in many studies reflect genetic differences between the two groups. Jensen's views are by no means widely accepted by his colleagues, and his article generated a large number of critical replies, challenging his interpretations of the evidence. Nevertheless, the article received a considerable amount of publicity, and it probably provided some scientific legitimation for those whites who find it convenient to believe in the intellectual inferiority of blacks.

Now, it can be argued that any black-white comparisons lend themselves to this or other kinds of use detrimental to the black community. Whether the comparison involves ability and achievement scores, or social attitudes, or life styles, it may well put blacks in a negative light—at least from the point of view of the white middle class. Often, the observed differences between blacks and whites may be spurious, being based on biased measures or indicators. For example, black children may perform more poorly on an aptitude test, not because they have less of the aptitude being measured, but because the test is more geared to the experiences of white middle-class children than to those of black ghetto children; the proportion of illegitimate births may be larger in the black community, not because there is a higher proportion of births out of wedlock among black women, but because there is a higher rate of reporting such births. If the observed differences are valid, their interpretation and evaluation may be subject to various biases. For example, differences in IQ may be interpreted (sometimes by psychologists themselves, and more often by nonspecialists) as reflecting innate differences in intelligence, even though such a conclusion is unwarranted by the data; differences in patterns of social behavior and attitudes may be taken as evidence of the immorality or disorganization of the black community because they are evaluated in terms of the white middle-class experience rather than the black ghetto experience. The unfavorable image of blacks presented by the research findings, though based on biases in measurement, interpretation, or evaluation, would become a "scientifically confirmed" reality. As such, it might reinforce negative stereotypes of blacks that already are held by the white population. It might further support negative expectations (often shared by blacks themselves) with respect to the performance of blacks, thus helping to produce a self-fulfilling prophecy. Finally, it might serve as a basis for policies that are irrelevant or detrimental to the interests of blacks, because they are derived from wrong assumptions about the capacities and needs of the black population.

The last set of problems has potentially very farreaching implications since it suggests that any study in which the psychological or social characteristics of a minority or disadvantaged group are assessed–no matter who carries it out, under what auspices, and within what frame of reference–may have damaging consequences for the groups studied. . . . The question is, How probable are such negative consequences? By contrast, what is the probability that the findings of the research may be used or usable in ways that would accrue to the advantage of the group under study? And, furthermore, what mechanisms are available and what steps have been taken to counteract the possibility of biased measures and the misinterpretation and misuse of the research findings? These are the kinds of questions that a social scientist must ask himself in each case before deciding to proceed with–or to abandon–a piece of research in a disadvantaged community. . . .

The wholesale indictment of social research or of entire areas within it is based on too undifferentiated a view of the establishment, of social scientists, and of the relationship between the two. To begin with, the notion that social scientists as a group are part of a vast conspiracy to manipulate oppressed populations in the interest of those in power is inconsistent with the facts, and an analysis that leans heavily on this notion is bound to be unproductive. The problem is far more complex and in some respects more serious since it is linked to systemic forces rather than to the machinations of evil men. To be sure, there are social scientists who are involved in deliberate manipulative activities–such as the counterinsurgency programs mentioned above–for various reasons and with varying degrees of awareness of the type of enterprise to which they are parties. No doubt, there are more social scientists involved in such activities than is commonly known, since by their very nature these activities are usually clandestine; and there is a danger that such involvements may increase if certain current trends in American society become even more pervasive. Such involvements, however, are by no means the norm among social scientists; in some fundamental respects, they go against the norms of the social science community, particularly if they involve secrecy, misrepresentation, and violations of confidentiality. Indeed, the major criticisms of such activities have come from within the social science community itself (see Horowitz, 1967; Wolf & Jorgensen, 1970).

The more sophisticated form of the indictment of social research is based on the notion that social scientists—both because they are beholden to the establishment agencies that sponsor their research and because of their own class positions—are bound to serve the interests of the elites. Therefore, whether or not they are engaged deliberately in manipulative and oppressive activities—and, in fact, even when they are oriented toward helping the poor and the powerless—the products of their research inevitably contribute to the disadvantage of these groups. This analysis, in my view, has a great deal of merit, but it remains too undifferentiated. First of all, the agencies that sponsor research—both governmental and private—cannot be described as monolithic service stations of the status quo. To be sure, they are usually not wellsprings of political revolution, but they have often (if not often enough) provided stimulation for or at least been responsive to research promotive of social change. . . . At its best, however, social research is an essential source of alternative perspectives and thus a potentially valuable tool in any effort to promote social change.

Social research has in fact made important contributions to social change and produced findings that strengthen the position of the disadvantaged and powerless groups. One of its major contributions has been in discrediting some of the commonly held myths that have provided support for white racism. Thus, while it is true that psychological data have on occasion been used in support of the notion of genetically based racial differences in intelligence, it should not be forgotten that it is the work of psychologists and anthropologists over a number of years that systematically has refuted this popular notion and made it scientifically unrespectable. Similarly, it is the work of sociologists and social psychologists that has refuted the popular tendency to attribute the disadvantage of blacks in America to some failing in their own character or social organization, by identifying the patterns of exclusion and oppression that are built into the institutions and attitudes of white America. To take another example, research on student protests and ghetto riots—even when it has focused on the characteristics of the participants—has helped to discredit the myths that student protesters are neurotics and that ghetto rioters are riffraff, thus making it necessary to look more carefully at the underlying causes of these actions.

All in all, then, I cannot accept the position that social research is inherently a tool of the establishment, nor do I feel that, on the whole, it has played that kind of role. Quite to the contrary, it would be self-defeating for those of us who identify with the powerless populations to reject or undermine social research, given its actual and potential contributions to the process of social change. At the same time, however, I feel that there is a very real and structural basis for the fear that some of the products of social research may be relatively disadvantageous for the powerless groups, given the power imbalance between those who sponsor and conduct the research and those who provide the data. . . .

Some Corrective Approaches

There are occasions when a piece of social research may damage so clearly the interests of the groups studied and violate their rights that it ought to be stopped. We do need to develop and extend mechanisms that will protect subjects against such abuses, without imposing political controls on the freedom of research. There are also occasions when an investigator may decide to refrain voluntarily from a particular line of research because he feels the probability that its products will be put to negative uses is too high. Such assessments must be left to the individual investigator. The most important corrective approaches, however, are not those designed to stop a particular line of research, but those designed to balance it—to make sure that all segments of the population have an opportunity to bring their perspectives to bear on the formulation of the problems, and to safeguard their interests in the interpretation and utilization of the results. At the level of the individual project, this means institutionalizing ways of involving representatives of the group under study both in the conduct of the research and in the utilization of the findings. At the level of research policy and the organization of research within the society, it means institutionalizing ways of diversifying the community of producers and users of social research. Such diversification would counteract the power imbalance by focusing on the research that is done rather than on the research that is prevented.

I examine here some of the institutionalized ways of correcting the current power imbalance in terms of mechanisms of accountability, patterns of research participation, and patterns of research utilization.

MECHANISMS OF ACCOUNTABILITY

Counterinsurgency research and its possible extensions to the domestic American scene underline the need for mechanisms to protect the groups under study against possible abuses. Mechanisms that might serve this purpose are basically similar to the mechanisms of protection and accountability that I discussed in connection with the *processes* of social research, since the ethical issues involved are directly continuous with the issues of deception, invasion of privacy, and deprivation of consent discussed in the earlier section. That is, serious ethical problems may arise because the investigator represents himself as an independent researcher when in fact his research is linked, directly or indirectly, to the mission of counterinsurgency agencies; or because the investigator violates the confidentiality of data by turning over information to such agencies; or because the investigator exposes the group he studies to possible harm or manipulation without informing them of these risks. However, the professional associations have found it even more difficult to deal with these problems than with the ethical problems arising in the usual investigator-subject relationship. The issues are more complicated than those involved in the one-to-one relationship of investigator and subject because they are intertwined closely with the sponsorship and political purposes of the research, and because they usually involve the possibility of harm to a group (such as an ethnic minority or a political faction) rather than to an identifiable individual.

Indeed, the imposition of controls and sanctions in this domain represents some very real dangers to the freedom of research from political constraints, since the line between ethical and political objections to a piece of research is often very hard to draw. Nevertheless, the line must be drawn. Violations of the rights of groups to voluntary informed consent and to the protection of their privacy, their confidences, and their interests cannot be countenanced on the basis of the investigator's legitimate right to freedom of research. Existing review committees and ethics committees must extend their functions—or special mechanisms of protection and accountability must be set up—to handle these types of violations. The challenge is to develop criteria and procedures that will make it possible to delegitimize research activities that are based on the systematic violation of the rights of subjects, without legitimizing the imposition of political controls on research. In general, I would follow the principle of reserving external controls and sanctions to those cases that involve fairly obvious abuses, while leaving it to other mechanisms to correct for the more subtle and remote disadvantages that social research may bring to powerless groups.

PATTERNS OF RESEARCH SPONSORSHIP

A necessary condition for achieving greater balance in the products of social research is to retain and in fact enhance the ability of social science to bring independent and diverse perspectives to bear on the study of social institutions and societal processes. In developing a national research policy, therefore, it is essential to work out patterns of research sponsorship and funding that are consistent with this principle. The sponsorship of social research, or of any area within it, must be diversified as much as possible; it should not be entirely in the hands of either governmental or private agencies and, within the governmental framework, no area of research should be monopolized by a single agency or set of agencies. Such monopolies are particularly dangerous when they are held by a mission-oriented agency—for example, the military, which has had a virtual monopoly in supporting certain areas of scientific work in the United States. Similarly, there is a need for diversity in the recipients of research funds. If research is carried out in different types of organizational settings, located in different areas, and staffed by investigators with different backgrounds, then the range of perspectives is likely to be broadened. It would be useful, for example, to carry out some research outside of a university context—perhaps by a community agency—in order to balance out the special bias that the university scholar usually brings to a problem.

Special care must be taken to preserve the autonomy of the organizations in which social research is carried out—particularly the universities, which are designed to serve as a major source of independent perspectives in the society. Sponsoring agencies, as well as the universities themselves, have the responsibility of avoiding the types of contracts that will undermine their autonomy. Secret research provides the most obvious example here; many kinds of operational research may also be inappropriate for the university setting. This is another reason for experimenting with a variety of organizational settings for research. Certain kinds of research—such as research that is designed specifically to facilitate or evaluate the functioning of an operational agency—probably can be carried out more effectively in an in-house research facility or in an independent (nonuniversity) research organization. When carried out within the university, on the other hand, such research well may weaken the university's unique capacity as an autonomous agency. A good way of testing the autonomy of a given research project is to examine systematically the assumptions that underlie it—if possible, with the help of colleagues who approach the problem from different cultural perspectives. In a truly independent piece of research, there should be no assumption that the investigator feels bound to leave unquestioned.

PATTERNS OF RESEARCH PARTICIPATION

Perhaps the most important way of counteracting current imbalances is to extend the range of participants in the conduct of social research. At the level of the individual research project, this goal can be accomplished partly by the development of participatory research patterns, as described earlier. In an action research program, for example, the subjects play an active role in the formulation and conduct of the research and the research is addressed to the problems with which their community is concerned. Even when the opportunities for active participation of the subjects are limited, it is often possible to extend the range of investigators who participate in the research. Whenever an investigator carries out research in a culture or subculture different from his own, it is particularly important to involve social scientists who are members of the community under study as colleagues in the planning, conduct, and analysis of the research. Such involvement is important, not only for ethical reasons (i.e., because it helps to protect the interests of the group under study), but also for scientific reasons (i.e., because it helps to balance the investigator's perspective as an outsider with those of colleagues who qualify as insiders).

At the level of research policy and the organization of research, the need is to broaden the base of participation in the research process, nationally as well as internationally. I like to speak in this connection of the *democratization of the research community*. The capacities and opportunities to carry out social research must be made available to all segments of the population. By the same token, all segments should participate equally in the role of subject; the pattern must be one of reciprocal exposure rather than of a sharp division between those who do the research and those who are researched upon.

There are some inherent limitations in the extent to which the disadvantaged segments of the population can be represented genuinely in the research process. Members of these groups who receive training as social scientists are, by definition, no longer "typical" of the groups they represent. Because of their high level of education and the financial and cultural conditions associated with it, their interests and perspectives are likely to diverge in at least some important ways from those of the most disadvantaged segments of the society. Nevertheless, the base of social research would be broadened considerably if more of its participants were recruited from the segments of the society that are now underrepresented. It would bring into the field individuals who—though not quite typical of the disadvantaged groups—would have a greater identification with their problems and a greater awareness of their perspectives.

In speaking of representativeness, I do not mean to imply that social research ought to be transformed into a political process, in which scientific truth is determined by who prevails in a power struggle. This view sometimes is conveyed by self-appointed spokesmen for disadvantaged groups, who try to use their power to exclude outsiders from research in minority communities or to determine the conclusions that can be drawn from such research. In evaluating this kind of tactic, we must keep in mind that there is considerable ambiguity about whom such spokesmen represent; they do bring their own special interests to the situation, and there is at least the possibility that they merely are replacing one form of oppression of the powerless with another. Though these tactics may be based on a genuine concern with the power imbalance that has characterized so much of social research, I see them as a distortion of the process of democratizing the research community, which can only have the effect of undermining the integrity of the research enterprise.

Democratization, as I see it, would enhance rather than endanger the integrity of social research. It aims for representativeness in the sense that the perspectives of the disadvantaged groups would be brought to bear more fully and fairly on the research process. Broadening the base of participation in social research would allow the interests and frames of reference of the disadvantaged groups a larger role in the formulation of the questions to which the research addresses itself and in the interpretation of the research findings. By bringing a variety of perspectives to bear on research problems, democratization would not only reduce the likelihood that the products of the research would give advantages to some groups at the expense of others, but it would also increase the overall validity of these products.

PATTERNS OF RESEARCH UTILIZATION

To counteract the current power imbalance, it is essential to extend not only the range of those who participate in social research but also the range of those who are able to utilize its findings. At the level of the individual research project, we must develop and institutionalize mechanisms of providing the individuals, groups, and communities that serve as subjects some meaningful access to the data they contributed. Findings that might be potentially useful to them, or that conceivably might be used against their interests, should be communicated to them in language they can understand. The purpose of such communication would be to indicate concrete ways of utilizing the findings to their own advantage and of protecting themselves against the possibly damaging uses to which others might put these findings. Furthermore, community organizations trusted by the subjects can be given access to the findings (which in most cases would not mean the raw data), so that they can take steps to utilize them in the community's interest and to protect the community against potentially harmful consequences.

At the level of research policy and the organization of research, there is a need for wider distribution among all segments of the population of the skills and resources needed to utilize the data of social research. Organizations representing the interests of the disadvantaged segments of the population must acquire the capabilities for using research findings in the development of their own programs and in their inputs to the debates around local and national policies. A major component of the requisite skills and resources is the capacity to counteract incomplete or faulty interpretations and applications of research data that might be detrimental to the interests of their group.

In the final analysis, the democratization of the community of research producers and research users must be seen as part of the process of redistributing power within our society at large. Social (and other) scientists, however, can contribute to this larger process by correcting the imbalances within their own spheres.

NOTES

1. There are some interesting exceptions to this generalization. Survey researchers often have noted that the rate of refusal encountered by interviewers ringing doorbells tends to be relatively higher among poor respondents. This tendency is probably due to the fact that the poor (and particularly the uneducated) respondent (*a*) is less likely to have a cognitive framework to which he can relate the request for an interview, (*b*) is more likely to feel that he has no opinions on the topic of the interview, and (*c*) is more likely to be suspicious of a middle-class stranger with pad and pencil in hand, who is reminiscent of a welfare investigator or other such official. For all of these reasons, when given the option, the poor respondent may prefer not to become involved. When research is carried out in an institutional context, however, he is likely to feel that he has no option and that his participation is one of the obligations of his dependent role—unless, of course, resistance is mobilized through an organized effort.
2. This analysis was developed by Elizabeth M. Douvan, Erasmus L. Hoch, and myself, while serving on the Psychology Subject Pool Committee at the University of Michigan.
3. Some critics of role-playing experiments (e.g., Freedman, 1969) have equated all role playing with this particular subtype of role playing. I tend to agree that this type of role playing is fairly limited in its usefulness, although I feel that for certain purposes it may be quite valuable and—depending on the particular procedures used—it may produce "real" behavior, not merely (as Freedman claims) "people's guesses as to how they would behave if they were in a particular situation." Beyond that, however, Freedman ignores all of the other forms of role-playing procedures which can generate levels of realism, spontaneity, and involvement far greater than those obtained in the traditional deception experiment.

REFERENCES

Bryan, J. H., and Test, M. A. Models and helping: Naturalistic studies in aiding behavior. *Journal of Personality and Social Psychology,* 1967, 6, 400–407.

Campbell, D. T. Prospective: Artifact and control. In R. Rosenthal and R. L. Rosnow (eds.), *Artifact in behavioral research.* New York: Academic Press, 1969.

Cook, S. W., Hicks, L. H., Kimble, G. A., McGuire, W. J., Schoggen, P. H., and Smith, M. B. Ethical standards for research with human subjects. (Draft, May 1972) *APA Monitor,* 1972, 3(5), I–XIX.

Erikson, K. T. A comment on disguised observation in sociology. *Social Problems,* 1967, 14, 366–373.

Flacks, R. The liberated generation: An explanation of the roots of student protest. *Journal of Social Issues,* 1967, 23(3), 52–75.

Freedman, J. L. Role playing: Psychology by consensus. *Journal of Personality and Social Psychology,* 1969, 13, 107–114.

Goffman, E. *Asylums: Essays on the social situation of mental patients and other inmates.* New York: Doubleday, 1961.

Hartmann, G. W. A field experiment on the comparative effectiveness of "emotional" and "rational" political leaflets in determining election results. *Journal of Abnormal and Social Psychology,* 1936, 31, 99–114.

Horowitz, I. L. (ed.) *The rise and fall of Project Camelot.* Cambridge: M.I.T. Press, 1967.

Jensen, A. R. How much can we boost IQ and scholastic achievement? *Harvard Educational Review,* 1969, 39, 1–123.

Kelman, H. C. *A time to speak: On human values and social research.* San Francisco: Jossey–Bass, 1968.

____. Patterns of personal involvement in the national system: A social-psychological analysis of political legitimacy. In J. N. Rosenau (ed.), *International politics and foreign policy: A reader in research and theory.* (Rev. ed.) New York: Free Press, 1969.

____. Comments on Wiesner's paper. In F. F. Korten, S. W. Cook, and J. I. Lacey (eds.), *Psychology and the problems of society.* Washington, D.C.: American Psychological Association, 1970. (a)

____. The relevance of social research to social issues: Promises and pitfalls. In P. Halmos (ed.), *The sociology of sociology* (The Sociological Review: Monograph No. 16). Keele: University of Keele, 1970. (b)

King, D. J. The subject pool. *American Psychologist,* 1970, 25, 1179–1181.

Latané, B. Field studies of altruistic compliance. *Representative Research in Social Psychology,* 1970, 1, 49–61.

Lear, J. Do we need new rules for experiments on people? *Saturday Review,* February 5, 1966, pp. 61–70.

Mead, M. Research with human beings: A model derived from anthropological field practice. *Daedalus,* 1969, 98, 361–386.

Milgram, S. Behavioral study of obedience. *Journal of Abnormal and Social Psychology,* 1963, 67, 371–378.

Miller, A. G. (ed.) *The social psychology of psychological research.* New York: Free Press, 1972.

Orne, M. T., and Evans, F. J. Social control in the psychological experiment: Antisocial behavior and hypnosis. *Journal of Personality and Social Psychology,* 1965, 1, 189–200.

Parsons, T. Research with human subjects and the "professional complex." *Daedalus,* 1969, 98, 325–360.

Piliavin, I. M., Rodin, J., and Piliavin, J. A. Good samaritanism: An underground phenomenon? *Journal of Personality and Social Psychology,* 1969, 13, 289–299.

Rainwater, L., and Yancey, W. L. *The Moynihan Report and the politics of controversy.* Cambridge: M.I.T. Press, 1967.

Ryan, W. *Blaming the victim.* New York: Pantheon, 1971.

Tomlinson, T. M. Ideological foundations for Negro action: A comparative

analysis of militant and nonmilitant views of the Los Angeles riot. *Journal of Social Issues,* 1970, 26(1), 93–120.
Warwick, D. P. Tearoom trade: A case study of ends and means in social research. Unpublished paper, York University, Toronto, 1971.
Wolf, E. R., and Jorgensen, J. G. Anthropology on the warpath in Thailand. *New York Review of Books,* 1970, 15(9), 26–35.

Life and Death of Project Camelot

Irving Louis Horowitz

In June of this year—in the midst of the crisis over the Dominican Republic—the United States Ambassador to Chile sent an urgent and angry cable to the State Department. Ambassador Ralph Dungan was confronted with a growing outburst of anti-Americanism from Chilean newspapers and intellectuals. Further, left-wing members of the Chilean Senate had accused the United States of espionage.

The anti-American attacks that agitated Dungan had no direct connection with sending U.S. troops to Santo Domingo. Their target was a mysterious and cloudy American research program called Project Camelot.

Dungan wanted to know from the State Department what Project Camelot was all about. Further, whatever Camelot was, he wanted it stopped because it was fast becoming a *cause célèbre* in Chile (as it soon would throughout capitals of Latin America and in Washington) and Dungan had not been told anything about it—even though it was sponsored by the U.S. Army and involved the tinderbox subjects of counterrevolution and counterinsurgency in Latin America.

Within a few weeks Project Camelot created repercussions from Capitol Hill to the White House. Senator J. William Fulbright, chairman of the For-

Irving Louis Horowitz, "Life and Death of Project Camelot," *Trans*-action 3 (November-December, 1965), 3–7, 44–47.

eign Relations Committee, registered his personal concern about such projects as Camelot because of their "reactionary, backward-looking policy opposed to change. Implicit in Camelot, as in the concept of 'counterinsurgency,' is an assumption that revolutionary movements are dangerous to the interests of the United States and that the United States must be prepared to assist, if not actually to participate in, measures to repress them."

By mid-June the State Department and Defense Department—which had created and funded Camelot—were in open contention over the project and the jurisdiction each department should have over certain foreign policy operations.

On July 8, Project Camelot was killed by Defense Secretary Robert McNamara's office which has a veto power over the military budget. The decision had been made under the President's direction.

On that same day, the director of Camelot's parent body, the Special Operations Research Organization, told a Congressional committee that the research project on revolution and counterinsurgency had taken its name from King Arthur's mythical domain because "It connotes the right sort of things—development of a stable society with peace and justice for all." Whatever Camelot's outcome, there should be no mistaking the deep sincerity behind this appeal for an applied social science pertinent to current policy.

However, Camelot left a horizon of disarray in its wake: an open dispute between State and Defense; fuel for the anti-American fires in Latin America; a cut in U.S. Army research appropriations. In addition, serious and perhaps ominous implications for social science research, bordering on censorship, have been raised by the heated reaction of the executive branch of government.

GLOBAL COUNTERINSURGENCY

What was Project Camelot? Basically, it was a project for measuring and forecasting the causes of revolutions and insurgency in underdeveloped areas of the world. It also aimed to find ways of eliminating the causes, or coping with the revolutions and insurgencies. Camelot was sponsored by the U.S. Army on a four to six million dollar contract, spaced out over three to four years, with the Special Operations Research Organization (SORO). This agency is nominally under the aegis of American University in Washington, D.C., and does a variety of research for the Army. This includes making analytical surveys of foreign areas; keeping up-to-date information on the military, political, and social complexes of those areas; and maintaining a "rapid response" file for getting immediate information, upon Army request, on any situation deemed militarily important.

Latin America was the first area chosen for concentrated study, but countries on Camelot's four-year list included some in Asia, Africa, and Europe. In a working paper issued on December 5, 1964, at the request of the Office of the Chief of Research and Development, Department of the Army, it was recommended that "comparative historical studies" be made in these countries:

> (*Latin America*) Argentina, Bolivia, Brazil, Columbia, Cuba, Dominican Republic, El Salvador, Guatemala, Mexico, Paraguay, Peru, Venezuela.
>
> (*Middle East*) Egypt, Iran, Turkey.
>
> (*Far East*) Korea, Indonesia, Malaysia, Thailand.
>
> (*Others*) France, Greece, Nigeria.

"Survey research and other field studies" were recommended for Bolivia, Columbia, Ecuador, Paraguay, Peru, Venezuela, Iran, Thailand. Preliminary consideration was also being given to a study of the separatist movement in French Canada. It, too, had a code name: Project Revolt.

In a recruiting letter sent to selected scholars all over the world at the end of 1964, Project Camelot's aims were defined as a study to "make it possible to predict and influence politically significant aspects of social change in the developing nations of the world." This would include devising procedures for "assessing the potential for internal war within national societies" and "identify(ing) with increased degrees of confidence, those actions which a government might take to relieve conditions which are assessed as giving rise to a potential for internal war." The letter further stated: "The U.S. Army has an important mission in the positive and constructive aspects of nation-building in less developed countries as well as a responsibility to assist friendly governments in dealing with active insurgency problems." Such activities by the U.S. Army were described as "insurgency prophylaxis" rather than the "sometimes misleading label of counterinsurgency."

Project Camelot was conceived in late 1963 by a group of high-ranking Army officers connected with the Army Research Office of the Department of Defense. They were concerned about new types of warfare springing up around the world. Revolutions in Cuba and Yemen and insurgency movements in Vietnam and the Congo were a far cry from the battles of World War II and also different from the envisioned—and planned for—apocalypse of nuclear war. For the first time in modern warfare, military establishments were not in a position to use the immense arsenals at their disposal—but were, instead, compelled by force of a geopolitical stalemate to increasingly engage in primitive forms of armed combat. The questions of moment for the Army were: Why can't the "hardware" be used? And what alternatives can social science "software" provide?

A well-known Latin American area specialist, Rex Hopper, was chosen as director of Project Camelot. Hopper was a professor of sociology and chairman of the department at Brooklyn College. He had been to Latin America many times over a 30-year span on research projects and lecture tours, including some under government sponsorship. He was highly recommended for the position by his professional associates in Washington and elsewhere. Hopper had a long-standing interest in problems of revolution and saw in this multimillion dollar contract the possible realization of a life-long scientific ambition.

THE CHILEAN DEBACLE

How did this social science research project create a foreign policy furor? And, at another level, how did such high intentions result in so disastrous an outcome?

The answers involve a network spreading from a professor of anthropology at the University of Pittsburgh, to a professor of sociology at the University of Oslo, and yet a third professor of sociology at the University of Chile in Santiago, Chile. The "showdown" took place in Chile, first within the confines of the university, next on the floor of the Chilean Senate, then in the popular press of Santiago, and finally, behind U.S. embassy walls.

It was ironic that Chile was the scene of wild newspaper tales of spying and academic outrage at scholars being recruited for "spying missions." For the working papers of Project Camelot stipulated as a criterion for study that a country "should show promise of high payoffs in terms of the kinds of data required." Chile did not meet these requirements—it is not on the preliminary list of nations specified as prospects.

How then did Chile become involved in Project Camelot's affairs? The answer requires consideration of the position of Hugo G. Nutini, assistant professor of anthropology at Pittsburgh, citizen of the United States and former citizen of Chile. His presence in Santiago as a self-identified Camelot representative triggered the climactic chain of events.

Nutini, who inquired about an appointment in Camelot's beginning stages, never was given a regular Camelot appointment. Because he was planning a trip to Chile in April of this year—on other academic business—he was asked to prepare a report concerning possibilities of cooperation from Chilean scholars. In general, it was the kind of survey which has mild results and a modest honorarium attached to it (Nutini was offered $750). But Nutini had an obviously different notion of his role. Despite the limitations and precautions which Rex Hopper placed on his trip, especially Hopper's insistence on its informal nature, Nutini managed to convey the impression of being an official of Project Camelot with the authority to make proposals to prospective Chilean participants. Here was an opportunity to link the country of his birth with the country of his choice.

At about the same time, Johan Galtung, a Norwegian sociologist famous for his research on conflict and conflict resolution in underdeveloped areas, especially in Latin America, entered the picture. Galtung, who was in Chile at the time and associated with the Latin American Faculty of Social Science (FLACSO), received an invitation to participate in a Camelot planning conference scheduled for Washington, D.C., in August 1965. The fee to social scientists attending the conference would be $2,000 for four weeks. Galtung turned down the invitation. He gave several reasons. He could not accept the role of the U.S. Army as a sponsoring agent in a study of counterinsurgency. He could not accept the notion of the Army as an agency of national development; he saw the Army as managing conflict and even promoting conflict. Finally, he could not accept the asymmetry of the project—he found it difficult to understand why there would be studies of counterinsurgency in Latin America, but no studies of "counterintervention" (conditions under which Latin American Nations might intervene in the affairs of the United States). Galtung was also deeply concerned about the possibility of European scholars being frozen out of Latin American studies by an inundation of sociologists from the United States. Furthermore, he expressed fears that the scale of Camelot honoraria would completely destroy the social science labor market in Latin America.

Galtung had spoken to others in Oslo, Santiago, and throughout Latin America about the project, and he had shown the memorandum of December 1964 to many of his colleagues.

Soon after Nutini arrived in Santiago, he had a conference with Vice-Chancellor Alvaro Bunster of the University of Chile to discuss the character of Project Camelot. Their second meeting, arranged by the vice-chancellor, was also attended by Professor Eduardo Fuenzalida, a sociologist. After a half-hour of exposition by Nutini, Fuenzalida asked him pointblank to specify the ultimate aims of the project, its sponsors, and its military implications. Before Nutini could reply, Professor Fuenzalida, apparently with some drama, pulled a copy of the December 4 circular letter from his briefcase and read a prepared Spanish translation. Simultaneously, the authorities at FLACSO turned over the matter to their associates in the Chilean Senate and in the left-wing Chilean press.

In Washington, under the political pressures of State Department officials and Congressional reaction, Project Camelot was halted in midstream, or more precisely, before it ever really got under way. When the ambassador's communication reached Washington, there was already considerable official ferment about Project Camelot. Senators Fulbright, Morse, and McCarthy soon asked for hearings by the Senate Foreign Relations Committee. Only an agreement between Secretary of Defense McNamara and Secretary of State Rusk to settle their differences on future overseas research projects forestalled Senate action. But in the House of Representatives, a hearing was conducted by the Foreign Affairs Committee on July 8. The SORO director, Theodore Vallance, was questioned by committee members on the worth of Camelot and the matter of military intrusion into foreign policy areas.

That morning, even before Vallance was sworn in as a witness–and without his knowledge–the Defense Department issued a terse announcement terminating Project Camelot. President Johnson had decided the issue in favor of the State Department. In a memo to Secretary Rusk on August 5 the President stipulated that "no government sponsorship of foreign area research should be undertaken which in the judgement of the Secretary of State would adversely affect United States foreign relations."

The State Department has recently established machinery to screen and judge all federally-financed research projects overseas. The policy and research consequences of the Presidential directive will be discussed later.

What effect will the cancellation of Camelot have on the continuing rivalry between Defense and State departments for primacy in foreign policy? How will government sponsorship of future social science research be affected? And was Project Camelot a scholarly protective cover for U.S. Army planning–or a legitimate research operation on a valid research subject independent of sponsorship?

Let us begin with a collective self-portrait of Camelot as the social scientists who directed the project perceived it. There seems to be general consensus on seven points.

First, the men who went to work for Camelot felt the need for a large-scale, "big picture" project in social science. They wanted to create a sociology of contemporary relevance which would not suffer from the parochial narrowness of visions to which their own professional backgrounds had generally conditioned them. Most of the men viewed Camelot as a bona fide opportunity to do fundamental research with relatively unlimited funds at their disposal. (No social science project ever before had up to $6,000,000 available.) Under such optimal conditions, these scholars tended not to look a gift horse in the mouth. As one of them put it, there was no desire to inquire too deeply as to the source of the funds or the ultimate purpose of the project.

Second, most social scientists affiliated with Camelot felt that there was actually more freedom to do fundamental research under military sponsorship than at a university or college. One man noted that during the 1950s there was far more freedom to do fundamental research in the RAND corporation (an Air Force research organization) than on any campus in America. Indeed, once the protective covering of RAND was adopted, it was almost viewed as a society of Platonist elites or "knowers" permitted to search for truth on behalf of the powerful. In a neoplatonic definition of their situation, the Camelot men hoped that their ideas would be taken seriously by the wielders of power (although, conversely they were convinced that the armed forces would not accept their preliminary recommendations).

Third, many of the Camelot associates felt distinctly uncomfortable with military sponsorship, especially given the present United States military posture. But their reaction to this discomfort was that "the Army has to be educated." This view was sometimes cast in Freudian terms: the Army's bent toward violence ought to be sublimated. Underlying this theme was the notion of the armed forces as an agency for potential social good—the discipline and the order embodied by an army could be channeled into the process of economic and social development in the United States as well as in Latin America.

Fourth, there was a profound conviction in the perfectibility of mankind; particularly in the possibility of the military establishment performing a major role in the general process of growth. They sought to correct the intellectual paternalism and parochialism under which Pentagon generals, State Department diplomats, and Defense Department planners seemed to operate.

Fifth, a major long-range purpose of Camelot, at least for some of its policy-makers, was to prevent another revolutionary holocaust on a grand scale, such as occurred in Cuba. At the very least, there was a shared belief that *Pax Americana* was severely threatened and its future could be bolstered.

Sixth, none of them viewed their role on the project as spying for the United States government, or for anyone else.

Seventh, the men on Project Camelot felt that they made heavy sacrifices for social science. Their personal and professional risks were much higher than those taken by university academics. Government work, while well-compensated, remains professionally marginal. It can be terminated abruptly (as indeed was the case) and its project directors are subject to a public scrutiny not customary behind the walls of ivy.

In the main, there was perhaps a keener desire on the part of the directing members of Camelot not to "sell out" than there is among social scientists with regular academic appointments. This concern with the ethics of social science research seemed to be due largely to daily confrontation of the problems of betrayal, treason, secrecy, and abuse of data, in a critical situation. In contrast, even though a university position may be created by federally-sponsored research, the connection with policy matters is often too remote to cause any *crise de conscience*.

THE INSIDERS' REPORT

Were the men on Camelot critical of any aspects of the project?

Some had doubts from the outset about the character of the work they would be doing, and about the conditions under which it would be done. It was pointed out, for example, that the U.S. Army tends to exercise a far more stringent intellectual control of research findings than does the U.S. Air Force. As evidence for this, it was stated that SORO generally had fewer "free-wheeling" aspects to its research designs than did RAND (the Air Force supported research organization). One critic inside SORO went so far as to say that he knew of no SORO research which had a "playful" or unregimented quality, such as one finds at RAND (where, for example, computers are used to plan invasions but also to play chess). One staff member said that "the self-conscious seriousness gets to you after a while." "It was all grim stuff," said another.

Another line of criticism was that pressures on the "reformers" (as the men engaged in Camelot research spoke of themselves) to come up with ideas were much stronger than the pressures on the military to actually bring off any policy changes recommended. The social scientists were expected to be social reformers, while the military adjutants were expected to be conservative. It was further felt that the relationship between sponsors and researchers was not one of equals, but rather one of superordinate military needs and subordinate academic roles. On the other hand, some officials were impressed by the disinterestedness of the military, and thought that far from exercising undue influence, the Army personnel were loath to offer opinions.

Another objection was that if one had to work on policy matters—if research is to have international ramifications—it might better be conducted under conventional State Department sponsorship. "After all," one man said, "they are at least nominally committed to civilian political norms." In other words, there was a considerable reluctance to believe that the Defense Department, despite its superior organization, greater financial affluence, and executive influence, would actually improve upon State Department styles of work, or accept recommendations at variance with Pentagon policies.

There seemed to be few, if any, expressions of disrespect for the intrinsic merit of the work contemplated by Camelot, or of disdain for policy-oriented work in general. The scholars engaged in the Camelot effort used two distinct vocabularies. The various Camelot documents reveal a military vocabulary provided with an array of military justifications, often followed (within the same document) by a social science vocabulary offering social science justifications and rationalizations. The dilemma in the Camelot literature, from the preliminary report issued in August 1964 until the more advanced document issued in April 1965, is the same: an incomplete amalgamation of the military and sociological vocabularies. (At an early date the project had the code name SPEARPOINT.)

POLICY CONFLICTS OVER CAMELOT

The directors of SORO are concerned that the cancellation of Camelot might mean the end of SORO as well as a wholesale slash of research funds. For while over $1,000,000 was allotted to Camelot each year, the annual budget of SORO, its parent organization, is a good deal less. Although no such action has taken place, SORO's future is being examined. For example, the Senate and House Appropriations Committee blocked a move by the Army to transfer unused Camelot funds to SORO.

However, the end of Project Camelot does not necessarily imply the end of the Special Operations Research Office, nor does it imply an end to research designs which are similar in character to Project Camelot. In fact, the termination of the contract does not even imply an intellectual change of heart on the part of the originating sponsors or key figures of the project.

One of the characteristics of Project Camelot was the number of antagonistic forces it set in motion on grounds of strategy and timing rather than from what may be called considerations of scientific principles.

The State Department grounded its opposition to Camelot on the basis of the ultimate authority it has in the area of foreign affairs. There is no published report showing serious criticism of the projected research itself.

Congressional opposition seemed to be generated by a concern not to rock any foreign alliances, especially in Latin America. Again, there was no statement about the project's scientific or intellectual grounds.

A third group of skeptics, academic social scientists, generally thought that Project Camelot, and studies of the processes of revolution and war in general, were better left in the control of major university centers and in this way kept free of direct military supervision.

The Army, creator of the project, did nothing to contradict McNamara's order cancelling Project Camelot. Army influentials did not only feel that they had to execute the Defense Department's orders, but they are traditionally dubious of the value of "software" research to support "hardware" systems.

Let us take a closer look at each of these groups which voiced opposition to Project Camelot. A number of issues did not so much hinge upon, as swim about, Project Camelot. In particular, the "jurisdictional" dispute between Defense and State loomed largest.

State vs. Defense

In substance, the debate between the Defense Department and the State Department is not unlike that between electricians and bricklayers in the construction of a new apartment house.

What "union" is responsible for which processes? Less generously, the issue is: who controls what? At the policy level, Camelot was a tool tossed about in a larger power struggle which has been going on in government circles since the end of World War II, when the Defense Department emerged as a competitor for honors as the most powerful bureau of the administrative branch of government.

In some sense, the divisions between Defense and State are outcomes of the rise of ambiguous conflicts such as Korea and Vietnam, in contrast to the more precise and diplomatically controlled "classical" world wars. What are the lines dividing political policy from military posture? Who is the most important representative of the United States abroad: the ambassador or the military attaché in charge of the military mission? When soldiers from foreign lands are sent to the United States for political orientation, should such orientation be within the province of the State Department or of the Defense Department? When undercover activities are conducted, should the direction of such activities belong to military or political authorities? Each of these is a strategic question with little pragmatic or historic precedent. Each of these was entwined in the Project Camelot explosion.

It should be plain therefore that the State Department was not simply responding to the recommendations of Chilean left-wingers in urging the cancellation of Camelot. It merely employed the Chilean hostility to "interventionist" projects as an opportunity to redefine the balance of forces and power with the Defense Department. What is clear from this resistance to such projects is not so much a defense of the sovereignty of the nations where ambassadors are stationed, as it is a contention that conventional political channels are sufficient to yield the information desired or deemed necessary.

Congress

In the main, congressional reaction seems to be that Project Camelot was bad because it rocked the diplomatic boat in a sensitive area. Underlying most congressional criticisms is the plain fact that most congressmen are more sympathetic to State Department control of foreign affairs than they are to Defense Department control. In other words, despite military sponsored world junkets, National Guard and State Guard pressures from the home State, and military training in the backgrounds of many congressmen, the sentiment for political rather than military control is greater. In addition, there is a mounting suspicion in Congress of varying kinds of behavioral science research stemming from hearings into such matters as wiretapping, uses of lie detectors, and truth-in-packaging.

Social Scientists

One reason for the violent response to Project Camelot, especially among Latin American scholars, is its sponsorship by the Department of Defense. The fact is that Latin Americans have become quite accustomed to State Department involvements in the internal affairs of various nations. The Defense Department is a newcomer, a dangerous one, inside the Latin American orbit. The train of thought connected to its activities is in terms of international warfare, spying missions, military manipulations, etc. The State Department, for its part, is often a consultative party to shifts in government, and has played an enormous part in either fending off or bringing about *coups d'état.* This State Department role has by now been accepted and even taken for granted. Not so the Defense Department's role. But it is interesting to conjecture on how matter-of-factly Camelot might have been accepted if it had State Department sponsorship.

Social scientists in the United States have, for the most part, been publicly silent on the matter of Camelot. The reasons for this are not hard to find. First, many "giants of the field" are involved in government contract work in one capacity or another. And few souls are in a position to tamper with the gods. Second, most information on Project Camelot has thus far been of a newspaper variety; and professional men are not in a habit of criticizing colleagues on the basis of such information. Third, many social scientists doubtless see nothing wrong or immoral in the Project Camelot designs. And they are therefore more likely to be either confused or angered at the Latin American response than at the directors of Project Camelot. (At the time of the blowup, Camelot people spoke about the "Chilean mess" rather than the "Camelot mess.")

The directors of Project Camelot did not "classify" research materials, so that there would be no stigma of secrecy. And they also tried to hire, and even hired away from academic positions, people well known and respected for their independence of mind. The difficulty is that even though the stigma of secrecy was formally erased, it remained in the attitudes of many of the employees and would-be employees of Project Camelot. They unfortunately thought in terms of secrecy, clearance, missions, and the rest of the professional nonsense that so powerfully afflicts the Washington scientific as well as political ambience.

Further, it is apparent that Project Camelot had much greater difficulty hiring a full-time staff of high professional competence, than in getting part-time, summertime, weekend, and sundry assistance. Few established figures in academic life were willing to surrender the advantages of their positions for the risks of the project.

One of the cloudiest aspects to Project Camelot is the role of American University. Its actual supervision of the contract appears to have begun and ended with the 25 percent overhead on those parts of the contract that a university receives on most federal grants. Thus, while there can be no question as to the "concern and disappointment" of President Hurst R. Anderson of the American University over the demise of Project Camelot, the reasons for this regret do not seem to extend beyond the formal and the financial. No official at American University appears to have been willing to make any statement of responsibility, support, chagrin, opposition, or anything else related to the project. The issues are indeed momentous, and must be faced by all universities at which government sponsored research is conducted: the amount of control a university has over contract work; the role of university officials in the distribution of funds from grants; the relationships that ought to be established once a grant is issued. There is also a major question concerning project directors: are they members of the faculty, and if so, do they have necessary teaching responsibilities and opportunities for tenure as do other faculty members?

The difficulty with American University is that it seems to be remarkably unlike other universities in its permissiveness. The Special Operations Research Office received neither guidance nor support from university officials. From the outset, there seems to have been a "gentleman's agreement" not to inquire or interfere in Project Camelot, but simply to serve as some sort of camouflage. If American University were genuinely autonomous it might have been able to lend highly supportive aid to Project Camelot during the crisis months. As it is, American University maintained an official silence which preserved it from more congressional or executive criticism. This points up some serious flaws in its administrative and financial policies.

The relationship of Camelot to SORO represented a similarly muddled organizational picture. The director of Project Camelot was nominally autonomous and in charge of an organization surpassing in size and importance the overall SORO operation. Yet at the critical point the organizational blueprint served to protect SORO and sacrifice what nominally was its limb. That Camelot happened to be a vital organ may have hurt, especially when Congress blocked the transfer of unused Camelot funds to SORO.

Military

Military reaction to the cancellation of Camelot varied. It should be borne in mind that expenditures on Camelot were minimal in the Army's overall budget and most military leaders are skeptical, to begin with, about the worth of social science research. So there was no open protest about the demise of Camelot. Those officers who have a positive attitude toward social science materials, or are themselves trained in the social sciences, were dismayed. Some had hoped to find "software" alternatives to the "hardware systems" approach applied by the Secretary of Defense to every military-political contingency. These officers saw the attack on Camelot as a double attack—on their role as officers and on their professional standards. But the Army was so clearly treading in new waters that it could scarcely jeopardize the entire structure of military research to preserve one project. This very inability or impotence to preserve Camelot—a situation threatening to other governmental contracts with social scientists—no doubt impressed many armed forces officers.

The claim is made by the Camelot staff (and various military aides) that the critics of the project played into the hands of those sections of the military predisposed to veto any social science recommendations. Then why did the military offer such a huge support to a social science project to begin with? Because $6,000,000 is actually a trifling sum for the Army in an age of multibillion dollar military establishment. The amount is significantly more important for the social sciences, where such contract awards remain relatively scarce. Thus, there were differing perspectives of the importance of Camelot: an Army view which considered the contract as one of several forms of "software" investment; a social science perception of Project Camelot as the equivalent of the Manhattan Project.

WAS PROJECT CAMELOT WORKABLE?

While most public opposition to Project Camelot focused on its strategy and timing, a considerable amount of private opposition centered on more basic, though theoretical, questions: was Camelot scientifically feasible and ethically correct? No public document or statement contested the possibility that, given the successful completion of the data gathering, Camelot could have, indeed, established basic criteria for measuring the level and potential for internal war in a given nation. Thus, by never challenging the feasibility of the work, the political critics of Project Camelot were providing back-handed compliments to the efficacy of the project.

But much more than political considerations are involved. It is clear that some of the most critical problems presented by Project Camelot are scientific. Although for an extensive analysis of Camelot, the reader would, in fairness, have to be familiar with all of its documents, salient general criticisms can be made without a full reading.

The research design of Camelot was from the outset plagued by ambiguities. It was never quite settled whether the purpose was to study counterinsurgency possibilities, or the revolutionary process. Similarly, it was difficult to determine whether it was to be a study of comparative social structures, a set of case studies of single nations "in depth," or a study of social structure with particular emphasis on the military. In addition, there was a lack of treatment of what indicators were to be used, and whether a given social system in Nation A could be as stable in Nation B.

In one Camelot document there is a general critique of social science for failing to deal with social conflict and social control. While this in itself is admirable, the tenor and context of Camelot's documents make it plain that a "stable society" is considered the norm no less than the desired outcome. The "breakdown of social order" is spoken of accusatively. Stabilizing agencies in developing areas are presumed to be absent. There is no critique of U.S. Army policy in developing areas because the Army is presumed to be a stabilizing agency. The research formulations always assume the legitimacy of the Army tasks—"if the U.S. Army is to perform effectively its parts in the U.S. mission of counterinsurgency it must recognize that insurgency represents a breakdown of social order. . . ." But such a proposition has never been doubted—by Army officials or anyone else. The issue is whether such breakdowns are in the nature of the existing system or a product of conspiratorial movements.

The use of hygienic language disguises the antirevolutionary assumptions under a cloud of powder puff declarations. For example, studies of Paraguay are recommended "because trends in this situation (the Stroessner regime) may also render it 'unique' when analyzed in terms of the transition from 'dictatorship' to political stability." But to speak about changes from dictatorship to stability is an obvious ruse. In this case, it is a tactic to disguise the fact that Paraguay is one of the most vicious, undemocratic (and like most dictatorships, stable) societies in the Western Hemisphere.

These typify the sort of hygienic sociological premises that do not have scientific purposes. They illustrate the confusion of commitments within Project Camelot. Indeed the very absence of emotive words such as revolutionary masses, communism, socialism, and capitalism only serves to intensify the discomfort one must feel on examination of the documents—since the abstract vocabulary disguises, rather than resolves, the problems of international revolution. To have used clearly political rather than military language would not "justify" governmental support. Furthermore, shabby assumptions of academic conventionalism replaced innovative orientations. By adopting a systems approach, the problematic, open-ended aspects of the study of revolutions were largely omitted; and the design of the study became an oppressive curb on the study of the problems inspected.

This points up a critical implication for Camelot (as well as other projects). The importance of the subject being researched does not *per se* determine the importance of the project. A sociology of large-scale relevance and reference is all to the good. It is important that scholars be willing to risk something of their shaky reputations in helping resolve major world social problems. But it is no less urgent that in the process of addressing major problems, the autonomous character of the social science disciplines—their own criteria of worthwhile scholarship—should not be abandoned. Project Camelot lost sight of this "autonomous" social science character.

It never seemed to occur to its personnel to inquire into the desirability for successful revolution. This is just as solid a line of inquiry as the one stressed—the conditions under which revolutionary movements will be able to overthrow a government. Furthermore, they seem not to have thought about inquiring into the role of the United States in these countries. This points up the lack of symmetry. The problem should have been phrased to include the study of "us" as well as "them." It is not possible to make a decent analysis of a situation unless one takes into account the role of all the different people and groups involved in it; and there was no room in the design for such contingency analysis.

In discussing the policy impact on a social science research project, we should not overlook the difference between "contract" work and "grants." Project Camelot commenced with the U.S. Army; that is to say, it was initiated for a practical purpose determined by the client. This differs markedly from the typical academic grant in that its sponsorship had "built-in" ends. The scholar usually *seeks* a grant; in this case the donor, the Army, promoted its own aims. In some measure, the hostility for Project Camelot may be an unconscious reflection of this distinction—a dim feeling that there was something "nonacademic," and certainly not disinterested, about Project Camelot, irrespective of the quality of the scholars associated with it.

The Ethics of Policy Research

The issue of "scientific rights" versus "social myths" is perennial. Some maintain that the scientist ought not penetrate beyond legally or morally sanctioned limits and others argue that such limits cannot exist for science. In treading on the sensitive issue of national sovereignty, Project Camelot reflects the generalized dilemma. In deference to intelligent researchers, in recognition of them as scholars, they should have been invited by Camelot to air their misgivings and qualms about government (and especially Army sponsored) research—to declare their moral conscience. Instead, they were mistakenly approached as skillful, useful potential employees of a higher body, subject to an authority higher than their scientific calling.

What is central is not the political motives of the sponsor. For social scientists were not being enlisted in an intelligence system for "spying" purposes. But given their professional standing, their great sense of intellectual honor and pride, they could not be "employed" without proper deference for their stature. Professional authority should have prevailed from beginning to end with complete command of the right to thrash out the moral and political dilemmas as researchers saw them. The Army, however respectful and protective of free expression, was "hiring help" and not openly and honestly submitting a problem to the higher professional and scientific authority of social science.

The propriety of the Army to define and delimit all questions, which Camelot should have had a right to examine, was never placed in doubt. This is a tragic precedent; it reflects the arrogance of a consumer of intellectual merchandise. And this relationship of inequality corrupted the lines of authority, and profoundly limited the autonomy of the social scientists involved. It became clear that the social scientist savant was not so much functioning as an applied social scientist as he was supplying information to a powerful client.

The question of who sponsors research is not nearly so decisive as the question of ultimate use of such information. The sponsorship of a project, whether by the United States Army or by the Boy Scouts of America, is by itself neither good nor bad. Sponsorship is good or bad only insofar as the intended outcomes can be predetermined and the parameters of those intended outcomes tailored to the sponsor's expectations. Those social scientists critical of the project never really denied its freedom and independence, but questioned instead the purpose and character of its intended results.

It would be a gross oversimplification, if not an outright error, to assume that the theoretical problems of Project Camelot derive from any reactionary character of the project designers. The director went far and wide to select a group of men for the advisory board, the core planning group, the summer study group, and the various conference groupings, who in fact were more liberal in their orientations than any random sampling of the sociological profession would likely turn up.

However, in nearly every page of the various working papers, there are assertions which clearly derive from American military policy objectives rather than scientific method. The steady assumption that internal warfare is damaging disregards the possibility that a government may not be in a position to take actions either to relieve or improve mass conditions, or that such actions as are contemplated may be more concerned with reducing conflict than with improving conditions. The added statements about the United States Army and its "important mission in the positive and constructive aspects of nation building . . ." assumes the reality of such a function in an utterly unquestioning and unconvincing form. The first rule of the scientific game is not to make assumptions about friends and enemies in such a way as to promote the use of different criteria for the former and the latter.

The story of Project Camelot was not a confrontation of good versus evil. Obviously, not all men behaved with equal fidelity or with equal civility. Some men were weaker than others, some more callous, and some more stupid. But all of this is extrinsic to the heart of the problem of Camelot: what are and are not the legitimate functions of a scientist?

In conclusion, two important points must be clearly kept in mind and clearly apart. First, Project Camelot was intellectually, and from my own perspective, ideologically unsound. However, and more significantly, Camelot was not cancelled because of its faulty intellectual approaches. Instead, its cancellation came as an act of government censorship, and an expression of the contempt for social science so prevalent among those who need it most. Thus it was political expedience, rather than its lack of scientific merit, that led to the demise of Camelot because it threatened to rock State Department relations with Latin America.

Second, giving the State Department the right to screen and approve government-funded social science research projects on other countries, as the President has ordered, is a supreme act of censorship. Among the agencies that grant funds for such research are the National Institutes of Mental Health, the National Science Foundation, the National Aeronautics and Space Agency, and the Office of Education. Why should the State Department have veto power over the scientific pursuits of men and projects funded by these and other agencies in order to satisfy the policy needs—or policy failures—of the moment? President Johnson's directive is a gross violation of the autonomous nature of science.

We must be careful not to allow social science projects with which we may vociferously disagree on political and ideological grounds to be decimated or dismantled by government fiat. Across the ideological divide is a common social science understanding that the contemporary expression of reason in politics today is applied social science, and that the cancellation of Camelot, however pleasing it may be on political grounds to advocates of a civilian solution to Latin American affairs, represents a decisive setback for social science research.

Dissection IX: Methods for What?

A Manifesto for Sociologists: Institution Formation – A New Sociology

Henry Etzkowitz and
Gerald M. Schaflander

Almost all of American sociology has abdicated the responsibility for finding solutions to the most urgent problems facing our society. What sociologists usually do is merely observe and ask questions as "objective" outsiders. They come to the people who are actually doing things in the world when they have a few moments to spare from doing laboratory-manipulated studies of students paid for by foundations and government and then use various techniques to find out what these people are doing in their groups or institutions, always looking in from the position of a neutral noninvolved observer.

We are nauseous over the continual replication of meaningless, microscopic quantifications of "what's wrong or right with American society" from sterile, neutral, noninvolved, objective research-sociologists!

We believe, as human beings and as sociologists, that we have a deep moral responsibility to go far beyond mere objective analyses of society (away from Parsonian-Mertonian Structural-Functionalism and Vidich-Stein Radical Nihilism).

Marshall Clinard, in his 1966 Presidential Address to the Midwestern Sociological Association on the responsibility of sociologists, said that they should

From Henry Etzkowitz and Gerald M. Schaflander, "A Manifesto for Sociologists: Institution Formation–A New Sociology" *Social Problems* 15: 4:399–408, 1968. Reprinted by permission of The Society for the Study of Social Problems and the authors.

go beyond routine survey research, get out into the world, get involved in crucial problems, and come back with recommendations for policy makers.

Although this is a significant call for sociologists to transcend their usual bounds, it still limits the area for sociological solutions to what might be accepted by government or policy makers, and does not consider the possibility of sociologists themselves organizing new institutions to implement their own proposals.

We believe it is imperative for sociologists to analyze precisely what is sick in American society and then to act to try to change and heal American society.

We call upon young sociologists and old sociologists (who are dying of "microscopic ennui") to join us in a macroscopic effort to return American sociology to a fundamental and basic institutional involvement in American society by exploring the life and death problem of slave-ridden Americans in the ghetto.

With race riots increasingly rampant in inner cities; with white-Negro cooperation at its lowest point in the civil rights movement; we moved to 1175 Bedford Avenue, Bedford-Stuyvesant (America's number one ghetto with nearly half a million residents) on January 9, 1967; and proceeded to build a Community Cooperative Center with a 50-50 white-Negro integrated Board of Directors. We put up our own money from our teaching salaries at Hunter and Brooklyn Colleges and rented a 20,000 square-foot building at 1310 Atlantic Avenue, Brooklyn; proceeded to renovate it with 30 young dropouts and delinquents and opened March 1, 1967, as a new Institution in Bedford-Stuyvesant.

As researchers we have found that when tape is used as an unobtrusive recorder of real-life interactions between people (building an institution together), the resources and materials are usually genuine and truthful.

When a sociologist is accepted as a partner by the people he is working with and studying, the taping is rarely a barrier or proscenium separating the sociologist from the respondent. In fact, most people tend to forget the recorder is on. The involvement and life-heat of the interaction consume the attention of both parties and insure an accurate reproduction of the responses of all the actors. Thus the Heisenberg principle is overcome in this type of sociological research because the research instrument rarely influences the process being studied! Isn't this one ultimate object of scientific research?

When an actor routinely acts, the proscenium in the theatre is the barrier between the actor and the audience. When the actor, however, breaks through the proscenium and becomes a person or character who is believable, identifiable, and full of verisimilitude, he and the audience are bound together in a common living experience and each forgets the presence of the proscenium. It's not artificial or stagey or contrived. It's real, genuine interaction!

It is our contention that routine survey research questions are generally unnatural; they set up a proscenium behind which the respondent acts out a role on cue (role plays) and in front of which the sociologist asks artificial, contrived questions. The resulting barrier often prevents truthful, believable interaction, i.e., did most people really admit sexual inadequacy to Kinsey; religious nonobservance to Lenski?

Some sociologists go beyond survey research and become participant observers, taking sociology a giant stride beyond the neutral quantifiers. Some become members of the institutions or groups they are studying, as for example, Erving Goffman, who went into an asylum in Washington, D.C. as a recreation director, watched the doctors and patients, and concluded that no one was sane! He found out how they role-played in their institution and how they got along.

A New School graduate sociology student, Gerald Levy, worked in the Welfare Department of New York City and came out with a fine report on how the bureaucratic system unconsciously worked to hurt and put clients off. In this instance a sociologist became part of an existing institution, but with no commitment to try to change what he saw as "sick."

C. Wright Mills will go down in sociological history as a brilliant and perceptive analyst of the power elite. He analyzed the power structure of the U.S. in the late fifties but, like Malcolm X, who also "told it like it is," Mills neither had a program for social change nor any hope at all for any coalition that could effectuate a change in the bureaucratic growth of the power elite.

In the final analysis, Mills saw no hope of changing present institutions nor did he believe new institutions could be built to stop the drift towards war and to restore democracy at home.

The pseudo-heirs to C. Wright Mills—Coser, Vidich, and Stein, leaders of the radical nihilists—write with vigor and refreshing passion about what's wrong with the Structural-Functional School of Parsons and Merton and the bureaucratic evils of American society. But Vidich tells his students to make the best deal they can within American society. He tells them to remain cool, detached, and objective—not to try to change or alter or fight bureaucracy, because if they do, they'll be corrupted through having to use the same tactics as the very bureaucrats they're struggling against. This nonprescription perpetuates the status quo because it serves as an ideology to rationalize and legitimate inaction for young sociologists, and graduate students (who come to sociology through Mills' perceptive critique—and are turned off by Vidich and Stein at the height of their desire to participate in social change).

We cannot opt out of American organization life with the analysis that bureaucracy inevitably corrupts. As the radical nihilists argue, if we do adopt this analysis it is likely to act as a self-fulfilling prophecy in influencing us to make deals or sell out to those organizations which we cannot avoid or must participate in.

To try to be an omniscient, rigidly objective, or value-free observer from afar is not only to abdicate from one's responsibilities as a citizen but to condemn oneself to be an essentially irrelevant critic; for it is only by participating in the most important and macroscopic areas of life in one's society (and in our society that means large and complex organizations) that one will have the relevant resources, data, and materials to develop a proper analysis of that society.

One social scientist who has gone beyond the noninvolved observer-participant role is Robert Coles, a psychiatrist. He went to study the Student Non-Violent Coordinating Committee in Mississippi during the summer of 1964. Once down there he found out that no one in SNCC was interested in talking to him. To them, he seemed to be just another social scientist asking what they thought were irrelevant questions. But instead of just asking his questions and getting "put-on" answers, he decided to stay for the summer and offered to become their doctor. Gradually he came to be trusted by them, enough to begin group psychotherapy.

Coles came to occupy a key position in their organization. As part of the inner circle, he helped to make decisions and then participated in the action they took. He thus knew what was going on from the inside. The insight and knowledge he gained thereby was far greater than that of the sociologist who flies down on the "Civil Rights Special" to ask Stokely Carmichael "How's it going, baby?" over a one night scotch-and-steak quiz session.

SNCC trusted Coles and he was able to tape record and take notes without having to ask any questions. He was interacting in a real life situation. His resources and materials were drawn from his daily life. He learned more about what was happening that summer than any sociologist could learn by any other sociological method. No outside observer, no one coming in with a questionnaire, or sending a questionnaire down, or coming down there to do depth interviewing, could learn as much as he did as part of the decision-making apparatus. Like any other social scientist, when he returned North he scientifically checked and evaluated his research. Yet he didn't innovate or initiate any basic institutional changes and SNCC's "Black Power" deterioration is history.

Many action sociologists (such as A. Shostak) counsel the poor and become grantsmanship experts within the government antipoverty structure—thus becoming coopted into a bureaucratic government program.

The expansion of the Viet Nam war and the accelerated growth of a Pax-Americana foreign policy has severely curtailed antipoverty funds as well as disrupted normal organizational expectations with sporadic "start and stop" funding. Moreover, social change was seriously inhibited because the Federal Government never could withstand the pressure from the big city political machines, and the local Congressmen who represented economic and political interests violently opposed to poor and grass roots organization which threatened their very economic and political control.

The experience of Mobilization for Youth in New York City, local congressional opposition to the grape workers' organizing struggle in California, and the cut-off of the independent Head Start Program in Mississippi are but a few of the many examples which illustrate the political schizophrenia of the government antipoverty program.

Another unique approach is that of Saul Alinsky, who left academic sociology to organize the poor. In the Woodlawn area of Chicago he connected existing organizations to each other in a new structure, The Woodlawn Organization. He gave it operational and tactical direction and prepared to confront Mayor Daley. Under Alinsky's leadership the residents of Woodlawn as members of T.W.O. marched on City Hall and demanded a say in urban renewal plans for their neighborhood. They were able to stop the proposed plans imposed from City Hall and get a reconsideration of urban renewal planning in the area so that they would be included in the planning process. However, after the initial confrontation with City Hall, the momentum of the T.W.O. slacked off. The marches to City Hall stopped and even the demonstrations in front of stores to lower prices dissipated.

Woodlawn is basically the same now as it was before Alinsky started. No fundamental institutional changes were achieved in Woodlawn nor in Syracuse, Rochester, or other communities where Alinsky's highly creative confrontations excite and motivate poor people, yet leave them in the same slums, with the same high cost of living and unemployment as when they started. They may have more self-esteem and self-identity but jobs, lower cost foods, and a decent place to live are no closer in any community served by Alinsky's noninstitutional approach to social change.

Many church, labor, and sociological groups have been attracted to Alinsky because of the dynamic excitement of his program and the potential increase in self-identity and self-esteem he develops among the poor. But we wonder if relative deprivation and disillusionment are not the end result of the Alinsky program when no fundamental institutional change occurs among the Alinsky-trained poor.

In the summer of 1948 Sol Tax, an anthropologist from the University of Chicago, took some of his students to study an Indian community in the Middle West. The students were appalled at the Indians' living conditions and wanted to change them. Tax, the anthropologist, first felt that they should remain outside as observers, but later, back at the University, changed his mind and the next time he brought the students back to the Indian community he was determined to act to change the situation.

In the Indian community there were two opposing factions and thus two views of what this situation was. One faction wanted to return to the old ways while the other wanted to discard the old ways and modernize. Tax's group proceeded to develop alternate solutions based on the views of these two Indian factions. Since they were commited to deriving their program for change from the ideas and wishes of the Indians, rather than suggesting new programs, the Tax group ended with a project to produce Indian *trinkets* for sale. This satisfied both factions: those who wanted to keep the old as well as those who wanted to act for economic improvement.

Thus, the Action–Anthropologist, feeling bound by the definition of the world of those he would help, was no more able to overcome the situation of debilitating poverty than the Indians.

The major difference between the program of the Tax Action Anthropologists and those of us who are "new" Institution–Formation sociologists[1] is that we feel that we must propose and/or develop new and unique institutional solutions to the situations people are in because there is no guarantee that poor people alone know how to solve their own problems—or that red or black voices necessarily speak with truth or clarity on the nature of their own appalling condition.

We cannot necessarily derive programs for social change from the very people who are victimized and desire change. They are usually limited in both knowledge and experience.

A social scientist who has recognized this is the late Allan Holmberg, a Cornell anthropologist, who went to the Indian community in Vicos, Peru, as a participant–intervener with a plan of action. In 1952, Cornell University, in association with the Indigenous Institute of Peru, rented Vicos, a hacienda of 2,000 Indians, and initiated a program for social change in education, community development, and involvement of the people in making decisions about what should be done. Yet Holmberg retained final veto power as an anthropological landlord.

Once people had a taste of modern life and education they often decided to leave for the cities while, with improvement of conditions in Vicos, some returned home. This can only be a temporary halt in the movement of people to cities, given the sociohistorical thrust towards urbanization.

Although Holmberg instituted a worthwhile effort to improve the lot of people in a rural area of Peru, he neglected consideration of macroscopic analyses of the long term trend towards the urbanization of Latin America. This would have shown him the difficulties of achieving significant changes in a traditional rural Institution and perhaps have led him to devote his efforts for social change towards urban Latin America.

Today in the ghettos we see a strong parallel between our sociological attempt to build new institutions and the CIO organizing drive in the late 1930s.

The CIO organizers didn't come to workers and ask them: "What's troubling you?" "What is your problem?" What they did was to say: "Look, you're getting picked off one at a time; you're being speeded up because you haven't got a union; because if one of you gets kicked around the rest of you don't go out. Here's a program we've got for you. . . . Sign this card. We're going to form an organizing committee; we'll sign everybody up that's inside the shop; we'll pull the shop out, and I'll tell you when to pull the shop out because that's what I'm an expert at. Here's the program we've got—if you don't like it, don't sign the card. If you like it, sign the card and we'll organize the plant."

People signed it or they didn't. If they did, the union organized. They wrote the leaflet, went out in front of the plant, pulled them out or sat down inside the plant until they got their contract.

When we came into Bedford-Stuyvesant (an area where more than one-half of the women are husbandless or unwed mothers; most of the rest of the population are unemployed, on welfare, narcotized or drunk; and young people are bitterly screaming for "black power" while they roam the streets) everybody said: "ask the community what they need." What community? Were we supposed to sit down and try to find some kind of consensus when Roy Wilkins doesn't agree with Martin Luther King and Martin Luther King rarely talks to Wilkins or agrees with Stokely Carmichael? They seldom get together, as Robert Penn Warren says, on any one issue. There is no one voice for the Negro—at the national or local level—as we have observed.

Therefore, it seemed very clear that it was up to us—because we have the knowledge and training—to propose new solutions. We could say, as did the CIO organizers, "This is the idea that *we* think is right. This is the program; we're going to come in as whites on a 50-50 basis. If you don't like it, OK!! If you do like it, come on and join us."

What we are proposing as sociologists is that we should initiate and organize totally new institutions where old ones are ineffective, and then study the institutions that we organize, as well as their relationships to other institutions that they will affect.

THE COMMUNITY CO-OP CENTER: A NEW AND UNIQUE INSTITUTION

As a first step, we analyzed what was essentially lacking in Bedford-Stuyvesant—an independent economic base for the Negro community. Without this economic base, Negroes could not build their own political power base or any other institution in the community, but instead were left dependent on the outside bureaucracy coming in—the welfare, the schools, the police, etc. They could present no defense against such bureaucracy without an economic base from which they could struggle. Because of plantation oppression and economic and educational discrimination, Negroes could not, through hard work alone, build up private enterprise as the Jews have done. Obviously, it's now too late! Economic opportunities and areas are no longer technologically open.

We felt it would take a new institution to accomplish this. So, we took an old institution, the cooperative, from another part of society and made basic and fundamental changes in it to make it effective in ghettos such as Bedford-Stuyvesant.

Excerpts from the following presentation to foundations and private individuals on January 25, 1967 started the fund raising and organization.

The proposal to create a new and unique Community Cooperative Center in Bedford–Stuyvesant is designed to achieve the following purposes:

Organize and study the effects of introducing a unique Community Cooperative Center in the slums of Bedford–Stuyvesant as a potential model for other urban ghettos to begin to solve their own economic, social, and political problems . . . through a *Self–Generating* and repetitive generating effort.

AS AN INITIAL OPERATIONAL SERVICE PROGRAM TO THE COMMUNITY

Simultaneously, the Project would initiate several levels of research to culminate in Ph.D. theses and/or books, as blueprints for the "Institution–Formation Sociology"–via foundation support (one time only) across the U.S.A.–with major concentration in ghettos of Boston, Philadelphia, Baltimore–Washington, Chicago, Detroit, Cleveland, Los Angeles, Oakland–San Francisco, Memphis, New Orleans, and Harlem in New York City.

Market research to determine precisely the "what and how much," daily consumption patterns of a validated cross–section of Bedford–Stuyvesant's ghetto community. Also what effects the mass media and the "outside consumer–oriented" society have on individual aspirations, desires and values.

An exhaustive continuing study of the effects existing institutions in the community have on Co–op members (churches, schools, police, welfare services, etc.) and what effect membership in a successful Co–op might have re institutional (long–range) influence on old and new members of the Community Cooperative Center.

UNIQUE INSTITUTIONAL PHILOSOPHY

The Project basically involves the transfer of an old, respected, and successful (rural and union–oriented) institution, the Co–op, from "developed" American society to the "underdeveloped," anarchic subsociety of the ghetto.

The venerable institution, the Co–op, is being drastically restructured and altered in order to become a *Self–Generating* source of continuing capital . . . to meet the continuing and growing needs of the specific ghetto . . . by *reinvesting profits in sorely needed community services.*

The basic and radical changes to be instituted are:

> 1. No membership fee will be charged to new members. The original organizing capital will be provided by foundation grants.
>
> 2. *Drastically reduced prices* (not competitive) on drugs, milk, butter, bread, meat, underwear, shoes, etc.; rather than the traditional "meet-competition" pricing approach of the old Co-op movement. Therefore, needless and often wasted time will be saved from recruiting large (absent) original membership fees; and endless educational efforts will be eliminated to keep members of the Co-op buying at competitive prices . . . in order to guarantee *Future* "divvies" and/or individual members dividends.
>
> 3. Total elimination of individual divvies or profits. A basic policy of reinvestment of the profits in social services to the membership and community will be substituted for the age-old (Rochdale) Co-op "divvy." Credit unions, camp and social scholarships, and job-training are early objectives of the project.
>
> 4. As services expand, more and more jobs at the CCC itself will be created—totally new and unexplored job and career images and opportunities will be fostered to develop dignity, self-respect, and to give hope and faith to the ghetto—to replace alienation.
>
> Above all, this Project should be supported because there is confusion and anarchy in the civil rights movement itself; there are arguments and deep differences over strategy and tactics and priorities and feuding between SNCC, SLC, NAACP, CORE, and the government and foundations. Here is a program that cuts through factionalism and ideological hangups.

In August of 1967, seven months after crankup, the new socioeconomic Institution, the CCC, presented itself in the following brochure:

> The Community Cooperative Center is a nonprofit, tax-free (filed for), biracial corporation at 1310 Atlantic Avenue in Bedford-Stuyvesant (Brooklyn, New York), the number one ghetto in the U.S.
>
> *The Community Cooperative Center operates a gasoline station, parking lot, drug store, and child care center.*
>
> The basic purpose of the Community Cooperative Center is that the profits from the business services—with drastically lower prices—are turned over to support the largest Child Care Center in New York City (107 children now attending, ranging from 3 months to 5 years) from 7:30 a.m. to 7:00 p.m. They are supervised by 4 certified teachers, 12 trained unwed mothers, 5 graduate nurses and 6 volunteer college students.
>
> Other health and social services will be added as profits increase.

The Community Cooperative Center has been organized as a Self-Help, Self-Generating, Self-Perpetuating, integrated institution that has received its original financing from teachers, students, wealthy individuals, and small foundations commited to integration.

The July 16, 1967, *New York Times* editorial puts it quite grimly and bluntly when it says: "As the trend towards violence grows among Negroes, so does its counterpart among frightened whites. More and more cries of black power evoke the echo of white power. . . . But it must be recognized that the threat of confrontation between Negro and white in the U.S. today is the most serious problem this nation faces, more serious even than Viet Nam . . ."

This rare bridge between blacks and whites is working here, and, this unique dialogue must be maintained and solidified with Newark and Detroit smoldering and Watts still festering.

This totally new and different institution might just be the key answer to the crises of our inner cities which, according to the New York Times, could tear this country apart.

The Bedford-Stuyvesant Community Cooperative Center is a model and, when successful, can be duplicated in your community.

If you want to join with us by contributing, or helping in any way, write to CCC Research and Development Corporation, 1310 Atlantic Avenue, Brooklyn, New York (467-1220).

Sincerely; Anna Copeland, Chairman (Girl Scout leader and youth religious leader); Gerald Schaflander, President (Instructor of Sociology, Boston University); John Bryan, Vice President (Graduate Student, Howard University); Clifford Etheridge, Vice President (Former Gang Leader); Rupert Vaughan, Vice President (Brooklyn College Student); Elliott Jeffries, Vice President (Contractor); and Henry Etzkowitz, Treasurer (Instuctor of Sociology, Northeastern University, Boston).

From a sociological research standpoint, the living proof of the correctness of this Institution-Formation or Involved Observer approach is what we have learned first hand about unwed mothers, dropout students, narcotics, unemployment, and the terrible void in verbal communication and interaction between Negroes and whites, through actually living and working together.

We have voluminous tape recordings of personality and organizational conflicts; hundreds of hours of tapes indicating significant, repetitive behavior patterns of young men and women involved in a life style and culture totally unknown to white America, which is only vaguely hinted at in Claude Brown's *Manchild in the Promised Land.*

Though Negroes in the ghetto aspire to achieve material possessions—status and educational goals—similar to those of white middle-class society; nevertheless their constant and repetitive failures to achieve these goals leave them alienated, frustrated, and then aggressive (J. Dollard). This inevitably leads to internal aggression of Saturday night knifings and cuttings; and external aggression of rioting, looting, intense exploitive sex (unwed mothers), alcohol, and narcotic gratification—all part of a secondary ghetto culture. For the dominant white middle-class culture—ever present through T.V.—stimulates a new, acute frustration level right in the ghetto apartment—every 15 minutes. They are tantalized, restimulated and refrustrated every 15 minutes with visual and auditory symbols of the white middle-class culture that they can never really "make."

So they turn inward in gratification and outward in aggression and establish a unique life style—a truly secondary culture. They are in schizoid conflict between the dominant culture they desire—and the secondary culture they are in.

Now, for the first time, white students and teachers have recorded sociologically the daily interaction, anxieties, fears, and hopes of a group of whites and Negroes together building a new Institution and a new way of life.[2]

Does anyone really believe this kind of material and resources could ever be derived from objective, neutral interviewing? It came through the confidence and trust we established by raising money, meeting payrolls, working in the cold together, and sharing mutual hopes, fears, and conflicts as this Institution is being built.

Only through naked confrontation, through daily living and working together could these conflicts be resolved and could we, as sociologists, begin to define the scope and true nature of the sociological and social psychological problems that threaten to erupt into race riots this summer unlike anything witnessed in America before.

We say nonsense to all of the separatist experts in the civil rights movement—when there's no "real" black power movement; when SNCC is going down the drain; when CORE is near dead; when the NAACP is ineffective in the ghetto, and when we've got more Negroes and whites working together in the CCC than anywhere else in the U.S.

Now we may run out of money and we may flop; but we've got a 20,000-square-foot building; we've got Negroes and whites working together. We refuse (truculently and belligerently) to let Negroes stereotype us as members of the "White Society" power structure.

We refuse to assume the guilt of white people who think like members of the White Citizens' Council and the KKK. We will not allow any Negro to judge us merely as whites. We are human beings and we'll judge them as human beings. There'll be no stereotypes. We will not accept it. We do not think that because they are Negroes they are good or bad. They are good or bad (just as whites) because they produce and they perform or they don't.

And that's our program; that's the institution we have, and this is a way to heal ghetto society.

We are acting in the tradition of the old CIO organizers. And we believe this is one way in which inner city slums in American society can be changed.

The information and data we have on sex, narcotics, educational insufficiency, family disintegration, and how Negroes respond to money or the lack of money is direct and personal and bears the imprint of the way it really is—which, we believe, can only flow from naturalistic field research.

We call for a return to the Chicago tradition of Albion Small's conception of the sociologist as "social agitator." We must form new institutions to heal the sickness in the ghettos through Community Cooperative Centers that are self-generating; new schools bereft of bureaucratic ponderousness; new social aid and protective institutions, free of spying but full of preventive social therapeutic tools; and other new institutions where the best elements in the so-called white society—artists, scientists, professionals, teachers, and students join hands with Negroes in the ghetto to rebuild American society from the heart of our key cities.

NOTES

1. Or "Involved Observers"; see Kenneth B. Clark, *Dark Ghetto,* New York: Harper, 1965, Introduction.
2. These tapes with analyses will be presented in a forthcoming book, *The Way It Really Is: A Socio-Historic Narrative Documentary,* Doubleday.